FIRST CENSUS
OF THE UNITED STATES
1790

NEW HAMPSHIRE

HEADS OF FAMILIES

AT THE FIRST CENSUS OF THE
UNITED STATES TAKEN
IN THE YEAR
1790

NEW HAMPSHIRE

Originally published: Government Printing Office
Washington, D.C., 1907
Reprinted: Genealogical Publishing Co., Inc.
Baltimore, 1966, 1973, 1992
Library of Congress Catalogue Card Number 73-8202
International Standard Book Number 0-8063-0571-1
Made in the United States of America

HEADS OF FAMILIES AT THE FIRST CENSUS
1790

INTRODUCTION.

The First Census of the United States (1790) comprised an enumeration of the inhabitants of the present states of Connecticut, Delaware, Georgia, Kentucky, Maine, Maryland, Massachusetts, New Hampshire, New Jersey, New York, North Carolina, Pennsylvania, Rhode Island, South Carolina, Tennessee, Vermont, and Virginia. The law which authorized this enumeration appears on page 6.

A complete set of the schedules for each state, with a summary for the counties, and in many cases for towns, was filed in the State Department, but unfortunately they are not now complete, the returns for the states of Delaware, Georgia, Kentucky, New Jersey, Tennessee, and Virginia having been destroyed when the British burned the Capitol at Washington during the War of 1812.

These schedules form a unique inheritance for the Nation, since they represent for each of the states concerned a complete list of the heads of families in the United States at the time of the adoption of the Constitution. The framers were the statesmen and leaders of thought, but those whose names appear upon the schedules of the First Census were in general the plain citizens who by their conduct in war and peace made the Constitution possible and by their intelligence and self-restraint put it into successful operation.

The total population of the United States in 1790, exclusive of slaves, as derived from the schedules, was 3,231,533. The only names appearing upon the schedules, however, were those of heads of families, and as at that period the families averaged 6 persons, the total number was approximately 540,000, or slightly more than half a million. The number of names which is now lacking because of the destruction of the schedules is approximately 140,000, thus leaving schedules containing about 400,000 names.

The information contained in the published report of the First Census of the United States, a small volume of 56 pages, was not uniform for the several states and territories. For New England and one or two of the other states the population was presented by counties and towns, that of New Jersey appeared partly by counties and towns and partly by counties only; in other cases the returns were given by counties only. Thus the complete transcript of the names of heads of families, with accompanying information, would present for the first time detailed information as to the number of inhabitants—males, females, etc.—for each minor civil division in all those states for which such information was not originally published.

In response to repeated requests from patriotic societies and persons interested in genealogy, or desirous of studying the early history of the United States, Congress added to the sundry civil appropriation bill for the fiscal year 1907 the following paragraph:

The Director of the Census is hereby authorized and directed to publish, in a permanent form, by counties and minor civil divisions, the names of the heads of families returned at the First Census of the United States in seventeen hundred and ninety; and the Director of the Census is authorized, in his discretion, to sell said publications, the proceeds thereof to be covered into the Treasury of the United States, to be deposited to the credit of miscellaneous receipts on account of "Proceeds of sales of Government property:"

Provided, That no expense shall be incurred hereunder additional to appropriations for the Census Office for printing therefor made for the fiscal year nineteen hundred and seven; and the Director of the Census is hereby directed to report to Congress at its next session the cost incurred hereunder and the price fixed for said publications and the total received therefor.

The amount of money appropriated by Congress for the Census printing for the fiscal year mentioned was unfortunately not sufficient to meet the current requirement of the Office and to publish the transcription of the First Census, and no provision was made in the sundry civil appropriation bill for 1908 for the continuance of authority to publish these important records beyond the present fiscal year. Resources, however, are available for publishing a small section of the work, and the schedules of New Hampshire, Vermont, and Maryland have been selected. In these states the names of heads of families in 1790 were limited in number, and the records are in a condition which makes transcription comparatively easy. In the following pages all the information is presented which appears upon these schedules, and the sequence of the names is that followed by the enumerator in making his report.

(3)

It is to be hoped that Congress will again grant authority and money for the publication of the remaining schedules, in order that the entire series, so far as it exists, may be complete. For several of the states for which schedules are lacking it is probable that the Director of the Census could obtain lists which would present the names of most of the heads of families at the date of the First Census. In Virginia, for example, a state enumeration was made in 1785, of which some of the original schedules are still in existence. These would be likely to prove a reasonably satisfactory substitute for the Federal list made five years later.

THE FIRST CENSUS.

The First Census act was passed at the second session of the First Congress, and was signed by President Washington on March 1, 1790. The task of making the first enumeration of inhabitants was placed upon the President. Under this law the marshals of the several judicial districts were required to ascertain the number of inhabitants within their respective districts, omitting Indians not taxed, and distinguishing free persons (including those bound to service for a term of years); the sex and color of free persons; and the number of free males 16 years of age and over.

The object of the inquiry last mentioned was, undoubtedly, to obtain definite knowledge as to the military and industrial strength of the country. This fact possesses special interest, because the Constitution directs merely an enumeration of inhabitants. Thus the demand for increasingly extensive information, which has been so marked a characteristic of census legislation, began with the First Congress that dealt with the subject.

The method followed by the President in putting into operation the First Census law, although the object of extended investigation, is not definitely known. It is supposed that the President or the Secretary of State dispatched copies of the law, and perhaps of instructions also, to the marshals. There is, however, some ground for disputing this conclusion. At least one of the reports in the census volume of 1790 was furnished by a governor. This, together with the fact that there is no record of correspondence with the marshals on the subject of the census, but that there is a record of such correspondence with the governors, makes very strong the inference that the marshals received their instructions through the governors of the states. This inference is strengthened by the fact that in 1790 the state of Massachusetts furnished the printed blanks, and also by the fact that the law relating to the Second Census specifically charged the Secretary of State to superintend the enumeration and to communicate directly with the marshals.

By the terms of the First Census law nine months were allowed in which to complete the enumeration.

The census taking was supervised by the marshals of the several judicial districts, who employed assistant marshals to act as enumerators. There were 17 marshals. The records showing the number of assistant marshals employed in 1790, 1800, and 1810 were destroyed by fire, but the number employed in 1790 has been estimated at 650.

The schedules which these officials prepared consist of lists of names of heads of families; each name appears in a stub, or first column, which is followed by five columns, giving details of the family. These columns are headed as follows:

Free white males, 16 years and upward, including heads of families.
Free white males under 16 years.
Free white females, including heads of families.
All other free persons.
Slaves.

The assistant marshals made two copies of the returns; in accordance with the law one copy was posted in the immediate neighborhood for the information of the public, and the other was transmitted to the marshal in charge, to be forwarded to the President. The schedules were turned over by the President to the Secretary of State. Little or no tabulation was required, and the report of the First Census, as also the reports of the Second, Third, and Fourth, was produced without the employment of any clerical force, the summaries being transmitted directly to the printer. The total population as returned in 1790 was 3,929,214, and the entire cost of the census was $44,377.

A summary of the results of the First Census, not including the returns for South Carolina, was transmitted to Congress by President Washington on October 27, 1791. The legal period for enumeration, nine months, had been extended, the longest time consumed being eighteen months in South Carolina. The report of October 27 was printed in full, and published in what is now a very rare little volume; afterwards the report for South Carolina was "tipped in." To contain the results of the Twelfth Census, ten large quarto volumes, comprising in all 10,400 pages, were required. No illustration of the expansion of census inquiry can be more striking.

The original schedules of the First Census are now contained in 26 bound volumes, preserved in the Census Office. For the most part the headings of the schedules were written in by hand. Indeed, up to and including 1820, the assistant marshals generally used for the schedules such paper as they happened to have, ruling it, writing in the headings, and binding the sheets together themselves. In some cases merchants' account paper was used, and now and then the schedules were bound in wall paper.

As a consequence of requiring marshals to supply their own blanks, the volumes containing the sched-

ules vary in size from about 7 inches long, 3 inches wide, and ½ inch thick to 21 inches long, 14 inches wide, and 6 inches thick. Some of the sheets in these volumes are only 4 inches long, but a few are 3 feet in length, necessitating several folds. In some cases leaves burned at the edges have been covered with transparent silk to preserve them.

THE UNITED STATES IN 1790.

In March, 1790, the Union consisted of twelve states—Rhode Island, the last of the original thirteen to enter the Union, being admitted May 29. Vermont, the first addition, was admitted in the following year, before the results of the First Census were announced. Maine was a part of Massachusetts, Kentucky was a part of Virginia, and the present states of Alabama and Mississippi were parts of Georgia. The present states of Ohio, Indiana, Illinois, Michigan, and Wisconsin, with part of Minnesota, were known as the Northwest Territory, and the present state of Tennessee, then a part of North Carolina, was soon to be organized as the Southwest Territory.

The United States was bounded on the west by the Mississippi river, beyond which stretched that vast and unexplored wilderness belonging to the Spanish King, which was afterwards ceded to the United States by France as the Louisiana Purchase, and now comprises the great and populous states of Louisiana, Arkansas, Indian Territory, Oklahoma, Missouri, Kansas, Iowa, Nebraska, South Dakota, North Dakota, and Montana, and most of Colorado, Wyoming, and Minnesota. The Louisiana Purchase was not completed for more than a decade after the First Census was taken. On the south was another Spanish colony known as the Floridas. Texas, then a part of the colony of Mexico, belonged to Spain; and California, Utah, Arizona, and New Mexico, also the property of Spain, although penetrated here and there by venturesome explorers and missionaries, were, for the most part, an undiscovered wilderness.

The gross area of the United States was 827,844 square miles, but the settled area was only 239,935 square miles, or about 29 per cent of the total. Though the area covered by the enumeration in 1790 seems very small when compared with the present area of the United States, the difficulties which confronted the census taker were vastly greater than in 1900. In many localities there were no roads, and where these did exist they were poor and frequently impassable; bridges were almost unknown. Transportation was entirely by horseback, stage, or private coach. A journey as long as that from New York to Washington was a serious undertaking, requiring eight days under the most favorable conditions. Western New York was a wilderness, Elmira and Binghamton being but detached hamlets. The territory west of the Allegheny mountains, with the exception of a portion of Kentucky, was unsettled and scarcely penetrated. Detroit and Vincennes were too small and isolated to merit consideration. Philadelphia was the capital of the United States. Washington was a mere Government project, not even named, but known as the Federal City. Indeed, by the spring of 1793, only one wall of the White House had been constructed, and the site for the Capitol had been merely surveyed. New York city in 1790 possessed a population of only 33,131, although it was the largest city in the United States; Philadelphia was second, with 28,522; and Boston third, with 18,320. Mails were transported in very irregular fashion, and correspondence was expensive and uncertain.

There were, moreover, other difficulties which were of serious moment in 1790, but which long ago ceased to be problems in census taking. The inhabitants, having no experience with census taking, imagined that some scheme for increasing taxation was involved, and were inclined to be cautious lest they should reveal too much of their own affairs. There was also opposition to enumeration on religious grounds, a count of inhabitants being regarded by many as a cause for divine displeasure. The boundaries of towns and other minor divisions, and even those of counties, were in many cases unknown or not defined at all. The hitherto semi-independent states had been under the control of the Federal Government for so short a time that the different sections had not yet been welded into an harmonious nationality in which the Federal authority should be unquestioned and instructions promptly and fully obeyed.

AN ACT PROVIDING FOR THE ENUMERATION OF THE INHABITANTS OF THE UNITED STATES.

APPROVED MARCH 1, 1790.

SECTION 1. Be it enacted by the Senate and House of Representatives of the United States of America in Congress assembled, That the marshals of the several districts of the United States shall be, and they are hereby authorized and required to cause the number of the inhabitants within their respective districts to be taken; omitting in such enumeration Indians not taxed, and distinguishing free persons, including those bound to service for a term of years, from all others; distinguishing also the sexes and colours of free persons, and the free males of sixteen years and upwards from those under that age; for effecting which purpose the marshals shall have power to appoint as many assistants within their respective districts as to them shall appear necessary; assigning to each assistant a certain division of his district, which division shall consist of one or more counties, cities, towns, townships, hundreds or parishes, or of a territory plainly and distinctly bounded by water courses, mountains, or public roads. The marshals and their assistants shall respectively take an oath or affirmation, before some judge or justice of the peace, resident within their respective districts, previous to their entering on the discharge of the duties by this act required. The oath or affirmation of the marshal shall be, "I, A. B., Marshal of the district of ———, do solemnly swear (or affirm) that I will well and truly cause to be made a just and perfect enumeration and description of all persons resident within my district, and return the same to the President of the United States, agreeably to the directions of an act of Congress, intituled 'An act providing for the enumeration of the inhabitants of the United States,' according to the best of my ability." The oath or affirmation of an assistant shall be "I, A. B., do solemnly swear (or affirm) that I will make a just and perfect enumeration and description of all persons resident within the division assigned to me by the marshal of the district of ———, and make due return thereof to the said marshal, agreeably to the directions of an act of Congress, intituled 'An act providing for the enumeration of the inhabitants of the United States,' according to the best of my ability." The enumeration shall commence on the first Monday in August next, and shall close within nine calendar months thereafter. The several assistants shall, within the said nine months, transmit to the marshals by whom they shall be respectively appointed, accurate returns of all persons, except Indians not taxed, within their respective divisions, which returns shall be made in a schedule, distinguishing the several families by the names of their master, mistress, steward, overseer, or other principal person therein, in manner following, that is to say:

The number of persons within my division, consisting of ———, appears in a schedule hereto annexed, subscribed by me this ——— day of ———, 179–. A. B. *Assistant to the marshal of* ———.

Schedule of the whole number of persons within the division allotted to A. B.

Names of heads of families.	Free white males of 16 years and upwards, including heads of families.	Free white males under 16 years.	Free white females, including heads of families.	All other free persons.	Slaves.

SECTION 2. And be it further enacted, That every assistant failing to make return, or making a false return of the enumeration to the marshal, within the time by this act limited, shall forfeit the sum of two hundred dollars.

SECTION 3. And be it further enacted, That the marshals shall file the several returns aforesaid, with the clerks of their respective district courts, who are hereby directed to receive and carefully preserve the same: And the marshals respectively shall, on or before the first day of September, one thousand seven hundred and ninety-one, transmit to the President of the United States, the aggregate amount of each description of persons within their respective districts. And every marshal failing to file the returns of his assistants, or any of them, with the clerks of their respective district courts, or failing to return the aggregate amount of each description of persons in their respective districts, as the same shall appear from said returns, to the President of the United States within the time limited by this act, shall, for every such offense, forfeit the sum of eight hundred dollars; all which forfeitures shall be recoverable in the courts of the districts where the offenses shall be committed, or in the circuit courts to be held within the same, by action of debt, information or indictment; the one-half thereof to the use of the United States, and the other half to the informer; but where the prosecution shall be first instituted on the behalf of the United States, the whole shall accrue to their use. And for the more effectual discovery of offenses, the judges of the several district courts, at their next sessions, to be held after the expiration of the time allowed for making the returns of the enumeration hereby directed, to the President of the United States, shall give this act in charge to the grand juries, in their respective courts, and shall cause the returns of the several assistants to be laid before them for their inspection.

SECTION 4. And be it further enacted, That every assistant shall receive at the rate of one dollar for every one hundred and fifty persons by him returned, where such persons reside in the country; and where such persons reside in a city, or town, containing more than five thousand persons, such assistants shall receive at the rate of one dollar for every three hundred persons; but where, from the dispersed situation of the inhabitants in some divisions, one dollar for every one hundred and fifty persons shall be insufficient, the marshals, with the approbation of the judges of their respective districts, may make such further allowance to the assistants in such divisions as shall be deemed an adequate compensation, provided the same does not exceed one dollar for every fifty persons by them returned. The several marshals shall receive as follows: The marshal of the district of Maine, two hundred dollars; the marshal of the district of New Hampshire, two hundred dollars; the marshal of the district of Massachusetts, three hundred dollars; the marshal of the district of Connecticut, two hundred dollars; the marshal of the district of New York, three hundred dollars; the marshal of the district of New Jersey, two hundred dollars; the marshal of the district of Pennsylvania, three hundred dollars; the marshal of the district of Delaware, one hundred dollars; the marshal of the district of Maryland, three hundred dollars; the marshal of the district of Virginia, five hundred dollars; the marshal of the district of Kentucky, two hundred and fifty dollars; the marshal of the district of North Carolina, three hundred and fifty dollars; the marshal of the district of South Carolina, three hundred dollars; the marshal of the district of Georgia, two hundred and fifty dollars. And to

obviate all doubts which may arise respecting the persons to be returned, and the manner of making the returns.

SECTION 5. Be it enacted, That every person whose usual place of abode shall be in any family on the aforesaid first Monday in August next, shall be returned as of such family; the name of every person, who shall be an inhabitant of any district, but without a settled place of residence, shall be inserted in the column of the aforesaid schedule, which is allotted for the heads of families, in that division where he or she shall be on the said first Monday in August next, and every person occasionally absent at the time of the enumeration, as belonging to that place in which he usually resides in the United States.

SECTION 6. And be it further enacted, That each and every person more than 16 years of age, whether heads of families or not, belonging to any family within any division of a district made or established within the United States, shall be, and hereby is, obliged to render to such assistant of the division, a true account, if required, to the best of his or her knowledge, of all and every person belonging to such family, respectively, according to the several descriptions aforesaid, on pain of forfeiting twenty dollars, to be sued for and recovered by such assistant, the one-half for his own use, and the other half for the use of the United States.

SECTION 7. And be it further enacted, That each assistant shall, previous to making his return to the marshal, cause a correct copy, signed by himself, of the schedule containing the number of inhabitants within his division, to be set up at two of the most public places within the same, there to remain for the inspection of all concerned; for each of which copies the said assistant shall be entitled to receive two dollars, provided proof of a copy of the schedule having been so set up and suffered to remain, shall be transmitted to the marshal, with the return of the number of persons; and in case any assistant shall fail to make such proof to the marshal, he shall forfeit the compensation by this act allowed him.

Approved March 1, 1790.

Population of the United States as returned at the First Census, by states: 1790.

DISTRICT.	Free white males of 16 years and upward, including heads of families.	Free white males under 16 years.	Free white females, including heads of families.	All other free persons.	Slaves.	Total.
Vermont	22,435	22,328	40,505	255	[1] 16	[2] 85,539
New Hampshire	36,086	34,851	70,160	630	158	141,885
Maine	24,384	24,748	46,870	538	None.	96,540
Massachusetts	95,453	87,289	190,582	5,463	None.	378,787
Rhode Island	16,019	15,799	32,652	3,407	948	68,825
Connecticut	60,523	54,403	117,448	2,808	2,764	237,946
New York	83,700	78,122	152,320	4,654	21,324	340,120
New Jersey	45,251	41,416	83,287	2,762	11,423	184,139
Pennsylvania	110,788	106,948	206,363	6,537	3,737	434,373
Delaware	11,783	12,143	22,384	3,899	8,887	[3] 59,094
Maryland	55,915	51,339	101,395	8,043	103,036	319,728
Virginia	110,936	116,135	215,046	12,866	292,627	747,610
Kentucky	15,154	17,057	28,922	114	12,430	73,677
North Carolina	69,988	77,506	140,710	4,975	100,572	393,751
South Carolina	35,576	37,722	66,880	1,801	107,094	249,073
Georgia	13,103	14,044	25,739	398	29,264	82,548
Total number of inhabitants of the United States exclusive of S. Western and N. territory	807,094	791,850	1,541,263	59,150	694,280	3,893,635

	Free white males of 21 years and upward.	Free males under 21 years of age.	Free white females.	All other persons.	Slaves.	Total.
S. W. territory	6,271	10,277	15,365	361	3,417	35,691
N. "						

[1] The census of 1790, published in 1791, reports 16 slaves in Vermont. Subsequently, and up to 1860, the number is given as 17. An examination of the original manuscript returns shows that there never were any slaves in Vermont. The original error occurred in preparing the results for publication, when 16 persons, returned as "Free colored," were classified as "Slave."

[2] Corrected figures are 85,425, or 114 less than figures published in 1790, due to an error of addition in the returns for each of the towns of Fairfield, Milton, Shelburne, and Williston, in the county of Chittenden; Brookfield, Newbury, Randolph, and Strafford, in the county of Orange; Castleton, Clarendon, Hubbardton, Poultney, Rutland, Shrewsbury, and Wallingford, in the county of Rutland; Dummerston, Guilford, Halifax, and Westminster, in the county of Windham; and Woodstock, in the county of Windsor.

[3] Corrected figures are 59,096, or 2 more than figures published in 1790, due to error in addition.

Summary of population, by counties and towns: 1790.

CHESHIRE COUNTY.

TOWN.	Number of heads of families.	Free white males of 16 years and upward, including heads of families.	Free white males under 16 years.	Free white females, including heads of families.	All other free persons.	Slaves.	Total.	TOWN.	Number of heads of families.	Free white males of 16 years and upward, including heads of families.	Free white males under 16 years.	Free white females, including heads of families.	All other free persons.	Slaves.	Total.
Acworth	117	160	197	348			705	Newport	132	187	198	389	4	1	779
Alstead	188	268	285	558	1		1,112	Packersfield	123	170	208	343	3		724
Charlestown	160	307	254	531	1	1	1,094	Plainfield	190	259	277	486	2		1,024
Chesterfield	315	441	532	928	2		1,903	Protectworth	46	56	49	104		1	210
Claremont	240	348	389	682	2	2	1,423	Richmond	221	332	368	680			1,380
Cornish	161	238	258	484	1	1	982	Rindge	188	276	306	554	7		1,143
Croydon	94	121	150	262	3		536	Stoddard	123	162	194	344		1	701
Dublin	157	227	223	444	5		899	Sullivan	37	48	68	103	1		220
Fitzwilliam	187	255	278	505			1,038	Surry	79	117	111	220			448
Gilsom	54	70	64	164			298	Swanzey	192	291	286	572	6		1,155
Hinsdale	86	127	142	251		4	524	Unity	88	133	139	265	1		538
Jaffrey	203	285	336	606	11		1,238	Walpole	195	327	335	589	1	2	1,254
Keene	208	319	318	663	5	2	1,307	Washington	97	137	135	273			545
Langdon	42	58	76	108	2		244	Wendell	51	70	64	133			267
Lempster	72	110	95	207	3		415	Westmoreland	299	473	524	998	4	1	2,000
Marlborough	138	175	219	392			786	Winchester	189	298	311	595	4	1	1,209
Marlow	64	73	90	156			319								
New Grantham	60	90	88	153	1	1	333	**Total**	**4,796**	**7,008**	**7,567**	**14,090**	**70**	**18**	**28,753**

GRAFTON COUNTY.

TOWN.	Number of heads of families.	Free white males of 16 years and upward, including heads of families.	Free white males under 16 years.	Free white females, including heads of families.	All other free persons.	Slaves.	Total.	TOWN.	Number of heads of families.	Free white males of 16 years and upward, including heads of families.	Free white males under 16 years.	Free white females, including heads of families.	All other free persons.	Slaves.	Total.
Alexandria	54	79	87	131			297	Landaff	55	75	80	137			292
Bartlett	51	55	57	135		1	248	Lebanon	225	375	282	515	8		1,180
Bath	85	117	136	239		1	493	Lincoln	5	8	5	9			22
Bridgewater	61	84	62	134		1	281	Littleton	19	28	26	42			96
Burton	23	34	45	62			141	Lyman	43	57	39	106			202
Cambridge (not inhabited)								Lyme	175	231	189	392	4		816
Campton	75	113	79	202		1	395	Millfield (not inhabited)							
Canaan	87	137	123	223			483	New Chester	50	70	103	139			312
Chatham	12	17	13	28			58	New Holderness	62	96	73	160			329
Cockburn	4	9	5	12			26	Northumberland	16	34	27	56			117
Cockermouth	70	94	104	175			373	Orange	22	32	37	61		1	131
Colburne	7	10	6	13			29	Orford	91	140	125	272		3	540
Concord (alias Gunthwaite)	65	91	75	147			313	Peeling (not inhabited)							
Coventry	17	21	20	47			88	Percy	8	14	11	23			48
Dalton	2	3	4	7			14	Piermont	72	103	113	206	1	3	426
Dame's Location	3	4	8	9			21	Plymouth	131	182	142	297		4	625
Dartmouth	21	34	25	52			111	Rumney	71	97	113	201			411
Dorchester	37	48	45	82			175	Senter's Location	3	5		3			8
Dummer (not inhabited)								Shelburne	6	12	5	18			35
Enfield (alias Relhan)	124	188	173	361	2		724	Stark's Location	6	8	5	16			29
Errol (not inhabited)								Sterling's Location	2	3	2	4			9
Franconia	16	22	18	32			72	Stratford	25	44	35	65			144
Grafton	69	99	110	194			403	Success (not inhabited)							
Hale's Location	2	3	2	4			9	Thornton	70	96	98	191			385
Hanover (including 152 students at Dartmouth College)	212	476	297	596	8	2	1,379	Trecothick (not inhabited)							
Hart's Location	3	3	4	5			12	Wales's Location	1	1	3	2			6
Haverhill	101	163	118	266	1	4	552	Warren	35	52	64	86	4		206
Kilkenny (not inhabited)								Wentworth	42	56	73	112			241
Lancaster	27	45	45	71			161	**Total**	**2,463**	**3,768**	**3,311**	**6,340**	**28**	**21**	**13,468**

HILLSBOROUGH COUNTY.

TOWN.	Number of heads of families.	Free white males of 16 years and upward, including heads of families.	Free white males under 16 years.	Free white females, including heads of families.	All other free persons.	Slaves.	Total.	TOWN.	Number of heads of families.	Free white males of 16 years and upward, including heads of families.	Free white males under 16 years.	Free white females, including heads of families.	All other free persons.	Slaves.	Total.
Amherst	384	571	575	1,205	18		2,369	Litchfield	57	99	87	166	17		369
Andover	111	166	167	312			645	Lyndborough	220	313	349	618			1,280
Antrim	97	138	144	244			526	Lyndborough Gore	8	11	8	19			38
Bedford	141	210	240	440	7		897	Mason	145	215	242	462	3		922
Boscawen	178	282	274	551	1		1,108	Merrimac	135	209	207	393	10		819
Bradford	45	56	60	101			217	New Boston	177	313	303	578	10		1,204
Campbell's Gore	23	28	35	57			120	New Ipswich	176	338	285	614	4		1,241
Dearing	148	213	264	459	2		938	New London	50	69	90	152			311
Derryfield	58	92	95	175			362	Nottingham West	188	267	246	544	7		1,064
Derryfield Gore	4	10	4	16			30	Peterborough	136	221	213	423	4		861
Dunbarton	134	209	244	448	20		921	Raby	60	86	89	160	3		338
Dunstable	115	179	146	306	1		632	Salisbury	215	335	385	640	2		1,362
Duxbury Mile-slip	27	39	45	85			169	Sharon	45	68	63	129			260
Fishersfield	60	68	105	152			325	Society Land	57	84	89	156			329
Francestown	173	232	234	517			983	Sutton	90	132	122	266			520
Goffstown	201	324	303	614	34		1,275	Temple	116	177	196	368	6		747
Hancock	117	156	160	315	3		634	Warner	148	220	195	448			863
Heniker	177	266	325	525	8		1,124	Weare	286	491	500	931	2		1,924
Hillsborough	141	193	211	393	1		798	Wilton	159	253	270	562	12		1,097
Hollis	242	340	378	723			1,441								
Hopkinton	269	445	417	852	1		1,715	**Total**	**5,331**	**8,145**	**8,392**	**16,168**	**176**		**32,881**
Kersarge Gore	18	27	27	49			103								

Summary of population, by counties and towns: 1790—Continued.

ROCKINGHAM COUNTY.

TOWN.	Number of heads of families.	Free white males of 16 years and upward, including heads of families.	Free white males under 16 years.	Free white females, including heads of families.	All other free persons.	Slaves.	Total.	TOWN.	Number of heads of families.	Free white males of 16 years and upward, including heads of families.	Free white males under 16 years.	Free white females, including heads of families.	All other free persons.	Slaves.	Total.
Allenstown	46	68	63	123	1	....	255	Newcastle	94	125	117	292	....	....	534
Atkinson	79	129	102	247	2	....	480	Newington	89	132	109	285	2	14	542
Bow	94	147	151	268	....	....	566	Newmarket	194	284	235	610	7	1	1,137
Brintwood	156	255	224	490	6	1	976	Newtown	99	126	132	271	....	1	530
Candia	167	246	273	521	....	....	1,040	Northampton	99	184	138	333	2	....	657
Canterbury	161	295	223	526	1	3	1,048	Northfield	114	154	155	295	2	....	606
Chester	343	490	449	960	1	....	1,900	Northwood	124	188	181	376	....	1	746
Chichester	82	137	118	237	....	....	492	Nottingham	178	275	249	530	4	11	1,069
Concor	279	494	405	828	7	4	1,738	Pelham	131	216	193	385	....	....	794
Deerfield	299	444	358	808	1	2	1,613	Pembrook	155	239	247	474	....	2	962
East Kingston	58	90	87	179	2	....	358	Pittsfield	147	204	220	444	4	....	872
Epping	223	338	256	654	2	5	1,255	Plaistow	94	134	123	259	....	....	516
Epsom	131	200	203	427	....	....	830	Poplin	78	136	104	251	1	1	493
Exeter	287	437	343	859	81	2	1,722	Portsmouth	893	1,158	973	2,487	76	26	4,720
Gosport (on Star Island)	20	32	22	39	....	....	93	Raymond	128	177	181	361	8	....	727
Greenland	105	170	141	309	12	2	634	Rye	152	226	189	439	8	3	865
Hampstead	121	195	157	370	2	1	725	Salem	207	287	294	626	9	2	1,218
Hampton	154	238	174	436	3	1	852	Sandown	105	138	115	309	....	....	562
Hampton Falls	91	150	96	291	3	....	540	Seabrook	132	178	178	357	2	....	715
Hawke	75	101	95	225	....	1	422	South Hampton	73	125	82	241	1	....	449
Kensington	146	222	147	435	....	....	804	Stratham	143	229	158	486	8	1	882
Kingston	167	244	188	470	3	....	905	Windham	102	156	173	328	1	5	663
Londonderry	422	676	573	1,325	25	5	2,604								
Loudon	166	272	274	521	5	2	1,074	Total	7,403	11,141	9,668	21,987	292	97	43,185

STRAFFORD COUNTY.

TOWN.	Number of heads of families.	Free white males of 16 years and upward, including heads of families.	Free white males under 16 years.	Free white females, including heads of families.	All other free persons.	Slaves.	Total.	TOWN.	Number of heads of families.	Free white males of 16 years and upward, including heads of families.	Free white males under 16 years.	Free white females, including heads of families.	All other free persons.	Slaves.	Total.
Barnstead	128	192	214	400	....	1	807	New Hampton	111	171	173	306	2	....	652
Barrington	420	608	650	1,221	2	....	2,481	Ossipee	69	86	82	171	....	....	339
Conway	98	149	146	279	....	....	574	Rochester	507	728	740	1,383	....	1	2,852
Dover	316	547	418	1,005	18	8	1,996	Sanbornton	293	415	424	748	....	....	1,587
Durham	230	336	271	634	2	3	1,246	Sandwich	155	216	243	446	....	....	905
Eaton	44	60	72	122	....	....	254	Somersworth	165	248	211	479	1	4	943
Effingham	31	42	43	67	....	1	153	Stark's Location	2	2	....	1	....	....	3
Gilmantown	441	615	682	1,290	22	1	2,610	Sterling's Location	9	10	13	25	....	....	48
Lee	180	277	224	533	2	....	1,036	Tamworth	47	67	72	126	....	1	266
Madbury	98	167	126	295	4	....	592	Tuftonborough	20	29	20	60	....	....	109
Merideth	153	248	211	419	4	....	882	Wakefield	115	158	195	293	....	....	646
Middleton	107	151	162	304	....	....	617	Wolfborough	78	110	120	217	....	....	447
Moultonborough	91	133	148	283	....	1	565								
New Durham	104	139	140	275	....	....	554	Total	4,087	6,012	5,918	11,594	64	21	23,609
New Durham Gore	75	108	118	212	7	....	445								

CHESHIRE COUNTY. [1]

ACWORTH TOWN.

NAME OF HEAD OF FAMILY.	Free white males of 16 years and upward, including heads of families.	Free white males under 16 years.	Free white females, including heads of families.	All other free persons.	Slaves.
Albree, Joseph	1	1	2		
Alexander, Jaben	1	3	4		
Archibald, Thomas	1	1	3		
Atwood, Amos	1		1		
Ayres, Christopher	1		2		
Barker, Josiah	1				
Blanchard, Aaron	2	3	4		
Blood, Edmund	1	5	3		
Blood, Phinehas	1		2		
Brigham, William	3	1	6		
Brown, Alexander	1		8		
Campbell, Daniel	1	2	2		
Campbell, James	1	2	4		
Carleton, Dean	1	3	2		
Chaffin, Samuel	1	1	5		
Chatterdon, Joseph	1	1	7		
Clarke, Elijah	1	3	4		
Clarke, John	1		1		
Clarke, Thomas	1	3	2		
Clarke, William	1	3	4		
Coben, Asa	1	2	1		
Coffin, David	1	1	2		
Coffin, Henry	1	5	3		
Coffin, Moses	1		2		
Copeland, Phinehas	1	2	2		
Davidson, John	3		3		
Dodge, Thomas	1	2	1		
Duncan, Isaac	2		4		
Duncan, John	1	5	3		
Finley, Joseph	3		5		
Finley, Samuel	1				
Foster, Isaac	2	3	5		
Gage, Abner	1	4	3		
Gates, Isaac	2	4	4		
Gates, Luther	1	3	2		
Gragg, John	1		1		
Gragg, Joseph	5		2		
Grout, Andrew	1		2		
Grout, Daniel	2	3	6		
Grout, Daniel, Junr	1		2		
Grout, Ebenezer	1				
Grout, William	1				
Haywood, Jacob	3	1	2		
Hewins, Peter	1	2	4		
Hill, Robert	1	1	5		
Hill, Thomas	1	5	4		
Holmes, Jonathan	1	2	2		
Houston, Alexander	3	1	6		
Humphry, Abel	1	2	2		
Hymes, Walter	1		5		
Ingalls, Amos	2	1	3		
Kenney, Amos	1		1		
Keyes, Amos	2		2		
Keyes, Edward	1	1	1		
Keyes, Ephriam	1	1	1		
Keyes, Jonas	2	1	4		
Keyes, William	2	4	3		
Kinnerson, George	1	2	2		
Lancaster, Moses	1	2	3		
McClure, James	2	4	4		
McClure, Robert	3	1	2		
McClure, Thomas	1		3		
McFarling, Joseph	1	3	2		
McKeen, Hugh	1	4	3		
McKeen, John	1	3	1		
McLaughlin, James	1	3	4		
Markham, Joseph	2	1	4		
Markham, William	2	1	3		
Mathewson, Charles	1	2	3		
Mayo, Isachar	1	4	3		
Merril, Nathaniel	2	1	1		
Miller, James	1	5	6		
Mitchel, William	3	3	4		
Nott, Thaddeus	1		3		
Nowland, John	1	1	1		
Orcott, Nathan	3		3		
Orcott, William	1		3		
Prowty, Johnson	1	2	4		
Reed, John	1	1	4		
Reed, Supply	1	2	4		
Robb, John	2	1	4		
Rogers, James	1	3	4		
Rogers, Jane	1		8		
Rogers, Jonathan	1		8		
Rogers, William	1	2	3		
Sawyer, Nathaniel	1		1		
Silsby, Eliphaz	4	2	5		
Silsby, Eusebius	1	3	3		
Silsby, Jonathan	1	4	4		
Silsby, Lasel	1	2	4		
Silsby, Samuel	1	4	3		
Silsby, Woodward Augustus	1		3		

ACWORTH TOWN—con.

NAME OF HEAD OF FAMILY.	Free white males of 16 years and upward, including heads of families.	Free white males under 16 years.	Free white females, including heads of families.	All other free persons.	Slaves.
Slader, Mehitable	2	1	4		
Slader, Thomas	1	2	3		
Smith, Edward	1	2	3		
Smith, Eli	1		3		
Smith, Hezediah	1		1		
Smith, Jedediah	1	3	3		
Stebbins, Mahumin	1	3	3		
Stowell, Alladuren	1		2		
Thornton, Stephen	1	3	2		
Tracy, Owen	1	2	3		
Turner, Joel	1	2	4		
Wallace, James	1	5	3		
Wallace, John	1		2		
Wallace, Mathew	2	2	4		
Warren, Moses	1	1	4		
Watson, Abraham	1	1	3		
West, Sprague	1		1		
Whitney, Nathaniel	1	1	3		
Williams, John	1	2	3		
Wilson, John	3		3		
Wilson, John, Junr	3	6	3		
Woodbury, Henry	1	4	3		
Woodbury, William	1	1	3		
Woodbury, Zachariah	1		3		
Woodbury, Zachariah, Junr	1	3	2		

ALSTEAD TOWN.

NAME OF HEAD OF FAMILY.	Free white males of 16 years and upward, including heads of families.	Free white males under 16 years.	Free white females, including heads of families.	All other free persons.	Slaves.
Abels, Simon	2				
Arch, James	1	1	1		
Ball, Samuel	1		2		
Banks, John	1	2	3		
Bartlett, Samuel	1	1	4		
Baxter, Benjamin	1	2	2		
Beckwith, Andrew	1	3	4		
Beckwith, Jason	1		4		
Beckwith, Martin	1	3	2		
Beckwith, Richard	1	1	2		
Beebee, Zaccheus	2	1	4		
Brigham, John	1	1	2		
Brimmer, John	1		4		
Brooks, Benjamin	2	1	1		
Brooks, John	1	3	3		
Brooks, Simon	1	1	3		
Brooks, Simon, Junr	2	3	2		
Brown, Abraham	3		1		
Brown, Abraham, Junr	1	4	4		
Brown, Elias	1	2	3		
Brown, James	1	1	1		
Brown, Nathaniel	1	3	3		
Brown, Spencer	1	3	6		
Bryant, John	2	2	2		
Burroughs, Daniel	1	4	3		
Burroughs, Elijah	2	1	3		
Burroughs, Joel	2	4	4		
Burroughs, John	1	2	6		
Burroughs, Timothy	1	1	5		
Butterfield, Benjamin	1	2	3		
Butterfield, John	2		3		
Buttrick, Abel	1	3	3		
Cady, Isaac	1		1		
Cady, Isaac, Junr	1	3	5		
Chandler, Joel	1	3	5		
Chandler, John	3	2	4		
Chapin, Justus	1		5		
Chapin, Oliver	1	1	2		
Chapin, Sarah		2	3		
Chase, Moses	4		1		
Cheever, Jacob	1		2		
Childs, Timothy	1		4		
Clarke, Andrew	2	1	5		
Comstock, Samuel	1	1	1		
Cook, Josiah	2		3		
Cooper, Nathaniel	2	3	5		
Crane, Joshua	3	3	4		
Crane, Zebulon	1	2	3		
Crosby, Josiah	2	2	3		
Currier, James	1		1		
Cutter, Benjamin	2		5		
Daniels, Moses	3		2		
Delano, Barnabas	2		2		
Delano, Gideon	2	3	5		
Druce, William	1		3		
Drury, Samuel	1		3		
Dutton, Abel	1	1	5		
Farnsworth, Moses	1	2	2		
Farnsworth, Thomas	4	1	2		
Fay, Nathan	3	2	6		
Fisher, Jonathan	1	3	5		
Fletcher, John	1	1	2		
Fletcher, Peter	1		3		
Fletcher, Timothy	1	4	3		

ALSTEAD TOWN—con.

NAME OF HEAD OF FAMILY.	Free white males of 16 years and upward, including heads of families.	Free white males under 16 years.	Free white females, including heads of families.	All other free persons.	Slaves.
Gale, Amos	2	3	4		
Gale, Elisha	2	3	4		
Gilman, Joshua	2	2	3		
Grant, Micheal	4	1	2		
Griffin, David	2		5		
Hale, David	2	3	3		
Hale, Joseph	1		2	1	
Hale, Moses	1	2	2		
Harrington, Benjamin	2	1	2		
Harrington, Eli	2	1	2		
Harris, Luke	1	1	1		
Hatch, Asa	1	3	3		
Hatch, Joseph	1	1	2		
Hatch, Judah	2		2		
Hatch, Phinehas	2	1	4		
Hatch, Reuben	1	2	4		
Heustis, Aristedus	1	5	2		
Holbrook, Elijah	2	2	4		
Holton, Abraham	1		3		
Hubbard, Abel	1	2	2		
Hubbard, Samuel	2	3	3		
Johnson, Isachar	1	4	4		
Kendall, Timothy	1	2	5		
Kent, Isaac	2	1	2		
Kidder, James	2	3	5		
Kidder, Samuel	1	4	4		
King, Jonathan	1		2		
Kingsbury, Absolam	2		2		
Kingsbury, Cyrus	1	2	2		
Kingsbury, Elisha	1		1		
Kingsbury, Ephriam	2		1		
Kingsbury, James	1	1	2		
Kingsbury, Obadiah	2		3		
Kingsbury, Samuel	1		2		
Kingsbury, William	1	1	1		
Ladd, John	1		1		
Ladd, Merriam	1	1	1		
Lankton, Levi	1		2		
Lummis, Eleazer	2	2	5		
Mack, Joseph	2	4	4		
Mann, Jacob	2	2	5		
Mann, Larnard	3	3	3		
Mann, Nathan	1	3	4		
Marrs, James	1	1	1		
Marvin, Giles	1	4	2		
Miller, Bathuel	1	1	3		
Miller, Eleazer	1		1		
Miller, Lemuel	2	5	4		
Moore, Jacob	1	1	3		
Morley, Daniel	1		3		
Morley, Elijah	1		2		
Morse, Nathan	1	1	4		
Newell, Daniel	1	1	2		
Newton, Jonas	1	3	3		
Newton, Jonathan	1		1		
Olds, Moses	1	2	4		
Olds, Phinehas	1		1		
Olds, Thomas	1	2	4		
Parker, Robert	1	2	3		
Perrin, Daniel	1		3		
Phelps, Abel	2	3	3		
Phelps, Joshua	1		5		
Prentice, Sartle	1	1	1		
Richardson, David	1	1	3		
Richardson, Samuel	3		3		
Richardson, William	2	1	3		
Robens, John	2	1	2		
Robertson, John	1	3	2		
Root, Thomas	1	1	2		
Rugg, Aaron	1	1	4		
Rust, Nathaniel	2	1	5		
Shephard, Amos	5		2		
Shephard, Joshua	1	2	2		
Shephard, Levi	1		2		
Shephard, Nathaniel	1	1	2		
Shephard, Simeon	1	3	5		
Shepherd, Oliver	3	2	2		
Simons, Mable			2		
Simons, William	1	2	2		
Slade, John	2	1	2		
Slade, John, Junr	1	1	5		
Slade, William	1	1	4		
Smith, Samuel	1	1	1		
Snow, Eli	1	3	4		
Snow, John	1		4		
Stevens, Elkanah	1		5		
Stevens, Elkanah, Junr	1	1	1		
Stone, Nathaniel	3	2	3		
Taylor, Thomas	1	6	4		
Temple, Isaac	2	1	5		
Thompson, David	1		2		
Thompson, Job	2	1	2		
Thompson, Job, Junr	2	3	3		

[1] No attempt has been made in this publication to correct mistakes in spelling made by the deputy marshals, but the names have been reproduced as they appear upon the census schedules.

CHESHIRE COUNTY—Continued.

NAME OF HEAD OF FAMILY.	Free white males of 16 years and upward, including heads of families.	Free white males under 16 years.	Free white females, including heads of families.	All other free persons.	Slaves.
ALSTEAD TOWN—con.					
Thompson, Samuel	3	2	4		
Thompson, William	2	3	6		
Tinney, John	1		6		
Twining, Nathaniel	1		2		
Vilas, Nathaniel	2	1	1		
Vilas, Noah	2		2		
Waite, John	1	2	4		
Waite, Thomas	1	2	3		
Waldo, Daniel	2	3	4		
Waldo, Edward	1	6	3		
Waldo, Elijah	1		2		
Wardner, Henry	1	5	4		
Wardner, Jacob	1	3	4		
Wardner, Phillip	1	1	1		
Watts, Jesse	1	1	3		
Watts, John	1		2		
Watts, Nathaniel	2		1		
Watts, Timothy	1	1	3		
Weatherhead, Jeremiah	1		2		
Wheeler, Peter	1	2	5		
Wheelock, Phinehas	1	2	3		
Whipple, Jeremiah	1	4	4		
Whitcomb, Asa	1	1	1		
Williams, Christopher	1		1		
Wood, Benjamin	1	4	5		
Wood, James	1	1	2		
Wood, John	2		6		
Wood, Joshua	1	5	3		
Wood, William	1	2	4		
Worster, John	1	2	2		
Yeamans, Stephen	1	2	3		
CHARLESTOWN TOWN.					
Adams, Daniel	1		4		
Allen, Nathan	2	2	6		
Arbuckle, Joseph	1	2	2		
Baker, Osman	5		4		
Baldwin, Joseph	1	1	5		
Bellows, Peter	4	2	5		
Billings, John	3	1	3		
Blood, Benjamin	1	3	6		
Bond, William	2	2	2		
Booty, Joseph	1		2		
Bowen, Charles	2	3	4		
Bowtell, James	2	2	3		
Brown, Aaron	1	1	3		
Brown, Daniel	1		2		
Brown, Joseph	3		2		
Brown, Joseph, Junr	1	1	1		
Brown, Levi	1	5	6		
Brown, Silas	1		2		
Burnham, Amos	1	5	3		
Burnham, Josiah	1	1	1		1
Carleton, Dean	1	3	5		
Carleton, Timothy	3	1	6		
Church, Simeon	1	1	4		
Clarke, Josiah	1				
Converse, John	1	2	2		
Cooley, Joel	1	2	2		
Coomes, Oliver	1	1	1		
Crosby, Samuel	1		2		
Cross, David	1	2	3		
Cushman, Paul	5	1	7		
Darling, William	1	3	3		
Decamp, David	1	2	3		
Dickenson, Elihu	5	1	4		
Dudley, David	1	1	1		
Dudley, John	1	1	3		
Ellsworth, Elijah	1	4	4		
Ely, Isaac H	2	2	6		
Enos, David H	2		2		
Farnsworth, Ebenezer	3	1	1		
Farnsworth, Thomas	3	1	2		
Farwell, Isaac	2		4		
Farwell, Isaac, Junr	1		2		
Farwell, Joseph	2	2	2		
Farwell, William	4		3		
Farwell, William, Jr	1	3	3		
Fuller, Benjamin	1	1	4		
Garfield, Samuel	3	1	4		
Geer, Shubael	1		2		
Geer, Thomas	2	3	4		
Glidden, Richard	1	3	2		
Grout, Elijah	4	2	9		
Grout, Johosophat	1	1	3		
Grout, Ruth		1	3		
Grow, John	2	1	4		
Hall, Oliver	2	4	3		
Harper, John	1	3	1		
Harper, Samuel	2	2	3		
Hart, Constant	1		1		

NAME OF HEAD OF FAMILY.	Free white males of 16 years and upward, including heads of families.	Free white males under 16 years.	Free white females, including heads of families.	All other free persons.	Slaves.
CHARLESTOWN TOWN—continued.					
Hart, John	1	2	1		
Hart, Josiah	2	1	2		
Hart, Simeon	1	1	3		
Hasham, Stephen	1		3		
Hastings, Joel	3		3		
Hastings, John	1		1		
Hastings, John, Junr	1	1	3		
Hastings, Oliver	3	1	1		
Hastings, Samuel	1		3		
Hastings, Sylvanus	2	2	5		
Hastings, Sylvanus, Junr	2	3	1		
Hastings, Willard	2	1	4		
Haywood, William	4	2	5		
Henry, Robert	1		2		
Henry, William	4	1	1		
Henry, William, Junr	3	1	4		
Hill, Jesse	1	1	1		
Hill, Tower	1				1
Hodgkins, John	1		1		
Holden, Timothy	1		3		
Holden, William	1	1	1		
Hooker, Seth	2	1	5		
Hubbard, David	1	5	3		
Hubbard, John	6	3	5		
Hubbard, Jonathan	5	2	4		
Hunt, Asahel	3	2	4		
Hunt, Samuel	7	1	6		
Indevine, Calvin	1	3	2		
Indevine, William	2	2	3		
Jewell, Silas	3	4	3		
Johnson, Jeremiah	1	1	3		
Johnson, Job	1		1		
Johnson, Sylvanus	2	3	3		
Jones, Benjamin	3	4	5		
Kimball, George	3	3	5		
Kimball, Levi	1	1	5		
Laberre, Benjamin	4	2	7		
Laberre, Rufus	1	2	3		
Lynes, David	1		1		
McClintic, William	1		5		
McMurphey, John	2	2	1		
Markham, Joshua	2	4	5		
More, Benjamin	3	2	4		
Newton, Timothy	1	4	3		
Nichols, Asa	3	2	5		
Nichols, Ebenezer	1	4	3		
Nichols, Knight	1	4	1		
Nichols, Phillip	2	1	2		
O'Brian, John	1		1		
Olcott, Bulkley	4	1	7		
Olcott, Simeon	2	3	2		
Page, Peter	2	4	5		
Page, Phinehas	1	1	2		
Page, William	1	2	6		
Parker, Elijah	4	5	6		
Parks, David	1	1	2		
Parks, Jonas	1	1	4		
Peas, Isaac	1	1	3		
Peirce, David	1		4		
Perkins, Henry	1		1		
Perry, Samuel	1	2			
Porter, William	1		2		
Powers, Cyrus	1	1	3		
Powers, Nathaniel	1	2	4		
Prowty, Caleb	1	2	4		
Putnam, Ebenezer	1	2	5		
Putnam, Samuel	1		1		
Putnam, Thomas	1	1	2		
Putnam, Timothy	3	1	3		
Putnam, Timothy, Junr	2	3	3		
Reed, Howard	2		2		
Remington, Samuel	2	2	2		
Royce, Durius	1		2		
Russel, John	2		4		
Sartwell, Simon	5	1	10		
Silsby, Julius	1	2	4		
Simons, Hazeal	1	3	4		
Simons, John	1		2		
Southworth, Rachal		3	4		
Spencer, Joseph	1	1	1		
Spencer, Joseph, Junr	1	2	3		
Sprague, Alden	2		4		
Stevens, Samuel	3	3	4		
Taylor, Thomas	1	1	3		
Taylor, Eliphalet	1	3	3		
Tucker, Isaac	1		1		
Walker, Abel	7	3	8		
Walker, Mathew	2	2	5		
Walker, Seth	6	3	5		
Weed, Samuel	1	4	4		
West, Benjamin	3		4		

NAME OF HEAD OF FAMILY.	Free white males of 16 years and upward, including heads of families.	Free white males under 16 years.	Free white females, including heads of families.	All other free persons.	Slaves.
CHARLESTOWN TOWN—continued.					
West, Timothy	3	1	8		
Wetherbee, Samuel	4	4	8		
Wheeler, Moses, Junr	2	1	5		
White, Elisha	2	1	3		
Willard, Francis Willoughby	3	3	6		
Willard, Jeremiah	1	2	1		
Willard, John	6	3	6		
Willard, Joseph	1		1		
Willard, Moses	4	1	3		
Willard, Samuel	3	3	4		
Wilson, Joseph	1	1	4		
CHESTERFIELD TOWN.					
Albee, Abner	1	1	3		
Albee, Peter	1	3	2		
Alexander, Ebenezer	1		2		
Ammidown, Jacob	1		3		
Atherton, Oliver	1	1	1		
Baldwin, Ephriam	1	1	1		
Baldwin, John	1		1		
Barrett, Zadock	2	2	4		
Bartlett, Zadock	1	4	3		
Bennett, Silas	2		1		
Bigelow, Isaac	1		1		
Bigelow, Isaac, Junr	2	1	3		
Bigelow, Russel	1		2		
Bingham, Chester	1	1	2		
Bingham, Gustavus	1	1	2		
Bingham, Nathaniel	3	1	5		
Bingham, Theodore	2	5	3		
Bishop, John	1	3	1		
Braley, John	1	5			
Brigham, Jotham	1		2		
Brigham, Oliver	1		1		
Britt, Seth	3	5	4		
Brown, John	2		3		
Brown, Oliver	1	1	1		
Buck, Elijah	1	3	4		
Bunker, Antipass	1		2		
Bunker, Antipass, 2d	2		3		
Burbee, Nicholas	1	1	3		
Caughlin, Richard	1	4	3		
Chaffin, Ephriam	1	2	2		
Chamberlain, Ithamer	2	3	4		
Chase, Abel	1	3	3		
Chase, Joshua	2	2	4		
Clarke, William	1	3	2		
Cobb, Sylvester	2	2	3		
Cobleigh, Eleazer	1	2	2		
Cobleigh, John	1	4	4		
Cobleigh, Jonathan	1	2			
Cobleigh, Oliver	3	1	3		
Coburn, Amos	2	3	4		
Coburn, Daniel	1	4	4		
Colburn, William	1	1	4		
Cole, Amasa	1	1	1		
Cole, Levi	1		2		
Coomes, Barhabas	1	2	1		
Cooper, Ebenezer	1	2	5		
Corban, Nathaniel	1	1	4		
Cressey, Aaron	1	2	5		
Cressey, Jonathan	1	3	3		
Cressey, Jonathan, 2d	1	2	4		
Cressey, Micheal	1		2		
Cutler, Lowamm	1		2		
Cutler, William	1	2	4		
Daby, Thomas	1	2	3		
Daniels, John	2	3	3		
Darling, John	1	5	1		
Davis, Amos	1	1	3		
Davis, Amos, 2d	2	2	4		
Davis, Ezra	2	2			
Davis, Hammond	1		1		
Davis, James	2	4	3		
Davis, Jonas	1	1	5		
Davis, Jonathan	1	4	4		
Davis, Joseph	1	2	1		
Davis, Reuben	1	2	3		
Davis, Simeon	2	1	4		
Davis, Solomon	1	6	2		
Davis, Thomas	2	3	3		
Davis, Zephaniah	1	1	2		
Day, Ezra	2	2	2		
Day, John	1	1	1		
Derby, Elnathan	1	1	3		
Dodge, Nathan	1	1	4		
Eager, Paul	1		4		
Eastman, James	1	2	6		
Emmons, Noah	2		1		

CHESHIRE COUNTY—Continued.

CHESTERFIELD TOWN—continued.

Name of head of family	Free white males of 16 years and upward, including heads of families.	Free white males under 16 years.	Free white females, including heads of families.	All other free persons.	Slaves.
Emmons, Noah, 2d	1	2	2		
Emmons, Sarah			4		
Evans, Zur	2		3		
Fairbank, Lucy		2	3		
Fairbank, Zenos	3	1	6		
Farnsworth, Edmund	2	1	4		
Farr, Aaron	2	2	6		
Farr, Abraham	1	1	2		
Farr, Asel	1	1	2		
Farr, Charles	1	1	2		
Farr, Daniel	2		4		
Farr, David	2		4		
Farr, Ebenezer	1	5	2		
Farr, Ephraim	3		4		
Farr, Isaac	1	2	4		
Farr, Jonathan	3		2		
Farr, Jonathan 2d	1		4		
Farr, Jonathan 3d	2	1	2		
Farr, Jonathan 4th	3	1	5		
Farr, Joshua	2	1	1		
Farr, Moses	1	2	4		
Farr, Samuel	1	2	2		
Farr, Samuel	2	1	3		
Farr, Thomas	1	1	1		
Farr, Thomas, 2d	1	1	3		
Farr, William	2	3	3		
Farwell, Benjamin	1	2	3		
Farwell, Calvin	1	1	1		
Farwell, Jonathan	2	3	6		
Farwell, Levi	1	1	5		
Farwell, Oliver	1	1	2		
Farwell, William	1	1	5		
Fisher, William	1		1		
Fisk, Aaron	1	5	2		
Fisk, Jacob	1		1		
Fletcher, Abel	3	4	2		
Fletcher, Ebenezer	2		2		
Fletcher, Samuel	1	2	5		
Fullum, Phinehas	1	2	5		
Gale, Asa	1	1	1		
Gale, Ebenezer	1		2		
Gale, Jonathan	2	2	4		
Garey, Sarah			2		
Gates, Jonathan	2	3	3		
Gould, Daniel	2	2	5		
Granger, Jonathan	2	2	3		
Green, John	1	1	1		
Green, Silas	1	2	1		
Hale, Jonathan R	1	2	2		
Hambleton, Samuel	1	6	2		
Harris, Abner	1		5		
Harris, John	1	4	3		
Harris, Pearly	1	1	3		
Harris, Thomas	1	1	2		
Hart, Samuel	2	2	3		
Harvey, Solomon	1		3		
Haskel, Benjamin	2	3	4		
Hastings, Andrew	2	4	4		
Hastings, Jonathan	1		1		
Hastings, Josiah	2	2	3		
Haywood, Ichabod	1	2	1		
Herrick, Shadrach	1	4	3		
Hervey, Ebenezer	4	2	3		
Hervey, Rufus	1	2	4		
Higgins, Charles	1	1	4		
Higgins, Joseph	1	3	2		
Higgins, Joseph	1	2	4		
Hildreth, Edward	3	2	6		
Hildreth, Isaac	1	3	3		
Hildreth, Jesse	1	1	1		
Hildreth, Joshua	1		3		
Hildreth, Lotan	1	1	2		
Hildreth, Martin	2	3	7		
Hildreth, Reuben	1	2	4		
Hildreth, Samuel	2	2	4		
Hildreth, William	2	4	2		
Hill, Torrent	2	2	2		
Holbrook, Daniel	1	1	2		
Holden, Lemuel	1	2	1		
Holmes, Calvin	1		1		
Holmes, Luther	1	1	2		
Holmes, Thomas	1		4		
Hooker, John	1	2	2		
Hopkins, Richard	2		1		
Hubbard, Amos	1	4	3		
Hubbard, Clarke	2		1		
Hubbard, Oliver	1	3	3		
Hudson, Benjamin	3	1	5		
Hutchinson, Benjamin	1		2		
Jackson, Eleazer	3	3	1		
Johnson, Abner	2	3	5		

CHESTERFIELD TOWN—continued.

Name of head of family	Free white males of 16 years and upward, including heads of families.	Free white males under 16 years.	Free white females, including heads of families.	All other free persons.	Slaves.
Johnson, Azel	4	1	1		
Johnson, Azel, 2d	1	1	1		
Johnson, Caleb	1	4	4		
Johnson, Charles	1	4	5		
Johnson, Isreal	1	4	3		
Johnson, Thomas	1	1	1		
Johnson, Zebediah	1	2	1		
Jordan, Amos	1		2		
Jordan, Eleazer	1	4	2		
Kimball, Mehitable	1	3	1		
Kingsbury, Abijah	1		2		
Kingsbury, Benjamin	1	2	1		
Kingsbury, Phillip	1	3	2		
Ladd, Timothy	3	1	3		
Latham, Auther	4	2	3		
Latham, James	1	3	1		
Lewis, Reuben	1	1	1		
Marble, Eleazer	1		2		
Marsh, Benjamin	1	2	4		
Marsh, Elisha	1	4	4		
Metcalf, Nathan	2	1	4		
Metcalf, Thomas	1	3	3		
Moore, Abner	2	2	4		
Morsman, Oliver	1	2	2		
Newhall, Josiah	1	1	2		
Newton, David	1		1		
Nichols, John	1		2		
Nichols, John, Junr	1	1	2		
Nichols, Samuel	1		1		
Oakham, Joseph	1		3		
Page, Daniel	2	3	5		
Parsons, Eliakim	1	1	2		
Partridge, Amos	1	2	4		
Partridge, Eli	4	3	3		
Partridge, Eli, 2d	3	2	3		
Partridge, Joseph	1	3	3		
Peacock, John	1				
Peacock, Samuel	1	2	7		
Peirce, John	1	4	1		
Phillips, John	1	2	7		
Phillips, Nathaniel	1	1	4		
Pomeroy, Eleazer	2	1	2		
Pomeroy, Solomon	1		4		
Powers, Ezekiel	2	5	3		
Powers, Mary	1	1	4		
Pratt, John	1	3	6		
Prentice, Joseph	2	2	7		
Pudney, Jonathan	1	4	2		
Randall, Antony	1		1		
Randall, Benajah	1	2	3		
Randall, Eleazer	1		4		
Randall, William	1	1	1		
Ray, Abel	2	3	5		
Ray, Reuben	1	1	3		
Reed, James	2	2	1		
Reed, James, 2d	1	1	3		
Reed, William	1	1	6		
Richardson, Silas	3	1	3		
Robens, David	2	2	2		
Robens, Robert	1		1		
Robertson, James	3	3	7		
Robertson, William	3	3	6		1
Rockwood, Elisha	1	3	3		
Safford, Ebenezer	1	3	1		
Sanderson, John	2		3		
Sanderson, John, 2d	1	2	2		
Sanderson, Thomas	2	2	3		
Scott, Ebenezer	1	2	1		
Scott, Nathan	3	1	6		
Scott, William	1	2	3		
Scovil, Ebenezer	2	2	2		
Secomb, Willis	1		8		
Shattuck, Jonathan	1	3	3		
Shurtliff, Asel	1	1	3		
Shurtliff, William	2		3		
Simons, William	2	1	2		
Smith, Aaron	2	1	3		
Smith, Amos	1	1	3		
Smith, Benjamin	1	2	3		
Smith, Daniel	1	2	2		
Smith, Joel	1	1	5		
Smith, Joseph	1	4	4		
Smith, Moses	2	2	4		
Smith, Reuben	1	1	3		
Smith, Thomas			1		1
Snow, Pliny	1	1	1		
Snow, Warren	2		3		
Snow, Zerubbabel	2	3	4		
Soper, Samuel	1	2	4		
Stearns, Abraham	2	4	2		
Stearns, Samuel	1	1	2		

CHESTERFIELD TOWN—continued.

Name of head of family	Free white males of 16 years and upward, including heads of families.	Free white males under 16 years.	Free white females, including heads of families.	All other free persons.	Slaves.
Stearns, Submitt	1	1	5		
Stockwell, Abraham	1	1	1		
Stoddard, David	1	6	3		
Stoddard, Eleazer	1		4		
Stoddard, Lemuel	1	2	1		
Stoddard, Thomas	1	2	3		
Stone, Benjamin	1	3	5		
Stone, Nathaniel	1	1	1		
Stone, Peter	2	3	3		
Streater, Amos	1	3	4		
Streater, Barzilla	1	2	4		
Streater, Benjamin	2	2	4		
Streater, Ebenezer	2		2		
Streater, Enoch	1	1	2		
Streater, Nehemiah	1	1	2		
Taft, Jonathan	1	1	5		
Tarbell, Nathan	1	3	5		
Thomas, Aaron	1		3		
Thomas, Amos	1	2	4		
Thomas, William	2		5		
Thompson, Silas	4	4	7		
Tinney, Daniel	2	1	2		
Titus, Joseph	1	5	6		
Tory, Josiah	1	3	2		
Tucker, Jonathan	1		1		
Tyler, Joshua	1	2	4		
Walker, Samuel	1	3	4		
Walton, Laurance	1		3		
Walton, Nathaniel	1	3	2		
Warden, Nathan	1	2	5		
Warner, Martin	1		5		
Welch, Rebecca			3		
Wetherbee, Hezekiah	1	3	4		
Wetherbee, Joab	1	2	4		
Wheeler, Benjamin	1	1	1		
Wheeler, Benjamin	2	2	4		
Wheeler, Ephraim	1	1	1		
Wheeler, Ephraim	2		3		
Wheeler, James	1		1		
Wheeler, James	2	4	3		
Wheeler, Jeremiah	1	1	4		
Wheeler, Joseph	3		2		
Wheeler, Peter	4	2	3		
Wheeler, Randell	1	1	4		
Whitney, Daniel	1	3	1		
Whitney, Ephraim	1		5		
Whitney, Ephriam	2	1	5		
Whitney, Joel	1	1	3		
Whitney, Micah	1		1		
Willard, Gipson	2	2	3		
Willard, Simon	5	2	9		
Witt, Artimas	1	2	3		
Wood, Abraham	1	3	5		
Wood, Ebenezer	1		1		
Wood, Eliphalet	1	2	4		
Wood, Silas	1	2	4		
Wyman, Silas	1	2	7		

CLAREMONT TOWN.

Name of head of family	Free white males of 16 years and upward, including heads of families.	Free white males under 16 years.	Free white females, including heads of families.	All other free persons.	Slaves.
Ainsworth, Edward	4		2		
Alden, Benjamin	1	3	3		
Alden, James	1	2	6		
Alden, John	2	2	5		
Allen, Moses	1	1	2		
Andrews, Elisha	3	1	1		
Andrews, Martin	1	2	1		
Andrews, Whiting	1	2	2		
Ashley, Luther	1	2	2		
Ashley, Oliver	3	1	4		
Ashley, Samuel	2		3		
Ashley, Samuel, Junr	2	2	5		
Atkins, Daniel	1	1	4		
Atkins, David	1	4	3		
Atkins, Elizabeth			1	3	
Atkins, John		1		3	
Atkins, Reuben	1		2		
Atkins, Samuel	1	3	2		
Atkins, Timothy	1	4	2		
Barnes, Bill	5	4	3		
Batchelor, Abel	1		2		
Belfield, Mary		1	2		
Blodgett, John	1	2	2		
Boldereye, James	2	1	3		
Bradley, Isaac	1	2	6		
Brooks, Barnabas	1	1	6		
Brooks, Cornelius	2	6	4		
Buckman, David	1	1	2		
Buckman, David, Junr	1	2	4		
Bunnel, Abel	1	2	2		
Carter, Thomas	1	2	2		

CHESHIRE COUNTY—Continued.

CLAREMONT TOWN—con.

NAME OF HEAD OF FAMILY.	Free white males of 16 years and upward, including heads of families.	Free white males under 16 years.	Free white females, including heads of families.	All other free persons.	Slaves.
Chaffin, David	2		2		
Chaffin, Timothy	2	2	2		
Clap, Roswell	1	1	2		
Clarke, Ethan	1	1	1		
Clarke, John	1	2	1		
Clarke, Joseph	1		2		
Clarke, Theophilus	2	1	2		
Cleveland, Benjamin	1	1	4		
Cleveland, Isaac	1	2	4		
Conant, Amos	1	3	4		
Cook, John	2	2	4		
Corey, Oliver	1	2	3		
Cossitt, Ambrose	1	3	6		
Cowles, Phinehas	1	1	3		
Cowles, Timothy	2	2	3		
Cushman, Ambrose	2		3		
Davis, Peter	1	3	2		
Derick, Ephriam	1	1	5		
Dickinson, Ashbel	6		2		
Dodge, David	3	1	4		
Dodge, David, Junr	1		1		
Duncan, John	1	1	4		
Dustin, Moody	1		3		
Dustin, Thomas	1	1	5		
Dustin, Timothy	1	7	3		
Dutton, John	2		4		
Edson, Ebenezer	1		2		
Ellis, Barnabas	3	5	3		
Ellis, Gideon	1	2	2		
Ellsworth, Oliver	2	1	4		
Erskine, Christopher	1		2		
Erskine, James	1	1	1		
Farrington, Ichabod	1	2	2		
Farrington, Samuel	1	3	2		
Field, Hannah			1		
Fielding, Ebenezer	2	1	5		
Fisher, Abraham	1	2	1		
Fisher, Jeremiah	1		1		
Fisher, Josiah	3	2	2		
Fisher, Timothy	1	2	3		
Ford, Daniel	1	2	4		
Geer, Shubael	4	2	4		1
Goodwin, James	1	2	5		
Goodwin, Thomas	2	1	1		
Goss, John	2	6	4		
Goss, Nathaniel	1	2	7		
Grandy, Asa	1	2	2		
Grannis, Timothy	2	4	3		
Green, Daniel	2	3	7		
Gregory, Dotty		1	1		
Gustin, Ezra	1	1	1		
Hawley, Richard	2		5		
Henderson, Gideon	3	3	2		
Hide, Gershom	2	1	5		
Higby, Charles	1	4	4		
Higby, Levi	1	3	1		
Higby, Stephen	1		1		
Hill, George	1		1		
Hitchcock, Icabod	1	3	4		
Hitchcock, John	1	5	3		
Hubbard, George	3	2	6		
Huntoon, Reuben	1	1	3		
Ives, Elizabeth	2	2	2		
Jones, Asa	2	4	4		
Jones, Asa, Junr	2	3	3		
Jones, Ezra	1	6	7		
Jones, Jabez	1		2		
Jones, Thomas	1	1	3		
Judd, Brewster	1	1	2		
Judd, Ebenezer	2		2		
Judd, Enoch	1		1		
Judd, Truman	1	2	1		
Kibberlinger, John	1	4	3		
Kibbey, Phillip	1	1	1		
Kilburn, Hannah	2		1		
Kingsbury, Richard	1	1	1		
Kingsbury, Sansford	3	1	3		
Kirtland, Gideon	2		2		
Knight, Amasa	2	2	5		
Laine, Samuel	1		2		
Lawrance, Benjamin	1	1	2		
Leach, Asa	1	4	2		
Leet, A. Rayner	1	2	2		
Leet, Asa	2		2		
Leet, Benjamin	1	4	5		
Leet, Ezekiel	1	1	1		
Livermore, Abraham	1	4	4		
McCoy, William	1		4		
Marsh, Isaac	1	1	1		
Mathews, Abner	2	2	4		
Mathews, David	1	1	3		
Mathews, Hubbard	1	2	2		

CLAREMONT TOWN—con.

NAME OF HEAD OF FAMILY.	Free white males of 16 years and upward, including heads of families.	Free white males under 16 years.	Free white females, including heads of families.	All other free persons.	Slaves.
Mathews, Jesse, Junr	1		3		
Mathews, Joel	1	2	2		
Mathews, Mary		1	2		
Meigs, Abner	2	4	1		
Mitcham, Asa	2	2	2		
Mitcham, James	4	1	4		
Moore, John	2	1	5		
Morgan, Isaac	1	2	5		
Murray, Beriah	5	5	3		
Nichols, Robert	1	3	3		
Norton, Levi	1	1	2		
Norton, Miner	1		1		
Osgood, William	2	5	4		
Pardy, Levi	1	1	1		
Parker, Jonathan	1	2	3		
Parker, Phinehas	1	1	1		
Parmala, Oliver	1	4	5		
Peake, John	3		3		
Peck, Jared	1	3	4		
Perkins, Alexander	1	1	4		
Perry, Thomas	1		4		
Peterson, Benjamin	1		1		
Peterson, Ephriam	1	2	4		
Petty, Reuben	2	1	7		
Plant, Ely	1	1	4		
Pollard, Abiather	1	1	3		
Putnam, Solomon	2	3	4		
Ralstone, Alexander	3	4	7		
Raymond, Benjamin	1		1		
Raymond, John	1	3	4		
Rice, Abel	1	1	8		
Rice, Ebenezer	4	1	2		
Rice, Hezekiah	2	3	5		
Rice, Jacob	1	1	1		
Rice, Josiah, Junr	1		2		
Rice, Nehemiah	2	3	4		
Rice, Reuben	1		1		
Rice, Shubael	1		2		
Rich, David	3		3		
Rich, Josiah	1	3	3		
Richardson, Jedediah	1	3	5		
Richardson, Oliver	1		2		
Robertson, Asher	1	1	3		
Robertson, Eliphalet	1		2		
Robertson, Robert	1		2		
Russel, Moses	1	3	4		
Scott, Abraham	1		1		
Scott, Ard	1	1	3		
Shaw, Jonathan	2	2	1		
Shaw, Jonathan, Junr	1		1		
Sheldone, Elisha	1	1	2		
Simes, William	2	4	5		
Smith, Levi	1	1	2		
Smith, Nathan	2	1	2		
Spafford, Amherst	1	1	2		
Spafford, Moses	1		1		
Spaulding, Abel	1	3	1		
Spaulding, Joseph	1	1	1		
Spencer, Jeremiah	2	2	6		
Spencer, Reuben	1	1	1		
Sperry, Ebenezer	1	5	2		
Sperry, Joseph	1	2	1		
Sprague, John	1	1	2		
Sprague, John, Junr	1	1	1		
Stebbins, John	1		5		
Stedman, David	1	2	3		
Sterne, Thomas	3	2	6	1	1
Sternes, Daniel	1	4	2		
Sternes, Samuel	1	1	2		
Stevens, Eliakim	1		2		
Stevens, Elihu	2		4		
Stevens, Elihu, Junr	1		5		
Stevens, Henry	3	1	1		
Stevens, Josiah	2	1	3		
Stevens, Meigs	1		1		
Stevens, Roswell	1	2	2		
Stevens, Ziba	1	1	3		
Steward, Jacob	2		4		
Steward, Jonas	1	6	3		
Stone, David	1		2		
Stone, Matthias	2	2	2		
Stone, Moses	1		2		
Stone, Samuel	1	1	3		
Strowbridge, George	1	2	2		
Strowbridge, James	1		2		
Strowbridge, John	3	2	4		
Strowbridge, William	2	4	1		
Sumner, Benjamin	4	3	5	1	
Sumner, Samuel	1		1		
Taylor, Robert	1	3	3		
Thomas, John	2		3		
Thomas, Zara	1	2	2		

CLAREMONT TOWN—con.

NAME OF HEAD OF FAMILY.	Free white males of 16 years and upward, including heads of families.	Free white males under 16 years.	Free white females, including heads of families.	All other free persons.	Slaves.
Thomas, Zina	1		1		
Tuttle, Gershom	1	1	3		
Tuttle, Oliver	2	1	6		
Tuttle, Solomon	1	2	1		
Tyler, Benjamin	4	1	2		
Tyler, Ephriam	1	3	4		
Walker, Samuel	1	1	2		
Warner, Daniel	1		2		
Warner, Daniel, Junr	1	1	4		
West, John	2	3	2		
Whiston, Joseph	1		2		
White, James	3	2	2		
White, Phillip	1	1	4		
Whitney, Abner	3	3	3		
Whittle, Samuel	1	4	4		
Wilkins, Andrew	1	2	2		
Wilson, Asa	1	1	2		
Wilson, Joseph	1	3	4		
Woodcock, Benjamin	1		2		
Works, Samuel	1	1	5		
Wright, Samuel	1	1	4		
York, David	1	1	1		
York, Jonathan	1	2	2		
York, Joseph	2		1		
York, William	1	1	4		
CORNISH TOWN.					
Aplin, Oliver	2		2		1
Ayres, Thomas	1		3		
Backus, Simon	1	3	5		
Barrows, Moses, Junr	2	1	2		
Bartlett, John	3		3		
Bartlett, Joseph	1	1	1		
Bartlett, Nathaniel	1	1	3		
Bingham, Elias	1	6	2		
Bingham, Elisha W	1	2	1		
Bingham, Jonathan	1	1	1		
Bryant, Isreal	1		1		
Bryant, Sylvanus	1	4	2		
Cady, Elias	2	1	5		
Cady, Nicholas	1	2	3		
Carpenter, Nathaniel	1	3	3		
Cate, Eleazer	1		1		
Cate, James	1	1	1		
Chase, Caleb	1	2	6		
Chase, Caleb, 2d	1		4		
Chase, Daniel	2	1	4		
Chase, Dudley	2	1	4	1	
Chase, John	2	1	2		
Chase, Jonathan	4	2	7		
Chase, Joseph	1	1	3		
Chase, Joshua	1	1	1		
Chase, Moses	4	2	4		
Chase, Moses, Junr	1	2	2		
Chase, Nahum	1	1	4		
Chase, Peter	2	2	5		
Chase, Samuel	1		1		
Chase, Samuel, Junr	4	3	10		
Chase, Simeon	2	1	3		
Chase, Solomon	3	3	4		
Chase, Stephen	1		3		
Chase, William	1	1	1		
Child, Stephen	2	2	6		
Choate, William	1	2	5		
Cobb, Ebenezer	1		2		
Cobb, Francis	1	3	3		
Colburn, Asa	1	4	2		
Colburn, Dudley	2	2	2		
Colburn, Merril	1	2	5		
Cole, Benjamin	1	1	2		
Cole, John	1	3	2		
Colton, Caleb	1	2	5		
Cotlin, Bybe L	2	1	1		
Cummings, Benjamin	2	5	4		
Cummings, Samuel	4	2	6		
Cummings, Warren	1		1		
Curtis, Nathaniel	1	1	2		
Davis, David	1	4	2		
Deming, Ebenezer	3		2		
Deming, William	2		1		
Dorr, Benjamin	1	1	2		
Dunlap, Robert	1	1	4		
Dustin, Nathaniel	1	3	3		
Fairbanks, Abel	1	6	1		
Fitch, Hezekiah	1	2	2		
Fitch, Samuel	2	1	5		
Fitch, Zebediah	1	4	4		
French, Ephraim	1	2	6		
Furguson, John	2	2	2		
Furnal, William	1	5	1		
Gibbs, Eliakim	1	3	3		

CHESHIRE COUNTY—Continued.

NAME OF HEAD OF FAMILY.	Free white males of 16 years and upward, including heads of families.	Free white males under 16 years.	Free white females, including heads of families.	All other free persons.	Slaves.	NAME OF HEAD OF FAMILY.	Free white males of 16 years and upward, including heads of families.	Free white males under 16 years.	Free white females, including heads of families.	All other free persons.	Slaves.	NAME OF HEAD OF FAMILY.	Free white males of 16 years and upward, including heads of families.	Free white males under 16 years.	Free white females, including heads of families.	All other free persons.	Slaves.
CORNISH TOWN—con.						CORNISH TOWN—con.						CROYDON TOWN—con.					
Hall, Benjamin	1	5	3			Wilson, Robert	1	1	3			Whipple, Aaron	1	1	2		
Hall, Moody	3	2	2			Woodward, Joshua	1	1	3			Whipple, Moses	3	3	4		
Hall, Nathaniel	1	2	3			Wyman, Jesse	2	2	3			Whipple, Moses, Junr	1		3		
Hall, Thomas	1		1			Young, Thomas	1		4			Whipple, Thomas	2	3	3		
Hall, Thomas, Junr	1	2	1									White, Constant	1	2	4		
Hambleton, Joseph	1	3	3			CROYDON TOWN.						Williams, William	1	1	3		
Harlow, James	1	3	2									Winter, Ebenezer	1	2	2		
Harlow, Robert	1		1			Bardeen, Moses	1	3	4			Woodcock, Jeremiah	1	1	3		
Haskell, John	1	1	5			Bowen, William	1	1	1								
Hildreth, Joel	1	2	1			Burdon, Simon	1	1	2			DUBLIN TOWN.					
Hildreth, Samuel	1	1	2			Burton, Bazaleel	2	2	4								
Hillyard, Luther	2		3			Burton, Benjamin	2	3	4			Adams, Isaac	1		1		
Hillyard, Samuel	3	2	3			Claflin, Timothy	2	2	1			Adams, James	4		1		
Huggins, David	1	1	8			Clarke, Nathaniel	3		1			Adams, Jonathan	1	1	5		
Huggins, Jonathan	2	2	5			Coit, Richard			1	1		Adams, Joseph	1		3		
Huggins, Nathaniel	2	3	2			Cooper, Barnabas	1	1	2			Adams, Moses	3	1	2		
Huggins, Samuel	3	3	3			Cooper, Ezra	3	3	5			Adams, Timothy	2		2		
Hunter, James	2	1	1			Cooper, Joel	1		3			Allen, Josiah	1	2	1		
Jackson, Benjamin	1	3	3			Cooper, John	1		1			Ames, John	1	2	2		
Jackson, Eleazer	2	4	2			Cooper, John, Junr	1	4	3			Ames, Jonathan	1	5	4		
Jackson, Micheal	1	2	5			Cooper, Samuel	1		5			Ames, Stephen	2		2		
Jackson, Perez	2		1			Cooper, Sherman	1	1	3			Appleton, Francis	1		1		
Jackson, Stephen	1		4			Cummings, Moses	2		2			Appleton, Isaac	1		2		
Jerould, Reuben	2		4			Cutting, Benjamin	1	2	5			Babcock, Amos	1	3	1		
Johnson, Abel	1	1	3			Cutting, Francis	1		1			Babcock, Ebenezer	1		3		
Johnson, Abraham	2		3			Cutting, John	1	1	3			Barrett, Jeremiah	1	1	6		
Johnson, Jesse	1		3			Cutting, Mary		2	4			Barrett, John	1	1	3		
Johnson, Joshua	2		1			Darling, Herculas	1		1			Bayley, Joseph	1	1	1		
Kimball, Edward	1	3	3			Davis, Solomon	1	4	5			Belknap, Nathaniel	1	3	5		
Kimball, Eliphalet	2		2			Dwinell, Amos	1	2	2			Bent, Stephen	2	1	2		
Kimball, Eliphalet, Junr	1		1			Dwinell, Archelus	1	3	3			Bigsby, Nathan	3	4	5		
Kimball, Lovewell	1		3			Eggleston, Timothy	1	1	3			Bond, Jonas	3		3		
Lucas, John	1	1	4			Elliot, James	1	3	5			Brown, Silas	1	3	2		
Lucy, Thomas	1	1	2			Elliot, John	1	1	5			Bullard, Simeon	1	3	5		
Lucy, William	1	2	4			Elliot, Thaddeus	2	2	2			Caldwell, John	1	2	2		
Luther, Caleb	1	5	4			Glidden, William	1		2			Chamberlain, James	2	1	3		
McCauley, Samuel	1		1			Gorden, Thomas	2		2			Clarke, William	1	1	2		
Machrees, Samuel	1	1	3			Green, Jesse	1	4	2			Cobb, Ebenezer	1	2	4		
Morse, Jeremiah	1		1			Hager, Amos	1	3	4	1		Cobb, Seth	1	3	1		
Morse, John	1	2	5			Hall, Abijah	1	4	1			Coffrin, James	3		2		
Nutter, Thomas I	1		1			Hall, Edward	1		1			Coffrin, John	1		1		
Page, Joshua	1	3	5			Hall, Edward, Junr	1	2	1			Eames, Ebenezer	1		8		
Paine, William	1	6	4			Hall, Emmerson	1	3	3			Elliot, David	3	1	4		
Parker, Stephen	1	1	2			Hall, Ezekiel	1	3	4			Ellison, Andrew	1	1	2		
Pike, Samuel	2		3			Hall, Ezra	1		1			Emory, Amos	2	2	3		
Plastridge, Caleb	1	5	3			Hall, John	1		3			Fairbanks, Asa	1	2	2		
Pratt, Stephen	1	1	1			Hall, Samuel R	1	3	6			Farnum, Joshua	1	1	5		
Putnam, Daniel	3		5			Hill, James	2		5			Fisher, Samuel	1	1	5		
Reecord, Lemuel	1	2	2			How, Mary	1		3			French, John	3		3		
Reed, Benjamin	1	1	2			Hudson, John	1	1	3			Gates, Oldham	1	1	3		
Reed, David	2	4	2			Humphrey, John	1	1	1			Gilchrist, Richard	2	2	5		
Reed, Elisha	1	2	3			Kimton, Ephriam	3	3	3			Gleason, Daniel	1	1	2		
Reed, Jonathan	1	1	4			Kimton, Jeremiah	1		1			Gleason, Phinehas	1		2		
Richardson, Jonas	1	2	3			Kimton, Rufus	1	1	3			Gowin, William	2		1		
Ripley, William	3		3			Leland, Jacob	2		7			Greenwood, Bela	1	1	1		
Roberts, Absolam	1	2	2			Marsh, Samuel	2	2	4			Greenwood, Eli	2	1	2		
Roberts, Daniel	1	2	4			Melendy, Ebenezer	1	3	3			Greenwood, Isaac	1	1	3		
Shapley, Jabez	2		4			Melendy, John	1	2	4			Greenwood, Joseph	1		1		
Shapley, Thomas	1	1	3			Metcalf, Abel	1		2			Greenwood, Joshua	1	4	3		
Smith, Benjamin	1		4			Metcalf, Obed	1		1			Greenwood, Joshua	1	1	4		
Smith, David	2		3			Metcalf, Samuel	2		2			Greenwood, Josiah	3		3		
Smith, Ichabod	1	3	2			Nelson, Moses	1	2	4			Greenwood, Moses	1	4	4		
Smith, Joseph	1	1	2			Newton, Phinehas	1	4	5			Greenwood, Nathaniel	1	2	3		
Smith, William	1	2	2			Noyce, John	1		2			Greenwood, William	1	1	4		
Spaulding, Abel	2		4			Parker, Henshaw	1	3	3			Guyer, Bartholomew	1	3	3		
Spaulding, Andrew	3		4			Partridge, Simeon	1		2			Hale, Ambrose	2	1	7		
Spaulding, Dier	3	1	2			Porter, Mathew	2	3	3			Hardy, Thomas	1	3	1		
Spaulding, Durius	1	3	2			Powers, Benjamin	1	1	2			Harris, Jason	1	2	1		
Spaulding, John	1	1	5			Powers, David	2	1	3			Haywood, Joseph	3	2	7		
Spicer, Jabez	1	4	3			Powers, Ezekiel	1	2	4			Haywood, William	1	2	4		
Stone, Josiah	1	4	3			Powers, Ezekiel, Junr	1		1			Hill, Ebenezer	4		5		
Taber, Phillip	2		2			Powers, John	1	5	4			Hoar, Jonathan	4				
Taylor, Joseph	1	1	5			Powers, Lemuel	1		1			Hogg, Samuel	1	2	7		
Thomas, Samuel	1	2	4			Powers, Samuel	2	1	3			Holt, Marston	2	1	3		
Thompson, Caleb	1	1	2			Powers, Stephen	3	2	3			Houghton, James	4	2	1		
Thompson, Loring	1	2	4			Powers, Uriah	1		1			Hunt, Isaac	1	2	1		
Thompson, Thomas	2		5			Putnam, Caleb	2	3	4			Hunt, Willard	1		3		
Tracy, Andrew	3	3	4			Putnam, David	1	1	6			Hymes, Abner	1	1	3		
Tucker, Abijah	3	1	3			Reccord, Abner	2	3	3			Jackson, Amos	1	1	2		
Tucker, Chester	1	1	1			Reed, John					1	Johnson, Simeon	2		3		
Vial, Abraham	1		1			Reed, Moses	1	2	2			Jones, Samuel	1	2	4		
Vincent, Richard	1		1			Rokes, Ezekiel	1	1	2			Kindell, Joel	1	1	1		
Vinton, John	2	3	4			Sanger, Phinehas	1	1				Knowlton, John	2	3	3		
Weld, John	3	4	5			Shirtliff, William	1	3	2			Knowlton, John, Junr	1	1	1		
Weld, Moses	1	1	6			Smart, Caleb	1	3	3			Knowlton, Solomon	1	1	1		
Weld, Walter	1	2	3			Sparhawk, Lucy	3	2	2			Larnard, Benjamin	3	4	3		
Wellman, James	2	1	2			Stockwell, David	1	5	3			Larnard, John	1	2	4		
Wellman, James, Junr	3	2	3			Stone, Uriah	1	4	2			Lewis, Mary			2		
Wellman, Solomon	1	1	1			Stow, Jonah	3	1	5			Little, Fortune				4	
Whiting, Nathan	1	2	3			Walker, Moses	1	2	2			Marshall, Aaron	1		3		
Whitten, John	2	2	9			Ward, Gershom	1	1	4			Mason, Bela	1	1	1		
Wickwire, Samuel	1		4			Wheeler, Nathaniel	1	4	4			Mason, Benjamin	1		1		
Williams, Benjamin	2	1	4			Wheeler, Seth	1	1	5			Mason, Benjamin, Junr	1	2	4		

CHESHIRE COUNTY—Continued.

NAME OF HEAD OF FAMILY.	Free white males of 16 years and upward, including heads of families.	Free white males under 16 years.	Free white females, including heads of families.	All other free persons.	Slaves.
DUBLIN TOWN—con.					
Mason, Joseph	2	2	7		
Mason, Moses	1	2	3		
Mason, Thaddeus	2	2	4		
Maynard, Abel	1	1	5		
Maynard, Isreal	1		2		
Mills, Phillip	2	2	2		
Morse, Amos	1	2	2		
Morse, Daniel	2	1	4		
Morse, Daniel, Junr	1		1		
Morse, Drury	1		2		
Morse, Eli	3		1		
Morse, Elizabeth			2		
Morse, Ezra	1	2	2		
Morse, Isaac	1		1		
Morse, John	2	1	3		
Morse, Reuben	2	3	4		
Muzzy, John	1	2	1		
Muzzy, Robert	1	1	1		
Muzzy, Robert, Junr	1	1	1		
Newton, Gideon	1	1	2		
Paine, John	1	3	4		
Parker, Abel	1	3	2		
Peirce, Silas	1		1		
Perry, Ivory	3	1	4		
Phillips, Richard	1	1	3		
Pratt, Asa	1	1	3		
Pratt, Moses	3		2		
Puffer, Jabez	2	1	2		
Rider, Moses	1	2	2		
Rollins, James	2	1	2		
Rollins, James, Junr	1	2	3		
Rollins, John	1	2	1		
Rollins, Joseph	1	1	4		
Rowell, Ichabod	2	1	2		
Russel, Amos	1	1	1		
Russel, Jonathan	1	1	3		
Russel, Simeon	1	2	2		
Russell, Stephen	1	3	3		
Sanger, Abner	1	2	2		
Simons, Daniel	3	1	2		
Smith, Benjamin	2	1	1		
Sprague, Edward	2		2		
Stanford, David	1		3		
Stanford, Josiah	2	1	4		
Stanford, Phinehas	1	2	3		
Stanley, Joshua	1	2	2		
Stone, John	2	1	4		
Strong, Richard	1	4	3		
Taggert, James	1	3	5		
Town, Gardner	2		2	1	
Townsend, David	2	4	5		
Twitchel, Abel	1	3	5		
Twitchel, Ebenezer	3	1	5		
Twitchel, Gersham	2		5		
Twitchel, Gersham, Junr	2	3	5		
Twitchel, Joseph	1	2	4		
Twitchel, Joshua	1	5	2		
Twitchel, Samuel	2	4	5		
Upton, James	1		2		
Upton, William	1		1		
Wakefield, Thomas	2	4	5		
Watkins, Zaccheus	1		2		
Wheeler, Lemuel	1	3	2		
White, Daniel	1	3	3		
White, Joel	2	2	4		
White, Thomas	1	2	6		
Whitney, Mercy			1		
Whittemore, Nathan	1		1		
Wight, John	2	1	5		
Wilder, Abel	1	3	4		
Wiley, Benjamin	1	3	3		
Wilkins, Jonathan	1		3		
Williams, Samuel	1	3	4		
Wright, John	2		3		
Yardly, William	1	2	4		
FITZWILLIAM TOWN.					
Adams, Daniel	1	4	3		
Adams, George	1		2		
Ammidown, Phillip	2	1	6		
Angier, Benjamin	1	2	1		
Angier, Silas	1	1	2		
Angier, Silas, Junr	2	3	1		
Babcock, Solomon	1	1	4		
Baker, Abel	1	1	1		
Barns, John	1	1	3		
Bellows, John	1	1	2		
Bent, Samuel	1	3	3		
Bigelow, Daniel	1		4		
Bigelow, Joseph	1	1	3		
Bishop, Agabus	2		6		

NAME OF HEAD OF FAMILY.	Free white males of 16 years and upward, including heads of families.	Free white males under 16 years.	Free white females, including heads of families.	All other free persons.	Slaves.
FITZWILLIAM TOWN—continued.					
Bishop, Agabus, Junr	3		1		
Bishop, Jesse	1	1	1		
Bowker, Bartlett	1	2	2		
Bowker, Charles	1	3	1		
Bowker, John	2	2	2		
Bowtell, Ebenezer	1	1	2		
Brewer, James	1	1	2		
Brigham, Benjamin	2	2	3		
Brigham, John	1	3	1		
Brigham, Levi	2	2	7		
Brigham, Mary			1		
Broadstreet, Jonathan	1		1		
Bulkeley, Nathaniel	2	1	1		
Burbank, Isaac	1		2		
Byam, Abel	2		2		
Byam, Benjamin	2	1	4		
Cameron, Duncan	2	2	5		
Camp, John	1		1		
Clarke, Calvin	1	2	4		
Clarke, Thomas	2	2	5		
Cobleigh, John	1	2	1		
Coburn, Silas	3	3	4		
Conant, Isaac	1		2		
Crane, William	1	2	5		
Crosby, Simon	1		2		
Cutler, John	1	2	1		
Cutting, Moses	1	2	6		
Davis, Samuel	1		3		
Davis, Zachariah	1		2		
Davison, Benjamin	2	1	6		
Deeth, Caleb	1		2		
Deeth, Pearly	1		1		
Deming, Oliver	1	2	1		
Drury, Moses	1	3	5		
Dunton, James	1	2	2		
Edey, Benjamin	1	1	2		
Estabrook, Abel	1	1	5		
Farrar, Daniel	2	3	4		
Farrar, John	1	1	3		
Farrar, William	2		2		
Fassett, John	4	1	3		
Fay, John	2	3	5		
Felton, Matthias	1	2	2		
Forrestall, Jesse	1	2	4		
Forrestall, Joseph	2	1	4		
Foster, Edward	2	2	3		
Foster, Joseph	2		1		
Freeman, Rufus	1	3	2		
Fullom, Francis	1	5	3		
Garfield, Dolly			1		
Gerry, James	1		2		
Goddin, John	1	1	3		
Goddin, Timothy	1		2		
Goodale, Asa	1	1	1		
Goodenough, Isaac	1		3		
Gould, Daniel	2		3		
Grant, Allen	1	4	2		
Griffin, Samuel	1	2	1		
Hall, Zaccheus	1	4	2		
Harrington, Joshua	2	3	5		
Harris, Stephen	2		2		
Hartwell, Josiah	1	1	2		
Haskell, Abner	2		2		
Haskell, Joseph	1		2		
Haskell, Josiah	1	4	2		
Haven, Jotham	1	6	1		
Hawkins, Abraham	1	4	2		
Hayden, Jesse	3	2	4		
Hayden, Joel	1	1	2		
Hemmenway, Joseph	1		1		
How, Daniel	1		1		
How, Nahum	1	1	3		
Jackson, Isaac	2	1	5		
Jackson, Isaac, Junr	1	2	2		
Johnson, Asa	1	4	3		
Johnson, Eliphalet	1	3	2		
Johnson, Susanah	1	1	1		
Kelly, Edward	1		2		
Kendall, Joshua	1	3	4		
Kendall, Samuel	4	2	5		
Knights, Jonas	2	3	6		
Lock, John	1	3	3		
Lock, William	1	2	6		
Mason, Eleazer	1	2	3		
Mellen, Pesah	1		3		
Miles, Joel	1	1	2		
Millen, Daniel	1		7		
Miller, Jacob	1	1	2		
Miller, Solomon	1		3		
Morse, Abner	1		1		

NAME OF HEAD OF FAMILY.	Free white males of 16 years and upward, including heads of families.	Free white males under 16 years.	Free white females, including heads of families.	All other free persons.	Slaves.
FITZWILLIAM TOWN—continued.					
Morse, James	1	3	3		
Morse, Joseph	1	4	2		
Muzzy, Nathaniel	1		4		
Nourse, Ebenezer	1	2	2		
Nourse, Joseph	1		1		
Nourse, Reuben	1	1	2		
Osgood, Mathew	1	3	2		
Parker, Ephriam	1	1	1		
Parker, Nahum	1	1	3		
Partrick, Samuel	2		3		
Patch, Samuel	2	2	3		
Patrick, Rufus	1	1	1		
Payson, Edward	2		4		
Peirce, Jonathan	1	1	6		
Perry, Micah	2	1	3		
Perry, Simeon	1	1	2		
Platts, Edward	2		3		
Potter, Ebenezer	1	3	4		
Pratt, Job	3	4	3		
Pratt, Reuben	3	1	4		
Pratt, Solomon	1	1	2		
Prescott, Hiram	2		1		
Pushee, David	2	1	2		
Reed, Joseph	1		4		
Reed, Phinehas	2		2		
Reed, Sylvanus	3	1	2		
Rice, Abraham	1		3		
Rice, David	1		1		
Richardson, Abijah	2	2	4		
Richardson, Stephen	2	1	2		
Rockwood, Samuel	1	1	3		
Sanders, David	2	4	4		
Sanders, Ebenezer	1	2	3		
Scott, Barachiah	2	2	1		
Scott, Benjamin	1		1		
Serjeant, Jacob	1	1	6		
Smith, Eli	1		1		
Smith, John	1	1	4		
Smith, Thaddeus	1	3	5		
Starkey, Peter	2	6	1		
Steward, Paul	1		1		
Stimpson, John	2		4		
Stockwell, Levi	1		2		
Stone, Abner	2	2	7		
Stone, Adam	1	1	2		
Stone, Hezekiah	1	3	3		
Stone, James	1	2	2		
Stone, Jason	2	1	2		
Stone, Joseph	1	1	4		
Stone, Samuel	1	3	4		
Sweetland, John	1	4	4		
Sweetser, Micheal	3	2	2		
Swift, David	1	1	1		
Toleman, Benjamin	1	3	1		
Toleman, Thomas	2	1	2		
Tower, Samuel	1	3	5		
Town, Elijah	1		1		
Townsend, Nathan	4	3	2		
Twitchell, Joshua	2	2	3		
Waite, Asa	2	3	3		
Wallace, Curwin	1	3	4		
Warner, Abijah	1	1	2		
Warren, Jonas	2	2	1		
Weare, Robert	1	2	2		
Wheeler, Silas	1	1	1		
Whitcomb, Francis	1		3		
Whitcomb, Oliver	1		2		
White, David	1	1	2		
White, Ezekiel	1	2	3		
White, Stephen	1		3		
Whitney, Joel	1	1	2		
Whitney, John	1	2	4		
Whitney, John, Junr	1	1	4		
Whitney, Jonathan	1	6	1		
Wilson, Artimas	1		2		
Wilson, Azariah	1	3	1		
Wilson, Nathaniel	2	1	1		
Wilson, Nathaniel, Junr	1		2		
Winch, Caleb	2	5	3		
Withington, William	2	4	5		
Wood, Jonas	1	4	4		
Woodbury, Peter	1	3	3		
Wright, Joel	2				
GILSOM TOWN.					
Adams, David	1	1	6		
Adams, Jonathan	1	1	2		
Ballard, James	1	1	2		
Bill, David	1		2		

CHESHIRE COUNTY—Continued.

NAME OF HEAD OF FAMILY.	Free white males of 16 years and upward, including heads of families.	Free white males under 16 years.	Free white females, including heads of families.	All other free persons.	Slaves.	NAME OF HEAD OF FAMILY.	Free white males of 16 years and upward, including heads of families.	Free white males under 16 years.	Free white females, including heads of families.	All other free persons.	Slaves.	NAME OF HEAD OF FAMILY.	Free white males of 16 years and upward, including heads of families.	Free white males under 16 years.	Free white females, including heads of families.	All other free persons.	Slaves.
GILSOM TOWN—con.						**HINSDALE TOWN—con.**						**JAFFREY TOWN—con.**					
Bill, Ebenezer	1	1	4			Frost, Joshua	2	2	3		2	Coleman, Aaron	1	2	4		
Bill, Samuel	2	1	4			Gardner, John	3	1	1		2	Crosby, Alpheus	1		2		
Bingham, John	1	4	2			Gay, Bunker	2	1	4			Cutter, David	1		1		
Blish, David	1	2	5			Gustin, Edward	1	3	2			Cutter, John	1	1	1		
Bliss, David	2	2	1			Gustin, Thomas	1		2			Cutter, Joseph	2	4	5		
Bliss, Jonathan	2	3	5			Hildreth, Edward	1	3	1			Cutter, Moses	1		3		
Bond, Elijah	1		2			Hill, Jesse	1	3	2			Cutter, Nathan	1	1	4		
Bond, Elisha	1		1			Hubbard, Ephriam	2	3	7			Darling, Amos	1		2		
Bond, Stephen	1	1	3			Jones, Lydia	1		6		2	Davidson, Charles	1	1	2		
Church, Jonathan	1		4			Lester, William	1	1	3			Davidson, John	2		2		
Clarke, Jonathan	1		1			Linkfield, Benjamin	2		3			Davidson, Thomas	1	2	1		
Clarke, Samuel	1	1	2			Linkfield, Edward	1		3			Davis, John	2		1		
Corey, Joshua	1	1	2			McCoy, Vine	1	1	1			Davis, John, Junr	1	2	4		
Corey, Samuel	1		2			Moore, Abel	1					Davis, John Gordon	2		1		
Crocker, Gershom	2	1	4			Morgan, Edward	3		2			Davis, Richard	2	6	4		
Dart, Ebenezer	1		2			Nettleton, Edward	1		2			Dean, Hiram	1	3	4		
Dart, Jesse	1	3	2			Peacock, John	2	1	1			Dean, Jonathan	1	1	6		
Dart, John	1		2			Perlin, John	1	3	1			Dole, Benjamin	2	2	4		
Dart, Roger	1		4			Robens, Samuel	1	4	2			Dunshe, Thomas	1	2	2		
Dart, Thomas	1		1			Rockwood, Micah	2	1	1			Dutton, Thomas	3	3	4		
Dart, Thomas, Junr	1	2	4			Rockwood, Thomas	1	3	5			Eaton, David	1	3	2		
Dart, Timothy	1	1	6			Sanger, Nathaniel	1	1	1			Eaton, John	1		1		
Davis, John	1	1	6			Sanger, Nathaniel, Junr	1	1	2			Emes, Moses	1	1	4		
Ellis, John	1		3			Shattuck, Cyrus	3	2	7			Emory, Daniel	3		2		
Hammond, Aaron	2	2	3			Shattuck, Gidion	1	2	1			Emory, Daniel	3	2	4		
Haywood, Sylvanus	1	4	4			Shattuck, Makepeace	1	1	3			Emory, Jonathan	1		1		
Holdridge, Jehiel	2	1	4			Shattuck, William	3	3	5			Emory, Noah	1	2	4		
Hurd, Ebenezer	1	1	4			Shephardson, Amos	1	3	1			Emory, Samuel	1		1		
Hurd, Justus	2		2			Smith, Jedediah	1	3	5			Emory, William	1	1	1		
Hurd, Robert L	1	1	1			Soule, Ivory	2	1	2			Etridge, George	1	2	3		
Hurd, Zadock	1	3	1			Stearns, Nathaniel	1	2	4			Fisk, Thomas	2	2	3		
Johnson, Jesse	1	1	2			Stebbins, Elihu	1		4			Fitch, Paul	3	1	6		
Kilburne, Ebenezer	3	3	5			Streater, John	1	4	3			Fortune, Amos					4
Mack, Bazaleel	1	1	2			Taylor, Hollis	1	4	4			Foster, Lucy			1	2	
Mack, Stephen	2		2			Taylor, Sarah	5	2	3			French, David	1	2	3		
Mark, John	1	3	5			Thomas, Daniel	1	2	2			French, James	1	1	4		
Peas, Peletiah	3	2	2			Thomas, Nathan	1	3	5			French, James, Junr	1	2	3		
Plumley, Joseph	1	1	3			Thomas, William	2	3	5			French, John	3		5		
Reding, Thomas	1	2	5			Tower, Benjamin	1		6			French, Thomas	1		3		
Reed, Josiah	2	1	6			Welch, John	1	1	1			Frost, Benjamin	1	3	3		
Severance, Ebenezer	1	1	2			Wilder, Tilley	1		6			Gage, James	3	1	3		
Severance, Phillip	1		1			Willard, Allyn	1	2	2			Gilmore, John	3	1	3		
Taylor, Simeon	2		1			Winslow, Luther	1	3	3			Gilmore, Robert	1	2	5		
Weare, Comfort	1	1	2			Wright, Aaron	2		4			Gilmore, Roger	3	2	4		
Weare, Moses	3	1	3			Wright, Durius	1		1			Goff, Thomas	1	1	1		
White, Turner	1	1	6			Wright, Eldad	4	1	4			Gould, Oliver	1	2	3		
Whitney, Samuel	1	3	3			Wright, Remembrance	1	3	1			Gould, Oliver, Junr	1	2	3		
Willcox, Eleazer	1	3	6									Gowin, James	2	2	2		
Wood, Joseph	1	1	2			**JAFFREY TOWN.**						Gragg, Hugh	1	2	5		
Wright, Daniel	1		3			Adams, Jonas	1	2	2			Green, Nehemiah	1	3	4		
						Adams, Phillip	2	1	4			Griffin, Dudley	1	6	2		
HINSDALE TOWN.						Adams, Samuel	1	3	4			Hale, John	1	2	4		
Allyn, Daniel	1	4	3			Adams, Thomas	1	1	2			Hale, Oliver	2	2	7		
Annis, Joseph	1	1	3			Ainsworth, Laban	1	1	3			Hall, Amos	1	2	4		
Barrett, Elijah	1	2	3			Avory, David	2	2	4			Hall, Nathan	2	3	5		
Barrett, John	2	2	2			Bacon, Oliver	1	2	2			Hardy, Nathaniel	1	3	4		
Barrett, Jonathan	1	5	1			Baldwin, Jacob	1		2			Harkness, Robert	2		1		
Barrett, Oliver	1	1	5			Bates, Joseph	3		3			Harper, John	1	3	6		
Barrett, Phillip	1	3	2			Bates, Joseph, Junr	1	4	1			Harrington, Seth	1		4		
Barrett, Silas	2	1	6			Bayley, David	2		2			Hathan, Ebenezer	1	2	1		
Barrett, Simeon	1		2			Bayley, Isaac	2		2			Hathan, Ebenezer	2	1	8		
Batchelor, Samuel	1		3			Bayley, Isaac, Junr	1		2			Hathan, Sarah	1	1	5		
Beebee, Timothy	1	7	2			Belknap, Josiah	2					Haywood, James	2	1	2		
Bellding, Elisha	2		5			Berdoo, Lois					6	Hedley, Abraham	1	3	3		
Blanchard, Aaron	1	1	2			Blodgett, Jonathan	2		1			Hogg, Joseph	1	2	7		
Burnham, Billy	2	3	2			Blodgett, Jonathan, Jur	1	2	3			Holt, Jonathan	1	3	2		
Butler, Josiah	2	2	11			Bowers, Benjamin	1	2	2			Holt, Thomas	1	2	3		
Butler, Thomas	2	1	2			Boynton, Amos	2	2	4			Horton, Joseph	1	3	3		
Butler, Valintine	1	1	1			Boynton, Nathan	1	4	3			Houghton, Abel	1		1		
Carver, Jonathan	1	1	2			Breed, Nathaniel	1		3			Houghton, James	1	1	2		
Chase, Ezekiel	1		4			Brigham, Alpheus	2	1	2			How, Adonijah	2	3	3		
Cooper, Aaron	1	4	3			Brooks, Joseph	1	1	6			Howard, Benjamin	2	4	1		
Cooper, Elijah	1	2	4			Brown, Daniel	1	3	2			Hunt, Nathan	1	1	2		
Darling, Dennis	1	2	2			Bryant, Daniel C	1	2	3			Ingalls, Josiah	1	3	4		
Delano, John	1	1	2			Bryant, John	2	1	6			Jacwith, Ebenezer	1	1	3		
Densmore, Gershom	2	2	3			Bryant, Kindall	1		2			Jacwith, Samuel	1		2		
Dewey, Widdow			4			Bryant, Samuel	2	1	3			Jewett, David	2	1	4		
Doolittle, Oliver	3	2	4			Bryant, Thomas	2		1			Jones, Abigal	1		3		
Eaton, Ephriam	2		2			Bulkeley, John	1	2	2			Joslin, John	1	2	3		
Elger, Waitsdel	1		1			Burpey, Moses	3	1	3			Joslin, Samuel	1	1	2		
Elmer, Hezekiah	2	1	3			Buss, Samuel	2	2	4			Kent, John	1	2	4		
Elmer, Hezekiah, Junr	1	2	1			Buttress, John	1	2	2			Lacy, David	1	1	2		
Elmer, John	1	1	3			Buttress, Simeon	1	2	2			Larrance, Benjamin	1	5	3		
Evans, Eldad	4	1	4			Carter, James	1	1	2			McAllester, William	3	2	4		
Evans, John	1	3	3			Carter, Oliver	1	3	4			Marshall, William	2	2	3		
Evans, Urial	1	5	5			Chadwick, David	1	1	4			Mathews, John	1	1	2		
Fisher, Daniel	4		2			Chamberlain, John	1	4	4			Maynard, Jesse	1		2		
Fisher, Ebenezer	2	2	4			Chamberlain, Joseph	2		2			Maynard, Lemuel	4	2	4		
Fisher, Jeremiah	1	2	2			Chaplin, Hezekiah	2		3			Moore, Thomas	2	1	5		
Fisher, William	1					Chaplin, Samuel	1	3	1			Mulligan, Alexander	2	1	4		
Flagg, Asa	1		1									Nourse, Peter	2	5	4		

CHESHIRE COUNTY—Continued

JAFFREY TOWN—con.

NAME OF HEAD OF FAMILY.	Free white males of 16 years and upward, including heads of families.	Free white males under 16 years.	Free white females, including heads of families.	All other free persons.	Slaves.
Nutting, Benjamin	2	3	1		
Page, Serjeant	1	3	4		
Parker, Abel	1	4	2		
Parker, Samuel	2		1		
Peabody, Moses	1	1	4		
Peirce, Jacob	1	3	5		
Peirce, Samuel	1	2	5		
Perkins, Joseph	3	2	4		
Perry, Daniel	1		1		
Pope, William	1		1	1	
Powers, Whitcomb	1		2		
Prescott, Benjamin	2	3	4		
Prescott, Oliver	1	2	2		
Priest, Daniel	2	4	4		
Priest, Jonathan	1	2	2		
Proctor, Oliver	1		1		
Pushee, John	1	3	2		
Rice, Caleb	1		1		
Richards, Edward	1	1	2		
Richardson, Tilley	1	1	4		
Rider, Aaron	2	3	5		
Ross, Abraham	2	1	4		
Russel, Joel	1		2		
Sanders, Samuel	1	2	1		
Sawyer, Rufus	1	1	1		
Serjeant, Lemuel	2		3		
Smiley, William	5		5		
Snow, Jesse	1		3		
Spafford, Eleazer	4	2	5		
Spaulding, Benjamin	3	1	3		
Spaulding, Phinehas	1	4	5		
Stacy, William	1		2		
Stanley, Jonathan	1		1		
Stanley, Lois	1	4	3		
Stanley, Samuel	1	3	7		
Stevens, James	2	1	5		
Stevens, William	1	4	5		
Steward, Joseph	2	1	1		
Steward, Simpson	3	4	3		
Stickney, Amos	2	1	4		
Stickney, Lemuel	1	2	4		
Stickney, Moses	1	3	3		
Stickney, Samuel	1	3	4		
Stone, John	1	3	2		
Stratton, David	1	2	2		
Taplin, John	1	1	4		
Taylor, Aaron	1	3	1		
Taylor, Nathan	1	1	4		
Taylor, Nathan	1	2	1		
Thompson, Asa	1		4		
Thompson, Ebenezer	1	2	2		
Thorndike, Joseph	2	6	5		
Thorndike, Joshua	1		1		
Turner, James	1	1	2		
Turner, Mary		2	5		
Turner, William	2	1	3		
Twist, Daniel	1	1	4		
Underwood, Jeremiah	1	2	2		
Warren, Simon	1	3	2		
Whipple, John	1	4	4		
Whitcomb, Ephraim	1	2	6		
Whitcomb, Simon	2		1		
Whiting, Cottin	1		4		
Whittemore, Benjamin	1	1	3		
Wilder, Ezra	2	1	3		
Wilder, Joseph	1	2	3		
Witt, Zaccheus	1	4	1		
Wood, John	1	6	4		
Worster, Moses	2	3	4		
Worster, William	2	1	3		
Wright, Francis	2	3	5		

KEENE TOWN.

NAME OF HEAD OF FAMILY.	Free white males of 16 years and upward, including heads of families.	Free white males under 16 years.	Free white females, including heads of families.	All other free persons.	Slaves.
Abbott, Joseph	1	2	1		
Abercrombie, Robert	1	1	4		
Archer, Benjamin	3		2		
Archer, Jonathan	1		6		
Archer, Zebina	1	1	1		
Baker, Ebenezer	1		2		
Baker, Elijah	2	3	3		
Baker, Thomas	4	2	4		
Balch, Benjamin	2	3	6		
Balch, David	3	1	3		
Balch, John	2	1	5		
Balch, John, Junr	2	1	6		
Banks, William	1		5		
Banks, William, Junr	1	1	2		
Bates, Betsy	2	1	2		
Bayley, Noah	1	2	4		
Bennett, Joseph	1	3	2		
Billings, Isaac	1	3	1		

KEENE TOWN—con.

NAME OF HEAD OF FAMILY.	Free white males of 16 years and upward, including heads of families.	Free white males under 16 years.	Free white females, including heads of families.	All other free persons.	Slaves.
Blake, Abel	2	1	2		
Blake, Asa	2	2	5		
Blake, John P.	1		1		
Blake, Nathan	2	2	5		
Blake, Nathan	1		2		
Blake, Obadiah	3	5	5		
Boynton, Solomon	1	3	3		
Bragg, Luther	3	4	5		
Bragg, William	3	1	4		
Briggs, Eliphalet	1	1	4		
Briggs, Elisha	1	1	1		
Briggs, Moses	1	1	3		
Brown, Joseph	1		3		
Butterfield, John	1	3	3		
Carpenter, Ebenezer	2	1	5		
Carpenter, Eliphalet	1		1		
Carpenter, Nathan	1	2	3		
Chandler, Alice	1	1	3		
Chase, Stephen	1	1	1		
Clarke, Cephas	2	4	3		
Clarke, Jesse	3	1	6		
Clarke, Sebia			2		
Clarke, Simeon	2		3		
Clarke, Simeon, Junr	1	3	3		
Connolly, John	2		3		
Crossfield, James	2	6	2		
Daniels, Aaron	1	2	2		
Daniels, Addington	1	2	4		
Daniels, James	1		1		
Daniels, John	3		1		
Daniels, Reuben	1	4	4		
Daniels, Samuel	1		1		
Day, Ebenezer	1	2	4		
Day, John	2	3	5		
Dickson, John	1	1	2		
Dix, Jonas	2	1	2		
Drake, Francis	1		2		
Dunbar, Elijah	2		2		
Dunbar, Mary	1		7	1	
Durant, Joshua	1	2	6		
Dwinnell, Bartholemew	2		2		
Dwinnell, Bartholemew, Junr	1	2	3		
Dwinnell, Isreal	1		1		
Dwinnell, Jonathan	2	1	7		1
Dwinnell, Thomas	2	1	5		
Eaton, Seth	3	2	4		
Edwards, Thomas	2	1	3		
Ellis, Benjamin	1		2		
Ellis, Caleb	1	1	3		
Ellis, Elisha	1		3		
Ellis, Gideon	1		1		
Ellis, Henry	1	2	3		
Ellis, Joshua	3	2	7		
Ellis, Josiah	2	3	4		
Ellis, Timothy	1	4	1		
Ellis, Timothy	1	1	2		
Emes, Calvin	1	3	2		
Emes, Luther	1		3		
Esty, Isaac	2		4		
Esty, Stephen	1		1		
Esty, William	1	4	4		
Eveleth, Zimri	1		3		
Field, Thomas	1	3	4		
Fisher, Thomas	2	2	3		
Foster, David	2	2	3		
French, Nathaniel	2		5		
French, Silas	2	3	5		
Geer, Walter	1		2		
Goodenow, Phebe			2		
Goodenow, Thomas	1	1	3		
Gray, Aaron	3	4	4		
Gray, William	1	1	2		
Griffith, James D	2	1	4		
Griswold, Stephen	2		5		
Griswold, Isaac	2	2	5		
Hall, Aaron	1	3	3		
Hall, Abijah	1	1	1		
Hall, Benjamin	1		2		
Hall, Hannaniah	1	2	3		
Hall, Jesse	3	2	3		
Hall, Susanah			2		
Harvey, Ezra	2	3	2		
Harvey, John	2	1	2		
Haywood, William	1	4	4		
Hill, Isreal	1		2		
Holbrook, Adin	1	2	3		
Houghton, Israel	1	1	3		
Houghton, John	1	7	1		
How, Gershom	1	1	3		
Howlet, Davis	1	2	4		
Hubbard, Peter	3	1	4		

KEENE TOWN—con.

NAME OF HEAD OF FAMILY.	Free white males of 16 years and upward, including heads of families.	Free white males under 16 years.	Free white females, including heads of families.	All other free persons.	Slaves.
Johnson, Moses	3	3	4		
Kingsbury, Daniel	3	3	5		
Kingsbury, Nathaniel	2	1	4		
Lampson, Phebe			2		
Le Bourveau, John	1	1	1		
Leonard, Noah	1	5	3		
Loveland, Isreal	1	1	2		
McGregory, Daniel	1	1	3		
Marsh, Moses	1	5	3		
Metcalf, Abijah	4	1	8		
Metcalf, Eli	1		1		
Metcalf, Ezra	1	3	4		
Metcalf, Jotham	2	1	9		
Metcalf, Luke	1	2	4		
Metcalf, Micheal	1	1	4		
Metcalf, Oliver	1		1		
Metcalf, Thaddeus	2	1	3		
Newcomb, Daniel	3	5	4		
Newell, Joseph	1	1	1		
Newton, Ebenezer	1		6		
Nichols, Levi	1	3	6		
Nims, Alpheus	3		3		
Nims, David	3	4	4		
Nye, Sylvanus	1	4	2		
Osgood, Benjamin	1	3	5		
Osgood, Jonas	2	1	3		
Osgood, Samuel	1		2		
Page, Ebenezer	1	2	3		
Page, Joseph	1		1		
Parker, Benjamin	1	3	1		
Parker, Joseph	1	2	3		
Parker, William	1	1	2		
Parker, William	1	1	5		
Partridge, Levi	2	2	6		
Patten, John	3		1		
Peabody, Moses	1	1	1		
Pemberton, Leonard	1	1	1		
Plumley, John	1	3	3		
Pollard, Joseph	3	1	4		
Pond, Abiather	3		2		
Pond, Jonathan	2	1	4		
Prescott, Jonas	1	1	4		
Reding, Thomas	2		2		
Reed, James	3		2		1
Reed, William				4	
Rice, Charles	1		5		
Richardson, Evi	2	3	5		
Richardson, Josiah	1	2	3		
Robens, Ebenezer	1	1	2		
Sanger, Rhoda			2		
Sawyer, James	1	2	6		
Shattuck, Stephen	2	1	2		
Simmons, David	1	2	4		
Slyfield, Andrew	1	1	4		
Smead, Simeon	1	2	3		
Snow, Caleb	2		2		
Snow, Daniel	3	1	2		
Snow, Hosea	1	3	2		
Sprague, Peleg	1	1	2		
Stertivant, Cornelius	2	1	2		
Stiles, Jeremiah	3	1	1		
Stiles, John	1	3	6		
Sumner, Clement	3		6		
Sylvester, Joseph	1	2	5		
Taylor, Isaac	1	2	5		
Thompson, Thomas	1	3	4		
Todd, William	3		2		
Town, Asa	1		2		
Town, Jacob	2	3	3		
Town, Nehemiah	1	2	4		
Town, William	1	3	5		
Tufts, Zachariah	1	2	3		
Walles, Robert	1	1	1		
Warner, Ebenezer	1		2		
Watson, Daniel	2	1	2		
Weare, Asa	2	1	3		
Wells, Thomas	1	5	3		
Wheeler, Abraham	1	1	2		
Wheeler, Abraham, Junr	2	2	6		
Wheeler, Jeremiah	2	2	2		
Wheeler, Jonathan	1	4	3		
Wheeler, Zadock	1	1	3		
Wilder, Abijah	4	2	6		
Willard, Josiah	3	2	3		
Willard, Lockhart	1	2	1		
Willis, Benjamin	1	1	2		
Wilson, Aaron	1	3	2		
Wilson, Abijah	1		1		
Wilson, Daniel	1	3	8		
Wilson, Joseph	3	2	3		
Wilson, Uriah	1		1		
Wood, Joshua	1		5		

CHESHIRE COUNTY—Continued.

KEENE TOWN—con.

NAME OF HEAD OF FAMILY.	Free white males of 16 years and upward, including heads of families.	Free white males under 16 years.	Free white females, including heads of families.	All other free persons.	Slaves.
Woods, William	2	3	3		
Wright, Ephraim	3		1		
Wright, James	2	1	4		
Wright, Phinehas	2	3	6		
Wyman, Isaac	3	3	3		
Wyman, Isaac, Junr	2	1	7		
Wyman, James	1	1	3		

LANGDON TOWN.

NAME OF HEAD OF FAMILY.					
Baker, John	2	3	4		
Baldwin, Joshua	1	1	2		
Egerton, James	2	2	3		
Fairbank, Levi	1	1	2		
French, Able	1	1	1		
French, John	2	1	2		
French, Thomas	1	2	1		
Gleason, Winsor	1		4		
Greenleaf, Isaac	1	1	3		
Harris, John	1		1		
Haywood, Jeremiah	1	3	4		
Henry, David	1	1	1		
Hoar, Leonard	1		3		
Huntington, Gamaliel	1	1	4		
Lamb, Nathaniel	1		2	2	
Palmer, Benjamin	1	1	3		
Prentice, John	2	1	2		
Prowty, Daniel	1	2	4		
Prowty, John	1	3	4		
Prowty, Samuel	2	4	2		
Putnam, John	1		3		
Reed, Ezra	1	1	2		
Richardson, Samuel	1	3	3		
Rockwell, Jabez	1	4	1		
Royce, John	3	1	1		
Royce, Lemuel	1	3	2		
Sartwell, John	1	4	4		
Sartwell, Obadiah	3	3	3		
Scripture, John	1	3	2		
Smith, Ebenezer	3	3	1		
Walker, Abel	2	4	4		
Walker, Asa	1	1	5		
Walker, Samuel	2	1	3		
Walker, Seth	1	2	2		
Wetherbee, Simon	1		2		
Wheeler, Joseph	2	1	1		
Wheeler, Samuel	1	3	2		
White, Buckminster	1	3	2		
Whitney, Joshua	1	2	2		
Willard, Jonathan	2	3	6		
Willard, Joseph	2	3	1		
Willard, William	1		4		

LEMPSTER TOWN.

NAME OF HEAD OF FAMILY.					
Abel, Elijah	2	3	5		
Abel, Phinehas	4	1	1		
Beckwith, Jabez	2	2	5		
Beckwith, Niles	1	3	4		
Bingham, Elijah	2		4		
Bingham, James	1	2	3		
Bingham, Roswell	1		1		
Booth, Epiphas	1	1	3		
Booth, Freegrace	1	3	4		
Booth, Joshua	1	3	1		
Booth, Oliver	2		1		
Booth, Oliver, Junr	1	2	1		
Branard, Elijah	1		5		
Branard, Jabez	1	1	2		
Bush, Benjamin	1	1	2		
Carey, Eliott	1		1		
Carey, Levina			2		
Carey, Olivet	1		2		
Carey, William	2	1	4		
Chapman, Richard	1	1	3		
Chappel, Daniel	1	2	3		
Dodge, Isaac	3	1	4		
Eggleston, Thomas	2	5	3		
Fisher, Elias	2		2		
Frink, Elijah	3		3		
Frink, Elijah, Junr	1		2		
Hibbird, Asa	1	1	4		
Hogg, Alexander	1	1	2		
Hogg, John	1	3	2		
Holt, Abner	1	2	4		
Huntley, Hezekiah	1	2	2		
Huntley, Moses	1		4		
Hurd, Jabez	1		3		
Hurd, Shubael	2	1	7		
Hurd, Uzzel	1	3	4		
Isom, William	3	3	2		
Jackson, Elizabeth		2	4		

LEMPSTER TOWN—con.

NAME OF HEAD OF FAMILY.	Free white males of 16 years and upward, including heads of families.	Free white males under 16 years.	Free white females, including heads of families.	All other free persons.	Slaves.
Loveridge, Amasa	1	2	1		
Lowell, Peter	1	3	3		
Martin, Luther	1	1	4		
Miner, Charles	2	2	4		
Miner, Timothy	1		1		
Nichols, Samuel	3	2	6		
Nichols, Timothy	1	2	6		
Noyce, Daniel	3	3	6		
Phelps, Barnabas	2	4	4		
Porter, Peter	2		2		
Prentice, Jonathan	2	4	5		
Rogers, James	4		2		
Rogers, James, Junr	1	1	2		
Roundey, Elven	1	1	2		
Roundey, Samuel	3		1		
Saybins, John	3	1	8		
Scott, John	1	4	5		
Smith, Isreal	1	1	2		
Spencer, Zaccheus	2	1	1		
Storey, William	1	1	6		
Tatten, Isaac				3	
Taylor, David	1		1		
Taylor, Jonathan	1		3		
Thatcher, Elisha	1	1	2		
Thatcher, John	2	1	4		
Way, John	4	2	1		
Way, Nathaniel	1	2	2		
Wheeler, Resolved	2	2	3		
Willcox, Comfort	2		1		
Willey, Allyn	2		1		
Willey, Allyn, Junr	1	3	2		
Willey, Benjamin	1		1		
Willey, Charles	1		2		
Willey, David	1	1	1		
Willey, Nathan	2		2		

MARLBOROUGH TOWN.

NAME OF HEAD OF FAMILY.					
Baker, Johnadal	1	1	2		
Ball, Daniel	1		7		
Ball, Jonathan	2	1	8		
Barker, Francis	1	1	1		
Barker, William	4		3		
Belknap, Ebenezer	1				
Bemis, David	1		3		
Bemis, James	1	2	3		
Bemis, Jeremiah	1	1	1		
Bemis, Jonathan	1		1		
Bemis, Timothy	2	1	1		
Benson, Benoni	2	4	4		
Blood, Joseph	1		8		
Brooks, Aaron	1	2	2		
Bruce, William	1	1	2		
Bullard, Ebenezer	2		2		
Buss, John	1	3	3		
Capron, Jonathan	2		4		
Capron, Jonathan, Junr	1	1	5		
Collins, Ebenezer	1	1	3		
Collins, Joseph	1		2		
Collins, William	1	2	2		
Converse, John	2		1		
Converse, Robert	1	2	2		
Coolidge, Abraham	1	1	1		
Cummings, Amos	1	1	2		
Cummings, Daniel	1	2	2		
Cummings, Peletiah	3		3		
Cutting, Daniel	1	3	4		
Cutting, Joseph	1	1	2		
Davis, Thomas	1		4		
Dean, James	1	1	6		
Dunfore, David	1	3	2		
Emerson, Caleb	1	4	3		
Emerson, Daniel	1	1	3		
Emes, Aaron	2	3	3		
Estabrook, John	1	3	2		
Farrar, George	1		2		
Farrar, Josiah	1		2		
Farrar, Phinehas	3	6	3		
Fife, Silas	2	5	3		
Fish, Alexander	1		1		
Flood, Betty	1	3	3		
Follet, Joseph	1	3	4		
French, Joseph	1	1	4		
Frost, Benjamin	1	1	1		
Frost, Jonathan	1	1	3		
Frost, Joseph	2	4	1		
Gage, Daniel	1	2	2		
Goodenough, Benjamin	2	5	2		
Goodenough, Calvin	1	3	2		
Gould, Daniel	1		2		
Greenleaf, Levi	1		2		
Greenleaf, Rebecca	2		2		

MARLBOROUGH TOWN— continued.

NAME OF HEAD OF FAMILY.	Free white males of 16 years and upward, including heads of families.	Free white males under 16 years.	Free white females, including heads of families.	All other free persons.	Slaves.
Grimes, Bartholomew	1	3	4		
Harvey, Timothy	1	2	5		
Hastings, Thaddeus	1	3	1		
Haywood, Theophilus	1	3	4		
Hemmenway, Ebenezer	1	2	1		
Hemmenway, Elias	1		4		
Hodgkins, Hezekiah	1	2	3		
Holman, Charles	1	1	2		
Hunt, Henry	1	1	1		
Jennings, Ebenezer	1	2	4		
Jewett, Benjamin	1	2	2		
Johnson, Timothy	1	2	2		
Joy, Nathaniel	1	1	1		
Lawrance, Daniel	1	2	4		
Lawrance, Jonathan	2	5	4		
Leeson, James	1	1	1		
Lewis, James	1		4		
Lewis, John	1	2	3		
Lewis, Josiah	1	1	2		
McAllester, Isaac	2		3		
McAllester, Samuel	1	1	1		
Mann, Theodore	1	3	4		
Mason, Ziba	1	1	3		
Metcalf, Asa	1	3	3		
Moffatt, William	1	2	1		
Moore, Lawson	1		2		
Moore, Thomas	1	1	1		
Newell, Jacob	3		1		
Newell, Jacob, Junr	1		4		
Newton, Luther	1	1	2		
Page, Lebbeus	1		2		
Page, Thomas	1	2	3		
Parkhurst, John	1	2	1		
Parmarter, Thaddeus	1		2		
Perry, Justus	1	1	2		
Phelps, Jacob	1	1	2		
Phelps, Putnam	1		1		
Phillips, Andrew	1		3		
Phips, Hannah	1	4	3		
Porter, Asa	1	1	3		
Porter, Joel	1	1	3		
Rhoades, Ebenezer	1	4	3		
Rhoades, Ebenezer, Junr	1		2		
Richardson, Isreal	1	1	2		
Robens, Isaac	1	1	3		
Roberts, Richard	2		3		
Robins, Benoni	1		1		
Rogers, John	3	1	3		
Rogers, John	3	2	4		
Sanders, Hannah		1	2		
Serjeant, Samuel	2	2	5		
Shaw, Ichabod	2	2	6		
Stone, Eliphalet	2	1	4		
Stone, John	1	1	2		
Swan, John	2	5	4		
Tayntor, Jedediah	1	2	2		
Temple, Ebenezer	1	3	3		
Tenny, William	2	6	4		
Thatcher, Benjamin	1	2	3		
Thompson, Samuel	1	4	2		
Thurston, David	3	1	2		
Tinney, Daniel	1	2	1		
Toleman, Joseph	1	2	2		
Tozer, Richard	2	2	4		
Tucker, Abijah	2		4		
Tucker, Moses	1	2	3		
Ward, Reuben	1	4	5		
Wheeler, David	1	3	7		
Whipple, Jonathan	1	2	5		
White, James	1	1	3		
White, William	2	3	5		
Whitney, Daniel	2	3	2		
Wilkinson, David	1	1	3		
Wiswell, John	1	4	4		
Woodward, Abel	1		1		
Woodward, Abijah	1		4		
Woodward, Daniel	1		3		
Woodward, Solomon	1	2	4		
Woodward, Stephen	1	3	3		
Worsley, Robert	1	2	5		
Wright, John	2		3		
Wright, Oliver	1	1	8		
Wright, Samuel	1	1	3		
Wyman, Joseph	1		3		

MARLOW TOWN.

NAME OF HEAD OF FAMILY.					
Beckwith, Amos	1	3	3		
Beckwith, Anson	1	2	1		
Beckwith, Eleazer	2	3	3		

CHESHIRE COUNTY—Continued.

NAME OF HEAD OF FAMILY.	Free white males of 16 years and upward, including heads of families.	Free white males under 16 years.	Free white females, including heads of families.	All other free persons.	Slaves.
MARLOW TOWN—con.					
Beckwith, Ira	1		5		
Bingham, John	1	3	1		
Bingham, Ripley	1	2	3		
Brigham, Ephriam	1	2	6		
Brown, Benjamin	1	2	1		
Brown, Francis	1	2	1		
Canfield, Samuel	1	2	3		
Chenney, Tristram	1		1		
Child, Abel	1	1	6		
Comstock, Cyrus	1		3		
Emes, Thomas	1	3	3		
Everett, Samuel	2	1	2		
Fisk, Simon	1	1	2		
Gee, Asa	1		2		
Gee, Laman	1	4	3		
Gee, Nathan	1	1	2		
Gee, Solomon	3	1	2		
Gee, Stephen	3	1	3		
Gustin, John	2	2	2		
Gustin, John, Junr	1		1		
Gustin, Josiah	1	3	5		
Haywood, Thomas	1	3	2		
Huntley, Aaron	1	3	1		
Huntley, Bathuel	1	1	2		
Huntley, Elisha	1		2		
Huntley, Isaiah	1	3	1		
Huntley, Jonathan	2		2		
Huntley, Luman	1	2	1		
Huntley, Nathan	1		1		
Huntley, Nathan, Junr	1	2	1		
Huntley, Rufus	1	2	2		
Huntley, Russel	1	2	2		
Huntley, Sylvanus	1	1	2		
Johnson, Hannah		2	5		
Kenney, Daniel	1	3	2		
Lanpher, Elizabeth	1	1	2		
Lewis, William	1	1	1		
Mack, Grace			4		
Mack, Silas	1	5	1		
Maynard, Banajah	1	1	1		
Messer, Oliver	1	1	1		
Messer, Timothy	1		2		
Messer, Timothy	1		2		
Miller, Sardis	1		5		
Munsil, Curtis	1	1	2		
Munson, James	1		2		
Parker, Samuel	1	4	2		
Preston, Thomas	1		4		
Rice, Andrew	1		3		
Rice, Samuel	2	1	4		
Richardson, Lemuel	1	1	3		
Sawyer, Hannah			2		
Shaw, Jacob	3	2	5		
Smith, Abner	1		4		
Smith, John	1	2	5		
Tubes, Abisha	2	2	4		
Tubes, Dan	1		3		
Tubes, Joseph	1	1	1		
Way, John	1		1		
White, Caleb	1	3	1		
Winch, Luther	1		2		
NEW GRANTHAM TOWN.					
Aldridge, Levi	1	1	4		
Bigsby, Amasa	1				
Burr, Ebenezer	2	3	3		
Church, Caleb	2		3		
Clemons, David	1	1	2		
Clemons, Isaac	1	1	3		
Cluff, Rachell		1	1		
Cotton, Lemuel	1				
Davis, Jeremiah	3	1	8		
Delino, Moses	1		2		
Dunkin, John	1	1	2		1
Dunkin, Samuel	5		4		
Dustin, Perley	1	1	1		
Dutton, Silas	4	2	3		
Easterbrooks, Experience	1	1	4		
Fuller, Mary			1		
Gage, Stephen	1				
Genney, Isaac	1	5	6		
Gennings, Stephen	2	2	3		
Ginney, James	2	3	2		
Gleason, Elijah	2	4	4		
Heriman, Leonard	2	2	2		
Hopkins, Phillip	2	3	5		
Hunter, William	1	3	3		
Huntington, William	2	4	2		
Johnson, Abnor	1	3	1		
Johnson, Elijah	2		2		

NAME OF HEAD OF FAMILY.	Free white males of 16 years and upward, including heads of families.	Free white males under 16 years.	Free white females, including heads of families.	All other free persons.	Slaves.
NEW GRANTHAM TOWN—continued.					
Joy, Silas	2	2	4		
Kan, Parker	3	3	4		
King, Peter	1	2	3		
Leach, Samuel	1	3	4		
Livermore, William	1	3	4		
Malaery, Abraham	1				
Massa, William	1	1	2		
Meeder, Reuben	1		2		
Merrel, John	1	2	3		
Merrel, Obediah	1		1		
Merrel, Obediah, Junr	2		2		
Parkhurst, George	1	2	2		
Pierce, Daniel	1	1	1		
Pierce, Job	1	1	2		
Pierce, John	2		3		
Pike, Ebenezer	1	1	1		
Pike, John	2		3		
Pike, John, Junr	1	1	3		
Read, Martin	1		1		
Rowel, Enoch	1	3	4		
Sawyer, Elias	1	1	2		
Scott, Robert	7		5	1	
Shartlaff, Lathrop	3		3		
Smith, Wadlough K	1	3	3		
Stebbins, Ebenezer	1	1	3		
Stephens, John	1				
Stonel, Jonathan	1	1	1		
Stonel, Samuel	1	2	3		
Taylor, Samuel	1	3	1		
Vernum, John S	1	3	3		
Young, Joab	1	1	4		
Young, Jonathan	2	4	2		
Young, Sebury		2	3		
NEWPORT TOWN.					
Ayres, John	1	3	1		
Bascom, Elias	3	3	6		
Bascom, Elias, Junr	1	2	3		
Bascom, Reuben	2	1	3		
Bayley, Jesse	1	2	6		
Bliss, Henry	1		4		
Bragg, Benjamin	1	1	3		
Britton, William	1		2		
Brown, David	2	3	5		
Brown, Elijah	1	2	3		
Brown, Jonathan	1	1	6		
Buell, Abraham	2	1	2		
Buell, Abraham	1	1	7		
Buell, Daniel	2	1	4		
Buell, Gurden	1	3	2		
Buell, John	1	1	1		
Buell, Joseph	2	2	6		
Buell, Joseph, Junr	1	1	1		
Buell, Mathew	1	2	2		
Buell, Mathew, Junr	1	1	5		
Buell, Simon	1	2	2		
Buell, Thomas	1	4	2		
Carpenter, Sorrell	2		1		
Chamberlain, Simeon	1	1	4		
Chapin, Daniel	2		1		
Chapin, Phinehas	1	1	3		
Church, James	2	1	2		
Church, Samuel	1	4	6		
Church, Whitman	1	1	1		
Colbey, Abner	1	1	5		
Comstock, Jonathan	2	3	3		
Cutting, David	1		2		
Cutting, Jonathan	1		2		
Dergy, Moses Paine	2	3	1		
Dexter, Stephen	2	4	5		
Drock, Simon					4
Dudley, Daniel	1		2		
Dudley, Daniel, Junr	1		2		
Dudley, Ezra	1	1	1		
Dudley, John	1		6		
Dudley, Josiah	2	2	5		
Dunham, Solomon	2	3	2		
Eastman, Benjamin	2	1	3		
Eastman, Johnson	2				
Ferring, Zebulon	1	2	1		
Fletcher, Joel	1	1	3		
Goodwin, Richard	1	1	8		
Goodwin, Theophilus	1		6		
Hall, Amos	3	3	1		
Hall, David	3	1	2		
Hall, Jared	1		2		
Hall, Levi	1	2	3		
Harrington, Timothy	1	3	2		
Harris, John	1	2	4		
Haven James	3		1		

NAME OF HEAD OF FAMILY.	Free white males of 16 years and upward, including heads of families.	Free white males under 16 years.	Free white females, including heads of families.	All other free persons.	Slaves.
NEWPORT TOWN—con.					
Haven, Joel	2	1	4		
Hayden, William	1	1	5		
Humphry, Arter	2	2	4		
Hurd, Nathan	3	2	4		
Hurd, Samuel	2	1	3		
Hurd, Samuel, Junr	1	2	3		
Hurd, Stephen	1	2	4		
Jinks, Jeremiah	1	3	3		1
Jones, Thomas	1	1	4		
Kelsey, Absolam	1	2	5		
Kelsey, Etham	1	3	2		
Kelsey, Isaac	1	3	2		
Kelsey, Jeremiah	1	2	3		
Kelsey, Jesse	2	3	3		
Kelsey, Joel	1	1	4		
Kelsey, Roswell	3	4	3		
Lane, Jesse	3	2	4		
Lane, Robert	2		2		
Lane, Thomas	1		1		
Lewis, John	2	1	1		
McGregory, Joel	1	1	2		
McGregory, John	2	3	1		
Mack, Aaron	1		3		
Mercey, Daniel	1	1	1		
Merritt, Ebenezer	2		2		
Messer, Theodore	3		2		
Metcalf, Elias	1	3	2		
Mott, Jared	1		1		
Nettleton, Jeremiah	4	2	5		
Newton, Christopher	4	2	5		
Newton, Isaac	2	1	6		
Noyce, Isaac	1	3	2		
Osgood, Thomas	1	2	4		
Osgood, William	1	3	2		
Parmala, Ezra	1	3	6		
Peck, Henry	1	5	1		
Peck, Hezekiah	1		4		
Perry, Stephen	1	2	7		
Phillips, William	1	2	5		
Pike, Jarvis	1		1		
Pike, John	1	2	1		
Pike, Moses	1	1	1		
Pike, Nathaniel	1		1		
Remele, John	1	3	3		
Reynolds, Jedediah	1	1	3		
Sholes, Aaron	1	1	2		
Sholes, Christopher	1	1	2		
Sholes, Hannah		1	2		
Sholes, Hutchinson	1		1		
Sholes, Levi	4	1	2		
Silver, John	1	3	1		
Silver, Samuel	1		1		
Spencer, Robert	1	3	1		
Stevens, Josiah	2	1	5		
Stevens, Josiah, Junr	1		2		
Stevens, Peter	1		1		
Stoddard, William	1	1	3		
Thayer, Mary		2	3		
Thompson, Samuel	1	3	1		
Tower, Ephriam	1	4	1		
Towner, Benjamin	1		1		
Wakefield, Jesse	1		2		
Wakefield, Jonathan	1	2	3		
Wakefield, Josiah	1		3		
Wakefield, Peter	2		2		
Warner, John	1	5	2		
Warner, Joshua	1	2	4		
Warner, Samuel	1	1	2		
Warner, Thomas	2		6		
Wheeler, Asa	1		1		
White, Enoch	2		1		
Wilcox, Uriah	2	4	5		
Willcox, Jesse	3	2	7		
Willcox, Phinehas	1	3	5		
Willmarth, Nathan	1		3		
Wines, Abijah	5		5		
Witcher, Thomas	1	2	4		
PACKERSFIELD TOWN.					
Abbott, Joseph	2	1	2		
Abbott, Joshua	2	1	2		
Adams, John	2	3	4		
Adams, Samuel	1	3	3		
Atwood, John	1		1		
Atwood, Josiah	1	1	3		
Atwood, Phillip	1	2	3		
Bancroft, James	1	3	4		
Bancroft, Timothy	1	3	2		
Banks, James	1	3	1		
Barker, William	4		5		
Barrett, Joseph	1	3	1		

CHESHIRE COUNTY—Continued.

NAME OF HEAD OF FAMILY.	Free white males of 16 years and upward, including heads of families.	Free white males under 16 years.	Free white females, including heads of families.	All other free persons.	Slaves.	NAME OF HEAD OF FAMILY.	Free white males of 16 years and upward, including heads of families.	Free white males under 16 years.	Free white females, including heads of families.	All other free persons.	Slaves.	NAME OF HEAD OF FAMILY.	Free white males of 16 years and upward, including heads of families.	Free white males under 16 years.	Free white females, including heads of families.	All other free persons.	Slaves.
PACKERSFIELD TOWN—continued.						PACKERSFIELD TOWN—continued.						PLAINFIELD TOWN—con.					
Barrett, Nathaniel	1	3	2			Wardwell, Solomon	2	4	2			Gates, Nathan	1	4	6		
Bassett, Samuel	1	3	3			Warren, Levi	1		2			Gates, Thomas	1	4	2		
Batchelor, Ruth	2		2			Warren, Samuel	4		4			Gikey, Sample	1	4	4		
Beard, David	4	3	4			Wesson, Nathan	2	3	1			Gilbert, John	1	3	6		
Beel, Aaron	1	1	4			Wheeler, Benjamin	1	1	1			Goodale, Moses	1	1	2		
Beel, Joseph	1	1	1			Wheeler, Jacob	1	3	5			Gothum, Henry	1	2	3		
Beel, William	1		1			Wheeler, Peter	1		1			Hall, Laban	1	1	3		
Beel, William, Junr	1		4			Whitcomb, Levi	1	2	4			Haywood, Eleazer	1		2		
Boynton, John	1	2	2			White, John	1	2	2			Hines, Nathan	2	2	2		
Breed, Allen	1	1	5			White, Samuel	1	3	4			Hovey, Daniel	1	6	2		
Breed, John	2	2	2			Whitney, Josiah	1	3	5			Hovey, Josiah	1	7	2		
Breed, Nathaniel	2	3	5			Whitney, Oliver	1	3	5			Hovey, Simeon	2	4	4		
Breed, Thomas K	1		1			Wilder, Levi	2	1	2			Huse, Perley	1	3	3		
Brewer, Isaac	1	1	3			Wilson, Archelus	1	4	6			Jorden, Benjamin	1	1	4		
Brigham, Jonas	1	2	2			Wright, Jesse	1	3	4			Joy, Benjamin	2		2		
Brown, Abijah	1	4	4			Wright, Nehemiah	1		4			Joy, Benjamin, Junr	1	3	4		
Brown, John	2	2	5			Wright, Oliver	1	3	2			Joy, David	1	3	4		
Brown, Joseph	3		3			Wright, Oliver	3	1	5			Joy, Ebenezer	1	2	2		
Bryant, James	1	4	2			Wyman, Mary	2		1			Kile, Ephraim	1		2		
Buckminster, Solomon	1	2	4			Wyman, Samuel	1		1			Kimball, Benjamin	1		3		
Chandler, Peter	1	2	1									Kimball, Benjamin, Jur	1	1	3		
Child, Amos	1	2	1			PLAINFIELD TOWN.						Kimball, Daniel	5	2	3		
Cobb, Stephen	3	2	4									Kimball, James	1	4	6		
Crosby, Solomon	1		2			Adams, Eliphalet	1		4			Kimball, Joseph	1	2	5		
Davis, Isaac	1		3			Adams, Micajah	2		1			Kimball, Joseph, Jur	2	1	5		
Davis, Jonas	1	1	3			Adams, Oliver	1	1	2			Kimball, Willes	1	2	1		
Day, Comfort	1	5	4			Adams, Simeon	1		2			Kingsbury, Oliver	1	2	5		
Day, Peletiah	2	1	3			Agur, Martin	1		2			Kinyon, Alexander	1	2	5		
Eames, Robert	1	3	4			Alexander, Arbe	1		2			Kinyon, Joseph	2	2	5		
Farwell, Absolam	1	2	3			Alexander, John	1	1	1			Kinyon, Joseph, Junr	1		1		
Farwell, John	3		6			Alexander, John, Junr	1		1			Lambert, Obed	2	4	2		
Farwell, Richard	2	6	2			Alexander, William	1		3			Leonard, Solomon	1	1	4		
Felt, Jonathan	2	4	5			Allen, Nathaniel	1		1			McNeal, John	1	3	2		
Felt, Joseph	1	2	1			Andrews, Nathan	2	5	2			Meader, John	1		1		
Felt, Samuel	2	1	2			Austin, John	3	3	6			Miller, Daniel	1				
Field, Mary		2	2			Avery, George	1	3	1			Miller, Robert	1	1	3		
Follet, William	1	1	4			Bachelor, Bhinehas	1					Miner, Eliphalet	1	3	4		
Foster, Jacob	3		3			Baker, Oliver	1	2	5			Miner, Roswell	1	3	3		
Fox, John	1		3			Baley, Joshua	1		2			Morgen, Nathaniel	1	1	2		
Goodenow, Abraham	2	2	6			Ballard, Daniel	1	3	1			Muxley, John	1	2	1		
Griffin, Samuel	1	3	3			Ballard, Israel	1	4	6			Nash, Littlefield	2		2		
Grover, James	1	3	2			Bean, William	1	3	5			Nichols, John	1		1		
Gurley, Betsy		2	2			Bill, Samuel	1	3	5			Otis, Robert	1	2	1		
Hall, Josiah	1	1	1			Blanchard, Joseph	1	1	2			Palmer, Aaron	1	4	4		
Hardy, Noah	1	2	2			Blanchard, Simeon	1		2			Payne, Edward	1	2	1		
Harris, Erastus	3		2			Bloss, Zadock	1	2	4			Payne, Jesse	1	2	2		
Heaton, Luther	2	1	3			Blunt, Andrew	1		1			Perkins, Samuel	1	2	1		
Holt, Daniel	2		2			Blunt, Jesse	1		3			Permont, Richard	2	7	3		
Holt, Enoch	1	1	2			Bridge, Benjamin	1		2			Perrey, David	3	1	4		
Holt, Joel	1		2			Cady, Reynolds	1	2	1			Perrey, Sylvanus	1	2	1		
Holt, Thomas	1		2			Cady, Robert	3		1			Pool, John	1		3		
Ingalls, Solomon	1	3	3			Carpenter, Abraham	1		2			Pool, Samuel	1		3		
Jacwith, John	1	1	2			Carpenter, Jesse	1	2	2			Quimby, Eleazer	1		3		
Jewett, Isaac	2	1	2			Cary, Jabez	3		4			Roberts, Abraham	2		1		
Kimball, David	1	1	3			Cary, Jabez, Junr	1		1			Roberts, Jesse	1				
Kimball, James	1		3			Cary, James	3		4			Roberts, Josiah	1		2		
Kitridge, Joshua	1		2			Chapman, Benjamin	1	2	3			Roberts, Perley	1	3	1		
Kitridge, Solomon	1	4	3			Chapman, Chester	1		2			Roberts, Ziba	1	3	2		
Lawrance, Joshua	1	5	2			Chapman, Joseph	1	4	1			Robinson, David	1	3	2		
Lawrance, Martin	1	4	2			Cheney, Thomas	1		2			Row, Jesse	1				
Le Bourveau, Zenos	1	3	2			Clarke, Cyrus	1		1			Shirtleff, Amos	1		3		
Maynard, Bannister	1		4			Clarke, Samuel	1	3	2			Smith, Aaron	1	1	3		
Melvin, Josiah	2		1			Cole, Daniel	2	3	2			Smith, Francis	4	3	6		
Neal, Amos	1		2			Cole, Ebenezer	1	1	3			Smith, Joseph	3	4	5		
Newhall, John	3		2			Cole, Ebenezer, Junr	1					Smith, Lemuel	1	1	4		
Nourse, Benjamin	1	2	5			Cole, Stephen	1					Smith, Lucy		1	2		
Osyer, Consider	2	1	4			Cook, Theophilus	2	2	4			Smith, Walter	1	1	2		
Paine, Zebediah	1	1	5			Corey, Isaac	1	3	4			Spalden, Amasa	1	3	3		
Peirce, Timothy	1	1	2			Corey, Manser	1		4			Spalden, Amos	3	4	3		
Phillips, James	2	1	3			Corey, Robert	1	1	1			Spalden, Bezaleel	1	3	3		
Priest, William	1	2	1			Corey, Simeon	1	3	4			Spalden, Champin	1	1	4		
Rice, Charles	1	2	3			Corey, Timothy	3	2	4			Spalden, Charles	2		5		
Richardson, Amos	1	1	2			Cotton, Job	1		2			Spalden, David	4	1	1		
Richardson, John	1	3	3			Cotton, Josiah	1	2	2			Spalden, Joseph	4		2		
Richardson, Thomas	1	1	2			Cutler, Benjamin	1	2	4	2		Spalden, Phillip	1	4	3		
Robins, Josiah	1	1	2			Cutler, Hodge	1	3	4			Spalden, Phinehas	1	1	2		
Rugg, Josephus	2		1			Cutler, Perley	2	2	5			Spalden, Ruluff	2	3	3		
Russel, Pompey					3	Cutler, William	1	1	2			Spalden, William	3	1	5		
Sawyer, Benjamin	1	6	2			Dean, Francis	1		2			Spencer, David	1				
Scripture, Samuel	1		1			Dowe, Gideon	2	1	4			Spiller, John	1		3		
Scripture, Samuel, Junr	1	3	2			Dyer, Moses	1		2			Squires, Moses	2	1	3		
Severance, Abby	1	4	2			Eagleston, Samuel	1	1	2			Stafford, Amos	2		1		
Sheldon, Ezra	1		2			Earl, Joseph	1	1	2			Stafford, Amos, Junr	2	1	3		
Skinner, Samuel	3	1	2			Foss, Walter	1	1	1			Stafford, Nathaniel	2	1	5		
Smith, Ezra	2	4	2			Freeman, Daniel	4	3	5			Stephens, David	1				
Smith, Jacob	1	1	2			French, Hezekiah	2	1	3			Stephens, David, Junr	1				
Sprague, John	1	3	2			Gallop, Asa	2	2	5			Stephens, Job	1	1	4		
Stoddard, Richard	2	1	6			Gallop, Thomas	2	4	2			Stephens, John	3		2		
Thomas, Odoardo	2	2	5			Gates, Beza	1		1			Stephens, John, Junr	2	1	3		
Toleman, Ebenezer	1	2	3									Stephens, Newhall	1		2		
Twitchel, Stephen	1	2	5									Stickney, Daniel	1	1	2		

CHESHIRE COUNTY—Continued.

NAME OF HEAD OF FAMILY.	Free white males of 16 years and upward, including heads of families.	Free white males under 16 years.	Free white females, including heads of families.	All other free persons.	Slaves.
PLAINFIELD TOWN—con.					
Stickney, James	1		3		
Stone, Abel	3	1	3		
Stone, Abel, Junr	1	1	1		
Stone, Ezekiel	1	2	1		
Stone, Levi	1				
Strate, Jeremiah	1	1	2		
Swan, Timothy	1	3	3		
Thomas, Ebenezer	1	1	1		
Tone, John T	1	2	3		
True, Benjamin	1	2	3		
True, Daniel	2		1		
True, Moses	1	1	1		
True, William	1	1	1		
Vincent, Timothy	1	1	5		
Ward, James	2		3		
West, Thomas	2	1	2		
Westgate, George	2		1		
Westgate, John	1	3	4		
Westgate, John, Junr	1				
Westgate, Joseph	1	4	3		
Wheeler, Rufus	1	1	6		
Whiteker, Gideon	1	1	3		
Whiteker, Phillip	1	3	2		
Williams, Atwood	1	2	3		
Williams, Charles	1		1		
Williams, Elisha	1	1	2		
Williams, Isaac	2	1	5		
Williams, Job	1	2	3		
Williams, Lemuel	2		4		
Wilson, Isaac	2	2	3		
Woodward, Gideon	1		5		
Wright, Ebenezer	3	4	4		
Wright, Phinehas	1	1	3		
PROTECTWORTH TOWN.					
Bean, Daniel	1	1	1		
Bean, David	1	1	3		
Choal, Benjamin	1		2		
Clark, Nathaniel	1	2	5		
Clay, Samuel	1	1	2		
Clefford, Israel	1		3		
Clefford, Israel, Junr	1	3	3		
Clefford, Trustham	1	1	1		
Colby, Isaac	1		3		
Colcord, Stephens	1		2		
Dudley, Jonathan	1				
Elkins, Moses	2	2	3		
Fillbrook, Daniel	1		2		
Hardy, Nicholas	2	2	3		
Hazzard, James	1		3		
Heath, Enock	1	1	3		
Heath, John	1	4	1		
Hogg, Robert	1	2	3		
Hoyt, Reuben	1	2	1		
Kinsman, Ephraim	1	4	4		
Loveran, John	1		3		
Lovran, Ebenezer	3		4		1
Morse, Theodore	1		2		
Noyes, Isaac	1		2		
Noyes, John	1	1	1		
Pilsbury, Joseph	1	1	2		
Quimby, Eliphalet	1	1	3		
Quimby, Elisha	1				
Quimby, John	3	2	2		
Quimby, Timothy	2	1	1		
Quimby, William	1				
Richardson, Daniel	1	1	2		
Richardson, Moses	1	2	3		
Riddle, James	1		2		
Riddle, James, Junr	1		1		
Roby, Samuel	1	3	3		
Samburn, Abraham	1		2		
Samburn, Jonathan	1		2		
Samburn, Reuben	1	3	4		
Sawyer, Stephen	1		2		
Stephens, Reubin	4	1	3		
Stephens, Samuel	1		1		
Stephens, Sarah	1	2	2		
Taylor, Joseph	1		2		
Taylor, Joseph, Junr	1	3	2		
Watson, Thomas	1	1	2		
RICHMOND TOWN.					
Aldrich, Aaron	1		1		
Aldrich, Abner	3	1	3		
Aldrich, Annanias	1	4	5		
Aldrich, Artimas	3	4	4		
Aldrich, Joseph	2	3	3		
Aldrich, Levi	3	4	4		

NAME OF HEAD OF FAMILY.	Free white males of 16 years and upward, including heads of families.	Free white males under 16 years.	Free white females, including heads of families.	All other free persons.	Slaves.
RICHMOND TOWN—con.					
Aldrich, Lott	1	1	6		
Aldrich, Nathan	1	4	5		
Aldrich, Nathanial	1	4	4		
Aldrich, Paul	1	1	4		
Aldrich, Phillip	1	1	6		
Aldrich, Royal	1	1	4		
Aldrich, Silas	1	1	5		
Aldrich, Solomon	1	3	4		
Aldrich, Uriah	1	1	2		
Allen, Moses	4		8		
Allen, Olven	1	1	1		
Amsbury, Alice	2	1	4		
Atherton, Jonathan	2	3	3		
Atherton, Solomon	3	1	2		
Ballou, Aaron	1		3		
Ballou, Abel	2	1	4		
Ballou, Daniel	1		2		
Ballou, David	2	2	2		
Ballou, James	2		1		
Ballou, James, Junr	1		1		
Ballou, Jared	1		6		
Ballou, Jesse	1	2	5		
Ballou, Nathan	1	2	3		
Ballou, Russel	1	1	4		
Ballou, Seth	1	1	1		
Ballou, Silas	1	1	6		
Barney, Joseph	1	3	3		
Barney, Martin	1		3		
Barras, Ebenezer	1		2		
Barras, John	3	1	4		
Barras, Michael	1	4	4		
Barras, Oliver	1	3	3		
Barrett, Jesseniah	1	3	2		
Bates, John	1	2	1		
Bennett, John	3	2	4		
Benson, Isaac	2	1	3		
Benson, John	1	1	1		
Blanding, Ebenezer	1	2	2		
Bollard, Stephen	2	1	4		
Bolles, David	3	2	2		
Bolles, David	1	1	1		
Bolles, John	1	2	5		
Bolles, Jonathan	3	3	3		
Bolles, Nathaniel	1	2	5		
Bolles, Solomon	1	3	2		
Bourn, Amos	5	2	5		
Bowen, Nathan	1	2	3		
Bowen, Nathaniel	1	1	1		
Bowen, Thomas	3	2	6		
Boyce, Cadis	1	2	3		
Boyce, John	1		3		
Boyce, Nathan	1	2	2		
Boyce, Paul	2	1	1		
Boyce, Stephen	1		1		
Brown, Abraham	1	2	3		
Brown, James	1	2	2		
Buffum, Benjamin	1		1		
Buffum, Caleb	1	1	3		
Buffum, Esek	1	1	2		
Buffum, George	1	2	3		
Buffum, Jedediah	4	2	5		
Buffum, Moses	2	1	3		
Buffum, Robert	3		3		
Bullock, Jeremiah	2	5	4		
Bump, Jacob	2	2	4		
Burlingame, Daniel	1	4	3		
Capron, Oliver	1	1	3		
Capron, Oliver, Junr	1	1	1		
Cargell, James	1	2	2		
Carpenter, Charles	1	1	1		
Carpenter, Daniel	1	1	2		
Carpenter, Samuel	2	1	3		
Cass, Daniel	2	2	2		
Cass, Daniel, Junr	1	3	2		
Cass, David	1	2	5		
Cass, Iddo	1	1	2		
Cass, Joel	1	3	4		
Cass, John	3		10		
Cass, John	1	3	3		
Cass, John	1		2		
Cass, Jonathan	2	3	5		
Cass, Joseph	1	3	4		
Cass, Joseph	3	3	4		
Cass, Luke	2	2	2		
Cass, Mordica	1	1	2		
Chase, Asa	1	1	1		
Chase, William	1	2	3		
Cook, James	1	1	2		
Cook, Jonathan	1	2	1		
Cook, Nicholas	1	2	2		
Cook, Priscilla	3		4		

NAME OF HEAD OF FAMILY.	Free white males of 16 years and upward, including heads of families.	Free white males under 16 years.	Free white females, including heads of families.	All other free persons.	Slaves.
RICHMOND TOWN—con.					
Cook, Sylvanus	1	1	4		
Cook, Zuriel	1	2	1		
Cooley, Aaron	1	2	1		
Corey, William	1	3	6		
Crane, Sarah	2	1	2		
Curtis, Luther	1		2		
Curtis, Noah	1	1	1		
Curtis, Samuel	1	6	3		
Day, Othenial	1	1	3		
Devenport, Elijah	1	2	2		
Ellis, John	1		1		
Ellis, Martin	1	3	3		
Garnsey, Amos	3	1	3		
Garnsey, Amos, Junr	1		1		
Garnsey, David	1	4	2		
Garnsey, Sourel	1	1	2		
Garnsey, William	2	5	5		
Gaskinn, Jonathan	2	1	3		
Gaskinn, Samuel	1	2	2		
Gaskinn, Varney	1		2		
Gerrish, John	2		1		
Gilson, Paul	2	2	4		
Gilson, Stephen	1	1	3		
Goddard, William	4	1	4		
Gorton, Amos	2	3	5		
Guile, Nepthali	1	1	4		
Hammond, Simson	1	3	5		
Handy, Paul	1	1	4		
Harkness, John	1	1	2		
Harkness, Nathan	3	4	4		
Harris, Abner	4	2	5		
Harris, Christopher	1		2		
Harris, Stephen	2	2	4		
Harris, Sylvanus	1	2	2		
Hewes, James	2		3		
Hicks, Ephriam	3	1	4		
Hicks, Oliver	1	4	4		
Holbrook, Peter	3	2	4		
Hunten, Samuel	2		2		
Ingalls, Edmund	2	2	3		
Ingalls, Henry	2		5		
Jillson, Jonathan	1		2		
Kimton, Stephen	1	3	4		
Kinsley, James	2	1	5		
McDaniel, Neals	1	3	2		
Mann, Abraham	1	3	5		
Mann, Daniel	1		4		
Mann, Elizabeth			4		
Mann, Gideon	2		5		
Mann, Gideon, Junr	1		3		
Martin, Amos	2	3	3		
Martin, George	2	4	2		
Martin, Jesse	2		1		
Martin, Peter	2	2	6		
Martin, Sarah	2	1	4		
Martin, Wilderness	1		1		
Millard, Ebenezer	1	1	3		
Morey, Levi	1		2		
Newell, Joseph	1	7	3		
Norwood, Francis	2		2		
Packer, Moses	1	2	4		
Page, Eli	1	4	2		
Parker, Reuben	2	3	3		
Parker, Silas	1	1	1		
Perry, Oliver	1	4	2		
Peters, Isreal	1		4		
Peters, Richard	2	1	5		
Phillips, Abraham	1	2	4		
Pickering, John	1	5	4		
Ramsdell, Aquilla	2	1	6		
Randell, Reuben	1	2	3		
Robertson, Timothy	1	2	3		
Robinson, John	1	1	3		
Robinson, Peter	1		2		
Russell, David	1	4	3		
Saybins, Isreal	2	3	7		
Scott, John	1	1	3		
Scott, Lemuel	2		2		
Scott, Luke	2	1	2		
Smith, Barnabas	1	1	1		
Smith, Holliab	1	2	3		
Snow, Ivory	1	3	2		
Starkey, Joseph	1	1	4		
Stockwell, Thaddeus	1	2	2		
Stoddard, Elijah	1	1	3		
Streater, Joseph	1	1	2		
Swan, Ebenezer	1	2	3		
Sweet, Antony	1	1	2		
Sweet, Jonathan	1		4		
Sweet, Jonathan, Junr	1	3	2		
Sweet, Richard	1	1	2		

RICHMOND TOWN—con. / RINDGE TOWN.

NAME OF HEAD OF FAMILY.	Free white males of 16 years and upward, including heads of families.	Free white males under 16 years.	Free white females, including heads of families.	All other free persons.	Slaves.
RICHMOND TOWN—con.					
Swift, Samuel	1	3	2		
Taft, Durias	1		2		
Taft, Ephriam	1	3	3		
Taft, Nathaniel	4		4		
Taft, Peleg	1		2		
Taft, Preserved	1		2		
Taft, Silas	1	1	1		
Thayer, Grindal	2	2	3		
Thayer, Jeremiah	2	1	2		
Thayer, Jeremiah, Junr	2	2	2		
Thayer, Levi	1		4		
Thayer, Simeon	4	1	3		
Thompson, Rachal	1	1	4		
Thrasher, Barnabas	2		1		
Thrasher, Benjamin	1	3	3		
Thurber, Hezekiah	1	3	3		
Thurber, Isaiah	3	2	3		
Thurbur, Sylvester	1		4		
Twitchel, Jonas	2		2		
Tyler, Moses	2	3	4		
Wheaton, Moses	1	3	2		
Whipple, Dan	1	4	5		
Whipple, Ichabod	1	4	4		
Whipple, Isreal	2	1	4		
Whipple, Rufus	2	3	4		
Whipple, Squire	2	1	3		
Whitaker, Silas	1	2	2		
White, Elijah	1	3	2		
Wing, John	1	3	5		
Wing, Joseph	2	3	3		
Woodward, Josiah	1	2	2		
Wooley, Nathan	1	2	2		
Works, Robert	4	1	2		
RINDGE TOWN.					
Adams, David	1	2	6		
Adams, Isreal	3	1	4		
Bancroft, Benjamin	2	3	4		
Bancroft, John	1	3	4		
Barker, Barnabas	2	1	2		
Barker, David	1		2		
Bigsby, Joseph	1	3	1		
Bowers, James	1	2	2		
Bowers, Nehemiah	1	1	4		
Busswell, John	2	2	7		
Carleton, James	4		4		
Carleton, William	1	3	2		
Carter, Abijah	1	5	1		
Chadwick, Joshua	1	1	5		
Challice, Timothy	1		2		
Chaplin, Michael	1	1	6		
Chapman, Jeremiah	3	5	4		
Colburn, Ebenezer	1	2	2		
Colburn, Ebenezer, Junr	1	1	1		
Converse, Zebulon	1	1	4		
Crombie, James	3	2	4		
Cummings, Abraham	1	1	3		
Cutler, Amos	2	2	2		
Cutler, Solomon	3		6		
Davis, Benjamin	4	2	3		
Davis, Ebenzer	1	3	5		
Davis, William	1	2	6		
Demary, Ezekiel	1	1	2		
Demary, John	1	1	2		
Demary, Thomas	1		3		
Eiles, John	2	1	10		
Emes, Thomas	2	1	3		
Emory, John	3	4	4		
Emory, Ziba	1	2	3		
Foster, Abner	1		1		
Foster, Benjamin	1		3		
French, Eunice		1	2		
Gardner, William	4	2	3		
Gibson, Isaac	1	2	2		
Gilson, Abel	1	1	1		
Goddin, Henry	1	1	1		
Goddin, Sarah			3		
Gould, Ebenezer	1		5		
Gragg, Daniel	2	4	6		
Hale, Abigal	1	2	2		
Hale, David	1	4	4		
Hale, Moses	1	1	2		
Hale, Moses, Junr	1	3	2		
Hartshorn, Ebenezer	1	1	2		
Henderson, John	1		2		
Houston, Caleb	1	1	2		
Houston, Priscilla			3		
Hubbard, Hezekiah	1	2	3		
Hubbard, Nathan	2	3	5		
Hunt, Ephraim	3		1		
Ingalls, Jonathan	1	1	3		

RINDGE TOWN—con.

NAME OF HEAD OF FAMILY.	Free white males of 16 years and upward, including heads of families.	Free white males under 16 years.	Free white females, including heads of families.	All other free persons.	Slaves.
Ingalls, Nathaniel	1		2		
Ingalls, Simeon	1	3	2		
Jewell, Abel	1	2	2		
Jewett, Edward	3		4		
Jewett, Ezekiel	1		3		
Jewett, Stephen	2		1		
Jewett, Stephen, Junr	3	2	7		
Johnson, Nathan	1	1	2		
Jones, Asa	1	1	2		
Keyes, Peabody	1	1	1		
Keyes, Uriah	1	2	5		
Kimball, Abigal	1	1	3		
Kimball, Andrew	1	1	4		
Kimball, Aquilla	2	2	3		
Kimball, William	1	2	3		
Lake, Daniel	3		2		
Lake, Enos	2	3	4		
Lake, Henry	2	3	2		
Lake, Jonathan	1	3	2		
Lock, Ebenezer	1	1	1		
Lovejoy, John	3		2		
Lovejoy, John, Junr	2	4	6		
Lowell, Nathaniel	1	1	1		
Mansfield, Levi	1	2	2		
Mason, Tilley	1	1	2		
Meeds, Joseph	3	4	4		
Metcalf, George	3		2		
Metcalf, Zatter	1	1	2		
Moore, Benjamin	1		4		
Moore, Joseph	1	1	1		
Mulligan, Joseph	1	3	2		
Muzzy, Ebenezer	1	4	3		
Newton, Charles	1	1	1		
Norcross, Jabez	1	2	2		
Norcross, Jeremiah	2	1	5		
Norcross, Page	2		1		
Page, Abijah	1	2	2		
Page, Daniel	2	3	2		
Page, Joseph	1		2		
Page, Lemuel	1	2	2		
Page, Nathan	1	1	3		
Page, Samuel	1	5	4		
Payson, Seth	3	4	5		
Peirce, Abraham	1	2	1		
Peirce, Benjamin	1	1	6		
Peirce, Josiah	1	3	3		
Perham, David	1		3		
Perkins, Abel	3	3	2		
Perkins, Jane		1	1		
Perry, John	1	3	4		
Philbrick, James	3	2	5		
Piper, Thomas	1	1	2		
Platts, Abel	2	3	4		
Platts, Abel, Junr	1	1	3		
Platts, Ebenezer	1	3			
Platts, Joseph	1		2		
Platts, Joseph, Junr	2	3	3		
Potter, Moses	2	1	1		
Priest, John	1	2	1		
Putnam, Jonathan	2	3	7		
Rand, Daniel	1	3	1		
Rand, Ezekiel	1	3	2		
Rand, Solomon	2	1	6		
Raymond, Joel	1	1	4		
Robins, David	1	2	2		
Robins, William	2	1	1		
Rugg, Amos	1	1	3		
Rugg, Levi	1	3	5		
Rugg, Solomon	1	1	1		
Rugg, Thomas	1	1	2		
Rugg, Thomas	1	3	4		
Russel, Samuel	1	2	6		
Russell, Nathaniel	4	1	4		
Russell, Nathaniel, Junr	1	2	2		
Sawtel, Hezekiah	1	2	4		
Sawtel, Jonathan	1	1	1		
Sawtel, Jonathan	1	3	5		
Sawtel, Josiah	1	1	1		
Shaw, Ebenezer	2	2	3		
Shed, Abel	4	5	2		
Sherwin, Asa	2	3	5		
Sherwin, David	2		3		
Sherwin, Jonathan	2		2		
Sloane, Isreal	1	2	2		
Smith, Henry	3		4		
Stevens, Oliver	1	1	1		
Steward, Benjamin	1	2	1		
Steward, Jack	1		2		
Stickney, William	1	1	2		
Stiles, Hezekiah	1	2	3		
Stone, Salmon	1	4	6		
Stratton, Ebenezer	1	4	2		

RINDGE TOWN—con. / STODDARD TOWN.

NAME OF HEAD OF FAMILY.	Free white males of 16 years and upward, including heads of families.	Free white males under 16 years.	Free white females, including heads of families.	All other free persons.	Slaves.
Streater, James	3		2		
Streater, John	1	2	1		
Swan, William	1	1	6		
Tarball, Samuel	2	1	2		
Thomas, Jethro	1		1		
Thomas, Moses	2	1	5		
Thomas, Moses, Junr	1	1	2		
Thomas, Nathaniel	2	1	6		
Thomas, Othnial	3	1	5		
Thompson, Richard	1	2	6		
Todd, Thomas	3	1	4		
Town, Amos	1	1	2		
Town, Francis	2	1	6		
Town, Francis, Junr	1		1		
Town, Jedediah	1	1	1		
Town, Jeremiah	2		5		
Town, John	2		4		
Tucker, Joel	2		4		
Tyler, Joshua	1	2	7		
Tyler, Parker	2	2	3		
Walker, Joshua	1	5	3		
Walker, Samuel	2	2	4		
Walton, William	1	4	4		
Wetherbee, Abraham	1	5	3		
Wetherbee, Daniel	1	3	3		
Wetherbee, John	1	3	4		
Wetherbee, Thomas	1		2		
Wetherbee, Thomas, Junr	1	1	1		
Wheeler, Jonas	1	1	1		
Wheelock, Luke	1	2	3		
Whiting, John	1		1		
Whiting, John, Junr	1	3	4		
Whitney, David	3	1	1		
Whitney, Isaiah	1	1	3		
Wilder, Silas	1	2	2		
Wood, Eliphalet	1	1	1		
Wood, Isaac	3	4	4		
Wood, James	2	1	3		
Woodey, William				7	
Wyman, Joseph	1	2	2		
STODDARD TOWN.					
Abbott, Nathaniel	1		3		
Abbott, Nehemiah	1	1	1		
Adams, Ephriam	2	3	5		
Adams, John	1	1	2		
Allen, David	1		2		
Baker, Timothy	1		2		
Bardeen, Phillip	1	1	4		
Barden, James	1	1	3		
Barrett, Isaac	1	3	1		
Blake, Eleazer	1	1	1		
Blazdel, Aaron	1				
Boynton, Benoni	2		1		
Brockway, Ephriam	2	2	2		
Brooks, Job	2	1	3		
Chandler, Asa	1	2	2		
Chandler, Jonathan	1	3	3		
Copeland, Jacob	2	4	4		
Copeland, Jacob, Junr	1		3		
Davis, Benjamin	1	2	4		
Dodge, Joseph	1	1	5		
Dun, Benjamin	1	4	3		
Dutton, William	1	2	2		
Eddey, Ward	2		1		
Edes, Samuel	1	4	4		
Emerson, Nathaniel	3	6	4		
Emerson, Richard	3	4	6		
Evans, Nathaniel	3	1	4		
Fairbank, Aaron	2		1		
Fairbank, Oliver	1	3	4		
Farlee, Ebenezer	1		2		
Farlee, John	1	4	4		
Farnsworth, Herber	1	3	5		
Farnsworth, Samuel	1	4	4		
Fisher, Isaac	1	1	1		
Flint, Joel	2		3		
Gerrett, James	1	2	4		
Gilson, Joel	2	5	2		
Gilson, Nathaniel	1	1	2		
Goodale, Enos	1	2	4		
Gould, Simeon	1		1		
Green, John	1	2			
Hardy, Auther P	1	1			
Hardy, Isaiah	2	2	4		
Hardy, Nathan	2	1	5		
Hardy, Stephen	1	2	2		
Haywood, Benjamin	1	2	4		
Haywood, Jesse	1	2	3		
Haywood, William	1	2	4		

CHESHIRE COUNTY—Continued.

STODDARD TOWN—con.

NAME OF HEAD OF FAMILY.	Free white males of 16 years and upward, including heads of families.	Free white males under 16 years.	Free white females, including heads of families.	All other free persons.	Slaves.
Henry, Bani	1		2		
Henry, John	1		2		
Henry, John, Junr	1	2	5		
Henry, Ziba	1		2		
Hodgman, David	2	2	6		
Hodgman, Oliver	1	2	3		
Hogg, Joshua	1		2		
Hunt, Caleb	4		2		1
Ingalls, Edmund	1	3	1		
Jenkins, Obadiah	2	3	5		
Jeruild, Samuel	1	1	2		
Joslin, David	1		4		
Joslin, Nathaniel	2		2		
Kemp, Susannah		2	4		
Kenney, Isaac	2	2	8		
Keyes, Daniel	1	1	3		
Lock, Daniel	1		1		
Lock, Enos	1	1	1		
McCloud, Samuel	1	3	3		
Mansfield, Willard	1	1	1		
Mansfield, William	1	1	1		
Messenger, Samuel	1	1	1		
Munroe, Nathan	1	4	1		
Nichols, Thomas	1	2	5		
Niles, Peter	1	2	5		
Osgood, John, Junr	3		4		
Osgood, William	2	2	2		
Parker, Phinehas	1	3	2		
Parker, Samuel	1	3	3		
Pearson, William	1	2	3		
Phelps, Edward	1		2		
Pike, William	1	2	3		
Pitcher, William	3	5	4		
Procter, Nathan	1	2	5		
Reed, Eliakim	1	1	2		
Reed, Elnathan	1		5		
Reed, Joshua	1	3	4		
Richardson, Nathan	1		2		
Richardson, Richard	2		3		
Richardson, Richard, Junr	1		1		
Robb, Andrew	3	2	2		
Robb, More	1		1		
Robb, Samuel	1		2		
Robb, Samuel, Junr	1	3	2		
Scott, Alexander	1		1		
Scott, David	1	3	3		
Scott, James	1	3	2		
Seaver, Samuel	2	4	3		
Shed, Jonathan	1	3	3		
Spaulding, Aaron	1		1		
Spaulding, John	1		6		
Spaulding, Levi	1	2	1		
Spaulding, Willard	1		2		
Spear, Allen	1	4	5		
Stevens, Daniel	1	2	4		
Stevens, Henry	1	1	1		
Taggert, John	4		1		
Tarball, Benjamin	1	1	1		
Thompson, Jonathan	1	1	3		
Thompson, Timothy	1	3	3		
Town, Benjamin	1		1		
Town, Isreal	4	1	2		
Town, Isreal, Junr	1	2	5		
Tuttle, Nathaniel	1		2		
Wells, Samuel	1	2	2		
Wheat, Joseph	1	3	1		
Wilson, James	2	4	5		
Wilson, Samuel	1	2	3		
Wood, Noah	1	2	2		
Wright, Caleb	2		2		
Wright, Ebenezer	1	3	4		
Wright, Joel	1		4		
Wright, Peter	1	1	3		
Wright, Silas	2	2	3		
Wright, Silas, Junr	1		2		

SULLIVAN TOWN.

NAME OF HEAD OF FAMILY.	Free white males of 16 years and upward, including heads of families.	Free white males under 16 years.	Free white females, including heads of families.	All other free persons.	Slaves.
Allen, Abel	2		3		
Baker, Jonathan	1	3	7		
Bolster, Nathan	1	3	3		
Brown, William	1	1	2		
Burdet, Ebenezer	1	3	1		
Burnham, Jonathan	1	4	2		
Caldwell, Daniel	1		1		
Carter, Elijah	1	2	1		
Chapman, Benjamin	1	1	3		
Chapman, John	1		2		
Chapman, John	3	3	3		
Demmick, John	2	3	6		

SULLIVAN TOWN—con.

NAME OF HEAD OF FAMILY.	Free white males of 16 years and upward, including heads of families.	Free white males under 16 years.	Free white females, including heads of families.	All other free persons.	Slaves.
Demmick, Timothy	2		4		
Eaton, Jonathan	1	1	5		
Ellis, Benjamin	1	1	1		
Ellis, Nathan	1		1		
Ellis, Simeon	1	2	2		
Farlee, John S	1	2	2		
Hubbard, Roswell	3	1	3		
Keith, Grindall	1	1	3		
Kemp, Benjamin	1	2	2		
McKinsie, William	1	3	2		
Mack, Abner	1		1		
Morse, Thomas	2	1	3		
Nims, Eliakim	1	1	2		
Nims, Zadock	1	3	3		
Osgood, Ezra	1	2	2		
Osgood, Joshua	1	7	3		
Reed, Hinds	1	3	4		
Row, James	2		3	1	
Row, John	1	1	2		
Sawtell, Micheal	1	3	3		
Seward, Josiah	1	3	4		
Seward, Samuel	1	3	3		
Wheeler, Jesse	1	2	3		
Wilson, Daniel	3	3	6		
Woods, Enoch	1		2		

SURRY TOWN.

NAME OF HEAD OF FAMILY.	Free white males of 16 years and upward, including heads of families.	Free white males under 16 years.	Free white females, including heads of families.	All other free persons.	Slaves.
Allen, Abel	2	1	3		
Allen, Abel, Junr	1	1	2		
Allen, Phinehas	1		3		
Barron, William	1		3		
Barron, William, Junr	1	1	2		
Baxter, Simon	3	2	5		
Benton, Abijah	1	1	4		
Bliss, Abner	1	1	5		
Britton, Phillip	1	3	2		
Brockway, Easter	1	1	1		
Brockway, John	1	2	3		
Brown, Moses	1	1	4		
Carpenter, Benjamin	2	1	2		
Carpenter, Benjamin, Junr	2	2	1		
Carpenter, Charles	1	2	1		
Carpenter, Jedediah	3		5		
Carpenter, Jedediah, Junr	1	1	2		
Carpenter, Jonathan	1		2		
Cram, Abiah	2	2	4		
Crandel, Edward	1	2	5		
Darling, David	1	1	3		
Dart, Eli	1	1	1		
Dart, Eliphalet	1	2	4		
Dart, Nathaniel	1	1	4		
Dasance, Jesse	1		1		
Delance, Dalavan	2	2	3		
Everett, Thomas	1	3	4		
Field, Moses D	1	5	5		
Fowler, Cheever	1	4	3		
Fuller, Levi	2	1	5		
Gilbert, Ebenezer	1	2	3		
Hancock, Asa	2	5	4		
Hannock, Levi	2		3		
Harvey, Thomas	4	2	1		
Haywood, Nathan	1	1	6		
Haywood, Peter	3	1	4		
Haywood, Sarah	2	2	2		
Hills, Samuel	1		3		
Holmes, Asa	1		1		
Holmes, Lemuel	3	1	4		
Humphry, James	1	4	5		
Isham, Benjamin	1	3	2		
McCordy, James	2	2	2		
McCordy, John	2	1	5		
McCordy, Samuel	1		1		
McCordy, Samuel, Junr	2		3		
Marrifield, Benjamin	1		1		
Marvin, John	2		1		
Marvin, John, Junr	2	2	2		
Munroe, Phillip	3	1	5		
Phillips, Reuben	1	2	4		
Prentice, Reuben	1	2	4		
Reding, John	1	2	2		
Reed, David	1	4	1		
Rice, Phinehas	1	1	3		
Riggs, Samuel	1	1	3		
Robertson, Jonathan	3	1	4		
Russell, William	1	1	3		
Scovel, Henry	1	1	3		
Skinner, Abner	2	2	2		
Smith, Abraham	1		1		

SURRY TOWN—con.

NAME OF HEAD OF FAMILY.	Free white males of 16 years and upward, including heads of families.	Free white males under 16 years.	Free white females, including heads of families.	All other free persons.	Slaves.
Smith, Abraham, Junr	1	1	1		
Smith, Daniel	1		2		
Smith, Ichabod	1	1	2		
Smith, Jonathan	2	1	2		
Smith, Samuel	3	3	5		
Smith, Stephen	2		2		
Smith, Thomas	2	1	2		
Smith, Thomas, Junr	1	2	2		
Streater, Zebulon	1	3	5		
Washburn, Caleb	1	2	3		
Washburn, Simeon	1		1		
Wetherbee, Tabitha		1	2		
Wilbore, Phillip	1		2		
Willcox, Asa	1	3	1		
Willcox, Obadiah	3		5		
Willcox, Obadiah, Junr	1	1	2		
Wright, Eleazer	1	1	2		
Wright, Oliver	1	2	2		

SWANZEY TOWN.

NAME OF HEAD OF FAMILY.	Free white males of 16 years and upward, including heads of families.	Free white males under 16 years.	Free white females, including heads of families.	All other free persons.	Slaves.
Aldrich, Amasa	3	3	4		
Aldrich, Benoni	1		2		
Aplin, Isaac	1		1		
Aplin, John	1	4	2		
Aplin, Thomas	3		2		
Aplin, Timothy B	1	1	2		
Battels, Jeremiah	1	2	5		
Battels, Thomas	1	1	1		
Beaverstock, Edward	1	2	4		
Bellding, David	1		2		
Bellding, David, Junr	2		3		
Bellding, Elijah	2	3	9		
Bellding, James	1		3		
Bellding, Moses	1	1	4		
Bellding, Samuel	1		3		
Bellding, Samuel, Junr	1	1	3		
Bishop, Timothy	1	3	5		
Brown, Abijah	1	3	3		
Brown, Benjamin	2		2		
Brown, Eleazer	1	2	3		
Capron, Nathan	2		4		
Capron, Otis		3	3		
Carpenter, Greenwood	1	5	5		
Carpenter, William	1	4	2		
Chamberlain, Samuel	3	2	5		
Chandler, Salmon	1	1	3		
Clemens, Abijah	1	6	2		
Cook, George	1	3	3		
Cresson, Guias	1		3		
Cresson, Nathan	1	3	2		
Cresson, Thomas	1	2	3		
Cross, Joseph	2	2	3		
Cross, Thomas	2	3	2		
Cummings, Enoch	2		3		
Cummings, Ephriam	2	4	3		
Cummings, Joseph	2	4	8		
Cummings, Nehemiah	3		2		
Cummings, Thaddeus	2	1	3		
Curtis, Amoriah	2		4		
Curtis, Calvin	1		2		
Darling, Aaron	1	1	2		
Day, Amos	1	2	2		
Day, Benjamin	1	1	5		
Day, Brier	1		5		
Day, Jonathan		1	2		
Dickinson, Joseph	2	3	4		
Dickinson, Nathaniel	3	5	4		
Dunton, Elijah	1	1	3		
Durant, Levi	2	3	3		
Eames, Jotham	1	1	1		
Farnsworth, Moses	1		2		
Farnsworth, Paul	1	2	2		
Farnsworth, Silas	1		1		
Flint, Daniel	1	2	3		
Franklin, John	1		2		
Freeman, Amos	1		3		
Freeman, Benjamin	1		2		
Frink, Calvin	1	1	3		
Gay, Seth	1		1		
Goddard, Edward	2	3	3		
Graves, Asahel	2	2	2		
Graves, Elijah	2		3		
Graves, Elijah, Junr	1	1	3		
Graves, Gad	1		3		
Graves, Joseph	1	2	2		
Graves, Josha, Junr	1		2		
Graves, Joshua	2	1	2		
Green, James	1	1	1		
Green, Samuel	1	1	5		
Green, Thomas	2	4	4		

NAME OF HEAD OF FAMILY.	Free white males of 16 years and upward, including heads of families.	Free white males under 16 years.	Free white females, including heads of families.	All other free persons.	Slaves.	NAME OF HEAD OF FAMILY.	Free white males of 16 years and upward, including heads of families.	Free white males under 16 years.	Free white females, including heads of families.	All other free persons.	Slaves.	NAME OF HEAD OF FAMILY.	Free white males of 16 years and upward, including heads of families.	Free white males under 16 years.	Free white females, including heads of families.	All other free persons.	Slaves.
SWANZEY TOWN—con.						**SWANZEY TOWN—con.**						**UNITY TOWN—con.**					
Griffith, David	1		4			Thompson, Samuel	2	3	5			Livingston, Isaac	1	2	4		
Griffith, William	1	1	3			Trask, Nicholas	2	1	2			Marshall, Moses	2		2		
Grimes, Charles	3	1	3			Trask, Stephen	1		3			Martin, Moses	1	1	6		
Grimes, James	2	2	1			Trowbridge, Thomas	2	1	3			Moody, Daniel	2	1	3		
Grimes, John	1	1	4			Tubs, Annanias	1	1	6			Moody, Josiah	1	3	4		
Grimes, William	3	2	7			Warner, Daniel	2	1	4			Moody, Josiah, Junr	1	4	3		
Guild, Dan	2	3	3			Warren, Timothy	2		4			Moody, Richard	1	3	3		
Gunn, Daniel	3	1	3			Weeks, William	1		2			Neal, William	3	3	4		
Gunn, William	1		1			Wetherbee, Abijah	1	3	2			Nott, Thomas	2	3	4		
Gunn, Wyatt	2		1			Wheelock, James	1	2	4			Peirce, Nicholas	3	1	3		
Hamlet, Josiah	1	2	3			Whitcomb, Elisha	3	4	5			Perkins, Jacob	1	2	1		
Hamlet, Phinehas	1	1	5			Whitcomb, John	3		3			Perkins, Joseph	3	1	3		
Hammond, Benjamin	1	1	5			Whitcomb, Jonas	2	1	2			Pike, Osteen	1	1	4		
Hammond, Isaac	3	2	5			Whitcomb, Jonathan	3	1	4			Procter, Jonathan	1	3	2		
Hammond, Jonathan	2		2			Whitcomb, Joseph, Jur	1	1	1			Samborn, Abraham	3	2	5		
Hammond, Joseph	3		1			Whitcomb, Philemon	2	4	6			Samborn, Phinehas	1				
Hammond, Joseph, Junr	2	1	3			Whitcomb, Silas	1	1	1			Sinclere, Barnabas	1	3	2		
Harvey, John	1		2			Whitcomb, Thomas	2	1	2			Sleeper, John	1	4	1		
Harvey, Kimbar	1	3	5			White, Stephen	1	2	1			Smart, Benjamin	1	2	1		
Hazen, Ame		2	2			Williams, Moses B	1	3	2			Smith, Hannah	1		1		
Hazen, Edward	1	3	3			Willis, Benjamin	1		2			Smith, Jacob	1	1	2		
Heaton, James	1	3	4			Willis, Maletiah	1		3			Smith, Thomas	1	1	7		
Hefferon, John	1	2	1			Wilson, Abel	1	1	1			Stockbridge, John				1	
Hefferon, Micheal	2		2			Wilson, Benjamin	3	3	5			Swett, Derbon	2		5		
Hewes, Benjamin	1		6			Wilson, Samuel	1	4	4			Thurber, Samuel W	1	3	3		
Hewes, George	2		2			Woodcock, Nathan	1	2	5			Thurstin, Moses	2	1	4		
Hibberry, Abner				6		Woodward, Isaac	1	1	2			Thurstin, Moses, Junr	1	4	3		
Hill, Nathan	1	1	3			Woodward, Isaac, Junr	1	1	1			Weed, David	2		3		
Hills, Ebenezer	3		3			Wright, Alpheus	1	1	2			Weed, Elijah	1	1	1		
Hills, Nathaniel	1	1	2			Wright, John	1	2	2			Weed, Joseph	1	2	2		
Hills, Nathaniel	2		5			Wright, William	3	1	2			Welch, John	1	1	1		
Hills, Samuel	3	1	2									Young, Hezekiah	1		3		
Hills, Samuel, Junr	2		5			**UNITY TOWN.**											
Howe, Simon	1	3	3			Barker, Ebenezer	2	1	1			**WALPOLE TOWN.**					
Hunt, William	1	1	1			Barron, Abel	1		1			Abbey, Mason	3		1		
Jones, Thankfull		1	2			Bartlett, Jacob	1	1	1			Alexander, Richard	2	1	2		
Kempton, Samuel	1		6			Bartlett, Joshua	3	1	2			Allen, Aaron	3	1	5		
Kimball, Eli	1	5	3			Bartlett, Matthias	1	3	5			Allen, Amasa	5		3		
Kimball, Jethro	1	4	5			Batchelor, Daniel	3	1	1			Allen, James	3	2	7		
Lane, Elkanah	2	1	2			Bodwell, Eliphalet	3	2	4			Allen, John	1	1	2		
Lane, Samuel	3	3	3			Bodwell, James	2		2			Ashley, Sarah			2		
Lawrance, Justus	1		2			Breed, Eliphalet	1	3	5			Baker, Nathaniel	2	1	2		
Lawrance, Paddock	1	1	1			Buckman, Amos	1		1			Beckwith, Bathuel	1		4		
Mann, Hezekiah	1	4	6			Buckman, Elias	1		3			Bellows, Benjamin	8	1	7		
Merril, Asa	3	1	2			Buckman, Stephen	1	3	4			Bellows, John	3	4	8		
Moore, Paul	1		3			Challice, Ezekiel	1	3	2			Bellows, Joseph	5	2	6		
Morse, Henry	2	1	5			Chase, Abner	2	1	5			Bellows, Josiah	4	2	2		
Nichols, Andrew	1	3	1			Chase, Amos	2	3	5			Bellows, Theodore	1	2	3		1
Olcott, Benjamin	2	1	3			Chase, Moses	1	1	1			Bellows, Thomas	4	1	3		
Olcott, Benjamin, Junr	1		2			Chase, Samuel	3		1			Bennett, Stephen	1	4	2		
Osgood, Elijah	3	1	3			Clough, Benjamin	1	3	3			Blake, Increase	1	2	1		
Osgood, Elijah, Junr	1		2			Clough, Cornelius	2	1	3			Brigham, Leonard	1	5	4		
Osgood, Ezekiel	1	1	2			Cram, Ephriam	1	1	3			Bundy, Asahel	2	2	5		
Page, Ephriam	1	1	2			Cram, Jacob	1	1	1			Bundy, Elias	1	2	6		
Page, Samuel	3	2	4			Cram, Sanborn	1	3	3			Bundy, Isaac	2	6	4		
Parker, John	1	1				Currier, Abner	1	2	6			Bundy, Nathan	2	3	5		
Parker, Jonathan	1	1	3			Dean, Jeremiah	1	2	2			Burt, Moses	2	3	5		
Parsons, Aaron	3	2	4			Dudley, James	2	1	3			Butterfield, Amos	1	1	4		
Parsons, Benjamin	1	2	3			Fifield, Moses	1		4			Carlisle, David	2	1	5		
Partridge, Amaziah	2	1	3			Gillman, Caleb	1	1	4			Chenney, John	1	4	2		
Peck, Amariah	1	4	3			Gillman, Stephen	1	3	4			Chenney, William	1	3	5		
Peirce, John	1		8			Glidden, Andrew	5	3	3			Churchill, Jonathan	1	2	4		
Pomeroy, Seth	1	2	3			Glidden, Jeremiah	2	1	4			Cockrin, John	1	1	2		
Prime, Joshua	1	1	4			Glidden, Jonathan	1	1	3			Crafts, John	2	2	3		
Prime, Josiah	2	1	1			Glidden, Jonathan, Junr	2	3	1			Davis, Ruth			2		
Puffer, Simeon	1		5			Glidden, Joseph	1	2	7			Debell, Alexander	1	1	1		
Ramsey, William	1	1	3			Glidden, Simeon	4	1	6			Dennison, Daniel	1		1		
Randall, Abraham	4	3	4			Hall, Amos	1	2	2			Dennison, Daniel, Jur	1	2	2		
Razey, Peletiah	2	1	3			Hart, Nathaniel	1	1	1			Dennison, Ebenezer	1		2		
Reed, David	1	2	4			Huntoon, Benjamin	4	2	4			Dennison, Jedediah	1	2	1		
Reed, Timothy	4	1	5			Huntoon, Caleb	1	1	7			Dennison, Lucy		3	2		
Rice, Josiah	1	4	2			Huntoon, Charles	2		1			Drury, Menoah	2	3	4		
Richardson, Amos	1		1			Huntoon, Charles 2d	1	2	5			Dunshed, Hugh	1	1	2		
Richardson, Wyman	1	5	4			Huntoon, Charles 3d	1	2	3			Eastman, Jonathan	1	1	2		
Sawyer, Abijah	2	1	2			Huntoon, John	1	2	1			Eaton, Ebenezer	2	3	4		
Sawyer, Isreal	1	3	4			Huntoon, Joseph	3	2	4			Eaton, Isaiah	3	2	4		
Scott, Ebenezer	3	2	1			Huntoon, Josiah	1	4	2			Eaton, Timothy	1	5	2		
Scott, Elisha	2		2			Huntoon, Moses	1	2	4			Emory, John	3	2	2		
Seaver, Shubael	2	3	3			Huntoon, Nathaniel	1		2			Emory, Joseph	1		5		
Sherman, David	1	2	1			Huntoon, Nathaniel, Junr	1	1	1			Engalls, Joseph		1	2		
Smead, Joseph	1	1	1			Huntoon, Phillip	1	3	5			Fairbank, Jonas	1	2	5		
Smead, Nims	2	2	3			Huntoon, Samuel	2		2			Farnham, Eber	1	4	3		
Stanley, Pentecost	2	1	6			Huntoon, Stephen	1		4			Farnham, Roger	1	2	5		
Starkey, Enock	1	5	3			Huntoon, T. Philbrook	1	2	3			Farnum, Ebenezer	2	2	4		
Starkey, John	1		2			Ladd, James	1	3	5			Fay, Joseph	1	1	3		
Stone, Ebenezer	1	1	4			Ladd, Mary	1	1	5			Fay, Levi	2	1	2		
Stratton, Richard	1	1	2			Ladd, Nathaniel	1	4	4			Fay, Lucy	1	1	2		
Taft, Nathan	1	4	2			Lampson, Amos	1		2			Fenton, Gamaliel	2		1		
Thompson, Ebenezer	1	4	5			Lampson, Asa	3		4			Fessendon, Thomas	2	4	5		
Thompson, John	3		5									Fish, Stephen	1	1	5		
Thompson, Roger	3	3	4														

CHESHIRE COUNTY—Continued.

WALPOLE TOWN—con.

NAME OF HEAD OF FAMILY.	Free white males of 16 years and upward, including heads of families.	Free white males under 16 years.	Free white females, including heads of families.	All other free persons.	Slaves.
Fletcher, Jonathan	3	1	4		
Fletcher, Samuel	1	3	3		
Flint, John	2	1	4		
Flood, Benjamin	2	1	3		
Fox, Eliphalet	3		3		
French, Andrew	7		2		
Gage, Asa	4	4	6		
Gates, Jonathan	2	1	4		
Gates, Jonathan, Junr	2	1	4		
Gates, Josiah	1	3	4		
Gates, Zaccheus	1	2	2		
Geer, George	1	1	2		
Gillchrese, Robert	1		2		
Gillchrese, Samuel	2		1		
Gillman, Constantine	1		2		
Gilson, Joseph	2	2	2		
Goldsmith, Josiah	1	1	7		
Graves, Aaron	2		2		
Graves, Aaron, Junr	1	1	1		
Graves, Abner	1		2		
Graves, Barnabas	1	2	1		
Graves, Durias	1	2	2		
Graves, Eliphaz	3	2	4		
Graves, Eliud	1		2		
Graves, Eliud, Junr	1	1	3		
Graves, Ezekiel	1	3	2		
Graves, John	1		1		
Graves, John, Junr	2	2	7		
Graves, John, 3d	1	1	2		
Griggs, Ephriam	1	3	2		
Griswold, Gilbert	1	1	1		
Griswold, Joseph	3		1		
Griswold, Josiah	2	2	6		
Hall, Abraham	1	1	5		
Hall, David	2	2	4		
Hall, Elisha	1		1		
Hall, John	1	4	2		
Hall, Jonathan	1		1		
Hall, Jonathan, Junr	1	3	5		
Hall, Recompence	1	2	5		
Hall, Roland	1	3	5		
Harrington, Antiphar	1	3	5		
Harwood, Ebenezer	1	2	3		
Hazleton, James	1				
Hoadley, Ithiel	1	2	4		
Hodgkins, Aaron	2	2	5		
Hodgkins, Aaron, 2d	2	2	4		
Hogg, David	1	7	4		
Holland, Abraham	2	2	2		
Hooper, Levi	2	2	3		
Hosmer, Jonas	3	1	3		
Hovey, Ichabod	1	1	2		
Huntington, Gurden	1		3		
Ingraham, Ephriam	1	2	1		
Jennison, John	4	2	6		
Jennison, Jonathan	1	5	4		
Jewett, Samuel	2	1	2		
Johnson, David	1	2	4		
Johnson, Isaac	1		1		
Johnson, Joseph	2	3	2		
Johnson, Moses	1	1	4		
Johnson, Thomas	2	2	4		
Joslin, Daniel	2	1	3		
Kilburn, John	3		3		
Kitridge, Francis	2	2	6		
Knap, James	2		1		
Lewis, James	1	3	3		
Lewis, John	1	2	2		
Lock, Phillip	1	3	4		
McLaughlin, William	1	1	1		
Martin, John	1	3	4		
Mason, Joseph	1	1	4		
Merriam, John	3		1		
Merriam, John, Junr	1	2	1		
Merriam, Richard	2	1	1		
Messer, Nathaniel	1	3	1		
Messer, Thomas	1	1	3		
Moore, William	4	1	2		1
Munn, Joseph	3	2	4		
Newton, Elnathan	1		3		
Nichols, Thomas	1	1	1		
Parker, Joseph	2	1	1		
Parker, Nathaniel	1		2		
Parker, Pearl	1	1	3		
Parker, Samuel	1		2		
Parker, Thomas	2	1	5		
Paul, James	3	5	2		
Prentice, Stephen	1	1	3		
Quintin, David	2	2	2		
Ramsey, William	1	5	2		
Randall, Ephraim	1	1	1		

WALPOLE TOWN—con.

NAME OF HEAD OF FAMILY.	Free white males of 16 years and upward, including heads of families.	Free white males under 16 years.	Free white females, including heads of families.	All other free persons.	Slaves.
Rice, John	1		3		
Rose. Elijah	1		3		
Royce, Aaron	1	1	4		
Royce, John	1	1	2		
Royce, Jonathan	3	2	5		
Russell, Aquilla	1	3	4		
Russell, Jadathan	2	3	6		
Russell, Thomas	1	3	1		
Salter, Samuel	2	2	4		
Sartwell, Benjamin	1	3	2		
Sikes, Nathaniel	1	1	4		
Smith, Benjamin	2	3	6		
Smith, John	1		2		
Spafford, Elijah	2	2	3		
Sparhawk, George	2	1	2		
Sparhawk, Thomas	2	3	4	1	
Sparhawk, Thomas, Junr	1	1	1		
Stearns, Aaron	2	1	5		
Stearns, Ephriam	1	5	2		
Stearns, Moses	1		4		
Sterling, Nathan	1	1	2		
Stevens, David	6		2		
Stocker, Ebenezer	1	4	3		
Stone, Lemuel	1	1	1		
Stowell, William	2	3	3		
Swan, Ebenezer	1		1		
Temple, Enos	1	1	3		
Thatcher, Joseph	1	1	3		
Titus, Sylvanus	3	1	2		
Townsley, Nacanor	2	1	2		
Trott, Samuel	1	2	1		
Usher, Daniel	1	1	3		
Wallcott, Roger	2	2	2		
Warren, Cornelius	2	1	4		
Warren, Jabez	2	2	4		
Warren, Winslow	1	1	1		
Watkins, Alexander	3	4	2		
Watkins, Edward	1	1	1		
Watkins, Nathan	4		3		
Weld, Joseph	1	3	2		
Wheeler, John	2	2	2		
Whipple, Daniel	3	2	4		
Willey, Barnabas	1	7	5		
Wire, Robert	1	5	4		
Wire, Samuel	3	4	7		
Wright, Moses	2	3	4		
Wyman, Uzziah	1	1	2		
Wyman, William	1	2	3		

WASHINGTON TOWN.

NAME OF HEAD OF FAMILY.	Free white males of 16 years and upward, including heads of families.	Free white males under 16 years.	Free white females, including heads of families.	All other free persons.	Slaves.
Babcock, Benjamin	1	1	1		
Bacon, Jeremiah	1	3	1		
Barney, John	1	2	4		
Barney, Levi	1	1	3		
Barney, Supply	2		1		
Barney, Thomas	2		2		
Brockway, Jonathan	3	2	1		
Brockway, Jonathan, Junr	1		2		
Brockway, Martin	1		4		
Brown, Thomas	2	1	4		
Burbank, Jacob	2	2	4		
Burpee, David	2		1		
Clarke, Jonathan	1	4	4		
Copeland, Samuel	2	3	3		
Crafts, Christopher	1		3		
Crane, Joseph	1	4	2		
Danforth, David	2	4	3		
Davis, Ebenezer	2		4		
Davis, Ephriam	1	4	4		
Davis, John	1	1	1		
Davis, Josiah	1	3	2		
Densmore, Eliphalet	4	1	2		
Draper, Jonathan	1	2	5		
Draper, Nathaniel	1	1	6		
Draper, Samuel	1	2	2		
Eaton, John	1	1	1		
Estabrook, Abraham	1	2	4		
Farnsworth, David	1	1	1		
Farnsworth, John	1	2	5		
Farnsworth, Joseph	1		5		
Farnsworth, Manasah	1	2	3		
Farnsworth, Simeon	2		4		
Farnsworth, Simeon, Junr	2	3	5		
Farwell, Ephriam	1		4		
Farwell, Thomas	1	1	2		
Farwell, Thomas, Junr	1		1		
Faxon, Francis	1	1	2		
Foster, Elijah	1	1	3		

WASHINGTON TOWN—continued.

NAME OF HEAD OF FAMILY.	Free white males of 16 years and upward, including heads of families.	Free white males under 16 years.	Free white females, including heads of families.	All other free persons.	Slaves.
Foster, Israel	1	1	7		
French, Elijah	3		1		
French, Isaac	1		3		
Graves, William	1	1	5		
Guile, Samuel	1	1	2		
Harris, David	1	4	3		
Harris, John	1		2		
Haynes, Joshua	1	1	2		
Healey, John	3	2	5		
Houghton, Adonijah	1	1	3		
Jackson, Asa	1		4		
Jacwith, Ebenezer	3	3	3		
Lee, Stephen	1	1	4		
Leslie, George	3		3		
Leslie, James	1	2	2		
Lewis, Samuel	1	4	3		
Lowell, Samuel	1	3	2		
Lowell, Simeon	1	3	5		
Lufkin, Jacob	1	2	1		
McMillen, John	1	1	3		
Meeds, Stephen	1	2	2		
Miller, Joseph	1		3		
Mills, Hezekiah	1	1	2		
Munroe, Joseph	1	1	2		
Pennyman, Thomas	4		1		
Petts, James	1	1	2		
Procter, Josiah	1		3		
Procter, Josiah, Junr	1		4		
Procter, William	2	3	5		
Putnam, Thomas	1		3		
Richards, Josiah	1	5	2		
Ross, Kneeland	1	2	3		
Rounsevel, Joseph	4		3		
Safford, John	1	3	3		
Safford, John, Junr	1		1		
Sampson, Abner	2		2		
Seaton, John	1		3		
Severance, Abel	1	2	1		
Severance, Daniel	1	4	1		
Severance, Ephriam	1		4		
Severance, Rufus	1	1	2		
Smith, Jesse	1	3	2		
Smith, Phillip	1		2		
Spaulding, Ebenezer	1	4	3		
Steel, James	1	2	1		
Steel, John	1		1		
Steel, Joseph	1		6		
Steel, William	1	1	2		
Stevens, Isaac	2	1	6		
Stevens, Jesse	1		3		
Tabor, Church	1	1	4		
Tabor, Joseph	4		1		
Tabor, Pardon	2		1		
Twiss, Samuel	1	1	3		
Vose, John	1	3	3		
Wheeler, Amos	2	3	2		
Wood, Ebenezer	1	3	5		
Woodward, Caleb	1	2	2		
Wright, Jacob	3	2	2		

WENDELL TOWN.

NAME OF HEAD OF FAMILY.	Free white males of 16 years and upward, including heads of families.	Free white males under 16 years.	Free white females, including heads of families.	All other free persons.	Slaves.
Angell, Eber	2	1	4		
Angell, Gideon	2	2	2		
Angell, Noell	1	1	2		
Angell, Stukeley	1	1	1		
Ayres, George	1		2		
Bartlett, Giles	1	1	3		
Bayley, Joel	1	4	5		
Bryant, Israel	1	1	5		
Bryant, James	1	1	3		
Clap, Job	1	2	6		
Cutt, Joseph	4	1	3		
Cutt, William	1		2		
Dam, Edward	1		1		
Freeman, Alden	1		4		
Freeman, Ebenezer	4	3	2		
Gage, Joshua	2	3	6		
Gardner, Christopher	1	6	5		
Grandell, Daniel	1		2		
Gunnison, Ephriam	3		2		
Gunnison, Nathaniel	1		2		
Gunnison, Samuel	1	1	1		
Haywood, Benjamin	1		1		
Kelsey, Giles	1	3	1		
Lang, Stephen	1		1		
Lang, William	1		2		
Lear, George W	1		3		
Lear, Joseph	1	1	4		
Libby, James	1	1	2		

CHESHIRE COUNTY—Continued.

NAME OF HEAD OF FAMILY.	Free white males of 16 years and upward, including heads of families.	Free white males under 16 years.	Free white females, including heads of families.	All other free persons.	Slaves.	NAME OF HEAD OF FAMILY.	Free white males of 16 years and upward, including heads of families.	Free white males under 16 years.	Free white females, including heads of families.	All other free persons.	Slaves.	NAME OF HEAD OF FAMILY.	Free white males of 16 years and upward, including heads of families.	Free white males under 16 years.	Free white females, including heads of families.	All other free persons.	Slaves.
WENDELL TOWN—con.						**WESTMORELAND TOWN— continued.**						**WESTMORELAND TOWN— continued.**					
McBritton, Jenny			1			Chamberlain, Job	1	1	1			How, Samuel	2	1	2		
Moses, Daniel	1	1	1			Chamberlain, John	2	2	5			How, Samuel 2d	2	2	4		
Perkins, Ichabod	3		3			Chandler, Aaron	1	1	4			How, Selah	1	2	1		
Rand, Benjamin	1	1	2			Chandler, John	1	2	3			Hutchins, David	1	3	2		
Rand, Benjamin, Junr	1	1	1			Church, Charles	2	3	3			Hutchins, William	2	2	6		
Rankins, Thomas	1		1			Church, Constant	2	2	3			Hynds, Patience			2		
Sherburne, Daniel	2	5	5			Clap, William	1	2	2			Isbel, Garner	1	1	5		
Tandy, Parker	1	2	4			Cobb, Daniel	4	1	4			Jenkins, Lemuel	1	1	1		
True, Moses	1	2	1			Cobb, George	1	5	4			Jinkins, David	1	2	2		
Wheeler, John	2	1	1			Cobb, Morgan	1	2	1			Johnson, Daniel	3	3	6		
Whitney, Joshua	1	4	4			Cobb, Richard	1	2	2			Johnson, Oliver	2		6		
Woodward, Elijah	1	1	2			Cobo, Samuel	4	3	5			Johnson, Samuel	1	4	2		
Woodward, Joshua	1	2	1			Cobb, Simeon	1	1	4			Jones, Dick				3	
Woodward, Nehemiah	2	2	3			Cole, Jonathan, 2d	2	4	6			Keep, Leonard	5	2	8		
Woodward, Richard	2		2			Crane, Ebenezer	1	3	3			Kendall, Peter	1		2		
Woodward, Squire	1	3	4			Craw, Jonathan	1	2	4			Kendall, Reuben	3	2	6		
Woodward, Thomas	1	1	3			Daggett, Durias	1		4			Kendall, William	1	5	4		
Young, Abiather	2	2	5			Daggett, Nathaniel	2	1	6			Kimball, Abel	1		2		
Young, Cornelius	1	1	2			Daggett, Reuben	1	2	6			Knight, Jonathan 2d	4		5		
Young, Edward	1	1	3			Daggett, Simon	1	3	5			Knight, Timothy	3	2	5		
Young, Esek	3		4			Daggett, William	3	1	5			Leech, Azariah	2		5		
Young, James	1	2	3			Daniels, Increase	3	2	6			Leech, Sherebiah	2	5	2		
Young, Robert	1	3	1			Day, Noah	1	1	3			Leech, Zephaniah	5	3	2		
						Dean, Samuel	2	2	3			Leving, Noah	1		1		
WESTMORELAND TOWN.						Demmon, Daniel	1	2	3			Lincoln, Abiather	1	1	5		
Albee, Ichabod	1	2	2			Derby, Abner	1		1			Lincoln, George	1		2		
Albee, Zuriel	2	3	4			Derby, Samuel	1		3			Lincoln, Mace	1		4		
Aldrich, Caleb	2	1	5			Derby, Squire	1	2	4			Lincoln, Samuel	1	3	7		
Aldrich, Caleb, Junr	1	1	2			Derby, Thomas	1	3	3			Livingston, John	1	4	3		
Aldrich, Ebenezer	1	1	2			Dodge, Josiah	3	3	2			Lord, Joseph	1		3		
Aldrich, George	3	2	4	1		Doolittle, John	3	3	4			Lord, Jotham	2	2	5		
Aldrich, Joel	2	1	4			Dors, Jepthah	2		2			McDonald, John	1	4	2		
Amsbury, Ebenezer	1	2	2			Dunham, Thomas	1	1	3			McMurphy, John	1	1	2		
Amsbury, Isreal	3	1	5			Dyer, Susanah			2			Macumber, Abiather	1	2	1		
Arnold, David	2		4			Edson, Jonah	2	4	5			Maherim, Ephriam	1	1	1		
Axtell, Benjamin	1	2	5			Estabrook, Samuel	1	1	7			Marsh, Benjamin	3	1	6		
Babbit, Nathan	1	3	4			Esty, Edward	1	4	1			Melven, Nathaniel	1		2		
Babcock, Amos	2	5	7			Esty, William	1		1			Millett, Ebenezer	1	3	4		
Baker, Elizabeth			3			Farmer, James	1	4	3			Mixer, Ezekiel	2	7	3		
Baker, John	2	5	2			Farnsworth, Ebenezer	1	1	2			Moore, Alpheus	5		1		
Baker, Peter	1	2	3			Feezee, John	1	3	8			Muzzy, Benjamin	1	2	4		
Bayley, Ebenezer	1	2	7			Felt, Joshua	1	2	3			Newton, Hannaniah	1	1	3		
Bayley, Jether	2	1	3			Finney, Nathaniel	1	2	3			Packard, Gideon	1	3	2		
Bennett, David	1	3	2			Fletcher, John	2	1	3			Packard, Joseph	2		1		
Bennett, Moses	3	1	3			Flint, Jonas	1	3	1			Pattin, Benoni	2	1	4		
Bennett, William	1	2	3			Franklin, Nathan	3	1	2			Peck, Ebenezer	1	1	4		
Benton, Joseph	2	2	1			French, David	2	3	4			Peirce, Amos	1	2	3		
Blanchard, Nathaniel	2	3	2			French, John	1	3	3			Peirce, Daniel	1	4	4		
Bowen, Ephriam	2	2	7			Fuller, Josiah	2	1	3			Peirce, Ebenezer, 2d	2	3	4		
Boynton, Joseph	2	3	5			Fuller, Noah	4	1	7			Peirce, Ezekiel	1		1		
Briggs, Caleb	2	1	1			Furguson, George	1	3	4			Peirce, Ezekiel, 2d	1	1	3		
Briggs, Ephriam	1		4			Garey, Seth	4	1	3			Peirce, Ezra	4	3	6		
Briggs, Joshua	1	1	4			Garey, Widdow			3			Peirce, John	1	2	5		
Britton, David	3	3	6			Gates, Elias	2	1	2			Pennyman, David	1		1		
Britton, Ebenezer	2	4	4			Gates, Paul	1		1			Pennyman, Paul	1	3	2		
Britton, Job	1	4	3			George, Benjamin	2	2	3			Phillips, Nehemiah	2	1	3		
Britton, Mary	1		2			Gilbert, Ebenezer	1		1			Pope, John	1	3	3		1
Britton, Samuel	1	1	7			Gilbert, Gideon	2	3	3			Pratt, Solomon	1	2	2		
Britton, Sarah	3	1	1			Gilson, Jonathan	1	1	1			Priest, Joel	1	2	7		
Britton, Seth	3	1	7			Gleeson, Benjamin	1	2	5			Prowty, Bela	3	2	5		
Britton, Stephen	1	2	1			Gleeson, Fortunatus	3	3	5			Reed, Abiah	3	2	5		
Brockway, William	3	2	10			Gleeson, James	3	5	5			Reed, Micah	3	5	4		
Brown, Aaron	1	2	4			Glinney, John	2		2			Robens, David	1	2	2		
Brown, Amos	2	4	2			Goodenow, Abel	1	1	1			Robens, John	4	3	1		
Brown, David	1		1			Goodenow, Israel	1	3	3			Robens, Jonas	3	1	5		
Brown, Ephriam, 2d	1	2	1			Goodenow, Jonathan	2	2	7			Robens, Solomon	1	2	4		
Brown, Joseph	4		7			Goodenow, Nathan	1	3	5			Russell, William	1	1	3		
Brown, Moses	2	1	1			Goodenow, Timothy	1	3	3			Sanderson, Ebenezer	1	1	3		
Brown, Nehemiah	2	5	1			Goodenow, William	1		3			Sawyer, Joseph	2		1		
Brown, Timothy	1	2	2			Graves, Nathan	2	2	6			Sawyer, Manasah	1	5	5		
Buffum, Joseph	2	2	2			Gray, Joseph	1	2	2			Scott, Waitsdell	3	4	3		
Bullock, Timothy	1	1	3			Hacket, Josiah	2	3	5			Shaw, Abiather	2	2	6		
Burt, Aaron	3	1	4			Harrington, Ebenezer	1	1	7			Silvester, Elijah	1		2		
Burt, Asa	3	1	4			Hartwell, Asahel	1	2	3			Silvester, Lemuel	1	2	2		
Burt, Enos	2	2	6			Harvey, Isaiah	2	4	4			Smith, Rufus	1	3	5		
Burt, Joseph	1	5	4			Haskins, Elkanah	2	4	4			Snow, Elijah	1		3		
Burt, Samuel	2		2			Hastings, Nathaniel	2	2	3			Stacy, David	3		4		
Butterfield, Isaac	4	2	4			Hatch, Edmund	1	3	6			Staples, Jacob	1	3	3		
Butterfield, Isaac, 2d	1	2	2			Hazleton, Richard	1	1	3			Stevens, Ebenezer	2	3	1		
Butterfield, James	1	1	5			Hazleton, Thomas	3		3			Stiles, Lincoln	1		1		
Butterfield, Jonas	4	4	3			Highland, Amasa	1	3	3			Stiles, Peleg	1	1	2		
Butterfield, Jonas, Junr	1	2	1			Hodges, Zebediah	1		3			Stoddard, Isaiah	1		1		
Butterfield, Timothy	1	1	3			Hodgkins, Peter	1	2	2			Stone, Allen	1		3		
Butterfield, Timothy	1	2	3			Hoskins, William	1		2			Stone, Daniel	1	2	6		
Carlisle, Daniel	2	3	5			Hoskins, William 2d	2	1	2			Stone, James	1	2	2		
Chamberlain, Amos	1	2	1			How, Abner	1		5			Stone, Keziah			3		
Chamberlain, Increase	2	2	4			How, Caleb	1	3	1			Streater, Samuel	1		3		
Chamberlain, Increase, Jnr	1	2	3			How, Daniel	1		3			Streater, Stephen	1	4	3		
Chamberlain, Jedediah	2		6			How, Edward	1	1	2			Telden, Joshua	1	3	5		
						How, Joseph	1	3	2			Temple, Archelus	2	1	2		
						How, Mehitable	1	2	2			Temple, John	1		2		

CHESHIRE COUNTY—Continued.

WESTMORELAND TOWN—continued.

NAME OF HEAD OF FAMILY.	Free white males of 16 years and upward, including heads of families.	Free white males under 16 years.	Free white females, including heads of families.	All other free persons.	Slaves.
Temple, Jonas	1		2		
Temple, William	1	1	4		
Thompson, Joseph	1	2	6		
Thompson, Moses	1	3	3		
Trotter, Alexander	2	2	1		
Tuell, Barnard	2		3		
Tuell, Charles	1	2	3		
Twitchel, Ephriam	1	1	1		
Waite, Jason	1	2	3		
Walker, Benjamin	1	3	4		
Walton, Hannah			4		
Ward, James	2	1	1		
Warner, Job	1	1	3		
Warner, John	2	1	4		
Warner, John, 2d	1	2	4		
Warner, William	2	2	5		
Washburn, Nathan	1		2		
Washburn, Seletiah	1	1	4		
Wetherell, Abiather	1		1		
Wetherill, David	2	3	6		
Wheeler, Abel	1	1	1		
Wheeler, Harriden	1	1	4		
Wheeler, John	2		1		
Wheeler, John, 2d	1	2	1		
Wheeler, Obadiah	1		3		
Wheeler, Silas	2	2	6		
Wheeler, Solomon	3	5	3		
White, John	2	2	4		
White, Joseph	2	1	5		
White, Moses	3	2	7		
White, Thomas	1	1	2		
Whitman, Daniel	1	6	3		
Whitman, Noah	1	2	4		
Whitney, Joseph	1	1	6		
Wilbore, David	1	2	2		
Wilbore, Elisha	2	2	3		
Wilbore, Job	2		6		
Wilbore, Joseph	1		1		
Wilbore, Nathaniel	1	3	3		
Wilbore, Phillip	1		1		
Wilbore, Phillip, 2d	2		7		
Willis, Jonathan	1	2	2		
Wilson, Ebenezer	1	4	1		
Winchester, David	1	1	4		
Winchester, Jonathan	2	4	2		
Wood, Ephriam	2	1	5		
Wood, James	1	3	5		
Wood, John	1		2		
Wood, Jonathan	2	2	1		
Woodward, Ezekiel	3	1	2		
Woodward, Ezekiel, 2d	1	2	1		
Woodward, Jacob	1	1	5		
Works, Samuel	4	2	5		

WINCHESTER TOWN.

NAME OF HEAD OF FAMILY.	Free white males of 16 years and upward, including heads of families.	Free white males under 16 years.	Free white females, including heads of families.	All other free persons.	Slaves.
Abbott, Moses	1	1	2		
Alexander, Asa	2	3	4		
Alexander, John	2	3	6		
Alexander, Reuben	5	3	4		
Alexander, Thomas	1	1	4		
Allen, Joseph	1	1	4		
Arbor, John Nicholas	1	1	1		
Ashley, Daniel	1	2	4		
Bancroft, Thaddeus	1	1	2		
Bannett, David	1	2	1		
Bartlett, Nathaniel	1		2		
Bartlett, Reuben	1	3	2		
Battels, Edward	4	1	7		
Belding, Joel	1	2	2		
Belding, Stephen	3	1	4		
Bishop, Joel	1	1	4		
Bond, Samuel	1	3	4		
Brigham, Abraham	1	3	2		
Brown, Samuel	2	2	4		
Burnham, Francis	3		1		
Butler, John	4	1	2		
Butler, John, Junr	1	1	5		
Cahoone, Daniel	4	1	3	1	
Chamberlain, Moses	2	1	7		
Chamberlain, Simon	4		4		
Coburn, Joseph	1	5	4		
Coller, Nathaniel	1		1		

WINCHESTER TOWN—continued.

NAME OF HEAD OF FAMILY.	Free white males of 16 years and upward, including heads of families.	Free white males under 16 years.	Free white females, including heads of families.	All other free persons.	Slaves.
Cook, Charles	2	1	3		
Cook, Charles, Junr	1		1		
Cook, Francis	1	1	4		
Coomes, Antony	2	2	5		
Corps, Joseph	1		1		
Cottin, Abijah	1	2	2		
Curtis, John	2	3	3		
Curtis, Thomas	1	3	1		
Darling, Stephen	1		2		
Dodge, Andrew	2	2	4		
Dodge, Ebenezer	1	2	3		
Dodge, Elijah	1	4	5		
Dodge, Nathaniel B	2	2	3		
Erskine, John	1	2	7		
Evans, Bedad	1	2	5		
Evans, Jeremiah	1		3		
Fassett, Adonijah	1	5	3		
Fassett, Samuel	2	1	4		
Field, Elihu	1	2	5		
Field, Guess	1		1		
Field, Guess, Junr	1	1	3		
Field, Waitsdel	1	4	3		
Field, Zachariah	2	3	5		
Follet, Benjamin	1	1	4		
Follet, John	1	8	3		
Foster, Henry	1	1	1		
Foster, Henry	2	4	3		
Foster, James	1		4		
Foster, James	1	2	2		
Foster, John	1	2	3		
Franklin, Daniel	1	1	3		
Franklin, Ichabod	1	2	3		
Franklin, Stephen	1	2	5		
Freelove, John	3		1		
French, Jonah	1	3	4		
Fuller, Benjamin	2	1	5		
Gale, Richard	1		3		
Garfield, Daniel	1	4	2		
Gordon, Stephen	1	1	1		
Goss, Phillip	3		1		
Goss, Phillip, Junr	1	1	4		
Gould, John	3	1	3		
Gould, Thomas	1	2	4		
Griggs, Ebenezer	2		1		
Griggs, Joseph	1	1	2		
Hammond, Abel	2	3	5		
Hatch, Asa	1	1	2		
Hatch, Jeremiah	2		2		
Hatch, John	1	3	3		
Hawkins, Daniel	4		6		
Hawkins, Stephen	1		4		
Haywood, Jonathan	1	1	3		
Haywood, Jonathan	2	2	3		
Healy, Daniel	1	1	2		
Healy, Ezra	2	1	4		
Healy, Nehemiah	1	2	3		
Healy, Samuel	1	2	5		
Higgins, John	1	4	4		
Hill, Jonathan	1	4	4		
Holbrook, Caleb	1	2	3		
Holmes, William	1		1		
Hoskins, Nehemiah	1	4	4		
Houghton, Elijah	2	1	3		
Houghton, Eunice	1		4		
Houghton, Solomon	1	2	3		
Humphry, William	3		2		
Hunt, Jonas	3	3	5		
Hutchins, Asa	2	2	2		
Hutchins, Isaac	1	3	5		
Hutchins, John	3	4	3		
Hutchins, Thomas	1		2		
Jewell, Justus	2	5	4		
Jewett, Hannah	1	4	5		
Jinks, Cynthia	1	1	2		
Joy, Michael	1		3		
Keyse, Nathaniel	1	2	1		
Killam, Ebenezer	1		1		
King, Nathaniel	3	1	5		
Kingman, Benjamin	1	1	5		
Knap, Elisha	3	1	3		
Larrance, Nathaniel, Junr	2	4	8		
Larrance, William	2	2	3		

WINCHESTER TOWN—continued.

NAME OF HEAD OF FAMILY.	Free white males of 16 years and upward, including heads of families.	Free white males under 16 years.	Free white females, including heads of families.	All other free persons.	Slaves.
Leech, Ephriam	2	2	2		
Leonard, Jonathan	1	1	1		
Long, Joseph	1	3	3		
Lyman, Joshua	1	2	1		
Lyman, Phinehas	1	1	1		
Lyman, Tarsius	1		3		
McDowell, Alexander	3	1	3		
Marble, Benjamin	2	1	2		
Marble, Joseph	1	3	4		
Marble, Levi	2	1	3		
Melven, Benjamin	3	2	5		
Miles, Henry	3	5	3		
Monroe, Nathaniel	1	1	8		
Moore, Theodosius	2	1	4		
Munroe, Joslin	2	4	3		
Narrowmore, Abiel	2	1	2		
Oldham, Abel	1		2		
Parker, Ezra	3	1	3		
Peirce, John	1		2		
Picket, Daniel Lock	1	2	1		
Plummer, Simeon	1	5	1		
Pomeroy, Peletiah	1	2	5		
Pratt, Jeremiah	4	2	8		
Price, William	1		1		
Putnam, Stephen	1		3		
Richardson, Paul	1		2		
Ripley, Eleazer	1	1	5		
Ripley, Nathaniel	1	4	4		
Rixford, Simon	1	1	1		
Rixford, William	1	4	2		
Roberts, Amasa	1		5		
Robertson, John	3	2	3		
Scott, Abel	2	1	2		
Scott, Abraham	2	1	4		
Scott, Ebenezer	4		4		
Scott, Rhoda			1		
Smith, Daniel	1	4	4		
Smith, Elisha	3	1	4		
Smith, Elisha, Junr	1				
Smith, Samuel	4		2		
Smith, Samuel, 2d	1		3		
Smith, Zimri	1				
Stearns, John	2	1	7		
Stebbins, Josiah	2	1	4		
Stedson, Job	1	1	2		
Stowell, Enoch	4	3	3		
Stowell, Joseph	3	2	4		
Taylor, Ebenezer	5	3	2		
Taylor, Samuel	1		6		
Thayer, Henry	1	3	5		
Thrasher, Benjamin	2	2	3		
Thurstin, Thomas	1	3	2		
Turner, Ishmael					3
Turner, Samuel	1	2	4		
Tuttle, Joseph	1	1	3		
Tuttle, Joseph, Junr	1	2	1		
Twitchel, Nathan	2		3		
Vary, Francis	3	3	4		
Vary, Samuel	1	2	3		
Vickery, Benjamin	1	3	4		
Wales, Roger	1	2	2		
Ware, Ziba	3	2	6		
Warren, Samuel	1	1	2		
Watkins, Theodore	1	1	4		
White, Greenfield	2		2		
Whittemore, Joshua	2	1	4		
Whitten, Solomon	1	2	3		
Wilder, Peter	1	1	2		
Willard, Amos	1	4	5		
Willard, Hannah		2	6		1
Willard, Seth	1	1	2		
Willard, Solomon	3	2	5		
Willis, Caleb	1	2	1		
Willis, Hezekiah	1	1	1		
Willis, Joshua	1	1	1		
Wise, Daniel	1	2	5		
Wood, Samuel	1	1	6		
Wooley, Asa	1		1		
Wright, Benjamin	1	5	3		
Wright, Mary		1	3		

GRAFTON COUNTY.

ALEXANDRIA TOWN.

NAME OF HEAD OF FAMILY.	Free white males of 16 years and upward, including heads of families.	Free white males under 16 years.	Free white females, including heads of families.	All other free persons.	Slaves.
Atwood, David	3	4	4		
Atwood, Joseph	1	1	1		
Bartlett, Christopher	1	1	3		
Basford, Benjamin	1	2	4		
Bradley, Ambros	1	2	2		
Burpee, Jonathan	2		6		
Case, Nason	1	3	4		
Clark, Jonathan	1	2	5		
Clufford, Ebenezer	2	6	4		
Colby, John	1	1	3		
Colton, Ebenezer	1	1	2		
Cook, Israel	1		1		
Cortless, Daniel	1	1	2		
Cortless, George	1	2	2		
Cortless, John M	1	1	6		
Emerson, Josiah	3		4		
Fellows, Abel	1		1		
Ferren, Enos	2	3	4		
Fevor, Isaac	1		2		
Fevor, Jacob	1	2	2		
Flanders, Levi	1	3	2		
Gale, Eliphalet	3	2	6		
Ingols, Nathaniel	1				
Ladd, Isaac	1	4	4		
Ladd, Jeremiah	2		2		
Ladd, Peter	1	1	2		
McMurphy, Daniel	2		2		
McMurphy, David	1				
McMurphy, John	2	1	4		
McMurphy, John, jr	1				
McMurphy, Saunders	1	1	2		
McMurphy, William	1	3	2		
Morrel, Simon	1	1	1		
Morrison, John	1				
Murry, Robert	1	3	4		
Niles, George	1	1	1		
Palmer, Jonathan	3	1	1		
Palmer, William	1				
Pingra, George	1		2		
Simonds, Ebenezer	2	4	2		
Simonds, John	1	1	1		
Simonds, Timothy	3	3	3		
Simonds, William	2	3	2		
Smith, Peter	1	2	2		
Taylor, Anthony	3	2	6		
Taylor, Ebenezer	1		2		
Taylor, James	1		1		
Taylor, Jonathan	1	6	2		
Tole, Jeremiah	3	2	4		
Tolford, John	1	5	2		
Tolford, Joshua	3	3	4		
Townsend, Ziba	1				
Williams, Ebenezer	2	1	2		
Winter, Benjamin	1	2	1		

BARTLETT TOWN.

NAME OF HEAD OF FAMILY.	Free white males of 16 years and upward, including heads of families.	Free white males under 16 years.	Free white females, including heads of families.	All other free persons.	Slaves.
Barnes, Ephraim	1		5		
Bassett, James	1	2	3		
Calton, Edward	1		2		
Calton, Samuel	1	1	2		
Chebuck, Levi	1	1	4		
Copp, Joseph	1		4		
Corkins, Thomas	1		2		
Eads, Peter	1		1		
Emery, Enoch	2	5	5		
Emery, Humphry	2	1	6		
Fall, Samuel	1	2	2		
Garlin, Richard	1	3	1		
Ginkens, Samuel	1	1	1		
Hall, Joseph	2	2	5		
Hall, Joseph, Jr	1		1		
Hall, Joseah	1	1	1		
Hall, Obed	1		2		1
Hunt, Richard	1		2		
Hutchins, Jonathan	1	1	4		
McColley, Flurrence	1		1		
Pendexter, John	1	3	9		
Pitman, Joseph	2	4	4		
Pitman, Mark	1		2		
Place, George	1		3		
Place, Jonathan	1	1	2		
Rockwell, Joseph	1				
Rogers, James	1	3	4		
Rogers, Samuel	1	1	5		
Rogers, Thomas	1				
Sanburn, Samuel	1	2	1		
Sevey, Jonathan	1		1		
Sevey, Joseph	1	1	2		
Sevey, Levi	1		3		
Sevey, Samuel	1	1	3		

BARTLETT TOWN—con.

NAME OF HEAD OF FAMILY.	Free white males of 16 years and upward, including heads of families.	Free white males under 16 years.	Free white females, including heads of families.	All other free persons.	Slaves.
Sevey, Simon	1		1		
Smith, Nathaniel	1		1		
Spring, Thomas	1	2	3		
Stanton, Elijah	1		2		
Stanton, Isaac	1	2	1		
Stanton, Samuel	1		2		
Taskell, Jonathan	1	2	4		
Taylor, John	1		1		
Thomson, Joseph	1				
Tomson, Miles	1				
Walker, Timothy	1	2	3		
Weeks, Josiah	1				
Weeks, John	1	4	2		
Whitham, Jeremiah	1	5	1		
Woodhouse, George	1	1	11		
Woodhouse, Samuel	1	3	6		
Worcester, John	1		5		

BATH TOWN.

NAME OF HEAD OF FAMILY.	Free white males of 16 years and upward, including heads of families.	Free white males under 16 years.	Free white females, including heads of families.	All other free persons.	Slaves.
Amy, George	1	1	2		
Amy, Heman	1	1	3		
Bacon, Ebenezer	2	1	2		
Baley, Aaron	1	3	3		
Baley, Daniel	1	4	5		
Baley, David	1	1	2		
Baley, Edward	1		3		
Barron, Jonathan	1	2	2		
Bartlet, Michael	3	1	2		
Bedle, Daniel	2	3	5		
Bedle, John	2	2	6		
Bedle, Joshua	1	2	5		
Buck, Amasa	1	4	2		
Buck, Thomas	1	2	2		
Calton, Jesse	1		1		
Chase, Abel	2	3	3		
Chase, James	2		2		
Chase, John	1	1	1		
Childs, Ezra	1	3	4		
Cleavland, Elisha	1	3	2		
Cleavland, Eliphalet	1	1	3		
Cleavland, John	2		1		
Cleavland, Solomon	1		2		
Clement, Simon	2	1	1		
Curror, Ichabod	1	3	4		
Curror, John	1	1	2		
Dam, Ebenezer	2	1	8		
Dodge, John	2	3	4		
Eastman, James	2	3	2		
Eastman, Obadiah	1	3	4		
Farman, John	4	4	3		
Hancock, Henry	2	2	3		
Hadlock, James	1	2	1		
Hamond, Mathew	1		3		
Hand, Oliver	1	1	4		
Hazelton, Maxi	1		2		
Hazelton, William	1		1		
Hardy, Jesse	1	1	3		
Hibbard, Timothy	1	2	3		
Henry, Joseph	1	3	2		
Herd, Jacob	3	2	5		1
Heriman, Jehiel	1	1	2		
Hinks, James	1		2		
Huggins, Jonathan	2		1		
Hunt, Henry	1	5	4		
Hunt, Zebulun	1	2	4		
Hutchinson, Jeremiah	4	1	6		
Lang, Samuel	1	3	4		
Lapish, John	2	1	2		
Morril, John	1	4	3		
Mitchel, James	1	5	2		
Moore, Isaac	1		1		
Morse, Uriel	1		3		
Noys, Timothy	1		2		
Petty, Zepheniah	1	1	2		
Pike, Moses	1		2		
Pike, Moses, Junr	1	2	1		
Powers, Aaron	2	2	3		
Powers, David	1	3	2		
Powers, Nahum	1		2		
Quimba, Daniel	1	5	1		
Ricks, Nathaniel	1	2	4		
Rowel, John	2		1		
Russel, Reuben	1		1		
Sanburn, Ebenezer	3	3	4		
Sanburn, Mark	1	2	7		
Sanburn, Richard	1	2	3		
Sanders, Joshua	2		1		
Salter, Bosinger	1	1	1		
Salter, Michael	1		3		
Sawyer, Oliver	1	1	5		

BATH TOWN—con.

NAME OF HEAD OF FAMILY.	Free white males of 16 years and upward, including heads of families.	Free white males under 16 years.	Free white females, including heads of families.	All other free persons.	Slaves.
Sergeants, Rogers	2	3	3		
Smith, James	1		1		
Smith, Joseph	3	3	3		
Smith, Stephen	1	4	4		
Stephens, Timothy	1	2	4		
Sticknor, James	1		3		
Sticknor, Mehitabel		2	3		
Sticknor, Reuben	1	1	3		
Turner, Solomon	2	2	4		
Waters, John	1	1	7		
Weeks, David	1	1	2		
Wheeler, Thomas	1	1	2		
Wilson, Gardner	1	1	1		
Wilson, Elijah	1	1	2		

BRIDGEWATER TOWN.

NAME OF HEAD OF FAMILY.	Free white males of 16 years and upward, including heads of families.	Free white males under 16 years.	Free white females, including heads of families.	All other free persons.	Slaves.
Boardman, Benjamin	1	3	1		
Boardman, Elias	1	2	2		
Brown, Stephen T	1	1	1		
Calton, Jonathan	1	3	3		
Clark, Ephraim	1		2		
Cleaveland, John	1		2		
Comings, Elisha	1	1	1		
Comings, Nathaniel	1		1		
Crafford, Ezra	3	2	4		
Crafford, Jonathan	2		2		
Crafford, Thomas	2		2		
Crague, Alexander	1				
Crague, David	1		1		
Crague, Mary			2		
Crague, Robert	1				
Drew, Moses	1	1	1		
Drew, Samuel	1	3	2		
Emmons, Benjamin	4	4	6		
Emmons, Joseph	1		2		
Fellows, Elizabeth			3		
Fellows, Jacob	1				
Fellows, John	1	1	2		
Fellows, Josiah	1	3	1		
Fellows, Moses	1	1	1		
Fuller, Chase	1	2	5		
Gorden, Jacob	2	1	3		
Gorden, Samuel	1				
Heath, James	1				
Heath, John	1	2	2		
Heath, Jonathan	1				
Heath, Josiah	2	1	1		
Heath, Peter	4		2		
Heath, Samuel	3	2	3		
Holt, Jonathan	1		1		
Ingals, Jonathan	3	1	4		
Ingals, Jonathan, Jur	1		4		
Jewet, Jonathan	1		2		
Kidder, Benjamin	1	1	2		
Kidder, Thomas	3	1	4		
Lock, Benjamin	1				
Lock, Thomas	2	2	4		
Mitchel, John	3	2	6		
Morse, Daniel	1	1	2		1
Moshure, Michal	3	2	5		
Ordway, William	1				
Peasley, Jacob	1	2	5		
Powers, William	3	2	3		
Samburn, Abraham	1	1	2		
Samburn, Elijah	1	1	2		
Senter, Isaac	1				
Sleeper, Daniel	1		1		
Sleeper, John	1	1	3		
Sleeper, Moses	1	1	4		
Speller, John	1	2	3		
Spencer, Seth	1	1	5		
Sterns, Samuel	1				
Tilton, John	1	1	1		
Turrel, Abel	1	2	4		
Turrel, Jonah	1	3	3		
Worthing, John	1				
Worthing, Samuel	1	2	3		

BURTON TOWN.

NAME OF HEAD OF FAMILY.	Free white males of 16 years and upward, including heads of families.	Free white males under 16 years.	Free white females, including heads of families.	All other free persons.	Slaves.
Allord, David	1	1	1		
Allord, Henry	5	2	3		
Brown, Theophilus	2	2	4		
Chase, John	1		1		
Crosby, Joseph	1	1	1		
Crosby, Samuel	1		2		
Gilman, Ezekiel	1	2	5		
Gilman, Jeremiah	3		4		
George, Isaac	2	4	2		
Head, Daniel	1		2		
Head, Nathaniel	1		2		

GRAFTON COUNTY—Continued.

NAME OF HEAD OF FAMILY.	Free white males of 16 years and upward, including heads of families.	Free white males under 16 years.	Free white females, including heads of families.	All other free persons.	Slaves.
BURTON TOWN—con					
Hefford, Nathaniel	1	1	2		
Herreman, David	1				
Hinks, Ambrose	2	5	2		
Jewel, John	1	1	1		
Jewel, John, Junr	1	2	5		
Meads, Benjamin	1	5	4		
Nealey, Andrew	1	3	5		
Noles, Nathaniel	1	3	4		
Payne, Hannah			1		
Weed, Benjamin	2	6	2		
Weed, Elisha	1	4	1		
Weed, Orland	3	2	5		
CAMBRIDGE TOWN.					
Not inhabited.					
CAMPTON TOWN.					
Adams, Isaac	1	1	2		
Baker, Moses	2	1	2		
Baker, Moses, Junr	1	1	1		
Baker, Sarah		1	3		
Baker, William	3		4		
Bartlett, Ebenezer	1	1	2		
Bartlett, Ebenezer, Junr	1		2		
Bartlett, David	1	1	4		
Bartlett, Moody	1		1		
Bartlett, Thomas	3	2	8		
Blasdal, Josiah	1	1	5		
Blasdal, Stephen	1				
Blasdal, Roger	1				
Branard, Cheleab	1	1	2		
Bump, James	1	1	7		
Burbank, Benjamin	1		3		
Burbank, Garshom	3		5		
Burbank, Jonathan	1	2	2		
Burbank, Urial	1				
Chase, Karr	1	3	5		
Cheney, Ebenezer	2	1	1		
Church, Jabez	2	1	5		
Church, Jered	1				
Church, Selden	2	3	4		
Church, Thomas	1				
Clark, John	1	1	2		
Cook, Cotting	1	1	2		
Cook, Ephraim	3				
Cook, Moody	2	2	5		
Cook, Samuel	1		4		
Fox, Isaac	1				
Fox, Urial	2	2	3		
Gideons, Stephen	2	3	2		
Goodhue, Stephen	1	3	2		
Hall, Jesse	1	1	1		
Homans, John	1	1	2		
Homans, Joseph	3	1	5		
Homans, Joseph, Jur	1	1	1		
Holmes, Chancy	1		1		
Holmes, John	2	2	2		
Holmes, Samuel	3	1	3		
Johnson, Ichabod	2	1	7		
Johnson, Jonathan	1	1	2		
Little, Ebenezer	4	1	4		
Little, Moses	6	3	6		1
Martin, Jirah	1	1	3		
Mash, Edmond	1	2	2		
Mash, John	1		3		
Merril, Enock	1	3	1		
Merril, James	2	2	4		
Mitchel, Isaac	1		2		
Nickals, George	1	2	3		
Noyes, Christopher	1				
Noyes, Samuel	2	2	2		
Palmer, Dudley	1	2	4		
Palmer, Joseph	1				
Palmer, Joseph, Junr	1		4		
Parseval, Ichabod	1		1		
Parseval, Rowland	2	4	2		
Parseval. Rowland, Jur	1	1	1		
Pulsepher, Joseph	2	3	4		
Rogers, Joshua	1				
Southmead, John	2	2	4		
Spencer, Amasa	1		2		
Taylor, Ebenezer	1		4		
Taylor, Ebenezer, Junr	1		3		
Taylor, Edward	1	1	3		
Taylor, Oliver	1		2		
Tupper, Ezra	1	1	2		
Tupper, Nathaniel	2	1	6		
Wait, Daniel	3	1	6		

NAME OF HEAD OF FAMILY.	Free white males of 16 years and upward, including heads of families.	Free white males under 16 years.	Free white females, including heads of families.	All other free persons.	Slaves.
CAMPTON TOWN—con.					
Willey, Abel	1	3	3		
Willey, Darius	3		6		
Willey, Jesse	1	1	2		
Worcester, David	1	1	1		
CANAAN TOWN.					
Ayer, William	2	3	3		
Barber, Joseph	1				
Barber, Robert	4	2	4		
Bartlett, Josiah H	1	2	2		
Bartlett, Nathaniel	1	1	4		
Bean, John	1	1	1		
Blasdal, Daniel	1	4	1		
Blasdel, Parot	2	1	4		
Blood, Enock	1				
Baldwin, Thomas	1	1	5		
Booth, Isaiah	1	2	2		
Bradbury, William	1		2		
Brdshan, Joshua	1	4	4		
Clark, Caleb	1		2		
Clark, Currier	2	1	1		
Clark, Josha	1		1		
Clark, Richard	2	1	4		
Clark, Richard, Junr	1		1		
Colby, Daniel	1	3	3		
Colkins, John P	1	4	4		
Currier, John	1	1	4		
Cushing, Joshua	1	1	2		
Duglas, William	1	5	2		
Dustin, Daniel	1	1	1		
Dustin, Jonathan	4		3		
Dustin, Jonathan, Jr	1	1	1		
Eastman, Stephen	1	1	2		
Finch, Henry	2	1	3		
Flint, Joseph	4	4	6		
Falsom, Joseph	1				
Fulsom, Josiah	4		1		
Fulsom, Samuel	1	3	3		
Gates, Rowland	1	2	1		
Gardner, Ezekel	1	1	3		
Gilman, Dudley	1	2	4		
Hadley, Abel	1	2	2		
Hadley, Simon	1		1		
Harris, Benjamin	1				
Harris, George	4	1	3		
Harris, George, Junr	1				
Harris, John	1	2	3		
Heath, Samuel	1		4		
Hovey, Jacob	1				
Jones, David	2	1	6		
Jones, Jehue	1	4	5		
Jones, Samuel	3	1	4		
Josland, Samuel	2	1	2		
Kimball, Asa	1	2	3		
Kenester, Francis	1	1	1		
Lathrop, Elias	1				
Lathrop, Thoddeus	1	3	2		
Micham, Samuel	4	4	5		
Miller, Jonathan	2		4		
Minor, Thomas	3	2	5		
Morse, Daniel	1	1	1		
Nichols, Ezra	1		1		
Norris, Eliphalet	1	3	3		
Noys, Samuel	1		1		
Otis, Richard	3	2	4		
Paddleford, Asa	1		3		
Richardson, Enock	2	3	2		
Richardson, William	2	2	3		
Roynalds, Hezekiah	1	3	1		
Samburn, Moses	1		8		
Sawyer, Benjamin	3	2	3		
Scofield, Eleazer	2	2	3		
Scofield, John	2	3	5		
Sergeant, Samuel	1	3	3		
Smith, Jabez	1				
Smith, Oliver	1		3		
Smith, William	1		2		
Springer, Henry	1	2	4		
Stevans, Amos	2	1	3		
Sticknor, Jonathan	1		1		
Stoddard, Clemont	1		2		
Webster, William	1	1	3		
Welch, Caleb	4	4	4		
Welch, Samuel	2	2	3		
Wells, Asahel	2	2	2		
Wells, Ezekel	2	2	4		
Wells, Joshua	2	2	4		
Weeker, Nathaniel	2	1	2		
Wheeker, Richard	2				

NAME OF HEAD OF FAMILY.	Free white males of 16 years and upward, including heads of families.	Free white males under 16 years.	Free white females, including heads of families.	All other free persons.	Slaves.
CANAAN TOWN—con.					
Willson, Warren	1	1	2		
Woodbury, James	1	1	2		
Worth, John	3	3	3		
Worth, Nathaniel	1		3		
CHATHAM TOWN.					
Cox, Isaac	1		2		
Cox, William	2		2		
Danford, Jacob	2		3		
Emes, John	1		2		
Emes, Nathan	2	3	4		
Fipp, Samuel	2	2	4		
Hazelton, Joshua	2		1		
Hazelton, Samuel	1	1	2		
Hereman, Amos	1	2	3		
Hutchins, Amos	1		1		
Knight, Joseph	1	4	2		
Robinson, Increase	1	1	2		
COCKBURN TOWN.					
Jorden, Philip	2	1	3		
Larnard, Abel	3		2		
Larnard, Roswell	1	1	2		
Wallis, William	3	3	5		
COCKERMOUTH TOWN.					
Ames, Stephen	2	1	3		
Ames, Stephen, Junr	2	1	2		
Atwell, John	1	2	2		
Atwell, Nathan	1				
Baley, Richard	2	3	4		
Ball, Nathaniel	1	3	5		
Bartlett, Evan	1	1	1		
Bartlett, Jonathan	1		3		
Bewel, Abraham	3	1	4		
Bewel, Asahel	1		4		
Blood, Asa	1				
Blood, Martha			1		
Blood, Timothy	1	2	3		
Blood, William	1	1	1		
Bowers, Jarathmel		2	4		
Case, John	1	2	2		
Colburn, James	1	2	3		
Colwell, Alexander	1	2	1		
Comings, William	3	3	6		
Crosby, Jeremiah	1	5	3		
Farling, Timothy	1				
Fletcher, Levi	1	2	1		
French, Silas	1				
Gilman, Timothy	1	1	1		
Goodhue, John	3	1	2		
Goodhue, Samuel	1		2		
Hale, David	2	2	1		
Hordy, Nehemiah	1	4	4		
Hazleton, Benjamin	1	2	1		
Hazleton, John	1				
Hazleton, Samuel	3	1	4		
Hazleton, Samuel, Jur	1		2		
Heath, Joshua	1	3	1		
Hubbard, Jonas	2	2	1		
Hubbard, Joseah	1		2		
Hubbard, Reuben	4		4		
Kemp, Zachariah	1	2	6		
Kindall, Ebenezer	4	1	2		
Lovejoy, Jacob	1	3	3		
Lovejoy, Abel	1		2		
Lovejoy, Simon	1	5	3		
Melvin, Ebenezer	1	4	5		
Medcalf, Ezekel	1	3	3		
Medcalf, Samuel	1	3	2		
Nevens, John	1	1	3		
Nevens, Thomas	1		2		
Nevens, Thomas, Junr	2	3	6		
Noys, Benjamin	1		2		
Noys, Elijah	1	2	3		
Noys, Enock	1		1		
Noys, Enock, Junr	1		2		
Page, Thomas	2	2	4		
Parker, Abraham	1		2		
Peasley, Francis	1				
Perkins, Jacob	1	3	5		
Pike, Daniel	1	2	2		
Pike, Druary U	1	2	2		
Phelps, Henry	1	3	2		
Phelps, Samuel	1	2	5		
Pool, Jonathan	1	2	3		
Powers, Abraham	1		3		

GRAFTON COUNTY—Continued.

NAME OF HEAD OF FAMILY.	Free white males of 16 years and upward, including heads of families.	Free white males under 16 years.	Free white females, including heads of families.	All other free persons.	Slaves.
COCKERMOUTH TOWN— continued.					
Powers, William	2	2	5		
Powers, William, Junr	1	1	3		
Rider, Asa	1		1		
Rose, Thomas	2	2	2		
Shattock, Edman	3	3	6		
Stewart, Joel	2	1	1		
Toylor, Jacob	1		2		
Wise, Ebenezer	1	2	5		
Woodbury, John	1	1	1		
COLBURNE TOWN.					
Hicks, David	2	3	4		
Larnard, Abijah	1	1	3		
Larnard, James	2	1			
McCollester, Andrew	1		4		
McCollester, William	1	1	1		
Merril, Roswell	1		1		
Smith, Moses	2				
CONCORD TOWN.					
Aldrick, Abner	2	3	3		
Aldrick, Jacob	1		2		
Aldrick, Moses	1				
Aldrick, Rue	1		2		
Aldrick, William	2	1	1		
Aldrick, William, Junr	1				
Appleby, Nathan	1	2	3		
Baley, Timothy	1	3	3		
Belknap, William	2	1	5		
Bishop, Josiah	3	1	5		
Burt, John	1	1	1		
Caswell, Ezra	1		2		
Caswell, Ozias	2	2	1		
Chapin, Daniel	1				
Chapin, Reuben	1		1		
Chase, Moses	1		2		
Daley, David	1	1	6		
Dexter, Caleb	1				
Dexter, Lemuel	1				
Dexter, Zenos	1				
Farman, Stephen	1	2	1		
George, Moses S	1		4		
Hayns, Joseph	2	2	2		
Hayns, Joseph, Junr	1	1	1		
Hazelton, John	1	2	2		
Hendreck, Marget			2		
Howland, George	1	4	2		
Ingals, Henry	1		1		
Jameson, Samuel	2	2	3		
Jesseman, Alexander	1		1		
Jesseman, George	1	1	1		
Jewet, John	2		3		
Jewet, Joseph	1		1		
Jewet, Nathaniel	1		3		
Judd, Levi	2	1	5		
Kay, Robert	1	4	3		
Major, Thomas	1	2	1		
Mardin, Edward	1	1	2		
Martin, Samuel	1		1		
Martin, William	1		8		
More, Amasy	1		1		
Northy, Eliphalet	1	1	2		
Okes, Simon	3		1		
Parker, Andrus	1	3	3		
Payne, Thomas	1		3		
Richardson, Sarah	2		2		
Richardson, Ebenezer	1	2	4		
Robins, Paul	1	3	2		
Sharmon, Jonathan	1	1	1		
Sharmon, Reuben	1	1	2		
Sharmon, Samuel	3		4		
Spooner, Beckford	1	3	6		
Spooner, Thomas	1				
Straton, Ebenezer	1	4	1		
Varbeck, John	1				
Varbeck, Philip	2	3	2		
Walker, Learnard	2	2	2		
Whitecomb, Benjamin	4		4		
Whitecomb, John	1	3	2		
Whitecomb, Josiah	1	1	2		
White, Samuel	1	1	6		
Young, John	2	5	2		
Young, Jesse	1	3	4		
Young, Robert	1	1	1		
Young, Samuel	7	1	6		
COVENTRY TOWN.					
Baley, Ebenezer	1	1	2		
Brown, Jeremiah	1	1	3		

NAME OF HEAD OF FAMILY.	Free white males of 16 years and upward, including heads of families.	Free white males under 16 years.	Free white females, including heads of families.	All other free persons.	Slaves.
COVENTRY TOWN—con.					
Bowley, John	1		1		
Bowley, Samuel	1		2		
Danford, Elkany	1	3	4		
Doley, Daniel	1	1	2		
Eastman, Obediah	2	4	3		
Eltol, Robert	1	2	5		
Flanders, Joseph	1	1	1		
Flanders, Seth	2		4		
Jackson, Samuel	2	2	1		
Lund, Ephraim	1		1		
Martin, Samuel	1	2	4		
Mead, Nathaniel	1	1	2		
Niles, Thankfull	2	1	4		
Noyes, Moses	1		3		
Whitecomb, Ebenezer	1	1	5		
DALTON TOWN.					
Blake, Moses	2	1	5		
Belew, Walter	1	3	2		
DAME'S LOCATION.					
Barber, Zebedee	2	3	3		
Clark, Joseph	1	1	4		
Larey, Daniel	1	4	2		
DARTMOUTH TOWN.					
Blasdar, John	2		1		
Danford, Samuel	1	2	3		
Felt, Robert	1		2		
Gorlin, Jabez	2	2	6		
Hart, Samuel	2	2	4		
Holmes, John	3	2	4		
Holmes, John, Junr	1		1		
Holmes, Lazareth	1	2	1		
Holmes, Samuel	1		2		
Hoyt, James	1		4		
Hyx, Benjamin	1	2	4		
Ingalson, William	4	3	4		
Mardin, James	1		3		
Mardin, John	3	1	3		
Moulton, Ezekel	2		3		
Moulton, William	1	1	1		
Plasted, Samuel	1	2	2		
Shoars, William	1	2	2		
Starbord, Richard	1	3	2		
Syms, Beming	1	1	2		
Webster, Benjamin	3	1	1		
DORCHESTER TOWN.					
Blood, Nathaniel	1	3	2		
Bridgeman, Gideon	1	3	3		
Burley, Gordon	1	3	2		
Burley, Joseph	3	1	4		
Clark, John	1	2	2		
Clefford, David	1	2	2		
Cole, Timothy	1				
Davis, Nicholas	2	1	4		
Fellows, Samuel	1	1	7		
Flanders, David	1		2		
Flanders, Jesse	2		2		
Flanders, Jesse, Junr	1	2	5		
Falsoru, William	1	1	4		
Gilman, Nathaniel	3		3		
Hubbard, Daniel	1		2		
Hubbard, John	2	2	1		
Hubbard, John, Junr	1		4		
Huckings, William	1		1		
Ingraham, Jeriah	1		2		
Ingraham, Jeriah, Junr	1	1	3		
Ingraham, William	1		2		
Norris, Andrew	1	1	3		
Norris, Benjamin	1	1	3		
Norris, Jacob	1		2		
Palmer, Joseph	3	1	3		
Piper, Samuel	1	3	3		
Piper, Benjamin	1		1		
Samburn, Edward	2	1	3		
Samburn, Ezekel	1	2	2		
Stickney, Joseph	1	1	2		
Willes, Jacob	1	2	2		
Winslow, Samuel	2	1	1		
Woodworth, Ebenezer	1	1	2		
Woodworth, Ezra	1	1	1		
Woodworth, Jabez	1	3	2		
Woodworth, John	1	6	1		
Woodworth, Sylvanus	1				

NAME OF HEAD OF FAMILY.	Free white males of 16 years and upward, including heads of families.	Free white males under 16 years.	Free white females, including heads of families.	All other free persons.	Slaves.
DUMMER TOWN.					
Not inhabited.					
ENFIELD TOWN.					
Adams, Henry	1				
Adams, William	2		2		
Ballows, Oliver	2	1	1		
Barker, Nathaniel	3	3	5		
Basford, Jonathan	1	1	2		
Bicknal, Nathan	3	1	3		
Bingham, Elisha	3	4	4		
Blasdal, Sergent	1	1	2		
Blodget, Abraham	2	2	2		
Bosworth, Jonathan	1		4		
Chapman, Samuel	1				
Choat, David	1	3	2		
Choat, Jacob	2	2	5		
Clark, David	1		2		
Clark, Richard	2		2		
Clough, Richard	1	3	3		
Clough, Theophilus	3	1	5		
Coffran, Jacob	3	3	6		
Coffin, Hannah			1		
Colby, Daniel	2	1	3		
Colby, Rowel	2	1	4		
Conant, Jonathan	1	2	1		
Corbit, Josiah	1	2	3		
Currier, Jonathan	3		1		
Currier, Richard	2	2	3		
Currier, Theophilus	1	1	1		
Curtis, David	1		1		
Dow, Thomas	1		3		
Dustin, Ebenezer	1	2	3		
Dustin, James	1	1	1		
Draper, Nathaniel	1		2		
Easterbrook, Josiah	1	1	2		
Eastman, Daniel	1	1	1		
Eastman, Ebenezer	2	2	3		
Eastman, Jonathan	1	1	1		
Eastman, Juda			1		
Eastman, Thomas	1		2		
Edson, Hosea	1	1	3		
Evans, William	1	3	1		
Farman, Baruciah	1		3		
Ferrin, Phineas	2	1	6		
Finch, Peter	1				
Flanders, Moses	1		1		
Folensby, Moses	3		5		
Folensby, John	1	1	4		
Fox, Elisha	1	1	4		
French, Jonathan	1		2		
Gage, David	2	2	6	2	
Goodall, Cornelius	2	1	2		
Goodhue, Joseph	3	3	3		
Gould, Christopher	1		1		
Green, Jonathan	1	1	3		
Guild, Hannah		3	4		
Guild, Noah	2	2	4		
Grow, William	1	1	1		
Hand, Ira	2		4		
Hannaford, Robert	1		2		
Harris, Joshua	2	3	4		
Heth, Daniel	1	3	1		
Heth, Jacob	3	1	3		
Holbrook, Ezekel	1	3	3		
Horton, Charles	1		3		
Howe, David	1		1		
Howe, Jonathan	1	2	3		
Hunter, Thomas	1	2	2		
Jackman, Samuel	1		3		
Jeffers, Stephen	2		3		
Jewet, James	2	4	5		
Johnson, James	1	1	3		
Johnson, Jesse	3	2	7		
Johnson, Jesse, Junr	1	1	1		
Johnson, Jonathan	1		1		
Johnson, Joseph	1	2	3		
Johnson, Peter	1	4	3		
Jones, Moses	2	1	8		
Kidder, Joseph	1		2		
Kidder, Thomas	1	3	3		
Kimbal, Ebenezer	1	5	3		
Lakeman, Askelus	1		2		
Lilly, John	2	4	4		
Lunt, Ezekel	2	1	3		
Lyman, Richard	1	1	3		
Lyon, John Fisker	1	1	3		
Mastin, Isaac	1	2	1		
Mastin, Nathaniel	1	2	3		
McDonald, James	2		3		
Mills, Hannah			5		
Mills, John	2	1	3		
Merril, Benjamin	2	2	10		

GRAFTON COUNTY—Continued.

ENFIELD TOWN—con.

NAME OF HEAD OF FAMILY.	Free white males of 16 years and upward, including heads of families.	Free white males under 16 years.	Free white females, including heads of families.	All other free persons.	Slaves.
Merril, Nathaniel	1	1	2		
Merril, Nathaniel, Jur	1	4	2		
Morgan, Edward	1		2		
Nayson, William	1	1	6		
Nicholds, Moses	1	1	2		
Paddleford, Abner	1	1	2		
Paddleford, Elijah	2	2	3		
Paddleford, Jonathan	1	4	3		
Paddleford, Philip	2	3	4		
Palmer, Jonathan	1		4		
Permot, Susany	1	3	1		
Petty, Asa	1	2	2		
Pierce, Caleb	1		2		
Powel, Moses	2		2		
Powel, Samuel	4		1		
Quimby, Benjamin	1	1	3		
Sawyer, Freeman	1				
Sawyer, Moses	1				
Smith, Richard	1	2	1		
Stanley, Joseph	3		5		
Stephens, Arkelus	1	1	3		
Stephens, Ezekel	3	3	5		
Stephens, James	1	3	3		
Stephens, Joshua	1	2	8		
Stickney, David	1		3		
Tole, Reubin	1	1	2		
Tolman, John	1	2	3		
Tucker, Jacob	2	3	4		
Warrin, Benjamin	2				
Webster, Levi	1	1	5		
Williams, Asa	1		2		
Williams, Robert	1	3	2		
Williams, William	1	3	1		
Worthis, Amos	4	3	4		
Wright, Zadock	10	5	16		

ERROL TOWN.

Not inhabited.

FRANCONIA TOWN.

NAME OF HEAD OF FAMILY.					
Aldridge, Edward	2		1		
Aldridge, John	1				
Applebe, Benjamin	1	4	4		
Applebe, Zebide	1	2	2		
Brown, Benjamin	1		1		
Drewery, John	2	2	1		
Gale, Henry	1	2	4		
Jesseman, George	1	1	4		
Night, Artebus	1	3	3		
Pierce, Superan	1				
Powers, Nicholas	1		3		
Slye, Stephen	1		1		
Snow, Nathaniel	4	1	2		
Taylor, Timothy	1		1		
Warren, Jonas	1		1		
Wheeler, Nathan	2	3	4		

GRAFTON TOWN.

NAME OF HEAD OF FAMILY.					
Aldrick, Jonathan	1	1	3		
Aldrick, Nathaniel	1	1	1		
Aldrick, William	1		1		
Barney, Aaron	3	1	2		
Barney, Aaron, Junr	1	2	3		
Bowen, Joseph	1	1	5		
Bowen, William	1	2	3		
Buffom, Jonathan	3	1	4		
Bullock, Benjamin	3		3		
Bullock, Hezekiah	1	2	3		
Bullock, Seth	1	3	1		
Castle, Daniel	1	6	3		
Castle, Joshua	1	3	3		
Clufford, Samuel	3	3	4		
Clufford, Stephen	1	2	2		
Coblins, Wentworth	1	2	2		
Dean, Isaac	1	1	3		
Dean, Isaac, Junr	1	2	3		
Demeranville, Charles	2	2	6		
Demeranville, John	2	1	3		
Drake, John	1	2	5		
Foords, Richard	1	2	2		
Foords, Robert	1	1	1		
Foords, William	3		1		
Foords, William, Junr	1	3	4		
Fox. Saintclair	1	1	1		
Hamilton, Joseph	1	1	3		
Horskin, Anthony	1	1	5		
Horskin, Ely	1		1		
Hoyt, Ebenezer	1	1	1		
Hoyt, John	1	2	3		

GRAFTON TOWN—con.

NAME OF HEAD OF FAMILY.					
Hoyt, Joseph	2	1	2		
Hilton, John	2	2	1		
Kimball, Amherst	1	1	2		
Kimball, John	2		3		
King, Daniel	1	2	4		
Martin, Levi	2	3	6		
Martin, Seth	2		1		
Martin, Silranus	1	1	2		
Mason, Nathaniel	1	2	3		
Mason, Perez	2	4	4		
Mason, Russel	2	1	1		
Peck, Mathew	1	2	4		
Peck, Israel	1	3	5		
Philip, Alkany	1	3	3		
Pixley, Alexander	2	1	3		
Reed, Moses	2	4	4		
Reed, Samuel	3		4		
Rowland, Daniel	2	2	3		
Rownald, Roger	1	4	4		
Sales, Solomon	1		2		
Sanders, Daniel	1	2	4		
Sanders, James	1	3	4		
Sevey, Joseph	1	1	1		
Sevey, William	1	2	2		
Sleeper, Gideon	2	3	2		
Smart, Charles	1	1	1		
Smith, Christopher	1	2	7		
Smith, Eleazar	5	1	1		
Smith, Shubal	1	2	2		
Stephins, Samuel	1	1	2		
Tucker, Samuel	1		2		
Weed, Daniel	1	1	3		
Weed, Joseph	1		5		
Wheeler, James	1		1		
Williams, Zebedee	1		2		
Williams, Mary	1	1	6		
Williams, Samuel	2	1	3		
Wright, Thomas	1	3	1		

HALE'S LOCATION.

NAME OF HEAD OF FAMILY.					
Johnson, Andrew	2	2	3		
Johnson, David	1		1		

HANOVER TOWN.

NAME OF HEAD OF FAMILY.					
Alvord, Aaron	1		1		
Ames, Jacob	1	3	3		
Babbet, Asa	1		2		
Babbet, Nathaniel	1	1	4		
Barrows, Jacob	1	1	5		
Bass, Jonathan	2	1	2		
Bascomb, Urial	1		1		
Benton, Stephen	1	2	3		
Bingham, Jabez	2		4		
Bridgeman, Abel	1	1	3		
Bridgeman, Isaac	1	1	6		
Bridgeman, John	3	3	5		
Brigham, Moses	1	1	2		
Brown, Eloida	1	2	2		
Brown, Joel	1	5	3		
Brown, Zadock	3	3	3		
Buck, Perley	1				
Buck, Reuben	1				
Burrows, Eden	1	1	4		
Burswell, John	1		1		
Camp, Israel	1	2	3		
Carpenter, Elijah	1		2		
Carpenter, Ezra	1	3	3		
Chandler, Daniel	1	3	3		
Chandler, David	3	4	5		
Chandler, William	2	1	2		
Chase, Caleb	1				
Church, Perley	1		2		
Cleaveland, Tyxhall	2		1		
Cobb, Nathan	2	2	2		
Conant, Edmond	1		2		
Conant, Nathaniel	1	1	1		
Collins, Samuel	2	2	4		
Colman, Zenos	1	1	3		
Cook, Samuel	1	1	3		
Cox, Jonathan	1	2	3		
Curtis, Ebenezer	1	1	1		
Curtis, Jonathan	1	2	3		
Curtis, Joseph	3	2	3		
Cushman, Joshua	2	2	3		
Davis, Benjamin	2	3	4		
Davis, Bezaleel	1	2	6		
Dewey, Benony	1	3	5		
Dewey, William	4	6	6		
Dowe, Lemuel	1		4		
Dowe, Lemuel, Junr	1		1		

HANOVER TOWN—con.

NAME OF HEAD OF FAMILY.					
Dowe, London				5	
Dowe, Salmon	1		2		
Duguet, Michal	1	3	5		
Durkee, Abijah	1		3		
Durkee, John	1	1	3		
Durkee, Thomas	2	1	1		
Easterbrook, Nehemiah	1	1	5		
Eaton, David	1	2	2		
Eaton, David, Junr	1	1	1		
Eaton, Jacob	1	2	1		
Edward, John	2	1	2		
Everit, Nathaniel	3	2	5		
Farrar, Humphry	3	4	4		
Fogg, David	3	1	1		
Forbes, Daniel	4		3		
Foster, George	1	2	2		
Foster, Jacob	1	2	7		
Fox, John	1	2	1		
Freeman, Jonathan	4	6	6		
Freeman, Otis	4	1	5		
Freeman, Russel	1	2	5		
Freeman, Solomon	1	1	3		
Fuller, Caleb	3	2	4		
Gates, Laban	1	1	2		
Gilman, Nicholas	1	1	5		
Goodrich, Eleazer	2	4	5		
Gould, Phinehas	1	1	6		
Green, Joseph	3	1	3		
Geen, Samuel	3	3	4		
Hall, Ithamar	1		1		
Hall, Webster	2	1	1		
Hall, William	3		3		
Hatch, Benjamin	2		2		
Haze, David	1	1	2		
Haze, Samuel	1	1	2		
Heaton, Joseph	1		3		
Heaton, Nathaniel	4		3		
Herrick, Stephen	1		4		
Heath, Jesse	1		2		
Hill, Eleazer	2	3	5		
Hill, Shadrick	3	4	4		
Holden, Abel	7	3	4		
Holt, Lemuel	3	2	4		
Hovey, Roger	2		3		
Huntington, Andrew	2	1	2		
Hurlbutt, Asher	1	1	3		
Hurlbutt, Eli	1		1		
Hurlbutt, Elijah	2	2	1		
Hurlbutt, Hezekiah	1				
Hurlbutt, Nathaniel	3		2		
Hurlbutt, Nathaniel, Jur	1		1		
Hustin, Isaac	4				
Hustin, James	1		1		
Ingals, Luther	1	2	3		
Jacobs, Solomon	2		3		
Jacobs, Solomon, Junr	1	1	2		
Karr, James	2		4		
Karr, Samuel	1	2	4		
Kellogg, Jabez	3	1	1		
Kent, Martin	1		2		
Kindrick, Anna	1		2		
Kindrick, Daniel	1	3	2		
Kindrick, John	1		2		
Kindrick, Samuel	1	5	2		
Kingsbury, John	1	1	1		
Kinsman, Aaron	1	1	4		
Kitcham, Joseph	3	3	5		
Kitcham, Nathaniel	1				
Kitcham, Zopher	2		5		
Knapp, Peter	2	4	4		
Lane, Ebenezer	7	3	3		
Lang, Richard	2	1			
Larkham, George	1		1		
Lee, Joseph	1	2	4		
Lavake, Augustus	1	2	3	2	
Levit, Freegrace	1	2	2		
Lincoln, Luther	1	1	3		
Lord, Nathaniel	2		4		
Mason, Robert	1	1	1		
McClure, Sammuel	1		2		
Morse, Noah	2	4	2		
Murch, James	3	3	5		
Ordway, John	2		2		
Owin, Timothy	2	2	1		
Page, Phinehas	1	2	5		
Parker, Asa	3		5		
Parker, Joseph	3	4	5		
Parks, Abel	1	4	5		
Pingry, Silvanus	2	1	4		
Porter, Eleazer	1	1	4		
Porter, Nathaniel	1	2	3		
Plumley, Alexander	1	2	6		

GRAFTON COUNTY—Continued.

HANOVER TOWN—con.

NAME OF HEAD OF FAMILY.	Free white males of 16 years and upward, including heads of families.	Free white males under 16 years.	Free white females, including heads of families.	All other free persons.	Slaves.
Plumley, Benjamin	1	4	3		
Putnam, Aaron	1	2	3		
Rice, Adam	2	2	4		
Rice, William	1	1	1		
Ripley, Nabby	1	2	5		
Risley, Asa	1	2	3		
Risley, Garshom	3	2	4		
Rude, Gideon	1	1	2		
Russel, John	1		1		
Slade, Samuel	2	3	6		
Slapp, Simon P.	2	1	6		
Smith, Aaron	2	4	3		
Smith, Abijah	2	4	4		
Smith, Anna	1		4		
Smith, Edward	3	2	4		
Smith, Elijah	1	4	1		
Smith, Gideon	1		2		
Smith, Gideon, Junr.	1		2		
Smith, Pastor John	1	2	6		
Smith, John	2	4	6		
Smith, Lowden	1	1	2		
Sprague, Polly		1	2		
Stearns, John	1		5		
Stoors, August	1	1	1		
Dartmouth College (students)	142	10			
Sweat, Stockman	1	1	1		
Tapliffe, Calvin	2	1	2		
Thomas, Jeremiah	1	2	2		
Tiffany, Benjamin	2	2	4		
Tiffany, Gideon	2	1	5		
Tiffany, James	1		2		
Timbalton, Samuel	1	1	6		
Tinney, Andrew	1	1	1		
Tinney, David	1	1	5		
Tinney, John	1	1	1		
Tinney, John, Junr.	1				
Tinney, Silas	1	3	3		
Tisdal, Barna	2	2	4		
Triscott, Jeremiah	1		2		
Triscott, Jerial	1				
Turner, Bela	1		4		
Turner, Habbackuk	1	1	2		
Wadaigh, Simon D.	2	3	2		
Walton, George	2	1	2		
Warner, Elisha	1		1		
Wills, Dyer	1	1	3		
Wills, Timothy	1	2	1		
West, Nathan	5	2	4		
West, Nathaniel	1	1	3		
Wheelock, Eleazer	3		6		
Wheelock, James	2	1	4		
Wheelock, John	3		2		2
Wheelock, Ralph	2		2		
Wilder, Jonas	1		1		
Williams, John	1		2		
Williams, John, Junr.	1	1	2		
Wood, John	1	5	5		
Woodward, Bezaleel	3	2	5		
Woodward, David	2	2	6		
Woodward, Deliverance	2	1	4		
Woodward, Jonathan	1	2	2		
Woodward, Titus	1	1	3		
Woodward, William	2	1	7		
Woodworth, Beriah	1	1	1		
Woolson, Ephraim	1	2	3	1	
Wright, Amasy	1		2		
Wright, Asa	1	1	1		
Wright, Barnard	1		1		
Wright, David	1	1	3		
Wright, Delino	1	1	1		
Wright, Elijah	1		1		
Wright, John	2	1	3		
Wright, Nathaniel	2	3	3		
Wright, Samuel	1	1	2		

HART'S LOCATION.

NAME OF HEAD OF FAMILY.					
Bassett, David	1	1	1		
Greanley, Nathan	1	2	1		
Hanson, Charles	1	1	3		

HAVERHILL TOWN.

NAME OF HEAD OF FAMILY.					
Abbot, William	1	3	7		
Adams, Paul	1	1	2		
Ash, David	1				
Barker, Samuel	1				
Barron, Timothy	2		2		
Beads, John	1	3	3		
Bedle, Moody	3	2	6		

HAVERHILL TOWN—con.

NAME OF HEAD OF FAMILY.	Free white males of 16 years and upward, including heads of families.	Free white males under 16 years.	Free white females, including heads of families.	All other free persons.	Slaves.
Bowley, Samuel	1		2		
Brooks, Samuel	6	2	2		1
Chapman, Amos	1				
Chase, Anne			1		
Chase, Marium			1		
Clark, Edward	1				
Clark, John	1		2		
Corless, James	2	3	6		
Corless, Samuel	2	2	5		
Crocker, Andrew	1	2	2		
Crocker, Benjamin	1				
Cross, Ephraim	1				
Cross, William	1	1	4		
Dow, Moses	4	2	10		
Duty, Moses	1	1	1		
Eastman, Abigal	2		2		
Elkins, Joseah	1				
Emes, Jonathan	2		1		
Emeson, Samuel	1				
Fifield, Elizabeth		4	3		
Fisk, Mary		1	3		
Flanders, Joseph	1	1	1		
French, Bezaleel	1		1		
Goodwin, Richard	1	2	5		
Goodwin, Semion	3		4		
Gould, Samuel	2		4		
Gray, Ebenezer	2	1	1		
Greenlief, David	3		3		
Harris, Jeremiah	2				
Hazelton, Robert	1	1	3		
Howard, John	1				
Howard, Joshua	3	2	3		
Hunt, Abnor	1	4	3		
Hunt, Daniel	3	1	3		
Hutchens, Joseph	4	1	5		
Jewel, David	1				
Johnston, Charles	2	1	4		
Johnston, Michal	1	1	4		
Kay, Bryan	1		1		
Kimbal, Amos	4	3	5		
Kindall, Edward	1				
Kenester, Benjamin	2	1	2		
King, James	1	1	2		
Knapp, George	1				
Ladd, Asa	1	2	3		
Ladd, David	2		4		
Ladd, Ezekel	4	2	3		
Ladd, James	1	2	7		
Ladd, John	1	4	6		
Ladd, Joseph	1	2	4		
Ladd, Samuel	4		2		
Lee, Samuel	1		1		
Lock, David	1	1	2		
Lock, William	1				
Luroy, James	1				
McCommic, Eles		1	2		
McKentush, Ebenezer	1	2	2		
Merril, Annis	1	3	3		
Merril, Nathaniel	1		10		
Montgomery, Iohon	1	1	2		
More, Moses H	1	2	4		
Morse, John	1	1	2		
Morse, Stephen	1	4	2		
Page, Jacob	1	2	6		
Page, John	4	3	2		
Pearson, Joseph	2	3	4		
Phelps, Martin	1	1	2		
Porter, Asa	8	1	6	1	3
Porter, Moses	1	4	2		
Porter, William	4	1	4		
Richardson, Daniel	1	1	1		
Ring, Jonathan	1	2	4		
Rodimon, Simon	1				
Russell, Moore	1				
Samburn, John	2	2	5		
Sanders, Avery	1	3	2		
Sanders, Jonathan	1		3		
Sayer, Enos	1				
Simpson, Mary			1		
Sly, John	1	1	6		
Staniford, Daniel	1				
Stephens, Daniel	3	3	4		
Swan, Israel	1				
Swan, Phinehas	1	2	5		
Thomson, Samuel	1	1	3		
Wesson, Peter	2		3		
Wheeler, Charles	1	3	3		
Whites, Samuel	1	1	2		
Whitecor, Ebenezer	1	1	3		
Windslow, John	1		1		
Wiser, Benjamin	2	4	6		

HAVERHILL TOWN—con.

NAME OF HEAD OF FAMILY.	Free white males of 16 years and upward, including heads of families.	Free white males under 16 years.	Free white females, including heads of families.	All other free persons.	Slaves.
Woodward, James	6	3	4		
Young, David	1	1	2		
Young, Joshua	4	1	4		

KILKENNY TOWN.

Not inhabited.

LANCASTER TOWN.

NAME OF HEAD OF FAMILY.					
Baker, Jonas	1	2	3		
Bracket, Joseph	3	2	2		
Bradley, John	1				
Brews, Phinehas	3		1		
Brown, Titus O.	1				
Buckman, Edward	2	2	4		
Chaney, Samuel	1	2	2		
Darby, Abijah	1		2		
Gotham, Robert	1		2		
Hartwell, Jonathan	1	3	4		
Hodgedon, Phinehas	1	1	3		
Howe, Daniel	1	1	1		
Johnson, Samuel	1	2	5		
Johnson, William	2	2	2		
Page, David	3	6	5		
Page, Moses	1	3	2		
Page, Samuel	1	3	2		
Spalden, Edward	1		1		
Stanley, Denis	3	2	4		
Stockwell, Emens	3	5	5		
Weeks, John	1	2	4		
Wilcox, Jeremiah	1	2	3		
Wilder, Elisha	4	1	3		
Wilder, Jonas	3	2	5		
Willson, Francis	2		2		
Willson, Stephen	1	2	2		
Winkley, John	1		2		

LANDAFF TOWN.

NAME OF HEAD OF FAMILY.					
Atwood, David	1	3	4		
Baley, Asa	2	5	6		
Brunson, Jonathan	2	1	5		
Carlton, Edmond	2	4	2		
Carlton, Peter	1	3	3		
Chandler, Ezra	1	1	3		
Clark, Ebenezer	1	1	1		
Clark, David	1		3		
Clark, John	3		2		
Clark, John, Junr.	1	1	3		
Clark, Levi	1				
Clark, Nathaniel	2	1	3		
Corey, Ephraim	2	3	6		
Couch, Stephen	2		3		
Currier, Benjamin	1	2	5		
Eastman, Simeon	1	2	1		
Eaton, Ebenezer	1		3		
Eaton, David	1				
Eaton, Samuel	1		2		
Edmans, George	1	4	1		
Farris, Gideon	1	2	1		
Grose, John	1	2	2		
Hodge, Alexander	1	3	2		
Hovey, Nathaniel	1		1		
Jackman, Moses	1	3	2		
Judd, Levi	2	2	5		
Judd, Nathaniel	1	1	4		
Kimball, Benjamin	1	4	2		
Kimball, Jonathan	1	1	3		
Libby, Luke	1		1		
Mann, Mathew	3	1	2		
Marshall, Samuel	1	1	1		
McKeen, Alexander	1	1	1		
Morse, Josiah	1	2	2		
Morse, Linus	1		1		
Night, Benjamin	1		4		
Night, Moses	1		1		
Noys, Jonathan	3	1	1		
Noys, Nathaniel	2	4	4		
Noys, Samuel	1		3		
Noys, Silvanus	1		1		
Noys, Thomas	1		1		
Page, John	1	3	4		
Petty, Jedediah	2	1	2		
Rice, Samuel	1		1		
Rice, Stephen	2	2	5		
Ricks, Nathaniel	1	2	1		
Rownals, Rowland	1	1	3		
Simons, James	1	1	1		
Snow, James	2	2	4		
Titus, Ebenezer	1	2	2		

GRAFTON COUNTY—Continued.

NAME OF HEAD OF FAMILY.	Free white males of 16 years and upward, including heads of families.	Free white males under 16 years.	Free white females, including heads of families.	All other free persons.	Slaves.
LANDAFF TOWN—con.					
Titus, Samuel	2	2	2		
Webber, Andrew	1	2	1		
Webber, Nathaniel	2	2	3		
Young, Caleb	2	1	5		
LEBANON TOWN.					
Abbot, Asahel	1				
Abbot, Beriah	2		2		
Abbot, Daniel	2	1	1		
Abbot, Jeremiah	1				
Alden, Daniel	2	2	1		
Alden, Zenos	1	2	4		
Aldridge, Andrew	3		3		
Aldridge, Clark	3		2		
Aldridge, Richard	1	2	2		
Atkens, Eleazer	1				
Allen, Asher	1	2	1		
Allen, Cady	1	3	2		
Allen, Diarca	2	1	2		
Auen, Phinehas	1	2	2		
Andrews, John	2	3	2		
Annis, Michal	1				
Annis, Solomon	1				
Aspenwill, Zalman	2	1	4		
Ayer, James	1				
Baker, Andrew	1				
Baker, Gideon	2	4	4		
Baker, Gideon, Junr	1	1	3		
Baldwin, Rufus	6		1		
Baldwin, Samuel	1				
Ballard, Sherebiah	1	3	4		
Baley, Samuel	1		2		
Barker, Daniel	1	1	2		
Ballows, James	1	2	4		
Basford, Joseph	1	3	4		
Belcher, Andrew	1				
Benet, Elisha	1				
Billings, Stephen	1	2	4		
Bingham, Samuel	3		1		
Bliss, Ebenezer	1	1	2		
Bliss, Azariah	2	2	2		
Bliss, Daniel	3		3		
Bliss, Isaiah	1	1	2		
Bliss, Jonathan	1	2	4		
Bliss, Stephen	3	3	3		
Blodget, Daniel	2	2	2		
Blodget, Ephraim	1				
Blodget, Nathan	1	4	1		
Bly, James	1				
Bosworth, Nathaniel	1	2	3		
Bosworth, Jonathan	2		3		
Brown, Ephraim	1	3	2		
Buck, Peletiah	1	1	2		
Burnham, Justus	1	1	1		
Calkins, Frederick	1	2	5		
Chandler, Daniel	2	1	2		
Chapman, John	1				
Church, Ichabod	1	1	1		
Colburn, Asa	1	4	3		
Colburn, John	1	2	3		
Colburn, Robert	3	2	5		
Colburn, Stephen	1	2	5		
Collin, Alexander	1				
Collin, Moses	1				
Cook, Frederick	1	2	1		
Cook, Jesse	3	2	3		
Cook, Pellum	1				
Cook, Simeon	3		1		
Cooper, John	1				
Corring, Richard	1				
Corring, William	1				
Crocker, David	1	3	3		
Crocker, James	3	3	5		
Crocker, Samuel	2		3		
Cushin, Daniel	1		1		
Dana, William	2	3	6		
Devanport, Lemuel	1				
Dewey, Elijah	1				
Dewey, Martin	1				
Dewey, William	1				
Downer, Joseph	1		3		
Downer, William	2		9		
Downer, Zacheus	2		4		
Durkee, Nathan	3	1	2		
Easterbrook, Aaron	1				
Easterbrook, Hibbard	1				
Easterbrook, Samuel	3	3	4		
Eldridge, John	1				
Eldridge, Zair	2	1	2		
Ellis, Oliver	1	3	5		
LEBANON TOWN—con.					
Fisher, Reubin		1	1		
Fitch, Asa	2	1	6		
Fox, John	2	1	4		
Freeman, Edman	3	2	3		
Freeman, Edman, Junr	1		1		
Freeman, Enock	1	3	4		
Fuller, Benjamin	3		2		
Fuller, Benjamin, Junr	1	3	1		
Garcy, Benjamin	1	2	4		
George, John	1	2	1		
Goodin, John	1				
Gould, Elijah	2	2	3		
Gray, John	1	3	4		
Green, Josiah	1	2	1		
Griswold, Jeremiah	1	2	2		
Griswold, John	3	2	6		
Griswold, Oliver	3		2	1	
Hall, Isaac	1	3	5		
Hall, Nathaniel	3	5	5		
Hamilton, Jonathan	2		1		
Hibbard, James	2	3	3		
Hibbard, John	1				
Hibbard, Moses	2	1	5	1	
Hibbard, Roger	1				
Hibbard, Roger, Junr	1	4	1		
Hinkley, David	1	4	4		
Hill, Charles	2	1	2		
Hough, Daniel	3	3	7		
Hough, David	5	2	6		
Hough, Lemuel	5	3	10	1	
Hough, Thomas	1				
Hough, Witherill	2	3	4		
Howe, Job	1				
Huntington, Hezekiah	1				
Huntington, James	3	3	4		
Huntington, Jeremiah	3		4		
Huntington, John	1				
Huntington, Roger	1				
Huntington, Theophilus	4	1	2		
Huntington, William	4	1	6		
Hutchins, Eleazer	1				
Hutchinson, Aaron	3	3	3		
Hyde, Elihu	5	1	4		
Hyde, Elihu, Junr	1				
Hyde, Levi	1		4		
Hyde, Silas	1				
Jakish, Amos	1				
Jay, Gideon	2				
Jones, James	4	5	5		
Johnson, Timothy	1	3	2		
Kimball, Amos	2		1		
Knox, Silvanus	1				
Lincoln, William	1	2	3		
Loomis, Ebenezer	1		1		
Loomis, Gamaliel	1		1		
Lathrop, Elijah	3	3	4		
Lathrop, Elisha	1				
Lathrop, Gideon	1				
Lathrop, Samuel	2	3	5		
Lathrop, Sluman	3	2	5		
Lyman, Richard	2	3	5		
Martin, Joseph	2	3	3		
Parkard, David	1	1	2		
Parkard, Ichabod	1	2	3		
Parkard, Nathaniel	2	2	3		
Parkard, Zacheus	1	1	2		
Parkis, Phinehas	6	2	4		
Patrick, John	1		1		
Payne, Elisha	4	1	3		
Payne, Elisha, Junr	1				
Payne, John	1				
Payne, Samuel	1	4	3		
Peck, Ebbe	1				
Peck, Simeon	4	1	4		
Peck, Simeon, Junr	1				
Peck, Walter	3	3	1		
Parsons, Moses	1				
Peterson, Turner	1	2	4		
Phelps, Daniel	2	5	4		
Pixley, Francis	1				
Ponto, Peter				4	
Porter, John	1	2	4		
Porter, Nathaniel	4	3	7		
Potter, Isaiah	1	3	3		
Putman, Reubin	1	1	3		
Raimont, Nathaniel	2	1	4		
Randall, John	1				
Redington, Enock	1	2	3		
Robinson, Eleazer	2	2	4		
Robinson, Daniel	2	1	6		
Root, Amos	1	1	2		
LEBANON TOWN—con.					
Saxton, Charles	2	2	3	1	
Searls, Josephus				1	
Simonds, Ared	3	3	4		
Smith, Jesse	1				
Smith, Oliver	1		1		
Smith, Peter	1		1		
Spiller, Joseph	1				
Sprague, Elijah	1				
Sprague, Elkana	1	1	2		
Sprague, Samuel	2	1	4		
Stoddard, David	2	1	2		
Stoddard, Solomon	1				
Storrs, Constant	6	6	4		
Storrs, John	1				
Storrs, Nathaniel	4	2	7		
Sumner, Clapp	3	1	3		
Sweatland, Jeremiah	2	1	5		
Simson, Robert	2	3	2		
Ticknor, Elisha	2	4	6		
Ticknor, John	2		3		
Ticknor, John, Junr	2		3		
Ticknor, Paul	1		2		
Tilden, Charles	1		2		
Tilden, Elisha	1	2	2		
Tilden, Joel	3	2	3		
Tilden, Joseph	1		1		
Tilden, Joseph, Junr	1	3	7		
Tilden, Stephen	2	1	2		
Tuck, Jeremiah	1				
Walbridge, Isaac	1	2	5		
Waterman, Silas	2		2		
Waters, Hezekiah	1	2	4		
Watkins, Amasa	1				
Wells, Thomas	2	1	3		
Wheatley, Andrew	1	1	2		
Wheatley, Nathaniel	3	3	4		
Whitney, Benjamin	1				
Whitney, David	1				
Willes, Abial	1	2	4		
Wills, Daniel	2	2	2		
Wills, Silvanus	1	3	4		
Wood, Ephraim	1	1	2		
Wood, Joseph	4	1	3		
Wood, Joseph, Junr	2	1	5		
Woodward, Henry	1	3	4		
Woodworth, Asa	1	2	3		
Woodworth, Isaac	1				
Woodworth, Jabez	1				
Wright, Abel	1	1	5		
Wyman, Solomon	1				
LINCOLN TOWN.					
Hatch, John	1		2		
Hatch, Thomas	1	1	2		
Kinsman, Nathan	2	3	2		
Wheeler, Amos	1	1	2		
Wheeler, Nathan	3		1		
LITTLETON TOWN.					
Baley, Ephraim	2	3	5		
Beman, Henry	1	4	2		
Caswell, Nathan	3	2	5		
Charlton, Robert	1		1		
Currier, Sergeant	1	1	2		
Eastman, Jonathan	3	1	2		
Hoyt, Samuel	1	3	2		
Larnard, Samuel	2		2		
Lewis, Jonas	1	3	5		
Minor, Isaac	1		2		
Minor, Thomas	2	1	2		
Nours, John	1	2	2		
Nours, Jonas	2		1		
Pingry, Ebenezer	1	2	1		
Powers, Whitecomb	1	1	2		
Wheeler, John	2	1	2		
Williams, James	1	2	1		
Williams, Peleg	1		2		
Williams, Providence	1		1		
LYMAN TOWN.					
Barber, John	1	1	2		
Bartlett, Robert	1	1	4		
Clough, William	5	2	3		
Davis, John	1	1	3		
Dexter, Joseph	2		5		
Eastman, Moses	1		1		
Fartington, Joseph	1		3		
Gilman, Jeremiah	1	1	2		

GRAFTON COUNTY—Continued.

NAME OF HEAD OF FAMILY.	Free white males of 16 years and upward, including heads of families.	Free white males under 16 years.	Free white females, including heads of families.	All other free persons.	Slaves.	NAME OF HEAD OF FAMILY.	Free white males of 16 years and upward, including heads of families.	Free white males under 16 years.	Free white females, including heads of families.	All other free persons.	Slaves.	NAME OF HEAD OF FAMILY.	Free white males of 16 years and upward, including heads of families.	Free white males under 16 years.	Free white females, including heads of families.	All other free persons.	Slaves.
LYMAN TOWN—con.						**LYME TOWN—con.**						**LYME TOWN—con.**					
Grimshaw, William	1	1	2			Fellows, Nathaniel	1					Sloan, John, Junr	1		3		
Hall, Elijah	2	1	3			Franklin, Jonathan	2	4	3			Sloan, Joseph	1		3		
Hodges, Lyman	1		2			Freeman, Silvanus	1		3			Sloan, Mathew	1	2	3		
Hodges, Nathaniel	2		2			Fuller, Daniel	1	1	1			Smith, Solomon	2	2	2		
Hunt, Moses	1	2	3			Gardner, Gideon	1					Starks, Ebenezer	1				
Knapp, Abial	3		2			Gardner, William	1					Starks, Joanna	1	2	3		
Knapp, Ephraim	1	1	1			Gilbert, Thomas	2	1	4			Starks, Jonathan	1		3		
Knapp, Jonathan	1	1	4			Gilbert, Thomas L	1		1			Starks, Jonathan, Junr	1		1		
Knapp, Lathrop	1	1	2			Goodell, Ezra	1		1			Starks, Moses	1		1		
Lang, Samuel	1		1			Goodell, Jacob	2		5			Starks, Phinehas	2	1	1		
Lang, William	1	2	3			Goodell, Jonathan	2		3			Sterdefent, Lemuel	2	5	3		
Locke, Elisha	1	1	2			Goodell, Jonathan, Junr	1					Strong, Jesse	1		1		
McPayne, Evan	1		1			Goodell, Luther	1					Strong, John	1	3	2		
Minor, William	1	3	1			Goodell, Thomas	2	2	3			Things, Samuel	1	1	4		
Moulton, Daniel	1		1			Grant, Benjamin	1					Thompson, John	2	3	5		
Moulton, David	2		3			Grant, Peter	2	1	6			Tinkham, Ebenezer	1	1	3		
Moulton, Job	1	1	5			Grant, Reuben	1	3	3			Turner, David	1	1	5		
Moulton, Jonathan	2		1			Hatch, Joseph	1	1	3			Turner, Jacob	1	2	3		
Moulton, Noah	1	2	2			Hill, Ebenezer	1					Warren, Asahel	2	2	4		
Olmsted, Joseph	1	3	3			Hovey, Abnor	1		1			Warren, Ezra	2	1	4		
Olmsted, Phinehas	1		2			Hovey, Daniel	1		2			Warren, Joshua	1				
Olmsted, Timothy	2		4			Hovey, James	1	2	3			Washburn, Libbeus	1	3	2		
Parker, Asa	1		3			Hovey, Samuel	3	4	5			Waterman, Seth	3		2		
Parker, David	1	1	1			Howard, Benjamin	1	1	4			Whitman, David	1				
Parker, Lemuel	1	4	4			Howard, Edward	2		4			Winslow, John	1				
Parker, Levi	1		3			Howard, Edward, Junr	1		2			Winslow, Samuel	1				
Parker, Isaac	2		1			Howard, Ellis	1					Wood, Benjamin	1				
Parker, Samuel	1	1	5			Howard, Enock	1					Wood, David	1	4	1		
Parker, Solomon	2		1			Howard, Daniel	1		3			Woodward, Nathaniel	1	2	2		
Parker, Solomon, Junr	1	2	6			Howard, Darius	1										
Sherburn, Daniel	1	1	1			Howard, Isaiah	2		3			**MILLFIELD TOWN.**					
Way, Samuel	1	2	2			Howard, Isaiah, Junr	1	3	4			Not inhabited.					
Wheathy, John	1	1	2			Howard, Joseph	1										
Wheeler, Abel	1		2			Howard, Solomon	1	2	1			**NEW CHESTER TOWN.**					
Williston, Silas	1	1	2			Howard, Uriah	1	1	2			Bennit, Tilton	2	6	4		
						Hubbard, Garshom	2	1	3			Boyd, William	1	1	4		
LYME TOWN.						Hews, Nathaniel	1		1			Buzwell, John	1	1	5		
Alden, Caleb	1	2	1			Hews, Nathaniel, Junr	1	3	5			Case, Chandler	1	1	2		
Baker, Thomas	3	3	3			Hews, Reuben	1	2	1			Case, Nason	3		2		
Baldwin, Josiah	1					Jenks, Zachariah	1	3	3			Chaplin, Caleb	1				
Beals, James	3	3	2			Kingsbury, Benjamin	3	3	6			Colby, Nathan	2	2	4		
Bell, John	1	2	5			Lamphier, John	1	2	3			Cook, Israel	1		1		
Bell, Reuben	1	1	1			Lane, Samuel	1		4			Crague, Alexander	1	2	4		
Bell, Samuel	1	3	3			Latham, Arthur	4	2	2			Emons, John	1	1	2		
Bell, William	1	1	3			Leecow, Samuel	1	1	2			Emerson, David	1		2		
Bingham, Jeremiah	1		1			Leonard, Humphry	1		1			Ferren, Ebenezer	1	3	3		
Bixby, Jonathan	1	1	3			Mason, Jonathan	1	2	2			Fevor, Cutting	1	2	5		
Bixby, Samuel	1	1	1			McCleave, Thomas	2		5			Fevor, Thomas	1	4	1		
Bixby, Walter	1					Moores, Ezra	1	4	2			Fuller, Thomas	1				
Brawton, Abijah	2	1	3			Morey, Benjamin	1	1	2			Golden, Windsor	1	1	2		
Brawton, Walter	2	1	3			Morey, Mace	1		3			Hastings, Asa	1	4	4		
Brewster, Ebenezer	2	1	6			Morey, Sylvester	1					Hoyt, Joseph	1	8	4		
Bugby, Martha	1	3	5			Nelson, Charles	1		1			Hunt, David	1	1	3		
Bugby, Timothy	1	1	1			Nelson, James	1	2	3			Hunt, Karr	2	4	4		
Buck, Thomas	1					Nelson, John	2		1			Huse, Thomas	1	1	1		
Carpenter, Jesse	2	2	4			Nelson, John, Junr	1					Murrel, Jonathan	4	2	4		
Carey, Christopher	1	3	2			Nelson, John, 3d	1					Morgan, John	1	1	2		
Chapman, Stephen	1	3	3			Parsons, Amos	1		3			Morrison, William	1				
Colburn, William	1					Parsons, Ebenezer	1					Murrey, William	2	4	4		
Comestock, Mary			1			Parsons, James	1	1	4			Nichals, Alexander	1		3		
Conant, David	1	1	3			Payne, Stoores	1	1	2			Nichals, John	1	1	2		
Conant, Josiah	1	1	3			Pelton, John	1		4			Nichals, William	1	2	4		
Conant, Jonathan	1	1	2			Pelton, Joseph	1	2	3			Pingra, William	1	1	2		
Conant, Rufus	4	2	4			Perkins, Abraham	2	1	3			Quimby, Jeremiah	3	1	2		
Conant, Solomon	1	2	4			Perkins, Isaac	1	3	5			Quimby, Jeremiah, Junr	1	1	3		
Conant, William	2		3			Perkins, Peter	1	2	4			Rowel, Thomas	1	2	5		
Convers, Joel	1	3	3			Perkins, Samuel	1	1	1			Samburn, Joseph	1	3	6		
Cook, James	2	2	3			Pingry, John	1		1			Samburn, Nathaniel	2		2		
Cook, Joshua	1	2	5			Pomery, Elisha	1	1	3			Samburn, Shurburn	1	2	1		
Cook, Lemuel	1					Porter, Calvin	2		2			Samburn, Theophilus	1	1	5		
Cook, Samuel	1		2			Porter, Thomas	2		2			Sergent, Phinehas	1	6	2		
Coult, Amherst	3	1	4			Porter, William	2	2	2			Sergent, Timothy	1	6	2		
Covel, Allen	1					Post, Joseph O	1	1	2			Searls, William	1	1	4		
Culver, John	1	1	3			Post, Peter	2	1	4			Sharlow, Daniel	1	1	3		
Cutting, Hezekiah	1	2	2			Preston, Isaac	2	2	3			Sleeper, Peter	3	7	2		
Cutting, Isaac	1		3			Rice, Benjamin	1		3			Smith, John	1	4	4		
Cutting, William	1					Rood, James	2		3			Straw, John	1	1	5		
Cutting, Zebedee	1	1	2			Rood, Oliver	1					Tilton, Sherburn	3	3	2		
Crosman, Elijah	1					Ross, Samuel	1					Tinney, Moses	1				
Daley, Reuben	1			1		Saple, Widow			1			Webster, Ephraim	3	3	3		
Davidson, William	1	2	2			Shepard, John					3	Wells, Peter	1	2	2		
Darby, Nathaniel	2	2	3			Shield, Alexander	1	2	4			Wells, Peter, Junr	1				
Delino, Jonathan	1		4			Simmons, John	1	1	4			Wells, Reuben	3	5	3		
Dimmick, David	1					Simmons, Samuel	1		2			Wells, Thomas	1	1	5		
Dimmick, John	1		2			Skinner, Abel	1	5	4								
Dimmick, Shubal	2	1	2			Skinner, Amos	1	2	2			**NEW HOLDERNESS TOWN.**					
Dimmick, Shubal, Junr	1	1	5			Skinner, Bariah	2		2			Baker, Andrew	2	2	4		
Dimmick, Samuel	1	1	1			Skinner, Ephraim	1	2	3			Baley, John	1	1	2		
English, James	3	3	4			Skinner, Jedediah	1	1	2								
Fairfield, John	1	1	5			Skinner, Joseph	2		2								
Fairfield, Walter	2	3	3			Skinner, Joseph, Junr	3	4	5								
						Sloan, John	3		1								

GRAFTON COUNTY—Continued.

NAME OF HEAD OF FAMILY.	Free white males of 16 years and upward, including heads of families.	Free white males under 16 years.	Free white females, including heads of families.	All other free persons.	Slaves.
NEW HOLDERNESS TOWN—con.					
Blair, David	1				
Blair, Elizabeth			5		
Blair, Samuel	1				
Blancher, Thomas	1		4		
Brickford, Samuel	1	2	2		
Clark, John	1	1	1		
Cockran, Joseph	1		5		
Cox, Charles	3	5	4		
Cox, Charles, Junr	1		3		
Cox, James	3		3		
Cox, John	1		3		
Cox, Robert	1		2		
Cox, Thomas	1				
Cox, William	1	4	3		
Curry, Samuel	1	3	3		
Curry, William	3	1	2		
Dorr, Samuel	1		1		
Drew, Levi	2	2	2		
Dwyer, Michal	1	2	4		
Ellison, Jacob	1	3	7		
Ellison, Thomas	1	2	3		
Fairfield, Benjamin	1	2	3		
Glins, Richard	1	3	2		
Hill, Robert	1	2	4		
Hill, Thomas	1		3		
Hix, John	1				
Hix, Joseph	1	3	4		
Hogen, Hugh	1				
Hogen, William	1		1		
Innes, Archalus	2		3		
Kinester, Rachel			4		
Livermore, Samuel	7	1	3		
Lowd, John	1	2	1		
Mooney, John	3	1	2		
Morse, Stephen	1	1	1		
Piper, William	3	2	5		
Ramsey, Hugh	3	1	3		
Shaw, John	2	2	3		
Shepard, Jacob	1	3	5		
Shepard, Joseph	2	3	3		
Shepard, Lucy		1	2		
Shepard, Richard	2		5		
Shepard, Samuel	2		5		
Shepard, Samuel, Junr	1				
Shepard, Samuel, 3d	1				
Shepard, Thomas	2	1	3		
Smith, Jeremiah	1		1		
Smith, John	1	3	3		
Smyth, Andrew	4	1	4		
Smyth, Caleb	1				
Smyth, James	1		1		
Smyth, Joshua	1				
Stanton, Isaac W	2	5	4		
Steward, William	1	1	1		
Swany, Bryan	2		4		
Thomson, John	4	1	3		
Thomson, Nathaniel	1		4		
Tobine, Samuel	2		2		
Webster, David	3	3	3		
Whitten, John	1	3	2		
NORTHUMBERLAND TOWN.					
Bennet, Abel	4	4	6		
Burnsides, Thomas	3	3	5		
Burnsides, James	1	2	2		
Clefford, Anthony	2	1	4		
Cole, Hannah			1		
Cole, Jonathan	1	2	1		
Day, Eliphalet	1	1	5		
Emes, Jeremiah	4	1	5		
Marshall, Anthropos	1	1	4		
Marshall, Caleb	5	2	5		
Meriham, Isaac	2	1	1		
Osgood, Abnor	2	4	4		
Peverly, Joseph	1	1	4		
Peverly, Thomas	2	1	3		
Spaldin, Daniel	3	2	2		
Herick, Nathaniel	2	1	4		
ORANGE TOWN.					
Arvin, William	1		1		
Bagley, Samuel	1	2	2		1
Barney, Jabez	1	5	2		
Briggs, Benjamin	1	1	3		
Briggs, Nathaniel	2	2	3		
Bulluck, David	1	2	3		
Bulluck, Sawyer	3	2	6		
Corlies, Elihu	1	3	2		
Corlies, John M	1				

NAME OF HEAD OF FAMILY.	Free white males of 16 years and upward, including heads of families.	Free white males under 16 years.	Free white females, including heads of families.	All other free persons.	Slaves.
ORANGE TOWN—con.					
Corlies, William	2	1	7		
Ellison, Joseph	1	1	2		
Gursha, Betsey			2	4	
Hall, Nicholas	1	2	2		
Hoyt, Benjamin	1				
Hoyt, Jonathan	1	5	4		
Knapp, Paul	3	2	4		
Pixley, Alexander	1	1	3		
Samburn, Samuel	1	1	2		
Sweat, Enock	4	1	1		
Sweat, John	1	1	2		
Tucker, Eshmel	1	2	2		
Waldo, Nathaniel	3	1	6		
ORFORD TOWN.					
Andrew, Theodore	1		3		
Avery, Simeon	5	2	3		
Bliss, Samuel	1		1		
Blood, Asa	1	1	4		
Blood, Stephen	1	3	2		
Carpenter, Eli	2	1	4		
Coggswell, Cibel			1		
Colburn, Daniel	1	2	5		
Cole, Daniel	1	2	3		
Cole, Jesse	1		1		
Cole, Samuel	1		5		
Corless, Jonathan	2	1	3		
Cross, Beteuel	2		2		
Darby, Ezra	1		2		
Darby, Jonathan	3		3		
Darby, Jonathan, Junr	1	2	4		
Darby, Pollas	1	1	1		
Darby, Simeon	1	1	4		
Dam, Theophilus	2	3	5		
Davis, Nathaniel	1	3	5		
Davis, Thomas	1		2		
Davis, Thomas, Junr	1	2	3		
Davis, Samuel	3	1	7		
Day, Samuel	1	2	2		
Dewey, Nathan	2				
Emery, Clemont	1	2	5		
Finney, Eleazer	1	1	2		
Fisher, Henry	1	1	2		
Follet, Benjamin	1		2		
Follet, Francis	1		3		
Follet, Jiles	1	1	2		
Fuller, William	1		2		
Hale, John	1	2	2		
Keys, Ezekel	1	3	2		
Loomis, William	1	2	4		
Lumbard, Stephen	1	1	3		
Mann, John	6	6	6		
Mann, John, Junr	3	2	2		
Mann, Solomon	1		4		
Marsh, Nathaniel	2	2	1		
Marston, Jeremiah	1	1	5		
Merril, Timothy	2	1	2		
Morey, Benony	1	4	2		
Morey, Israel	1	2	2		
Morey, John	2		5		
Morey, Samuel	4		3		
Morse, Enos	1		2		
Muchemore, James	1	2	4		
Newhall, Jeremiah	3	1	2		
Palmer, Abraham	1				
Palmer, Ichabod	1		1		
Palmer, Ichabod, Junr	1	1	2		
Palmer, Moses	1		2		
Palmer, Moses, Junr	1	1	1		
Palmer, Nathaniel	3	4	3		
Parkhurst, John	4	2	3		
Parkhurst, Josiah	1		3		
Phelps, Ephraim	2	2	6		
Phelps, Joel	1		2		
Phelps, Nathaniel	2	1	1		
Phelps, Samuel	1	3	5		
Phelps, Samuel, Junr	1	1	2		
Porter, Alexander	1		3		
Quaint, Benjamin	1		3		
Quaint, Thomas	1	3	1		
Rogers, Nathaniel	1	1	2		
Rowel, Benjamin	1	3	9		
Sawyer, Abel	1	2	3		
Sawyer, Ichabod	3	2	6		
Sawyer, John	2	1	4		
Sawyer, Jonathan	2	4	5		
Sergents, Timothy	1	4	4		
Simpson, William	3		4		
Sloaper, Henry	1		4		
Smith, Joseph	1		4		
Smith, Joseph, Junr	1		1		
Stickney, Nathan	1	1	3		

NAME OF HEAD OF FAMILY.	Free white males of 16 years and upward, including heads of families.	Free white males under 16 years.	Free white females, including heads of families.	All other free persons.	Slaves.
ORFORD TOWN—con.					
Strong, Alexander	1	1	2		
Strong, Jonathan	1		1		
Simons, John	2	3	2		
Tainter, Michal	2	3	3		
Tilloson, Daniel	1		2		
Tilloson, Daniel, Junr	3	3	5		
Todd, Samuel	3	3	4		3
Tylor, Asa	2		3		
Warren, Benjamin	1		2		
Ware, Joseph I	2	2	3		
Ware, Nathaniel	1	2	2		
Webster, Nathan	1	2	5		
Williams, Moses	2	2	5		
Woodbury, James H	1	3	4		
PEELING TOWN.					
Not inhabited.					
PERCY TOWN.					
Blake, Elisha	3	2	4		
Cole, Barnet	1	1	2		
Levit, Peter	2	3	1		
Lunn, Joseph	1	1	2		
Rowel, Daniel	3	3	3		
Smith, Benjamin	2		3		
Smith, Caleb	1	1	5		
Smith, Isaac	1		3		
PIERMONT TOWN.					
Abby, Hezekiah	1	1	3		
Allen, John	1	1	2		
Andrew, Jason	1				
Andrew, Miles	1	1	1		
Andrew, Miles, Junr	1				
Bachellor, Isaiah	1	1	5		
Baley, Solomon	2	2	3		
Barret, Lemuel	1				
Bean, Benjamin	1	1	3		
Blancher, Joseph	1	4	2		
Blinn, James	1		3		
Carter, Noah	1		4		
Case, Zenos	3	2	3		
Chandler, Abnor	2	1	3		
Chandler, Jonathan	4	1	3		
Chopp, Moses	1	2	4		
Crook, Andrew	2	1	3		
Crook, Andrew, Junr	1	1	3		
Crook, Hezekiah	1		1		
Crook, Samuel	1	2	2		
Erwin, David	1	2	4		
Erwin, John	1	2	3		
Fisk, Amos	1				
Foord, Amos	1		1		
Foord, Hezekiah	1	5	3		
Foord, Hezekiah, Junr	1	2	4		
Foord, Joseph	1	2	4		
Foord, Noah	1		2		
Foord, Seth	1	2	5		
Forbis, John	1		2		
Holmans, Ezekiel	1	1	2		
Huggins, Samuel	1	2	2		
Jones, Samuel	1		1		
Jones, Solomon	1	3	3		
Karr, John	2	1	5		
King, Peter	1	1	1		
Lacy, William	1		3		
Lock, Elisha	2	2	4		
McConnell, Moses	1	4	3		
Metcalf, Burges	4	3	7		
Moulton, James	4	1	4		
Patterson, Isaac	4	2	3		1
Phelps, Devanport	3	1	4		1
Richard, John	2		1		
Richard, John, Junr	1	2	2		
Richard, Russel	1	1	2		
Root, Ephraim	1	6	3		
Root, Samuel	1	4	4		
Russel, Thomas	2	1	4		
Sanders, Jonathan	1	1	3		
Sawyer, Dill	1	2	5		
Sawyer, Edward	1	1	5		
Sinclair, Joseph	1		2		
Sleeper, Joseph	1	1	5		
Stephens, Francis	1	4	6		
Stephens, Moses	1	5	3		
Stephens, Parker	3	3	4		
Stone, Benjamin	1		1		
Stone, Benjamin, Junr	1				
Stone, John	1	2	3		
Stone, Samuel	1		1		

NAME OF HEAD OF FAMILY.	Free white males of 16 years and upward, including heads of families.	Free white males under 16 years.	Free white females, including heads of families.	All other free persons.	Slaves.
PIERMONT TOWN—con.					
Stone, Uriah	1	3	4		
Talton, William	1	4	5		
Tarbox, William	1	1	2		
Taylor, Jonathan	1	1	3		
Tilton, John	1		1		
Tylor, David	1	4	4		
Tylor, Ebenezer	2	2	5		
Tylor, Jonathan	1	2	5		
Webb, Azariah	3	3	3	1	
Wellman, Lemuel	1				
Young, Richard	3	2	3		
PLYMOUTH TOWN.					
Ales, David	1		1		
Baley, Richard	2	3	4		
Baley, Solomon	2	3	2		
Barnard, Currier	1	2	2		
Bartlett, Stephen	1	3	2		
Bean, Darbin	1	1	2		
Bean, Elisha	2	3	2		
Blodget, Elliot	1		2		
Blodget, Ebenezer	2		3		
Blodget, James	1	2	4		
Blodget, James, Jur	1		3		
Blodget, Josiah	1				
Blood, Amos	1				
Brown, Josiah	3	3	7		
Brown, Lucy	2	1	2		
Brown, Nathaniel	1				
Brown, Patty			2		
Brown, Silas	1				
Burbeck, James	1	1	2		
Buzwill, Caleb	1				
Buzwell, Richard	1		1		
Clark, Ephraim	1		1		
Crofford, William	2	1	2		
Cummings, Henry	1				
Cummings, Jothum	3	6	3		
Cummings, Jothum, Jur	1				
Davis, Moses	1	1	5		
Dearbin, Peter	2	1	2		
Dearbin, Samuel	3	2	9		
Draper, Jacob	1	5	2		
Emerson, Nathaniel	1		4		
Emerson, Samuel	2	5	3		
Evans, Edwards	1		1		
Fernam, John	2	1	1		
Fletcher, Joshua	1	7	1		
French, Moses	1	3	3		
George, William	4		3		
George, William, Junr	1	1	1		
Gould, Benjamin	3		4		
Greeney, Peter	1	2	2		
Greanlief, Samuel	1	2	2		
Greenough, William	1	1	10		
Hay, Edward	1				
Harrit, James	2	1	2		
Heath, Darbin	1		1		
Hecox, Andrew	1	2	4		
Herrick, Joseph	1		1		
Herman, Thomas	2	2	6		
Hews, Richard	1	1	2		
Hoburt, David	1				
Hull, George	3		2		
Hull, Moses	1				
Kemp, John	1	2	3		
Keyes, Ephraim	1		3		
Keyes, Ephraim, Jur	1	2	4		
Keyes, Jonas	1		3		
Keyes, Peter	1	2	2		
Lovejoy, Samuel	1				
Marsh, Ephraim	2	2	3		
Marsh, Jacob	3	1	3		
Marsh, John	1				
Marsh, Oresiphros	2		3		
Marsh, Samuel	2	1	3		
McClure, Thomas	2		2		
McIntire, Hugh	1		2		
McQuestion, Peter	2				
Melvin, Ebenezer	3		2		
Merrill, David	1				
Merrill, Jacob	1		1		
Merrill, Jacob, Junr	1		1		
Morse, Jonathan	1		3		
Morse, Samuel	1	3	2		
Mullokin, Nathan	1				
Nevens, John	1	2	3		
Parker, Zachariah	2	1	3		
Pennyman, Jonathan	2		2		
Pennyman, Nathan	1				
Phillips, Amos	2		3		

NAME OF HEAD OF FAMILY.	Free white males of 16 years and upward, including heads of families.	Free white males under 16 years.	Free white females, including heads of families.	All other free persons.	Slaves.
PLYMOUTH TOWN—con.					
Phillips, John	1	1	4		
Phillips, Joseph	1				
Phillips, Paul D	1				
Porter, John	1	1	7		
Pratt, David	1	1	1		
Rayn, James	2	2	4		
Rayn, Joseph	1				
Read, John	1	1	9		
Rideout, Benjamin	1	1	3		
Rideout, John	1		2		
Robins, Jonathan	1	2	4		
Robins, Jonathan, Junr	1	3	2		
Rogers, Enock	1	3	3		
Rogers, John	1	3	6		
Senter, David	1	3	5		
Senter, Edward	1		2		
Senter, Joseph	3	1	3		
Sergents, Asa	1				
Sergents, Christopher	1	1	1		
Sergents, Moses	1				
Siphros, John	1	4	4		
Smith, Jacob	1		2		
Snow, Benjamin	1	2	2		
Snow, Marium			1		
Snow, Nehemiah	1		2		
Sterns, Aaron	1				
Stearns, Nathan	2	1	1		
Stearns, Samuel	2		2		
Taylor, Joel	2	2	1		
Taylor, Peter	1				
Therlow, Moses	1		2		
Thornton, Joshua	1				
Ward, Benjamin	1				
Ward, Daniel	1		1		
Ward, Enock	1	4	4		
Ward, Isaac	1	1	2		
Ward, Nathaniel	1		3		
Webber, John	3	3	6		
Webster, David	4	2	4		4
Webster, Daniel	1	3	4		
Webster, Edward	1				
Webster, Eliphalet	1		1		
Webster, Hannah		3	4		
Webster, Peter	1				
Webster, Stephen	2		2		
Welloughby, John	1	3	2		
Welloughby, John	2	3	5		
Wells, Benjamin	1		3		
Wells, Stephen	4	2	3		
Wells, Wentworth	2		4		
Worcester, Francis	1		2		
Worcester, Francis, Junr	2	2	3		
Wright, Abijah	1	2	2		
RUMNEY TOWN.					
Berrey, Aaron	1		3		
Berrey, Zebedee	1		3		
Blodget, Jonathan	1	2	3		
Braynard, Asahel	1	4	4		
Braynard, Bezaleel	2	1	4		
Braynard, Daniel	2				
Braynard, Ebenezer	1		4		
Burnham, Abraham	4	3	4		
Burnham, Joseph	1		2		
Clark, Charles	3	1	3		
Clark, Jonathan	2	2	4		
Clark, Joseph	1		4		
Chamberlin, John	1				
Chamberlin, Jonathan	1		3		
Clensey, Jeremiah	1	1	4		
Clefford, Isaac	1		2		
Clefford, John	1	3	4		
Clefford, Nathaniel	1	3	5		
Clefford, Samuel	1	1	1		
Clefford, Zachariah	1	1	4		
Crague, Alexander	3	3	4		
Crague, David	1		1		
Crague, David, Junr	2	5	3		
Cross, Isaiah	1	2	1		
Dearben, Michal	1		3		
Doe, John	2		3		
Easterbrook, Joseph	1	2	1		
Fuller, John	1	1	6		
Fuller, Hannah			3		
Hall, John	1	5	2		
Hall, Jonathan	2	3	7		
Howard, James	1	3	2		
Haynes, Cutting	2	3	6		
Haynes, Cutting, Junr	1		1		
Heth, James	6	5	6		
Heth, William	2	5	3		

NAME OF HEAD OF FAMILY.	Free white males of 16 years and upward, including heads of families.	Free white males under 16 years.	Free white females, including heads of families.	All other free persons.	Slaves.
RUMNEY TOWN—con.					
Hodge, Thomas	1	1	3		
Hutchinson, Gardner	2	1	5		
Johnson, David	1	1	1		
Johnson, Samuel	1	2	1		
Jones, Joseph	1	4	3		
Kimbal, Sarah	1	1	2		
Keyes, Ebenezer	1	3	4		
Keyes, Samuel	1		2		
Kimball, Thomas	1	2	2		
Kimball, Timothy	1	2	3		
Lucus, Thomas	2	1	1		
Mastin, John	1	1	2		
Myhew, Peter	1	2	3		
Norris, Benjamin	1				
Phelps, Paul D	1				
Pitts, Thomas	1	1	5		
Preston, William	1	5	2		
Ramsey, Hugh	1	3	2		
Ramsey, James	2	2	4		
Ramsey, Mathew	1	1	4		
Ramsey, Thomas	1	4	3		
Richardson, David	1				
Samburn, Josiah	2	1	3		
Samburn, Josiah, Junr	1		1		
Smart, Daniel	1				
Smart, Elisha	1	1	2		
Smart, Moses	1	3	2		
Smart, Richard	2	1	1		
Smart, Richard	1	2	3		
Smart, William	1	1	2		
Webber, John	1	1	5		
Webber, William	3	2	5		
Webber, William, Junr	1				
Weeks, John	1	2	1		
Wyman, Levi	1	3	3		
SENTER'S LOCATION.					
Gentleman, Philip	1				
Herriman, Nathaniel	3		3		
Pike, Robert	1				
SHELBURNE TOWN.					
Austin, Hopstill	1	1	4		
Ingols, Daniel	5		1		
Ingels, Moses	1	1	3		
Messer, Jonathan	2	2	5		
Peabody, John	2	1	2		
Stephens, John	1		3		
STARK'S LOCATION.					
Evens, John	1		3		
Ordway, John	1	2	3		
Ordway, Jonathan B	2	2	1		
Ordway, Joseph	1		2		
Ordway, Joseph, Junr	1	1	6		
Starks, Samuel	2		1		
STERLING'S LOCATION.					
Sterling, Hugh	2		1		
Walker, Joseph	1	2	3		
STRATFORD TOWN.					
Baldwin, Heath	1	1	6		
Baldwin, Jabez	2	2	4		
Barlow, Joseph	3				
Blodget, Elijah	1		4		
Blodget, Josiah	1		3		
Blodget, Mary	3	1	3		
Brown, James	2	1	5		
Curtis, James	1	4	3		
Curtis, Stephen	3		1		
Curtis, William	1	2	3		
French, Charles	1	1			
Fuller, Hezekiah	2	3	7		
Gamsby, George	1		1		
Gamsby, John	3	1	3		
Hinman, Elijah	2	1	3		
Holbrook, Evans	2	1	2		
Holbrook, Joseph	1		2		
Johnson, Isaac	2	3	5		
Lamkin, Joshua	3	1	2		
Lamkin, Sally		4	2		
Lambkin, Thomas	1	4	3		
Shuff, Jacob	1	3	3		
Smith, John	2		1		
Strong, Charles	4				
Webster, Elisha	1	2	2		

GRAFTON COUNTY—Continued.

NAME OF HEAD OF FAMILY.	Free white males of 16 years and upward, including heads of families.	Free white males under 16 years.	Free white females, including heads of families.	All other free persons.	Slaves.
SUCCESS TOWN.					
Not inhabited.					
THORNTON TOWN.					
Bagley, Winthrop	1		3		
Bacon, Benjamin	1	2	2		
Blake, Isaac	1		1		
Blake, Israel	3	3	3		
Blake, Israel, Junr	1		1		
Blake, John	1				
Brown, James	2	3	4		
Bracket, Jacob	1				
Brown, Daniel	1		1		
Brown, John	1	3	5		
Brown, John, Junr	2	2	2		
Cheaney, Elias	1	2	4		
Cheaney, Elias, Junr	1		2		
Cheaney, Paul	1		1		
Colley, Enock	1	2	4		
Colby, Abnor	1	1	1		
Colby, Samuel	1	3	1		
Cone, Jonathan	2	1	4		
Dustin, Jonathan	1		1		
Dustin, Richard	2	1	3		
Elliot, Edmond	2	4	4		
Elliot, Ephraim	2		2		
Elliot, Ezekiel	3	3	9		
Farren, Jonathan	1	1	4		
Foss, John	1	1	3		
Foss, Moses	3	3	5		
Fox, Silas	1	2	3		
Gorden, Peter	2	1	2		
Hatch, Anseln	1				
Hatch, Joseph	1	3	1		
Hubbard, William	2	2	4		
Hutchins, Hannah		1	4		
Ingols, Timothy	2	1	3		
Linsey, David	2	1	4		
Linsey, Ephraim	2	1	3		
Linsey, Thomas	1		1		
McCarter, John	1	3	5		
McClannel, John	1	2	5		
McDamet, Archebald	1		5		
McNorton, Widow	1	1	3		
Nichals, Moses	1	3	3		
Osgood, John	1	3	5		
Perkins, David	2	1	4		
Petty, James P	2	1	5		
Petty, Loammi	1		3		
Petty, Richard	1	4	5		
Prescott, Edward	1	2	2		
Ranker, James	2	4	2		
Robinson, John	2		1		
Russell, Moses	1				
Serbethud, John	1				

NAME OF HEAD OF FAMILY.	Free white males of 16 years and upward, including heads of families.	Free white males under 16 years.	Free white females, including heads of families.	All other free persons.	Slaves.
THORNTON TOWN—con.					
Seargent, Jacob	1	2	6		
Smith, Stephen	1	4	3		
Sterns, Peter	1	2	3		
Stearns, Peter, Junr	1		1		
Sulingham, Jacob	1	5	1		
Thornton, William	2	2	4		
Thornton, William	1	2	2		
Torcy, James	2		1		
Walker, Thomas	1		2		
Walker, Thomas, Junr	1				
Wells, John	1	1	1		
Webster, Joseph	1		3		
Webster, Nathaniel	2	2	2		
Willey, Abel	4	3	3		
Willey, Abel, Junr	1		4		
Willey, Jared	1	2	2		
Willey, Patience			2		
Willey, Seth	1		3		
Worcester, Noah	2	2	5		
TRECOTHICK TOWN.					
Not inhabited.					
WALES'S LOCATION.					
Genison, Hopestill	1	3	2		
WARREN TOWN.					
Bachelor, Reuben	2	2	3		
Bowles, Charles			1	4	
Butler, William	2	2	7		
Clemons, Jonathan	1	2	3		
Clemens, Obediah	4	3	5		
Clough, Nathaniel	1		4		
Copp, Eliphalet	1		2		
Copp, Joshua	3	7	6		
Fellows, Jonathan	2				
Fellows, Samuel	1	2	1		
French, Joseph	1		1		
Gardner, James	1		1		
Holmes, Caleb	1		2		
Knight, Samuel	1	1	4		
Little, Amos	1		3		
Lufkin, Levi	1		1		
Lund, Silas	1		1		
Lund, Stephen	1	5	4		
Merrel, Abel	2	3	2		
Merrel, Jonathan	2	2	4		
Merrel, Joseph	1	3	1		
Merrel, Joshua	1	1	1		
Merrel, Stephen	3	1	4		
Patch, Joseph	1	5	2		
Pilsbury, Richard	3	2	1		

NAME OF HEAD OF FAMILY.	Free white males of 16 years and upward, including heads of families.	Free white males under 16 years.	Free white females, including heads of families.	All other free persons.	Slaves.
WARREN TOWN—con.					
Richardson, Stephen	1	1	4		
Samburne, Henry	1	3	3		
Sweat, Elisha	1	1	2		
True, Ephraim	1	3	2		
Welch, Aaron	1	1	1		
Whicher, Chase	2	3	3		
Whicher, John	3	4	2		
Whicher, Joseph	2	4	3		
Witman, William C	1		1		
Witman, William C., Junr	1	3	1		
WENTWORTH TOWN.					
Akin, James	1	1	1		
Akin, John	2		3		
Akin, John, Junr	1		3		
Ames, Amos	1				
Boyanton, Asa	2	1	4		
Boyanton, Thomas	1	3	4		
Chase, Nicholas	1	3	2		
Clark, Daniel	1	3	4		
Clark, Thomas	2	1	5		
Clefford, Isaac	3	5	2		
Cupper, Joseph	1	1	1		
Colton, Benjamin	1	2	3		
Cross, Experience	1		3		
Currier, Samuel	2		1		
Eaton, Job	1	1	2		
Elsworth, Samuel	1	6	3		
Grove, Ebenezer	1	3	3		
Heard, Amos	1	1	2		
Heaton, Ebenezer	1	2	1		
Heaton, Jonathan	1		2		
Hooper, Samuel	1	1	3		
Keeser, Lemuel	2		1		
Kimball, Joseph	2	3	3		
Leicester, John	1	3	3		
McClaron, Hugh	1	4	1		
Page, Enock	1	5	2		
Page, Ephraim	3	1	4		
Peten, Absalom	2	2	3		
Pilsbury, Josiah	1	1	2		
Pilsbury, Merril	1	1	3		
Putney, Aron	1	2	2		
Putney, Asa	2		4		
Smart, Samuel	1	1	2		
Smith, Benjamin	1	2	3		
Smith, John	1	1	2		
Smith, Joseph	2		2		
Smith, Molly		2	3		
Stephens, Peter	2	4	6		
Weeks, Benjamin	1	2	4		
Whicher, Reuben	2	4	3		
White, Nathaniel	2		3		
Worcester, Louis		1	4		

HILLSBOROUGH COUNTY.

NAME OF HEAD OF FAMILY.	Free white males of 16 years and upward, including heads of families.	Free white males under 16 years.	Free white females, including heads of families.	All other free persons.	Slaves.
AMHERST TOWN.					
Barnard, Jeremiah	5	1	5		
Wilkins, Samuel	4	2	6		
Barker, Ephraim	4	3	6		
Lovejoy, Joshua	1	3	5		
Means, Robert	3	4	11	1	
Warner, Daniel	3	1	5		
Wilkins, John	3	2	4	1	
Atherton, Joshua	2	1	6	1	
Ellenwood, Ralph	2	2	5		
Spiller, Thomas	1	1	3		
Henchman, Nathaniel	1	1	6		
Kendall, Nathan, Jr	1	2	5		
Keef, Rachel		2	4		
Baldwin, Tabitha		1	3		
Dana, Saml	3	2	6		
Wiet, Saml	1	2	3		
Nichols, Hannah	2	2	5	1	
Watson, John	3		3		
Curtis, Saml	2	3	4		
Stewart, David	2	1	3		
Fletcher, Robt	3	1	4		
Baldwin, Isaac	2		4		
Brown, John	1	1	1		
Brown, William	1			5	
Wilkins, Jona., Jr	1		3		
Ray, James	5	3	6		
Odell, Ebenr	1	2	4		
Taylor, Ebenr	5		1		
Gordon, William	1	1	1		

NAME OF HEAD OF FAMILY.	Free white males of 16 years and upward, including heads of families.	Free white males under 16 years.	Free white females, including heads of families.	All other free persons.	Slaves.
AMHERST TOWN—con.					
Curtice, Jacob	2	1	3		
Farnum, Joseph	1	3	7		
Holt, Thomas	2	1	3		
Blanchard, Joseph	1		2		
Stewart, John, Junr	1	2	5		
Dodge, Barthl	3	2	4		
Ellenwood, Rolinson	1	2	2		
Kitteridge, John	1	3	4		
French, Ephraim	2	4	3		
Smith, Timothy	1		2		
Melendy, William	1	1	2		
Eaton, John	1	3	5		
Boutell, Reuben	1	2	2		
Read, William	3	1	2	1	
Kendall, Nathan	2	1	2		
Weston, Ebenr Jr	3		2		
Weston, Ebenr	2	1	3		
Boutell, Joseph, Jr	2		3		
Boutell, Kendall	1		2		
Odell, William	1		3		
Odell, John	1	1	5		
Smith, Marverick	1	1	1		
Boutell, Joseph, 3d	1	3	3		
Boutell, Joseph, 4th	2		1		
Fields, Saml	1	2	3		
Gilmore, James	2	1	4		
Usher, Eleazr	1	3	2		
Colburn, Joseph	1	3	1		
Stearns, John	3	1	3		

NAME OF HEAD OF FAMILY.	Free white males of 16 years and upward, including heads of families.	Free white males under 16 years.	Free white females, including heads of families.	All other free persons.	Slaves.
AMHERST TOWN—con.					
Danforth, David	4	4	7		
Delaway, John	1	2	4		
Ellsworth, Jona	1	1	1		
Ellsworth, Lucy			2		
Hobson, Jeremiah	3	2	5		
Cleavs, Nathan	1	3	6		
Wheeler, John	1	3	3		
Jones, Phineas	2	2	2		
Prince, Joseph	2	3	4		
Prince, Elizabeth	2	1	1		
Barron, Moses	2	3	6		
Bradford, William, Jr	1	2	6		
Burnam, Joshua	2	3	4		
Burnam, Stephen	1		1		
Seaton, John	2		2		
Odell, William, Jr	1	2	5		
Lovejoy, James	1	5	2		
Jones, Timothy	1	2	3		
Wacher, Stephen	1	1	3		
Jewet, Joseph, Jr	1	1	1		
Melendy, Nathl	1	3	2		
Melendy, Thomas	1	3	2		
Arbuckle, John	2	1	6		
Lovejoy, Hezekh	1		3		
Lovejoy, Jona	1	1	2		
Underwood, Ths	1	4	4	1	
Taylor, Jona	1	1	3		
Dutton, John	1	1	5		
Stevens, Danl, Jr	1	2	5		

HILLSBOROUGH COUNTY—Continued.

AMHERST TOWN—con.

NAME OF HEAD OF FAMILY.	Free white males of 16 years and upward, including heads of families.	Free white males under 16 years.	Free white females, including heads of families.	All other free persons.	Slaves.
Merril, Ben	1	3	3		
Goss, Ephraim	1	1	2		
Roby, James	1		4		
Maning, Isaac	1	1	2		
Kidder, Danl	1	1	4		
Jewet, Joseph	1	1	2		
King, William	1	2	3		
Low, William	1	3	5		
Ellenwood, Ebenr	1	1	3		
Boutell, Amos	1	1	2		
Kimball, Ebenr	2	1	2		
Mussey, Dimond	1	3	5		
Lyon, Jona	1		1		
Lyon, Jona., Jr	1	1	2		
Henry, Saml	1	2	6		
Harvell, John	3		3		
Goodwin, Matthew	1	4	4		
Dunkle, Thad	1	3	5		
Hosea, Robt	2		2		
Prince, Abel	1	2	3		
Robertson, Peter	1	2	4		
Clark, Joseph	1	2	2		
Kittridge, Zeph	4	1	7		
Hartshorn, John	1	2	7		
Smith, Jona, Jr	3		3	1	
Peacock, William	2	2	4		
Abbot, Isaac	2	3	4		
Davis, Benja	1		4		
Davis, Andrew	1	2	6		
Codman, Henry	1	1	6		
Truel, Amos	2	2	6		
Melendy, William, Jr	5	5	4	1	
Hazeltine, Susanna		2	3		
Smith, Jona	3	1	2		
Clark, Timo	3	4	2		
Douglas, William	1		1		
Boutell, Aaron	1	1	6		
King, William	1	1	3		
Wilkins, Benja	1		1		
Clark, Lydia		1	2		
Shannon, Andrew	2	2	4		
Hutchinson, Ebenr	2	6	2		
Wilkins, Ben	2	1	3		
Wilkins, David	1		2		
Swininton, Asa	1		1		
Goss, Peter	1	1	3		
Fetton, Elisha	2	2	2		
Fisk, William	1	4	5		
Stewart, William	1	2	6		
Dammon, John, Jr	1				
Stewart, John	1		1		
Campbell, Danl	2	2	6		
Dammon, Benja	1	2	3		
Lund, Jona	3	3	4		
Shepard, Saml	2	5	2		
Standley, Abel	1	1	1		
Standley, Jacob	1		1		
Standley, Jacob, Jr	1		4		
Kimball, Henry	1	2	2		
Seaton, Saml	2		2		
Hildreth, David	1	1	3		
Dodge, Susanna		1	4		
Wakefield, Ebenr	1	1	3		
Howard, Pitmun	1	1	4		
Holt, Reuben	1	3	5		
Pike, Benja	1		1		
Pike, Benja, Jr	1	3	3		
Pike, Enoch	1	1	2		
Maning, John	1	2	3		
Kendall, Danl	1	1	4		
Kendall, Jacob	1	2	3		
Rollings, Joseph	1	1	2		
Jaqueth, Isaac	1	1	4		
Barrons, William	1	3	2		
Stearns, Saml	1	2	2		
Stearns, Saml, Jr	1	1	2		
Coggin, Joseph	3		5		
Stearns, Benja	1	2	2		
Herrick, Josh	3	2	6		
Clark, H. Ward	1	2	4		
Campbell, Henry	1				
Williams, Mary	1	1	2	1	
Carlton, John	1	1	5		
Goodridge, Allen	1	3	5		
Lynch, Catharine	4	1	3		
Carlton, Oliver	2		4		
Fuller, Nathan	2		1		
Fuller, Nathan, Jr	1	1	2		
Dunckle, John	2		8		
Averill, Thomas	1		1		
Averill, Thomas, Jr	1	5	3		
Phelps, Nathan	3	1	6		

AMHERST TOWN—con.

NAME OF HEAD OF FAMILY.	Free white males of 16 years and upward, including heads of families.	Free white males under 16 years.	Free white females, including heads of families.	All other free persons.	Slaves.
Cole, John	2	1	3		
Green, Amos	1	2	6		
Flint, Amos, Junr	1	1	3		
Steel, Joseph	2	1	2		
Rea, Ebenr	2	6	5		
Standley, Saml	1	2	5		
Hildreth, Jacob	3	2	2		
Wakefield, Thomas	1	1	2		
Tolbert, Philo	1	1	1		
Wakefield, William	1	2	1		
Ellinwood, Jedidiah	2		4		
Howard, William	4	1	3		
Sercomb, John	1	3	5		
Howard, Josiah	1	1	3		
Shepard, John	1	1	2		
Nichols, Joseph	1	1	2	1	
Bacheldor, Ebenr	2	2	6		
Batcheldor, John	1	3	4		
Hill, Timothy	1	4	3		
Spaulding, Henry	1	1	3		
Russell, Peter	3	1	4		
Peabody, Thomas	1		1		
Peabody, Hannah	2		4		
Flint, Amos	1		1		
Trevit, Henry	1	3	2		
Stevens, Danl	3	1	3		
Hutchinson, Elisha	1	2	4		
Elliot, Francis	1	1	3		
Elliot, Amos	1	1	3		
Levit, Andrew	3	2	5		
Mills, John	2	1	3		
Crosby, William	2		1		
Buxton, Jona	1	1	2		
Lummus, Porter	1		2		
Crosby, Josiah	4		2		
Crosby, Josiah, Jr	2	5	3		
Hopkins, Solo	1	1	3		
Hutchinson, Nathan, Jr	1	3	3		
Blanchard, Augustus	3	3	6		
Foster, Moses	1		1		
Burns, John	2	1	1		
Burns, John, Junr	1	2	2		
Burns, Danl	1	1	1		
Crosby, Samson	2		3		
Gilman, James	1	2	4		
Kindrick, Benja	1	3	3		
Carter, Michl	1	1	2		
Blunt, John	1	1	5		
Wallace, James	1	1	3		
Conant, Benja	2		4		
Dunkle, David	3	3	5		
Hutchinson, Timo	1	2	2		
Woods, Peter	1	2	2		
Lovejoy, Saml	1	2	3		
Hall, Jesse	1		1		
Sargent, Ebenr	1	2	3		
How, Isaac	1	2	3		
Lund, Willard	1		1		
Towne, Barthl	2		2		
Lovejoy, Jona	1	1	5		
Towne, Moses	2	2	1		
Southwark, Isaac	4	1	1	1	
Lakeman, Joseph	1		2		
Sevey, Nathl	1	2	2		
Hutchinson, Abner	2		2		
Boynton, John	1	1	2		
Roby, John	1	1	2		
Fick, Ebenr	1	2	3		
Taylor, Benja	1	3	2		
Curtice, Jacob, Junr	1	3	3		
Wilkins, Abijah	3	1	3		
Lovitt, Simon	1	2	3		
Weston, Thomas	3		3		
Lamson, William	2	2	5		
Hastings, William	1	2	2		
Marvell, James	1	2	5		
Abbot, Ephraim	2		2		
Willson, Hannah			3		
Perkins, Joseph	1		4		
Perkins, Joseph, Jr	2	2	5		
Bruse, John	1	2	3		
Averill, John	1	2	4		
Beckford, Joseph	1	1	2		
Langdoll, Joseph	1	1	7		
Woodbury, James	3		3		
Cole, Nathan	1	5	4		
Kittridge, Solo	2	2	3		
Carlton, Enoch	1		1		
Fick, John	1		1		
Trow, Joseph	2	4	5		
Hopkins, James	1	1	3		
Shepard, Jothm	3	2	3		

AMHERST TOWN—con.

NAME OF HEAD OF FAMILY.	Free white males of 16 years and upward, including heads of families.	Free white males under 16 years.	Free white females, including heads of families.	All other free persons.	Slaves.
Bradford, John	3	3	4		
Bradford, Andrew	1		1		
Hogg, William	2	1	3		
Hartshorn, James	2		4		
Hartshorn, John, Jr	1	2	2		
Hartshorn, Edward	1	1	1		
Woolson, Thomas	3	1	4		
Wallace, Joseph	3	1	3		
Wallace, John	1	3	3		
Hartshorn, William	1		4		
Holt, Ebenr	1		1		
Lamson, Jona	1		2		
Lamson, Jona, Jr	1	1	1		
Peabody, Saml	1	3	2		
Peabody, Moses	1	1	1		
Lovejoy, Joseph	1	1	3		
Flint, Hutchinson	1	1	3		
Flint, Nathan	1		2		
Flint, Nathan, Jr	1	4	2		
Simonds, Benja	1		4		
Dodge, Josiah	1	2	4		
Wilkins, Mirriam			2		
Averill, Elijah	1	1	3		
Wheeler, Timo	2	5	4		
Rider, Ebenr	1		1		
Beckford, Joseph	1	1	2		
Smith, Timo, jr	1	2	3		
Tuck, Joseph	1		4		
Hopkins, Williams	1		2		
Hopkins, Hannah			2		
Hopkins, Martha	2	1	1		
Bradford, William	2		2		
Bradford, Enos	2	1	2		
Cochran, John	1	2	7		
Carlton, Oliver, Jr	1	2	3		
Gould, Stephen	1	2	3		
Gould, Richard	1	1	3		
Goodwin, Thomas	1		4		
Howard, William	1		2		
Harwood, John	2	2	5		
Kimball, Moses	1		2		
Kimball, Moses, Jr	1	3	1		
Nichols, Knight	2	2	4		
Parker, Robt	2	1	4		
Smith, Jacob	2	3	1		
Smith, James	1	5	2		
Smith, Danl	2	2	1		
Steele, Saml	1		2		
Symond, Danl	1		1		
Tuttle, Nathan	1	1	4		
Upton, Enos	1	3	3		
Upton, Ezekiel	2	2	5		
Wilkins, Aaron	1	2	3		
Wilkins, Eli	1	3	2		
Woodbury, Peter	2		3		
Wilkins, William	4	4	5		
Wilkins, Lydia			2		
Ward, Richard	1	4	3		
Jones, Nathan	1		3		
Jones, Nathan, Jr	1	2	7		
Jones, Peter	1	1	3		
Abbot, Stephen	1	1	5		
Averill, Ebenr	1	5	2		
Averill, Elijah	1	1	3		
Bowers, Oliver	1	2	2		
Bradford, Andrew, Jr	1	2	2	1	
Burns, Moses	2		2		
Burns, George	2	1	6		
Smith, Isaac	1		2		
Burns, Thomas	3	2	6		
Burnam, Andrew	1		2		
Cole, Eliphalet	1	3	4		
Clark, Benja	1	2	3		
Clark, Ebenr	1		4		
Clark, Danl	1	2	2		
Chandler, David	1	2	5		
Crosby, Stephen	1	1	3		
Campbell, Robt	1	2	1		
Cunings, John	1	3	7		
Clark, Joshua	2	2	2		
Clark, Joshua, Jr	1		2		
Hutchinson, Asa	1	2	3		
Holt, Obadiah	1	1	3		
Handley, Henry	1	1	2		
Hutchinson, Nathn	4	2	6		
Hutchinson, Benja	2	1	3		
Hopkins, Peter	1	2	3		
Hale, Ambros	1	2	3		
Hoar, Joseph	2		2		
How, Stephen	1	3	3		
Hopkins, William	1		2		
Hopkins, Hannah	1		2		

HILLSBOROUGH COUNTY—Continued.

AMHERST TOWN—con.

NAME OF HEAD OF FAMILY.	Free white males of 16 years and upward, including heads of families.	Free white males under 16 years.	Free white females, including heads of families.	All other free persons.	Slaves.
Hopkins, Martha	2	1	1		
Hartshorn, Benja	1	2	2		
Kidder, Josiah	1	3	4		
Melvin, David	1	2	2		
Merril, Nathan	1	1	1		
Osgood, Josiah	1	1	2		
Pettingill, Joshua	2	1	4		
Peabody, William	3	2	6		
Purple, John	1		2		
Small, William	1	2	3		
Smith, Danl., Jr	1	3	4		
Small, Joseph	1	1	2		
Wilkins, Robt. B	1	1	2		
Whitney, Elijah	1	1	5		
Wilkins, Benja., Jr	1	2	3		
Temple, Benja	2	3	4		
Taylor, William	2	1	4		
Towne, Israel	2	1	3	1	
Upham, Phineas	3	1	4		
Wilkins, Aaron	1	3	2		
Weston, Isaac	1	2	5		

ANDOVER TOWN.

NAME OF HEAD OF FAMILY.	Free white males of 16 years and upward, including heads of families.	Free white males under 16 years.	Free white females, including heads of families.	All other free persons.	Slaves.
Row, John, Jr	2	2	5		
Fellows, Joseph	2		2		
Fellows, Ezekiel	3	1	3		
Marsten, Paul S	2	3	2		
Rollings, Simeon	1	2	4		
Fuller, James	1	4	3		
Morral, Jabez	1	2	4		
Row, Nathan J	1	2	3		
Page, Joshua	1	3	2		
———, William	4	2	4		
Scribner, Ebenr	1	3	4		
Fifield, Edward	1		2		
Scribner, Samuel	1		1		
Scribner, Josiah	1	5	3		
Conner, Simeon	2	3	5		
Hanes, Josiah	1	2	4		
Morey, William	2		1		
Morey, William, Jr	1	3	3		
Row, John	1	2	1		
Row, Nathl	2		3		
Clough, Moses	1	2	6		
Clough, Wadley	1	1	1		
Cilley, John	1	1	5		
Fellows, Joseph	2	3	3		
Ash, William	1	1	1		
Ash, John	2		2		
Blake, William	3	1	3		
Brown, Joseph	3		3		
Blake, Samuel, Jr	1		4		
Blake, Thomas	2		2		
Barnard, Silas	1		2		
Blake, Bradley	1	2	2		
Blake, Samuel	2		1		
Brown, William	1	4	1		
Bailey, John	1	1	2		
Brown, Caleb	1	2	2		
Brown, Abby	1	3	4		
Brown, Moses, Jr	1	1	3		
Brown, Joseph, Jr	1	1	3		
Blake, Theoph	1	1	3		
Brown, Isaac	1	1	4		
Batchelder, Josiah	1	2	3		
Batchelder, Mark	2		2		
Barber, Jethro	1	2	1		
Brown, Moses	3	1	1		
Call, Stephen	2		1		
Call, John	2	3	4		
Colby, John	1	1	2		
Call, Nathl	1	1	2		
Corlas, Patetiah	1				
Danforth, Joshua	1	2	3		
Dier, William	2	3	4		
Danforth, Nathl	1		3		
Dudley, John	1	2	2		
Dudley, Stephen	1		2		
Day, Saml	1		1		
Dudley, Jacob	1		1		
Flanders, Nathl	1	4	3		
Green, Stephen	1		2		
How, Jona	1		1		
Hilton, Charles	1	4	4		
Hall, Henry	1	2	4		
Hillard, Weare	1				
Hoyt, Reuben	1		2		
Hoyt, Benja	2	1	4		
Ladd, Edward	4	2	3		
Ladd, Thing	1	1	5		
Morrison, David	1		2		

ANDOVER TOWN—con.

NAME OF HEAD OF FAMILY.	Free white males of 16 years and upward, including heads of families.	Free white males under 16 years.	Free white females, including heads of families.	All other free persons.	Slaves.
Mitchel, Philip	1	4	5		
Nuton, Richard	1	3	4		
Philbrick, Joseph	2	5	3		
Roberts, John	4	3	2		
Rollings, Eliphalet	1	3	1		
Danforth, Josiah	1		3		
Rowel, John	2		5		
Roberts, Jona	3		4		
Row, John	2	2	4		
Rains, Saml	2		1		
Samborn, Richard	1		2		
Sanders, John	1	1	1		
Sanborn, Eliphalet	1		4		
Stevens, Jona	3	2	2		
Cilley, Benja., Jr	1	1	1		
Cilley, John	1	3	3		
Symonds, James	1	1	4		
Cilley, Saml	1	1	6		
Sanborn, David	1	3	4		
Sleeper, Thomas	2	2	5		
Cilley, Danl	2	2	2		
Cilley, Aaron	2	3	6		
Cilley, Benja	3	3	2		
Cilley, Elisha	1	1	1		
Cilley, Benja. 3d	2				
Scribner, Thomas	2		3		
Swett, John D	3	1	2		
Sawyer, John	2	2	6		
Sleeper, Jedidiah	1	2	3		
Trew, William	2	1	2		
Tilton, Ebenr	1	4	3		
Tucker, James	1	2	1		
Tuker, Ebenr	3		6		
Turrell, John	1	1	4		
Welch, Thomas	1	1	1		
Welch, Archelaus	1		4		
Welch, Moses	1	1	1		
Weare, Peter	1	1	2		
Weare, Jona	1	4	6		
Badcock, Josiah	1	1	3		
Frazier, Benja	1	1	2		
Fuller, David	2	3	2		
Clough, Moses	2	2	7		

ANTRIM TOWN.

NAME OF HEAD OF FAMILY.	Free white males of 16 years and upward, including heads of families.	Free white males under 16 years.	Free white females, including heads of families.	All other free persons.	Slaves.
Boyd, Joseph	1	4	3		
McCluer, David	1	1	3		
Cochran, Isaac	2	1	4		
Dunlap, Thomas	3	1	3		
Raley, Majr	1	2	2		
Cochran, Michl	4	4	3		
Chenee, Elias	1	4	1		
Aaten, Nathl	1	4	3		
McCoy, John	1	4	1		
Jemerson, Hugh	1	1	2		
Jemerson, Thomas	1	2	2		
Nichols, Danl	2	1	4		
Nichols, Adam	1	3	1		
Brown, John	2		5		
Butler, Tobias	2	3	4		
Ladd, Jona	2		1		
Dickey, Adam	1		3		
Aiken, John	3		5		
Nesmith, Arthur	1				
Seaton, Andrew	1	1	1		
Wright, David	2	3	1		
Smith, Robt	4		1		
Jimerson, Alexander	1	2	4		
McFarland, Danl	2	3	3		
Gilmore, James	3	2	3		
Duncan, James	1	3	2		
Nichols, Thomas	2	1	7		
Steele, James	2	2	3		
George, Michael	1	2	2		
Downing, Saml	1		4		
Downing, Danl	2	1	2		
McAlvin, John	2		1		
Brown, William	1	4	2		
Barker, Peter	2	2	3		
Karr, William	1	2	2		
Wood, Charles	1	1	1		
Campbell, John	1	2	1		
Barker, Abijah	1	2	1		
Holms, William	2	1	3		
Kidder, Ebenr	1	2	3		
Wyer, Jeremiah	1	2	4		
McAllaster, James	1	2	2		
McClary, William	2	1	2		
Stewart, Francis	2		3		
Stewart, Thomas	1	2	3		
Warren, John	2	2	3		

ANTRIM TOWN—con.

NAME OF HEAD OF FAMILY.	Free white males of 16 years and upward, including heads of families.	Free white males under 16 years.	Free white females, including heads of families.	All other free persons.	Slaves.
Moor, Saml	3	3	7		
Wallace, James	1	2	2		
Stewart, John	1	1	4		
Stewart, Thomas, Jr	1	1	1		
Gragg, Alexander	1	1	3		
Dunlap, Adam	1	2	2		
Curtice, Stephen	1		3		
Curtice, Leml	1	1	4		
Holms, William, Jr	1	1	2		
Boutels, Reuben	1	2	2		
Dunsmore, Saml	1		1		
Day, Thomas	1		1		
Steele, James, Jr	1	1	3		
Bums, Robert	1	2	2		
Stewart, John, Jr	1	2	2		
Carr, James	1	5	2		
Carr, John	1	1	2		
Weston, Southwark	2	2	3		
Taylor, Nathl	1		1		
McAllaster, Richard	2	2	5		
Nesmith, James	1	1	3		
Dow, Perry	1	1	5		
Patch, Thomas	1	2	1		
Cristy, Saml	1	1	1		
McAlvin, Robt	1	2	5		
McAlvin, John	1	2	2		
Steele, James, 3d	1		2		
Flanders, Jona	1	1	1		
Gragg, Saml	3	2	7		
Alexander, John	1				
McMaster, Saml	1		1		
Gragg, Benja	3		2		
George, Moses	2		3		
Bydell, William	1	2	2		
Duncan, John	2	1	6		
Boyd, William	2	3	3		
McDole, Alexander	1				
Boyd, James	2				
Parker, William	1	1	2		
Miltimore, Daniel	1	1	3		
Nesmith, Jona	1	3	2		
Moor, Jehorda	1				
Duncan, Robt	1		1		
Hopkins, James	1	1	3		
Patten, Samuel	1	2	5		
Vose, Samuel	2				
Butterfield, Benja	1	3	5		
Wallace, John	1		1		
Houston, William	1	1	4		
Goodhue, Ebenr	1	2	4		
George, Simon	1		1		

BEDFORD TOWN.

NAME OF HEAD OF FAMILY.	Free white males of 16 years and upward, including heads of families.	Free white males under 16 years.	Free white females, including heads of families.	All other free persons.	Slaves.
Pickle, William	1	1	1		
Houston, John	4	1	1		
Moor, Saml	1	4	5		
Bennet, James	2	2	6		
Stevens, Abiel	1		1		
Stevens, David	1	5	2		
Moor, James	2	5	6		
English, Agnes	1	2	4		
Gardner, John	1		4		
McIntosh, John	1	5	2		
Burns, William	1	3	3		
Cutler, Nathan	1		1		
Gerrish, Saml	2	1	3		
Boyes, Thomas	1	1	3		
Dole, Stephen	2	4	3		
Moor, William	3	2	3	1	
Rand, John	3	2	3		
Morrison, John	1	2	3		
Buxton, Benja	1		2		
Headen, William	1				
Riddle, Hugh	1	1	2		
Smith, Benja	1		3		
Smith, Adam	2	1	3		
Moor, John	1	2	7		
Walker, Andrew	1	4	3		
Boyes, John, Jr	3	2	3		
Kenedy, William	1		3		
Henry, Saml	1	3	2		
Wallace, John	2	1	4		
Wallace, Josiah	1		3		
Lincoln, Ezekiel	3	1	4		
Lincoln, Elisha, Jr	1	3	4		
Gordon, John	2	4	5		
Cuningham, Jonh	2	2	5		
Twirel, Saml	2	1	2		
Moor, John	1	4	3		
Alexander, Robt	3	4	3		
Wallace, Jos	1	2	4		

HILLSBOROUGH COUNTY—Continued.

BEDFORD TOWN—con.

NAME OF HEAD OF FAMILY.	Free white males of 16 years and upward, including heads of families.	Free white males under 16 years.	Free white females, including heads of families.	All other free persons.	Slaves.
Wallace, John, Jr	1	5	3		
Martin, Amos	1		1		
Walker, James	1	3	4		
McQuig, Jacob	3	1	3		
Man, Rebecca		3	3		
Wallace, Jane			2		
Barnet, Hannah			1		
Kenedy, Anna			1		
Martin, Jona	1	1	3		
Goffe, Greggs	2		5		
Whittle, Thomas	1	3	2		
Goffe, John	2	1	4		
McIntoch, John, Jr	1	3	3		
Gilmore, James	1	2	4		
Parker, John	1	1	2		
Harvell, Joseph	1	4	3		
Parker, William	4	2	2		
Sherley, Pherez	1	1	1		
Powers, Whitcomb	1	1	3		
McLaughlin, Thomas	1	2	5		
McKeen, Bennet	2	1	3		
Whitman, John	1	3	4		
Morrell, Robert	1		1		
Dow, Benja	3	2	5		
Underwood, James	1	3	3		
Vose, James	2	1	5		
Dickey, Adam	2	1	2	1	
McLaughlin, Joseph	1	2	1		
Gardner, Amos	1	1	2		
Dole, Silas	2	2	6		
Lincoln, John	1	1	3		
Lincoln, Elisha	1	1	1		
Harris, Thomas	1	3	3		
Lincoln, Robt	1		1		
Vickery, John	3	1	2		
Patten, John	1	1	3		
Chandler, Ezeekah	3		4	1	
Laughlin, James	1	3	3		
McDefee, Mathew	1	3	2		
McLaughlin, John	4	1	1		
Patten, Saml	1	1	4		
Patten, Joseph	2		1		
Martin, James	4	2	4		
Houston, James	1		3		
French, Stephen	3	3	5		
Moor, John, 3d	1	3	4		
Vase, Saml	3		2	1	
Reed, James	1	2	3		
Chubbuck, Simon	1	4	3		
Bell, John	1	1	2		
Moor, Danl	3		1	3	
Burns, John	1	1	4		
Wallace, James	1	3	4		
Patten, Matthew	3	1	4		
Laughlin, Nathl	1	1	3		
Aikin, John	1		2		
Miller, Matthew	4	2½	7		
Barron, Benja	2	1	3		
Swett, Moses	3		5		
Coker, Wm	1				
Lyon, Edward	1	3	2		
Campbell, James	1		3		
Barnes, Asa	2	3	4		
Richardson, John	1	1	2		
Worcester, Jesse	1	2	4		
French, Mary	1	2	4		
Sprague, Nicholas	2		1		
Sprague, Benja	1	3	4		
Barnes, John	2		3		
Patten, Robt	1	1	3		
McLary, David	2		6		
Gilchrist, Robert	2	2	3		
McFarson, John	1	2	4		
Dunlap, John	4	5	4		
Leach, James	1	1	3		
Gilmore, Margaret		4	4		
McKenny, John	2	2	6		
Sargent, Daniel	1				
Houston, Joa	1	3	6		
Pratt, John	1				
Walker, Robt	1	5	3		
Fugard, Saml	1	2	3		
Bell, Jos	1	4	3		
Riddel, John	1	2	5		
McDuffee, Matthew	1		2		
McDuffee, Wm	2	2	3		
Patterson, Saml	4	1	4		
Orr, George	1		6		
Orr, John	1	4	5		
Willet, Benja	1	2	4		
Nesmith, James	1	1	4		
Gardner, Ezekiel	1	3	4		

BEDFORD TOWN—con.

NAME OF HEAD OF FAMILY.	Free white males of 16 years and upward, including heads of families.	Free white males under 16 years.	Free white females, including heads of families.	All other free persons.	Slaves.
Attwood, Isaac	2	2	4		
Townsend, Thomas	1	2	2		
Riddle, Isaac	1	2	2		
Riddle, Mary	1	1	1		
McAlaster, Jerusha		1	4		
McAlaster, John	1	3	5		
Riddle, William	3		3		
Walker, William	2	2	5		
Aiken, Mary	1	1	7		
Larkin, Partrick	1	4	1		
Wallace, Jane			2		

BOSCAWEN TOWN.

NAME OF HEAD OF FAMILY.	Free white males of 16 years and upward, including heads of families.	Free white males under 16 years.	Free white females, including heads of families.	All other free persons.	Slaves.
Sargent, Michael	1	4	5		
Rolph, Benja	4		3		
Bean, Joseph	2	1	2		
Scales, Matthew	1	1	4		
Goggins, Nathl	2	4	5		
Pillsbury, Daniel	2	2	1		
Elliot, Nicholas	1	3	2		
Bean Peter	1		1		
Elliott, Thomas	3	2	5		
Call, Silas	2	2	3		
Call, David	1	1	5		
Kimball, Peter	2	1	7		
Mussey, John	2	3	4		
Corser, Saml	2	2	3		
Corser, Stephen	1	1	1		
Rolph, John	1	2	1		
Eastman, Timothy	3	2	5		
Call, Moses	2	3	3		
Calf, Moses	1		2		
Couch, Benja	1	4	3		
Swett, John	2	1	4		
Little, Joseph	3		1		
Swett, Benja	1	4	3		
Stone, George	1		2		
Danforth, Joshua	2	2	2		
Cuch, Joseph	1	1	3		
Hale, Joseph	1	1	2		
Kilburn, Nathl	1		1		
Morse, Saml	1		5		
Kilburn, Eliph	1	2	5		
Gerrald, Edward F	1	1	7		
Gerrald, John	1	1	4		
Eastman, Timothy	3	1	3		
Gerrish, Joseph	3		4		
Beverly, Saml	1	2	1		
Little, Enoch	4		2		
Day, Benja	2		2		
Cass, Benja	1		3		
Cass, Joseph	2		4		
Jackman, John	3	4	5		
Jackman, Samuel	1	3	4		
Jackman, Samuel, Jr	1	1	3		
Atkinson, Samuel, Jr	1	1	3		
Dunlap, James	1		1		
Turssell, James	1	3	4		
Elliot, Thomas	1	2	4		
Grant, Joseph	1		3		
Corser, Thomas	1	2	5		
Corser, William	1	5	3		
Fick, Benja	1	2	2		
Barnard, Trustrinn	3		2		
Barnard, Nathl	1	1	1		
Austin, John	1	2	1		
Warthin, Ezekiel	1		2		
Stevens, Nathl	1	2	3		
Roby, Saml	1	3	2		
Gordon, Thomas	1		3		
Little, Friend	1	3	3		
Little, Thomas	1		3		
Noyes, Isaac	2	1	3		
Noyes, Cutting	1	5	5		
Jackman, Benja	3	1	7		
Jackman, Joshua	1	1	1		
Flanders, Ezekiel	1	3	6		
Cochran, Rebecca		2	4		
Flanders, Aaron	2	5	7		
Flanders, John	3	1	2		
Bohonon, Jacob	2	1	1		
Noyes, Trustrim	1	1	4		
Atkinson, Nathl	4		2		
Plummer, Priscilla	2		2		
Atkinson, Benja	1	2	2		
Jackman, Saml	1	1	5		
Hale, John	2	3	1		
Coggwell, Nathl	2	2	7		
Gerrish, Enoch	3	2	4		
Wood, Saml	1	1	2		
Mannuel, John	2	1	5		

BOSCAWEN TOWN—con.

NAME OF HEAD OF FAMILY.	Free white males of 16 years and upward, including heads of families.	Free white males under 16 years.	Free white females, including heads of families.	All other free persons.	Slaves.
Choat, Thomas	3		3		
Ames, Saml	2		4		
Shepard, Danl	1	3	2		
Pillsbury, Porter	1	4	3		
Elsy, John	1		1		
Richard, Danl	1	2	3		
Farnum, John	2	3	2		
Morrall, John	3	3	3		
Brown, Francis	1	3	1		
Willey, Ezekiel	1	2	5		
Austin, Benja	1		1		
Little, Noah	1	1	2		
Gerrish, Moses	2	1	1		
Danforth, William	2	2	3		
Vowley, John	1	2	3		
Severance, Benja	1		3		
Robertson, James	2	3	4		
Swett, Benja	1		2		
Severance, Nicholas	1		1		
Corser, David	2	3	5		
Corser, John	1	7	3		
Thurstin, Jona	2	1	4		
Colby, Danl	1		3		
Corser, Jona	3	3	4		
Kilburn, Nathl	2	3	2		
Fick, Elizabeth		1	2		
Fick, Isaac	1		1		
Corser, Simeon	1	2	1		
Danforth, Jedidiah	2	3	5		
Corser, Nathan	1	1	1		
Flanders, Enos	2		2		
Flanders, Enos, Jr	1		2		
Jackman, Humphrey	1	3	4		
Flanders, John	1	3	3		
Mussey, Saml	4		4		
Chadwick, Eedmund	2	3	2		
Knolton, John	4	1	2		
Atkinson, Nathl	1	2	2		
Gerrish, Henry	4	3	4		
Flanders, Jacob	1		1		
Bettee, Thomas	3	2	3		
Noyes, Benja	4		3		
Atkinson, Thom	3	2	3		
Atkinson, Saml	1	3	4		
Greenfield, Thomas	1	1	4		
Hudden, Ebenr	1		2		
Hudden, Joseph	1	3	6		
Avlin, John	1	3	3		
Persons, Isaac	2	1	2		
Parsons, Sumsbrey	1	1	2		
Carter, Winthrop	2	1	6		
Peterson, Danl	3	4	4		
Clark, Danl	4	1	2		
Richardson, Zachariah	2		2		
Clough, Benja	1	2	3		
Burbank, David	1	4	3		
Lunt, Joseph	1	1	4		
Green, Nathl	1	2	3		
Vaney, Sarah	1		3		
Fowler, Anna	1		2		
Urin, James	1	1	4		
Jackman, George	1	1	6		
Jackman, William	1	2	2		
Webster, Benja	1	3	4		
Ilsley, William	2		2		
French, James	1	1	1		
Moody, Ebenr	1	2	2		
Jackman, Moses	1	3	4		
Gerrish, Joseph	3	1	7		
Burbank, Moses	2		2		
Burbank, Wells	1	2	3		
Burbank, Saml	2	4	6		
Morse, Nicholas	1		1		
Morse, Moses	1	1	5		
Heath, Dorithy			4		
Merril, Roby	2	1	3		
Morril, Saml	1	1	2		
Flood, Richard	1	2	6		
Urine, John	1		2		
Hoyt, Jedidiah	1	4	3		
Chandler, Isaac	3		3		
Chandler, John	2	4	7		
Webster, Stephen	1		2		
Fowler, Saml	1		2	1	
Dunlap, James	1		4		
Picket, James	1	1	1		
Day, Asa	2		6		
Day, Daniel	1		3		
Gerrish, Jeremiah	2		2		
Carter, Danl	1	2	3		
Corser, James	1		2		
Knight, Caleb	2		4		

HILLSBOROUGH COUNTY—Continued.

NAME OF HEAD OF FAMILY.	Free white males of 16 years and upward, including heads of families.	Free white males under 16 years.	Free white females, including heads of families.	All other free persons.	Slaves.
BOSCAWEN TOWN—con.					
Jackman, Sam¹	2		3		
Sherley, Thomas	2	6	3		
Ahers, John	1	1	3		
Burbank, Moses	3	2	3		
Burbank, Dan¹	1	1	4		
Little, Thomas	1	1	3		
Little, Friend, Jr	1	3	3		
Little, Benjᵃ	4		3		
BRADFORD TOWN.					
Abbot, Asa	1		2		
Abbot, Paul	1	1	2		
Ward, Stephen	1	2	1		
Ward, Ephrᵐ	1		3		
Clough, Samuel	1	3	1		
Whitcumb, Reuben	3	5	2		
Dustin, Asa	1				
Baley, Moses	1		2		
Hough, Peter	1	2	6		
Davis, Isaac	1	1	3		
Davis, James	1		4		
Davis, Dan¹	1	1	1		
French, Orphon	2				
French, Abraham	1	2	5		
Cressey, Dan¹	3		3		
Andrews, Joshua	1	2	4		
Brown, Eliphalet	1		2		
Hoyt, Enoch	1	5	1		
Hoyt, Stephen	3	2	6		
Eaton, Ebenʳ	2	1	2		
Hildreth, Simᵃ	2		1		
Colby, Ebenʳ	1	1	2		
Presby, William	2		4		
Presby, George	1		3		
Brown, John	2	4	3		
Brown, William, Jr	1		1		
Chenee, Sam¹	1	2	2		
Young, Dan¹	1	2	2		
Brown, William	1	2	4		
Trumball, Nath¹	1				
Presby, James	1	2	3		
Presby, Nath¹	1		1		
Presby, Nath¹., Junʳ	1		1		
Presby, Joseph	1	3	4		
Ward, Abner	1	2	3		
Cresey, Edward	1		2		
Sweatt, Abner	1	3	1		
Blanchard, Jacob	1	2	1		
Brockway, Asa	1	4	2		
Batchelder, Uzzie	1	2	5		
Crane, Samuel	1	1	2		
Stiles, Barnet	1		1		
Swett, David	1	1	1		
Ingals, David	1	2	2		
Blanchard, Peter	1				
CAMPBELL'S GORE.					
Curtice, Isaac	1		4		
Curtice, Ebenʳ	1	3	1		
Carter, Isaac	1	1	1		
Morrison, David	1	1	1		
Sweet, Jonᵃ	1	3	4		
Wyman, Stephen	1		2		
Rock, John	2				
Rock, John, Jr	1		5		
Gibson, Dan¹	1	3	4		
Jones, Joshua	1		3		
Dresser, Asa	1	2	6		
Perkins, David	2	1	4		
Bagley, Henry	1	3	1		
Andrews, Isaac	1		1		
Goodale, John	1		1		
Barker, Nath¹	1	2	1		
Richards, Joel	1	1	2		
Sweet, Jonah	3	2	3		
Jones, Sam¹	2	4	4		
Prockter, Isaac	1	1	3		
Gordon, Daniel	1	1	1		
Jones, James	1	4	2		
Jones, William	1	3	3		
DEARING TOWN.					
Aiken, Thomas	2	2	4		
Aiken, William	1	4	6		
Anderson, Joseph	1				
Aiken, Matthew	2				
Anderson, Sam¹	2		3		
Bailey, Thomas	1	1	2		
Bailey, Jonᵃ	2	1	1		

NAME OF HEAD OF FAMILY.	Free white males of 16 years and upward, including heads of families.	Free white males under 16 years.	Free white females, including heads of families.	All other free persons.	Slaves.
DEARING TOWN—con.					
Bartlett, John	4		4		
Bartlett, Jacob	1	4	5		
Blood, Lem¹	1	2	5		
Mills, James	1	1	5		
Masterman, James	1	4	2		
Newman, Thomas	1	4	3		
Newman, Ebenʳ	1		6		
Newman, Josiah	1	3	2		
Obrion, Matthew	1	3	2		
Peasley, Amos	1		3		
Patterson, Sam¹	1	4	1		
Putney, John	1	5	4		
Richardson, Thomas	1	1	2		
Shattuck, William	2	2	1		
Swetser, Nath¹	1	3	3		
Straw, Jonᵃ	1	3	7		
Spear, Thomas	2		2		
Smith, Jacob	1		3		
Stewart, John	1	2	2		
Philbrick, David	2	1	4		
Thompson, Seth	1	2	4		
Townshend, Aaron	2	1	4		
Vose, Robert	1	2	3		
White, John	2	2	3		
Whiteker, James	1	4	4		
Waugh, William	1		4		
Wilson, Alexander	1	3	2		
Wilson, David	3	3	8		
Weatherspoon, Alexⁿ	1	1	4		
Wilkins, Phineas	1		2		
Wilkins, Hezekiah	2		2		
Alcock, Robt	2	6	5		1
Alcock, Mansel	1	1	2		
Aiken, Ninian	3		5		
Aiken, Andrew	1	1	5		
Aiken, Sam¹	1	2	2		
Blood, Ebenʳ	3	3	5		
Blood, Abel	1	4	2		
Blood, James	1		3		
Bradford, Benjᵃ	2	3	4		
Bradford, William	2	1	3		
Brown, Benjᵃ	1	1	2		
Codman, William	2	3	4		
Brown, Ebenʳ	2	2	1		
Brown, William	1	4	3		
Bartlett, Solomon	1		3		
Chase, William	3		3		
Clough, David	1	1	3		
Clark, Ephraim	1	2	3		
McCluer, David	3	1	3		
Eaton, James	1	4	4		
Farmer, Joseph	1	2	3		
Fulton, Robt	3	3	5		
Forsith, William	3	4	3		
Farson, William	1	3	4		
Farson, Joshua	1	1	1		
Forsith, Matthew	1	1	2		
Flanders, John	1	4	4		
Fuller, Thomas	1	1			
Gibbins, Filch	1		2		
Gibson, John	1	2	3		
Gragg, Alexander	1	5	3		
Gragg, John	1	4	3		
Gragg, Reuben	1	2	3		
Gould, William	1	3	5		
Gove, Robt	1	1	2		
Griffin, Partrick	3		4		
Hogg, Robt	2		1		
Hellery, John	1	2	4		
George, Francis	2	1	4		
Grimes, James	1	1	3		
Kelly, Moses	1	1	7		
Kelly, Richard	1	3	3		
Kelly, Ebenʳ	1	5	5		
Lyon, John	1	3	3		
Lock, Benjᵃ	1	2	1		
Lock, Jonᵃ	1		2		
Lock, Ebenʳ	2	1	1		
Lock, Stephen	1		5		
Merril, Thomas	2	2	4		
Morse, Parker	1	4	3		
Mears, Dan¹	2	1	3		
Mills, Joseph	3	3	4		
Mills, Robt	1	3	4		
Chase, Amos	1	3	3		
Karr, Nathan	2		2		
Currier, Isaac	1	2	2		
Clark, Benjᵃ	2	3	3		
Dow, Even	2	2	3		
Dow, Stephen	1	1	4		
Durrant, Jonᵃ	2	1	5		
Fulsom, Joshua	2	3	4		

NAME OF HEAD OF FAMILY.	Free white males of 16 years and upward, including heads of families.	Free white males under 16 years.	Free white females, including heads of families.	All other free persons.	Slaves.
DEARING TOWN—con.					
French, Jonᵃ	1	1	1		
Fogg, Jeremiah	1	1	2		
Gove, Abraham	1	4	5		
Gove, Nath¹	1	4	1		
Goodwin, Matthew	1		2		
Grimes, Francis	4	1	2		
Hogg, Alexander	1		4		
Heath, Timothy	1	2	3		
Hogg, William	1	1	5		
Hassel, Elias	1		2		
Hanson, Sam¹	1	1	2		
Hadlock, Levi	1	2	6		
Hadlock, Hezekiah	1	2	2		
Holt, Jabez	2	1	3		
Lovering, Reuben	2		4		
McKeen, William	5	4	5		
Newman, Benjᵃ	1	3	4		
Patten, Sam¹	1	2	3		
Patten, Jonᵃ	1	1	2		
Peasley, Humphrey	3	1	3		
Pope, Simon	1	3	2		
Prescott, James	2	1	6		
Rolf, Benjᵃ	2	2	3		
Robertson, William	1	1	3		
Smith, Ichabod	3	1	1		
Smith, Moses	2	4	3		
Sherer, David	1		2		
Sherer, Sam¹	3		3		
Sherer, William	1		1		
Sherer, James	1	1	3		
Travis, Asa	2	2	1		
Travis, Asa, Jr	1	1	5		
Wheeler, Jacob	1	1	1		
Wyman, Jonᵃ	3	1	3		
Wyman, Timothy	1		1		
Wyman, Timothy, Jr	2	4	5		
Wilson, Robt	1	3	3		
Wikins, Bray	1	2	6		
Farson, Robert	1	2	5		
Ellsworth, Thomas	1	2	6		
Hadley, Enos	1		3		
Abbot, Timothy	1	2	3		
McAdams, Mary		2	1	1	
Hart, Jesse	1	1	2		
Summers, George	1	1	2		
McLaughlin, John	1	4	1		
Kelly, Jonᵃ	1	1	1		
Read, Joel	1		3		
Bartlett, Solᵒ	1				
DERRYFIELD TOWN.					
Merril, Abraham	1	2	2		
Stevens, Ezekiel	2	1	7		
Merril, David	2	4	2		
Merril, Nath¹	1	2	4		
Baker, Nath¹	1	1	3		
Dustin, John	1		2		
Hall, John, Jr	1	1	2		
Hall, John	1		4		
Hall, Dan¹	2	5	2		
Little, John	2	1	6		
Pendergrass, Sarah			2		
Huse, Abel	3	1	3		
Hazeltine, Asa	4	3	3		
Pingry, Stephen	1	4	2		
Symond, Elizabeth	1	1	3		
Woods, Bridget			1		
McClintock, Michael	1		1		
Evering, Alexander	1	1	1		
Merril, Moses	1	1	3		
Peirce, Oliver	1	2	3		
Stark, John	2	4	7		
Ray, John	1	5	3		
Stevens, Timothy	1		3		
Rust, John	1	2	5		
Merril, Abraham, Jr	1	2	2		
Rowel, David	4	1	1		
Farmer, Joseph	3	1	1		
Webster, John	4	1	2		
Green, John	1	1	5		
Brown, Israel	1	1	5		
Davis, Abigail			1		
Young, E. Clark	1	1	5		
Griffin, Theodore	1	1	5		
Griffin, John	2	2	4		
Nutt, William	2		7		
Nutt, James		1	2		
Webster, Enos	2	2	2		
Moor, Sam¹	2	3	3		
Goffe, John	2	3	3		
Garmin, James	1	3	6		

HILLSBOROUGH COUNTY—Continued.

NAME OF HEAD OF FAMILY.	Free white males of 16 years and upward, including heads of families.	Free white males under 16 years.	Free white females, including heads of families.	All other free persons.	Slaves.	NAME OF HEAD OF FAMILY.	Free white males of 16 years and upward, including heads of families.	Free white males under 16 years.	Free white females, including heads of families.	All other free persons.	Slaves.	NAME OF HEAD OF FAMILY.	Free white males of 16 years and upward, including heads of families.	Free white males under 16 years.	Free white females, including heads of families.	All other free persons.	Slaves.
DERRYFIELD TOWN—con.						DUNBARTON TOWN—con.						DUNSTABLE TOWN—con.					
Blodget, Joshua	2	4	3			Burnam, John	2	4	3			Harris, Ebenʳ, Jr	1	2	4		
Peckham, John	1	1	5			Clement, James	3	2	6			Brown, Jos	1	4	3		
Emerson, Charles	1		1			Wright, John	1	2	4			Butterfield, Abel	3	2	8		
Emerson, Peter	1		3			Burnam, Nathˡ	1	5	7			Killnut, Reuben	1	1	2		
Emerson, Abijah	1	1	2			Caldwell, Thomas	4	1	5			Whitney, Silvanus	1		2		
Davis, Danˡ	1		1			Wrider, Ebenʳ	1	4	4			Searles, Thomas	1	4	2		
Perham, William	1	4	4			Stinson, William	5		5			Lund, John	2	3	6		
Greeley, John	1	1	1			Jemerson, Alexander	1	3	3			Combs, Medad	1		3		
Ammy, Abraham	3		4			Jemerson, Danˡ	2		2	1		Alld, David	2	3	6		
Hazeltine, Jonª	4	1	2			Allison, Samˡ	2	5	5			Sergent, Joshua	1	2	4		
Gamble, Archibald	2		4			Davis, Edmund	1	2	3			Swallow, Joseph	1		2		
Stevens, Ephraim	1	3	3			Harris, Walter	1	1	3			Swallow, Silas	1	2	1		
Young, Israel	2	9	4			Dugle, William	1	2	6			Turrel, Edward	1	2	3		
Young, James	1	1	1			Smith, William	1	5	2			Kemp, Nathˡ	1	1	1		
Stevens, Ebenʳ	4		2			Garvin, Samˡ	2	2	3			Fisk, Nathan	1	1	2		
Thompson, Hugh	1		2			Hadley, Amos	2	3	3			Whitney, Phineas	2	3	3		
Thompson, James	1	3	4			Storey, Danˡ	2	1	6			Harris, Jonª	1	2	3		
Smith, Samˡ	1	2	4			Page, Jeremiah, Jr	3	3	6			Moors, Asa	2	1	5		
						Perkins, Archeus	1	3	3			Lowell, Stephen	2		2		
DERRYFIELD GORE.						McGuin, Danˡ	3		3			Lawrence, Nathˡ	1	2	2		
Whiteker, Thomas	4		4			Foster, Andrew	1	3	3	3		Fisk, Eleazar	2		1		
Stark, Samˡ	3		5			Hogg, Samˡ	1	2	3			Gilson, David	1	1	1		
Emerson, James	1	4	3			Bassett, John	1	2	4			Gilson, John	1		2		
Stevens, Henry	2		4			Stewart, Samˡ	1	1	1			Gilson, Jeremiah	1		3		
						Stickney, Thomas	2	1	3			Lowell, Jacob	1		3		
DUNBARTON TOWN.						Healy, Paul	2		4			Robins, John	6		3	1	
Davis, Francis	1	2	1			George, Thomas	1	3	4			Adams, Richard	1	2	3		
Colby, Kimball	1		3			Burk, Samˡ	1	5	6			Robinson, John, Jr	1	2	3		
Colby, Jacob Sargent	1	2	4			Palmer, Simeon	2		5			Robinson, John, 3d	1	1	3		
Elliot, Richard	1	1	1			McGregore, David	1	2	3			Honey, Elijah	1	1	2		
Austin, Caleb	1	3	4			Ayres, Stephen	1	2	5			Robins, Joseph	2	1	5		
Emory, Amos	1	2	2			George, Austin	1	3	3			Jewell, Nathˡ	1		1		
Putney, Asa	1	1	3			Church, John	2		8			Elliot, William	1	4	2		
Putney, James	1	3	3			Stinson, Archibald	3	3	5			Hale, Abner	2	1	2		
Putney, Henry	2		4			Hammond, David	3	1	3			Landigal, Partrick	1		3		
Putney, David	1		1			Stinson, James	2	5	3			Jewell, Samuel	1	5	2		
Moor, William	1	3	4			Jemerson, John	1	2	3			Lovewell, Jonª	1	1	2		
Merril, John	2	2	2			Hogg, Robt	1	3	4			Hale, Henry	1	1	1		
Merril, Richard	1	1	1			Tewkbury, Thomas	2	4	4			Searles, Danˡ	1				
Messer, Danˡ	1	2	2			Trimey, William	4	2	4			Honey, Shepard	1	1	2		
Bailey, Phineas	2	4	4			Mills, Thomas	1		1			Taylor, Martha	1		2		
Mitchel, Francis	1	1	4			Mills, Caleb	3	1	1			Lovewell, Rachel			2		
Ring, Benjª	2	1	2			Holmes, John	4		6			Woods, Oliver	2		1		
Davis, Jonª	1	2	4			Trussell, Moses	1		3			Woods, Benjª	1	1	1		
Combs, John	1	1	2			Mills, Thomas, Jr	2	1	4			Merrel, David	1	2	3		
Hacket, Ebenʳ	2		3			Mills, John	2	2	2			Shurtliff, Simª	3	2	3		
Hacket, Danˡ	1	4	3			Wuse, Thomas	2	2	5			Harris, William	1		4		
Hassey, Samˡ	1	3	5			Hammon, Thomas	1	4	6			Lovewell, Noah	2	3	5		
Hacket, James	3		2			McCalley, James	1	4	4			Fletcher, Philip	1	1	2		
McCurdy, John	5	1	4			Beard, William	1	1	4			Fletcher, Philip	1		1		
Stewart, James	1	3	4			Hazeltine, Daniel	1		2			Fletcher, Ruth	2	4	3		
Wheeler, Stephen	1	2	4			Lord, Samˡ	1	4	2			Fosgat, Ebenʳ	1	4	2		
Brown, Isaac	1		3			Buntoon, John	1	4	4			Wright, John	1	3	2		
Wheeler, Danˡ	1		1			Fulton, John	1	4	4			Wright, John, Jr	1	3	2		
Wheeler, William	1	2	2			Chesemore, Jacob	3	1	5			Persons, Thomas	1	4	5		
Wheeler, William, Jr	2	1	1			Farson, James	1	6	2			Adams, Eda	1	3	2		
Sanders, Oliver	1		1			Sargent, Abel	1	4	5			Searles, Elizabeth	5		2		
Sanders, David	1	2	3			Sargent, Enoch	3	1	4			Honey, William	2		1		
Bailey, Oliver	1	1	1			Sargent, Winthrop	1	2	3			Taylor, Jacob	2	1	2		
Bailey, Elijah	1	2	2			Hoyt, Thomas	2	1	4			Adams, Jacob	1	1	2		
Miller, John	1	1	5			Hoyt, Timothy	1	3	2			Wright, Wincol	2		4		
Sargent, Noah	1		2			King, James	1		1			Lund, Thomas	3	3	4		
Colby, Sargent	2		2			Bailey, Isaac	1	3	4			Adams, Ephraim	1		1		
Woodbury, Hezekiah	2	3	4			Stark, Archibald	2	2	8			Whiting, Joseph	1	1	2		
Woodbury, Hezekiah, Jr	1	1	1			Gould, John	3	3	1			Blanchard, Rebecca	2	1	6		
Woodbury, Ebenʳ	1	2	1			Colby, Hugh	1	2	4			Farewell, Eleazer	1	2	4		
Colby, Archelaus	2	1	3			How, John	1	1	3			Seavy, John	2	1	1		
Fever, Danˡ	1	2	2			Page, Sip					3	French, Benjª	3	1	3		
Page, Caleb	2	2	5			Moor, Samson					8	Clutler, Nathan	2	1	2		
Bailey, Simon	4	2	5			Porter, Ceasar					5	Searles, John	2		3		
Stark, Caleb	2	1	3									Smiley, David	2		2		
Ladd, Timothy	1	3	4			DUNSTABLE TOWN.						Roby, Hannah	2		3		
Clefford, Israel	1	6	5			Kidder, Joseph	2		5			Lund, Augustus	2		2		
Page, Jeremiah	2		4			Whittle, William	1		1			Lund, Levi	1	1	1		
Page, Jeremiah, 3d	1		1			Butterfield, William	1	3	3			Hunt, William	4		3		
Page, William	1	2	9			Adams, Silas	1	2	7			Hunt, Zachariah	2		1		
Hamlet, William	1	1	2			Jewell, James	1					Pollard, Samˡ	3	1	4		
Swain, Joseph	1		2			Breed, Aaron	1	2	2			Blanchard, Nathanˡ	1		1		
Sawyer, Sims	2	1	1			Alexander, Zach	1		4			Lund, Jonª	3	1	3		
Abbot, Joshua	1	2	5			Powers, Jonª	3	2	4			Smith, Benjª	4		5		
Smith, Samˡ	2		3			Hall, Joseph	2	6	4			Lund, Danˡ	1		3		
Cochran, Thomas	2	2	3			Blodget, Oliver	2	1	2			Lund, Joel	2		4		
Wicomb, Thomas	1	2	2			Jewell, James	1	3	3			Woods, Ebenʳ	1	3	2		
Mitchel, Francis	1	1	4			Snow, John	2		3			Fletcher, Robt	1		5		
Head, James	1		2			Harris, Ebenʳ	5	1	3			French, Rebecca	1	2	4		
Story, David	3	2	6			Honey, Permeter	1	3	5			Baldwin, Cyrus	3		3		
Wells, Philip	1		1			Jewell, Benoni	2		3			Moor, David	1	4	2		
Burnam, Asa	1	5	5			Butterfield, Mary			3			Wright, Zebedee	1	1	4		
Burnam, Abraham	2	1	3			Butterfield, John	2		3			Sharwin, Elnathan	2	1	3		
Burnam, Samˡ	4	2	9			Roby, Thomas	2	3	3			Peirce, Daniel	1	2	2		
						Foot, Isaac	1	1	2			Chambers, Matthew	1	1	1		
												Butterfield, Henry	1	3	1		

HILLSBOROUGH COUNTY—Continued.

NAME OF HEAD OF FAMILY.	Free white males of 16 years and upward, including heads of families.	Free white males under 16 years.	Free white females, including heads of families.	All other free persons.	Slaves.
DUNSTABLE TOWN—con.					
Butterfield, Sarah			4		
Jaquith, Daniel	1	1	1		
Giles, Ebenr	2		1		
Harris, Joseph	1		2		
DUXBURY MILE-SLIP.					
Blanchard, John	1		1		
Blanchard, Stephen	1	4	2		
Blanchard, Lucy		2	5		
Blanchard, Joseph	1		3		
Chandler, Danl	1	2	5		
Cheney, Jedidiah	1	1	2		
Gutterson, Saml	4	4	4		
Moor, Joshua	1	3	4		
Blanchard, Isaac	1	1	2		
Wright, Benja	1	4	4		
Peabody, Aaron	2	5	2		
Blanchard, Amos	1	1	2		
Brown, Caleb	1	2	3		
Badger, James	3		5		
Shed, Simon	1		4		
Jones, Caleb	3	1	6		
Lewis, Benja	3	4	4		
Boynton, Richard	1	1	6		
Hubbard, Jeremiah	1	1	2		
Martin, Nathan	1	2	1		
Jones, Jona	2		4		
Howard, Nehemiah	2	1	2		
Blanchard, Simon	1	4	4		
Boynton, Richard, Jr	1		1		
Upton, Rebeca			2		
Pearson, Saml	2		4		
Flinn, Jacob	1	2	2		
FISHERSFIELD TOWN.					
Whiteker, Abner	1	2	2		
Wells, Abraham	1	3	4		
Dudley, Bailey	1	2	4		
Baker, Benja	3		1		
Baker, Benja, Jr	1	1	5		
Little, Bond	2	4	3		
Atwood, Caleb	1	1	1		
Hastings, Jonas	1		1		
Harvey, John	1		1		
Leach, William	1	2	1		
Amery, David	1		1		
Nance, David	1	1	3		
Tole, Ebenr	1	2	1		
Cross, Ephraim	2	4	2		
Wells, Eleazar	1	1	3		
Mayhall, Ebenr	1	1	2		
Farmer, David	1	2	4		
Webster, Joseph	1	4	4		
Corning, George	1				
Lane, John	1	3	5		
Cutter, John, Jr	1	4	4		
Harvey, John, Jr	2	4	4		
Vance, John	1	4	3		
Merril, Jona	1	2	7		
Harvey, Ichabod	1	2	5		
Emery, Josiah	1	2	3		
Cutter, Josiah	2		1		
Gillingham, James	1	4	4		
Stevens, Jacob	1	1	3		
Cross, Joseph	2	4	3		
Chandler, Joseph	1	4	3		
Marshal, Joseph	1	1	3		
Emery, Joel	1	3	3		
Baker, Jesse	1		2		
Ainger, Jesse	1	2	2		
Vance, James	1	1	1		
Gordon, John	1	1	3		
Dodge, William	1	5	3		
Hastings, Levi	1		3		
Harvey, Lemuel	1	2	4		
Whitecar, Moses	1	1	2		
Tole, Paul	1		1		
Little, Saml	1	1	1		
Stevens, Timothy	1	1	1		
Parmer, Samuel	1		2		
Gunnison, Samuel	1	3	1		
Atwood, Saml	1		2		
McWilliams, Thomas	1	1	3		
Clemmons, Timothy	1	3	5		
Little, Thomas	1				
Tole, William	1	6	2		
Emery, William	1	3	4		
Cochran, William	1	1	3		
Brown, William	1		2		
Clark, Zephaniah	1	1	2		
Gitchel, Zebulon	2	2	3		
Emerson, Charles	1		2		
FISHERSFIELD TOWN—continued.					
Britton, William	1		2		
Maxfield, John	1		1		
Dow, Jesse	1	4	2		
FRANCESTOWN TOWN.					
Bradford, Moses	1				
Bixby, Asa	1		3		
Bixby, Thomas	1	1	3		
Bixby, Edward	1	2	4		
Brown, Thomas	1		2		
Butterfield, Robt	1	1	2		
Butterfield, William	2		4		
Butterfield, William, Jr	2	1	4		
Abbot, Solo	1				
Bradford, Robt	2	3	5		
Boyd, Nathl	1		3		
Boyd, Saml	1		3		
Brewster, James	1	1	4		
Brewster, Isaac	2		3		
Balch, Israel	2	3	4		
Batchelder, Isaac	1		2		
Batten, Richard	2		4		
Batten, Richard, Jr	1		2		
Batchelder, Amos	1	1	1		
Brown, Matthew	2				
Burns, John	2		3		
Burns, Saml	1	2	2		
Bullard, Ebenr	1	2	2		
Austin, Jona	2	1	5		
Barnard, Saml	1	1	2		
Bullard, Oliver	1		3		
Carson, John	1		5		
McCluer, Joseph	1		3		
Campbell, William	1	1	3		
Cockran, Nenian	2		2		
McCoy, William	1	1	3		
Clark, Nathl	1	1	4		
Clark, Danl	1	4	3		
Costen, Bishop	1		1		
Carson, William	1		1		
Caldwell, William	2	1	5		
Cockran, Robt	1	2	2		
Dane, Danl	2	1	3		
Dane, Benja	1		5		
Dane, John	1	3	2		
Dickey, John	2	6	6		
Dickey, William	1	2	3		
Dickerman, Saml	1	3	6		
Dawson, Timothy	1		3		
Dodge, Simon	1	3	4		
Durrant, David	1	2	4		
Dustin, Eliphalet	2	3	5		
Dimond, Francis	1	2	2		
Eaton, Moses	3		3		
Ewell, Peleg	1		4		
Everett, Eleazar	1	2	3		
Fish, John	2	4	4		
Feltch, Benja	2	2	3		
Fuller, Stephen	1	3	3		
Fuller, Rufus	1	2	1		
Furbanks, Elias	2	1	2		
McFarson, Henry	2		2		
McFarson, James	1		2		
Fisher, James	1	4	3		
Fisher, Abner	1	3	1		
Fisher, David	1	1	3		
Fuller, Jason	1	1	2		
Farrington, Nathl	2	2	1		
Farrington, Hezekiah	1		3		
Fisher, Nathl	2	2	6		
Fisher, Thomas	1	1	2		
Fuller, Danl	1	3	1		
Follensbee, William	1	1	4		
Denerson, John	1	1	2		
Fisher, Moses	1	1	2		
McFarson, Saml	2		2		
McFarson, John	2	1	2		
McFarson, James	1	1	2		
Fisher, Seth	1	1	2		
Fuller, Seth	1	1	3		
Farnum, Peter	2	1	1		
Green, John	3	3	4		
Montgomery, Hugh	1	4	5		
Gould, Joseph	1		1		
Gilbert, Laraford	1	1	3		
Hilands, John	1	2	2		
Huntington, John	2	1	5		
Hopkins, William	2	1	4		
Holmes, Enoch	2	2	3		
Hall, Joseph	1		5		
Holmes, Oliver	2	1	3		
Holmes, Jabez	1	2	1		
FRANCESTOWN TOWN—continued.					
Hogg, James	1	2	3		
Hopkins, Boyd	2	1	4		
Hopkins, James	1	2	4		
Johnson, Saml	1	1	1		
Johnson, John	1	1	3		
Knight, John	1	1	3		
Johnson, Joseph	1	4	1		
Lewis, David	2	1	4		
Lewis, Isaac	1	2	2		
Lewis, Asa	1	2	2		
Lord, William	1	1	3		
McLane, Mather	2	3	5		
Lampson, Joseph	1	1	3		
Loley, Saml	1		2		
Lakin, Winslow	1	2	3		
Lewis, Nathl	1		3		
Kimball, Joseph	1		3		
Kittridge, Stephen	1	1	1		
Martin, Saml	1	2	8		
McMurphy, Archibald	1	2	4		
Merrill, Phineas	1		6		
Munihan, John	2	2	4		
Mitchel, Thomas	3	2	4		
Mitchel, John	1		4		
Morse, Timothy	2	1	4		
Martin, Jesse	1	2	2		
Millen, Robert	2	1	3		
Moor, William	1	1	3		
Munihan, Adam	1				
McMillan, Saml	1		1		
Nutt, Saml	4	3	5		
Nichols, Saml	2	1	2		
Nichols, John	1	2	5		
Nutt, William	1	2	2		
Patch, Jona	2	3	3		
Pettee, Abner	1	2	3		
Perry, Joseph	3	2	4		
Potter, Samuel	1	1	2		
Quigley, Thomas	1		2		
Quigley, Hannah	1		2		
Richardson, Zachh	1	4	3		
Scobey, David	2	4	4		
Sleeper, Benja	1	2	3		
Sleeper, Nathl	1	4	4		
Sleeper, Moses	1	2	1		
Smith, John	1	2	3		
Starret, David	2	4	6		
Starret, William	3	3	7		
Starret, William, Jr	1	2	4		
Spaulding, Abel	2	1	1		
Spaulding, Abel, Jr	1	1	3		
Savage, Nathl	1	4	1		
Thorp, Saml	1	1	5		
Thompson, Saml	1	1	3		
Templeton, Thomas	1	1	4		
Thompson, Luther	1		4		
Thompson, Alexanr	1		2		
Todd, James	2	2	2		
Whitny, Zachh	3	3	5		
Wetherspoon, Danl	1	3	4		
Wetherspoon, James	1		2		
Wetherspoon, Alexd	1		2		
Wetherspoon, James, Jr	2	1	2		
Wilkins, Amos	1	1	4		
Wilson, Thomas	1		5		
Wilson, James	1		2		
White, Saml	1	2	1		
Woodbury, Peter	3	2	3		
Whitney, James	1	1	3		
Whitney, Joseph	1		3		
Winchester, Lemuel	1	2	3		
Vose, Francis B.	1	2	2		
Shattuck, Stephen	1	2	4		
Townshend, Aaron	1	1	2		
Butterfield, Isaac	2	3	5		
Barnes, Joseph	1		3		
Eastman, Olive			7		
Alld, Sarah		1	2		
Patch, Thomas	1	1	1		
Standley, Richard	2		3		
Alld, Joseph	1		5		
McClench, Robt	1		1		
Kemp, Asa	1	1	4		
Ross, James	1		2		
Fuller, Thaddeus	1	2	2		
Wilson, William	1	1	3		
GOFFSTOWN TOWN.					
Waters, Cornelius	1	1	4	1	
Adderson, William	1		1		
Adderson, James	1	1	2		
Ayers, James	1		2		

HILLSBOROUGH COUNTY—Continued.

NAME OF HEAD OF FAMILY.	Free white males of 16 years and upward, including heads of families.	Free white males under 16 years.	Free white females, including heads of families.	All other free persons.	Slaves.
GOFFSTOWN TOWN—con.					
Ayers, William	2	2	2		
Annis, Saml	2	1	3		
Blodget, William	2	2	2		
Adderson, Sarah			2		
Bradbury, Winthrop	2		1		
Burwell, David	1	1	2		
Burnam, Thomas	1	1	5		
Blasdel, Henry	2	1	4		
Barr, James	2	4	3		
Black, Edward	1		3		
Burwell, Joseph	1	3	4		
Burwell, John	1	1	1		
Butterfield, John	2	1	8		
Butterfield, John, Jr	3	5	7		
Bell, Jona	1	4	2		
Butterfield, Peter	2	3	4	1	
Allen, David	1	2	3		
Chubbuck, Ensign	1	2	1		
Clement, Phillip	2	4	6		
Crage, John	3		3		
Clogstone, John	3	1	3		
Clerk, Nathl	2	2	2		
Clogstone. William	1	1	1		
Colby, Richard	2	1	2		
Colby, John	1		1		
Colby, John, Jr	1		3		
Conery, John	2	1	2		
Cochrim, George	2	1	5		
Chenee, Dan	1	1	2		
Chenee, Joseph	1	2	4		
Cushing, John	1		2		
Chandler, Josiah	2		3		
Cunningham, George	3	1	4	1	
Davis, Saml	1	3	1		
Davis, Mabica	1	1	3		
Dunkler, Joseph	1	2	3		
Dow, Job	4	1	7		
Dow, Peter	3		4		
Davis, Joseph	1	5	4		
Dunlap, Joseph	2	4	3		
Densmore, John	2	2	5		
Dodge, Antipas	3	3	5		
Eley, Israel	2	2	2		
Emerson, Obadiah	1	2	3		
Eaton, Saml	1	1	4		
Eaton, Enoch	1	1	3		
Eaton, James	2	1	1		
Ferrin, Philip	3	2	8		
Foster, Jeremiah	1	1	5		
Flanders, Stephen	1	2	2		
Flanders, Simeon	1	5	1		
Goff, Saml	1	3	4		
George, John	2	2	3		
George, John, Jr	1	2	3		
Gilmore, Mary	1		1		
Gilcrest, Alexanr	4	1	4		
Gilcrest, Jane			1		
Howard, Nathl	1		2		
Hadley, Ebenr	4	4	7		
Harwood, John	1	1	3		
Hubbard, John	1		1		
Hubbard, Isaac	1		4		
Hoyt, James	1	1	3		
Herryman, Peter	1	4	3		
Flaws, Obediah	2		1		
Hale, David	2		4		
Hart, Charles W.	2		3		
Hadley, Plummer	3	1	4		
Hadley, John	1		2	1	
Hardy, Moses	1	4	2		
Jones, John	2	2	6		
Jones, Philip	2	4	3		
Jehonet, Prince				9	
Johnson, Timo	2	1	3		
Kittridge, Danl	1	1	2		
Kittridge, James	1		2		
Kidder, Eliphalet	2	2	1		
Kennedy, Thomas	3	1	4		
Kidder, Job	5	4	8		
Kittridge, Nathl	1		2		
Kerr, William	2		1		
Kerr, Thomas	1	2	3		
Kelly, Rebecca	2	1	4		
Kemp, Reuben	1	2	2		
Kittridge, Asa	1	2	3		
Kelly, Moses	3	3	4		
Kennedy, Saml	3		3	1	
Kennedy, Robt	3		7		
Kennedy, Jane	1		2		
Kimball, Timo	2	1	5		
Little, Caleb	1	3	1		
Little, George	2	1	3		
Little, John	1	4	1		
Little, Moses	2	1	5		
GOFFSTOWN TOWN—con.					
Laughlin, Saml	2		1		
Laughlin, Allen	2		1		
McIntire, Timo	2		1		
McCoy, Alexanr	3	1	7		
Martin, Joshua	2	3	7		
McAlaster, Margaret	1		2		
Moor, James	1	1	3		
Moor, Robt	2	5	5		
McFarson, William	2	2	3		
McDougle, William	1	2	3		
McDole, John	3	1	2		
Moor, Abraham	1	1	5		
Moor, Robert, Jr	2	1	2		
McGregore, Robt	8	2	4		
Nichols, William	2	3	1		
Noyes, Philip	1		2		
Oneal, John	1	5	3		
Ordway, John	2	2	3		
Pike, James	1	2	4		
Page, Enoch	2	1	2		
Orr, John	4		3		
Page, James	3		6		
Page, Moses, Jr	2	2	5		
Page, William	2	3	3		
Pettee, John	3	3	5		
Poor, George	1	3	1		
Poor, Saml	1	4	2		
Pollard, John	2		3		
Ordway, Saml	2	2	3		
Quimby, John	2	2	5		
Russel, James	1	5	2		
Richard, James	1		2		
Richardson, Matthew	1		2		
Roby, Saml	2	2	3		
Ring, Isacher	2	1	3		
Richards, David	1	2	5		
Richardson, Robt	3	2	5		
Rollings, John	1	2	3		
Richards, Benja	2	2	2		
Ross, John	1	1	3		
Richard, Amos	2	2	4		
Richard, Eliphalet	1	2	2		
Saltmarsh, John	1	1	2		
Stevens, Thomas	1		1		
Smith, John	2	1	2		
Sergent, James	1		3		
Sergent, Enoch	1	1	4		
Sergent, John	2	3	5		
Sergent, Charles	1	2	3		
Stevens, David	1		3		
Stevens, Nathl	1	3	2		
Stevens, Jacob	1	2	4		
Sawyer, David	1	2	5		
Stearns, Elijah	2	1	1		
Sergent, Timo	1	1	2		
Sergent, Joseph	1	2	2		
Sergent, Truworthy	2		2		
Stevens, Benja., 3d	1	3	2		
Stark, Stephen	3	1	2		
Aderson, Ruth			2		
Small, Simeon			1	7	
Small, Jona			1	7	
Small, Aaron			1	4	
Sawyer, Enoch	2	2	4		
Stevens, Benja., Jr	1	2	3		
Stevens, Jona	3	3	4		
Stevens, Benja	1	1	2		
Stevens, Timo	1	3	3		
Sherley, Thomas	1		2		
Sherley, James	1	2	4		
Spear, Robt	1	1	3		
Sergent, Elias	1	1	2		
Story, William	2	2	5		
Saltmarsh, Thomas	4	2	3		
Tyler, Dudley	1		1		
Todd, Alexander	3		2		
Taggart, John	1	5	3		
Tuttle, Symond	1	2	5		
Wells, Aaron	1		2		
Wells, Prude	1		2		
Wheeler, Samson	1	2	3		
Wells, Silas	1	2	3		
Walker, Alexander	4	1	4		
Warren, Thomas	2	3	4		
White, Saml. G	1	3	2		
Wyman, Seth	1	1	4		
Woods, Jona	1	1	2		
Wright, Thomas	1		1		
Wright, Abel	2	3	5		
Wells, Timothy	2		3		
Workley, Timothy	2	4	4		
Webster, Saml	2	4	4		
Walker, Silas	1	3	7	2	
Walker, Esther			2		
GOFFSTOWN TOWN—con.					
Wright, Ephraim	1	1	6		
Wyman, Joseph	1		1		
Wheeler, Benja	1		1		
Wells, Robert	1		2		
Warren, John	1	3	2		
Whitney, Elnathan	2	1	6		
White, William	1	1	5		
Teel, Aaron	1	1	1		
Hawse, Nathl	1	1	4		
HANCOCK TOWN.					
Lakin, Lemuel	1	3	3		
Boutell, William	2		4		
Washburn, Elisha	1	5	2		
Morrison, Moses	2		2		
Morrison, John	2		2		
Duncan, Robt	3		5		
Davis, James	3	1	4		
Russel, Joel	2	4	4		
Spaulding, Bezeleel	1	2	2		
Kelso, Peter	1	4	3		
Washburn, Joseph	1	1	2		
Lakin, William	2		4		
Grimes, Arthur	1	3	2		
Grimes, James	1	1	1		
Preston, Abner	1	1	3		
Ames, Saml	2		4		
Aames, Eleazar	1	1	1		
Kimball, Dan	1	3	1		
Baker, Jesse	1		1		
Whiting, Saml	1	1	2		
Foster, John	1	2	4		
Ames, David	5	2	4		
Dennis, Moses	1	3	4		
Moor, Abraham	1	2	4		
Cumings, Peter	1	1	2		
Cuming, John	2	3	4		
Lawrence, Nicholas	1	1	3		
Davis, Asa	2	1	1		
Dodge, Joseph	1	3	5		
Davis, Edmund	2	3	2		
Tuttle, Samson	2	1	1		
Sawyer, Jona	2	5	2		
Lawrence, Oliver	1		1		
Lawrence, Dan	1		1		
Davis, Edmund	1	1	1		
Bowers, John	1	2	3		
Moors, Timothy	1	3	5		
Jones, Thomas	1	2	4		
May, Thomas	1	2	2		
Williams, William	1	1	3		
Duncan, James	2	3	5		
Wheeler, Noah	1	1	3		
Knights, Benja	1		1		
Wood, Solo	2	2	3		
Weare, Jason	1	1	3		
Hosea, David	1		1		
Nay, William	1	1	2		
Spaulding, Thomas	2	1	4		
Tinney, Amos	2	3	3		
Stone, Josiah	1	1	3		
Hazeltine, Nathl	1		1		
Tenny, Asa	1		1		
Tenny, Silas	1		2		
Gowing, Ebenezer	1	2	3		
Davis, Elijah	1	3	3		
Grimes, Hugh	3	1	7		
Holden, Asa	1		3		
Fuller, Dan	1	3	1		
Majury, Jona	1	1	2		
Mather, Robert	3	3	6		
Davis, Elijah	1	1	5		
Davis, Isaac	1	1	2		
Miller, John	1	2	4		
Symond, Joseph	2	2	3		
Barker, Jesse	1	1	1		
Turrel, Saml	2	3	3		
Davison, Nathl	1	1	5	1	
Ball, Benja	1		4		
Blodget, Josiah	1		2		
Blodget, Solomon	1		1		
Smith, James	1		2		
Smith, James, Jr	1	1	2		
Willey, Robt	1		2		
Knights, Enos	1	2	3		
Knights, David	2	2	4		
Crag, Thomas	2	2	2		
Miller, Thomas	1		2		
Whitcomb, John	1		1		
Priest, Levi	1	2	3		
Woods, Stephen	1	1	2		
Whitcomb, Abner	1		2		
Whitcomb, Saml	1		3		

HILLSBOROUGH COUNTY—Continued.

NAME OF HEAD OF FAMILY.	Free white males of 16 years and upward, including heads of families.	Free white males under 16 years.	Free white females, including heads of families.	All other free persons.	Slaves.
HANCOCK TOWN—con.					
Hubbard, David	1	3	4		
Boynton, Thomas	1		1		
Lakin, Simeon	1	1	2		
Peirce, Nehemiah	1	4	2		
Hubbard, Solomon	1	2	3		
Bonnor, John	1		3		
Merrill, Moses	1		4		
Whittemore, Zebedee	1	1	4		
Boutell, William	2	4	3		
Gates, Sam¹	2	1	4		
Horley, James	2	2	3		
Brooks, William	1	1	4		
Parker, Stephen	1	2	3		
Brooks, John	2	1	2		
Abbot, William	1	2	3		
Ames, Phineas	1	2	2		
Cross, Sam¹	2	1	1		
Cross, Nath¹	1		5		
Ellenwood, John	1		2		
Hadley, Seth	2	2	3		
Hills, Joseph	1		1		
Hills, James	1	2	2		
Hadley, Jacob	1	2	3		
McMaster, Thomas	1		2		
Orr, Hugh	2	2	6		
Ober, Hezekiah	2				
Parker, Aaron	1	2	1		
Tenny, Sam¹	2	3	4		
Spaulding, Edward	2		2		
Whittemore, Collins	1	1	1		
Whitcomb, Sam¹	1		2		
Tucker, David	1		2		
Stevens, Jon^a	1	2	5		
Barker, David	1		5		
Drew, James					2
HENIKER TOWN.					
Adams, Aaron	4	2	2		
Adams, Moses	1	1	1		
Adams, Giddeon	1		4		
Archer, Michael	1	1	3		
Alexander, Jonas	2	2	6		
Amsden, Uriah	1		1		
Amsden, Joseph	2	5	3		
Amsden, Noah	1	1	3		
Arnald, Joseph	2	2	3		
Adams, Stephen	2	2	3		
Abbot, Tim^o	3	2	2		
Borman, Francis	2	1	4		
Borman, Jon^a	5	2	5		
Borman, Abiathar	1	4	2		
Borman, Jon^a	1	1	1		
Brown, Thomas	2		5		
Barns, Elisha	1	1	4		
Barr, Sam¹	1	4	3		
Baley, Joseph	1	2	1		
Campbell, Robt	1	4	4		
Clough, David	1	4	5		
Clough, Oliver	2		3		
Clough, Benj^a	3	1	5		
Chadwick, John	1		2		
Chadwick, Joseph	1	4	2		
Campbell, John	1	4	1		
Campbell, John, Jr	1	1	1		
Campbell, Jesse	1		2		
Campbell, Phineas	1	2	2		
Conner, John T	2	2	2		
Chase, Nath¹	1	3	2		
Colby, Dan¹	1	3	4		
Cheles, Sol^o	2	3	3		
Campbell, David	2	5	4	1	
Conner, David	3	2	4		
Conner, Moses	2	4	5		
Colby, David	1	1	2		
Colby, Levi	1	4	3		
Colby, Eliph^t	1	2	4		
Colby, Nich^s	1	1	3		
Chase, Enoch	1	1	2		
Dustin, Moses	1	6	2		
Dow, Aaron	1	1	2		
Dunlap, Sam¹	5	4	3		
Eastman, Aaron	2	2	6		
Eastman, Jon^a	1	2	2		
Eager, Joseph	1		4		
Edwards, Oliver	1	3	2		
Eager, Luke	2	1	5		
Edwards, Benj^a	1	2	3		
Eaton, John	1		2		
Eastman, Sam¹	1	3	3		
Flanders, Tim^o	1		4		
Frissel, Sam¹	2	2	3		
HENIKER TOWN—con.					
Fifield, Moses	1		3		
Goss, Ephraim	2	2	3		
Gibson, Thaddeus	1	3	3		
Gitchel, Zebulon	1	1	3		
Gordon, Abel	1		3		
Greanleaf, Charles	1	2	4		
Gould, Amos	1		4		
Gould, William	1	2	2		
Goodenow, John	4	3	2		
Gibson, Joseph	1	4	5		
Gibson, Tim^o	2	6	2		
How, Eliakim	2	1	4		
How, Eliakim, Jr	1		2		
Hunter, Edward	2	2	2		
How, Eben^r	1		2		
How, John	1	3	3		
House, Moses	2	1	5		
Heath, Sargent	2	2	1		
Howlett, Joseph	1	1	4		
Howlett, John	1	1	3		
Harriman, Eben^r	2	3	3		
Hoyt, Moses	1	3	4		
Hoyt, Benj^a	1	1	1		
Herriman, Joshua	1	3	6		
How, William	1		2		
How, Michael	1	3	3		
Hartshorn, Eben^r	4	3	5		
Hartshorn, John	1	1	2		
Heath, Matthias	1	3	4		
How, Eli	1	3	2		
How, Peter	1	1	2		
How, Nehemiah	1	4	3		
How, Phebe	1		2		
Hager, Joel	1		2	1	
Johnson, Sol^o	1	1	2		
Joslin, Nath¹	1		2		
Joslin, Sarah	1	2	6		
Johnson, Enoch	1	1	3		
Karr, Sarah	1		2		
Kimball, Sam¹	2	4	5		
Kimball, Joshua	1	4	5		
Kimball, William	2		2	4	
Kemp, Levi	1		2		
Lewis, Joseph	3		1		
Lesley, George	1		3		
McKillop, David	1	3	3		
McKillop, Sam¹	1	5	4		
Mansfield, David	2	1	1		
Mansfield, Samuel	2	3	4		
Morrison, Samuel	3	1	5		
Morrall, Ephraim	2	3	4		
Morrall, David	1				
Marsh, Joseph	1	2	3		
Mitchel, William	1	1	2		
Morrison, Sam¹., Jr	1	6	2		
Morrison, Abim^k	3				
Mirrick, William	2		2		
Newton, Jonah	1	2	3		
Newton, Nahum	1	3	4		
Noyes, Oliver	1		4		
Purrington, Wintrop	1		1		
Pope, Thomas	1		1		
Pope, David	1	2	8		
Patrick, William	1		2		
Putney, Thomas	2	3	2		
Putney, John	1		1		
Pingry, Thomas	1	2	3		
Plummer, Thomas	2		5		
Pattington, Eleaz^r	2		1		
Patterson, Josiah	2	3	4		
Patterson, Joseph	1	1	4		
Patterson, Eleazar, Jr	1		4		
Pike, Zechariah	1	5	1		
Phillips, Eben^r	1				
Rice, Dan¹	2	2	6		
Rice, Jacob	2	3	3		
Ross, Jon^a	1	2	5		
Rice, Christopher	2		4		
Rice, Elijah	1	3	2		
Ray, Jon^a	1	3	4		
Smith, Ezekiel	2	2	3		
Smith, Sam¹	2	3	6		
Sawyer, Jon^a	1	2	3		
Sargent, Eben	1	1	1		
Sargent, William	1	2	2		
Stone, Thomas	1	1	1		
Stewart, Thomas	1	3	2		
Smith, John	1	1	3		
Stone, Thomas, Jr	1	1	3		
Smith, John, Jr	2	3	4		
Symonds, Sam¹	2				
Symonds, Simeon	2	1	5		
HENIKER TOWN—con.					
Tucker, John	2		1		
Tyler, James	1	3	3		
Tucker, Ezra	2	2	6		
Temple, Jasper	1				
Tucker, Benoni	1	4	2		
Whitman, John	1	1	2		
Ward, Josiah	3	1	7		
Ward, Phineas	5	4	3		
Ward, Jesse	1		1		
Witherinton, Francis	3	3	6		
Wallace, Robt	2	5	1	1	
Wallace, William	1	1	1		
Wallace, James	3	1	3		
Willson, Thomas	1	4	3	1	
Prat, Joseph	1		5		
Rogers, Simon	1	1	4		
Silver, Timothy	1	5	2		
Wadsworth, Sam¹	2	3	3		
Whitney, Joshua	1	2	1		
Wood, Jon^a	1	2	5		
Wood, Joseph	1	1	4		
Whitney, Alexan^r	1	2	6		
Whitcomb, Charles	3	4	5		
Whitcomb, Benj^a	1	5	3		
Whitman, Daniel	4		1		
Whiteker, Moses	2				
Witherington, Elias	1		2		
Whitney, Isaac	1	2	2		
Brown, Enoch	3		2		
Heath, Joshua	1	4	4		
Hoyt, George	1	3	4		
HILLSBOROUGH TOWN.					
Bames, Jon^a	2	7	2		
Andrews, Isaac	5		2		
Andrews, Isaac, Jr	1	2	4		
Abbot, Darius	3	1	4		
Bradford, Sam¹	2	4	3		
Bradford, Eliphalet	2	1	5		
Burnam, Tim^o	1		4		
Bradford, Sam¹., Jr	1	2	3		
Blanchard, David	1	3	3		
Beard, Elijah	2	1	4		
Baldwin, Genison	2		1		
Baker, Ephraim	1	2	5		
Booth, George	1		3		
Booth, William	2		3		
Butler, Bala	1		4		
Bradford, Tim^o	2	2	3		
Coolage, Nath¹	3	1	2		
Chandler, Isaac	2		3		
Chandler, Isaac, Jr	1	2	2		
Chambers, William	2	2	1		
Carter, James	2		2		
Curtice, John	1	1	3		
Dutton, John	2		4		
Dutton, Benj^a	1	2	2		
Dutton, James	2	1	5		
Dodge, Sam¹	2		4		
Danforth, Jon^a	1	1	3		
Danforth, Sam¹	1	2	3		
Easty, Joshua	3	2	2		
Eaton, James	1		1		
Ellinwood, Sam¹	1	2	4		
Flint, Jacob	1	3	4		
Gannee, William	1	2	6		
Gould, Benj^a	1	1	1		
Gray, Tim^o	1	2	3		
Griffin, Dan¹	2	2	1		
Gerry, Nath¹	1	2	3		
Hartwell, Tim^o	1		3		
Heywood, Nath¹	1				
Hall, John	1	2	6		
How, Otis	2	7	2		
Hartwell, John	1	2	6		
Dix, John	1				
Cooledge, Paul	1	3	1		
Hartwell, Sam¹	1	3	3		
Jones, Moses	1	1	2		
Kendall, Joshua	1		2		
Killum, Dan¹	2	3	1		
Kimball, Benj^a	2	3	5		
Little, Ezekiel	1		1		
Little, George	1	2	5		
Lacy, Sam¹	1		1		
Morrill, John	1	3	1		
Munro, Thaddeus	1	1	2		
Medes, Benj^a	1		2		
Medes, John	1		3		
Murdough, Sam¹	1	3	3		
McNeill, Jane			5		

HILLSBOROUGH COUNTY—Continued.

HILLSBOROUGH TOWN—continued.

NAME OF HEAD OF FAMILY.	Free white males of 16 years and upward, including heads of families.	Free white males under 16 years.	Free white females, including heads of families.	All other free persons.	Slaves.
McNeill, Danl	1	2	2		
Nelson, Moses	1	1	4		
Nichols, John	2		2		
Nichols, Joseph	1	2	5		
Preston, Jedidiah	2	3	3		
Parmiter, Nathl	1	2	4		
Robins, Peter	2	1	2		
Robbins, Zacheus	1	2	2		
Rolph, Danl	1	1	2		
Robinson, Saml	1		1		
Richardson, Jonas	1	1	3		
Simonds, Joseph	1	1	6		
Simonds, Nathl	1				
Sargent, Jona	1	3	5		
Sprague, John	1	1	1		
Shattuck, Abiel	1		3		
Taggart, William	2	2	4		
Taggart, James	1	3	3		
Train, Ephraim	1	3	1		
Wilkins, Nehemiah	1	3	5		
Jones, Joel	2	2	3		
Wilkins, Andrew	2	3	4		
Wheeler, Oliver	1	4	5		
Wilkins, Asaph	1	1	2		
Andrews, Solo	1	2	1		
Barnes, Asa	1	2	5		
Bixbee, Andrew	3		1		
Bixbee, John	1	1	2		
Elliot, Roger	1		1		
Fick, Elijah	1	3	1		
Gibson, John, Junr	2				
Gibson, John	2	3	5		
Goodale, David	2	2	3		
Gray, Ephraim	3	1	3		
Green, David	1		3		
Hutchinson, William	2	1	3		
Jones, Benja	3	3	4		
Jones, Abel	1		3		
Karr, James	1	2	3		
Karr, Thomas	1		2		
Karr, Thomas, Jr	1		2		
Livermore, David	1	1	2		
Love, William	1	1	2		
Little, William	1	2	3		
McCalley, John	1	1	4		
Miller, Thomas	2	2	6		
McNeill, John	2	2	2		
McCalley, James	3		3		
Murdough, Thomas	1		2		
Marshall, David	1	1	4		
Peirce, Benja	1	1	3	1	
Parker, William	1	2	2		
Patten, Robt	1		1		
Preston, Saml	2	2	4		
Pope, Saml	1	3	2		
Parker, Silas	1	1	1		
Richardson, Parker	2	2	3		
Stow, Mary		1	3		
Stevens, Calvin	1	4	4		
Smith, John	1	1	3		
Shed, John	1	1	2		
Steel, Moses	2		2		
Taylor, Saml	1	3	4		
Towne, Enos	1	2	2		
Taggart, Archibald	2	1	6		
Tolbert, William	1	1	5		
Tagart, Joseph	1	2	4		
Temple, Benja	1	1			
Wheeler, Fortunatus	1		3		
Miller, Farrar	1	2	3		
Wiley, George	1		1		
Karr, Robt	1		1		
Jones, William	1		1		
Wiley, John	1	1	2		
Kerr, Robert	1		1		
McClary, John	1	2	5		
McClintock, John	1	5	5		
McClintock, Alexander	1	2	4		
Wiley, Timo	1	3	4		
Taggart, Robert	1	2	1		
Eaton, Abrathn	1		3		
Clark, Silas	2	1	2		
Eayrs, William	1	4	3		

HOLLIS TOWN.

NAME OF HEAD OF FAMILY.	Free white males of 16 years and upward, including heads of families.	Free white males under 16 years.	Free white females, including heads of families.	All other free persons.	Slaves.
Emerson, Danl	2		2		
Austins, Benja	2		3		
Ames, Jeremiah	2		2		
Atwell, John	2	2	1		
Adams, William	1	2	3		

HOLLIS TOWN—con.

NAME OF HEAD OF FAMILY.	Free white males of 16 years and upward, including heads of families.	Free white males under 16 years.	Free white females, including heads of families.	All other free persons.	Slaves.
Abbot, Benja	1	2	2		
Barker, Nehemiah	2	1	3		
Bowers, Oliver	1	1	2		
Boynton, Abraham	1	2	5		
Burge, David	1	1	2		
Brooks, William	2	2	4		
Blood, Francis	1	4	3		
Bailey, Danl	1	1	2		
Bailey, Danl., Jr	1		4		
Bailey, Joel	1	1	2		
Bailey, Aaron	1	1	2		
Baldwin, Ezra	1	1	2		
Colburn, Robt	1	5	4		
Colburn, Nathl	1	1	4		
Colburn, Benja	2	1	7		
Clark, Elijah	1	2	3		
Colburn, James	1	1	3		
Cumings, Benja	2	2	4		
Chamberlin, Wilder	1	1	1		
Clark, Richard	1		2		
Danforth, Jona	2	4	4		
Dix, Jona	1		2		
Darrah, Robt	1	2	2		
Eastman, Amos	2		2		
Eastman, Amos, Jr	2	5	4		
Eastman, Jona	2	1	3		
Emerson, Timothy, Jr	1	4	3		
Emerson, Thomas	3	4	1		
Emerson, Timothy	1		1		
Emerson, Moses	1				
Eames, David	1		1		
Farmer, Abigail	1		3		
Farley, Ebenr	2	3	7		
Farley, Stephen	1	3	4		
French, William	1	1	6		
French, Nehemiah	1	1	5		
Farley, Ruth		4	4		
Dumlee, David	1		1		
Flagg, Jonas	3	1	4		
Flagg, Eleazar	1				
Foster, Edward	2	3	5		
Green, Jonas	1	2	3		
Hood, Joseph	2	2	4		
Hale, John	2	2	4		
Hobbard, Shabriel	1	1	2		
Hardy, Phineas	2		1		
Hardy, Phineas, Jr	1	2	3		
Hardy, Jesse	1		3		
Haden, Saml	2		1		
Hardy, Levi	2	2	3		
Hardy, Moses	1		1		
Holden, David, Jr	1	1	1		
Harris, Job	1		2		
Jewett, James, Jr	2	1	1		
Jewett, Enoch	1	3	4		
Kendrick, Hannah	1	1	2		
Kendrick, Mary	1	2	2		
Keyes, Abner	1	2	8		
Leeman, Nathl	1	1	3		
Lawrence, Oliver	4	1	3		
Lawrence, Peleg	1		1		
Leeman, Abraham	1		3		
Lesley, Joseph	2	1	3		
Lovejoy, Asa	1	1	5		
Lund, Ephraim	1	2	4		
Lea, Abigail	1		3		
Merrill, Danl	2	1	2		
Moor, Jacob	1	2	3		
May, Zebulon	1	2	3		
Needham, Stearns	2	2	3		
Nevins, Benja	1	2	3		
Nevins, Joseph	1	2	7		
Nutting, John	1	2	4		
Peirce, Solomon	3	3	4		
Prockter, Syas	1	3	4		
Prockter, Moses	2	2	2		
Pike, Joseph	1	2	5		
Parker, Josiah	4	1	2		
Parker, Eleazar	3		1		
Patch, Thomas	2	3	5		
Powers, Thomas	1	1	3		
Parker, Benja. W	1	1	1		
Parker, Jona	2		2		
Read, William	2	3	4		
Read, Joshua	1	2	4		
Rogers, Benja	1	2	1		
Read, William, Jr	1		1		
Smith, Saml	1	2	3		
Spaulding, Jona	3	3	5		
Spaulding, Silas	1	2	3		
Shed, John	1	1	4		
Tinney, William	3	3	5		

HOLLIS TOWN—con.

NAME OF HEAD OF FAMILY.	Free white males of 16 years and upward, including heads of families.	Free white males under 16 years.	Free white females, including heads of families.	All other free persons.	Slaves.
Wright, Noah	2	3	1		
Waltingsford, David	2	4	6		
Wheeler, Ebenr	2	1	2		
Wheeler, Thads	2	5	2		
Wright, Benja	1	2	5		
Woodbury, Joseph	1				
Whiting, Leonard	2	1	5		
Willoughby, Oliver	1	2	1		
Youngman, Saml. W	1	2	1		
Abbot, Saml	1		2		
Ames, Busby	1	5	4		
Abbot, George	1	1	2		
Ames, John	2	3	5		
Boynton, Moses	2		5		
Burge, Ephraim	1	2	3		
Blood, Solomon	3	4	6		
Blood, Josiah	2	3	4		
Blood, Elnathan	3	1	6		
Ball, Ebenr	1		1		
Ball, Ebenr, Jr	2	3	4		
Ball, William	1	2	1		
Ball, John	1	2	4		
Brown, David	2		1		
Brown, William	1	1	2		
Brown, William, Jr	2	1	1		
Brown, Eliphalet	1	5	1		
Blood, Jacob	1		5		
Brown, Abel	1	2	3		
Boynton, Joshua	2	3	1		
Boynton, Benja	1	5	5		
Bradley, Thomas	1	3	4		
Blood, John	1	1	3		
Blood, Danl	2	5	4		
Conant, Josiah	2	3	7		
Conant, Abel	1	2	3		
Connery, Saml	1	2	4		
Cook, Timothy	1		1		
Connery, Stephen	1	1	4		
Craft, Saml	1	2	2		
Douglas, Phineas	1				
Davis, Joshua	1	4	3		
Dow, Reuben	3		2		
Emerson, Ralph	2		4		
Emerson, Danl	1	3	3		
Farley, Caleb	3	1	3		
Farley, Caleb, Jr	1	6	2		
French, Timothy	2		2		
French, Isaac	2	2	5		
Ghoss, John	1	4	5		
Goodhue, John	1	1	5		
Goodhue, Sarah	1	1	1		
How, Ephraim	1	3	3		
Holden, David	1	2	2		
Hobbard, Jona	1		6		
Haskell, Joseph	1	3	2		
Hardy, Nehemiah	2	3	2		
Hardy, Isaac	1	1	1		
Holt, Eifield	1		2		
Holt, Fifield, Jr	2	1	4		
Jewett, Nathl	2	1	2		
Jewett, Stephen	2		3		
Jewett, Stephen, Jr	1	1	5		
Jewett, Saml	1		2		
Jewett, James	1		1		
Jewett, Jacob	2	2	6		
Jewett, Jacob, Jr	1	2	3		
Johnson, Saml	1	1	5		
Jaquith, Thomas	1	4	3		
Kenny, Israel	2	2	7		
Lovejoy, Danl	2	1	4		
Moor, Danl	1	3	3		
Phelps, Nathn	1	2	4		
Phelps, John	1	3	5		
Pool, William	2		3		
Peirce, Richard	3	2	4		
Powers, Samson	1	4	5		
Powers, Francis	2	3	4		
Runnels, Saml	1		1		
Rideout, James	2	1	6		
Rideout, James, Jr	1	1	2		
Rideout, Nathl	1	3	3		
Ranger, Nehemiah	2	3	2		
Shattuck, Zachh	3		2		
Shattuck, Zachh, Jr	1	4	2		
Stearns, Joseph	1	3	3		
Spaulding, Edward	1		2		
Spaulding, Jacob	1		2		
Shipley, Abel	2	4	5		
Smith, Emerson	3	2	5		
Smith, John	1	2	4		
Sanders, Benjamin	2	4	3		
Sanders, Jona	1				

HILLSBOROUGH COUNTY—Continued.

HOLLIS TOWN—con.

NAME OF HEAD OF FAMILY.	Free white males of 16 years and upward, including heads of families.	Free white males under 16 years.	Free white females, including heads of families.	All other free persons.	Slaves.
Shattuck, Nathl	1	2	3		
Senter, John	1		1		
Taylor, Edward	2		3		
Twist, Asahel	1		1		
Thurston, Moses	1	1	2		
Wyman, Jesse	2	1	2		
Willoughby, Saml	1	4	6		
Worcester, Noah	3	3	5		
Wood, Nehemiah	2		3		
Woods, Jonas	1	1	4		
Wright, Lemuel	1	5	2		
Wright, Uriah	2	3	3		
Wright, Saml	1	3	5		
Wheat, Joseph	2	1	8		
Wood, William	1	3	5		
Wheat, Solomon	3	2	3		
Wright, Elisha	1		3		
Wheat, Thomas	2		3		
Wheat, Josiah	1		2		
Willoughby, John	1		1		
Willoughby, James	2		2		
Willoughby, Jonas	1	1	2		
Warren, Benja	1	1	2		
Youngman, Nicholas	1		1		
Youngman, Jabez	1	2	1		
Runnils, Stephen	1	1	5		
Parker, Benja	1		1		
Heywood, Joseph	1		2		
Farley, Benja	1	1	2		
French, Saml	1		2		
French, Isaac B	1	2	4		
Hunt, Sarah	1	1	5		
Mosher, Unice	1	1	5		
Blood, Priscilla	1		2		
Bills, Abner	1	3	2		
Woods, David	1	3	4		
Estherbrooks, Joseph	1		1		
Merril, Danl., Jr	1		1		
Leeman, Saml	1		1		
Stedman, Mary			3		
Pool, Wm. Walsted	2	2	4		
Sawyer, Timothy	1		2		
Emerson, David	1	1	2		
French, Mary	1	2	4		
Bailey, Timothy	1	2	3		
Stearns, John	1	2	3		
Kemp, Thomas	1	2	3		
Parker, Saml	2	1	1		
Conrick, Martha		1	2		
Hale, Jona	1	1	1		
Stevens, Richard	1	3	3		
Lovejoy, Christopr	1		1		
Prockter, Cotton	1		1		

HOPKINTON TOWN.

NAME OF HEAD OF FAMILY.	Free white males of 16 years and upward, including heads of families.	Free white males under 16 years.	Free white females, including heads of families.	All other free persons.	Slaves.
Allen, Jona	1		2		
Allen, Jona., Jr	5	1	5		
Allen, Jona., 3d	1	2	2		
Boynton, John	1		4		
Allen, Andrew	3	3	5		
Boynton, Joel	1	1	3		
Bailey, Isaac	3	1	4		
Bailey, Joshua	3		4		
Bailey, John	1	1	1		
Burrows, Josiah	1	2	2		
Burwell, James	3		3		
Blake, Henry	2		4		
Brown, Ensley	2	3	7		
Barnard, Joseph	3	1	3		
Burwell, Benja	1		2		
Burwell, Ezra	1		2		
Burnam, Joseph	1	2	4		
Babson, Isaac	1		5		
Currier, John	1		3		
Chadwick, John	1	2	2		
Chenee, Isaac	1	4	3		
Colby, Eliphalet	1		1		
Colby, Ephraim	2	3	6		
Colby, Nehemiah	2	1	3		
Collins, Jona	1	2	4		
Colby, Anthony	3		5		
Colby, William D	2	5	2		
Clement, Nathl	2		2		
Bear, Hannah			2		
Chase, Jona	3	1	5		
Clement, Richar	1	1	3		
Currier, Edmund	1		1		
Chandler, Isaac	2	3	4		
Chandler, Joseph	2	2	6		
Darling, John	1	1	1		
Darling, Benja. B	2	1	2		
Darling, Timothy	4	5	4		

HOPKINTON TOWN—con.

NAME OF HEAD OF FAMILY.	Free white males of 16 years and upward, including heads of families.	Free white males under 16 years.	Free white females, including heads of families.	All other free persons.	Slaves.
Darling, Peter	1	5	2		
Darling, Moses	1	4	4		
Darling, Onesimus	1		1		
Durgan, Elijah	2	3	4		
Durgan, Bening	1	1	2		
Emerson, Moses	3	3	3		
Eastman, Simeon	1	5	2		
Farington, Saml	2	4	4		
Fellows, Isaac	1	1	2		
French, Green	2		4		
Flanders, Michael	1	1	6		
Gould, Elias	1	3	2		
Gage, John	2	3	6		
Gould, Gideon	3	2	6		
Godfry, Meriam			3		
George, John	1	5	5		
Herrick, Jona., Jr	2	2	4		
Herrick, Danl	3	1	3		
Hildreth, Levi	1	2	2		
Hills, Moses	3		4		
Hart, John	2	4	2		
Herris, Saml	2		3		
Gill, William	1		1		
Holmes, Elijah	2		6		
Holmes, Benja., Jr	1	4	2		
Hoyt, Ezra	3		7		
Hoyt, John, Jr	1		2		
Jewett, John	2	1	1		
Jewett, Saml	1	3	3		
Judkins, Jona	1	1	5		
Judkins, Joseph	1		1		
Kimball, Abrm	3	2	3		
Kimball, Saml	3	5	4		
Kimball, Nathl	1	2	4		
Kimball, John	3	1	4		
Kimball, Smith	1	3	1		
Kimball, Job	1	1	3		
Kimball, Abel	2		2		
Kimball, David	1	1	2		
Knowlton, Roba	2	3	1		
Knowlton, Ezekiel	3	3	4		
Kimball, Aaron	1	2	4		
Long, Enoch	3		2		
Long, Enoch, Jr	2	1	4		
McLaughlin, Lawrence	2	1	2		
Morral, Mark	3		3		
Merrill, Richard	2	1	3		
Morse, Joshua	2	1	5		
Norris, Zebalon	1		4		
Prockter, Jona	1	4	2		
Quinby, Jona	2		2		
Quinby, Isaac	1	1	3		
Row, Josiah	1	1	2		
Storker, Saml	1	3	3		
Smith, Moody	1	4	5		
Smith, Morse	1		5		
Smart, Benja	1	1	3		
Smart, Joseph	1	1	3		
Smith, Josiah	1		2		
Smart, Elijah	1	3	2		
Straw, James	1	1	2		
Straw, Jona	1		2		
Straw, Jacob, Jr	1	2	5		
Straw, Saml	1	1	4		
Straw, Moses	1	2	4		
Swain, Benja	2	2	3		
Standley, Jacob	1	2	3		
Story, Jeremiah	2		1		
Story, Jeremiah, Jr	2	3	3		
Story, Thomas	2	2	6		
Story, Nathl	1	2	5		
Sargent, Nathl	4		5		
Sargent, Elizabeth			4		
Smith, James	1	2	2		
Titcomb, Moses	2	1	2		
Thompson, Benja	2	1	4		
Tewkbury, John	1	3	2		
Trussell, John	4	3	4		
Trussell, Danl	1		1		
Taylor, Adonijah	3	1	2		
Tenny, Danl	4	1	4		
Wager, Hannah			4		
Webber, John	1		2		
Webber, Richard, Jr	1	3	3		
Webber, Richard	1		4	1	
Webber, Thomas	1	3	3		
Titcomb, Benja	1		2		
Wiggin, Benjamin	4	1	5		
Burt, Caleb	4	2	2		
Brown, Abraham	2	4	2		
Rickford, Thomas	3		6		
Burbank, Ebenr	1		5		
Bailey, Thomas	2		5		

HOPKINTON TOWN—con.

NAME OF HEAD OF FAMILY.	Free white males of 16 years and upward, including heads of families.	Free white males under 16 years.	Free white females, including heads of families.	All other free persons.	Slaves.
Bailey, Levi	3		2		
Bailey, Amos	1	1	1		
Currier, Abraham	3		5		
Currier, Henry	1	2	4		
Currier, Reuben	1	1	3		
Choat, Joseph	2		2		
Currier, Samuel	1	2	4		
Cresee, Richard	3	3	1		
Cross, Ralph	2	2	3		
Clement, Joshua	1	1	1		
Clough, James	2	2	2		
Daw, Simeon	3	1	4		
Daw, Simeon, Jr	2	1	4		
Emerson, Saml	1	1	2		
Eastman, Joseph	1		3		
Eastman, Joseph	1	3	4		
Eastman, Benja	1	3	4		
Eastman, Enoch	1	2	7		
Eastman, Joseph, Jr	1		1		
Eastman, Thomas	1	3	2		
Eastman, Timothy	2	2	4		
Eastman, John	1	2	2		
Eastman, Ezra	1	1	2		
Eaton, John	3	1	5		
Emerson, Jeremiah	2	2	3		
Eastman, John	1		1		
Flanders, Jeremiah	1	4	3		
Fowler, David	2	2	3		
Fowler, Jona	1	3	2		
Farnum, Timothy	1		2		
Gould, Moses	2	3	1		
Gould, Nathl	2	1	3		
Gould, Christopher	1		2		
Gunison, Daniel	1	1	1		
Gould, John	1		3		
Herriman, Stephen	2	1	3		
Herriman, Stephen, Jr	1	2	4		
Hunt, Eonos	1	3	2		
Hadley, Ezekiel	1				
McHard, James	3				
Hastings, Moses	2		1		
Hastings, Joseph	1	4	3		
Holmes, John	3		7		
Kimball, Moses	1	1	7		
Kart, Sarah	1		2		
Ladd, Thomas	1		4		
Long, Moses	1	3	4		
Merrill, David	1	2	4		
Ordway, Ebenr	1	1	3		
Ordway, John	1	1	4		
Ordway, John, Jr	1	2	2		
Putney, Thomas, jr	3	3	4		
Putney, William	1	2	2		
Putney, Stephen	1	1	3		
Peters, William	1	1	3		
Person, Noah	1	4	2		
Philbrick, Joseph	1		2		
Poor, Eliphalet	3	3	6		
Rowell, Ephraim	3		8		
Rowell, Nathan	2	3	5		
Rowell, Abel	1		2		
Silver, Saml	2	2	3		
Sargent, Benja	1	1	2		
Standley, John	1	1	5		
Standley, Saml	1		4		
Standley, William	1	1	3		
Young, David	8	2	8		
Annis, David	1	2	5		
Wood, Giddeon	1	1	2		
Dolph, Henry	1		1		
Mackey, Benja	1	2	1		
Choat, John	1		2		
Bayford, Elizabeth			2		
Hunt, Jonathan	1	1	1		
Hammond, Phineas	1	1	1		
Taylor, William	1		3		
Standley, Sarah			3		
Adams, Saml	2	1	3		
Brackenbury, Saml	1		2		
Blasdell, Saml	1		2		
Blasdell, John	2		2		
Burbank, John	1	1	2		
Burbank, Saml, Jr	2		2		
Clement, John	2		3		
Currier, John, Jr	4	1	4		
Clement, David	2		4		
Clough, David	2	3	2		
Clark, Joseph	1	5	2		
Clark, Jacob	2	2	4		
Chase, Danl	2	2	2		
Chase, Ambros	2	2	1		
Davis, Abraham	2	2	3		
Fellows, David	3	2	7		

HILLSBOROUGH COUNTY—Continued.

NAME OF HEAD OF FAMILY.	Free white males of 16 years and upward, including heads of families.	Free white males under 16 years.	Free white females, including heads of families.	All other free persons.	Slaves.
HOPKINTON TOWN—con.					
French, Henry	4		4		
Flanders, Daniel	3		2		
Greeley, Aaron	2	4	6		
Greeley, Philip	2	3	6		
Gordon, Jonᵃ	3	4	3		
Gordon, Amos	2	2	5		
Hoyt, Samˡ	3	1	5		
Hoyt, Eastman	2	4	5		
How, David	1	4	2		
How, Peter	3		2		
Hale, John	1	4	3		
How, Jotham	3	1	6		
Hoyt, Jacob	1	3	5		
Blasdel, John	1		2		
Hoyt, Benjamin	1	3	2		
Hoyt, John	1	3	3		
Jewell, Moses	3	3	5		
Jones, John	2	4	4		
Jones, Moses	2		2		
Murry, Daniel	2	2	8		
Moor, John	3	2	5		
Marsh, Joseph	1	2	4		
Morgan, Nathˡ	1	2	2		
Morgan, Nathan	1	1	1		
Osgood, John	1	2	2		
Person, Oliver	2		3		
Parley, Isaac	2		1		
Page, Samˡ	1	3	4		
Quimby, Benjᵃ	1		1		
Quimby, Jonᵃ	1	3	3		
Rogers, Richard C	2	1	4		
Rogers, Samˡ	1	2	1		
Rogers, Robᵗ	1	1	3		
Rogers, Aaron	1	1	3		
Rogers, Paul	1	1	2		
Sawyer, Samˡ	2	2	5		
Sawyer, Joshua	1	1	2		
Stickney, Sarah	1	1	4		
Sawyer, Sarah			2		
Sibley, Jacob	2	5	4		
Straw, Ezekiel	3		6		
Straw, Jacob	4	2	4		
Straw, Samˡ, Jr	1	1	3		
Story, Joseph	1	4	4		
White, John	1	2	7		
Tinney, Moses	1		1		
KERSARGE GORE.					
Urine, Daniel	2	1	4		
Bean, John	1	1	1		
Elliot, Dudley	1		2		
Cross, Thomas	1	2	1		
Knoles, Joseph	1	2	2		
Parmer, Jonathan	2		1		
Quimby, Joshua	1	1	3		
Parmer, Jeremiah	1	6	1		
Wells, Thomas	3	2	4		
Annis, Daniel	2	2	6		
Shepard, Ebenʳ	3	2	5		
Smith, David	1	2	3		
Smith, Elisha	1	1	3		
Watkins, Jason	2		2		
Parmer, John	1	2	4		
Parmer, James	2	2	4		
Cross, Nathˡ	1	1	1		
Quimby, Samuel	1		2		
LITCHFIELD TOWN.					
Cotton, Samˡ	4		3		
Barker, William	1		3		
Chase, Enoch	1	1	1		
Gare, David	1	1	2		
Read, William	1	3	5		
Humblet, Hezeʰ	1	1	1		
Whedden, John	1	1	2		
Stewart, John	1		1	2	
Richardson, Josiah	1	2	4		
Blodget, Daniel	2	4	2		
Cochran, Samˡ	2		3		
Parker, Matthew	5	1	6		
Keef, Matthew	1		1		
Parker, Matthew	2	4	6		
Parker, Jonᵃ	2	4	2		
Parker, Robᵗ	2	1	2	3	
Whdden, William	1		1		
Quegg, David	3	3	4		
MᶜQueton, David	2	3	2		
MᶜQueston, James	2	1	2		
Truel, David	2	3	4		

NAME OF HEAD OF FAMILY.	Free white males of 16 years and upward, including heads of families.	Free white males under 16 years.	Free white females, including heads of families.	All other free persons.	Slaves.
LITCHFIELD TOWN—con.					
MᶜQueston, William	4		5		
MᶜQueton, John	1		1		
Clagett, Clifton	2	3	3		
Kendall, Sarah	1	2	3		
Clagett, Wentworth	2		4		
Whittemore, Jacob	2	7	3		
Harrell, Gershom	1	3	2		
Kendall, Timᵒ	2	5	5	1	
Vose, Jonah	2		1		
Chase, Ebenʳ	3	2	4		
French, Asa	1	2	3		
Hildreth, William	2		3		
Chase, Samˡ, Jr	2	1	2		
MᶜQueston, Simon	3	2	2	1	
Bixby, William	4	4	5		
Parker, Mary			2	1	
Nahor, James	2		1		
Nahor, James, Jr	3	1	2		
Chase, Samˡ	3	2	4		
Chase, Simeon	2	1	3		
Chase, Joseph	3	4	8		
Campbell, David	1	2	5		
Page, Jacob	1	3	2		
Whitle, Thomas	1	1	1		
Caldwell, James	1	2	2		
Barnes, Jehannah			3		
Barnes, Joseph	1	2	4	1	
Darrah, Robᵗ	3	1	2		
Whitle, John	1		5		
Sprake, Samˡ	1	2	4		
Cross, John	2		2		
Hills, Eliphᵗ	1		3		
Underwood, James	3	2	6		
Blanchard, Cesar				3	
Blanchard, Peter				3	
Rand, Jack				2	
LYNDBOROUGH TOWN.					
Goodridge, Sewell	2	3	6		
Abbot, Kneland	2	5	3		
Averill, David	1	2	5		
Abbot, Lemuel	1		1		
Averill, Daniel	1	2	2		
Abbot, Peter	1	1	1		
Batchelder, Carlton	1		1		
Batchelder, Nathan	1	2	4		
Batchelder, Molten	1	1	1		
Blaney, William	1	3	4		
Barron, William	3		3		
Badger, Robᵗ	1	1	6		
Badger, Lucy	1	1	2		
Badger, David	1		1		
Batton, Richard	1	2	3		
Buffee, John	2	2	3		
Brown, Jeremiah	3	3	4		
Besom, John	1	1	4		
Burnam, Stephen	2	1	4		
Burnam, Nathˡ	1	4	2		
Burnam, James	2	2	6		
Bullard, Edward	1	1	2		
Beckford, Edmund	3	1	2		
Boutell, James	3		5		
Butler, Jonᵃ	1	2	4		
Blazdel, Samˡ	3		3		
Blanchard, Jotham	2	3	5		
Barnes, Henry	1	1	1		
Barker, Theophilus	1		2		
Baldwin, Jeremiah	1	3	1		
Badger, Stephen	1				
Burnam, William	1	2	4		
Bullard, David	1	3	6		
Case, John	1		2		
Carson, William	4		3		
Batchelder, Joseph	3	3	4		
Bevens, Mary			2		
Cram, Solomon	1	1	1		
Carlton, Jeremiah	2	2	7		
Carkin, John	1	1	3		
Cram, Uriah	2	3	3		
Cram, David	3	2	6		
Cram, Jacob	2		4		
Chamberlin, Jonᵃ	2		2		
Chamberlin, Jonᵃ, Jr	3	2	4		
Chamberlin, John	1	2	4		
Chamberlin, Samˡ	1	3	5		
Cram, Benjᵃ	1	1	2		
Cram, Benjᵃ, Jr	3		1		
Cram, David	1		1		
Clark, Peter	4	1	4		
Clark, John	1	1	2		

NAME OF HEAD OF FAMILY.	Free white males of 16 years and upward, including heads of families.	Free white males under 16 years.	Free white females, including heads of families.	All other free persons.	Slaves.
LYNDBOROUGH TOWN—continued.					
Cresey, Andrew	1	3	4		
Cram, John	1	1	1		
Cram, Jacob, Jr	1	1	2		
Cram, John, Jr	1	1	1		
Carlton, Thomas	2	3	3		
Crosby, Jacob	1		2		
Campbell, John	1		1		
Dutton, Josiah	3		1		
Dutton, Benjᵃ	2	3	3		
Dutton, Jacob	1	2	3		
Dutton, Asa	1		4		
Dutton, Ezra	1	2	2		
Dutton, William	1	2	3		
Day, Susanna			4		
Day, Robᵗ	2	3	4		
Dankler, Hezekiah	1	5	1		
Dascombe, Jacob	1	1	4		
Dodge, Jesse	2	3	3		
Draper, William	1	2	2		
Dodge, Esther		1	2		
Ellenwood, Sarah			3		
Ellenwood, Joseph	1	3	3		
Ellenwood, Samuel	1	1			
Ellenwood, Jacob	1	1	1		
Epes, Francis	2	1	5		
Epes, Benjᵃ	2		1		
Epes, Joseph, Jr	1	2	1		
Fuller, Andrew	1	3	1		
Fletcher, Caleb	2	1	8		
Fletcher, Simeon	2		1		
Flint, Elijah	1	3	3		
Farnum, Stephen	1	2	2		
Gould, Daniel	3	3	5		
Gardner, Ebenʳ	1	3	3		
Grant, John	1	3	5		
Gould, Stephen	1	3	1		
Gould, Daniel, Jr	1	3	5		
Giddings, Isaac	1	2	4		
Houston, Samuel	2	4	3		
Hutchinson, Nehemiah	1	2	3		
Hutchinson, Nathˡ	1		1		
Hutchinson, Thomas	1	5	2		
Hutchinson, Ebenʳ	1	2			
Hadley, Joshua	3		3		
Hadley, Joshua, Jr	1		2		
Herrick, Joseph	2	1	6		
Hutchinson, Sarah		1	2		
Hutchinson, Samˡ	1	2	3		
Hagget, Matthew	1		2		
Hagget, John	1	1	1		
Hager, Isaac	1		3		
Epes, John, Jr	1	2	2		
Epes, Joseph	1		1		
Hutchinson, Deborah			3		
Hartshorn, John	1	4	2		
Holt, William	1				
Holt, William, Jr	2	2	2		
Holt, Benjᵃ	1		3		
Hobbs, Joseph	1		3		
Hazeltine, Nathˡ	1	3	5		
Hazeltine, David	1	2	3		
Hardy, Daniel	1	2	3		
Hopkins, Ebenʳ	1				
Holt, Daniel	1		1		
Hildreth, Ephraim	2		4		
Hutchinson, Ebenʳ	1				
Howard, Silas	1	3	4		
Jones, Benjᵃ	2	4	5		
Johnson, William	1		1		
Kidder, John	1	1	2		
Kidder, Jonas	4	3	3		
Kidder, John, Jr	1	3	5		
Kidder, Phineas	1	2	2		
Kidder, Ephraim	1	1	1		
Kidder, Joseph	1	1	1		
Killum, Samuel	1		2		
Killum, Benjᵃ	4	3	3		
Kenny, Josiah	1	1	2		
Kimball, Ebenʳ	1	1	1		
Kerr, James	1				
Lewis, Benjᵃ	1		2		
Lewis, Moses	1		3		
Lewis, Aaron	2	1	8		
Lund, Phineas	1		3		
Low, Simon	1	2	3		
Lawrence, Noah	1	1	2		
MᶜMaster, Samˡ	2		4		
MᶜAdams, Samˡ	1	3	4		
MᶜAdams, Hugh	1	1	1		
Manuel, Joel	2	1	2		

HILLSBOROUGH COUNTY—Continued.

NAME OF HEAD OF FAMILY.	Free white males of 16 years and upward, including heads of families.	Free white males under 16 years.	Free white females, including heads of families.	All other free persons.	Slaves.
LYNDBOROUGH TOWN— continued.					
McIntire, Timo	1	4	5		
McIntire, Jacob	1	1	2		
McCloud, John	2	1	3		
Ordeway, John	4	1	2		
Ordway, Enoch	1	1	3		
Ordeway, Trustum	1	1	4		
Osgood, David	1		3		
Phelps, Nathl	1	4	5		
Persons, Jona	1		1		
Persons, Timothy	1	2	1		
Persons, George	3	2	6		
Putnam, Ephraim	3	1	3		
Putnam, Ephraim, Jr	2	3	3		
Putnam, David	2	2	5		
Putnam, Aaron	1	5	2		
Perhum, Oliver	1	3	1		
Persons, Joseph	1	1	2		
Persons, Jona, Jr	1	1	2		
Parker, William	1	3	3		
Persons, Daniel	1	1	3		
Punchard, James	2	2	2		
Peabody, Isaac	2	2	3		
Parker, Robert	1	3	2		
Rand, Nehemiah	2	1	3		
Ross, Walter	2	1	3		
Richardson, Thomas	2		4		
Richardson, John, Jr	1	1	1		
Runnalds, John	2	2	6		
Russel, Daniel	2	3	2		
Richardson, Joseph	2	4	3		
Read, Jotham	1		3		
Russel, Nathl	1	3	5		
Mansfield, Mary		1	1		
Persons, Jonathan	1	2	2		
Richardson, John	1	1	1		
Smith, John	2	2	4		
Smith, Benja	1	2	1		
Stiles, Joshua	1	5	3		
Stiles, Moses	3	1	3		
Stiles, Moses, Jr	1	1	2		
Savage, John	2	2	3		
Stratten, David	1	3	3		
Spaulding, Edward	3	1	2		
Spaulding, Levi	2	2	3		
Senter, Benja	1	5	4		
Stewart, Saml	1	2	3		
Spaulding, Joseph	1	2	4		
Stephenson, John	2	1	4		
Sargent, Joshua	1	1	1		
Stearns, Josiah	1	1	4		
Smith, John, Jr	1	2	2		
Thompson, John	3		4		
Towne, Sarah			3		
Towne, Richard	1		4		
Towne, Thomas	1	4	3		
Towne, Thomas, Jr	1	4	4		
Taylor, William	1		1		
Wellman, Jacob	2		1		
Wellman, Jacob, Jr	1	3	4		
Wilkins, Amos	3	2	5		
Woodard, Eleazar	4	1	5		
Woodard, Ithamar	2	3	3		
Woodard, John	1	3	3		
Whittemore, Amos	3	4	3		
Whittemore, Sarah		2	4		
Stiles, John	1	3	2		
Stiles, Samuel	2		2		
Whittemore, Samuel	1	3	6		
Whittemore, Aaron	1	2	2		
Thompson, Thomas	1		2		
Willson, Abiel	1	2	1		
Whitemarsh, Charles	1		4		
White, Moses	1		5		
Walton, Reuben	1	1	3		
Wilkins, Asa	3		3		
Abbot, Josiah	1	4	1		
Willson, Simeon	1		1		
Freeman, Hampn					
LYNDBOROUGH GORE.					
Holt, John	2		1		
Holt, Joshua	1	2	3		
Batchelder, Joseph	2	1	6		
Blunt, William	1	1	2		
Severance, John	1		1		
Lovejoy, Nathl	1	2	3		
Pevee, Peter	2	2	3		
Fletcher, John	1				

NAME OF HEAD OF FAMILY.	Free white males of 16 years and upward, including heads of families.	Free white males under 16 years.	Free white females, including heads of families.	All other free persons.	Slaves.
MASON TOWN.					
Allen, Abijah	3	3	5		
Adams, John	2	4	4		
Adams, Abel	2	2	2		
Ames, Simon	2	3	3		
Barrett, Joseph	2	2	6		
Batchelder, Jona	1	2	2		
Ball, Joseph	2	2	7		
Blodget, John	2	2	5		
Ball, Eleazer	2	1	5		
Bullard, Joseph	1		1		
Bullard, Silas	2	4	1		
Blood, Ebenr	2		4		
Blood, Thomas	1	3	3		
Cumings, John	1	1	3		
Davis, Zachh	1	2	4		
Blood, Asa	2	1	3		
Dakin, Amos	1	2	5		
Dakin, Sarah	1		4		
Dakin, Timo	2	1	2		
Elliot, William	1	3	4		
Elliot, Andrew	1	2	4		
Flagg, Isaac	1	2	5		
Fisk, Eleazar	1	4	3		
Fay, Jonas	1	4	4		
Holding, Amos	1		6		
Hall, Nathl	3	1	2		
Hosmore, William	2	1	2		
Hodgman, Reuben	3	2	5		
Hodgman, Benja	1		2		
Hodgman, Thomas	1		5		
Wheelock, Timothy	1		2		
Hosmer, Reuben	1	1	1		
Jeffs, John	4	3	2		
Kendall, Reuben	1	3	3		
Kendall, Benja	1	1	4		
Knowlton, Benja	1	3	4		
Knowlton, Henry	1	4	3		
Russel, Joseph	3	1	3		
Lawrence, Richard	1	2	4		
Lawrence, Enos	2		2		
Lawrence, Stephen	2	1	8		
Merriam, Abraham	1	4	3		
Mann, Benja	3	1	6		
Brown, Isaac	1	2	1		
Merriam, Joseph	3	1	5		
Merriam, Ezra	1	1	2		
Parker, Obadiah	4	1	5		
Pike, William	1	2	3		
Russel, Saml	1	1	1		
Robbins, Thomas	1	4	1		
Scripture, Oliver	1	1	7		
Searle, Jona	2	4	5		
Wait, John	1	1	1		
Townshend, Saml	1	2	8		
Willson, David	1	2	2		
Warren, Henchman	1	1	5		
Whipple, Nathl	1	1	5		
Stone, Asa	1	2	5		
Shattuck, Ebenr	1	2	3		
Wheeler, Aaron	2	2	4		
Whiteker, John	2	3	5		
Wheeler, Timothy	2	1	7		
Woods, Saml	2	3	3		
Woods, James	2	3	5		
Woods, Joseph	3	3	5		
Weston, Roger	1	2	2		
Abbot, Joseph	1	2	2		
Barrett, Reuben	2		3		
Barrett, Reuben, Jr	1	6	2		
Barrett, Benja	1	1	4		
Barret, Jesse	1	3	1		
Barret, William	1	1	2		
Barrett, Zacheus	1	4	4		
Barrett, William, Jr	1	2	3		
Blood, Amos	2	1	3		
Brown, David	2	2	4		
Boynton, Jeremiah	1		2		
Chambers, William	2	2	3		
Crane, Benja	1				
Austin, Thomas	1	1	2		
Elliot, John	1	1	2		
Elliot, Josiah	1		2		
Elliot, Oliver	3		1		
Elliot, Elias	2	2	7		
Elliot, Saml	1		2		
Haven, Clerk	3	3	6		
Eaton, Abijah	1	2	2		
Giles, Joseph	2	2	4		
Goodard, John	1		3		
Green, Saml	1	1	1		

NAME OF HEAD OF FAMILY.	Free white males of 16 years and upward, including heads of families.	Free white males under 16 years.	Free white females, including heads of families.	All other free persons.	Slaves.
MASON TOWN—con.					
Herrick, Amos	1		1		
Hall, John	1	4	3		
Elliot, Hannah	1		3		
Kemp, Abel	1	4	3		
Campbell, John	2		2		
Grimes, John	1	2	1		
Lawrence, John	1	1	7		
Miles, Sarah	1		7		
Merriam, Silas	1	2	2		
Merriam, Abraham	1		2		
Fisk, Simon	1	2	3		
Russell, Jason	2	5	2		
Russell, John	2	3	5		
Russel, Robert	1	3	5		
Ross, Andrew	1	1	4		
Robbins, Seth	1	4	3		
Smith, Saml	3	1	2		
Smith, Nathl	3		2		
Smith, Nathl, Jr	1		2		
Shed, William	1	4	3		
Scripture, John	1	1	1		
Swallow, John	3	1	7		
Swallow, John, Jr	1	4	2		
Scripture, James	1	2	7		
Stewart, Jeremiah	2	3	1		
Tarbel, Thomas	2	3	3		
Tarbel, John	1	2	5		
Tarbel, Saml	1	1	3		
Tarbel, Edmund	1		2		
Tarbox, Danl	1		2		
Wheeler, James	1	1	2		
Wheeler, James, Jr	1	5	1		
Williams, Jona	1		4		
Webber, Jotham	1	4	3		
Winchop, John	3		4		
Winchop, Noah	1	1	2		
Willson, Edward, Jr	1		2		
Wetherbee, Jacob	1	1	3		
Wetherington, Elisha	3	2	1		
Wait, John, Jr	1	3	4		
Williams, Nathl	1	1	2		
Wetherbee, David	1		1		
Lawrence, Danl	1	1	3		
Sanders, Joseph	1	1	2		
Sanders, William	2		1		
Levere, Peter	1	3	2		
Farewell, Edward	1	3	2		
Gray, Joseph	1	3	2		
Crossman, James	2		1		
Pratt, John	1				
Dunster, Jason	3		3		
Herrick, Amos	1		1		
Read, Thomas	1		2		
Worer, Danl			1	3	
Parkhurst, William	1	1	7		
MERRIMAC TOWN.					
Bennup, Jacob	1	3	7		
Cumings, Simn	3	2	5		
Danforth, Solo	1	2	3		
Stearns, Zechah	2	1	2		
Fields, Martin	2	2	3		
Chubbuk, Ensign	2	1	4		
Cumings, James	1	1	2		
Tarbel, Cornls	2	1	2		
Nurse, Benja	1	2	3		
Colburne, Jerathl	1	3	1		
Hassel, Jason	1	3	5		
Barret, Jonas	1		1		
Heath, Reuben	1	2	4		
Breed, Abigail			5		
Cumings, Jona	1	1	4		
Chubbuck, Elijah	1		3		
Whitmun, John	1	1	2		
Breed, Nehemiah	1		2		
Chamberlin, Joseph	2		1		
Wilkins, Stephen	2	2	4		
Wilkins, Andrew	1	2	2		
Usher, Robt, Junr	1	1	3		
French, Nicholas	1	3	2		
Fields, Joshua	1	4	2		
Fields, Henry	3		4		1
Combs, John, Jr	1	4	2		
Davis, Gideon	2	4	4		
Hills, Ebenr	2		2		
Hills, Ebenr, Jr	1	1	2		
Hills, Stephen	1	1	5		
Prockter, Reuben	2	1	7		
Peirce, Willard	1		2		

HILLSBOROUGH COUNTY—Continued.

NAME OF HEAD OF FAMILY.	Free white males of 16 years and upward, including heads of families.	Free white males under 16 years.	Free white females, including heads of families.	All other free persons.	Slaves.	NAME OF HEAD OF FAMILY.	Free white males of 16 years and upward, including heads of families.	Free white males under 16 years.	Free white females, including heads of families.	All other free persons.	Slaves.	NAME OF HEAD OF FAMILY.	Free white males of 16 years and upward, including heads of families.	Free white males under 16 years.	Free white females, including heads of families.	All other free persons.	Slaves.
MERRIMAC TOWN—con.						MERRIMAC TOWN—con.						NEW BOSTON TOWN—continued.					
Stearns, Danˡ	3		2			Cowin, Thomas	1		4								
Farewell, Oliver	3	3	5			McClench, Joseph	2	2	5			Smith, Thomas	1	1	1		
Clure, John	1	1	1			Willson, Jonᵃ	1	2	4			Smith, Johnson	1	1	2		
Wheeler, James	2	2	4			Carlton, Tim.	1					Smith, James	1	1	1		
Killecutt, Othnˡ	1	1	1			Cumings, Thomas	2	1	7			Stewart, John	1		1		
Chamberlin, Joseph	1	3	2			Fields, John	1	1	1			Stickney, Samˡ	1	1	3		
Goodwin, Nathˡ	1	1	2			Reterbush, Christopher	1	2	3			Thompson, David	2	1	3		
Wentworth, Rebecca	1		4	4		Davis, Abel	1	1	2			Thompson, John	1	2	1		
Thornton, Matthew	4		3	1		Spaulding, Samˡ	5		2			Thompson, David, Jr	1		2		
Wakefield, John	1	1	4			Spaulding, Samˡ, Jr	1	2	4			Towne, Joseph	4	2	4		
McCluer, William, Jr	1	3	3			Spaulding, Danˡ	3	3	1			Walker, Andrew	2	2	1		
Lund, Stephen	2	2	3			McCluer, William	1	1	5			Walker, Andrew	2	2	2		
Lund, Charity	7	1	4			Wheeler, James	1	2	5			Walker, James	1	1	1		
Ayres, Joseph	3	2	7									Waugh, Margaret		3	1		
Conant, Israel	3	1	3			NEW BOSTON TOWN.						White, William	1	2	5		
Spaulding, Oliver	1	1	2									Whipple, John	4	3	3		
Bodwell, John	2		3			Andrews, Joseph	1	3	2			Willson, Robᵗ	4	4	2		
Gillis, Hugh	1	1	3			Astin, Hezekh	1	1	2			Willson, Samˡ	1	5	4		
Barnes, Thomas	1		1			Beard, Joseph	1	1	2			Woodbury, William	2	1	3		
Barnes, Corneˢ.	1	3	3			Beard, William	2		2			Wilkins, Eliphalet	1	1	2		
Vickery, Thomas	4		2			Betty, William	2	2	4			Abbot, Asa	1				
Barnes, Reuben	1	3	3			Betton, Samˡ	2	1	3			Alexander, Sarah	2		3		
Buxton, Elijah	1	1	2			Blearr, William	4	1	8			Boyd, Robᵗ	2	1	3		
Chamberlin, John	2		4			Brown, Samˡ	2	3	5			Boyd, Samuel	2	1	1		
Roby, Silas	2	3	2			Burns, John	1	3	5			Caldwell, David	1		3		
Stevens, John	1	1	1			Bailey, John	2	1	2			Campbell, William	1		5		
Chamberlin, Thomas	1	1	2			Bennet, Jacob	2	1	2			Cristy, Moses	2	2	1		
McGilvery, John	2	4	3			Bootman, Nathˡ	1	1	4			Cristy, Thomas	1	1	3		
Hay, Thomas	4	2	4			Cochran, John	2	3	7			Cochran, John, Jr	2	4	3		
Toothaker, Roger	1	4	5			Carnes, James	1	3	5			Cochran, Nathˡ	1		2		
McGaw, Jacob	4	4	6			Cochran, Elijah	1	4	4			Cochran, James	2	2	5		
Thomas, Joseph	2	3	3			Clark, William	4		4			Caldwell, James	3	2	4		
Nesmith, Robert	2	1	3			Clark, Ninian	2	5	4	1		Campbell, Robert	3	6	3		
Wallace, William	2	4	3			Clark, Ephraim	2	2	5			Cochran, Thomas	2	1	4		
Scoby, Joseph	1	2	2			Cristy, Jesse	2	3	3			Cochran, Peter	3	4	4		
Jackson, Samˡ	3	2	3			Cristy, Jesse, Jr	2	3	1			Cristy, Margaret	1	1	2		
Vickery, Benjᵃ	1		6			Cromby, James	3	3	2			Dodge, Enoch	2		2		
Bell, James	1		3			Dane, Daniel	3	3	6			Dodge, James	2	3	6		
Vickery, Moses	2		5			Cochran, Jannet	2		3			Dodge, James, 3ᵈ	2	3	7		
Darrah, James	1	5	2			Dickey, Elias	1	3	2			Dodge, Noah	2	4	7		
Fisk, David	1		2			Dodge, Nehemiah	2		4			Dodge, Elisha	2	6	4		
Butterfield, Charles	1	1	4			Dodge, Nehemiah, Jr	1	5	3			Dodge, Benjᵃ	2			1	2
Townsend, Oliver	1	3	1			Dodge, Nathˡ	1	4	3			Dodge, Benjᵃ, Jr	2		5		
Gilmore, James, Jr	1	2	2			Dodge, Simon	2	4	4			Dodge, Gidⁿ	1	1	2		
Gilmore, James	1					Dodge, Soloᵒ	2	2	4			Dodge, Ammi	1	2	3	1	
McKeen, Samˡ	1	2	4			Dodge, William	2	1	4			Dennis, Arthur	1	3	6		
Combs, John	2		3			Dodge, Jacob	1		2			Davis, John	2	3	4		
Combs, James	1	2	3			Dodge, Jacob, Jr	1	4	4			Farefield, Nathˡ	2	6	3		
Roby, Benjᵃ	1	1	3			Donovan, Christian	1		2			Farefield, Matthew	2		6		
Barron, William	1	2	7			Dodge, David	1	1	2			Hooper, Jacob	1	3	3		
George, Thomas	1		1			Dodge, Daniel	2	1	2			Hazeltine, Joseph	1	2	6		
Langer, William	2	1	1			Farson, James	3	1	2			Henderson, David	1	1	2		
Barnes, Robᵗ	1	3	2			Farson, James, Jr	2	3	2			Jones, Joshua	1	2	3		
McConnuk, John	1	3	3			Gragg, James	3	3	4			Jones, Ephraim	3		5		
McConnuk, Samˡ	2	3	2			Gragg, Lesley	2		6			Kelso, William	1	2	5		
Walker, Zach	2	3	6			Gragg, Samˡ	3		2			Kelso, Danˡ	3	7	4		
Whalen, John	1	1	2			Gragg, Alexanʳ	1		1			Kelso, Alexander	1	1	5		
Miller, William	2		1			Gragg, Samˡ, Jr	1	4	3			Kennedy, John	1	2	5		
Pine, Joseph	1	3	2			Griffin, Jonᵃ	1	1	3			Lamson, Joseph	1		4		
Gout, John	1	3	3			Gordon, John	1		8			Leach, Joseph	2	1	5		
Alld, John	2		2			Gove, Jonᵃ	4		3			Leach, Joseph, Jr	1		2		
Alld, John, Jr	1	2	1			Griffin, Thomas	2		2			Moor, Allen	2		1		
Hartshorn, Benjᵃ	2	2	6			Hogg, Abner	1	1	3			Moor, Solomon	1	1	4	4	
Foster, Samˡ	1		2	2		Hogg, Robᵗ	3	1	3			Macmullen, Archᵈ	2	1	2		
Usher, Robᵗ	1	2	3			Hogg, William	1		3			McMullen, Hugh	5	2	1		
West, Enos	4	1	7			How, Aaron	1					McMullen, John	2	3	7		
How, Mark	1	2	2			Henry, John	2	1	3			McMullen, John, Jr	2		1		
Gage, Phineas	1	2	4			Jacks, Martha	2	3	4			McMullen, Danˡ	2		1		
Gage, Moses	2	1	3			Gordan, John	1	3	3			McMullen, James	2	1	3		
Gibson, Samˡ	1	2	3	1		Johnson, William	1	1	5			McMullen, William	2	2	5		
McCalley, Alexandʳ	2	2	7			Langdel, Livermore	2	1	7			McAllaster, Archᵈ	4	1	9		
Barron, Samˡ	1	3	2			Levingston, John	1	1	1			McLaughlin, David	1	2	5		
Parker, Ebenʳ	2	4	3			Levingston, William	2	1	2			McLaughlin, John	5	3	4		
Roby, Oliver	1	1	1			Little, Taylor	1		2			McLaughlin, Eliza	1		2		
Nichols, Samˡ	1		1			Morgan, Josiah	1	1	6			McNeill, William	1	3	4		
Nichols, Joseph	1	1	1			McNeill, Danˡ	1	1	5			Maden, Lemuel	2	5	3		
Nichols, Mary	1		1			McKensey, Joseph	3	2	3			McCollum, Ebenʳ	2	3	3		
Mirrick, Moses	1	2	3			Ober, Jacob	2	5	3			Patterson, Robᵗ, Jr	3	2	5		
Gage, Aaron	1	4	5			Patch, Samˡ	1		1			Patterson, Robᵗ, 3ᵈ	1	3	5		
Trisker, Josiah	1	1	2			Patch, Reuben	1		2			Parrot, John	2	1	5		
Brown, Benjᵃ	1	2	4			Patch, Stephen	1	3	2			Richards, John	1		1		
Dickey, James	1		1			Patterson, William	1		4			Roles, Samˡ	1	2	4		
Hassel, Abel	1		3			Peabody, Isaac	2	3	3			Stevens, Ephraim	1	1	4		
Hutchinson, Soloᵒ	1		1			Perkins, Philemon	2	2	2			Stevens, David	1	2	4		
Hutchinson, Soloᵒ, Jr	1	2	5			Patterson, Robᵗ	3		2			Wells, John	1	6	4		
Arbukle, William	1		1			Read, Zadock	1	1	4			Waters, Samˡ	2		2		
Arbukle, William, Jr	1	1	1			Stinson, David	1	3	4			Willson, James, Jr	2	3	4		
Taylor, Timothy	3	2	4	1		Shepley, Oliver	1	1	3			Willson, James	3	3	3		
Gillis, Jonᵃ	1	2	1			Smith, John	4	3	5			Willson, Alexander	2	3	3		
Hale, Richard	2	2	2			Smith, Samuel	1		3								

HILLSBOROUGH COUNTY—Continued.

NEW BOSTON TOWN—continued.

NAME OF HEAD OF FAMILY.	Free white males of 16 years and upward, including heads of families.	Free white males under 16 years.	Free white females, including heads of families.	All other free persons.	Slaves.
Willson, Thomas	4	1	1	2	
White, Robt	3	2	3		
Warren, Josiah	3	1	7		
Gragg, Mehitabel			2		
Cree, Samuel	1	2	1		
Redington, Daniel	1	1	2		
Curtice, Dudley	1		4		
Vernum, Prescot	1				
Moor, Allen, Jr	3		2		
Abbot, Saml	2	1	1		
Munro, Susanna		1	3		
Abbot, Daniel	1	1	2		
Shed, Nathan	2	5	6		
Kennedy, James	1	1	2		
Putnam, Jacob	2	2	4		

NEW IPSWICH TOWN.

NAME OF HEAD OF FAMILY.	Free white males of 16 years and upward, including heads of families.	Free white males under 16 years.	Free white females, including heads of families.	All other free persons.	Slaves.
Farrar, Stephen	8	6	8	1	
Blanchard, Simon	1	4	5		
Burrows, William	2		5		
Burrows, William, Jr	1	1	1		
Bartlett, Saml	2	1	5		
Brown, Asa	1	3	2		
Benney, John	1	1	2		
Chandler, James	3	2	6		
Chamberlin, Aaron	1	4	5		
Campbell, Robt	3	1	5		
Conant, Zeba	1	3	6		
Champney, John	1	2	4		
Davis, Jona	2	3	5		
Davis, Josiah	2	4	4		
Fletcher, Saml	2	4	3		
Fletcher, Ebenr	2	4	2		
French, James	1	2	3		
Fox, Timo	1		3		
Fox, Timo, Jr	3	3	5		
Faro, Nathl	2	3	5		
Gibs, Benja	1	1	3		
Gowing, John	1		1		
Gowing, John, Jr	1	1	3		
Hildreth, Stephen	1	2	3		
Hildreth, Ephraim	1	1	3		
Hildreth, Hannah		1	3		
Heald, Thomas	1	3	4		
Holden, Saml	3		3		
Hoar, Jotham	2	2	4		
Hodgkins, William	3		3		
Knight, Enos	2	1	4		
Knight, Benja	1	1	1		
Hodgins, Nathl	1	1	1		
Knight, Elijah	1	2	3		
Knight, Ebenr	1	1	5		
Morse, Elijah	1		3		
Kimball, Ezra	3	1	6		
Lee, Jona	1	3	3		
Miles, Abraham	2		3		
Newhall, Onisimus	2	1	4		
Newhall, Elijah	1	1	1		
Parker, Joseph	3	2	5		
Pratt, Phineas	2	2	5		
Preston, James	2	1	4		
Preston, Isaac	2	1	3		
Pratt, John, Jr	1	2	5		
Peirce, Stephen	3	3	5		
Peirce, Benja	1	1	4		
Russel, Ezekiel	1	1	2		
Rumnill, David	3	3	8		
Stone, Joel	1	1	4		
Shea, Saml	1	2	2		
Spear, Saml	2	1	4		
Statton, Nicholas	1	1	3		
Shattuck, Peter	2		3		
Stearns, Joshua	1		2		
Stone, Jonas	1				
Spaulding, Thomas	2		2		
Spafford, Benja	3	1	5		
Shattuck, John	1	1	4		
Taylor, Reuben	2	2	4		
Twiss, Jona	4	4	2		
Taylor, Thaddeus	2	2	4		
Bacon, Retire	1		2		
Tenny, Joseph	2	3	2		
Tucker, Moses	3	1	4		
Whittemore, Saml	2	2	3		
Willson, Jonas	1		1		
Willson, Jonas, Jr	1	2	3		
Wheeler, Jonas	1		1		
Wheeler, Seth	4	1	7		
Walker, Silas	1				
Walker, John	1		4		

NEW IPSWICH TOWN—continued.

NAME OF HEAD OF FAMILY.	Free white males of 16 years and upward, including heads of families.	Free white males under 16 years.	Free white females, including heads of families.	All other free persons.	Slaves.
Walker, Jesse	2		4		
Wheeler, Saml	1				
Warren, Joseph	2	3	5		
Wheeler, Richard	1	6	2		
Wright, Sarah	1		2		
Wilkins, John	1	1	2		
Wilkins, Josiah	1	3	3		
Wheeler, John	1		2		
Wheeler, John, Jr	1	1	3		
Gould, Adam	1		1		
Adams, Stephen	1		2		
Farr, Eunice		1	3		
Robins, Nathan	2		3		
Walker, Nathan	1		2		
Whiting, Mary			2		
Tillick, Lucy			1		
Adams, Ephraim	3	1	3		
Adams, Benja	3	1	3		
Appleton, Isaac	4	3	6		
Briant, Hamma		1	1		
Appleton, Francis	4	1	4		
Ames, Eli	2	1	4		
Adams, Ephraim, Jr	2	2	8		
Atherton, Jona	6	2	4		
Amsden, Jonas	1	1	5		
Barrett, Charles	8	3	6		
Brown, John	4	1	4		
Brown, Josiah	6	4	6		
Brown, Ebenr	2	2	6		
Batcheldor, Joseph	4	1	5		
Batcheldor, Josiah	2	2	3		
Brooks, Solomon	1	3	5		
Batcheldor, Saml	2	2	2		
Blood, David	1	2	5		
Champney, Ebenr	3	2	4		
Cumings, Eleazar	3		3		
Cutter, John	1	1	1		
Carlton, Nathl	3	1	1		
Cleary, William	2	1	3		
Davis, Stephen	3	2	2		
Davis, Silas	2	2	4		
Emerson, John	1	3	4		
Farrar, Timo	3	3	4		
Foster, Danl	3		7		
Fletcher, Thomas	2		2		
Fletcher, Thomas, Jr	1	2	1		
Fletcher, Jonah	2	2	3		
Fletcher, Peter	4	1	3		
Cook, Noah	2	2	3		
Fletcher, Francis	2	3	2		
Gould, Nathl	1	1	1		
Gould, Simeon	2		4		
How, Isaac	2	4	3		
Hills, David	6	3	6		
Hartwell, Ephraim	9	1	8	1	
Heywood, Saml	3	3	2		
Hale, Ephraim	1	3	3		
Hubard, John	1				
Kidder, Rachel			4		
Kidder, Aaron	4	1	5	1	
Mansfield, Daniel	2	4	5		
Mansfield, Ezra	2	3	3		
Meriam, Nathl	2	1	2		
Preston, John	4	5	10	1	
Pritchard, Jereh	5	3	3		
Prentice, Nathl	2	3	3		
Parker, Asa	2				
Prockter, Benja	1		3		
Prockter, Joseph	1	1	2		
Pitts, John	1	1	4		
Pritchard, Benja	1	3	4		
Robinson, David	1	2	4		
Swain, Daniel	1	3	4		
Smith, Abigail		3	7		
Start, George	3	4	5		
Spear, William	2	2	2		
Stickney, Joseph	2	1	2		
Stratton, Danl	2	3	5		
Towne, Ezra	2	4	7		
Towne, Edmund	2	1	3		
Williams, Benja	1	3	6		
Knouton, Benja	3	1	5		
Morse, Elijah	1		2		
Pritchard, John	2		4		
Walton, Josiah	2	1	4		
Walton, Josiah, Jr	1		3		
Wheeler, William	2		4		
Whelock, Joseph	1	2	2		
Whelock, Ithamar	1		1		
Willson, Suply	1	3	4		
Warner, John	3	3	5		

NEW IPSWICH TOWN—continued.

NAME OF HEAD OF FAMILY.	Free white males of 16 years and upward, including heads of families.	Free white males under 16 years.	Free white females, including heads of families.	All other free persons.	Slaves.
Bigelow, Silas	2	6	4		
Briant, Josiah	1	2	2		
Brooks, John	2	4	3		
Breed, Jane	1	1	6		
Breed, Allen	3	2	4		
Barr, James	1	2	3		
Russel, Saml	3		2		
Bacon, Jonas	1	1	3		
Kimball, Martha			4		
Clary, Catharine			5		
Ball, Saml	1	2	2		
Davis, Hannah			2		

NEW LONDON TOWN.

NAME OF HEAD OF FAMILY.	Free white males of 16 years and upward, including heads of families.	Free white males under 16 years.	Free white females, including heads of families.	All other free persons.	Slaves.
Currier, Thomas	1	2	4		
Pike, Thomas	2	2	4		
Jewett, Jedidiah	1	2	1		
Goodwin, Nathl	1	4	4		
Lyon, John	2	1	2		
Sargent, Ebenr	1	4	2		
Sargent, Anthony	2	1	1		
Sargent, Ebenr., Jr	2		1		
Sargent, Peter	1	1	1		
Davis, Josiah	1	1	3		
Herrick, Jona	1	2	1		
Austins, John	1		1		
Austin, John, Jr	1	4	2		
Lamb, James	1	4	2		
Morgan, John	3		2		
Morgan, John, jr	1	5	2		
Gile, Ephraim	1	1	6		
Brinklebank, Saml	2	1	8		
Knolton, Ezekl	1	1	1		
Messer, James	3	1	5		
Messer, Nathl	1	3	2		
Adams, Benja	2	2	3		
Burpee, Thomas	1		1		
Burpee, Thomas, Jr	2	2	6		
Burpee, Asa	1	2	3		
Messer, James H	1	1	3		
Dole, John	1	1	5		
Adams, Solomon	1	1	5		
Adams, Jona	1		2		
Adams, John, Jr	1	1	5		
Adams, John	1		1		
Adams, Moses	1		1		
Brucklebank, James	2	3	4		
Everout, Jona	2	2	4		
Sargent, Peter	3	3	3		
Simonds, Job	2	2	7		
Crickett, Benja	1	2	3		
Hays, Zebedee	1	3	2		
Knolton, Robert	1	1	3		
Colby, Joseph	2	1	2		
Gay, Eliphat	1	3	4		
Everout, Penuel	1	1	4		
Everout, Jeremiah	1		1		
Everout, Levi	1	1	3		
Slack, John	1	1	3		
Woodbury, Benja	1	4	5		
Hunting, Israel	1		1		
Hunting, Ebenr	1	5	3		
Hales, Nathl	1	5	2		
Harvey, Levi	3	3	8		

NOTTINGHAM WEST TOWN.

NAME OF HEAD OF FAMILY.	Free white males of 16 years and upward, including heads of families.	Free white males under 16 years.	Free white females, including heads of families.	All other free persons.	Slaves.
Merrill, Nathl	2		2		
Merrill, Henry	1		2		
Davis, Jacob	1	2	2		
Smith, Page	1	2	7		
Page, Abner	2	1	2		
Richardson, Ebenr	2	1	5		
Melvin, James	1	1	1		
Butler, Gideon	1	1	2		
Charlis, James	1	1	1		
McIntire, Asa	1	2	4		
Hadley, Moses	1	4	3		
Read, Abijah	1	1	3		
Peirce, Nathl	1	1	2		
Marsh, Saml	1		2		
Marsh, Ebenr	1	1	2		
Peirce, Joshua	3		2		
Marshal, Richard	3	1	6		
Hills, Saml	1	1	3		
Hills, Philip	2	4	3		
Hardy, Richard	1	2	4		
Spaulding, Reuben	2		1		
Spaulding, Reuben, Jr	1	2	4		

NOTTINGHAM WEST TOWN—con.

NAME OF HEAD OF FAMILY.	Free white males of 16 years and upward, including heads of families.	Free white males under 16 years.	Free white females, including heads of families.	All other free persons.	Slaves.
Cumings, Eben	2	3	2		
Cross, Peter	2		2		
Cross, Peter, Jr	1		2		
Cumings, Ebenr	2	3	4		
Andrews, James	1				
Peas, William	2		2		
Kenny, Hannah			2		
Andrews, Levi	2		3		
Andrews, Levi, Jr	1		2		
Greeley, Ezekiel	2	1	2	1	
Marshal, Danl	2	1	3		
Marshal, Saml	1	2	1		
Hills, Nathl	3		2		
Hills, William	2	3	2		
Hills, Jereh	3	3	3		
Butterfield, Jona	1	2	3		
Hills, Hannah	1		2		
Hills, Thomas	1	3	5		
Hills, Elisha	2	1	5		
Davis, John	1		1		
Marsh, Thomas	1	1	2		
Tarbel, David	1	4	3		
Marsh, Jona	1	1	1		
Barrett, Simeon	1	2	5		
Barrett, Isaac	1	3	5		
Barrett, Joel	1	5	4		
Glover, David	1	3	2		
Barrett, James	1	1	3		
Barrett, Rebecca	1	2	2		
Marshal, Elijah	1	2	5		
Marshal, Nathl	2	1	6		
Hale, John	1		1		
Smith, Hugh	2		5		
Hale, Thomas	1	1	3		
Hale, Henry, Jr	2		2		
Campbell, David	2	6	6		
Smith, John	2	1	5		
Lawrence, David	2	2	5		
Lawrence, Jona	1	1	3		
Marshall, Philip	1	2	1		
Page, Isaac	1	4	3		
Barrett, Moses	2		4		
Graham, William	2	4	3		
Eastman, Eleaner		1	2		
Richey, James	1		3		
Burroughs, Benja	2	3	5		
Robinson, Andrew	1	1	3		
Robinson, Sim	2	3	3		
Peabody, David	1		4		
Peabody, David, Jr	1	3	1		
Kidder, Benja	2	1	2		
Hobs, Joseph	2	1	4		
Merrill, Joshua	1	2	1		
Robinson, Peter	1	3	3		
Robinson, John	2	1	2		
Cutler, Thomas	1	1	3		
Sargent, Reuben	1	1	1		
Greele, Zacheus	1	5	4		
Tarbox, Mehitabel	1	2	4		
Tarbox, Sarah	1		6		
Marshal, John	1	4	2		
Marshal, Lot	1	1	2		
Senter, Thomas	1	1	9		
Burrows, Joseph	2		3		
Burrows, William	1	1	4		
Greele, Moses	2		3		
Andrews, Joel	1		3		
Steel, Joseph	1	1	4		
Wason, Saml	2	1	4		
Davis, Asa	2	1	3		
Caldwell, Joseph	1	2	3		
Caldwell, James	1	2	6		
Wason, James	1		1		
Cumings, David	2	1	4		
Hamlet, Thomas	1	1	4		
Stewart, Robert	2	3	2		
Ford, James	4	1	5		
Gould, Joseph	1	1	2		
Gould, Jona	1	1	5		
Sevey, Andrew	2	1	2		
Merrill, John	1	1			
Merrill, Theo	2		2		
Johnson, Moses	4	1	6		
Merrill, Isaac	1	3	3		
Burns, George	2	3	5		
Moody, Friend	1	1	2		
French, Saml	1	1	3		
Hardy, Benja	1	1	4		
Colburn, Zacheus	2		2		
Chase, Henry	2		2		
Watkins, Abner	2	1	4		

NOTTINGHAM WEST TOWN—con.

NAME OF HEAD OF FAMILY.	Free white males of 16 years and upward, including heads of families.	Free white males under 16 years.	Free white females, including heads of families.	All other free persons.	Slaves.
Hardy, Isaac	1	2	4		
Butler, John	1		1		
Butler, John, Jr	1	1	4		
Caldwell, John	3	2	3		
Heywood, Sl. Smith	2		2		
Burns, William	2	3	4		
Pollard, Thomas	1	1	3		
Hendy, Jona	1	2	5		
Willson, Joseph B	2	1	4		
Brown, Robertson	1		1		
Burbank, Saml	2		2		
Burbank, Jona	1	1	1		
Pollard, John	2	4	3		
Marshal, Benja	1		2		
Chase, Stephen	3		2		
Colburn, Isaac	1		5		
Merrill, Benja	1	2	1		
Winn, Joseph	1		1		
Winn, Joseph, Jr	1	2	2		
Underwood, Phineus	1	6	2		
Chase, Joshua	1	3	5		
Pollard, Asa	2	1	1		
Chase, Benja	1	1	2		
Pollard, Benja	3	1	3		
Blodget, Beniah	1		2		
Blodget, Jerem	1		2		
Blodget, Asa	1	3	3		
Blodget, Joseph	1		2		
Blodget, Joseph, Jr	1	1	3		
Greele, Joseph	1	4	4		
Tenny, Edward	2	1	4		
Blodget, Jona	1	3	3		
Blodget, Jabez	1		3		
Pollard, Tim	2	1	3		
Winn, Nathan	1	1	2		
Atwood, John	1	1	2		
Marshal, Henry	1	4	1		
Pemberton, James	1		2		
Brown, Saml	1		1		
Kelly, Joseph	1	2	3		
Cutter, Richard	2	1	2		
Gibson, William	1	1	3		
Burrows, George	1		1		
Smith, Tim	2	2	3		
Hadley, Parrett	1	1	3		
Hadley, Eliph	1		1		
Hadley, Eliphalet, Jr	1	1	3		
Hadley, Stephen	2	4	4		
Douglas, Robert	1	1	1		
Hadley, Enos	1	1	2		
Caldwell, Alexander	1	1	5		
Farmer, Jonas	1	1	2		
Willson, Thomas	1	2	4		
Chase, John	1		3		
Caldwell, Saml	1	3	3		
Searles, Elnath	3		4		
Tenny, Jona	1	2	3		
Duty, Mark	1	1	2		
Huey, Mansfield	1				
Glover, Robt	2	2	6		
Hardy, Jonas	1	1	4		
Blodgett, Phin. W	1		3		
Gould, Isaac	2	1	3		
Wiman, Seth	2		3		
Hazeltine, John	1		1		
Ayres, John	1		1		
Smith, Saml, Jr	1		2		
Smith, Saml	3	1	4		
Smith, Thomas	3	2	6		
Bancroft, Caleb	1	2	1		
Morse, Benja	1	2	1		
Bradley, Joseph	1	1	2		
Marsh, John	1	2	3		
Duty, Mary				5	
Braddish, Ceasar					6

PETERBOROUGH TOWN.

NAME OF HEAD OF FAMILY.	Free white males of 16 years and upward, including heads of families.	Free white males under 16 years.	Free white females, including heads of families.	All other free persons.	Slaves.
Evens, Asa	3	3	4		
Gray, Matthew	1	2	6		
Evens, Heman	1	1	2		
Evens, Nathl	1	1	2		
Fergusson, Henry	2	2	5		
Fields, John	1	4	2		
Felsh, Oliver	2		2		
Foster, Isaac	1	1	3		
Finch, Richard	1	1	4		
Gragg, John	3		4		
Gragg, John, Jr	2		1		
Gragg, Saml	2	2	6		
Gragg, Hugh	1	1	1		

PETERBOROUGH TOWN—continued.

NAME OF HEAD OF FAMILY.	Free white males of 16 years and upward, including heads of families.	Free white males under 16 years.	Free white females, including heads of families.	All other free persons.	Slaves.
Gragg, Kelso	5	2	4		
Gragg, Robt	1	2	3		
Gray, John	1	1	3		
Gordon, Saml	3	3	7		
Houston, Saml	1	3	5		
How, Joel	1	3	2		
How, Saml	1	1	4		
Holt, Nehemiah	1	1	1		
Hockley, James	1	3	3		
Hogg, Simson	1	1	3		
Hovey, David	1		1		
Hovey, Richard	1				
Holmes, Abraham	3	6	4		
Haggett, Abner	1	1			
Holt, Israel	1		2		
Hammell, Joseph	1	1	3		
Holt, Saml	1		2		
Hunt, Eli	2	1	3		
Holms, Nathl	3	2	2		
Little, Thomas	2	1	1		
McAllaster, Randell	1		2		
Miller, James	3	2	4		
Miller, William	3	2	2		
Miller, Saml	1	2	6		
Moor, Abraham	1	2	2		
Moor, John	1		2		
McCoy, Christopher	2		3		
Holt, Joshua	3		2		
Holten, James	1		4		
Mullican, William	1	4	3		
McCoy, William	1		5		
Morrison, Samuel	1	1	3		
Miller, Samuel, Jr	1	2	3		
Mitchel, Samuel	1	2	3		
Morrison, John	2	2	2		
Moor, William	3	2	7		
Morrison, Robt	3	3	3		
Morrison, Thomas	3	1	5		
Morrison, Sarah	1		4		
Mitchel, Saml, Jr	1	1	3		
Mitchel, John	1	3	4		
Mitchel, Benja	1	4	2		
Moor, Saml	2	1	2	1	
Moor, Saml, Jr	1	2	4	1	
Mitchel, Isaac	2	2	3		
McCloud, Thomas	3	5	6		
Nay, William	4	2	3		
Nay, Sarah	2		4		
Nay, James	3	5	3		
Parker, Sarah	1		5		
Osgood, Kendal	1	1	3		
Powers, William	1	3	6		
Patterson, Isaac	1		2		
Porter, Francis	1	3	4		
Parker, Giddeon	1	1	2		
Porter, James	1	4	4		
White, John	1	2	4		
Pearce, Nathl	1		6		
Richey, Robt	1				
Richardson, Abijah	1	1	2		
Robertson, Amos	1	1	1		
Richey, James	2	3	3		
Miller, Saml	1		4		
Robbe, William	1	1	5		
Robbe, Alexanr	4	3	2	1	
Swan, John	1	2	4		
Spafford, Amos	1	1	1		
Swan, William	2	3	4		
Swan, Robt	1	2	3		
Swan, Jeremiah	1	1	1		
Steele, Thomas	1	1	3		
Smiley, David	1	1	5		
Smith, John	3		7		
Smith, Saml	3		1		
Scott, John	1		3		
Scott, William, Jr	1	3	2		
Shattuck, Ezekiel	1	1	3		
Stewart, Charles	3	3	8		
Scott, John	1	1	3		
Spear, Saml	1				
Spring, Chiles	3		1		
Steele, David	3	1	4		
Smith, John, Jr	2		1		
Smith, Ephraim	1	2	4		
Smith, Ephraim, Jr	1		2		
Stewart, Thomas	2	2	4		
Smith, William	6		3	1	
Smith, James	2	1	3		
Smith, Robt	2	2	3		
Smith, Martha			1	2	
Todd, John	1		1		

HILLSBOROUGH COUNTY—Continued.

NAME OF HEAD OF FAMILY.	Free white males of 16 years and upward, including heads of families.	Free white males under 16 years.	Free white females, including heads of families.	All other free persons.	Slaves.
PETERBOROUGH TOWN—continued.					
Taylor, Isaiah	3	1	2		
Templeton, William	1	2	2		
Templeton, Matthew	2	1	4		
Stone, David	1	3	1		
Thayer, Barthl	2	1	2		
Thayer, Christor	2	3	2		
Taylor, Aaron	1	1	2		
Turner, Thomas	5		4		
Treadwell, Saml	1	2	5		
Taggart, Saml	1		2		
Turner, Thomas	5		4		
White, William	1	2	4		
White, William, Jr	1	1	5		
Woodcock, John	2	1	2		
Willson, Robt	3	2	5		
Warren, Danl	2	4	3		
Whittemore, Nathl	1	4	1		
White, John, 3d	1		2		
White, John, Jr	1	4	4		
White, Charles	1	5	5		
Whittemore, Paul	1	1	2		
Willson, Saml	1	5	3		
Wiley, Saml	1	1	4		
White, David	1	1	2		
White, Thomas	1		2		
White, Partrick	2	2	3		
White, John, 4th	1	2	4		
Young, John	1	2	4		
Taylor, Abraham	1	2	3		
Waight, Nathl	1	1	1		
Pevey, Thomas	1	2	3		
Pevey, Peter	1	1	3		
RABY TOWN.					
Shannon, R. Cutts	2	2	6		
Chadwick, Benja	1	2	4		
Farnsworth, Samson, 3d	3		3		
Hall, William, Jr	1		1		
McDonald, Randel	2	2	5		
Sever, Robert	1	3	3		
Dukey, James	1	3	2		
Brown, Clerk	2		5		
Douglas, Saml	1	2	2		
Emery, Ebenr	3	1	2		
Gowing, Ezekiel	1		2		
Graham, William	1	1	3		
Gilson, Ebenr	3	1	4		
Gilson, Eleazar	1	3	3		
Hall, William	1	2	1		
Lesley, Jonas	1	3	4		
McDonald, James	1		3		
Procktor, Ezekiel	2		2		
Parker, Abijah	1	1	2		
Perkins, Jesse	1	2	1		
Senter, Simeon	1	2	3		
Shattuck, Isaac	2		2		
Sartell, Ephraim	3	1	3		
Sawyer, Jona	1	1	3		
Wheeler, Abiezer	1	2	1		
Wetherbee, Oliver	1	1	1		
Austin, Phineas	1	4	2		
Austin, Bulah	1		6		
Brooks, Benja	1	1	4		
Bennet, Phineas	1	3	4		
Campbell, James	5	1	3		
Davidson, David	1	1	2		
Emerson, John	1	1	1		
Farley, Benja	2	3	5		
Blood, Reuben	1		2		
Green, Saml	1	2	3		
Grace, Benja	1	2	2		
Hdgman, Joseph	2	1	1		
Hodgman, Abel	1		2		
Hodgman, Abraham	1	2	1		
Lawrence, Ezekiel	1	2	2		
McIntosh, Alexander	3		4		
McIntosh, James	2		3		
McIntosh, Archibald	1	1	5		
Patten, Nathl	1	1	1		
Patten, Nathl., Jr	1	3	2		
Russel, George	1		3		
Russel, Saml	2	1	3		
Russel, Andrew	1	1	3		
Spaulding, Danl	1	1	4		
Smith, Joshua	1	3	2		
Smith, Joshua, Jr	1	3	2		
Tucker, Swallow	3	1	3		
Sanders, Isaac	1	3	3		
Kirk, Charles	1	3	3		
Wetherbee, Timothy	1	3	4		

NAME OF HEAD OF FAMILY.	Free white males of 16 years and upward, including heads of families.	Free white males under 16 years.	Free white females, including heads of families.	All other free persons.	Slaves.
RABY TOWN—con.					
Turrel, William	1	2	2		
Wood, John	1	2	1		
Emery, Ebenr	2	2	2		
Boston, Philip				3	
SALISBURY TOWN.					
Batchelder, Benja	1		1		
Bohonon, Jacob	1		2		
Baker, Benja	2	3	3		
Bean, Joseph	3	2	4		
Bohonon, Andrew, Jr	3	2	3		
Bean, Jeremiah	2		2		
Bowen, John	2	4	4		
Blasdell, Philip	1	3	1		
Bailey, George	1	1	2		
Bailey, John	1		1		
Barker, Robert	1		3		
Bartlett, Joseph	1	5	3		
Bean, John	1	2	4		
Blasdell, Isaac	1	2	4		
Bean, Betty		1	2		
Brucklebank, Danl	1	5	2		
Bean, Saml	1	2	6		
Bean, Phineas	2	4	4		
Bean, Sinclear	1	1	2		
Bean, Benaiah	1	1	7		
Bohonon, Ananiah	1	5	2		
Bean, Nathl	1	1	2		
Busswell, Edward	2	4	2		
Clefford, Benja	1		1		
Clay, James	3	3	4		
Clay, William	1				
Colby, Enoch	1	2	1		
Collins, Charles	1		4		
Cushing, Caleb	1	1	2		
Colby, Philip	3	1	5		
Collins, John	3	3	4		
Cross, Stephen	2	6	4		
Chellis, Thomas	1	4	3		
Calf, William	2	3	3		
Clefford, Richard	1	1	2		
Calf, William, Jr	2	1	3		
Colby, Ephraim	2	6	2		
Cram, Jona	2	3	2		
Austin, Saml	1		3		
Barker, Peter	1	1	1		
Bohonon, John	1		2		
Bohonon, Andrew	1		1		
Calf, Joseph	3	1	6		
Clement, John	1	3	5		
Chase, Enoch	2		4		
Chase, Thomas	1	1	1		
Chase, Bala	1		1		
Clement, Moses	1	1	1		
Couch, John	1	5	4		
Chellis, John	1	4	5		
Chellis, Enos	1		3		
Chilley, Moses	1	1	2		
Clefford, Edward	1	1	3		
Danforth, Jona	1	2	3		
Danforth, Benja	1	4	1		
Eastman, Joel	2		2		
Eastman, Edward	3	1	3		
Eastman, Benja	2	1	1		
Evens, Edward	2	2	4		
Eaton, Levi	1	1	3		
Elkins, Abiel	2	1	4		
Eaton, Samuel	1	1	5		
Eastman, Peter	1	3	4		
Elkins, Saml	2	4	4		
Elkins, Jeremiah	1	1	1		
Eastman, William	3		3		
Fellows, Danl	2		6		
French, Joseph	4	3	5		
Fifield, John	1	1	3		
Fifield, Winthrop	1	2	1		
Fellows, Richard	1	1	1		
Fellows, Moses	1	5	1		
Fellows, John	1	1	3		
Fellows, John, Jr	1	1	1		
Foster, Richard	1	3	2		
Foster, Hezekiah	1	1	2		
Fifield, Obediah	1	2	5		
Fifield, David	1		3		
Fifield, Benja	1	4	2		
Fifield, Josiah	1		3		
Fifield, Edward	2	3	6		
Fifield, Joseph	3	3	5		
Fifield, Jona	3	4	3		
Foster, Jona	1	2	3		
Flanders, Ezra	3	3	4		

NAME OF HEAD OF FAMILY.	Free white males of 16 years and upward, including heads of families.	Free white males under 16 years.	Free white females, including heads of families.	All other free persons.	Slaves.
SALISBURY TOWN—con.					
Fifield, Abner	1	2	3		
Flanders, Jacob	1	3	4		
Farnum, John	2	6	3		
Fifield, Sherburn	1	1	3		
Frazer, Benja	1	1	5		
Fowler, Robt	1	3	2		
Greele, Benja	1		1		
Gale, John	4	2	7		
Gilman, Danl	1	4	3		
Greele, Richard	1	1	4		
Gale, James	1	4	1		
Greele, Shubal	2	4	6		
Greeleaf, Stephen	2		3		
Graves, Israel	1	4	3		
George, Ezrea	1	3	2		
George, Levi	1				
Garland, Moses	1	3	6		
Greele, Matthew	1	4	1		
Greenough, Richard	1	5	4		
Greele, Benja, Jr	1	4	4		
Gillman, John	1	1	2		
Garland, Jacob	3	3	6		
Huntoon, Danl	1	2	3		
Huntoon, Benja	4		3		
Howard, Benja	1	2	4		
Heath, Nehemiah	3		3		
White, John	2		3		
Heath, Job	2	2	3		
Hall, David	2	3	4		
Huntoon, Danl, Jr	1	1	1		
Huntoon, Phineas	1	1	1		
Huntoon, Jona	1		1		
Judkins, Obadiah	1		3		
Judkins, Saml	3	3	3		
Judkins, Leonard	4	2	1		
Judkins, Caleb	2	2	4		
Johnson, Ebenr	2	1	4		
Razer, William	1	3	4		
Samson, John	2		4		
Lowell, Joseph	1	2	2		
Lovrin, Saml	1	4	2		
Lowell, Danl	1	2	2		
Lowell, James	3		1		
Lowell, Nehemiah	1	1	2		
Lovekin, Abigail	1		3		
Morril, Abel	2	1	3		
Mason, Joseph	2	3	1		
Mussey, John	1		1		
Meloon, Nathl	1	2	6		
Meloon, Joseph	2	1	3		
Morse, Moses	1	2	1		2
Mason, John	1	1	3		
Newton, William	2		6		
Norris, John	2	1	2		
Norris, Saml	1	1	2		
Osburn, William	1	3	1		
Page, Onesophus	3	4	5		
Pettingill, Joseph	3	1	4		
Pingry, Aquilla	2		4		
Pettingill, Carlton	2	1	1		
Patterson, Williot	3	2	5		
Parin, Thomas	2		2		
Parin, Stephen	1		1		
Pillsbry, Saml	1	2	5		
Pettingill, David	1	2	5		
Parker, Danl	1	2	3		
Pettingill, Benja	3	1	3		
Pettingill, Amos, Jr	1	1	3		
Pettingill, Benja, Jr	1	3	3		
Pettingill, Benja, 3d	1	1	1		
Quimby, Ebenr	1	2	5		
Quimby, Trustrim	2	2	4		
Quimby, Joseph	1		1		
Richardson, Saml	1	2	1		
Reddington, Thomas	1				
Runlett, Theoph	1	1	3		
Roberts, Jeremiah	1	3	3		
Scrivner, John	1		3		
Stevens, Hubbard	1		3		
Scrivner, Saml	3	3	5		
Sawyer, Stephen	4	1	3		
Sawyer, Edward	1		1		
Sanburn, John	1		2		
Severance, William	1	2	2		
Sweet, John	3	2	7		
Sanborn, Benja	3		3		
Smith, Sarah	3	3	5		
Smith, John	1	6	1		
Scrivner, Edds	2	6	2		
Scrivner, Edward	1	3	4		
Scrivner, Edward, Jr	2	2	5		
Sanborn, Winthrop	2		3		

NAME OF HEAD OF FAMILY.	Free white males of 16 years and upward, including heads of families.	Free white males under 16 years.	Free white females, including heads of families.	All other free persons.	Slaves.
SALISBURY TOWN—con.					
Sallaway, William	1	1	3		
Sweet, Joseph	2		1		
Stevens, Cutting	1	1	9		
Stevens, Danl	1	3	3		
Stevens, Isaac	1		1		
Sawyer, Moses	2	2	4		
Scrivner, Benja	2	2	3		
Severance, Peter	1	2	6		
Sanborn, Abraham	1	2	3		
Severance, Joseph	2	6	3		
Smith, Stephen	2		1		
Searle, Jona	2	3	5		
Tandy, Abel	1	1	1		
Tandy, Saml	1	1	3		
Trew, Jacob	2	3	4		
Thompson, Benja	1		3		
Trew, Reuben	3	1	4		
Tucker, Ebenr	2	4	4		
Tucker, Jacob	1	3	3		
Trew, Reuben, Jr	2		2		
Sweet, Peter	1		2		
Tucker, Nathl	2	1	3		
Watson, Abijah	1	1	4		
Watson, Caleb	1	3	2		
Wadley, Benja	2		3		
Webster, Humphrey	1	2	3		
Woodman, Benja	1	3	2		
Webster, Jeremiah	1	4	3		
Webster, John	3	2	7		
Webster, Stephen	2	3	6		
Wilder, Luke	3		2		
Webster, Esther	1	3	5		
Webster, Israel	1	2	4		
Webster, Joseph	1	1	3		
Whittemore, Peter	1	3	3		
Webster, John	1				
West, Edward	2	2	1		
Ginerson, John	2		4		
SHARON TOWN.					
Taggart, John	3	1	5		
Hennary, John	2		5		
Densmore, Thomas	1	2	1		
Piper, Thomas	1		2		
Lays, Reuben	1	3	4		
Templeton, Matthew	2	2	3		
Atwood, Joshua	2		2		
Spafford, Abijah	1	2	3		
Brown, John	1	3	5		
Law, James	2	1	2		
Barrett, Nathl	1	1	1		
Gragg, Saml	3	2	5		
Swan, John	2	2	5		
McCoy, Gilbert	2	2	3		
Auborn, William	1	2	2		
Bamer, Jona	3		2		
Nay, Robert	1		4		
Sawyer, Josiah	3	3	5		
Miller, Joseph	1	2	3		
Perry, James	2		1		
Taggart, John, Jr	1	2	2		
Cumings, Reuben	1	5	5		
Cumings, Mary			3		
Conn, George	1	1	1		
Moor, David	3	1	2		
Moor, James	1		5		
Andrews, Jereh	1		2		
Briant, Edward	1		2		
Carlton, Moses	2	2	3		
Ames, David	1	1	2		
Ames, Walter	1		1		
Mullian, James	2	4	2		
Clark, James	1		2		
McAlaster, John	2	1	2		
Amsdel, Abraham	2	2	5		
Smith, Edward	3		7		
Mullican, Saml	1	3	1		
Bevenstock, John	1	1	3		
Parkman, Ezekiel	1	2	3		
Adams, Joel	1	2	4		
Melven, Ethan	1		1		
Chamberlin, Nathl	1	2	1		
Mace, Joseph	1	1	3		
Taggart, John, 3d	2	3	3		
Taggart, William	1	2	1		
SOCIETY LAND TOWN.					
Colby, John	1	2	2		
Straw, Danl	1	3	2		
Fitch, John	1	2	3		
Gibson, Matthew	1	2	4		
Puffer, Matthias	2	2	2		

NAME OF HEAD OF FAMILY.	Free white males of 16 years and upward, including heads of families.	Free white males under 16 years.	Free white females, including heads of families.	All other free persons.	Slaves.
SOCIETY LAND TOWN—continued.					
Dodge, Giddeon	1	2	2		
Hoyt, Jona	1	1	1		
Putnam, Joseph	2	2	7		
Killum, Benja	2		2		
Huntington, Joseph	1	3	4		
Feser, Moses	1		3		
Nutting, Ezekiel	1	1	3		
Bailey, James	2				
Eaton, Joseph	1	2	3		
Butterfield, Saml	1	4	1		
Rogers, Robt	3	8	3		
Parker, Alexander	5	1	5		
Hacy, Henry	3	3	4		
Willson, William	1	2	3		
Farmer, Saml	1		3		
Dutton, John	1	2	4		
Hoyt, Jona	1	1	1		
Dustin, Zachariah	1	1	3		
Willson, Thomas	1	1	3		
Johnson, John	1	3	3		
Alexander, Robert	1		1		
Ramsey, James	1	3	3		
Edwards, Thomas	1		1		
McMaster, John	1	2	3		
Holt, Oliver	1		1		
Holt, John	1		2		
Waugh, John	2	1	5		
Herrick, Pram	1	1	2		
Ramsey, John	3		4		
Weeks, Saml	2	2	1		
Codworth, Timothy	2	3	3		
Pollard, Benja	3	2	7		
Ramsey, William	1	2	2		
Farrington, Ebenr	2	2	2		
Cavender, Charles	1	2	4		
Chase, John	1		2		
Atchason, Thomas	1	3	3		
Robertson, Douglas	2	4	3		
Darrah, William	1		1		
McCray, William	1	2	2		
Gills, John	1		3		
Hirkinson, Joseph	1	1	2		
Putnam, Joseph, Jr	1	1	2		
Corton, Ebenr	3	1	3		
Gould, Stephen	1	3	3		
Lund, Jesse	1		1		
Corton, Ebenr, Jr	2		3		
Codworth, Timothy	1		2		
Codworth, Saml	1	2	2		
Dustin, John	2	2	4		
Dunsmore, Robt	2	2	5		
Armer, Jane	2		3		
SUTTON TOWN.					
Ray, Reuben	1	2	1		
Harvey, Matthew	2	4	3		
Kezer, Ebenr	1		1		
Eaton, David	3		4		
Hutchinson, William	1	1	2		
Woodard, Eliphalet	1	3	3		
Woodard, Stephen	1	3	2		
Nichols, Josiah	1	2	1		
Sagar, Caleb	1	1	5		
Dustin, Peter	1		1		
King, John	1	1	2		
Bean, William	2	2	3		
Hills, Moses	1	2	4		
Merrill, Nathl	1	1	2		
Hutchinson, James	1	2	3		
King, James	2	2	3		
Pressey, William	1	1	4		
Pressey, Amos	1	1	1		
Nelson, Asa	1	1	5		
Nelson, Philip	1	2	3		
Presley, Abraham	2	1	6		
Sargent, Philip	1	2	1		
Quimby, Moses	2		5		
Nelson, Jona	1		1		
Bean, Samuel	2	4	4		
Gile, Ephraim	1	1	1		
Gile, David	1		2		
Davis, Jona	3	1	6		
Stevens, Daniel	1	1	1		
Emery, Danl	1		1		
Fellows, Jesse	1	1	1		
Wadley, Benja	1	4	4		
Wadley, Thomas	1	2	2		
Keezer, Simon	3	6	8		
Peasley, John	1		2		
Davis, Jacob	1		3		
Hildreth, Ephraim	1	1	2		

NAME OF HEAD OF FAMILY.	Free white males of 16 years and upward, including heads of families.	Free white males under 16 years.	Free white females, including heads of families.	All other free persons.	Slaves.
SUTTON TOWN—con.					
Fowler, Benja	1		2		
Whiteker, Francis	2		2		
Messer, Danl	5	1	6		
Gile, Reuben	1	1	2		
Parker, Hezekiah	5	1	6		
Walker, Thomas	2		2		
Marsten, Jacob	1	2	4		
Flanders, Ezekl	1	1	6		
Kimball, John	1	2	2		
Nelson, Stephen	1	4	6		
Page, Jona	1		1		
Johnson, Jona	1	1	2		
Urine, Joseph	1	2	3		
Crosby, Ebenr	1		3		
Little, Lot	1		2		
Jones, Ezra	2	2	3		
Roby, Ichabod	1	2	2		
Peasley, Peter	1	2	2		
Kimball, Caleb	3	1	7		
Colburn, Jona	2		3		
Kendrick, Dudley	3	1	3		
Rowell, Jona	3	1	2		
Rowell, Thomas	1		2		
Chase, Abner	1	2	2		
Wheeler, Plumr	1	2	4		
Williams, Benja	1		1		
Roby, Jona	1	4	3		
Scales, William	1		4		
Stevens, Phineas	1	3	5		
Cheene, Nathl	1	3	3		
Hastings, Philemon	1	1	1		
Johnson, Joseph	1	4	2		
Russel, Silas	1	2	4		
Roby, Saml	2		1		
Littlehale, Ezra	1	1	4		
Peasley, Saml	2	3	5		
Andrews, Saml	2	2	5		
Colburn, Leonard	1		5		
Wadley, Joseph	1	5	3		
Peasley, Isaac	1	2	2		
Philbrick, Benja	2	2	4		
Chase, John	2				
Andrews, Danl	2		1		
Hoyt, Ephraim	1		2		
Davis, Jacob, Jr	1	1	3		
Davis, John	1		2		
Davis, Jesse	1		2		
Wadley, Moses	1				
Bean, Cornelius	2	1	4		
Ambrus, Saml	1	3	5		
Wills, Benja	4		7		
Downing, John	1	1	2		
Como, Francis	1	3	3		
TEMPLE TOWN.					
Miles, Noah	2	1	3		
Averil, Jona	4	1	2		
Adams, Levi	1	2	2		
Austin, Timothy	2	2	2		
Blood, Francis	4	2	2		
Bancroft, Caleb	1		3		
Brown, Ephraim	2	2	5		
Burnap, John	4	1	2		
Burnap, Saml	1	1	5		
Ball, Nathl	1		3		
Ball, Nathl, Junr	1	5	1		
Ball, John	1	1	4		
Boynton, Elias	2	3	3		
Brown, Jonas	1	3	3		
Craggin, John	3	1	2		
Craggin, Benja	2	2	2		
Craggin, Francis	3	4	3		
Cutter, Benja	2	2	7		
Cumings, Archelaus	2	2	6		
Colburn, Elias	1	2	5		
Conant, Ephraim	1	7	2		
Chamberlin, Asa	1	1	2		
Densmore, Ephraim	1		2		
Densmore, Zebh	1	3	3		
Drury, William	1	4	5		
Drury, Garshom	2	1	3		
Drury, Ebenr	2	2	6		
Durkee, Silas	2	2	2		
Emery, Zachh	1	2	5		
Everout, John	3	4	2		
Edward, Ebenr	3	2	5		
Foster, Hannah	1	1	6		
Foster, Joshua	1		4		
Fletcher, Robt	2	2	4		
Felt, Aaron	1	6	4		
Felt, Peter	2	2	5		

HILLSBOROUGH COUNTY—Continued.

NAME OF HEAD OF FAMILY.	Free white males of 16 years and upward, including heads of families.	Free white males under 16 years.	Free white females, including heads of families.	All other free persons.	Slaves.	NAME OF HEAD OF FAMILY.	Free white males of 16 years and upward, including heads of families.	Free white males under 16 years.	Free white females, including heads of families.	All other free persons.	Slaves.	NAME OF HEAD OF FAMILY.	Free white males of 16 years and upward, including heads of families.	Free white males under 16 years.	Free white females, including heads of families.	All other free persons.	Slaves.
TEMPLE TOWN—con.						WARNER TOWN—con.						WARNER TOWN—con.					
Farrar, Oliver	3	1	2			Bartlett, Simᵒ	1		2			Pettee, Danˡ	1		3		
Farrar, Ephraim	1	2	1			Barnard, Thomas	1	1	4			Person, John	1	3	3		
Butterfield, Samˡ	1		2			Badger, Stephen	2		3			Person, Samˡ	2	2	5		
Brown, John	1	1	1			Bagley, Ebenʳ	1	2	2			Pressey, Pasky	2		4		
Farrar, Charles	1	1	1			Bagley, Peter	1	2	3			Pressey, James	1		3		
Fuller, Elias	1		2			Burnap, Joseph	1	1	1			Peabody, Jedidiah	2	1	2		
Fuller, David	1	2	4			Currier, Joseph	2	3	6			Putney, Asa	1	2	2		
Fick, Jonah	2	2	3			Currier, John	2	2	5			Peters, John	2	1	3		
Fletcher, Samˡ	1	1	2			Currier, Danˡ	1	4	5			Perker, Daniel	2	1	3		
Goodale, Ezekiel	3	3	2			Currier, Abraham	1		2			Ring, William	1	3	4		
Gould, Abijah	1	2	1			Colby, Roger	3	1	3			Rand, Israel	1		3		
Griffin, Sarah	1		5			Colby, Moses	1	3	2			Richardson, Stephen	1		1		
Howard, Samˡ	4	2	3			Colby, Elliot	2	3	4			Ordway, Bradshaw	1	3	6		
Holt, Samˡ	2	3	3			Colby, Ezekiel	1					Sawyer, Joseph	3	1	6		
Holt, Abiel	1	3	4			Colby, Stephen	1	1	3			Sawyer, Edmund	2		2		
Hale, Ephraim	2	1	5			Colby, John	1		3			Smith, Jonᵃ	2		3		
Hale, Peter	1	1	4			Colby, Nathˡ	1		2			Straw, Jonᵃ	2	1	3		
Hale, Joseph	1	3	1			Colby, Levi	1	1	4			Straw, Richard	2	4	4		
Hale, Danˡ	2	1	4			Colby, Hezekiah	1	3	2			Sargent, Benjᵃ	3	5	5		
Hale, Joseph, Jr	1		2			Colby, Jonˡ	1	2	3			Sargent, Joseph	1	6	1		
Hale, Peter, Jr	1	3	1			Chase, Isaac	1		2			Sargent, Abner	3	3	4		
Jewett, Ezekiel	2	1	3			Clement, Moses	4	1	4			Sargent, Ebenʳ	1	1	3		
Jewett, Nathˡ	2	2	1			Clark, Moses	3	2	6			Stevens, Moses	1	2	3		
Kidder, Joseph	2		3			Call, Moses	2	1	5			Stevens, Jonᵃ	2	2	5		
Kimball, Isaac, Jr	2	1	1			Clough, Reuben	1	3	4			Samburn, William	1		3		
Kimball, Isaac	3	2	6			Annis, Moses	1	1	2			Trumbal, Samuel	2	2	6		
Kendall, John	1	4	6			Currier, William	2		2			Tucker, Eben	1	1	4		
Lovejoy, Jonᵃ	1	1	3			Clough, Thomas	2	1	5			Thurber, Benjᵃ	1		1		
Lowell, Joseph	1	4	1			Coggswell, Joseph	1		2			Thurber, Francis	1		2		
Marshall, Jonᵃ	2	2	4			Davis, Zebulon	1	3	8			Walton, Abigail	1	2	2		
Marshall, Thomas	2	1	2			Davis, Aquilla	1	1	2			Walden, Isaac	1	4	6		
Manser, William	2	2	2			Davis, Wells	1	3	3			Whitcomb, Jacob	1	2	4		
Manser, William, Jr	1	1	3			Davis, Francis	1	3	1			Whitcomb, Benjᵃ	1		2		
Manard, Caleb	2	1	4			Davis, Nathˡ	1	1	3			Watson, Parmenus	1	1	4		
Moor, John	1	2	3			Davis, Gideon	1		2			Watson, Daniel	1	2	2		
Pearce, Levi	1	2	5			Davis, Gideon, Jr	1	3	3			Watson, Jonᵃ	1		4		
Powers, Gideon	2	2	2			Davis, Robert	1	4	3			Walker, Isaac	1	1	3		
Putnam, Stephen	1	2	6			Davis, Francis, Jr	1	3	3			Ward, Simon	1		3		
Patten, John	2	4	6			Davis, Amos	1		2			Walden, Ezra	1		2		
Parlim, Stephen	1		1			Davis, John	1		2			Dolton, Isaac	1	1	1	2	
Powers, Sarah			2			Danforth, Phineas	1		2			Elliot, Isaac	1		3		
Piper, Solomon	1	1	3			Edmund, Stephen	2	1	2			Osgood, Philip	2	5	2		
Richard, Joseph	1		2			Evens, Tappen	3		5			Kelley, Caleb	1		3		
Richardson, Abijah			4			Evens, Nicholas	2	1	5			Sevey, Andrew	1	1	3		
Spafford, Aldad	3	2	7			Flood, Daniel	3	1	4			Kimball, Reuben, Jr	1		3		
Severance, Abby	1		4			Flanders, James	2	1	3			Weed, Priscilla	1		4		
Severance, Asa	1	1	4			Flanders, Philip	1	1	2			Flood, Amos	1	3	3		
Stickney, S. Richard	1	2	3			Flanders, Zebulon	1	6	1								
Searle, David	1	1	3			Flanders, Christian	1	2	3			WEARE TOWN.					
Searle, William	1	1	4			Flanders, Philip, Jr	1	2	2								
Searle, William, Jr	1	1	4			Flanders, Moses	1	2	2			Atwood, Joshua	4	3	4		
Searle, Joseph	1	3	5			Flanders, Isaiah	1	1	6			Atwood, Jonᵃ	1	1	3		
Stickney, Moses	2		2			Flanders, Hopk	2	3	4			Adams, Richard	2		2		
Stone, Abigail			2			Fifield, Jonᵃ	3	1	2			Ayers, Samˡ	2	3	3		
Steart, John	1	3	3			Farren, Francis	2	2	6			Atwood, Caleb	2	4	6		
Shelden, Abraham	3		3			Davis, Joseph	1	1	1			Brown, Moses	1	2	3		
Stiles, Asa	2	1	4			Foster, Joseph	3		1			Barnard, Edward	1	3	3		
Shattuck, Nathˡ	2	2	5			Foster, Benjᵃ	1		3			Barnard, David	2	2	3		
Stevens, Jonᵃ	1		3			Foot, Charles	1		5			Brown, Elisha	1		1		
Searle, Danˡ	2	1	2			Foot, Thomas	1	3	3			Baker, Samˡ	1	1	7		
Searle, David, Jr	1	1	3			Goodwin, Ezekiel	1	2	3			Bowls, Stephen	1				
Savage, Jube					3	Goodwin, Seth	3		4			Bean, Samˡ	3	2	4		
Tinney, Benjᵃ	2	2	7			Gould, Robert	2		2			Butler, Elijah	1				
Tinney, Benjᵃ, Jr	2	7	4			Gould, Jonᵃ	1	1	3			Burnam, Jabex	1		4		
Todd, Joshua	2		4			Gilmore, David	2	1	3			Brown, Deborah	2	2	4		
Upton, Anna		1	5			Greele, Joseph	2		2			Bailey, Ebenʳ	5	3	3		
Walker, Samson	1	2	7			Heath, Nehemiah	2		3			Blasdel, Mariah	2	2	4		
Whiting, Oliver	3	2	5			Hall, John	1	1	4			Brackenbury, Danˡ	2		3		
Wheeler, Abijah	4	5	5			Hadley, Samuel	1		1			Bailey, Jesse	2	5	2		
Wheeler, Nathˡ	1	4	5			Harvey, David	1		3			Buxton, James	2	2	2		
Venton, Benoni	1	3	2			Harvey, Abner	1		3			Bailey, Danˡ	1	4	6		
Howard, Nathˡ	1		1			Hunt, Joseph	2	1	1			Breed, Zephᵇ	2	1	2		
Powers, Paul	1		1			Haggett, Thomas	1	2	4			Breed, Ebenʳ	4	3	6		
Stickney, Paul	1	1	1			Hunt, Nathˡ	3	1	3			Archelaus, Henry	1	1	3		
Rice, Amos	1	1	1			Hoyt, Joseph	1					Breed, Ebenʳ	1	1	1		
Searles, John	1		2			Hensman, Asa	2		3			Blake, John	1		3		
Stowell, John	1	4	2			Jones, Jonᵃ	1	3	2			Blake, Jesse	1		3		
Parkhurst, Andrew	1	1	2			Jones, Caleb	1		3			Blake, Winthrop	1	2	4		
Searlet, John					3	Kimball, Reuben	3		4			Blake, John, Jr	2	4	4		
Sanders, Susanna		1	2			Kelley, John	1	1	1			Brown, Elijah	1		1		
						Lowell, William	1	1	4			Brown, Elijah, Jr	2	2	5		
WARNER TOWN.						Lowell, William, Jr	1		2			Brown, Eliphalet	4	3	2		
						Morrall, Danˡ	2		4			Brown, James	1	2	3		
Kelley, William	3	3	3			Morrall, John	1	1	3			Bailey, Samˡ	1	5	5		
Annis, Thomas	1	3	4			Morrall, Zebulon	1	2	2			Boynton, Moses	1	5	4		
Annis, Solᵒ	1	1	2			Morrall, William	1	3	4			Collins, Dustin	3		1		
Ballard, William H.	2		2			Morrall, Ephraim	3	1	6			Caldwell, Samˡ	1	3	4		
Bagley, David	2	1	4			Morrall, Enoch	1	1	2			Caldwell, Samˡ, Jr	1	2	3		
Bean, Nathˡ	4	4	5			Morrall, Richard	1	1	2			Caldwell, William	6	1	3		
Barnard, Charles	1	2	6			Merrill, William	2	1	2			McNeill, John Caldwell	1	2	2		
Bartlet, Richard	2		2			Norton, John	2		1			Caldwell, James	1	2	2		
Bartlett, Joseph	1		1			Pettee, Asa	3	1	6			Chase, Nathan	1	2	3		

WEARE TOWN—con.

NAME OF HEAD OF FAMILY.	Free white males of 16 years and upward, including heads of families.	Free white males under 16 years.	Free white females, including heads of families.	All other free persons.	Slaves.
Chase, Dudley	2	3	5		
Chase, John	1	4	5		
Collins, Tristram	1	4	4		
Chase, Abraham	2	3	4		
Colby, Levi	1	4	3		
Colburn, Thomas	1	2	4		
Karr, Jacob	1	6	2		
Cilley, John	5	2	3		
Cilley, Thomas	1	3	3		
Collins, Benja	4		1		
Collins, Stephen	1		1		
Collins, Moses	1	3	2		
Karr, Ezekiel	1	2	4		
Clough, Winthrop	2	3	3		
Cilley, Benja	2	2	4		
Colby, Ezekiel	1		2		
Clement, Jesse	1	1	1		
Clement, Ezra	2	2	3		
Clement, Henry	1	4	5		
Carlis, Timothy	3	4	6		
Clough, Nathan	1	3	4		
Karr, Zebulon	1		4		
Colburn, Charles	1	1	2		
Collins, Jeremiah	1	1	1		
Colburn, Matthew	1		3		
Currier, Moses	3	2	3		
Cooper, Solomon	2		2		
Cram, Thomas	1	2	4		
Cram, Ezekiel	2	6	3		
Colby, Winthrop	1	2	5		
Cram, Nathan	2	4	8		
Cross, Thomas	1		2		
Coleman, Solomon	1	4	2		
Davis, Thomas	1	1	1		
Dustin, William	2	1	5		
Dow, Winthrop	2	1	3		
Dow, David	2	3	4		
Dustin, Paul	3	1	3		
Dow, Jedediah	2	3	4		
Dow, Jona	5	1	6		
Dustin, Saml	1	1	3		
Emery, Danl	1		1		
Eastis, Jona	2	1	1		
Emery, Sylvanus	1	1	7		
Emery, Caleb	2	2	3		
Emerson, Marden	2	4	3		
Emerson, Jona	1		1		
Emerson, Danl	3	1	3		
Emerson, Thomas	2		2		
Evens, Thomas	3	3	6		
Eaton, Humphrey	1	3	3		
Eaton, Ithamar	5	3	3		
Eaton, Obadiah	3	4	7		
Emerson, Moses	1		3		
Emerson, James	3	2	4		
Emery, Jesse	1		2		
Eastman, Thomas	3	2	4		
Eastman, Saml	2	4	6		
Emerson, Stephen	1	2	3		
Eastman, Moses	1	3	4		
Eastman, Ichabod	3	3	6		
Follinsbee, Thomas	2	4	3		
Fever, John	3	5	4		
Fifield, Nathl	1	3	8		
Fifield, Edward	1	1	2		
Fever, John, Jr	1		1		
Flanders, Benja	1		1		
Feltch, Joseph	3	1	2		
Feltch, Jabez	1		3		
Flanders, Thomas	2	1	3		
Flood, Mark	1		2		
Flood, Danl	1	2	5		
Foot, Isaac	3		3		
Flood, Joseph	1	2	3		
George, Charles	1	1	1		
George, Elijah	1	2	2		
Gove, Jona	1	1	6		
Green, Levi	1	2	4		
Gove, William	1	1	4		
Gove, Edmund	1	1	3		
Gove, Danl	1	6	4		
Gove, Danl, Jr	1	1	1		
Gove, David	3		4		
Gove, Mark	2	2	4		
Gove, John	4	2	4		
Gove, Elisha	1	3	3		
Green, Michajah	1		4		
Green, Jeremiah	1	2	3		
Green, Isaiah	2		2		
Green, David	1		2		
Green, Moses	1		2		
Gale, Benja	2		3		

WEARE TOWN—con.

NAME OF HEAD OF FAMILY.	Free white males of 16 years and upward, including heads of families.	Free white males under 16 years.	Free white females, including heads of families.	All other free persons.	Slaves.
George, Timothy	2	1	4		
Gould, Danl	2		6		
Gould, Jona	1	1	2		
Gale, James	2	1	5		
George, Moses	1	1	1		
Gove, Jona	1	2	1		
Green, Isaiah, Jr	1	1	1		
Goodhue, Joseph	2		1		
Gove, Nathl	2	1	5		
Gove, Obadiah	1		4		
Gove, David, Jr	1	2	2		
Goodwell, Robert	2		3		
Gove, Elijah	1	4	5		
Graves, John	3	2	4		
Graves, William	1	2	1		
George, Joseph	3	2	5		
Gove, Nathan	1	1	5		
Griffin, Richard	1	2	5		
Griffin, Jona	1	1	1		
Graves, Calvin	1	2	4		
Goodale, Stephen	1	1	2		
Gove, Stephen	1	1	2		
Hadlock, Richard	1	1	2		
Hadley, Danl	1	5	6		
Huntington, Benja	1	1	4		
Hutchinson, John	1	3	3		
Huse, Joseph	1	6	2		
Huntington, John	1	4	2		
Harwood, James	1	2	3		
Hoyt, Abner	2	1	3		
Hogg, James	3		7		
Hook, Danl	1		1		
Hazen, Moses	2	4	6		
Hardy, Oliver	3	3	5		
Hadlouk, Jona	2	3	6		
Hodgden, Jona	3	1	4		
Hadley, George	2	4	2		
Hadlock, Joseph	2		2		
Johnson, Robert	1	1	2		
Johnson, Edmund	3		3		
Johnson, Enoch	2	6	3		
Jones, Joseph	1	1	2		
Jones, Natha	2	1	5		
Jones, Ephraim	2	2	6		
Jones, Mary			3		
Johnson, Amos	1	2	1		
Kimball, Nathn	2		2		
Kelley, Isaac	1	2	3		
Kimball, Hannah	2		2		
Kimball, Ezekiel	2	3	5		
Kimball, Danl	1	1	3		
Kimball, Joseph	1	1	3		
Kinson, John	3		3		
Kelly, Langley	4		4		
Lull, David	1	3	3		
Lull, Moses	2	1	3		
Mansfield, Joseph	3	2	3		
Melvin, Abraham	3	1	3		
Marshal, Moses	3	4	4		
Marshal, Benja	1	1	1		
Mudgett, Moses	1	4	2		
Martin, Jona	3	1	4		
Maxwell, Joshua	2	2	6		
Marshal, Asa	1	1	2		
Martin, Saml	1	1	3		
Mudgett, John	2		2		1
Morril, Jabez	2	3	5		
Mussey, John	3	3	4		
Nichols, Thomas	2	1	2		
Nichols, Humphrey	1	3	3		
Noyes, Joseph	1	2	5		
Osborn, Jonathan	1	3	2		
Page, Eliphalet	2	2	4		
Page, Johnson	1	1	3		
Philbrick, Richard	1	2	4		
Purington, Chase	1	3	3		
Peasley, Caleb	1	2	5		
Page, John	2	1	5		
Peasley, Silas	3	2	5		
Peasley, Nathl	3		2		
Peasley, Nathl, Jr	1		1		
Peasley, Benja	1		2		
Peasley, Jona	3	1	2		
Purington, Hezekiah	1	4	3		
Purington, Elisha	2		4		
Purington, Elisha, Jr	1		2		
Perkins, Solomon	1		2		
Palmer, Benja	1	2	2		
Peasley, Ebenr	3	3	6		
Philbrick, Jona, Jr	1	1	2		
Pettingill, Dudley	1	3	3		

WEARE TOWN—con.

NAME OF HEAD OF FAMILY.	Free white males of 16 years and upward, including heads of families.	Free white males under 16 years.	Free white females, including heads of families.	All other free persons.	Slaves.
Philbrick, Saml	5	1	4		
Philbrick, Jona	1	3	3		
Perkins, Joseph	1	3	4		
Person, Danl	2	2	4		
Pillsbury, Ezra	1	1	1		
Peasley, Jona, Jr	3	1	2		
Page, Jona	2	4	2		
Page, John, Jr	2	1	1		
Page, Saml	1		1		
Page, Saml, Jr	2	3	6		
Peasley, John	2	2	2		
Day, John	1	1	2		
Quimby, Moses	3	1	3		
Colby, Philip	1	2	3		
Crocker, Richard	1		1		
Page, Lemuel	3	4	2		
Philbrick, Thomas	1	1	1		
Rowel, Saml	1	2	4		
Rogers, William	1	2	4		
Rowel, Job	2	1	3		
Roby, John	1	2	6		
Ring, Nathl	2	4	3		
Stoning, Amos	2	1	7		
Shaw, Benja	1	3	1		
Shaw, Isaac	2	2	3		
Stevens, Thomas	1		7		
Straw, Saml	3		1		
Sargent, Philip	1	2	6		
Sargent, Isaac	1	1	3		
Sargent, Asa	2		1		
Sargent, Jacob	1		2		
Shaw, Thomas	1	1	1		
Shaw, Follinsbee	1	3	3		1
Tuttle, Jotham	4	2	1		
Twiss, John	1	5	3		
Tuxbury, Henry	1	3	5		
Toby, Saml	2	1	3		
Turrel, Seth	1		2		
Tuxbury, Jacob	1	3	9		
Webster, Joseph	5	2	4		
Worthen, Saml	4	4	7		
Worthly, Thomas	2	1	2		
Worthly, Jona	3	4	7		
Woodbury, Jesse	4	1	6		
Watson, Nicholas	2		3		
Watson, Ithamar	1		1		
Worthly, Nathl	1		1		
Whiteker, Asa	1	4	7		
Reed, Artemus	2	1	5		
Wood, Benja	1	2	5		
Whiteker, William	2		4		
Watson, John	4	1	5		
Whiteker, Caleb	1	2	4		
Philbrick, John	2	3	5		
Kilburn, Mehitabel			2		
Gove, John, Jr	1		2		
Gove, Ezekiel	1		2		
Cram, Jedidiah	2	2	3		
Osborn, David	1	1	1		
Webster, Abraham	1		3		

WILTON TOWN.

NAME OF HEAD OF FAMILY.	Free white males of 16 years and upward, including heads of families.	Free white males under 16 years.	Free white females, including heads of families.	All other free persons.	Slaves.
Fisk, Abel	2	1	3		
Abbot, Abiel	5	1	7		
Abbot, William, Jr	2	4	4		
Abbot, Jeremiah	2	2	5		
Abbot, Jacob	2	2	6		
Abbot, William	1	1	6		
Abbot, Barachias	3	2	3		
Abbot, Natha	2	1	5		
Ballard, Natha	2	1	6		
Blanchard, Joshua	3	2	5		
Blanchard, Benja	1	3	4		
Blanchard, David	1	1	2		
Blanchard, Jeremiah	1	3	5		
Batchedor, Asch'l	1	1	2	1	
Batcheldor, Daniel	3	2	6		
Baker, Joseph	2	2	4		
Burse, Silas	2	3	4		
Ballard, Uriah	2	2	3		
Burton, Jona	1	3	5		
Brown, Isaac	1	1	2		
Betty, William	2	2	1		
Buxton, John	2	1	2		
Hood, Danl	2	3	4		
Burnam, Jeremiah	1		1		
Burnam, Jeremiah, Jr	1		3		
Ballard, Elisha	1		4		
Cram, John	1	1	4		
Holt, Oliver	1	1	4		
Cram, Jona, Junr	1		2		

HILLSBOROUGH COUNTY—Continued.

WILTON TOWN—con.

NAME OF HEAD OF FAMILY.	Free white males of 16 years and upward, including heads of families.	Free white males under 16 years.	Free white females, including heads of families.	All other free persons.	Slaves.
Colburn, George	1	3	8		
Eaton, Thomas	2	3	2		
Fry, Isaac	3	4	5		
Greeley, Saml	1		1	1	
Greeley, Saml, Jr	1	4	3		
Gage, Peirce	2	2	4		
Greeley, Nathl	3	6	6		
Goldsmith, William	1	5	4		
Gray, Timothy	1		2		
Gray, Timothy, Jr	2	3	3		
Gray, Joseph	1	2	2		
Hartshorn, Jona	1	2	3		
Hartshorn, Saml	2	2	2		
Hoit, Joseph	2	2	5		
Holt, Timothy	1		2		
Holt, Timo., Jnr	1	2			
Holt, Elias	1		2		
McIntire, John	1	3	1		
King, Richard	2		2		
Livermore, Jona	2	2	5		
Lovejoy, Danl	3	3	2		
Lovejoy, Moses	1	3	3		
Lovejoy, Saml	1	6	4		
Laney, George	1				
Lovejoy, Henry	2	2	3		
Martin, Jona	4	1	3		
Martin, Chrisa	1	3	4		
Morgan, Ashby	2	4	4		
Parkhurt, Jona	2	1	1		
Parkhurt, Jona., Jr	1	1	2		
Parkhurt, Jesse	1		4		
Perry, Abigail	1		2		
Peirce, William	1		3		
Peirce, Benja	1	1	3		
Peirce, William, Jr	1	2	5		
Parker, Sarah			4		
Parker, Benja	2	1	3		
Parker, Josiah	1	1	1		
Phelps, Abigail		1	3		
Peabody, Ephraim	2	2	6		
Perry, Abijah	3	3	3		
Pettingill, William	1	1	4		
Russell, Thomas	4	3	4	1	
Rideout, Benjamin	2	3	4		

WILTON TOWN—con.

NAME OF HEAD OF FAMILY.	Free white males of 16 years and upward, including heads of families.	Free white males under 16 years.	Free white females, including heads of families.	All other free persons.	Slaves.
Rockwood, Ebenr	2	5	6		
Stevens, John	2	2	5		
Steel, Benjamin	1	2	4		
Spaulding, Abijah	1		3		
Snow, Joseph	1	3	4		
Smith, Uriah	3	4	4		
Sawyer, Nathl	1	1	5		
Simonds, Joseph	1		4		
Whitney, Richard	3	5	5		
Wood, David	1		2		
Abbot, George	3	3	6		
Abbot, Job	1	2	4		
Averill, Moses	1	1	3		
Baldwin, John	1	2	3		
Burton, John	1	1	6		
Burton, David	1	2	5		
Burton, Abraham	3	3	8		
Bale, William	1		1		
Bale, William, Jr	2	2	6		
Burse, Stephen	2	2	5		
Baldwin, Timo	1		3		
Butterfield, Abraham	3	1	8		
Barker, Phineas	1	2	3		
Bridges, Abiel	1		1		
Bridges, John	2	1	3		
Cram, John	1	1	3		
Cram, John, Junr	4	2	5		
Cram, Zebulem	1		5		
Cram, Ebenr	1	2	5		
Cram, Humphrey	1	1	1		
Chandler, Ebenr	2	3	5		
Colburn, Amos	3		2		
Dale, Timo	2		3		
Dale, John	1	2	7		
Davis, Saml	3	2	3		
Dascomb, James	3	2	3		
Farrington, John	1	2	6		
Farrington, Phineas	1		5		
Fletcher, Charles	1	2	4		
Fletcher, Oliver	1	1	1		
Fuller, Enoch	1	5	2		
Fuller, Joseph	3		3		
Hall, Timothy	1	3	4		
Herrick, Edward	3	4	3		

WILTON TOWN—con.

NAME OF HEAD OF FAMILY.	Free white males of 16 years and upward, including heads of families.	Free white males under 16 years.	Free white females, including heads of families.	All other free persons.	Slaves.
Hazeltine, Nathan	1		1		
Hutchinson, Saml	2	4	6		
Hutchinson, George	2		4		
Holt, Amos	2	2	5		
Holt, Jeremiah	1	2	3		
Holt, Simeon	1	2	5		
Hawkins, William A	2	3	3		
Holt, Barachias	1	1	3		
Holt, Volintine	1	1	2		
Hutchinson, Ebenr	1	4	2		
Johnson, Ephraim	1	1	4		
Johnson, Ezra	2		1		
Johnson, James	1		2		
Kenney, Daniel	1	2	3		
Kenney, David	2		2		
Keyes, Symond	3	4	5		
Lewis, Thomas	1	3	4		
Milliam, Alexander	3		1	1	
Peabody, Isaac	1	2	3		
Putnam, Moses	2	2	2		
Putnam, Jacob	2	2	5		
Putnam, Mary	1	1	3		
Putnam, Archelaus	1	2	3		
Putnam, Philip	1	1	6		
Putnam, Archelaus, Jr	2	3	8		
Putnam, Archelaus, 3d	1	1	1		
Parker, Hannaniah	2	1	5		
Puram, Saml	1	1	2		
Russel, Jedidiah	1	4	3		
Read, Peter	1	1	4		
Stiles, Joseph	3	2	2		
Snow, Phebe			1		
Stiles, Abner	2		3		
Shelden, Saml	3	1	4		
Warren, Peter	1	5	4		
Wilkins, Archelaus	1		1		
Wilkins, Uriah	1	1	6		
Lowell, Timo	1	3	5		
Taylor, Hannah			2		
Perry, Jame	1		4		
Butterfield, Mary	1		4		
Blanchard, George					8

ROCKINGHAM COUNTY.

ALLENSTOWN TOWN.

NAME OF HEAD OF FAMILY.	Free white males of 16 years and upward, including heads of families.	Free white males under 16 years.	Free white females, including heads of families.	All other free persons.	Slaves.
Sargent, Starten	2	1	3		
Buntin, James	1	1	2		
Buntin, Robert	1	1	4	1	
Webster, Samuel	1	3	3		
Webster, David	1		5		
Colton, Amos	1		1		
Gout, William	1	1	1		
Shackford, Theod	2		2		
Leonerd, John	2	1	3		
McCoy, Charles	2	2	6		
Row, Samuel	2	4	2		
Sergent, Jona	1	2	4		
Durgin, Roger	2	1	3		
Burgin, Eli H	3	1	3		
Smith, Burliegh	1	2	3		
Farnum, Joel	1				
Clark, Ichobad, junr	1	3	1		
Kenistone, Samuel	4		3		
Leonerd, John	1		1		
Colby, Peter	1		1		
Clak, Ichobad	2	1	3		
Benson, Thomas	1		1		
Nelson, James	1		4		
Kenistone, Samuel, jr	1	2	2		
Allen, Isiah	1	3	4		
Dowse, John	1	2	2		
Marden, Israel	1		2		
Trithefethren, John	2	4	4		
Robbison, John	1	2	2		
Leavitt, Moses	1	2	3		
Cate, Joshua	3	1	3		
York, Samuel	1	2	1		
Davis, Zebulon	1	1	3		
Davis, William	1		3		
Jonson, Jeremiah	1		2		
Davis, Daniel	1	1	3		
Bumford, Charles	2		3		
Smith, Nathl	2		3		
Harford, John	2	2	3		
Evans, George	2	6	5		

ALLENSTOWN TOWN—con.

NAME OF HEAD OF FAMILY.	Free white males of 16 years and upward, including heads of families.	Free white males under 16 years.	Free white females, including heads of families.	All other free persons.	Slaves.
Hoyse, John	1	2	6		
Fisk, Samuel	2	4	3		
Thurstin, Jesse	1		2		
Jonson, John	3	2	1		
Luis, Fredrick	1	1	2		
Goodhue, Samuel	1	1	2		

ATKINSON TOWN.

NAME OF HEAD OF FAMILY.	Free white males of 16 years and upward, including heads of families.	Free white males under 16 years.	Free white females, including heads of families.	All other free persons.	Slaves.
Dow, James	1	1	2		
Knight, Joseph	2	2	6		
Knight, Daniel	1		2		
Merrill, John	2	1	4		
Noyes, Peter	1	1	1		
Noyes, Joseph	2		1		
Grenough, Moses	1		5		
Little, Nathl	1	3	4		
Clemmens, Peter	4		3		
Noyes, Stephen	1		4		
Page, Asa	3		7		
Page, Stephen	3	3	2		
Noyes, James	3		2		
Peabody, Nathl	2	1	2		
Noyes, Caleb	2	2	4		
Noyes, Enoch	1	1	2		
Noyes, James, jr	1	2	3		
Knight, James	1		3		
Knight, Joseph, jr	2		2		
French, Joseph	2	3	6		
Little, Saml	1		1		
Little, Saml. N.	1	2	3		
Noyes, Humphry	1	4	4		
Whitaker, Jona	1	1	3		
Sawyer, Jona	1	1	3		
Sawyer, Benja	1	1	1		
Sawyer, Jesse	2	1	3		
Stone, Benja	1	1	4		
Poor, Danl., jr	2	1	5		
Poor, Jona	3	1	7		

ATKINSON TOWN—con.

NAME OF HEAD OF FAMILY.	Free white males of 16 years and upward, including heads of families.	Free white males under 16 years.	Free white females, including heads of families.	All other free persons.	Slaves.
Knight, John	2		2		
Knight, John, jr	1	4	5		
Atwood, John	1	2	6		
Knight, Enoch	2	2	6		
Cogswell, Wm	2	1	3	2	
Bassett, John	1	2	2		
Nichols, Jona	2		3		
Dow, John	2	4	4		
Page, Danl	2	2	4		
Peabody, Revd.Stephen	1	1	2		
Richards, Benja	4	1	5		
Page, Sarah	1	2	5		
Page, Wm	1	1	2		
Grover, Joseph	2		2		
Pearse, Rebecca		2	3		
Dole, Parker	2	1	3		
Dole, Stephen	2		1		
Dole, Stephen, jr	1	1	3		
Little, Thos	2	2	5		
Johnson, John	2	3	5		
Mills, Reuben	1		2		
Mills, Reuben, jr	1		1		
Emery, Benja	1		1		
Emery, Moses	1		4		
Chandler, Joseph	2	1	6		
Palmer, Joseph	2	1	7		
Goodwin, Saml	2	2	3		
Belnap, Ezekiel	2	1	4		
Belnap, Joshua	1	1	1		
Little, Joseph	2		2		
Page, Jona	1	1	3		
Rowell, Jona	1		2		
Wood, Thos	1	1	3		
Morrill, Priscilla		2	2		
Ingals, John	2	4	3		
Park, Edward	4	1	5		
Dustin, Nathl	1	4	2		
Webster, Moses	2	1	1		
Merrill, James	3	5	2		
Webster, Jona	2	5	3		

ROCKINGHAM COUNTY—Continued.

NAME OF HEAD OF FAMILY.	Free white males of 16 years and upward, including heads of families.	Free white males under 16 years.	Free white females, including heads of families.	All other free persons.	Slaves.
ATKINSON TOWN—con.					
Knight, Elipt	2	1	3		
Poor, Daniel	1	1	1		
Poor, Jeremiah	2	2	1		
Webster, John	1		3		
Webster, Joseph	1	4	4		
Webster, Wm	2		1		
Webster, Saml	2		3		
Emery, Benja	2		2		
White, Sarah	1		1		
BOW TOWN.					
Thompson, Benjamin	1	3	4		
Bryent, John Esr	3	2	6		
Currier, Ruben	2		3		
Currier, Jona	1	2	5		
Walker, William	1	1	3		
Green, Jacob	1	5	4		
Deeks, Timothy	2	1	3		
Emerson, George	1	3	4		
Rogers, Samuel	2	4	5		
Rogers, Joseph	1		1		
Norris, Moses	1	2	4		
Meanwell, Anthony	1		1		
Robbison, Thomas	3		4		
Clough, David	2	4	2		
Clough, Jona	1	5	3		
Rowell, Eliphalet	1	3	2		
Dow, Samuel	1	1	2		
Eastman, Stephen	1	2	4		
Dow, Richard	2		4		
Dow, Sollomon	1	1	1		
Clemmons, Jona	1	3	5		
Gughshey, Jno	2		2		
Benson, Henery	3		3		
Welch, Samuel	1	3	3		
Clemment, Amos	1		3		
Ordway, Samuel	1	1	1		
Dow, Emersay	1		2		
Stevens, Barthoniel	1	4	5		
Morrill, John	1	3	1		
Robbison, William	2	3	5		
Robbinson, John	3		5		
Buzell, James	1	1	3		
Clough, Levi	1				
Dow, John	1		2		
Hamphell, Henery	5	1	4		
Hamphell, John	1	1	2		
Brown, Molley	2	2	3		
Heath, Simeon	2	2	7		
Clemmett, Samuel	2	1	2		
Buzell, Edward	3	1	4		
Holt, Nathl	2	2	2		
Heath, Sollomon	2	3	6		
Covis, Nathl	1	3	3		
Walker, Samuel	1				
Walker, Abiel	1				
Sergent, Simeon	1	1	3		
Clough, Richard	2	1	2		
Stevens, David	1	1	1		
Nicholas, John	3		2		
Rogers, Samuel	1	1	3		
Welch, Samuel	3	1	3		
Harvey, Barronet	1	1	3		
Colby, John	3		2		
Colby, Abraham	2	4	3		
Elliott, Rachel	1	2	2		
Colby, Willebe	3	1	3		
Colby, Thomas	1	3	4		
Sullivan, John	1	3	1		
Luflin, David	1	1	1		
Saunders, James	1	1	2		
Siliver, David	1	3	1		
Whipple, Benjn	1	4	2		
Silver, Nathan	1				
Farnham, Joel	1				
Silver, John	2	3	1		
Siliver, Samuel	1	1	1		
Sanders, Samuel	1				
Noyes, Nathan	1	5	1		
Nois, Benjn	5	1	8		
Nois, Enoch	1	3	6		
Nois, John, junr	1	1	1		
Nois, John	1	4	5		
Banton, Richard	1	1	4		
Alexander, Samuel	2	1	3		
Moors, Ephm., jr	1	2	3		
Moors, Ephm	2	1	5		
Moor, Moses	1		2		
White, Isaac	3	4	6		
Moor, James	1	3	2		
Merrill, Nehemiah	1		3		

NAME OF HEAD OF FAMILY.	Free white males of 16 years and upward, including heads of families.	Free white males under 16 years.	Free white females, including heads of families.	All other free persons.	Slaves.
BOW TOWN—con.					
Badger, Ezr	2	3	2		
Clough, Elijah, jr	1	1	3		
Backer, Joseph	4	3	3		
Backer, John	2	2	2		
Hamphell, Elizabeth	1		2		
Garvin, John, jr	2	2	5		
Garvin, John	2		2		
Carter, John	1	1	3		
Hay, William	1				
Robbison, James	1	4	5		
Gout, Samuel	1	1	3		
Dustin, Moses	1	1	1		
Grafhon, John	2	1	2		
Colby, Elijah	1	1	7		
BRINTWOOD TOWN.					
Allsworth, Jeremiah	3		7		
Safford, Joseph	2		3		
Weights, Thomas	1	2	3		
Thing, Petter	2		3		
Colbee, Ichabod	1	2	3		
Thing, Eliphlet	1	3	3		
Thing, Josiah	1		1		
Thing, Samuel	2	2	3		
Thing, John	1	4	2		
Thing, Bartholomew	2	1	3		
Philbrick, John	2	2	1		
Wormall, Samuel	3		1		
Dudley, John	1	3	2		
Kimbal, Dudley	1		3		
Dudley, Mary		1	4		
Dudley, Wintrope	1	3	4		
Smith, Elaxandrew	2	1	3		
Dudley, Josiah	2	2	4		
Wilson, Humphry	3	1	3		
Marshall, Hawley	2		3		
Levet, Gillman	2	1	4		
Marshall, Henery	1	2	2		
Roberson, Dudley	3	3	3		
Stowraney, Thomas	1		1		1
Swain, Caleb	2	3	2		
Levet, Seven	2	2	4		
Wilson, John	2	1	4		
Thustin, Oliver	2	1	4		
Dollar, Noah	2	1	3		
Thing, John	1		1		
Thing, John	3		3		
Hook, Jacob	1	1	2		
Ward, Andrew	1	1	3		
Prescut, Nathaniel	3	2	5		
Thing, Levi	1	3	2		
Taylor, Jonathan	2	4	5		
Cram, Jonathan	2	1	3		
Row, Arators	1	3	3		
Cram, Benjamin	1	1	3		
Row, Jeremiah	2	4	5		
Lifard, Jonathan	1	2	2		
Lifard, Frances	1		1		
Lifard, Moses	1	1	3		
Shaw, John	3	3	6		
Sinkler, James	2	2	6		
Row, Jeremiah	2	3	2		
Sinkler, James, ju	2	2	6		
Marston, Jonathan	1	1	2		
Sanborn, Coffin	2	1	3		
Brook, William	2		2		
Peavey, Samuel	1	1	2		
Dearborne, Daniel	1				
Shepard, Samuel	1	2	7		
Shaw, Samuel	2	2	4		
Judkins, Ruth	5	2	5		
Tuck, John	2	1	5		
Tuck, Edward	1	3	5		
Goarding, Timothy	2		3		
Smith, Caleb	1	2	1		
Smith, John	1	4	3		
Smith, Joseph	1		1		
Woodbrey, John	1	2	3		
Quimbee, Moses	1		3		
Merrill, William	6		3		
Quimbee, John	1	1	3		
Fifeld, Abigail			2		
Morrill, Abraham	1		1		
Quimbee, Edward	2	1	2		
Witcher, Isaac	2	2	5		
Levet, Thomas	2	2	4		
Robards, Benjamin	1		1		
Dollar, John	1	2	4		
Robards, Thomas	2		2		
Hook, Josiah	2	2	3		
Goarding, Thomas	2	2	8		

NAME OF HEAD OF FAMILY.	Free white males of 16 years and upward, including heads of families.	Free white males under 16 years.	Free white females, including heads of families.	All other free persons.	Slaves.
BRINTWOOD TOWN—con.					
Been, Jeremiah	1	2	2		
Gorge, Gedion	1	1	3		
Perry, William	1	1	1		
Been, Loami	1	2	4		
Dowling, William	2		1		
Been, Jepthy	1	2	2		
Burbank, Abner	4	1	4		
Been, Richard	3	2	5		
Chase, Ebenesar	1		3		
Been, Eevi	1	4	4		
Wezey, Thomas	1	2	3		
Sleeper, Benjamin	1	3	3		
Clielford, John	1	2	1		
Liffard, Bilard	2	1	3	2	
Been, Jeremiah	3	1	3		
West, Nehemiah	1	2	2		
Fellows, Stevens	3	2	1		
Coloney, William	1	1	3		
Ladd, Steven	3	1	5		
Jewel, Joseph	4	2	5		
Sanborn, Elishar	2		6		
Sleeper, Jonathan	2	3	3		
Megoon, Moses	1		3		
Fifeld, Moses	1	1	3		
Sanborn, Edward	1	3	2		
Sanborn, Lydeia			1		
Grase, Nathaniel	2	2	5		
Graves, William	1	3	4		
Morrill, Abraham	1	2	2		
Morrill, Levi	1	2	4		
Sanborn, Daniel	2	1	5		
Drake, Simeon	1	2	2		
Smith, Jabish	3	2	5		
Duse, Sipp				4	
Fesy, Jonathan	2		2		
Fesy, Jonathan, ju	1	2	2		
Kimball, Porter	1	1	2		
Pulsipher, Benjamin	1	3	2		
Goarding, James	3	1	5		
Marstone, Wintrope	2	3	3		
Fifeld, David	2		2		
Roberson, Joseph	2	6	8		
Trask, Jonathan	1	3	1		
Lock, Samuel	2	1	2		
Goarding, Jonathan	1	1	2		
Dollar, David	2		6		
Gording, Scribner	3	1	4		
Colcord, Ebeneazer	3	1	3		
Colcord, Ebeneazer, ju	1	2	2		
Stevens, Nathaniel	1	3	6		
Stevens, Edward	2		2		
Stevens, Samuel	1	2	3		
Clafford, David	4	1	11		
Wadley, Joseph	2	5	3		
Clark, Daniel	2		3		
Smith, Joshua	1		3		
Smith, Robert	1	1	2		
Smith, Ruben	1		2		
Roberson, James	3	1	3		
Roberson, Samuel	1		3		
Trask, Samuel	1	1	5		
Roberson, David	1	1	6		
Roberson, Jonathan	2		3		
Quimbee, Jonathan	1	2	7		
York, Joseph	1	2	3		
Jacks, Nancy			1		
Judgkins, Mary			2		
Ward, Sarah	2	3	2		
York, Richard	3	1	1		
Been, Joseph	3		4		
Rolling, Joseph	1	2	1		
Moody, Jonathan	1		2		
Smith, Nicholas	4	2	6		
Laberee, Petter	1	1	3		
York, Richard	1	4	4		
Fesy, George	1		1		
Watson, Jonathan	1	4	5		
Judgkins, Sarah			3		
Egley, Samuel	1		3		
Judgkins, Samuel	1	1	1		
York, John	2	2	3		
CANDIA TOWN.					
Moore, Samuel	2	1	2		
Moore, Saml., Jr	1	2	5		
Smith, Chase	1	2	3		
Smith, Chase, Jr	1	1	3		
Mores, Peter	1	3	4		
Mores, Joshua	1	2	2		
Miller, William	1	2	2		
Morrel, Saml	2	3	3		

ROCKINGHAM COUNTY—Continued.

NAME OF HEAD OF FAMILY.	Free white males of 16 years and upward, including heads of families.	Free white males under 16 years.	Free white females, including heads of families.	All other free persons.	Slaves.	NAME OF HEAD OF FAMILY.	Free white males of 16 years and upward, including heads of families.	Free white males under 16 years.	Free white females, including heads of families.	All other free persons.	Slaves.	NAME OF HEAD OF FAMILY.	Free white males of 16 years and upward, including heads of families.	Free white males under 16 years.	Free white females, including heads of families.	All other free persons.	Slaves.
CANDIA TOWN—con.						CANDIA TOWN—con.						CANTERBURY TOWN— continued.					
Marden, Stephen	1	2	2			Bean, Nathan	1	3	3								
Pilsbury, Abijah	1		2			Bean, Phinehas	1	1	3			Chase, Edward	1	1	1		
Palmer, Benjᵃ	1	3	5			Bean, Reuben	1	3	4			Cogswell, Ebenzʳ	1	1	2		
Prince, Caleb	1	1	3			Buswell, Samˡ	2	4	3			Colcord, Nathˡ	1	1	4		
Pilsbury, David	1	1	6			Brown, Sewall	1	3	3			Cogswell, Moses	1	3	3		
Palmer, Joseph	2	4	4			Burpee, Nathan	1	1	2			Clough, Ezikle	1	3	2		
Pilsbury, Jonᵃ	2	1	8			Burley, William	1	1	2			Chandler, Ebenzʳ	1	2	4		
Prescott, John	2	1	3			Burley, Wm., Jʳ	1	1	2			Currier, Simeon	1		3		
Pearly, Jacob	1	2	2			Cass, Benjᵃ	2	4	4			Clough, Obediah	4	2	7		
Patten, Robᵗ	2	1	4			Colby, Enoch	1	2	3			Clough, Jeremiah	3		3		
Prince, Joseph	1		1			Cram, Edward	1	1	2			Clough, Jeremiah, junʳ	2		1		
Palmer, Stephen	2	1	4			Clark, Henry	2		3			Carter, Olendo	2		4		
Patten, Thoˢ	2	2	5			Clark, Henry, Jʳ	1	3	3			Carter, John	1	1	6		
Pearsons, Taylor	1	2	3			Critchet, James	2	1	3			Clough, Joseph	2		2		
Quimby, Jeremiah	3	3	6			Clifford, John	1	1	4			Clemment, Nathˡ	3	1	3		
Roby, John	2	2	6			Clifford, Jacob	2	3	3			Carter, Daniel	1	2	2		
King, Jonᵃ	1	4	2			Clay, John	1	3	3			Carter, Nathanˡ	2	1	2		
Rowe, Jonᵃ	1	3	1			Camet, John	2	3	2			Curry, Thoˢ	3	1	7		
Rowe, Josiah	2	1	9			Clay, Stephen	1	1	2			Clough, Nehemiah	2	2	4		
Roby, Levi	1	1	1			Clough, Samuel	2		1			Davis, Samuel	1	3	2		
Rowel, Miriam			1			Clark, Stephen	3	4	3			Davis, Stephen	1	1	1		
Rowe, Sherburne	2	4	3			Colcord, Samˡ	2	1	2			Dearborn, Thomas	3	1	3		
Roby, Walter	2		6			Cutler, Wm	1		2			Daniels, Samuel	1	1	4		
Roby, Walter, Jʳ	1		2			Clifford, Zachariah	2	1	3			Davis, Jonᵃ	1	2	3		
Rand, Nathˡ	2	1	2			Dolbear, Daniel	2	1	4			Dwendell, Henery	1	3	3		
Smith, Betsy	2	1	7			Dolbear, Israel	1		3			Danford, Jere	1	2	2		
Smith, Benjᵃ	2	3	3			Dustin, Moses	3	2	4			Danford, Moses	1	1	3		
Smith, Jonᵃ	1	3	4			Clay, John, Jʳ	1	3	3			Davis, John	3	1	4		
Sevey, Jonᵃ	1	1	2			Dearborn, Samˡ	1	6	4			Danford, Simeon	1	3	4		
Sargeant, John	3	1	3			Dalbear, Wm	1		1			Durgin, Joseph	2	2	6		
Sargeant, John, Jʳ	1	2	2			Eaton, Abigail	1		2			Flitcher, Daniel	4		3		
Miller, James	3	2	6			Eaton, Benjᵃ	1	1	1			Foster, James	1		2		
McClure, James	1	2	4			Eaton, Ephraim	1	2	4			Foster, Jacob	2	1	5		
Sargeant, Moses	1	2	5			Edmonds, Edward	1	1	2			Forrist, William	1	1	4		
Smith, Obadiah	2	1	2			Eaton, John	1	1	1			Foster, Jonᵃ	2		4		
Smith, Obadiah, Jʳ	1	1	1			Eaton, Jesse	1	1	5			Foster, Asa	3		4		
Smith, Oliver	1	2	2			Emerson, Moses	1	1	2			Foster, Daniel	2	1	5		
Scribner, Samˡ	2	2	4			Emerson, Nathˡ	2	2	6			Foster, Daniel, junʳ	1		2		
Sargeant, Thoˢ	2	1	1			Eaton, Paul	2	1	3			Forrist, John	2	1	1		
Towl, Benjᵃ	2	2	6			Fith, Abraham	2	3	2			Foster, Abiel, Esqʳ	5		6		
Turner, Moses	1	1	3			Fith, Daniel	1	1	2			Fowler, Abner	1	1	3		
Towl, Wm	1	1	1			French, Moses	2	3	4			Garrish, Samuel	4	1	1		
Towl, Wm., Jʳ	1	1	4			French, Nick	2	3	4			Gibson, James, junʳ	2				
Vernum, James	1	1	4			Foster, Samˡ	1		2			Glines, William	3	2	4		
Tyler, John	1	3	3			Fifield, Stephen	1	3	3			Gibson, James	1		3		
Thorn, Nathˡ	1	2	2			French, Simon	1	3	2			Gibson, Thomas	1	2	4		
Towl, Samˡ	3	2	5			Goodwin, Ebenezer	1	1	2			Gaut, William	2	2	3		
Turner, Wm	1		3			Gibson, James	1	1	1			Glover, John	1	3	1		
Whitaker, Anna	1		3			Hallbert, Benjᵃ	2	1	3			Glines, Nathˡ	1	3	3		
Wadley, Benjᵃ	1		1			Hall, Benjᵃ	1	1	2			Ham, John	1				
Worthen, Jacob	1	2	2			Hills, David	2	1	6			Ham, Joseph	1	1	1		
Worthen, Jacob, Jʳ	1	1	1			Hills, John	1	3	5			Hogsdon, Miles	1		2		
Wiggen, John	2	3	4			Hills, Jonᵃ	2	2	2			Haynes, Samuel	2	4	3		
Woodman, Jonᵃ	2	1	8			Hills, Jethro	2	2	6			Haynes, Richard	1	1	4		
Wason, John	2		2			Hall, Nathˡ	3	1	4			Heath, Caleb	2	1	5		
Wauson, Robert	2	4	2			Hall, Obededam	3	4	4			Hoit, Abner	2	3	3		
Wilson, Robert	2	3	2			Hardy, Samˡ	2		5			Haseltine, William	2	2	3		
Worthen, Samˡ	3	2	5			Judkins, John	1	4	2			Hall, Obediah	1	3	6		
Wason, Thoˢ., Jʳ	1	1	5			Knowles, Amos	1	1	3			Hacket, Jeremiah	4	1	3		
Wadley, Widow Poley		1	2			Knowles, Ephraim	1	3	4			Heath, Daniel	1	1	3		
Currier, Thoˢ	1		2			Karr, John	2	1	6			Hacket, Wᵈ Sarrah			1		
Miller, Willm	1	1	1			Knowles, Seth	1	1	2			Heath, Simon	1				
Rowe, Thoˢ	1		1			Libbey, Arthur	2	3	4			Hoit, Abner, junʳ	1	2	3		
Long, Benjᵃ., Jʳ	1	1	2			Long, Benjᵃ	1	3	3			Ingalls, John	5		2		
Whitaker, Danˡ	3	3	3			Lane, John	2	3	4			Jackson, Moses	2	2	2		
Calden, Thoˢ	1	2	2			Lane, Peter	1	2	2			Jonson, John	2	1	5		
Wilson, Thoˢ	1	1	5			Knowles, Amos	2	1	3			Jones, Benjᵃ	1	3	2		
Wilson, Thoˢ., Jʳ	1		4			Collins, John						Jackson, Samuel	3	1	4		
Foot, Samˡ	1		5									Kent, John, junʳ	3		1		
Wadleigh, Danˡ	1		1			CANTERBURY TOWN.						Kimball, Ebenezʳ	2	2	4		
Burbank, Thomas	1		5			Aras, Joseph	2		4		3	Kimball, John	2	3	2		
Anderson, Thomas	1	1	1			Ames, Samuel	4	3	6			Lange, Jonᵃ, junʳ					
Anderson, Thomas, Jʳ	1					Ames, Simon	2		2			Liford, James	4	3	3		
Anderson, Wm	1		1			Asten, Thoˢ	1		1			Liford, John	3		2		
Batchelder, Benjᵃ	2	2	4			Asten, Peter	3	1	2			Lange, Jonᵃ	1	1	1		
Bagley, Jonᵃ	3	2	5			Biglow, Stedmon	1	1	2			Lange, Simeon	1	1	1		
Bagley, Samuel	2	2	5			Bracket, Simeon	1		1			Lange, Edmund	2		1		
Bagley, Jacob	2	4	7			Beck, Henery	2	2	4			Lange, Moses	1	2	1		
Brown, Aaron	1	1	1			Boynton, Joshua	2	1	2	1		Luis, Thomas	1		8		
Bean, Abijah	2	1	2			Blake, John	1	2	3			Morill, Ezekle	14	4	22		
Brown, Caleb	2	2	7			Bartlet, Gideon	2	1	5			Marthews, Elijah	1	1	4		
Brown, David	2	2	2			Bracket, Ichobad	1		3			Moore, Archelus	1		1		
Bean, Jerᵉʰ	1	2	3			Bradley, Benjⁿ	1		3			Moor, Joseph	1	2	4		
Bean, Jonᵃ	2		3			Brier, John	1	6	4			Moore, William	2	4	4		
Bean, Joseph	2	2	6			Bradley, Jonᵃ	2	2	4			Moore, John	3	3	1		
Brown, Jonᵃ	2	6	5			Bean, John	3	4	4			Mann, James	1	1	1		
Brown, Jonᵃ., Jʳ	2	3	5			Blanchard, Benjⁿ	4	3	4			Morrill, Laban	4	2	5		
Buswell, Moses	1	1	2			Brown, Simeon	2	2	5			Moore, Ezikle	1		1		
Brown, Nathˡ	1	1	3			Blanchard, Stephen	1		4			Meloony, James	1	1	2		
Burpee, Nathˡ., Jʳ	1	1	2			Clough, Leavitt	1	1	3			Morrill, Marstin	2	1	5		
Burpee, Nathan	2		3									Mooney, Obediah	1	1	3		

ROCKINGHAM COUNTY—Continued.

CANTERBURY TOWN—continued.

NAME OF HEAD OF FAMILY.	Free white males of 16 years and upward, including heads of families.	Free white males under 16 years.	Free white females, including heads of families.	All other free persons.	Slaves.
Moore, Samuel	1	3	3		
McCrillis, David	4	1	7		
Marden, Josiah	1		1		
Morrill, David	2	1	6		
Merriner, Nicholas	1		1		
Peverly, Nathˡ	4	3	2		
Pallett, Nathˡ	2	2	5		
Rawlings, Joshua	1	2	3		
Randall, Richard	2	1	4		
Ralph, William	1	2	7		
Small, John	1	1	2		
Small, Ephriam	1	1	2		
Shannon, John	1				
Small, Isaac	1		4		
Sandborn, Joseph	3	4	12		
Sargent, Samuel	2	4	5		
Stephens, Jesse	1	1	3		
Sandborn, Benjamin	2		4		
Sargent, Elijah	4		2		
Shepard, Morrill	2		2		
Soper, Joseph	1		2		
Shepard, James	2	1	5		
Sutton, John	1	1	2		
Stephens, Simon	1	4	2		
Simonds, William	1				
Sinkler, Noah	1	3	4		
Sutton, Michael	2	2	3		
Schales, Edwᵈ	1		3		
Tibbits, Henery	3	3	6		
Tallent, Margret		2	2		
Whidden, Nathˡ	1	1	3		
Watson, Josiah	1		2		
Wiggin, Chase	2	2	5		
Whitcher, Benjⁿ	10	6	19		
Ward, Thoˢ	2	2	5		
Williams, Jonᵃ	1		8		
Whidden, Person	1	1	2		
Weeks, Joshua	3	2	5		
Walker, William	1	3	3		
Weeks, Samˡ	1	1	1		
Young, Joseph	1		1		
Young, Winthrop	1	4	5		
Glines, Nathˡ	1	2	2		
Foss, Josiah	1				
Randall, Danˡ	1	2	2		
Foster, David	2	3	2		
Coggswell, John	1	1	2		
Runnels, Enoch	1	2	1		
Bardeen, Nathˡ	1	1	4		
Whitcher, Jeddediah	2	1	1		
Heath, Jonathan	1		2		

CHESTER TOWN.

NAME OF HEAD OF FAMILY.	Free white males of 16 years and upward, including heads of families.	Free white males under 16 years.	Free white females, including heads of families.	All other free persons.	Slaves.
Sargeant, Abraham	2	2	8		
Shirley, William	2		3		
Shirley, Hugh	2	2	2		
Shirley, John	3	1	2		
Cops, Joseph	1	1	2		
Hall, Peter	2	4	3		
Jack, Jonᵃ	1		2		
Cops, Joshua	1	1	1		
Towel, Anthony	1		2		
Wilson, Wᵐ	2	1	3		
Jack, Samˡ	3	3	4		
Hazeltine, Moses	1	4	2		
Hazeltine, John	1	3	4		
Hazeltine, Peter	1		2		
Forshlith, Robert	2	4	6		
Hazeltine, Benjᵃ	1	3	3		
Tolford, Hugh	3	1	3		
Davis, Ichabod	1	4	4		
Sever, Thoˢ	1		3		
Mills, David	1	5	2		
Campbell, Alexⁿ	1	6	2		
Chase, Pearley	1	1	3		
Fuller, Benjᵃ	1		1		
Hoit, Jabez	3	1	2		
Dearborn, Joseph	2	1	5		
Hills, Benjᵃ	1	2	4		
Wilson, John	2	4	3		
Crawford, James	2	1	2		
Green, Jacob, Esq	1	3	5		
Rowel, Samˡ	1		3		
Dearborn, Sherburne	1	2	2		
Smith, Wᵐ	1	2	1		
Emerson, John	1	1	4		
Mills, Benjᵃ	1	2	2		
Dearborn, John	1	2	9		
Buck, Moses	1	2	2		

CHESTER TOWN—con.

NAME OF HEAD OF FAMILY.	Free white males of 16 years and upward, including heads of families.	Free white males under 16 years.	Free white females, including heads of families.	All other free persons.	Slaves.
Waddel, James	1		4		
Hills, Jacob	2	1	5		
Webster, Nathan	2	2	7		
Wilson, Benjᵃ	1		2		
Wilson, Wᵐ	1	2	1		
Wilson, James, Jr	3	1	2		
Wilson, Samˡ	2		3		
Colby, Jethro	2	1	4		
Merril, Amos	1				
Sleeper, Edmund	1	1	3		
Richardson, Thoˢ	1		1		
Severance, Ruth		1	3		
Roby, Edward	1	3	5		
Page, Benjᵃ	2	3	5		
Richardson, Pierson	2	1	2		
Dearborn, Benjⁱ	1	4	2		
Wiggins, Joseph	1		3		
Bell, Willᵐ	4	1	3		
Greenough, Danˡ	1	2	2		
Townsend, Ebenzʳ	3	3	5		
Towl, Simon	2	4	2		
Glitton, Nathˡ	1	1	2		
Mills, Willᵐ	2	3	4		
Folensby, Nathan	1	2	2		
Tolford, William	2				
Hazeltine, Richᵈ	1	3	4		
Emerson, Samˡ	1		2		
Mills, John	1	3	2		
Grimes, John	2		3		
Grimes, Robert	1		4		
Silver, Abraham	2	1	2		
Sargeant, Phebe			1		
Gilchrist, Wᵐ	1		1		
Miller, Robert	1				
White, Willᵐ	3	3	6		
Wier, Daniel	1	2	4		
Long, Benjᵃ	2	4	3		
Shaw, David	2	3	2		
Dearborn, Asa	2	2	5		
Dunlap, James	1	1	2		
Dearborn, Jonᵃ	2	2	5		
French, Jabez	2		3		
Worthen, Ezekiel	2	2	3		
Clay, Stephen	1	3	3		
Worthen, Michael	3	1	5		
Hills, Isaac	4	1	3		
Hills, Stephen	3	1	3		
Curtis, George	1	1	2		
Hills, Benjᵃ, Jr	2		2		
Hills, Benjᵃ	1	2	2		
Long, Joseph	1	1	3		
Wilson, David	1	4	4		
Richardson, Daniel	1	2	3		
Wilson, Robert	2		6		
Wilson, John	1	1	2		
Bruce, Moses	2	1	5		
Moor, Henry	2	1	2		
Moor, Charles	1				
Knowles, John	1	1	1		
Hoit, John	2		3		
Hoit, Benjᵃ	2		7		
True, Joseph	3		2		
True, Benjᵃ	2		2		
Furnel, Thoˢ	1	1	3		
McLelen, Joseph	2	1	3		
McLelen, Andrew					
Lock, Willᵐ	2	1	4		
Knowles, Nathan	2		2		
Basford, Jacob	1	1	3		
Webster, Nathan, Jr	1	1	2		
Wason, Thomas	1				
Wason, James	2	3	4		
Brown, Samuel	1		1		
Brown, Joseph	1	3	2		
Knowles, John	3	2	3		
Knowles, John, Jr	1		2		
Basford, John	2				
Basford, Ebenezer	2	3	3		
Prescott, Daniel	1	2	3		
Prescott, Minilims	1	1	2		
Hills, Abner	2	2	1		
French, Mary		2	3		
French, Benjᵃ	3	1	4		
Currier, Benjᵃ	3	2	8		
Currier, Gideon	2	2	5		
Hills, Peter	2		2		
Knowles, Joseph	2		3		
Marden, George	1	2	3		
Dolbar, Israel	2		2		
Lane, John	2		1		
Lane, Isaac	2		6		

CHESTER TOWN—con.

NAME OF HEAD OF FAMILY.	Free white males of 16 years and upward, including heads of families.	Free white males under 16 years.	Free white females, including heads of families.	All other free persons.	Slaves.
Butterfield, John	1	1	2		
Libbey, Benjᵃ	1		4		
Hall, Joshua	3		2		
Hall, Moses K	1		2		
Hall, Reuben	1				
Brown, Richard	1	1	7		
Nudd, Samˡ	1	1	5		
Norton, Joseph	3		3		
Norton, Jonᵃ	1	2	2		
Barrey, Jonᵃ	3	2	4		
Forsaith, Matthew	1		2		
Forsaith, Josiah	2	3	3		
Shackford, Samˡ	2		2		
Quimby, Bradbury	1		1		
True, Benjᵃ	1		3		
True, Joseph	1	1	1		
Richardson, Danˡ	3	1	1		
Morse, Joseph	1	4	4		
Morse, Josiah	2	3	4		
West, Wilks	3	3	4		
Flagg, Revᵈ Mʳ	1				
Flagg, Josiah, Esqʳ	2	3	4		
Melven, Benjᵃ	1	5	2		
Dearborn, Ebenezer	1	2	1		
Seargeant, Doctʳ Thoˢ	2	1	3		
Webster, John	2	1	5		
Blasdel, Isaac	2		4		
Webster, Toppan	2	1	5		
Hicks, William	1				
Sandborn, Moses	1	1	1		
Roby, Edward, Esqʳ	1	2	3		
Elliot, Benjᵃ	2		3		
Killy, Ezekiel	1	1	3		
Brown, Benjᵃ	1	1	6		
Runnels, Robert	1	3	2		
Underhill, Moses, Jr	1	1	2		
Underhill, John, Jr	1	1	3		
Pierce, James	2	3	6		
Hodgkins, Daniel	1	1	3		
Luftkin, Stephen	1	4	2		
Chase, Jacob	2	1	2		
Chase, Stephen	1	1	3		
Underhill, John	3		2		
Underhill, Samˡ	1	3	2		
Preson, Edward	2	3	2		
Heath, Levy	2		1		
Preson, Moses	1	1	3		
Clark, Reuben	1	1	2		
Merril, Thoˢ	1		2		
Hall, Joseph	1	4	3		
Hall, Jonᵃ	1		1		1
Hall, Benjᵃ	2	4	2		
Towle, Isaac	1		1		
Towle, Abraham	2	1	2		
Underhill, Hezekiah	1		2		
Underhill, Josiah	1	3	2		
Hills, Benjᵃ	1	2	2		
Lanecy, Robert	1		2		
Hall, Nathˡ	1		3		
Calfe, Joseph	3		1		
Blunt, Joshua	1	1	1		
Grimes, John		1	2		
Patten, John	1	1	4		
Leach, Wᵐ	1	2	4		
O'Donovan, Denis	2	3	4		
Shirley, Samˡ	2	2	5		
Shirley, James	1	1	1		
Shirley, Alexʳ	2	1	2		
Blanchard, Joseph	2	3	5		
Currier, David	1	1	2		
Wilson, Adam	1		1		
Wilson, William, Jr	1		2		
Crawford, John	1	1	5		
Crawford, John, Jr	1				
Underhill, Moses	2		2		
Crombie, Moses	1	1	2		
Underhill, Nathˡ	1	1	2		
Crombie, Benjᵃ	2		1		
Fields, John	1				
Davis, Jonᵃ	1		5		
Davis, Samˡ	3	2	3		
Porter, Samuel	1	1	4		
Willson, John	1	1	3		
Smith, Joseph	1	1	2		
Griffin, Philip	1		1		
Griffin, John	1		3		
Shannon, John	1		2		
Shannon, Thoˢ	1		2		
Shannon, William	1	2	4		
Leavitt, Nathˡ	1	1	1		
Leavitt, Jeremiah	1	2	1		

ROCKINGHAM COUNTY—Continued.

CHESTER TOWN—con.

NAME OF HEAD OF FAMILY.	Free white males of 16 years and upward, including heads of families.	Free white males under 16 years.	Free white females, including heads of families.	All other free persons.	Slaves.
Rand, John	1		1		
Rand, Jerem^h	1	1	3		
Pain, John	1		3		
Griffin, Abij^h	1	2	1		
Barney, Ithamar	1	1	2		
Barney, Moses	1		2		
Griffin, Nathl	1	2	4		
Sevey, John	1	2	1		
Sever, El^h	1		1		
Morse, Abraham	2		4		
Smith, Benjn	1		3		
Poor, Eliph^t	1		5		
Barney, Anna			3		
Carr, Joseph, Jr	1		1		
Pilsbury, Elijah	2		3		
Weeks, W^m	2	3	4		
Richardson, Moses	3		3		
Carr, Joseph	2		5		
Lane, Benaiah	1		3		
Moor, Charles	2	4	2		
Prescutt, John	2	1	2		
Griffin, Jerem^h		2	3		
Grose, William	1	1	2		
Ran, John	1		1		
Payne, John	1		2		
Rand, Jerem^h	1	1	4		
Morrel, Adam	2	3	5		
Lynn, Joseph	2	1	7		
Silver, James	2		5		
Fowler, Thos	1		7		
McDuffee, Archibald	2	2	6		
Worthen, Stephen	1	4	1		
Worthen, Aquila	1		1		
Hoit, W^m	1	2	2		
Hall, Joshua	1	1	3		
McDuffee, Mansfield	1		2		
McDuffee, Hugh	1		4		
McDuffee, James	1	2	3		
Layker, Saml	1	1	4		
Moors, Stephen	3		3		
Moors, Joshua	2		1		
Emerson, Amos	3	1	5		
Emerson, Jonath^n	1		2		
Gage, Saml. H.	1	4	3		
Currier, Simeon	2	3	2		
Lynn, Joseph			3		
Moors, Amos	1	2	5		
Brown, W^m	1	1	3		
Towl, Francis	2	2	5		
Lehead, Robert	1		3		
Dinsmore, Arthur	2	3	3		
Aiken, Peter	1	3	4		
Aiken, Daniel	1		2		
Aiken, Mary	1	1	2		
Weatherspoon, David	1	4	2		
Northen, Saml	1	3	3		
McKinley, Robert	1	2	5		
Dinsmore, Robert	1	4	2		
Templeton, Matthew	1		1		
Burbank, Arthur	1	6	1		
Shirley, Thos	1	2	3		
McMaster, Thos	1		2		
Hunter, James	2		4		
Presson, Robt	1	2	1		
Eaton, Alexander	1		3		
Patten, David	1	1	2		
Griffin, John	1	3	2		
Archibald, John	1	1	2		
Bangan, John	1		3		
Brown, Benj^a	1	1	2		
Wells, James	1	2	3		
Brown, William	1	1	3		
Pierce, Saml	1		2		
Brown, Joshua	1		3		
Merril, Stephen	1		2		
Merril, Barnard	1	2	2		
Grimes, Mary			4		
McFarland, James	1	1	2		
Crombie, Hugh	2	1	3		
McMurphy, James	1	1	3		
Dustin, Mavey			4		
Orr, John	1		1		
Orr, James	1	1	3		
Craige, John	2		1		
Weatherspoon, Robert	1	1	1		
Wawson, James	1		3		
McFarland, James	1	1	3		
White, Saml	2		3		
Emery, Jon^a	1	5	4		
Harper, Daniel	1	1	1		
March, Stephen	2		4		
Martin, Nathl	1	4	4		

CHESTER TOWN—con.

NAME OF HEAD OF FAMILY.	Free white males of 16 years and upward, including heads of families.	Free white males under 16 years.	Free white females, including heads of families.	All other free persons.	Slaves.
Karr, Simeon	2		4		
Karr, David	1	3	3		
Davis, Robert	1	1	1		
Herriman, Rufus	2	5	2		
Gordon, Robert	1	4	3		
Otterson, James			4		
Brown, Saml	3		6		
Brown, W^m	2	3	3		
Brown, Joseph	3	2	4		
Head, Nathl	2	3	4		
Gott, Nathl	1	2	3		
Mores, Anthony	2	1	4		
Martin, Daniel	2	1	7		
Dalton, John	1	1	2		
Stevens, Henry	1	1	4		
Kimball, Jesse	3	4	2		
Emerson, James	1	4	3		
Laykin, John	3	1	3		
Allen, Danl	1	2	2		
Hall, Caleb	2		3		
Dearborn, Stephen	1		3		
Dearborn, Rich^d	1		3		
Chase, Moody	3	4	4		
Chase, Wells	1		1		
Chase, B. Pike	1	2	1		
Wood, Nathl	2	1	2		
Underhill, Jerem^h	1	4		2	
Dearborn, Stephen	1		3		
Dearborn, Rich^d	1		3		
Murray, Saml	1	2	3		
Clark, John	1	2	3		
Bracket, Barnett	2	1	4		
Moors, Abraham	2		4		

CHICHESTER TOWN.

NAME OF HEAD OF FAMILY.	Free white males of 16 years and upward, including heads of families.	Free white males under 16 years.	Free white females, including heads of families.	All other free persons.	Slaves.
Seavey, Mark	1		1		
Seavey, George	4	1	2		
Green, Jabish	2		3		
Marden, James	3	2	7		
Shaw, Hilyard	3	2	4		
Sergent, George	1	2	4		
Davis, Caleb	1	3	3		
Stonning, Mary			2		
Hook, Peter	1	1	1		
Hook, Dier	1	1	3		
Brown, David	1	1	5		
Cram, Stephen	1	1	2		
Robey, Samuel	2	1	4		
Hilyard, Simeon	1	3	5		
Hilyard, John	1	3	5		
Jackson, Samuel	1		2		
M^cfield, John	2	2	4		
Jackson, Benjamin	2	2	5		
Sandborn, Abra^m	1	2	4		
James, Samuel	3	3	5		
Lake, Thos	2	1	3		
Sandborn, Joseph	1	2	1		
Sandborn, Jeremiah	2	1	3		
Fellows, Joseph	1	1	3		
Hilyard, Zebulon	3	3	5		
Prescoot, James	2	2	3		
Smith, David	1	3	4		
Dow, Parley	1	2	3		
Mason, Benjn, jr	2	2	2		
Mason, Benjn	5	3	4		
Mason, Joseph	2		5		
Kenny, Joseph	1	3	2		
Green, Simon	1	1	4		
Dow, Joseph	1	2	2		
Loin, Joshua	2		2		
Miller, David	3	2	4		
Brown, Nathan	4	1	2		
Tilton, Danl	1		3		
Sergent, Richard	1	3	3		
Brown, Amos	1	2	2		
Towel, Joshua	1	1	2		
Lion, Asa	1		2		
True, Abra^m	1	3	3		
Tilton, Asa	1	1	2		
Moses, William	1	2	2		
Purrington, Joseph	1	1	1		
Shaw, Benjn	1		1		
Sandborn, Jacob	1	1	1		
Prevear, Nathl	1	1	1		
Morill, Joses	2	1	3		
Lake, Thomas, jun^r	1		2		
Sanborn, Levi	1	3	2		
Morrill, Smith	1	5	2		
Edmans, Edward	2		4		
Edmans, William	1		1		
Rand, Edward	1	2	3		

CHICHESTER TOWN—continued.

NAME OF HEAD OF FAMILY.	Free white males of 16 years and upward, including heads of families.	Free white males under 16 years.	Free white females, including heads of families.	All other free persons.	Slaves.
Langmaid, John	3	2	5		
Edmans, Jon^a	1	3	3		
Hook, Frances	4	3	3		
Drake, Thomas	5		2		
Stonning, John	1	1	2		
Stonning, Jacob	1	1	1		
Sandborn, Theophilus	3	3	3		
Davis, Samuel	1		1		
Davis, Samuel, jun^r	1	1	2		
Leavitt, Edmund	1	2	3		
Hook, Thos	1		2		
Stonning, Jedediah	1		2		
Stonning, Levi	1	1	3		
Leavitt, Jon^a	3	2	3		
Prevear, Benjn	1	1	3		
Sandborn, Dudly	2	2	9		
Morrill, Joseph, jun^r	1		2		
Moulton, Joseph	3		4		
Sevea, William	5	1	2		
Bachelder, Nathl	1	2	4		
Morrill, Paul	4	1	3		
Wilkerson, Benning	1	1	3		
Haines, Meline	1	2	4		
Hanes, Benjn	1		1		
Knox, Tim^o	1	3	4		
Morrill, Malchijah	2	1	2		

CONCORD TOWN.

NAME OF HEAD OF FAMILY.	Free white males of 16 years and upward, including heads of families.	Free white males under 16 years.	Free white females, including heads of families.	All other free persons.	Slaves.
Abbott, Joseph	2	2	3		
Abbott, Nathl	2		3		
Abbott, Isaac	2		1		
Abbott, Edward	5	3	4		
Abbott, Benjn, jun^r	3	1	5		
Abbott, Nathl. C.	1	2	5		
Ayers, Richard	4	4	3		
Abbott, Amos	3		3		
Abbott, Jabez	2	1	5		
Abbott, Nathan	3		5		
Abbott, Jesse	3	1	3		
Abbott, Ruben	2	1	9		
Abbott, Elias	1	1	3		
Abbott, Daniel	1	3	4		
Abbott, Moses	1	4	3		
Abbott, Ezra	2		4		
Abbott, Nathaniel, Jr.	2	1	3		
Abbott, Joseph, jun^r	1				
Abbott, Joshua	3	2	3		
Andrews, Thomas	1		1		
Ambrose, Robert	4	1	3		
Ambrose, Jon^a	1		1		
Ambrose, Nathl	2		3		
Austin, Aron	1		1		
Abbott, Jacob	1				
Bradley, John	2	4	4		
Buzell, Caleb	1	4	2		
Bunker, Abel	1	1	3		
Badger, John	1				
Bradley, Moses	2		1		
Bradley, Jeremiah	3				
Bradley, Samuel	1	1	4		
Butler, Samuel	2	3	2		
Blanchard, John	2	1	2		
Brown, Enoch	1				
Bradley, Timothy	2	2	6		
Chandler, Jeremiah	1				
Carter, Ezikle	2		1		
Carter, David	1	1	1		
Carter, Ezra	2	1	7		
Coffin, William	3		4		
Colby, John	1	2	5		
Carrigan, Phillip	4		2		
Claiasby, Joseph	1	4	2		
Carter, Ephriam, jur	1		2		
Colby, John	1	4	3		
Corlis, George	2		2		
Chase, Daniel	2		1		
Chase, Isaac	1	1	3		
Carter, Daniel	3	3	4		
Carter, Joseph	2	2	4		
Carter, Moses	1	3	2		
Currier, William	2	1	6		
Currier, Joshua	1	1	3		
Currier, John					
Currier, Nathl	2	4	3		
Colby, John, jun^r	2	1	6		
Clough, Joseph	2	2	5		
Chandler, Thomas	1		3		
Carter, Ephriam	2	1	5		
Chandler, Timothy	3	1	3		
Chandler, John	2		3		

ROCKINGHAM COUNTY—Continued.

NAME OF HEAD OF FAMILY.	Free white males of 16 years and upward, including heads of families.	Free white males under 16 years.	Free white females, including heads of families.	All other free persons.	Slaves.	NAME OF HEAD OF FAMILY.	Free white males of 16 years and upward, including heads of families.	Free white males under 16 years.	Free white females, including heads of families.	All other free persons.	Slaves.	NAME OF HEAD OF FAMILY.	Free white males of 16 years and upward, including heads of families.	Free white males under 16 years.	Free white females, including heads of families.	All other free persons.	Slaves.
CONCORD TOWN—con.						CONCORD TOWN—con.						CONCORD TOWN—con.					
Chandler, Joseph	1	2	2			How, George	3	1	2			Chase, Joseph, jr	1	1	2		
Crosman, Stephen	2	2	4			Hartshorn, Jeremiah	2	1	2			Elliott, Jonᵃ, junʳ	1	4	2		
Carter, Jacob	1	1	5			Heath, Amos	1	1	5			Eastman, Joseph, junʳ	2		5		
Caulton, Gideon	1					Heath, Amos, junʳ	1					Eastman, Moses	4		4		
Colby, Joseph	1	3	5			Heath, Elias	1					Farnham, Ebenezʳ	1	1	3		
Davis, Robert	3	1	6			Hoit, John	2	3	5			Farnam, Ephriam, junʳ	1	1	5		
Davis, Benjamin	1					Jonson, James	1	1	2			Foss, Ebenzʳ	1	2	3		
Dow, Timᵒ	1	4	4			Jonson, Jonᵃ	1	3	5			Hoitt, Joseph	2		3		
Dow, Ebenezʳ	4	1	2			Kimball, John	3		2			Morse, Stephen	1		1		
Davis, Samuel	2	1	5			Kimball, Stephen	1	5	3			Marten, Henery	3	3	4		
Dimond, Ruben	1	3	4			Kimball, Timothy	2	1	3			Evans, Isᶜ	1	1	2		
Dimond, John	1	2	3			Kent, William A	2					Framble, John	1	2	4		
Davis, Nathan	1	2	3			Kimball, Capt. Ruben	4		7			Kimball, Benjᵃ	1	1	2		
Dimond, Ezikle	1	2	5			Kimball, Asa	3	2	3			Virgin, Ebenzʳ, junʳ	2	1	2		
Dimond, Jacob	1					Kimball, Phineas	2	3	3			Frambell, John	1	2	4		
Dimond, Isaac	1					Kimball, Benjᵃ	4	1	5			Hoitt, John, junʳ	1		2		
Dimond, Abner	1					Kimball, Mellin	1		2			Colby, Joseph	1	2	4		
Dimond, Israel	1					Livermore, Daniel	3	1	1			Sattin, Sollomon	1				
Duncan, Majʳ. Wᵐ	4	2	4			Livermore, Edward S	3	3	4			Chandier, Joshua	2	1	5		
Emery, Benjᵃ	2	4	3			Ladd, Dudley	1	3	1			Ralph, Nathˡ	2	2	4		
Emerson, Jonᵃ	2	2	5			Lovejoy, Henery	1		1			Parker, Enoch	1	2	4		
Eaton, Thomas	3	1	6			Lovejoy, Chandler	2	1	3			Hoitt, Joseph	1		2		
Eastman, William	1	2	4			Lovejoy, John	1		1			Abbott, Samuel	1	1	2		
Elliott, John	4		6			Morse, Benjᵃ	2	2	5			Abbott, Nathan, 3ᵈ	1		2		
Elliott, John, jur	1	4	1			Moulton, Henery	2		4			Dimond, Ezeikle	5		3		
Elliott, Bernerd	1	3	3			Moulton, Jonᵃ	1		1			Bradley, Rufus	1	1	1		
Elliott, Jonᵃ	2		4			Odlin, John	3		2			Chase, Daniel	2	3	4		
Emerson, Elizer	1					Osgood, Richard F	2	1	2			Abbott, Timothy	1	2	5		
Eastman, Robert	2	1	2			Parker, Enoch	1	1	6			Patridge, Toby	1	1	2		
Eastman, Jonᵃ	3	4	2			Parker, Asa	2	3	2			Dustin, Ebenzʳ	4	2	2		
Eastman, Stetson	1	1	1			Page, Job	1	1	3			Colbey, Sol				4	
Eastman, John	3	3	4			Powell, Benjᵃ	1	1	2			Stone, Andrew	1	1	2		
Eastman, Ebenʳ	1		1			Page, Daniel	1	3	4			Stone, David	1	4	1		
Eastman, Peasley	2		2			Potter, Ephriam	1	3	6								
Eastman, Caleb	1		1			Potter, Richard	2		2			DEERFIELD TOWN.					
Eastman, Moses	2	2	5			Potter, Anthony	1		1								
Eastman, Nathˡ	2	2	5			Ralph, Nathˡ., junʳ	2	3	4			Morrill, Adonijah	1	1	1		
Eastman, Jacob	2	1	4			Ralph, Benjᵃ	1	2	3			Prescott, Abraham	1	2	3		
Eastman, William	1	2	4			Rowell, Cristopher	2		1			Nealey, Andrew	1	4	3		
Eastman, Jeremiah	1	1	2			Runnells, Joseph	1	4	3			Bartlett, Abiel	2	3	4		
Eastman, Henery	1					Roach, John	1	1	2			Prescott, Anna	1	1	3		
Eastman, James	1					Runnels, Jonᵃ	3	3	3			Hoitt, Enoch	1				
Farnham, Benjᵃ	3	4	5			Rogers, Daniel	2		2			Towl, Benjᵃ	1		2		
Farnham, Ephram	2		4	1		Rollins, David	1	2	2			Sandborn, Benjᵃ	3		8		
Farnham, Sarah	1		4			Rix, James	1					Fellows, Benjᵃ	1	3	3		
Farnham, Joseph	2		3			Stickney, William	1	3	3			Griffin, Benjᵃ	1				
Farnham, Stephen	2	2	3			Sweatt, Benjᵃ	1					Sargent, Benjᵃ	2	1	6		
Farnham, Joseph, jr	2		4			Sweatt, Benjᵃ, junʳ	1					Mudget, Bennonia	1	1	2		
Farnham, Daniel	1	1	2			Stickney, Thomas	3	1	4			Prescott, Chase	1	1	2		
Farnham, Abner	2	5	2			Stevens, John, Esqʳ	1	4	4			Leavitt, Dudly	3		3		
Farnham, John	2	3	5			Stickney, Jonᵃ	3	4	5			Bachelder, David, jur	1		3		
Farnham, Josiah	3		2			Shute, John	3	4	3			Bachelder, David	3	1	3		
Fisk, Ephriam	2	5	6			Shute, John, junʳ	1	2	2			Leavitt, Dudley, jʳ	1				
Fisk, Ephriam, jr	1	2	3			Souther, John	1	2	2			Moulton, David	1		1		
Flanders, Richard	2	2	3			Stone, David	2	5	4			Hains, David	1	3	5		
Fiffield, Benjᵃ	1		3			Stone, Andrew	1		1			Prescott, Enoch	1				
Fiffield, William	1	4	2			Sheppard, Isaac	3					Chadwick, Edmund	3	3	5		
Flanders, Abner	1	5	2			Stickney, Danˡ	1	2	3			Griffin, Eliphalet	1		1		
Flanders, Oliver	2	4	2			Smith, Joseph	1	1	2			Eastman, Ephriam	1	3	4		
Fuber, Nathˡ	1	1	2			Stevens, James	4	3	9			French, Enoch	3		2		
Fiffield, Paul	1					Shaw, Thomas	1		2			Robbie, Enoch	1		3		
Foss, Timothy	2		5			Scales, James	2	2	4			Bachelder, Ephᵐ	2		3		
Green, Peter	2	3	5			Tuttle, Stephen	1	4	1			Eastman, Ephᵐ, junʳ	1				
George, David	4	3	7			Towle, Jacob	3	4	5		1	Brown, Enoch	1	4	3		
George, David, junʳ	2	1	2			Thompson, wᵈ Sarah			2		1	Sandborn, Enos	2		2		
Green, Peter, Esqʳ	4	2	5			Turner, William	1					Smith, Edward	2	1	3		
Gale, Daniel	4	1	5			Thopson, Joshua	1		2			Ham Gideon	1				
Gage, John	1	1	3			Thopson, Samuel	1	3	3			Wallis, George	2		3		
Graham, George	2		3			Tucker, Eliphalet	1		2			Seavey, George	2		3		
Graham, Joshua	1	3	2			Virgin, Phineas	2	1	2			Morris, Henery	1				
Godwin, Samuel	1	2	6			Virgin, Ebenʳ	3	2	2			Eastman, Henery	1	1	3		
Gage, Sollomon	2	1				Virgin, William	2	1	7			Chase, Hannah		2	1		
Herbert, Richard	3	2	5	1		Virgin, Jonᵃ	2	2	3			Leavitt, Joshua	3	2	2		
Hannaford, Benjᵃ	4		4			Virgin, Danˡ	1		2			Morse, John, jᵘʳ	1	1	1		
Hall, David	3		3			Virgin, Betty		2	3			Morse, John	1				
Hoitt, Oliver	1	3	6			Walker, Timᵒ	3	2	9	1		Wiggin, William	3		3		
Hardy, Asa	1	2	3			Walker, James	3	3	3			Prescott, Jese, jr	1				
How, Phineas	2	2	4			Walker, Bruce	1	4	2			Eastman, Jeremiah	2		4		
Hoitt, Moses	1					West, John	2	2	3			Eastman, Jeremiah, jr	1				
Hall, Joseph, & Wilkins, M	5		5		2	Wood, Richard	1		2			Ham, Joseph	2	1	4		
Hall, Ebenezʳ	1		2			Wheeler, Jeremiah	2	1	4			Langley, James	4	4	4		
Hall, Stephen	3	3	6			Whitney, Leonerd	1	2	2			Morrison, James	2		4		
Haseltine, Lt. Joseph	2	2	3			Wilson, Thomas	8	1	5			Avery, John	1		2		
Haseltine, Richard	3	1	4	1		Weeks, John	1		4			March, Joseph, Esqʳ	2		3		1
Hazetine, James	3	2	5			Worthen, Jacob	1					Parsons, John	1		2		
Harris, Robert	4	1	5			Young, Hezekiah	1	2	3			Phillbrick, Jonᵃ	3	2	4		
Houston, Isaac	3		3			Cain, John	1		1			True, Jacob	1	1	6		
Hall, Daniel	1	7	3			Perkison, Henery	1	4	3			Gove, Jeremiah	2	1	1		
Hutchins, Abel & L	2	3	5			Chase, Claleb	1	3	7			Prescott, James	1		4		
Hoig, Andrew	1	1	5			Abbott, Ezra, jr	2	3	1			Neasey, Joshua	1	2	3		
Harrick, Asa	1	3	4			Abbott, Aron	2		2			Thompson, John	1	3	3		
						Bradley, Phillbrick	1	2	6			Bean, Joseph	1	3	1		

ROCKINGHAM COUNTY—Continued.

DEERFIELD TOWN—con.

NAME OF HEAD OF FAMILY.	Free white males of 16 years and upward, including heads of families.	Free white males under 16 years.	Free white females, including heads of families.	All other free persons.	Slaves.
Judkins, Jonᵃ	2	1	3		
Sandborn, John P	2		4		
Paulisher, Jonᵃ	1	1	2		
Prescott, John	2	3	3		
Mead, John	3	4	4		
Phillbrick, James, junʳ	1				
Thrasher, Jacob	1	3	3		
Gove, John	1	3	4		
Thustin, Jonᵃ	1				
Bernerd, Moses	4	1	5		
Seavey, Moses	5		3		
Leavitt, Moses	1				
McClure, Mary			1		
Stevens, Moses	2		3		
Bartlett, Moses	2	3	2		
French, Moses	2	1	2		
Nutter, Nathˡ	1	2	2		
Moulton, Nathˡ	1		2		
Towle, Nathan	2	1	3		
Lane, Noah	1	4	4		
Griffith, Nathan	2	1	3		
Prescott, Nathan	1	1	5		
Bacheldʳ, Nathaniel	2	3	5		
Simpson, Patten	1	1	4		
Sandborn, Peter	2	2	2		
Prescott, Wd. Ruth			3		
Goodhue, Robert W	2	1	6		
Merrill, Robert	2	4	4		
Langley, Samˡ	1	1	3		
Robie, Samˡ	1				
Chase, Stephen	1	2	5		
Goodhue, Samuel, jᵘʳ	2		7		
Bachelder, Samuel	1	1	5		
Palsiepher, Samuel	1		2		
Wille, Stephen	2	1	5		
Collins, Samuel	1				
Prescott, Stephen	3	1	4		
Hendrick, Sarah		3	3		
Neasey, Simon	1	4	2		
Thurstin, Stephen	1	2	3		
Batchelder, Simon	1	1	2		
McClure, Samuel	1	2	6		
Prescott, Stephen	2		4		
Blasdle, Thomas	2	2	5		
Robie, Thomas	1		3		
Rand, Thomas	2		5		
Cram, Tristram	1	2	6		
Pearson, Timothy M	2	3	6		
Upham, Timothy	1	2	2		
Griffin, Thomas	1	1	2		
Sandborn, Tristram	2		5		
Moulton, Thomas	1		1		
Tirrell, Wᵐ	2		3		
Smith, William	3		4		
Mudget, William	2		1		
Mudget, William, jr	1	1	3		
Chase, Parker	1	2	1		
Hinnes, William	2	2	1		
Langley, Isiah	1				
Rollings, Aron	1		2		
Rowlings, Aron, junʳ	1	2	1		
Marshall, Aron	1	1	2		
Carrier, Benjⁿ	1		1		
French, Benjⁿ	2	4	3		
Stevens, Benjⁿ	2		4		
Novies, Benjⁿ	1				
Currier, Daniel	3	5	4		
Robbison, David	3	2	3		
Ladd, Danˡ	3		3		
Brown, Ebenezer	3	1	3		
Merrill, Elipᵗ	1	1	3		
Gilman, Ezikle	1	2	4		
Rawlings, Elijah	1	2	1		
Rawlings, Francis	1	2	1		
Tucker, Henery	3	3	4		
Daniels, Jonᵃ	1		1		
Brown, John	2	2	1		
Brown, John, jr	1	3	1		
Jenness, Jonᵃ	2	2	2		
Cram, Josᵃ	1	2	3		
Eastman, John	1		1		
Hoitt, Joseph	3		2		
Merill, Joseph	1		1		
Merrill, John	3	1	4		
Prescott, Jesse	3		2		
Prescott, Jesse, jr	1	3	2		
McCoon, Jonᵃ	1				
Prescott, Joseph	1	3	2		
Simpson, John	1	2	1		1
Chase, Joseph	1	2	2		
Merrill, Jeremiah	1		1		
Ladd, Jeddediah	1				
Currier, Joseph	1	5	2		
Robbinson, Jonᵃ	1	3	5		
Judkins, Joel	1	3	2		
Meloon, Jeremiah	1	1	2		
Phillbrick, Jonᵃ, jr	3	1	1		
Young, James	1	2	4		
Daniels, John	2	2	5		
Young, John, jr	1	1	1		
Young, John	1		3		
Kenistone, James	1	1	4		
Bean, Jeremiah	2	4	5		
Bean, Levi	2	1	2		
Marshall, Moses	2		5		
Megoon, Moses	1	2	3		
Chase, Moses, jr	2	1	4		
Chase, Moses	2		4		
Blasdle, Nehemiah	1	1	2		
Robbison, Nathˡ	1	5	2		
Rollings, Nathˡ	1				
Sandborn, Nathan	2		3		
Daniels, Nathˡ	1				
McCoon, Nathˡ	3		3		
Rynes, Nathˡ	2	1	2		
Phillbrick, Nathan	2	4	4		
Ladd, Peter	1	1	3		
Jenness, Richard, Esqʳ	3	2	5		
Beady, Reviah	1	1	3		
Hannes, Gideon	1	2	1		
Leavitt, Peter	1				
Norton, Simon	1	1	2		
Smith, Samuel	2	3	5		
Brown, Simon	1	1	1		
Bachelder, Samˡ	1		3		
Hoitt, Samuel	1	1	1		
Ladd, Benjⁿ	1	2	3		
Jenness, Thomas	5	3	4		
Robbison, Thomas	2	2	6		
Mathews, Thomas	1	1	2		
Stevens, Theophilus	1	1	2		
Brown, Ebenezʳ, junʳ	1				
Cram, William	2	1	4		
Allen, Wᵈ					1
Long, William	1	2	2		
Folsom, William	1				
Currier, Benjⁿ, jr	1				
Freeze, Andrew	1	3	3		
Kenistone, Andrew	1		4		
Frew, Abraham	3		8		
Fellows, Adonjah	1	1	2		
True, Ezra	1		4		
Dame, Ezra	1				
Buttler, Benjamin	1	1	3		
Page, Benjⁿ	2	2	3		
Neal, Capt	1		1		
Tilton, Danˡ	1		2		
Marstin, Danˡ	2		2		
Moor, Danˡ	1		3		
Marstin, David	1	1	3		
Page, Danˡ	1	4	2		
Burbank, David	1	5	2		
Sawyer, David	1				
Cram, Ephraim	1	3	5		
Tilton, Ebenzʳ	1	2	2		
Eastman, Ezikle	1	1	4		
Knowles, Ezikle	1	1	2		
Dearborn, Edward	2	4	6		
Lord, Eliphalet	2	3	3		
Bachelder, John	1	1	4		
Batchelder, Josiah	1	3	3		
Bachelder, Increasᵉ	2	2	3		
Brown, James	1	2	1		
Dearborn, James	1	2	6		
Griffin, Joseph	1	1	4		
Godpee, John	1	3	2		
Kenistone, Joseph	3	1	2		
Lucy, John	2	1	2		
Palmer, Joseph	3		3		
McCrillis, John	2	1	3		
Moulton, John	1	2	5		
Shepherd, Isaac, jr	1	3	2		
Tilton, Josiah	2	1	4		
Cass, Jonᵃ	1	4	5		
Mills, Joseph, Esqʳ	3	1	6		
Avery, Jeremiah	2				
Blue, Jonathan	1		1		
Batchelder, James	1		2		
Sawyer, Josiah	3		3		
Hilton, Joseph	3	4	6		
Cram, John	2	3	2		
Bartlett, John	2		2		
Pevere, Joseph	1		6		
Avery, John	2		7		
Ash, William	1		1		
Griffin, Lydia			4	1	
Dame, Levi	2		6		
Clark, Moses	2	2	3		
Thompson, Moses	1	2	1		
Avery, Nathˡ	1	2	2		
Grast, Nathˡ	1	1	2		
Prescott, Nathˡ	1	2	6		
Nutter, Nathˡ	1	2	2		
Page, Onesophorus	1	2	5		
Dowse, Ozen	2		3		
Gove, Nathan	2		6		
Tilton, Phineas	2	1			
Brown, Ruben	1		5		
Batchelder, Stephen	1	2	3		
Hobbs, Samuel	2		2		
Blue, Samuel	1	1	2		
Wedgwood, Samuel	2		2		
Leavitt, Samuel	1		3		
Marstin, Simon	4	2	6		
Green, Timothy	1	1	1		
Perkins, Samauel	2	2	2		
Woodman, Samuel	1	2	5		
Folsom, Samuel	2	1	1		
Wallis, Simeon	1				
Brown, Truworthy	1				
Taylor, Truwᵗ	1	3	4		
Savage, Thomas	1	2	2		
Thompson, William	1	2	2		
Ring, Zebulon	1	4	4		
Prescott, Samuel	1		4		
Mason, Joseph	1				
Hilton, John	2	1	2		
Trefethren, George	1		1		
Bachelder, Stephen	1	1	3		
Tuston, John	1	2	2		
Rawlings, Jeremiah	1	1	1		
Coffin, John I	1		1		
Lord, Samuel	1				
Whitcher, Wᵈ Lidia			3		
Langley, James, jr	1				
Marten, Moses	4	2	4		
Masons, Robert	1		2		
Marstin, Robie	3	1	6		
Phillbrick, James	1		2		
White, Joseph	1		2		
Ash, John	1		2		
Blue, Edward	1		2		
Young, Joseph	2	2	3		
Bedy, Azariah	1	1	3		
Sleeper, Robert	1	1			
Webster, Edey	1		3		
Wallis, James	1		3		
Young, Joshua	1	1	3		
Leavitt, Thomas	1	1	4		
Tandy, Richard	1	3	6		
Phillbrick, James	1		2		
White, Joseph	1	2	2		
Upham, Timoth	1	2	2		

EAST KINGSTON TOWN.

NAME OF HEAD OF FAMILY.	Free white males of 16 years and upward, including heads of families.	Free white males under 16 years.	Free white females, including heads of families.	All other free persons.	Slaves.
Carter, John	2	2	2		
Whittier, Nathˡ	1	6	4		
Morrill, Phillip	2		3		
Blaisdell, John	1	2	3		
Rowell, Jacob	2	2	8		
Cooper, Wᵐ	1	1	3		
Currier, Jacob	1	3	4		
Eastman, Barnard	1	1	4		
Eastman, Timothy	1	2	1		
Currier, Ezra	2	2	5	1	
Morse, Abner	2	2	5		
Currier, Jeremiah	2	2	5		
Gale, Abigail	2	1	2		
Blasdell, Moses	2	1	1		
Cooper, Wᵐ	1		1		
Defoché, Peter	2	1	7	1	
Mase, Andrew	1	2	4		
Currier, John	2	2	4		
Shepherd, Abner	3		2		
Bean, Joseph	1	3	4		
Emerson, Ithamore	1		1		
Chelsey, Christʳ	1	1	3		
Bachellor, Nathˡ	3		4		
Ordway, Jacob	1	1	4		
Sanborn, John	1	4	4		
Barwell, James	2	2	4		
Cram, John	2	2	3		
Sanborn, Trutram	1	2	2		
Bachellor, Nathˡ G	3	4	3		
Webster, Elipᵗ	2	1	6		

ROCKINGHAM COUNTY—Continued.

NAME OF HEAD OF FAMILY.	Free white males of 16 years and upward, including heads of families.	Free white males under 16 years.	Free white females, including heads of families.	All other free persons.	Slaves.
EAST KINGSTON TOWN—continued.					
Webster, Jonᵃ Ladd....	2	2	6		
Tilton, Josiah........	1		2		
Tilton, David........	2		2		
Tilton, Phillip........	3	2	4		
Greeley, Edward......	2		1		
Sanborn, John........	1		1		
Sanborn, Enoch......	1	1	2		
French, Richard......	1		3		
Philbrick, David......	1	1	1		
Greeley, Andrew......	1	1	2		
Greeley, Reuben......	1	1	1		
Greeley, Jonᵃ........	3		3		
Smith, Richard........	4	1	2		
Fifield, Ebenʳ........	1	3	4		
Brown, Widow........	2	2	4		
Clough, Elijah........	1		1		
Webster, Caleb.......	2	3	7		
Webster, Widow......			1		
Fifield, Joseph.......	1	5	2		
Thomson, Widow.....			3		
Greeley, Moses........	1	1	2		
Greeley, Mary.......	1	2	3		
Woodman, Joshua.....	2	1	3		
Stevens, Edward......	1	1	1		
Toppan, John.......	1	2	4		
Patten, James.......	1		3		
Morrill, John........	2	4	3		
Stickney, Moses.....	2	1	2		
EPPING TOWN.					
Bachelder, Nathan.....	1		1		
Barber, Daniel........	1		4		
Barber, Daniel, junʳ....	1	2	2		
Barker, John........	1		4		
Barker, Jonᵃ........	4	3	5		
Bartlett, John........	1	2	5		
Bartlett, John, junʳ.....	1	1	1		
Blake, Theophilus......	2	2	5		
Blake, Ebenezʳ.......	1	1	1		
Blake, Paine........	1	2	4		
Blake, Dearborn.....	1	1	1		
Blake, Joseph........	3		3		
Blasdell, Jacob........	5	4	7		
Blocket, Amos......	2	1	1		
Brown, Joshua........	2	2	5		
Brown, Benjⁿ........	1	2	4		
Burleigh, Thoˢ........	2		2		
Bunker, John........	1	2	1		
Brown, Wᵈ........			2		
Brown, Paul........	1	2	2		
Brown, Joshua, junʳ....	1	1			1
Bickford, Samuel.....	1		3		
Chase, Josiah........	1	3	3		
Clifford, Benjⁿ.......	3		2		
Clark, Jonᵃ........	1	3	2		
Coffin, Moses........	1		1		
Coffin, Enoch........	5	1	3		1
Carr, John........	1		1		
Carr, John, jur........	1	2	2		
Carrier, Moses......	1	2	2		
Chase, James........	1		4		
Clark, Stephen......	3	1	1		1
Clifford, Stephen.....	1	2	4		
Cilley, Eliphalet......	1	1	2		
Coalman, Joseph......	1	1	3		
Croket, Chase........	2	4	6		
Clark, Samuel........	1	1	6		
Clough, Ezikle......	2	1	4		
Clark, Josiah........	1		3		
Dow, Samuel........	1	2	3		
Dalton, Moses........	1	1	1		
Dearborn, Molley......	1		2		
Dow, Daniel........	3	3	5		
Dow, Josiah........	2	1	5		
Davis, Moses........	3		7		
Dimond, Isaac........	2	4	4		
Drake, Simon........	2	1	4		
Dow, Withrop........	2	4	6		
Dow, Zebulon........	1	1	4		
Dow, Benjⁿ........	1		3		
Dow, Beniah........	2		4		
Edgerly, Zebulon.....	2		2		
Dow, John........	3		2		
Dorothy, Charles.....	1	4	8		
Elkins, Ebenezʳ.....	1		1		
Elliot, Jonᵃ........	2	2	4		
Fogg, Seth........	4		4		
French, Joseph......	2		1		
Folsom, Joshua......	2	2	8		
Folsom, Abraham.....	1		2		
EPPING TOWN—con.					
Folsom, David........	5	1	4		
Farrar, Jonᵃ........	1		3		
Farrar, Jnᵒ........	1				
French, John........	1		4		
Folsom, Thoˢ........	1	1	1		
French, Samˡ........	1	2	4		
Fogg, Jonᵃ........	2	1	4		
French, Ezra........	2		2		
French, Braziller.....	1	1	8		
French, Gould........	2	2	3		
Folsom, Josiah......	1	2	3		
French, Amos........	1		2		
French, Ruben......	1	1	1		
Freeze, Jacob........	1		2		
Freeze, Gordon......	1				
French, Abraham.....	1				
Folsom, Samuel.....	1	1	4		
Gordon, Jonᵃ........	1		2		
Gale, Danˡ........	1	1	6		
Greenleaf, Samˡ.....	1		5		
Gordon, Dudly......	2		2		
Gordon, Joana......	1	1	1		
Gilman, Chase........	1	1	1		
Hanson, Andrew......	1	4	2		
Hanson, Sarah......		2	2		
Hacket, Judah......	2		2		
Hoit, Benjⁿ........	2	3	4		
Huse, Sargent........	2	1	4		
Hains, Lewis G........	1	1	1		
Haley, Thoˢ........	1		1		
How, Mark........	1	1	5		
Hoag, Nathan........	3	2	1		
Hook, Ezikle........	1	1	2		
Hill, Josiah........	1		3		
Hook, Wᵐ........	1	2	2		
Hacket, Judah......	1	1	3		
Harry, Phillip........	1		2		
Jenness, Joseph.....	1	3	3		
Jonson, Benjⁿ......	1		2		
Jonson, Benjⁿ, Jr.....	1	3	3		
Jonson, James........	1	1	6		
Jonson, Timᵒ........	3	1	2	1	
Jonson, Jeremiah.....	1		1		
Jonson, Samˡ........	1		1		
Jones, John........	1	2	3		
Lane, Joshua........	2	3	3		
Ladd, Paul........	1		3		
Ladd, Nathˡ........	1		3		
Lawrence, David.....	1	1	2		
Lawrence, David, junʳ..	2	2	3		
Lawrence, Edward....	2	6	3		
Lawrence, Gordon.....	2	5	3		
Lowell, David........	1	1			
Ladd, Dudley........	2		3		
Lock, Asa........	1	2	4		
Marden, John........	1	2	6		
Martin, John........	1		1		
Morrill, Oliver........	3	2	1		
Morrill, Wᵐ........	3		2		
Morrill, Samuel.....	3	3	3		
Maxfield, Nathˡ....	3	4	5		
Morrill, Levi........	1		2		
Norris, Joanna........			4		
Norris, Jonᵃ........	1		2		
Norris, Josiah........	1	2	2		
Norris, Simeon......	2	3	3		
Norris, James........	1	3	2		
Norris, James, junyer..	2	3	4		
Norris, Thomas......	2	2	6		
Norris, James, 3ᵈ....	1	1	1		
Norris, Israel........	1	3	4		
Norris, Joseph........	1	2	1		
Norris, Theophilus....	1		2		
Norris, Anna........			1		
Osgood, Chase........	2	1	7		
Osgood, Ruben......	2	1	5		
Brown, Molley........			2		
Prescott, Samuel, jun..	1		2		
Perkins, Abraham....	1		2		
Prescoot, John........	2		4		
Prescoot, Samˡ......	1	3	4		
Prescoot, Mich........	1	1	4		
Prescott, Nathan G...	2	1	3		
Prescott, Jonathan.....	2	2	4		
Pike, John........	2		2		
Page, John........	1	2	2		
Page, Benjⁿ........	3		5		
Persons, John........	1		6		
Purrington, George....	1	1	3		
Purkins, John........	2		2		
Plumer, Samˡ........	3		4		
EPPING TOWN—con.					
Perkins, Abraham, junʳ.	1	1	2		
Persons, Samuel........	2	1	2		
Pease, John........	3		3		
Purrington, Joshua....	1	3	3		
Pipper, John........	1	1	2		
Pike, John, Jʳ........	1		1		
Plumer, Wᵐ........	2	1	3		
Purkins, Jonᵃ........	1		5		
Peasley, Joseph........	2	1	4		
Page, Wᵐ........	1	2	6		
Purrington, Joseph.....	1	3	4		
Pease, Eliphalet......	1	4	3		
Purkins, James......	1				
Rundlet, Jonathan.....	1		1		
Rundlet, Josiah........	2	2	4		
Rundlet, Jacob........	2	3	4		
Rundlet, James........	2		4		
Rundlet, James, junʳ...	1				
Rundlet, James, 3ᵈ.....	1	2	2		
Rundlet, Daniel......	1	2	6		
Robbinson, Nicholas...	2	2	3		
Rowel, Wᵈ........	3	4	5		
Robbinson, Jonathan..	2		2		
Robbinson, Simeon....	1		5		
Rundlet, John........	1				
Smith, Samuel........	1				
Sweft, Betty........		1	1		
Smith, John........	1				
Shepard, Joseph.....	2		2		
Sandborn, Tristram....	1	1	3		
Straw, Ebenezʳ........	3		8	1	
Straw, John........	1		2		
Sandborn, Nathan....	1	2	7		
Sandborn, Danˡ......	2	1	2		
Sandborn, Jeremiah...	2	1	2		1
Stevens, Theophilus...	3	1	5		
Smith, Benjⁿ........	1	1	1		
Swaine, Nathan.....	1	1	3		
Smith, Jeremy........	1	2	2		
Sandborn, Henery....	3	4	5		
Straw, John........	1	1	2		
Straw, Margret......	1		3		
Smith, Stephen......	1	3	2		
Stevens, William.....	1	1	3		
Stevens, Sarah......	1		5		
Stickney, Amos......	1		2		
Sleeper, John........	1	1	2		
Towl, Lewi........	2	3	3		
Taylor, David........	1				
Tilton, Abraham.....	3		3		
Towl, John........	3	2	4		
Tilton, Josiah........	3	2	3		
Tilton, Jethroe......	1		2		
Tilton, Daniel........	1	4	2		
Towl, Thomas........	1	4	3		
Taylor, Jeremiah.....	1	1	3		
Taylor, James........	1				
Towl, Jenness........	1		2		
Taylor, Joˢ., Junʳ.....	1				
True, Elijah........	1	1	5		
Taylor, Joseph........	1		3		
Taylor, David........	1				
Wadliegh, Enoch.....	1	1	2		
Wiggin, Henery......	4		2		
Winslow, Jonᵃ........	3	1	6		
Wheeler, Nehemiah....	2	1	3		1
Wiggin, Elijah........	2	1	4		
Watson, Danˡ........	1		2		
Wiggin, Wᵐ........	2		2		
Watson, Nathan.....	1	2	3		
Wilkinson, Samuel....	2		2		
Wille, Robert........	1	2	3		
EPSOM TOWN.					
Allen, Jude........	1	2	4		
Ame, Joel........	1	1	7		
Ames, Samˡ........	1		3		
Ames, Samuel, Junʳ...	2	3	4		
Babb, Thoˢ........	2		7		
Bickford, Mary......			3		
Bickford, Hannah....		2	1		
Bickford, Samuel.....	1	1	5		
Bickford, Thomas....	1	2	5		
Blake, Samuel........	1	2	5		
Bracket, Ebenezer....	2	2	5		
Bartlett, Jonᵃ........	1	1	5		
Brown, Joseph........	1	2	3		
Brown, James........	1		1		
Brown, Enoch........	1	3	2		
Brown, Levi........	1	2	2		

ROCKINGHAM COUNTY—Continued.

EPSOM TOWN—con.

NAME OF HEAD OF FAMILY.	Free white males of 16 years and upward, including heads of families.	Free white males under 16 years.	Free white females, including heads of families.	All other free persons.	Slaves.
Cate, John	3	1	4		
Cass, John	1		1		
Cass, Simon	1	7	1		
Cass, Thomas	1	1	2		
Cass, Levi	1	2	3		
Chapman, Simeon	3	1	7		
Clifford, Israel	1	2	2		
Critchet, Edward	2	1	3		
Critchet, John	1		1		
Davis, Ephream	1	2	4		
Dickey, David	3	3	4		
Dennett, Joseph	2		4		
Drew, Sollomon	1		4		
Fowler, Simond	3	1	5		
Goss, Samuel	2	1	3		
Goss, Joseph	2	1	5		
Gray, James	4	1	4		
Goodwin, Benjn	3	3	6		
Grant, John	1	4	3		
Hogan, John	1	1	3		
Haynes, John	2	2	4		
Ham, Benson	2	1	5		
Ham, John	1		3		
Howe, David	1	1	2		
Hutchins, John	1		1		
Hutchins, Saml	4		3		
Kenistone, Nathl	1	2	6		
Knowles, Josiah	2	1	2		
Lamprey, Morris	2		2		
Libbe, Isaac	3	1	2		
Libbe, Job	1	3	1		
Libbe, Jethroe	1	4	3		
Libbe, Bennett	1	3	3		
Lock, Moses	2		2		
Lock, Ephriam	1	2	5		
Lock, Jona	2		2		
Lock, Francis	1	1	4		
Lock, Samuel	1		4		
Lock, Abraham	2	3	4		
Lock, Simeon	1	2	2		
Drake, Josiah	1		2		
Acreman, Peter	1	4	2		
Marden, Nathan	1		1		
Marden, Nathan, jr	1	2	5		
Moses, James	3	3	4		
Moses, Sylvanus	2	3	3		
McClary, John	1		2		
McClary, Michl	2	3	4		
McClary, James F	3	1	6		
McCrillis, Wm	1	3	2		
Moulton, Saml	2		3		
Morrill, Amos	2	5	3		
Marden, Joseph	2	3	1		
Mann, Wd	1	1	3		
Nason, William	2	1	6		
Osgood, Samuel	1	2	5		
Osgood, Moses	2	2	6		
Osgood, Abraham	1		3		
Page, Jeremiah	2	3	3		
Pettingill, Ephriam	2		4		
Page, Simeon	1	1	1		
Pettingall, Jethroe	1	2	1		
Pearsons, Jona	3		4		
Pearsons, Caleb	1	1	2		
Phillbrick, Daniel	2	1	7		
Phillbrick, Samuel	2	2	3		
Prescot, Jeremiah	3	3	3		
Prescoot, Jeremiah, junr	1		2		
Robertson, Levi	1	4	2		
Robertson, Benjn	1	2	2		
Rand, Wm	2	2	6		
Rand, Richard	1	2	7		
Rand, Saml	1	1	3		
Sandborn, Elipht	2	3	4		
Sandborn, Josiah	1	1	1		
Sandborn, Ruben	3		2		
Sandborn, Moses	1	3	3		
Sandborn, Thos	1		3		
Sanders, George	2	1	3		
Seavey, Jos	1	2	2		
Sherburne, Jos	3	2	6		
Sherburne, William	1	2	5		
Sherburne, Nathl	1		3		
Towle, Jona., junr	2		3		
Towle, Saml	2		4		
Towle, Joseph	1	3	4		
Towle, Semion	1		3		
Tucke, Wd Mary	2		3		
Tripp, Richard	3		3		
Wallis, George	1				
Wallis, Ebenezer	1	3	4		
Wallis, Abraham	2	1	9		

EPSOM TOWN—con.

NAME OF HEAD OF FAMILY.	Free white males of 16 years and upward, including heads of families.	Free white males under 16 years.	Free white females, including heads of families.	All other free persons.	Slaves.
Wallis, Wm. W	1	2	5		
Wallis, Nathl	2	6	3		
Wallis, Joseph	1	4	3		
Wood, James	2		3		
Yeaton, William	1	4	1		
Berry, Thos	1	3	5		
Gordon, Alexander	2	1	4		
Shaw, Daniel	1		2		
Ames, Sollomon	1	4	5		
Blake, Jethroe	1	1	1		
Brown, Jona	1		2		
Davis, Samuel	2	2	2		
Hains, Jeremiah	1		4		
Haines, Elisha	1	2	1		
Knowles, Isaac	1	1	5		
Moses, Saml	2	4	3		
Phillbrick, Perkins	1	2	3		
Rand, Dowse	1	1	1		
Drake, Josiah	1		2		
Haseltine, Ebenezer	1	2	2		
Brown, Job	1	3	2		
Urin, George	2	1	4		
Barton, Wm	2	2	4		

EXETER TOWN.

NAME OF HEAD OF FAMILY.	Free white males of 16 years and upward, including heads of families.	Free white males under 16 years.	Free white females, including heads of families.	All other free persons.	Slaves.
Atherton, Matthew	1	2	1		
Adams, Mary	1	1	3	1	
Arms, Edward	1		1		
Acres, Joseph	1	1	3		
Brooks, Samuel	3		2		
Bond, John	1		2		
Bennet, William	1	2	3		
Barker, Josiah	3	1	2		
Beckett, Deborah	1	2	5		
Boardman, Benjamin	5		4		
Beal, James	1	3	3		
Burleigh, James	2	1	3		
Bennet, Joseph	1	2	1		
Bickford, Dennis	1	1	1		
Boardman, Joseph	4		3		
Bond, Mary			1		
Cram, Benjamin	1		1		
Colcord, Edward	3		2		
Connor, Jonathan	3		3		
Connor, John	3		2		
Currier, Isaac	1		3		
Calfe, James	1	1	7		
Calfe, Oliver	2	1	7		
Cram, Joseph	2	2	4		
Connor, Benja	2	1	2		
Chamberlain, Esther	4		4		
Chamberlain, Samuel	1	1	4		
Cross, Nathl	2	6	4		
Colcord, Jonathan	2		2		
Creighton, Elizabeth	1	3	4		
Currier, Ephraim	1	2	2		
Cass, Jonathan	1	3	4	1	
Cook, John	1	1	2		
Colcord, Samuel	1	4	4		
Carter, Jacob	3	2	4		
Connor, Benjamin, Junr	3	1	3		
Cushing, Peter	1	1	3		
Creighton, Dorothy		1	1		
Carty, John	1	1	3		
Dollof, Joseph	1	1	2		
Dutch, Arthur	1		2		
Durant, William	1	1	5		
Dolloff, Thomas	2		1		
Dean, Ward Clark	2		3		
Dean, John	2	3	3		
Dean, Thomas	5	2	7		
Daniels, Minas	1		2		
Dodge, Jabez	2	3	4		
Dutch. Samuel	1	1	4		
Dearborn, Benjamin	1	1	3		
Dean, Eliphalet	1	2	3		
Dollof, Abner	1	2	1		
Daniels, Samuel	1	1	4		
Eastman, Francis B	2		3		
Emery, Noah	3	4	4		
Eldridge, Joseph	1	2	3		
Emery, Joanna	1	1	5		
Eastman, Edward	1	1	3		
Flood, Widow			1		
Folsom, Mary	1		3		
Folsom, Elizabeth		1	6		
Folsom, Peter	2	1	3		
Folsom, Thomas	3		6		
Folsom, James	3		3		
Fogg, David	2	1	4		
Folsom, James	4	2	4		

EXETER TOWN—con.

NAME OF HEAD OF FAMILY.	Free white males of 16 years and upward, including heads of families.	Free white males under 16 years.	Free white females, including heads of families.	All other free persons.	Slaves.
Folsom, Trueworthy	1	1	1		
Fogg, Seth	1	1	4		
Folsom, Jonathan	2	3	2		
Folsom, James, Junr	2	2	3		
Fogg, Shuah			3		
Fuller, George	3	5	3		
Fogg, Stephen	3	1	4		
Folsom, James, 3d	1	2	2		
Folsom, James, 4th	2	2	3		
Fowle, Robert L	1	1	5		
Flood, Joseph	1	1	1		
Giddings, Mehitabel	1	2	5		
Gilman, Josiah	1	2	3	1	
Gilman, Trueworthy	1	1	3		
Gilman, John Ward	2	3	4		
Gilman, Josiah, Junr	2		5		
Gilman, Theophilus	3	1	1		
Gilman, Biley	3		4		
Gilman, Sarah		1	4		
Gilman, David	1		1		
Gilman, Nehemiah	3		2		
Gilman, Zebulon	2	1	5		
Gilman, Sarah, Junr			2		
Gidding, Eliphalet	3	2	3	1	
Gilman, John Taylor	4	1	9		
Gidding, John	2	1	3		
Gordon, James	1		2		
Grant, Daniel	2	1	2		
Graves, Benjamin	2		2		
Gordon, Elizabeth	2	1	2		
Gilman, Samuel	1	3	2		
Gilman, Eliphalet	1	2	5		
Gordon, Benjamin	2	1	2		
Gilman, James	1	2	3		
Gilman, Nathaniel	3	1	8	1	
Gilman, Olive		1	4		
Gilman, Benja Clark	3	1	1		
Gilman, Mary		1	2	1	
Gidding, Nathaniel	2	1	5		
Gardner, William	1	1	3	1	
Gilman, Thomas	1		3		
Gill, Joel				3	
Gordon, Joseph	1		1		
Gilman, Shuah		2	3		
Hopkinson, John	2	2	3		
Haley, Benjamin	1	7	3		
Hale, Eliphalet	4		6	3	
Hackett, James	2	3	4		
Hackett, William	1		4		
Hobart, Samuel	6		3		
Hall, Kinsley	5	2	4		
Hopkinson, Moses	1	1	4		
Hopkinson, Dorothy	1		4		
Henderson, Joseph	1	3	3		
Herrick, Nathaniel	1	1	2		
Hale, William	2		2		
Haven, John	2	1	2		
Hoag, Joseph	2	2	4		
Hains, Thomas	1	1	3		
Hill, Jonathan	2	1	3		
Hoit, Joseph	1	2	5		
Hilton, Benjamin	1	2	3		
Hall, Elizabeth		1	2		
Hilton, Andrew	1	1	1		
Jones, Daniel	4	1	5		
James, Kinsley Hall	1				
Jewett, Paul	1	2	2		
Jordan, Richard	1	4	3		
Judkins, John	1	2	3		
Johnson, John	1	2	6		
Johnson, Bradbury	1	2	1		
Kimball, Dorothy			2		
Kimball, Robert	2	1	2	2	
Kimball, Nathaniel	2		3		
Kelly, William	1	2	1		
Kimball, Dudley	1		2		
Lougee, Jonathan Folsom	2	1	5		
Lary, Jonathan	1	1	2		
Lamson, Gideon	1	2	4		
Lamson, Elizabeth	1		3		
Lamson, Benjamin	4		6		
Lamson, Joseph	1		2	1	
Lyford, Anna	1	2	9		
Lyford, Theophilus	4		6		
Lougee, Joseph	2	2	5	2	
Leavitt, James	2	3	6		
Lawrence, Joseph	1				
Lord, Robert	2	2	5		
Leavitt, John	3		2		
Lovering, Joseph	2	2	6		

ROCKINGHAM COUNTY—Continued.

NAME OF HEAD OF FAMILY.	Free white males of 16 years and upward, including heads of families.	Free white males under 16 years.	Free white females, including heads of families.	All other free persons.	Slaves.
EXETER TOWN—con.					
Lovering, Benjamin....	4	2	3		
Leavitt, Jeremiah......	5	3	6	1	
Ladd, Eliphalet........	3	4	8	1	
Lovering, Jonathan....	1	1	3		
Ladd, Simeon.........	1		4		
Leavitt, Benjamin.....	1	3	4		
Leavitt, Josiah........	1	2	2		
Lakeman, Peletiah....	2	3	4		
Lamson, Jane.........			1		
Lampson, Joseph, Junr	1	3	2		
Lord, John...........	1		2		
Lampson, Samuel.....	1		1		
Mitchel, Caleb........	1	2	5		
Mead, William........	1	4	3		
Morrison, Alexander...	1		2		
McCluer, James.......	2	4	4		
Mason, Francis.......	1	1	3		
Marsh, Zebulon.......	1	2	2		
Moore, William.......	1	1	1		
Moses, Theodore.....	1	1	3		
Moulton, Nathaniel....	2	1	2		
Marsh, Samuel........	1	3	3		
Mace, Joseph........	1		1		
Mansfield, Isaac......	3	3	2		
Marshall, Widow......			1		
Magoon, Abigail......			1		
Marsh, Henry........	1		1		
Nelson, Josiah.......	1	1	5		
Nicholl, Dudley.......	1	1	2		
Nutter, Mark........	1	2	1		
Nicholl, John........	1	2	2		
Nicholl, Nicholas.....	1		3		
Odlin, Woodbridge....	3	1	5	1	
Odlin, Winthrop......	1	1	3		
Odlin, Judith........			3		
Odiorne, Thomas.....	4	2	6		
Odlin, Samuel........	1		2	1	
Osborne, Joseph......	1	3	3	1	
Odiorne, George......	3	1	2		
Pearson, Jacob......	6	3	5		
Parker, William......	4	1	3		
Parker, William, Junr..	3	1	4		
Parks, Robert........	1	1	3		
Pickering, James.....	2		3		
Phillips, John........	3		2	1	
Poor, Martha........			4	1	
Pearson, Edmund.....	2	3	5		
Peabody, Oliver......	1	1	6	1	
Philbrook, Samuel....	1	2	3		
Pearson, Dole.......	2	2	4		
Philbrook, John......	1		3		
Rundlett, Charles.....	2	1	3		
Rundlett, James.....	2	3	6		
Rundlett, Benjamin...	1	1	1		
Robinson, Caleb......	1		3		
Robinson, Ephraim....	3	2	7		
Rundlett, John......	1	4	4		
Robinson, Joseph.....	2	1	5		
Rawlings, Josiah.....	2	4	5		
Robinson, Josiah.....	1		1		2
Rust, Samuel........	1	2	5		
Rundlett, Jonathan....	1		3		
Robinson, Trueworthy.	1	3	1		
Robinson, Jeremy....	1	1	3		
Randell, Jacob......	1	1	3		
Rundlett, Henry.....	3		4		
Rundlett, James, Junr.	1	2	2		
Rundlett, Joseph.....	1	1	2		
Robertson, Daniel....	3	2	4		
Row, Enoch........	1	2	1		
Robinson, Mary......		1	1		
Swazey, Joseph......	1		2		
Smith, Daniel........	2	1	2		
Smith, Mary........	1	1	2		
Shurtliff, Abraham....	1		3		
Smith, Benjamin.....	1		4		
Safford, Benjamin....	1	4	3		
Swazey, Ebenezer....	1		3		
Sanborn, Deborah....	2		3		
Smith, Theophilus....	2	3	5		
Sanborn, John......	2		6		
Sanborn, Abraham....	2	1	3		
Smith, Dorothy......			3		
Swazey, Ebenezer, Junr	1	1	3		
Shaw, John........	2	2	3		
Swazey, Joseph, Junr..	2	2	5		
Sheriff, Peirce......	1	1	1		
Smith, Joseph......	1	1	3		
Smith, Josiah Coffin...	1		1		
Speed, Thomas......	1	3	3		
Sleeper, Sanborn.....	1	3	2		
Swazey, Thomas.....	1	1	2		
EXETER TOWN—con.					
Stickney, Levi........	1	1	3		
Stevens, Edward......	1		1		
Steele, John........	1		3		
Tilton, Joseph.......	3	2	7		
Thing, Winthrop.....	2		3		
Taylor, Daniel.......	2		1		
Thing, Stephen......	1	1	4		
Thurston, Caleb.....	1	1	2		
Thurston, James.....	4	1	5		
Tenney, Samuel.....	1	1	4		
Watson, Abigail.....			4		
Vickery, Elijah......	2	3	3		
Webb, Samuel.......	1		3		
Wiggin, Joshua......	3		5		
Wiggin, Joseph......	2	5	2		
Wallace, Spencer....	1	1	2		
Wiat, Josiah........	1	3	4		
Williams, Isaac.....	2	1	2		
Webster, Thomas....	2		2		
Wiggin, Simon......	1		2		
Watson, Joseph.....		1	3		
Wiggin, Joseph, Junr..	1	1	1		
York, John Carr.....	1	2	5		
York, Jonathan Young.	1	1	5		
Young, Joseph......	1	2	3		
Young, Mary........	1		4		
Hall, Judas........					5
Sampson, John......				1	1
White, Archelaus....					2
Dailey, London.....					5
Fisk, Cato........					5
Fogg, Fortune......					7
Deuce, Bob Bombaway.					4
Fogg, Scipio.......					2
Tash, Oxford......					6
Oakland, Jaques....					5
Light, Prince......					6
Diamond, Susanna...					4
Holland, Hannah....					4
GOSPORT TOWN.					
Mace, John........	4	1	4		
Caswell, Martha.....			2		
Caswell, Robert.....	2		3		
Down, William......	3		1		
Pearse, William.....	3	2	2		
Pusley, John.......	1		1		
Caswell, Samuel....	1	1	2		
Down, Samuel......	2	1	1		
Shapley, James.....	1	2	1		
Caswell, John, Junr..	1		1		
Robinson, John.....	2	4	2		
Rendall, Richard....	2	2	2		
Robinson, John, Junr.	1	1	2		
Bragg, John.......	2		4		
Rendall, John......	1	2	2		
Mace, Thomas......	1		2		
Down, Edward......	2	3	2		
Rendall, William....	1	2	1		
Webber, Elizabeth...			1		
Nuton, John.......	2	1	3		
GREENLAND TOWN.					
Ayers, Mary........			1		
Ayers, Phebe.......	2		2		
Ayers, Pelatiah.....	2		3		
Ayers, Eliphalet....	2		5		
Ayers, Joshua......	1	2	3		
Ayers, Samuel.....	1	4	1		
Beck, William......	1	1	4		
Blazo, Thomas.....	1	1	3		
Bailey, Jonathan....	2	3	4		
Barker, Philip......	1	2	5		
Berry, Thomas.....	2	2	3		
Berry, Thomas, Junr.	3	2	3		
Berry, Isaiah......	1	2	1		
Brackett, Elizabeth..	1		2		
Brackett, James....	1		2		
Brackett, George....	5	1	7		
Brackett, Joshua....	2	2	6		
Brown, Moses......	1	1	3		
Cate, Samuel......	3		3		
Cate, Joshua......	1		3		
Cate, Jeremy......	1	1	2		
Cate, Joseph......	1	5	4		
Cate, Andrew......	1	2	2		
Cate, Eliphalet.....	1		3		
Chapman, Job......	2	4	3		
Clark, Enoch......	2	3	5		
Dearborn, Abraham....	2	1	3		
GREENLAND TOWN—con.					
Downing, Jonathan....	1	2	5		
Dockum, Jonathan.....	1	3	2		
Clark, Joseph.......	4		1		
Gerrish, Sally......			1		
Gotum, Mercy......		2	2		
Foss, Josiah.......	2		2		
Goss, Nathaniel.....	1		2		
Goss, Nathaniel.....	2	1	1		
Haynes, William.....	3	1	2		
Haynes, Matthias....	2		1		
Haynes, John......	1		1		
Haynes, Josiah.....	1				
Haynes, Nathaniel...	1	3	4		
Haynes, John, Junr..	3	5	4		
Haynes, Matthias, Junr	2	3	3		
Haynes, Samuel.....	1	2	2		
Haynes, Lewis......	1		3		
Hatch, Samuel......	2	2	3		
Huggins, Samuel....	1		3		
Huggins, Susanna...			2		
Jenkins, William....	2		1		
Jenkins, Mark......	1		2		
Johnson, Nathan....	2		4	1	
Johnson, Ebenezer..	4	1	4		
Johnson, Joshua....	2		2		
Johnson, Mary.....			1		
Johnson, Thomas...	1	2	3		
Johnson, David....	2	1	4		
Johnson, Joshua McCris.	1	4	2		
Kenniston, Stacey...	1	1	1		
Kenniston, Bickford..	1	4	3		
Lang, Thomas......	1	3	7		
Lang, Thomas, Junr..	1	2	2		
Lang, George......	3	3	4	1	1
Lang, Josiah.......	2	2	4		
Libbey, George.....	2		2	1	
Lunt, Mary........			1		
McClintock, Samuel..	1	2	4		
March, Clement.....	4	6	4		
March, Stephen.....	3		4		
Marston, Thomas....	2	1	8		1
Marston, Nathaniel..	1		2		
Marston, Nathaniel, Junr	1	1	2		
Marston, Matthias...	1	1	1		
Marston, Elijah.....	1	3	2		
Maloon, Mark......	1	3	1		
Norton, Benjamin...	4	1	3		
Norton, Simeon....	3		2		
Norton, James.....	1	1	2		
Nudd, Samuel.....	1	1	3		
Nudd, Benjamin....	1	1	5		
Nudd, Thomas.....	1	1	4		
Packer, Thomas....	3	3	3		
Pattinson, Garvin...	2		2		
Philbrook, Robert Tufton.	2		2		
Philbrook, George....	1	1	2		
Philbrook, Samuel...	1	1	2		
Pickering, Samuel...	3		4		
Pickering, William...	3	5	5		
Pickering, Daniel...	3	2	4		
Piper, John.......	2		4		
Robinson, Shadreck..	1	3	2		
Rollins, John......	1		5		
Sanborn, Jabez.....	1		2	1	
Simpson, Sarah....	2	2	3		
Simpson, David....	1	2	8		
Simpson, George....	1		2		
Tarlton, Richard....	2		3	1	
Warner, Jack......				4	
Weeks, Abigail.....			2		
Weeks, Ichabod....	8	1	5		
Weeks, William, Junr.	2	2	4		
Weeks, Joshua.....	1	2	5		
Whidden, Hannah....			1	3	
Whidden, John.....	2		3		
Wiggin, David.....	1	1	3		
Wiggin, Levi......	2	3	3		
HAMPSTEAD TOWN.					
Adams, Caleb......	2		2		
Abraham, John.....	1		3		
Atkins, John......	1		2		
Atwood, Moses.....	1	2	3		
Atwood, James.....	2	4	5		
Adams, John......	2	2	1		
Atwood, John......	1		3		
Atwood, John, jr....	2	3	3		
Briant, Andw......	2	4	3		
Bond, Joseph.....	3	1	3		

ROCKINGHAM COUNTY—Continued.

HAMPSTEAD TOWN—con.

NAME OF HEAD OF FAMILY.	Free white males of 16 years and upward, including heads of families.	Free white males under 16 years.	Free white females, including heads of families.	All other free persons.	Slaves.
Bond, John	2	4	5		1
Brown, John	1	4	4	1	
Brown, Sam¹	1	3	6		
Brown, James	1	2	2		
Brown, Moses	3	1	6		
Clark, Amos	1	2	2		
Corliss, Joshua	2	1	5		
Collins, Jonª	2	2	5		
Calf, John	2	2	3		
Currier, Ezekiel	2	2	5		
Currier, Sam¹	1	1	3		
Carlton, Jonª	1		1		
Copps, Ebenʳ	1	1	2		
Dexter, David	1	1	4		
Darling, John	1	2	5		
Davis, Josiah	2	1	2		
Emerson, Benjª	2	3	3		
Emerson, Robert	4	3	3		
Emerson, Walls	2	1	6		
Emery, Thomas	2		2		
Eastman, Joshua	1	3	2		
Eastman, Edmᵈ	1		1		
Emerson, Benjª	1		2		
Eastman, Jonª	1	1	2		
Eastman, Peter	1		2		
French, Joshua	3	1	4		
French, Joseph	1		2		
George, Augustine	2		4		
George, Jonª	1	1	1		
Gorden, John	3	2	3		
Gooden, Timothy	1	1	6		
Gooden, Smith	1	1	3		
Heath, Isaac	1	3	9		
Hutchins, Hezekʰ	3	1	2		
Huriman, Reuben	1		2		
Herriman, Laban	2	4	4		
Hadley, Nathˡ	1	1	1		
Heath, Benjª	2		2		
Heath, Jesse	1	5	1		
Herriman, John	1		4		
Herriman, John, jr	1	4	4		
Howard, Amos	2		2		
Huse, James	3	3	5		
Hogg, John	1		2		
Hogg, John, jr	3	3	3		
Hoit, Thoˢ	1	2	2		
Johnson, Sam¹	1		2		
Johnson, Sam¹, jr	1	2	3		
Johnson, Joseph	1	2	2		
Johnson, Henry	2	1	3		
Johnson, Caleb	2	2	4		
Johnson, Noah	1	1	4		
Johnson, Abramᵐ	1	1	1		
Kent, Job	1	2	6		
Kimbal, Dudley	2	1	3		
Kimbal, Joseph	2		2		
Kelley, Sam¹	1		3		
Keaser, David	1	1	2		
Kimbal, Benjª	4		3		
Kimbal, John	1	1	5		
Kiaser, Sam¹	1	2	2		
Little, Moses	2		1		
Little, Michael	1		4		
Little, Danˡ	1	3	4		
Little, Jonª	2	1	3		
Little, Sam¹	1		1		
Moore, Edmᵈ	2	2	3		
Merrick, Josiah	2	2	6		
Moulton, Davᵈ	1	1	1		
Mills, Amos	1	1	1		
Muzzy, Thoˢ	2	1	7		
Marshal, Wᵐ	4		5		
Morse, Peter	2	3	3		
Morse, Edmᵈ	5		3		
Moulton, Wᵐ	1		4		
Moulton, Wᵐ., jr	1	1	2		
Noyes, Joseph	1	1	2		
Noyes, Joshua	2	1	3		
Ordway, John	2		3		
Poor, Hannah			2		
Page, Sam¹	2	1	1		
Plumer, John	1		1		
Poor, David	3	1	3		
Quimby, Stephen	1	3	3		
Quimby, Jacob	2	1	2		
Reed, Thoˢ	3	2	2		
Richardson, Jonª	1		6		
Richardson, Wᵐ	2	1	2		
Rogers, Abner	3	3	2		
Stevens, Timothy	2	1	2		
Shepherd, Sam¹	3	1	2		
Sawyer, Abner	1		2		
Sawyer, John	1	1	1		

HAMPSTEAD TOWN—con.

NAME OF HEAD OF FAMILY.	Free white males of 16 years and upward, including heads of families.	Free white males under 16 years.	Free white females, including heads of families.	All other free persons.	Slaves.
Tewksbury, Benjª	3	1	5		
True, Jonª	2	1	5		
Wadley, Aaron	1		2		
Webster, Joshua	2	1	4		
Williams, Moses	1	4	2		
Williams, John	1	2	3		
Webster, Caleb	1	3	5		
Weave, John	3	1	6		
Worther, Oliver	3		4		
Dolloy, Sarah			1		
Woodward, Mary			1		
Stevens, Sam¹	2		1		
Purkins, Mary	1		4		
McLain, Ceasar				2	
Hoit, Ebenʳ	1	3	3		
Stevens, Josiah	1	2	3		
Ayers, Joseph	1	1	4		
Shannon, Thoˢ	2	1	5		

HAMPTON TOWN.

NAME OF HEAD OF FAMILY.	Free white males of 16 years and upward, including heads of families.	Free white males under 16 years.	Free white females, including heads of families.	All other free persons.	Slaves.
Brown, Samuel	2	3	7		
Brown, Samuel, Junʳ	3	3	2		
Brown, Nathan	2	2	2		
Brown, Moses	1		4		
Brown, Zacheus	1	1	3		
Bachelor, Benjamin	2		5		
Bachellor, Carter	1		1		
Blake, Samuel	1	4	4		
Blake, Nathan	1		1		
Blake, Jonathan	2	2	3		
Blake, Jethro	2	1	5		
Bachellor, Nathaniel	2	2	5		
Bachellor, Levi	1	2	1		
Brown, Samuel, 3d	1	1	1		
Burdoe, Philip				2	
Currier, Jacob	2	3	5		
Coffin, Amos	4		2		
Collinet, Charles Joseph Gabriel	1	1	2		
Crosby, Anna			2		
Dow, Samuel	2	2	4		
Dow, Joseph	3	1	1		
Dow, Simon	1	2	3		
Drake, Robert	2	1	4		
Drake, Robert, Junʳ	1	3	3		
Drake, Samuel	2	2	4		
Dearborn, Josiah	3	2	3		
Dearborn, John	3	3	4		
Emery, Willard	1	2	4		
Elkins, Henry	3	4	5		
Elkins, Moses	3	1	4		
Fellows, Ephraim	2	1	2		
Fogg, John	2		11		
Fifield, Mary			2		
Garland, Jonathan	2	3	5		
Godfrey, Jonathan	1	1	3		
Godfrey, Jonathan, Jr	1	1	2		
Godfrey, Tristam	1	1	3		
Green, John	1		2		
Garland, Joseph	2		3		
George, Henry	1	2	1		
Godfrey, Isaac	1	1	3		
Hobbs, Morris	1	2	4		
Howell, Hannah			2		
Johnson, Joseph	1				
Johnson, Ezra	1		4		
Johnson, Nathaniel	1	1	2		
Jenness, Thomas	1		1		
James, Joshua	1	2	2		
Jenness, Richard	1	2	3		
Johnson, James	2		1		
Knowles, Amos	4	1	2		
Knowles, Jeremiah	1				
Knight, Joseph	2	1	2		
Lamprey, John	2		5		
Lamprey, Reuben	3	1	7		
Lamprey, Daniel	1	2	5		
Lamprey, Daniel, Junʳ	2	1	2		
Locke, Jonathan	2		3		
Leavitt, Thomas	2	3	3		
Leavitt, Thomas, Junʳ	3	1	4		
Lane, William	2		1		
Lane, John	2		2		
Lane, Simon	2		2		
Lane, Ebenezer	3	2	3		
Lane, Josiah	2	3	4		
Lane, Ward	1	3	3		
Lane, William, Junʳ	1	5	1		
Leavitt, Nathaniel	1	1	4		
Leavitt, James	1	1	6		
Lane, James	1	1	2		
Leach, Joseph	1				1

HAMPTON TOWN—con.

NAME OF HEAD OF FAMILY.	Free white males of 16 years and upward, including heads of families.	Free white males under 16 years.	Free white females, including heads of families.	All other free persons.	Slaves.
Marston, Jeremiah	2		5		
Marston, Jonathan	3		1		
Marston, Simon	2		3		
Marston, Samuel	1	1	4		
Marston, Jacob	2		2		
Moulton, John	2		2		
Moulton, John, Junʳ	1		1		
Moulton, John, 3d	1	1	5		
Moulton, John Mob	2		7		
Moulton, Jeremiah	2	1	3		
Moulton, William	1		1		
Moulton, Elisha	1		1		
Moulton, Benjamin	1	2	2		
Moulton, Small	2	1	3		
Mace, Samuel	3		3		
Moulton, Josiah	1	1	2		
Mason, Benjamin	2		2		
Mason, Josiah	1	3	2		
Moulton, Robert	2	1	5		
Marston, Philip Smith	2	3	4		
Marston, Elisha Smith	2	3	2		
Marston, Jonathan, Jr	1		5		1
Marston, Josiah	1	1	2		
Marston, Ephraim	3		3		
Mace, Deborah			4		
Moulton, Mary			2		
Nudd, Simon	1	3	2		
Nudd, Thomas	1	2	1		
Philbrook, James	2		1		
Perkins, Moses	2	3	3		
Palmer, Joseph	3		1		
Page, Samuel	1	2	4		
Page, Abner	2	3	3		
Page, Stephen	2		3		
Philbrik, Daniel	1	1	4		
Philbrick, Jonathan	1	1	2		
Philbrick, Joseph	1		2		
Philbrick, Joseph, Junʳ	1	2	3		
Philbrick, John	1		2		
Philbrick, James, Junʳ	1		2		
Page, Tabitha			5		
Redman, Sarah	2		5		
Redman, Joseph	1		2		
Shaw, Benjª Brown	2	1	3		
Shaw, Joshua	1	2	1		
Sanborn, Winthrop	1		2		
Shaw, Simeon	1		2		
Shaw, Josiah	1		2		
Shaw, Benjamin	1	1	3		
Sanborn, Simon	3	2	2		
Sanborn, James	1	3	2		
Sanborn, Abner	1	2	2		
Sanborn, Jonathan	1		1		
Souter, John	1	3	2		
Thayer, Ebenezer	1	2	5		
Toppan, Christopher	5	2	7		
Towle, Philip	3		2		
Towle, Joseph	1	1	1		
Towle, Amos	2		3		
Towle, Abraham Perkins	1	1	5		
Towle, Elisha	2	2	4		
Towle, Lemuel	1		3		
Towle, Ann			3		
Towle, Jeremiah	1		2		
Towle, Amos, Junʳ	2	2	3		
Towle, Josiah	1		3		
Towle, Samuel	3		6		
Towle, Joshua	1		2		
Towle, Joshua, Junʳ	1	5	3		
Towle, Jabez	1	4	1		
Tucke, John	1		3		
Tucke, John, Junʳ	1	3	6		
Tucke, James	1	4	1		
Tucke, Hulda	1	2	2		
Tucke, Anna			3		
Towle, Abigail			3		
Taylor, John	4	1	6		
Taylor, John, Junʳ	2	2	3		
Tilton, Ebenezer	1	2	1		
Towle, Nathˡ	1		2		
Ward, Cotton	2		1		
Weare, Daniel	2	1	2		
Yeaton, Christian	1		2		

HAMPTON FALLS TOWN.

NAME OF HEAD OF FAMILY.	Free white males of 16 years and upward, including heads of families.	Free white males under 16 years.	Free white females, including heads of families.	All other free persons.	Slaves.
Brown, Abraham	4		5		
Brown, John	1	4	3		
Burnham, Jonathan	2	1	3		
Brown, Nathan	5		2		
Brown, Nathan, Junʳ	1	2	3		
Blake, Henry	2	2	3		

ROCKINGHAM COUNTY—Continued.

NAME OF HEAD OF FAMILY.	Free white males of 16 years and upward, including heads of families.	Free white males under 16 years.	Free white females, including heads of families.	All other free persons.	Slaves.
HAMPTON FALLS TOWN—continued.					
Brown, Rachel			3		
Blake, Jeremiah	2	1	3		
Bachellor, David	3	2	7		
Blasdell, Leonard	1	1	2		
Bragg, Robert	1	1	3		
Blake, Christopher	1	1	2		
Brown, Michael	1	1	1		
Cram, Nehemiah	1	1	3		
Cram, Jonathan, Jr	1		3		
Cram, Jonathan	2	2	5		
Dow, Judah	3	1	3		
Dow, Zebulon	1	2	1		
Dodge, Nathl. Hubbard	3	4	4		
Dodge, Nathaniel	2	1	5		
Eaton, Timothy	1		2		
Fifield, George	2	1	9		
Green, Isaac	2	3	5		
Green, Eaton	1	1	2		
Hillyard, Benjamin	1		1		
Healey, Levi	2	1	5		
Hoag, Hussey	1	3	3		
Hillyard, Stephen	1	1	2		
Healey, Nathaniel	4	1	2		
Fifield, Margaret			1		
Knowles, Nathan	2	1	2		
Knowles, Gamaliel	4		2		
Lane, Jeremiah	5		2		
Lane, Isaiah	2		3		
Lane, Samuel	1	2	4		
Lane, Jonathan	1		3		
Leavitt, Elizabeth		1	2		
Locke, Josiah	2		5		
Leach, John	1		3		
Mace, Richard	1		1		
Marshall, Francis	1		1		
Moulton, Redman	2	1	11		
Melcher, Samuel	1		2		
Melcher, Samuel, Jr	2	1	4		
Moulton, Thomas	1	1	4		
Miller, Robert				3	
Marshall, Gideon	1	1	3		
Merrill, Aaron	1	3	6		
Marshall, Robert	1	2	3		
Nason, Richard	3		4		
Nason, Richard, Junr	1	2	8		
Norton, David	2	1	2		
Langdon, Samuel	1	2	5		
Prescott, James	3	1	4		
Prescott, Samuel	1	1	1		
Prescott, James, Junr	2	2	5		
Pervear, Josiah	1	4	2		
Perkins, David	3	1	5		
Pike, Benjamin	4	4	4		
Page, William	1		2		
Row, Paine	1	3	3		
Raymond, Joseph	2		3		
Rollins, John	1	1	2		
Sleeper, Ruth			2		
Weare, Thomas	1	1	2		
Sanborn, Benjamin	2		3		
Sanborn, Benjamin, Jr	1	1	3		
Sanborn, James	2		4		
Sanborn, Caleb	2	1	2		
Sanborn, Abner	2		2		
Sanborn, Meshech	1		4		
Sanborn, Theophilus	1	2	1		
Swain, Stephen	1	1	1		
Tilton, Jonathan	3	1	6		
Tilton, Nathan	4		2		
Tilton, Stephen	1	1	3		
Tilton, Caleb	1	1	5		
Tilton, Benjamin	3		2		
Tilton, Michael	1		3		
Vickery, Joshua	1	1	2		
Tilton, Samuel	2	5	6		
Wells, Aaron	2	1	2		
Ward, Melcher	1	1	3		
Wadleigh, John	1		2		
Weare, Samuel	2	1	3		
Wells, Joseph	2	1	6		
Worth, Timothy	3	1	5		
Wells, Moses	1	2	3		
Downs, John	1		3		
Stanyan, Keziah		1	3		
Chase, Charles	1		1		
HAWKE TOWN.					
Thorn, James	1	1	4		
Bartlett, George	3	3	5		
Bean, Jeremiah	1	3	5		
Sanborn, Joseph C	1	3	4		
HAWKE TOWN—con.					
Page, Thomas	3	1	4		
French, Jona, 3d	1	4	2		
Philbrick, Mary	1	1	6		
Sanborn, Josiah	1	1	1		
Sawyer, Gideon	1		2		
Sawyer, James	1		1		
Woodward, Wm	1		1		
Bachellor, David	1	1	1		
Sanborn, John	1	2	3		
Sanborn, Jethro	1		2		
Sanborn, Obediah	1	1	1		
Sanborn, Jona	1	1	3		
Page, Simon	1		2		
French, Jona	1		2		
Chase, Simon	1		5		
Hook, Humphry	2	1	3		
French, Jona, jr	2	1	2		
Hook, Israel	2	3	3		
Towle, Jeremy	1	1	6		
Towle, James	1	3	3		
Towle, Caleb	2		2		
Dearborn, Henry	3	2	3		
Spafford, Benja	1	1	5		
Hills, Reuben	2	5	2		
Page, Benja	1	2	1		
Eastman, Edward	3		3		
Campbell, Annis	1	2	4		
Quimby, David	2		3		
Quimby, Samuel	2	1	3		
Quimby, Aaron	2	1	4		
Burwell, Wm	3		5		
Tewksbury, Josiah	1	4	6		
Williams, Joseph	3	2	8		
Fellows, Joseph	1	2	1		
Woodman, Moses	1	2	2		
Sargeant, Saml	1	1	1		
Collins, Richard	2	1	6		
Barnard, Stephen	1		3		
Quimby, Paul	1		1		
Colby, Enos	2	1	4		
Dimond, Israel	1		2		
Dimond, Israel, jr	1	2	5		
Blake, Jona	1		2		
Blake, Hezekiah	1	2	5		
Morrill, Henry	2		1		
Morrill, Nathl	1	1	3		
Sleeper, Nehemiah	3	2	5		
Collins, Joseph	1	1	5		
Chase, Caleb	1		5		
Sleeper, Martha	1		2		
George, Wm	2	4	1		
Eaton, Joseph T	1		2		
Eaton, Jabez	1		1		
Bean, Elisha	2	4	5		
Brown, Nathl	1	4	5		
Eastman, Saml	1	1	3		
Jones, Nathan	1		1		
Jones, Jona	1	2	5		
Plummer, Samuel	3	2	3		
Collins, Benja	1	3	1		
Eastman, Jona	1	2	2		
Clough, Zaccheus	1		2		1
Baechellor, Elisha	3		3		
French, Joanna			2		
Merrill, Samuel	1	1	2		
True, Jabez	1	3	4		
Bradley, Joseph	1	1	2		
Fellows, Molly			1	3	
Darling, Elizabeth			1		
Page, Jona			2		
Blake, Lucy			1	2	
KENSINGTON TOWN.					
Brown, Joseph	3	4	4		
Wood, Aaron	2		1		
Eastman, Benja	2		4		
Eastman, Abner	1		2		
Dow, Caleb	1	1	4		
Brown, Benja, jr	1	1	3		
Worthen, Enoch	1	2	7		
Brown, Jona	2		3		
Brown, Abel	1		2		
Sherburn, Joseph	2	1	3		
Ward, Elizth			1		
Purington, Jona	2	1	5		
Wear, Lucy	1		1		
Dow, Jabez	1	1	3		
Weare, Nathl	3	4	3		
Dow, Jona	3		3		
Dow, Abihal	1	2	3		
Brown, Patience			4		
Palmer, Jona	1	2	6		
KENSINGTON TOWN—continued.					
Brown, Benja	1		2		
Brown, David	2	2	4		
Brown, Stephen	2	3	3		
Gove, Nathl	2	1	3		
Loverin, Ebenr	3		2		
Page, Nathl	3		2		
Clifford, Saml	1		1		
Clifford, Saml, jr	1	3	3		
Clifford, Joseph	1		3		
Dow, Nathan	1	1	3		
Dow, Benja	1		1		
Conner, Benja	2	5	4		
Conner, John	1		1		
Prescutt, Robt	1		2		
Johnson, Josiah	1	1	1		
Chase, David	1	2	4		
Blake, Elisha	1	1	2		
Blake, Elisha, jr	1	2	2		
Prescutt, Marstin	1	2	3		
Blake, Mesheek	1	2	2		
Shaw, Abram	1	2	4		
Rowe, Joseph	2	1	5		
Lock, Edwd	1	1	2		
Shaw, Moses	1		1		
Shaw, Moses, jr	2		4		
Shaw, David	1	3	2		
Shaw, Nathan	1	2	6		
Dearborn, Saml	3	1	3		
Dearborn, Jereh	2	1	4		
Brown, Josiah	1		2		
Brown, Caleb	1	3	2		
Dow, Reuben	4	1	4		
Blake, Josiah	1		1		
Blake, Hezekiah	1	2	4		
Gove, Nathan	2	2	3		
Gove, Widow	1		2		
Purkins, Widow			2		
Chase, Stephen	2	1	2		
Chase, Elihu	2	2	4		
Steward, Abigail	1		1		
Green, Abram	1		4		
Green, Jona	1	1	1		
Johnson, Obediah	2	2	3		
Green, John	1		1		
Green, Stephen	3	4	5		
Flanders, Jona	2		3		
Lamper, Saml	2	1	4		
Page, Stephen	2		3		
Burnham, Lemuel	1		2		
Palmer, Philbrick	1		4		
Palmer, Joseph	1	2	3		
Palmer, John	1		1		
Hilliard, Ann	2	3	6		
Lamper, Ruth	1		3		
Lamper, John	1		4		
Dow, Joseph	1	3	3		
Dow, Nathan	1		1		
Dow, Benja	1	1	4		
Cook, Thomas	2		4		
Blake, Jereh	2		5		
Fellows, Jereh	1	2	2		
Fogg, Jereh	2	1	7		
Sanborn, Moses	1		1		
Sanborn, James	2	3	2		
Tucke, Jesse	2	5	4		
Healey, Nathl	1		2		
Healey, Newhal	3	1	2		
Sanborn, Abram	2		2		
Sanborn, Jewell	1		2		
Wadley, Joseph	3	1	3		
Wadley, Joseph, jr	1	2	5		
Prescutt, Jona	1		2		
Prescutt, Jona, jr	1	2	3		
Blake, John	1		1		
Blake, Philemon	2		3		
Rowe, Jona	2	2	2		
Rowe, Benja	2	4	8		
Melcher, Benja	1		5		
Melcher, Edwd	3		5		
Clifford, Ebenr	4	3	6		
Tilton, Jona	2	1	3		
Rowe, Winthrop	2		4		
Bachellor, John	1	1	2		
Prescutt, Saml	3		2		
Lane, Joseph	2		3		
Lane, Joshua	1	1	2		
Fellows, Jereh	2		1		
Fellows, Jona	1		3		
Fellows, Nathan	1		2		
Potter, Ebenr	2	1	5		
Tucke, Widow	1		4		
Sherburn, Widow	1	1	2		

ROCKINGHAM COUNTY—Continued.

KENSINGTON TOWN—continued.

NAME OF HEAD OF FAMILY.	Free white males of 16 years and upward, including heads of families.	Free white males under 16 years.	Free white females, including heads of families.	All other free persons.	Slaves.
Shaw, Caleb	1	1	1		
Shaw, Elijah	2	2	3		
James, Moses	1		3		
James, David	1		5		
Morgan, Parker	4	2	3		
Fogg, James	2	1	5		
Hodgedon, Hanson	1	2	3		
Sanborn, Richd	3		1		
Green, Widow	1		2		
Page, Elizth	1	1	6		
Page, Aaron	2	3	4		
Moulton, Benja	3	1	5		
Hudd, Weare	1	1	3		
Bachellor, Josiah	2		2		
Bachellor, Benja	1	1	2		
Bachellor, John	1		2		
Bachellor, John, jr	1		3		
Bachellor, Jereh	2		3		
Prescutt, Benja	1		1		
Prescutt, Simon	2	2	3		
Hobbs, Noah	1	1	5		
Sanborn, Theop	1	4	3		
Sanborn, Widow	1		1		
Sanborn, Henry	1		4		
Brown, Wm	1	2	3		
James, Benja	1		1		
James, Benja, jr	1	2	4		
Hilliard, Joseph Chase	1	1	1		
Hilliard, Theops	1	1	3		
Tilton, Jereh	5	1	2		
Tilton, Benja	2	3	4		
Prescutt, Joseph	1		1		
Perrere, Saml. Noyes	1	1	4		
Conner, Widow			3		
Green, Abraham	1		4		

KINGSTON TOWN.

NAME OF HEAD OF FAMILY.	Free white males of 16 years and upward, including heads of families.	Free white males under 16 years.	Free white females, including heads of families.	All other free persons.	Slaves.
Beede, Hezikiah	1	1	3		
Sanborn, Peter	1		1		
Woodman, Joseph	1	2	4		
Sanborn, Isaac	1	3	3	1	
Magoon, Benja	2	1	3		
Smith, Danl	3	2	2		
Sleeper, Richd	1	3	4		
Sleeper, Benja	3	1	3		
Sanborn, Wm	4	1	3		
Judkins, Esther	3		3		
Fefield, Peter	2	2	4		
Judkins, Joseph	1	1	3		
Sanborn, Hannah	1		2		
French, Saml	1		1		
French, Saml	2	3	3		
French, Abraham	3	3	6		
Fefield, Jna. Clifford	1	1	1		
Filbrick, Sarah	1		2		
Long, Ebenr	2		4		
French, David	1		2		
French, John	2	1	1		
Fefield, Saml	2		1		
Fefield, Saml., junr	1		2		
Eastman, Ebenr	3		3		
Stevens, Saml	1		2		
Sanborn, Mary	1	1	4		
Stevens, Benja	4	1	5		
Judkins, Henry	1	2	6		
Bartlett, Seth	1		5		
Bartlett, John	1	2	2		
Gale, Amos	5	2	7		
Gale, Gilman	1		1		
Calf, John	3		2		
Huntoon, John	2	1	3		
Procter, Ebenr	1		1		
Procter, Abigail	1		1		
Griffin, Ebenr	2				
Dutch, George	1		3		
Colcord, Mehitabel			3		
Colcord, Danl	1	2	6		
Caruth, James	1	1	2	1	
Pattin, Wm	1	3	5		
George, Gideon	2	3	2		
Loverin, Benja	1		2		
Garland, Nathl	2	1	5		
Sanborn, Timothy	1		3		
Sanborn, David	1	3	2		
Tande, Wm	1		2		
Sanborn, John Q	1	1	1		
Young, Aaron	2	3	6		
Favor, Daniel	1	1	4		
Fefield, Peter	1		3		
Davis, Saml	1	2	7		
Chase, Nathl	1	3	4		

KINGSTON TOWN—con.

NAME OF HEAD OF FAMILY.	Free white males of 16 years and upward, including heads of families.	Free white males under 16 years.	Free white females, including heads of families.	All other free persons.	Slaves.
Thorn, James	1		3		
Thorn, John	1				
Thorn, Jacob	2	4	4		
Elkins, Ann	2		2		
Eastman, John	2	2	6		
Elkins, Thomas	1	1	2		
French, Henry	2	3	2		
Sanborn, Saml	1		1		
Webber, John	1	1	1		
Tucker, Benja	1		1		
Tucker, John	2	1	1		
Calf, Saml	1		1		
Singelton, John	1		1		
Sivett, Nathan	1		3		
Sivett, Widow	1	1	2		
Huntoon, Aaron	1	4	2		
Hook, Jacob, Esqr	2		3		
Bartlett, His Excely, Josiah	4	1	5		
Calf, John, jr	1		3		
Abbott, Peter	1	3	1		
Brown, Benja	1	1	4		
Calef, Joseph	2	1	3		
Chase, Charles	2	1	5		
Bartlett, Joshua	1		2		
Cooper, Benja	1	2	4		
Thayer, Revd Elihu	2	2	5		
Wheeler, Solomon	1	2	3		
Secombe, Simmons	1	1	6		
Stevens, Benja, 3d	1		2		
Sivett, Stephen	4	2	7		
Graves, Jacob	2		2		
Stevens, Ebenr	4	1	2		
Stevens, Ebenr, jr	2	2	1		
Clough, Benja	1		7		
Davis, Nehemiah	1		1		
Eastman, Ebenr, jr	1		1		
Foot, Jacob	1	3	6		
Woodman, Joshua	1		1		
Woodman, Saml	2	4	2		
Buswell, Danl	1	2	4		
Thomson, Thomas	1	1	6		
Bartlett, Nathan	3		4		
Thomson, Saml	3	1	2		
Tongue, Widow	1		3		
Blasdel, Ralph	1		1		
Greenfield, Elizth			1		
Webster, Jacob	2	2	6		
Webster, Benja	1	3	1		
Quimby, Betty			2		
Winslow, John	1	2	2		
Badger, Stephen	3	3	3		
Davis, Phineas	1	4	1		
Fellows, Josiah	1				
Blasdel, Daniel		3	2		
Fellows, Nathl	1	3	8		
Sanborn, Jona	1		1		
Nicholls, Nicholas	2	2	2		
Collins, Wm	1	5	3		
Severance, Saml	1	1	5		
Silloway, Benja W	2	2	4		
Sleeper, Edwd	1		2		
Sleeper, Jona	1		2		1
Winslow, Jacob	1	1	4		
Favour, Saml	1	2	3		
Stevens, Mary			1		
Severance, John	2		2		
Davis, John	1	3	4		
Winslow, Ephm	2		6		
Sleeper, Wm	1		2		
Sleeper, John B	1	2	2		
Collins, Jona	1	3	5		
Wadley, Daniel	1	1	1		
Wadley, Widow	1		6		
Peasley, Jacob	1	4	4		
Huse, Samuel	1	2	2		
Hubbard, Elizth	1	1	2		
Severe, Thomas	3		1		
Davis, Phillip	1		2		
Davis, Webster	1		2		
Silloway, Greeley	1	3	3		
Bootman, Thomas	1	2	1		
Flanders, David	2		2		
Bootman, Sarah			2		
Webster, Gideon	1	1	3		
Hoit, Elipt	1		1		
Peasley, Timothy	3	1	4		
Davis, Reuben	2		2		
Noyes, Widow	3	1	2		
Severe, Caleb	1	1	1		
Webster, Isaac	2		1		
Webster, John	1	2	7		
Pollard, Jona	1	1	6		

KINGSTON TOWN—con.

NAME OF HEAD OF FAMILY.	Free white males of 16 years and upward, including heads of families.	Free white males under 16 years.	Free white females, including heads of families.	All other free persons.	Slaves.
Pollard, Isaac	2		1		
Johnson, Jeremh	2	1	5		
Hunt, Henry	2	1	5		
Hunt, Nehemiah	3	1	3		
Colby, Thomas	1	1	3		
Carter, Mary			1		
Carter, Jacob	1		4		
Stewart, Saml	1	3	3		
Sargeant, Saml	1		1		
Welsh, Joseph	1		1		
Welsh, Moses	2	1	4		
Stewart, Stephen	1	3	2		
Collins, Benja	1		2		
Hunt, Moses	1	3	2		
Dearborn, Nathl	1		2		
Stevens, John	1	3	1		
Tucker, Joseph	1	1	1		
Homans, Joseph	1	1	1		
Eastman, Jacob	1	2	3		
Davis, Hannah			1		
Beede, Azeriah	1		2		

LONDONDERRY TOWN.

NAME OF HEAD OF FAMILY.	Free white males of 16 years and upward, including heads of families.	Free white males under 16 years.	Free white females, including heads of families.	All other free persons.	Slaves.
Moore, Robert	4	1	5		1
Wilson, Robert	2	3	3		
Morrisson, Jona	1	1	3		
Hopkins, John	2	2	5		
Hughs, John	2	3	7		
Sargeant, Chillis	1	4	2		
Nesmith, John	3		3		
Nesmith, Benja	1	3	2		
Tadd, Samuel	1		6		
Alexander, John	1	2	5		
Wilson, Saml	3		4		
Carlton, John	1	1	4		
Clark, George	2	1	6		
Alexander, Wm	1		2		
Alexander, Mary			2		
Alexander, Hugh	2	1	5		
Cochran, Saml., jr	3		3		
Cochran, Saml	3	2	6		
Anderson, Thos	2	1	3		
Montgomery, Hugh	2	5	7		
Gregg, Wm	1	1	4		
Gregg, Ebenr	1	1	1		
Gregg, George	2	1	2		
Hemphill, Nathl	1	1	3		
Kelley, Peter	3	1	2		
Nesmith, John	4	1	2		
Moore, James			2		
Miltemore, Wm	4		4		
Wilson, James	2	1	4		
Currier, John	1	1	4		
Savory, Saml	1	3	1		
Barnard, James	1	3	3		
Humphry, James	2	4	4		
Steel, John	3	3	4		
Paul, James	1		1		
Mitchell, Thos	2		3		
Procter, Jacob	1	4	3		
Reed, George	4		3		
Reed, John	3		6		
Morrisson, Joseph	2		5		
Morrisson, Abraham	2	4	3		
Clendenin, Robert	2	4	4		
Paul, David	1	5	7		
Taylor, John	1	1	2		
Taylor, James	1	1	2		
Taylor, Wm	3		5		
Adams, Joseph	1	4	3		
Bond, John	1		1		
Bond, Gilbert	1		3		
Hovey, Joseph	1	3	3		
Johnson, Stephen	1	5	3		
Davidson, David	2		2		
Davidson, Thos	2		1		
Page, Abraham	2	2	3		
Taylor, David	4	2	3		
Colby, David	2	1	2		
Morrisson, Saml	1	1	4	1	
Wilson, Thomas	1	1	5		
Morrisson, Samuel	1	3	3		
Davidson, Revd Wm	2	4	4	2	
Morrisson, Revd Wm	3	3	8		
Clendenin, Jenny	1		2		
Humphrys, Wm	1	2	6		
Taylor, Adam	1	1	3		
Taylor, Samuel	1	3	4		
Thomson, James	1	3	4		
Morrisson, Saml	1		2		
Adams, John	1		3		
Prentice, John	5	1	5	3	

ROCKINGHAM COUNTY—Continued.

LONDONDERRY TOWN—continued.

NAME OF HEAD OF FAMILY.	Free white males of 16 years and upward, including heads of families.	Free white males under 16 years.	Free white females, including heads of families.	All other free persons.	Slaves.
Allisson, Saml	4	1	5		
Allisson, James					
Platts, James	2		6		
Cochran, James	1		1		
Cross, John	2	2	2		
Runnels, Daniel	4	2	5		
McKeen, John	2		3		
McKeen, Daniel	1		1		
Morrisson, Robert	2	1	4		
Carr, Samuel	1	1	2		
Kelso, Agnis	3		3		
Warner, John	1		2		
Warner, John, jr	1	4	2		
Carr, Mary	1	1	6		
Ferrin, Timothy	2		1		
Moore, Andrew	1		1		
Patten, James R	1		2		
Stinson, Nathan	1	3	5		
Sargeant, Volantine	1	1	2		
McKenzie, Phillip	1	4	3		
Moore, Parker	1	1	3		
Dalton, Hannah		1	3		
Spear, Ebenr	1		1		
Taylor, John	1	1	3		
Alexander, James	4		4		
Johnson, Lemuel	1	6	3		1
McCollum, Robert	2	4	6		
McNeal, Josiah	1	2	4		
Ralph, Ann			2		
Ralph, Moses	1	3	1		
Dinsmore, James	3	4	3		
Blair, David	2	2	2		
Wood, George	1	2	5		
Clark, Widow	1	3	3		
Ayers, Wm	1		1		
Ingals, Moses	1	3	2		
Wallis, John	1		1		
Wallis, Jona	2	2	4		
Palmer, John	1	1	1		
Palmer, James	3	2	2		
Moore, John	3	2	7		
Fulton, Robert	2	1	3		1
Clark, John	4	2	4		
Waddle, James	1	1	2		
Waddle, John	2	1	4		
Morrisson, James	1	1	5		
Nesmith, Jona	1	4	5		
Smith, Nathl	3		1		
Chase, Jacob	4	3	4		
Nesmith, James	2		1		
Boyes, Samuel	5	1	3		
Boyes, James, jr	1	3	4		
Boyes, Margeret	1	2	5		
Boyes, James	1	1	4		
Page, Wm	2	1	4		
Adams, David	2	2	4		
Morrisson, Robert	2	1	2		
Patingale, Phineas	2	3	3		
Sawyer, Amos	1	2	7		
Osmond, Henry	1	1	2		
Sawyer, Reuben	1	1	1		
McAllister, George	1	3	3		
White, Samuel	1		2		
White, Ephraim	1	2	2		
Cornin, John	3	1	2		
Lions, Wm	4	2	2		
McClary, Saml	1		2		
Adams, Jona	4		2		
Brown, Nathl	1	1	2		
Carlton, David	1	6	2		
Hunter, John	2	4	4		1
Parkinson, Wm	1	3	4		
Chiney, Benja	5		2		
McNeal, Robert	1	2	6		
Ayers, James	2		3		
Allisson, John	1		4		
Safford, Abraham	3	2	4		
Holman, Stephen	3	2	4		
Adams, David	3	3	6		
Clark, Matthew	2	1	4		
Gunnior, Agnis	1		2		
Miltimore, James	4		3		
Fisk, Joseph, jr	1		2		
Fisk, Joseph	4		4		
Jackson, Joshua	1	3	3		
Barker, James	1	2	3		
Barker, John	2	1	5		
Danforth, Joseph	2	1	2		
Wallis, James	2	1	3		
Gregg, Joseph	3	4	5		
Gregg, Benja	3				

LONDONDERRY TOWN—continued.

NAME OF HEAD OF FAMILY.	Free white males of 16 years and upward, including heads of families.	Free white males under 16 years.	Free white females, including heads of families.	All other free persons.	Slaves.
Danforth, John	1	1	3		
Gregg, James	2	1	3		
Gregg, John	1	1	2		
Martin, Jacob	4		7		
Thom, Isaac	4	3	7		
Clendenin, Wm	1	2	4		
Belton, John	2		1		
McMurphy, Robert	2	1	1		
McMurphy, Robert, jr	1	2	3		
McFarland, Robert	2		2		
Archibald, Robert	2	1	3		
Burwell, Abel B	1	4	3		
Chapman, Joanna		2	4		
Choat, William	2	3	5		
McGregore, James	3	2	5		1
McDuffee, Daniel	4	3	8		
Adams, Edmund	3	3	3		
Steward, Saml	1	1	2		
Orr, James	1		3		
Senter, Abel	1	1	5		
Moore, John	3	1	3		
Morrisson, John	1	3	2		
Choat, James	1	2	3		
Barnett, Robert	1		3		
Cherry, Saml	1	4	4		
Morrill, Simeon	1		4		
Morrill, Barns	1		4		
Morrisson, David	3		6		
Kelso, Alexander	1	3	3		
Ela, John	1		1		
Cheney, Nathl	1		1		
Ela, David	2	3	5		
Wallis, Robert	2	3	1		
Nichols, Alexander	2				
Nichols, James	1	2	2		
Dodge, Agnis		2	3		
Boyes, Alexander	1		3		
Dodge, Parker	2	1	8		
Plummer, Bunsley	2		5		
Chapman, Dudley	2	1	4		
McCurdy, John	1	1	3		
Kelso, Jona	1	3	4		
Dodge, Saml	2	1	2		
Nourse, Nathl	3		2		
Martin, Nathl	3		2		
Stevens, John	2	1	4		
Gilmore, Wm	2		1		
Shute, Benja	1	1	3		
Moore, John	2		5		
Hill, Moses	1				
Chase, John	1		3		
Christy, Thomas	2	1	4		
Boyes, Sarah			1		
Doake, James	1	3	7		
McKeen, John	1	5	5		
Cochran, John	1	1	4		
Ramsey, James	3		2		
Cox, Elizabeth		3	4		
Jewett, Nathl	1	3	5		
Cox, Charles	1		1		
Patterson, David	1	3	3		
Patterson, Peter	1	1	3		
Cochran, John	2		3		
Anderson, John	1	1	4	1	
Anderson, James	1	3	5		
Wallis, Wm	1	1	3		
Danforth, Wm	2	1	5		
Neal, Widow	3	2	5		
Holmans, John	1	2	6		
Reed, Jona	2	1	4		
Ewins, John	2	1	3		
Akin, James	3	5	4		
Chiney, Thomas	1	3	3		
Wallis, Rebecca			3		
Pinkerton, James			3		
Morrisson, Saml	1	4	4		
Bell, John	3	2	3		
Pinkerton, John	4	2	3		
Dickey, Matthew	4		2	1	
Dickey, John					
Sessions, Samuel	2	3	5		
Dunkan, Abraham	2		2		1
Dunkan, John	3	1	3		
Dunkan, Wm	2	1	4		1
Cochran, James	2		2		
Nichols, Matthew	1				
Giles, John	2	1	3		
Corning, George	3		2		
McClary, Thomas	1	3	2		
McClary, John	1	1	1		
Hogg, James	2	2	4		

LONDONDERRY TOWN—continued.

NAME OF HEAD OF FAMILY.	Free white males of 16 years and upward, including heads of families.	Free white males under 16 years.	Free white females, including heads of families.	All other free persons.	Slaves.
McClinch, John	2	1	3	1	
Senter, Saml., jr	1	3	3		
Watts, John	1	1	5		
Hogg, Wm	1		2		
Donalson, James	2	1	1		
Highland, Thomas	1	1	6		
McMurphy, James	2	1	8		
Smith, Elias	2		2		
Craigie, James	1	1	2		
Craigie, Robert	3		3		
Clark, Saml	3		5		
Morrisson, Abraham	1	2	3		
Carlton, Thomas	1	1	2		
Page, Paul	1	2	4		
Burkley, Lawrence	1	1	6		
Ela, Edward	2	4	2		
Lennon, Thomas	1	2	2		
Holmes, Thos	1	4	9		
Anderson, Wm	3	3	4		
Hourre, John	2	3	2		
Rogers, James	2	3	3		
Boyd, Robert	2	1	2		
Graham, Saml	2		2		
Plummer, Abel	3		3		
Anderson, Saml	2		1		
Leach, Joseph	1	1	3		
Watts, Moses, jr	1	2	3		
Anderson, John	1	1	6		
Moore, Wm	1	2	3		
Anderson, Allen	1	1	2		
Anderson, Saml	2	1	2		
Anderson, Saml., jr	1	2	5		
Boyd, Alexr	1	2	3		
Anderson, Wm., jr	1	2	4		
McAdams, Wm	1	1	2		
Dwinnell, Thos	2	1	5		
Towns, Moses	1	3	2		
Burbank, Ezra	1		1		
Towns, Elijah	1		4		
Towns, Elijah, jr	1	1	1		
Nichols, Jacob	4	2	6		
Woodburn, David	1	3	5		
Clark, John	2		2		1
Gould, Amos	2		4		
Foster, David	2	2	8		
Thomson, John	2	1	5		
Chapman, Joseph	1	3	2		
Thomson, Saml	1	1	1		
Jones, Josiah	3	1	5		
Clark, Matthew	1	2	4		
Chase, Stephen	1		1		
Hamlet, Ezekiel	1	2	3		
Jones, Jesse	1	1	2		
Patterson, Thos	2	5	5		
Patterson, Peter	1		1		
Patterson, John	1	2	2		
Dickey, Wm	1	2	3		
Dickey, Adam	1		2		
March, John	4	1	4		
Gregg, James	2		3		
Durnnell, Elijah	3		5		
Senter, Reuben	1		5		
Senter, Ebenr	1	3	3		
Senter, Saml	1		2		
Nichols, James	1	1	2		
Senter, Aaron	1	1	4		
Alexander, Wm	1	2	2		
Smith, Saml	1		2		
Abbott, Benja	1	2	2		
Richardson, Jacob	1	2	3		
Gerrish, Benja	2		1		
Thomson, James	1	6	6		
Dimond, Ephrm	2	1	3		
Jones, Josiah, jr	1	1	3		
Thomson, Robert	2	1	1	1	
Boyd, John	3				
Anderson, John	1		3		
Bailey, Joseph	1	2	3		
McAllister, Rebecca		3	6		
Herriman, Jona	1		2		
Mack, Andrew	1	4	5		
Thom, Wm	1	1	1		
Campbell, Henry	1		2		
Burbank, Enoch	1	2	2		
Dwinnell, John	3	1	7		
Ames, Noyes	1		1		
Lesley, Alexr	1	2	4		
Walls, Margt			2		
Fisher, Saml	2		3	1	
Fisher, Ebenr	2				
Crowall, Saml	2		3		

ROCKINGHAM COUNTY—Continued.

LONDONDERRY TOWN—continued.

NAME OF HEAD OF FAMILY.	Free white males of 16 years and upward, including heads of families.	Free white males under 16 years.	Free white females, including heads of families.	All other free persons.	Slaves.
Merrill, David	1		1		
Barnett, Ann	2	1	4		
Crowall, David	1	3	2		
Plummer, Nathan	1	2	3		
Wallis, James	1	1	2		
Sargeant, Widow	1		3		
Kimball, John	2	1	1		
Gage, Wm	2		1		
Dodge, Isaac	1		1		
Corning, John	1		2		
Duncan, George	2	1	3		
March, Saml	2		3		
Hogg, Joseph	2	1	3		1
Hogg, James	1		1		
Watts, Moses	1		3		
Watts, James	1	1	1		
Corning, Joshua	2		2		
Corning, Saml., jr	1	1	1		
Boyes, Robert	1	4	3		
Dickey, Adam	2	2	3		
Griffin, Jona	3		6		
Wilson, Robert	4	3	5		
Reed, Abraham	3	2	4		
Pearse, Oliver	1	2	2		
McMurphy, Archibald	3	2	9		
Alls, Saml	1		1		
McMurphy, Saml	1	1	1		
Brewster, David	1	1	2		
Adams, Saml	2		5		
Adams, Wm	1	2	2		
Pinkerton, Mattw	2	1	6		
Craigie, Grenvat			5		
Stinson, Martha	1		1		
Weare, Wm	2		3		
Dickey, Robert	1	4	5		
McDuffee, John	1	4	3		
Sherburn, Pompey				5	
Adams, Masey	2		2		
McGregore, James	2	2	7		
Scoby, Mary			1		
Tear, Joseph	1	1	2		
Clark, Elizabeth			3		
Cochran, Robert	3	1	3		
McGraw, Roger	2	3	3		
Cheney, James	1	2	3		
Kilcade, John	1		2		
Whidden, Saml	1	2	1		
Dunshee, Martha		1	2		
Cohoon, James	1		1		
White, Levi				5	
Cummins, Ann			2		
Emery, Elipt	1	1	6		
Boyes, John	1	1	5		
Hunter, Saml	1	1	2		
Gaites, Mary		1	1		
Dickey, Jane			1		
Patterson, Wm	1		3		
Akin, Elizabeth	2	1	4		
Russel, George	1	2	3		
Matthews, Widow			4		
Chase, Moses	1	2	1		
Watts, Hugh	1	1	5		
Corning, Benjs	1	2	1		
Abbott, Doctr	2		3		
Wilson, David	1	4	3		
Allen, John	1	3	1		
Palmer, Jona	1	2	4		
Emery, Jesse	1	3	3		
Low, Nathl	1		2		
Oliver, Andrew	1		3		
Warner, Nathl	1	1	1		
Clark, Saml., jr	1				
Nichols, Joseph	1	2	3		
Fisher, William	1	5	2		
Rankin, Wm	1	1	5		
Anderson, Robert	2		1		
King, Jenny			1		
Crombie, John	1	1	3		
McKeen, Robert	1	1	2		
Boyd, Thomas	1	1	3		

LOUDON TOWN.

NAME OF HEAD OF FAMILY.	Free white males of 16 years and upward, including heads of families.	Free white males under 16 years.	Free white females, including heads of families.	All other free persons.	Slaves.
Bachelder, Abraham	2		3		
French, Abel	1	1	2		
Stevens, Abiel	1	4	4		
Bacheleder, Abraham 3d	1	3	3		
Bachelder, Abraham, 2d	2	6	3		
Chamberlain, Abiel	2	3	6		
Moor, Archelus	2		2		
Clough, Abner	1		1		

LOUDON TOWN—con.

NAME OF HEAD OF FAMILY.	Free white males of 16 years and upward, including heads of families.	Free white males under 16 years.	Free white females, including heads of families.	All other free persons.	Slaves.
Muffet, Agilea	1	1	4		
Lovring, Osgood	1	1	2		
Holden, Abraham	1	2	3		1
Stevens, Aron	1		2		1
Buzell, Cornelious	1	1	2		
Pilsbury, Caleb	2	5	6		
Stevens, Caleb	3	1	3		
Sargent, Charles	2		1		
Drew, Clemet	1	1	1		
True, Danl	1		2		
Eastman, David	1	3	3		
Ordway, Danl	2	3	3		
Fowlers, Danl	1	1	3		
Greely, David	1	2	3		
Furnald, Demind	1	4	5		
Hutchins, David	1	1	3		
Leavitt, Daniel	2	2	1		
Smith, Danl	1		3		
Bagley, David	1	1	2		
Ladd, Danl	3	1	6		
Moulton, Elijah	1	1	1		
Bickford, Eli	1	2	3		
Wood, Enoch	4		1		
Rawlings, Eliphalet	5	1	4		
French, Eziekle	1	1	6		
Sandborn, Ebenezer	2	1	1		
Blasdell, Ezery	1	2	2		
Carr, Elliot	1	2	6		
Buzell, Elijah	1		4		
French, Ebenezer	1	2	2		
Parker, Ebenezer	1	1	2		
Mathes, Gashorn	3	1	3		
Parker, Green	1		3		
Moor, Henery	1		3		
Blasdell, Henery	2	1	6		
Hoit, Hanson	2	1	4		
Bachelder, Jethroe	1		1		
Glines, Israel	1	4	3		
Rogers, Isaac	1	2	2		
Harvey, Isiah	1	1	5		
Clifford, Isaac	1	1	4		
Lowell, Isaac	3		3		
Pilsbury, Isaac	2	2	2		
Dimond, Isaac	1	2	3		
Ordway, Joses	1				
Moulton, Joseph	3		7		
Sargent, Jacob	1		2		
Bachelder, Jethroe, Junr	3	1	3		
Morrill, James	2	1	4		
Hoit, Jonathan	2	2	3		
Berry, Joshua	1	2	3		
Osborne, Jacob	1	3	4		
Thompson, James	2	3	4		
Rines, Joshua	1	2	4		
Sandborn, John	2	4	6		1
Smith, Jona	3	2	3		
Sargent, John	2	1	3		
Drew, John	2	6	7		
Smith, Joseph	2	3	4		
Silver, James	2	2	2		
Sargent, Joshua	1	2	2		
Perkins, Jona C	1	1	1		
Tilton, Joseph	2	2	6		
Randall, Jona	1	2	1		
Brown, Jeremiah	1		2		
Sporfield, John	1	3	4		
Clough, John	1				
Chase, Jona	2	1	3		
Hutchins, Jos	2		2		
Mason, Jos	1		2		
Clough, Jona	4		4		
Bennett, Joseph	1		2		
Bennett, Jeremiah	1	2	5		
Chase, James	1	5	4		
Wells, James	1	1	4		
Sandborn, Jeremiah	4	3	8		
Clough, Jeremh	4		3		
Stevens, John	1	1	3		
Moors, John	1	4	6		
Sargent, Josiah	1		5		
Abbott, John	1	4	2		
Moor, Jno	2	2	4		
Pipper, Jona	1		2		
Stoniel, Jonathan	2	1	2		
Bachelder, Libbey	1	1	5		
French, Levi	2	3	2		
Weeks, Leonerd	1	1	3		
Morris, Moses	1	2	3		
Chamberlin, Moses	1	2	3		
Ordway, Moses	1		2		
Ordway, Moses, Junr	1	3	4		
Rowel, Moses	3	3	7		

LOUDON TOWN—con.

NAME OF HEAD OF FAMILY.	Free white males of 16 years and upward, including heads of families.	Free white males under 16 years.	Free white females, including heads of families.	All other free persons.	Slaves.
Morill, Moses	1	4	3		
Lovring, Moses	2	5	4		
Stevens, Moses	2	1	2		
Bachelder, Nathl	3	1	5		
Rawlings, Nathl	2	1	1		
Bachelder, Nathan	3	2	4		
Bachelder, Nathan, Jr	2	3	5		
Bachelder, Nath., Jr	3		5		
Tilton, Nathan	2	2	3		
Weeks, Nathl	1	1	1		
Hill, Nathl	3	1	3		
Moors, Nathl	1	2	2		
Emery, Nathl	2	2	5		
Clough, Nathan	2	3	2		
Wiggin, Noah	1	2	3		
Blasdell, Oliver	2	2	2		
Morrill, Oliver	2		1		
French, Obediah	1	2	5		
Lovring, Osgood	1	1	1		
Brown, Phillip	2	4	2		
Rawlings, Peter	1	1	2		
Page, Phineas	1	2	1		
Bachelder, Phineas	1	1	2		
Stevens, Phineas	1	4	2		
Drew, Robert	4	2	4		
Bachelder, Richard	1	3	4		
Collins, Ruben	1	1	3		
Floud, Richard	1		4		
Ayers, Saml	1	1	3		
Chamberlin, Saml	1	1	5		
Chamberlin, Saml, Junr	1	1	5		
Fiffeald, Stephen	2	1	1		
Purkins, Stephen	2		4		
Long, Stephen	1		1		
Jacobs, Saml	2	1	2		
Carter, Saml	3	2	3		
Wells, Stephen	2	2	3		
French, Saml	3	2	4		
Piper, Saml	2	2	5		1
Hill, Saml	2	2	4		
Cate, Stephen	2	7	3		
Cate, Saml	2		3		
Morrill, Saml	4	2	5		
Bachelder, Thos	1	1	2		
Proctor, Thos	2	2	5		
Swett, Thos	3	1	4		
Sergent, Thos	1	5	4		
Palmer, Truworthy	1	4	5		
French, Timo	2	1	4		
Moor, Thomas	2		4		
Gleeson, Timothy	2	2	4		
Emery, Thos	1	1	3		
Moress, Wm	1		4		
Tilton, Wm	4	1	5		
Worth, Wm	3	1	7		
Lovring, Willebe	1	1	2		
Going, Wm	1	4	2		
Boyton, Wm	2	4	3		
Wheeler, Wm	2	1	2		
Clifford, Wm	1	3	2		
Buzdeal, Wm	1	1	2		
Bachelder, Wm	1	2	1		
Bachelder, Wm., Junr	1	2	1		
Gibson, Wm	1	1	1		
Winslow, Zeblon	1	3	3		
Quaso, Pompay				4	

NEWCASTLE TOWN.

NAME OF HEAD OF FAMILY.	Free white males of 16 years and upward, including heads of families.	Free white males under 16 years.	Free white females, including heads of families.	All other free persons.	Slaves.
Simpson, John	1	1	4		
Prescott, Henry	4	1	5		
Blunt, John	5	1	3		
Frost, George	1	4	7		
Tarlton, John	1	3	4		
Bell, John	2		4		
Vennard, William	2	3	4		
Tredick, William	1	2	4		
Trefethen, Abraham	1	2	5		
White, Robert	1	3	4		
Randell, Paul	3		3		
Neal, William	1		1		
Neal, John	1		3		
Batson, Stephen	2		1		
Shannon, John	1	2	2		
White, Joshua	4		5		
White, Nathan	1	1	3		
Amazeen, John	2	1	3		
Amazeen, Ephraim	4	1	2		
Amazeen, Joseph	2	1	2		
Amazeen, Christopher	2	5	3		
Jones, William	2		6		
Mitchel, David	3		6		

ROCKINGHAM COUNTY—Continued.

NAME OF HEAD OF FAMILY.	Free white males of 16 years and upward, including heads of families.	Free white males under 16 years.	Free white females, including heads of families.	All other free persons.	Slaves.	NAME OF HEAD OF FAMILY.	Free white males of 16 years and upward, including heads of families.	Free white males under 16 years.	Free white females, including heads of families.	All other free persons.	Slaves.	NAME OF HEAD OF FAMILY.	Free white males of 16 years and upward, including heads of families.	Free white males under 16 years.	Free white females, including heads of families.	All other free persons.	Slaves.
NEWCASTLE TOWN—con.						**NEWINGTON TOWN— continued.**						**NEWMARKET TOWN— continued.**					
Bell, Abednego	3	3	3			Pickering, John Gee	1	2	6		2	Bordman, William	1	3	5		
Tarlton, Elias	2	3	7			Fabyan, Samuel	1	1	5			Burleigh, Mehitabel			5		
Smith, Isaac	1		2			Pickering, Richard	2	2	8		1	Bracket, Benning	3	2	10		
Pridham, Isaac	1	2	4			Pickering, Ephraim	5	1	6	1		Branscomb, Arthur	1	3	2		
Stocker, William	2	2	4			Dame, Timothy	3	1	1			Bryent, Walter, Junr	1	2	3		
Frost, Joseph	1	1	3			Pickering, Nicholas	1	2	3			Bracket, Jeremy	2	2	4		
Bell, Sampson	3		6			Thomas, Stephen Jones	3	1	5			Bartlett, Joseph	1	1	4		
White, Edward	1	4	3			Furber, Jethro	2	1	5			Badger, Thomas	1	3	1		
Odiorne, Benjamin	2	4	3			Dame, Abigail		1	3			Burleigh, Henry	1		1		
Kennear, John	1	3	6			Furber, William	1	2	4			Chapman, Paul	1	1	2		
Yeaton, Andrew M	2	2	5			Coleman, Phinehas	2		3	1		Chapman, David	2	4	5		
Tredick, Henry	1	3	5			Coleman, Martha	1		2			Cheswill, Wentworth	3	1	7		
Goudy, Samuel	1		3			Coleman, Joseph	2	2	3			Cook, John	1		2		
Neal, William, Jr	1	2	4			Coleman, John	3	1	3			Chapman, Benjamin	1		2		
Neal, James	1	1	4			Trickey, Jonathan	2		4			Cram, James	3		3		
Yeaton, John C	2	3	6			Peavey, James	1	4	5			Chapman, Smith	1	3	4	2	
Pearce, William	1					Patterson, Temperance			1		3	Churchill, Thomas	3		3		
Bell, Mary			2			Nutter, Matthias	2	2	5			Churchill, Thomas, Jun2	1	1	1		
Tredick, Edward	1	1	4			Downing, Bartholomew	1	3	2			Churchill, Ichabod	1	2	1		
Simpson, John, Jr	1	1	5			Adams, Joseph	1	2	2			Churchill, Samuel	2	1	4		
Amazeen, William	1	2	4			Hodgdon, Benjamin, Jr	1	3	3			Colcord, Gideon	3		7		
Yeaton, Richard	1	1	7			Nutter, Thomas	1	1	4			Colcord, Jeremy	2	1	1		
Mullen, James	1	3	2			Nutter, Jona Warner	1	1	2			Colcord, Joseph	2	3	4		
Furnald, Archelaus	1	3	4			Nutter, Hatevil, Junr	1	2	6	1		Colcord, David	3	7	3		
Meloon, Abraham	1	1	2			Pickering, Valentine	2	1	3			Colcord, John	1	4	4		
Meloon, Benjamin	1	1	1			Downing, Joshua	1	2	3			Colcord, Edward	1		4		
Tarlton, George	1	2	3			Willey, Zebulon	1	1	2			Coffin, William	1	3	4		
Vennard, William, Junr	1		3			Dame, Benjamin	2	2	1			Carpenter, Anthony W		2	3		
Amazeen, Nathaniel	1	1	2			Dame, Joseph	3		2			Carlo, William	2		2		
Bell, Shadrech	3		3			Hodgdon, Benjamin	1	2	2			Chapman, Levi	1	1	3		
Tarlton, Richard	1	1	1			Fabyan, John	1	2	5			Carlton, Theodore	1	2	4		
Martin, Edward	1	1	2			Huntress, Nathan	2	3	3			Chapman, Solomon	1	1	2		
Yeaton, William	1	2	2			Colebath, Joseph	2	1	2			Doe, Joseph	2	3	6		
Yeaton, Benjamin	1	3	2			Bickford, Ichabod	2	3	4			Doe, Zebulon	3	1	4		
Trefethen, Sampson	1	2	1			Nutter, John	1	1	1			Doe, Zebulon, Junr	1		4		
Amazeen, Joseph, Jr	1	2	1			Downing, Josiah	3	1	2			Doe, Andrew	1	1	1		
Bell, George, Junr	1	2	4			Rawlings, Samuel	2		5			Duda, Zebulon	3		4		
Neal, Richard	1	1	1			Rawlings, Paul	2	1	4			Dow, Simon	1		4		
Batson, Stephen, Junr	1		4			Huntress, Joseph	3		2		1	Durgin, Francis	1	1	2		
Tredick, William, Jr	1	1	3			Brasbridge, Edward	1	1	3			Durgin, Francis, Junr	1	1	2		
Bell, George	1	2	2			Quint, Thomas	1	1	5			Doe, Reuben	3	2	2		
Allen, William	1		4			Furber, Levi	1	3	6			Folsom, William	1	1	6		
Sheafe, Sampson	2	2	3			Pickering, Benjamin	1	1	1			Fowler, Philip	3	1	3		
Rand, Samuel	1	4	2			Walker, Daniel	2		2			Fowler, Philip, Junr	1	1	5		
Bickford, Joshua, Jr	1		2			Nutter, Hatevil	3		3			Fowler, Jacob	1	1	2		
White, William C	1	1	2			Leighton, Joel	2	4	6			French, Benjamin	1	1	2		
Yeaton, Philip	1		1			Hight, William	1		2			French, William	1	3	5		
Jenkins, Benjamin	1	1	3			Bickford, Nathan	1	4	2			Folsom, Jeremiah	1	1	1		
Tredick, Henry, Junr	1		3			Hight, Dennis	3	1	3			Folsom, John	4	2	4		
Card, Edward	1		2			Downing, Samuel	1	1	2			Folsom, Jacob	1	1	2		
Amazeen, Joseph, 3d	1	1	1			Huntress, Noah	2	2	5			Folsom, Ephraim	2		3		
Bell, Jane	1	1	4			Hodgdon, John	2	2	3			Folsom, Mary	2	1	3		
Vincent, Thomas	1	2	3			Nutter, Jethro	1		2			Gilman, Nathaniel	1	1	3		
Pinner, Joseph	2	1	3			Nutter, James	4		8			Goodwin, Robert	3		4		
Odiorne, Lydia		1	3			Quint, Benjamin Roe	2		2			Graves, Joseph	1	2	2		
Wilkinson, Luke	1		1			Nutter, William	1		2			Gilman, Andrew	1	1	4		
White, Nathan, Junr	1		2			Huntress, George	1	1	4			Gilman, Broadstreet	4	3	8		
Jones, Mary			3			Pickering, Nehemiah	1	2	4			Hunniford, Thomas	2		2		
Card, Martha		1	4			Huntress, Seth	1	1	5			Hearsay, Nicholas	2	2	2		
Lawry, Joanna	1		4			Dame, Issachar	1		2			Hearsay, Peter	2		2		
Bell, Matthew	1	1	4			Nutter, Henry	1	1	4			Hilton, Ichabod	2	1	3		
Noble, Oliver	1		5			Hight, Jonathan	3	1	2			Hilton, Daniel	3		2		
Martin, Wilmot	1		2			Downing, Susanna			2			Hilton, Daniel, Junr	1		2		
Oliver, Hannah	1	1	3			Adams, Samuel	1	2	2			Hill, Daniel	1	1	4		
French, ——	1	1	3			Huntress, Susannah		2	2			Hill, James	3	4	11	1	
Yeaton, Martha		1	2			Brasbridge, John	1		4			Hilton, Edward	3		3		
Clark, Mary			1			Huntress, Mark	1	1	2			Hilton, Josiah	3	1	4		
White, William	1	1	3			Colebath, Pitman	1		2			Hodge, John	1	2	1		
Loudon, William	1		3			Brasbridge, William	2		1			Hilton, Winthrop	1	1	2		
Rendall, James	1		3			Nutter, Anna			2			Hall, Elizabeth			4		
Hodgdon, Charles	1		3			Nutter, Mary			3		1	Judkins, Sarah		1	2		
												Kidder, Nathaniel	1	3	4		
NEWINGTON TOWN.						**NEWMARKET TOWN.**						Kenniston, Widow		2	2		
Furber, Mary		1	2			Adams, Josiah	1		6			Kenniston, Jonathan	2	1	3		
Hart, Lois	1	3	3			Ames, Daniel	2	1	1			Kenniston, Aaron	2	1	5		
Downing, Jonathan	1	1	4			Ames, Jacob	1		1			Lyford, Francis	2	2	2		
Shackford, Samuel	3		5			Baker, Samuel	1	1	3			Lyford, Stephen	3		5		
Shackford, John	4	2	5			Badger, William	2	2	3			Lord, Nathaniel	2	3	6		
Thompson, John	1	2	4			Burleigh, Andrew	1	1	2			Mead, Benjamin	1		5		
Walker, Mark	1		2			Bean, Joseph	1	1				Mead, Jeremiah	4		3		
Rawlings, Noah	1		3			Burleigh, Jacob	2	3	5			Mighils, John	1	3	3		
Rawlings, Esther			3			Burleigh, Josiah	2	4	6			Marstes, John	1	3	3		
Nutter, Anthony	1		3			Burleigh, Samuel	3		1			Mighils, Eliphalet	1		3		
Downing, Richard	2		2		2	Burleigh, Moses	4		6			Mitchel, Robert	1		3		
Pickering, William	2	2	2			Burleigh, James	2	1	5			Medar, John	1		7		
Hodgdon, Richard	1		3			Burleigh, William	2	2	4			Mason, Samuel	1		1		
Pickering, Mary		1	3			Bryant, Walter	2		3			Neal, Samuel	2	4	3		
Pickering, James	1	4	7			Bennet, John	2	1	2			Neal, Walter	2	1	3		
Downing, John	2	1	3			Bennet, Cotton	1	1	2			Neal, John	2	1	2		
Adams, Benjamin	1	1	1	1	2	Bennet, Josiah	1	3	3			Neal, Zebulon	1	3	2		
Adams, Nathan Webb	1	4	3									Neal, Hubartus	2		3		

ROCKINGHAM COUNTY—Continued.

NAME OF HEAD OF FAMILY.	Free white males of 16 years and upward, including heads of families.	Free white males under 16 years.	Free white females, including heads of families.	All other free persons.	Slaves.
NEWMARKET TOWN—continued.					
Neal, Hubartus, Junr	1	3	5		
Pike, Robert	1	3	4		
Perkins, John	1	1	2		
Peas, Nathaniel	3		5		
Presson, Richard	1	3	1		
Perkins, John, Junr	2	1	3		
Pickering, Samuel	1	1	1		
Pickering, Winthrop	1	2	2		
Pickering, James	1		3		
Robinson, Jonathan	2	3	4		
Rogers, Nathaniel	2	2	9		
Smith, Daniel	2		3		
Smith, Joseph, Junr	1	1	3		
Stevens, William	1		3		
Smith, Edward	1	1	4		
Savage, Job	2		3		
Smart, Joseph	2	2	7		
Smith, Winthrop	4	1	5		
Smith, Eliphalet	2		2		
Smith, James	1	2	1		1
Smith, Joseph	3		5		
Shute, William	1		1		
Shute, Walter	2	2	2		
Stockman, Benjamin	1	3	2		
Shute, John	1	1	3		
Smith, Joseph, 3d	1	1	2		
Smart, Hilton	1	1	3		
Smart, Charles	2	2	3		
Smart, Samuel	1		3		
Smith, John Moody	4	1	8		
Speed, John	1	4	3		
Smart, David	1		5		
Speed, Ebenezer	1		2		
Sanborn, Jonathan	2		4		
Smart, Josiah	1	3	4		
Sargent, Mary			2		
Smart, Robert	1		1		
Smith, Samuel	1	1	2		
Tilton, Daniel	3	1	3		
Taylor, Benjamin	1		4		
Torr, Vincent	1	2	3		
Tarlton, Stilman	2	1	6		
Tash, John	1	2	6		
Wilson, Ebenezer	1		2		
Watson, Dudley	1	1	4		
Wiggin, Michael	1		1		
Wiggin, Henry	4	2	6		
Wiggin, Chase	2		2		
White, William	1	2	4		
Wedgwood, John	2	2	6		
Wiggin, Jonathan	2	1	5		
Watson, John	1	1	2		
Young, Joseph	2	3	6		
Young, John	1	3	3		
Young, John, Junr	1	1	4		
Young, Jeremiah	1	1	5		
Hart, George	1	2	3		
Ratcliff, Roger	1		1		
Thurston, Widow			3		
Cabot, James	1		2		
Shute, Abigail			2		
Odiorne, Elizabeth			2		
Folsom, Polly		3	2		
Roberts, Reuben			1	1	
Mighels, Samuel	1	1	2		
Folsom, Benjamin	1	1	3		
Perkins, William			2		
Perkins, William, Jr	1	3	1		
Folsom, Jonathan	1		1		
Ayers, Miriam		1	2		
Pinner, Benjamin	1		1		
Parsons, Mary			3		
Hamilton, Phebe		1	2		
Hearsay, James	1	1	2		
Presson, Elizabeth			3		
Solum, Jane				3	
Cheswill, Thomas	1	1	3		
Durgin, Stephen	2		3		
Ham, Thomas	1	2	1		
Bryant, John	1	2	1		
Sanborn, Sarah		2	2		
Weeks, Joseph	2		3		
Skriggens, Widow		1	2		
Crosby, Hannah		2	1		
Urin, Paul	1		2		
Ewers, Nathaniel	2		3		
NEWTOWN TOWN.					
Carter, Benja, jr	1	1	3		
Carter, Benja	1	1	2		
Carter, Abram	1		4		

NAME OF HEAD OF FAMILY.	Free white males of 16 years and upward, including heads of families.	Free white males under 16 years.	Free white females, including heads of families.	All other free persons.	Slaves.
NEWTOWN TOWN—con.					
Carter, Ephm	1	3	2		
Colby, Danl	2		1		
Colby, Nathl	1		1		
Hoit, Benja	1		4		
Hoit, Benja, jr	1		2		
Hoit, Saml	1		3		
Goodwin, Thos	1		4		
Goodwin, Danl	1		1		
Gould, Nathan	2	3	4		
Goodwin, Danl, jr	1	3	5		
Peasley, Wm	2	3	1		
Colby, Jacob	2	4	2		
Colby, John	1		5		
Ames, Revd Jona	1	2	3		
Bartlett, Gideon	1		1		
Bartlet, Gersham	2	1	3		
Sargeant, David	2	2	5		
Sargeant, Jesse	1		3		
Bartlett, Joseph	3	3	4		
Favor, Timothy	1	1	6		
Favor, Micah	1		4		
Morre, Daniel	1	4	3		
Rowell, Hannah	2	2	4		
Brown, Enoch	2	1	1		
Morse, Wm	1	1	1		
Heath, Sargeant	2		5		
Steward, Robert	3	3	3		
Backston, David	1	3	3		
Peasley, Mary	2	1	4		
Peasley, Edmund	2	2	2		
Hogg, Silas	1		1		
Peasley, Stephen	1		2		
Peasley, Micajah	1	2	1		
Chase, Francis	2		1		1
Chase, Francis, jr	1	3	4		
Colby, Barzillai	1	1	3		
Peasley, John	1	1	4		
Hobbs, Jacob	1		3		
Bartlett, Matthias	1	1	3		
Bartlett, Joseph	1		1		
Bartlett, Richd	2		3		
Whittier, Isaac	1	4	2		
Whittier, Mark	2	3	4		
Whittier, Asa	1	2	3		
Carlton, Wm	1	1	3		
Carlton, Moses	1		2		
Peasley, Paul	2	4	2		
Whittier, Timoty	1	2	5		
Whittier, Andw, jr	1	2	2		
Whittier, Sarah	1		4		
Whittier, Andw	2		2		
Bagley, David	1		1		
Bagley, Elijah	1	3	3		
Bagley, Joshua	1		8		
Currier, Thos	1		1		
Bartlett, Elipt	3	3	2		
Eliott, Thos	1	3	2		
Sanborn, Worster	1	2	4		
Hoit, Reuben	1	4	5		
Hoit, Jedidiah	1	2	3		
Gould, Thos	3		3		
Fowler, Margt			1		
Currier, John	1		3		
Rowell, Jacob	2		4		
Eliott, Edmund	1	2	1		
Gould, Wm	1	1	3		
Gould, Mary			4		
Hoit, Moses	3	2	3		
Carter, John	1		2		
Carter, Nathl	1	2	2		
Carter, Sarah		2	2		
Currier, Richd	1	2	5		
Currier, Aaron	1		3		
Currier, Aaron, jr	2		3		
Collins, Charles	1	2	4		
Kimbal, Abraham	1		2		
Palmer, Benja	1		2		
Kimbal, Lidia			1		
Eastman, Roger	1		1		
Eastman, Isaac	1	6	2		
Currier, Phillip	1	3	2		
Currier, Jona	1	3	4		
Kimbal, Hanh	1		2		
Kimbal, Jona	1	1	1		
Eliott, Timothy	2	3	2		
Currier, James	1	3	3		
Ferrin, Aquilla	1	4	3		
Colby, Thos	3	4	2		
Chellis, Ann			2		
Tewkesbury, Jacob	1	1	2		
Goodwin, David	1		1		
Hoit, Micah	2		4		
Goodwin, Timoty	2	2	5		

NAME OF HEAD OF FAMILY.	Free white males of 16 years and upward, including heads of families.	Free white males under 16 years.	Free white females, including heads of families.	All other free persons.	Slaves.
NEWTOWN TOWN—con.					
Beatte, Sarah			1		
Goodwin, Sarah			1		
Norris, Benja	1	2	3		
NORTHAMPTON TOWN.					
Haines, Abner	2	3	2		
Davis, Samuel	1		2		
Loverin, Ebenezer	4		8		
Loverin, John	1	3	3		
Marston, Benjamin	3		4		
Marston, Thomas	2		7		
Dearborn, Reuben Gove	2	3	4		
Rundlett, Noah	2	1	4		
Nudd, James	3	2	2		
Brown, Joseph	1	2	3		
Lamprey, Simon	2	1	6		
Jenness, Isaac	1	2	3		
Drake, Jonathan	1	1	4		
Leavitt, Moses	2	1	6		
Brown, Benjamin	4	3	4		
Wingate, John	3	2	3	2	
Swett, Benjamin	1	3	3		
Dearborn, Levi	2		2		
Mason, Benjamin	2	2	2		
Dow, Simon	2		3		
Knowles, David	3		3		
Marston, Mary			3		
Johnson, John	2		3		
Chapman, Samuel	1		3		
Ayers, John	1	1	3		
Brown, Joshua	1		1		
Leavitt, Thomas	5	2	5		
Brown, Simon	2	1	2		
Leavitt, Benja	3	1	2		
Thurston, Benja	3	5	7		
Hobbs, Benjamin	2		2		
Bachellor, Henry	3	2	3		
Dearborn, Reuben	1	4	5		
Dearborn, John	1	2	5		
Dearborn, Samuel	1	5	2		
Dalton, Josiah	2				
Dalton, Michael	1	2	1		
Godfrey, William	3	1	3		
Garland, Joseph	3		5		
Jenness, Samuel	1	2	4		
Marston, Isaac	5	1	6		
Marston, Simon	1	4	8		
Nudd, John	1		5		
Page, Jonathan	2		2		
Page, Simon	1		2		
Page, Stephen	4		4		
Page, Christopher	1		3		
Robie, John	2	1	9		
Fogg, Dearborn	3		5		
Smith, Samuel	3		4		
Towle, Zachariah	3	1	4		
Marston, Levi	1	1	2		
Page, Dudley	1		2		
Page, Benjamin	1		4		
Dearborn, Joseph	2	3	3		
Leavitt, Simon	1	2	3		
Sanborn, William	2	3	4		
Sanborn, Thomas	4		3		
Shaw, John	1	3	3		
Kimball, Abraham	1	1	4		
Smith, Deacon	2	1	3		
Smith, Rachel			2		
Taylor, John	2		4		
Hobbs, Morris	2	2	3		
Fogg, Jeremiah	1	1			
Moulton, Joseph	2	2	4		
Marston, John	2	3	4		
Page, Francis	2		3		
Page, Coffin	1	2	2		
Page, John	1	1	2		
Redman, Tristram	1		2		
Drake, Abraham	1	2	5		
Bachellor, James	3		7		
Bachellor, Josiah	2	3	6		
Brown, Jacob	2	1	4		
Brown, John	1	5	2		
Cotton, Thomas	1	3	2		
Dearborn, Reuben, Jr	4		4		
Fogg, Abner	4	1	2		
Fogg, John	1		2		
Fogg, Samuel Robie	1	1	3		
Hobbs, Joseph	1	1	2		
Hobbs, Benjamin	3		3		
Hobbs, Thomas	2	2	4		
Philbrick, Benjamin	2	1	3		
Philbrick, Page	1	3	3		
Jenness, Isaac, Junr	2	1	4		

ROCKINGHAM COUNTY—Continued.

NAME OF HEAD OF FAMILY.	Free white males of 16 years and upward, including heads of families.	Free white males under 16 years.	Free white females, including heads of families.	All other free persons.	Slaves.	NAME OF HEAD OF FAMILY.	Free white males of 16 years and upward, including heads of families.	Free white males under 16 years.	Free white females, including heads of families.	All other free persons.	Slaves.	NAME OF HEAD OF FAMILY.	Free white males of 16 years and upward, including heads of families.	Free white males under 16 years.	Free white females, including heads of families.	All other free persons.	Slaves.
NORTHAMPTON TOWN— continued.						**NORTHFIELD TOWN— continued.**						**NORTHWOOD TOWN— continued.**					
Knowles, Jonathan	2		1			Purkins, Robert	1	2	3			Jonson, Benjn., Junr	2	1	4		
Lamprey, John	2	2	4			Rowen, John	1	2	2			Dudy, Epha	2	4	3		
Wedgwood, Jonathan	1		3			Robbinson, Simeon	2	4	2			Nealey, John	2	3	5		
Wedgwood, James	2	1	3			Sandborn, Wm	2	2	2			Bacheldor, David	1	1	2		
Bachellor, Samuel	2	2	4			Sandborn, Mathew	1	1	2			Bachelder, John	2	3	6		
Dearborn, Simon	2	1	2			Sandborn, Jonathan	1	1	3			Bachelder, Simon	1	2	5		
Drake, Nathaniel	1	1	3			Smith, Richard	1	2	2			Jonson, Simon	1	1	1		
Ques, William	1	5	2			Shepard, Phillip	1	1	1			Pilsbury, Enoch	3		2		
Palmer, William	1	4	4			Sargent, Zebedah	1		4			Durgin, Jona	1				
Taylor, Joseph	1	5	3			Simonds, John	2	1	3			Carr, Archelous	1		2		
Lamprey, Morris	1	1	1			Stephens, Aron	2	2	2			Clough, Wm	2	1	5		
Bachellor, Zachariah	1					Smith, William	3	2	3			Benick, Arter	1	1	1		
						Sherburne, Thomas	1		1			Hoit, Benjn	1	1	1		
NORTHFIELD TOWN.						Sherburne, James	1	3	4			Wiggin, Paul	1	1	3		
Arlen, Samuel	2	1	3			Sawyer, Jotham	1	4	2			Hill, Jona	1	2	2		
Ash, Joseph	1		2			Sawyer, Gideon	1	2	6			Hill, Nicholas D	1	3	3		
Bartlett, Samuel	1		2			Smith, Edward	1	3	2			Sherburne, Saml	3	3	4		
Blanchard, Edward	5	5	3			Turrill, William	2	1	1			Sherburne, John	1		4		
Blanchard, Richard	3	3	5			Whitcher, Nathl	1	2	6			Hoit, Moses	2		4		
Colby, Nathan	1	3	1			Whitcher, Ruben	2		2			Bennick, Thomas	1	2	3		
Cross, John	1	2	3			Whitcher, Jona	1	3	5			Pipper, Thomas, junr	1	1	2		
Cross, James	2	2	3			Whitcher, William	1	3	1			Knowles, David	2	3	4		
Cross, Thomas	3	1	3			Wadliegh, Jonathan	2	3	4			Knowles, Simeon	1		4		
Cross, Jesse	2	6	4			Welch, Benjn	1	3	4			Duddy, Nicholas	1	1	3		
Cochran, John	2	4	4			Welch, Jona	2		2			Benick, Ebenezer	2	1	6		
Currey, Robert	1					Wille, Ezikle	2		2			Hill, Benjn	1		1		
Clough, Lewi	1					Clough, Gilman	2		2			Blasdell, Peter	1	2	1		
Clough, Thos	1	1	2			Wille, Isaiah	1	1	3			Sandborn, Jona	1	1	3		
Clough, Thos., junr	1		1			Williams, William	1	2	4			Mead, Levi	2		3		
Collins, Benjamin	2	5	4			Rines, William	1				2	Clark, Jona., Esqr	2	2	5		
Cilley, John	1	1	2			French, Elisha	1	1	1			Wille, John	1	2	2		
Dolaff, David	1		2			Dearborn, Shubal	1	2	1			Crokes, John	3	1	3		
Danforth, Henery	1		3			Purkins, Wd Anna		2	2			Watson, Eleazer	2	2	2		
Davis, Hezekiah	1	2	1			Bowles, Wm H	1	1	2			Wiggin, John	1	1	2		
Dearborn, Shubal	1		3			Davis, Samuel	1	2	5			Pipper, Tho'	2	2	4		
Dearborn, Nathl	1	3	6			Foss, Isaac	1		3			Pipper, Nathl	1	2	2		
Dearborn, Abraham	1		3			Cross, Wd Hannah			1			Kelley, Benjamin	1	2	4		
Dearborn, John	1	3	3			Gessions, Lydia			4			Kenistone, Volintine	2	2	4		
Dearborn, Jona	1	1	1									Edgerly, Samuel	1		3		
Dyer, Edwd. St	1					**NORTHWOOD TOWN.**						Crokes, John, Junr	1	2	2		
Melloony, Hannah	1		3			Demeritt, Joseph, Esqr	4	1	3			Harvey, John	3	1	3		
Ellison, Richard	1	2	4			Chelsle, John	2		3			York, Joseph	1	1	1		
Forrist, William	2	3	5			Hull, Richard	3	1	3			Blake, Sherburne	2	1	3		
Forrist, John	1	2	2			Stokes, Benjn	1	2	1			Shute, Jos	1	3	2		
Forrist, James	1	1	1			Knight, John	1	1	5			Norris, Moses	1	1	5		
Fiffield, Jona	2		3			Bachelder, Saml	2	1	5			Foss, Jona	1	2	2		
French, Sollomon	2					Knowlton, Tho	1	4	6			Blake, Jona	1	2	2		
Foss, Robert	1		4			Knowlton, Jona	2	1	4			Swaine, Jacob	1	1	2		
Foss, Thos	3		4			Shaw, Jos	1	2	2			Rawlings, David	2	1	5		
Gilman, Thos	1		5			Randall, Job	2		4			Mathews, Volintine	1	1	1		
Glines, John	1					Durgin, Joseph	1	1	4			Swaine, Phineas	1	2	3		
Gilman, Saml. T	1		5			Durgin, John	2		3			Jonson, Saml	2		3		
Gilman, Jona	1		1			Durgin, Ebenezer	1		3			Jonson, Moses	3	2	3		
Glines, Benjn	1	1	2			Knowlton, Ebenezer	1	1	3			Bickford, John	1	2	2		
Gile, Jona	1	4	3			Knowlton, Wm	1	1	2			Bickford, Sollomon	3	2	4		
Glidden, Charles	5	2	6			Gile, John	1	1	2			Bickford, Soloman, Jur	1		3		
Glines, William	1		6			Mathews, Gideon	1	2	1			Bickford, John	2	5	3		
Glines, William, junr	1	4	2			Giles, Charles	1					Bartlett, Saml	1	4	4		
Gibson, James	1		3			Morrison, Robert	1	3	2			James, James	2	1	4		
Glines, Job	1					Watson, James	2	1	6			Hoit, Joshua	1	3	2		
Heath, Jacob	2	5	2			Smith, Wm	1					Hoit, Stephen	1	3	6		
Heath, Ezikle	1	3	3			Clough, Caleb	2	1	5			Woodman, Archbd	2		2		
Hancok, George	1	3	6			Morill, Nathl	2		2			Calley, Jona	1	1	2		
Hancock, Joseph	1	2	2			Griffin, Theophilus	2	3	4			Brown, Saml	1	2	5		
Hancock, William	1	2	3			Bartlett, Nathan	1	1	5			Brown, Ruben	1		1		
Hains, Stephen	1		3			Wille, Wm	1	2	1			Buzzel, Wm	1	2	2		
Hodgsdon, Edmund	2		2			Brown, Joseph	1	3	2			Morrill, Hibbard	1	2	3		
Hills, David	1		1			Brown, Benjn	1	2	5			Griffin, Jno	1	4	3		
Hills, Daniel	2		2			Emerson, Samuel	1		4			Chesle, Sawyer	2	1	4		
Hills, Timothy	1					Rawlings, Thomas	1	2	4			Cram, David	1		4		
Jonson, Dole	1	1	4			Furbur, Joshua	4	5	2			Gough, James	1	1	3		
Jon's, George	1	1	3			Garland, Nathl	2		4			Knoles, Joseph	1		1		
Kenistone, Jonathan	1	1	1			Jenness, Jona	1	1	4			Wille, John	2	1	2		
Kenistone, William	2		3			Jonson, Jno	2	1	7			Watson, Wm	1		2		
Kezer, Edmund	1	4	2			Shaw, Benjn	2	1	4								
Kinistone, William, Jr	1		2			Bachelder, Henery	2	1	6			**NOTTINGHAM TOWN.**					
Kenistone, David	1	1	3			Bachelder, Abraham	1	5	5			Arnold, Robert	2		4		
Leavitt, Joseph, Jr	2	1	2			Cate, Joseph	1	1	1			Butler, Benjamin	1				1
Leavitt, Jonathan	1	1	3			Caswell, Richard	2	1	1			Butler, Henery	1	4	4		
Leavitt, Jonathan, jr	1		3			Caswell, Elijah	1	4	3			Brown, John	3	2	4		
Leavitt, Gideon	1	3	6			Caswell, Thomas	1	1	2			Bean, James	3	2	4		
Leavitt, Wadliegh	1					Buzreal, Sollomon	1		4		1	Bartlett, Thomas	3	6	3		
Lyford, John	2		3			Marsh, Saml	1	1				Banfild, John	2	2	1		
Mason, David	2		4			Bachelder, Increas	3	2	5			Brown, Nichl	1	2	2		
Mills, Archelus	2	2	7			Godfree, Moses	3	1	5			Burnam, Saml	2	1	4		
Mills, Ruben	1	1	1			Wallis, Wm	3	2	3			Butler, Zephaniah	4	1	3		1
Mann, Joseph	1	1	1			Taylor, Elipt	2	1	4			Burnam, Jacob	1	3	3		
Morgin, David	1					Morrill, Green	1	4	4			Bartlett, Nehemiah	2	3	3	1	
Purkins, James	2	3	4			Morrill, Benjn	1	4	4			Bartlett, Love			2		
Pike, Perkins	1					Hoit, Daniel	3	3	5			Burnam, Silas	1	1	3		

ROCKINGHAM COUNTY—Continued.

NAME OF HEAD OF FAMILY.	Free white males of 16 years and upward, including heads of families.	Free white males under 16 years.	Free white females, including heads of families.	All other free persons.	Slaves.
NOTTINGHAM TOWN— continued.					
Barker, Philbrick	3	2	6		
Bachelder, Josiah	1	3	2		
Bartlett, Jonn	1	1	2		
Burnam, Ebenezer	2	3	4		
Bickford, John	2	3	3		
Burnam, Joseph	1		1		
Brasy, Saml	2		3		
Beverly, Margret			4		
Chaney, Moses	2	1	5		
Cilley, Else			1		2
Cilley, Brady	1				1
Colcord, Saml	1	4	4		
Cilley, Joseph	3	1	4		4
Cilley, Cutting	3	4	2		
Carter, Sollomon	1	3	4		
Chelse, Andrew	2	2	4		
Cilley, Jonathan	2	3	3		
Cilley, Greenleaf	1		2		
Cram, Theophilus	1	4	5		
Cate, William	1		1		
Cate, Daniel	1		1		
McCoy, Charles	2	3	6		
Dearborn, Samuel	1		3		
Dame, Moses	1	1	2		
Davis, Moses, Junr	2	3	5		
Davis, Moses	3	1	4		
Davis, Jonathan, Jr	1	3	2		
Drew, Joshua	1	2	6		
Davis, Abner	3	2	3		
Dame, Samuel	2	1	5		
Davis, Jona	2	1	4		
Davis, Jacob	1	1	5		
Davis, John, Jr	1		2		
Dalton, Moses	1		3		
Davis, Sollomon	1	1	2		
Elliot, John	1	1	2		
Emerson, Mark	2	1	5		
Fox, Andrew	2	1	4		
Furnald, Thomas	1	4	3		
Furnald, Charles	1	3	2		
Furnald, Mary	1		2		
Ford, John	3	3	6		
Follet, John	1	1	1		
Follet, Caleb	1	3	3		
Fox, John	1	1	1		
Gove, Jona	3	3	8		
Gove, Saml	1	3	6		
Gile, Asa	1		1		
Garrish, Paul	1	3	5		
Gile, John	2	2	6		
Glass, James	3		3		
Goodhue, Nathl	2	3	6		
Garland, Simon	1	1	1		
Gile, Saml	1	1	2		
George, Joseph	1	1	3		
Glass, Thos	2		2		
George, Thos	1		2		
Harvey, Jona	1	5	5		
Harvey, Frances	2		2		
Hill, Robert	1	3	3		
Harvey, James	1	2	2		
Goodride, Barnard	1				
Harvey, Thos	1		2		
Harvey, James, Jr	1	2	2		
Harvey, Joseph	1				
Harvey, Frances, Jr	1	1	2		
Harvey, John	2	3	5		
Hines, Thomas	2		1		
Hayes, Aron	2	1	4		
Hayes, Aron, Jr	1		1		
Huntoon, Saml	1		3		
Harvey, Saml	1				
Hall, Joseph	1				
Hill, Jno	1				
Hayes, Solloman	1	2	1		
Harvey, Anny			3		
Jones, Saml	1				
Jones, Robbert	1		1		
Kelse, James	4	1	2		
Knight, Wm	1	1			
Knight, Wd. Hannah			4		
Kenistone, John	3		2		
Lawrey, William	1	3	2		
Langley, Eldad	1		3		
Langley, Jonathan	1	3	5		
Leathers, Abendigo	2	2	6		
Lucy, Allexander	2	1	5		
Leathers, Nowel	2	2	3		1
Libbey, Ham	1	1	3		
Ladd, Semion	1	2	6		
Lucy, Benjn	1	1	1		
NOTTINGHAM TOWN— continued.					
Leathers, Abel	1	4	3		
Leathers, Nicholas	1		4		
Langley, Winthrop	1	2	2		
Langley, Job	1	1	3		
Libbey, James	1	1	1		
Leathers, Joseph	2	2	3		
Langley, Benjn	1	1	5		
McCrillis, John	2	1	5		
Magner, Jno	2	2	3		
Marston, John	2	2	4		
McDaniel, Danl	1	1	3		
McCoy, Charles	2	3	6		
Norris, Benjn	3		3		
Nealey, John	3		4		
Nealey, Joseph	1	5	2		
Norris, Wm	1	2	2		
Odle, Thomas	2	3	6		
Priest, Joseph	1	2	3		
Priest, Quick	1	1	2		
Pribble, Joseph	1		1		
Pickering, Anthony	1	1	2		
Page, David	1	2	4		
Palmer, Groth	1	1	2		
Randall, Shadrick	1	1	1		
Rawlings, Jona	2	1	2		
Randall, Jona	1	1	1		
Rowel, Rice	2	1	9		
Rowell, Abraham	1	1	1		
Rowe, Ichobad	4	3	6		
Randall, Nathl	2	2	3		
Randall, Joseph	1	1	2		
Rogers, Thos	1		1		
Row, Elijah	1		2		
Robbinson, Jno K	1		3		
Simpson, Andw	4	1	3		1
Stevens, Joshua	4		3		
Scales, Abraham	1	1	2		
Stokes, Benjn	2	2	3		
Simpson, William	2	2	6		
Spencer, Ebenezer	1	2	3		
Shaw, Benjn	1	1	1		
Stringer, Wm	1				
Stevens, John	1	1	2		
Scales, Ebenezer	1		2		
Snell, George					3
Spencer, Isaac	1		4		
Tuffts, Thos	1	4	4		
Tuttle, Stoten	2	4	3		
Tuttle, Benjn	2		5		
Tuttle, Joseph	1	1	2		
Trickey, Saml	1	2	3		
Thurstin, James	4	2	5		
Tukesbury, Thos	1	3	3		
Trickey, Joshua	1	1	2		
Winslow, Elisha	3		3		
Williams, John P	3	4	3		
Watson, Benjn	3	2	5		
Winslow, Benjn	2	1	5		
Watson, John	1		1		
Watson, James	4	3	3		
Whitcher, Benjn	2	1	2		
Whitcher, Joseph	2	1	3		
Wille, Jona	4	1	4		
Welch, William	4		4		
Witham, Peltiah	1	1	2		
Whidden, Mark	1	1	3		
Welch, John	1	1	5		
Wille, Charles	1	3	5		
Welch, Thos	1	1	3		
Wiggin, David	1	3	4		
Whitehorn, Saml			4		
Whitehorn, John	2		4		
Young, Elizabeth			2		
PELHAM TOWN.					
Smith, Jese	1	2	6		
Tallant, Hugh	5	2	2		
Wyman, Josiah	1		3		
Hutchinson, Saml	4	1	6		
Hebbes, James	1	2	4		
Richardson, Philip	1	1			
Gorrel, Hannah			1		
Campbell, Saml	1		1		
Hardey, Thos	1	1	1		
Wyman, Abijah	1	1	1		
Richardson, Philip	3		4		
Atwood, Joshua	1		3		
Atwood, Paul	1	1	2		
Quantars, Robt	1	1	2		
Gage, James	2	1	1		
PELHAM TOWN—con.					
Gage, Isac	1	1	5		
Wyman, Danl	1		2		
Little, John	3		2		
Farguson, John	6	2	4		
Mudy, Amos	2		3		
Handy, Asa	1	1	6		
Wyman, John	1	1	3		
Kemp, Jacob	1	1	2		
Handy, Wm	1	2	2		
Kemp, Jessa	1	2	2		
Kemp, Jessa, Jr	1	1	1		
Wyman, Wm	1	1	3		
Wyman, Joshua	1	2	1		
Stickney, Asa	2	1	5		
Wyman, John, Jr	1	1	2		
Buttler, John, Jr	2	3	2		
Fargurson, James	3	1	2		
Hamblett, Benjn	1		1		
Buttler, Jacob	2	3	2		
Handey, Edward	1	1	3		
Buttler, Danl	2	3	5		
Buttler, Jacob, Jr	1	4	5		
Sparford, Thomas	2	5	3		
Cutter, Seath	1	4	2		
Richardson, Joseph	2	3	4		
Tenney, Danl	1	2	3		
Barker, Danl	2	2	4		
Marchel, Isac	1	1	3		
Buttler, Josiah	1	2	4		
Buttler, Marcy	2	1	3		
Wyman, Ester	2	2	3		
Johnson, Davd	2	4	3		
Baldon, Joseph	1	1	2		
Hall, Rapha	1	4	2		
Gibbins, James	2	5	4		
Gibbins, John	3	4	4		
Gibbins, Barnabus	3	1	4		
Barker, Ebenzr	3	1	4		
Norris, Robt	3	2	3		
Handey, Elipt	2	2	5		
Mussey, John	1	2	5		
Peabody, Abram	1	1	1		
Buttler, Caleb	3	3	5		
Buttler, Davd	1	5	4		
Nevens, John	1	2	3		
Buttler, John	1		1		
Davis, Saml	1	2	6		
Tarbox, John	1	1	3		
Wells, John	1		2		
Handey, Joseph	2	2	3		
Buttler, Jonathan	1	3	2		
Griffen, Saml	1	1	3		
Griffen, Jonathan, Jr	2	4	3		
Spaldan, Lot	2		6		
Gauld, Mark	2		3		
Sherborn, Benjn	2		4		
Hamblet, Jonathan, Jr	3		3		
Richardson, Asa	1	1	1		
Hamblett, Jonathan	1	1	1		
Richardson, Danl	2	2	2		
Palmer, Ebenr	2		1		
Palmer, Ebenr, Jr	1	2	4		
Cross, Abel	1	3	4		
Parsons, Stepn	1	2	3		
Merrell, Nathl	2	4	3		
Coborn, Marcy	1	1	4		
Gage, Jonathan	1	2	5		
Bradford, Josiah	1	2	3		
Gage, Amos	1		4		
Gage, Nathl	3		7		
Gage, Benjn		1	2		
Garden, Marcy		1	2		
Gage, Josiah	2	1	2		
Petingill, Asa	1	1	2		
Hall, Richard	3		6		
Willson, James	2	2	4		
Clark, Timothy	2	1	4		
Titcomb, Moses	2	2	6		
Gage, Davd	1	4	4		
Patterson, Joseph	2		3		
Webester, Ebenr	2	3	4		
Webester, Jonathan	1	2	3		
Burk, Isac	1	1	4		
Grimes, Alexander	1	1	2		
Gage, Asa	1	2	5		
Atwood, John	1		2		
Noys, Moses	1				
May, Ezekl	2	1	3		
Foster, James	3	2	4		
Clark, Timothy	1	1	4		
Atwood, Jonathan	4		4		
Griffin, Jonathan	1	1			

ROCKINGHAM COUNTY—Continued.

PELHAM TOWN—con. / PEMBROOK TOWN

NAME OF HEAD OF FAMILY.	Free white males of 16 years and upward, including heads of families.	Free white males under 16 years.	Free white females, including heads of families.	All other free persons.	Slaves.
PELHAM TOWN—con.					
Willson, Danl	2	2	4		
Davies, Timothy	1	2	6		
Willson, Isac	4	1	6		
Pedengill, Jonathan	2	1	3		
Webber, Wm	2	1	4		
Johnson, Thomas	1	1	1		
Hardey, Philip	2		1		
March, Jacob	1				
Marsh, Ralf	2		3		
Webber, Abbet	1	2	2		
Hardy, Job	1	4	1		
Richardson, James	3	3	2		
Coburn, Benja	1	5	3		
Write, Sarah		2	2		
Ried, Henney	1	1	1		
Richardson, Abel	1	1	2		
Carlton, Asa	2		3		
Barker, Abel	3		2		
Hayward, Edward	1		2		
Abbet, Uriah	1				
Curren, Nathl	3	2	4		
Corborn, Edward	2		2		
Bowls, Amos	1	2	4		
Atwood, Danl	1	2	5		
PEMBROOK TOWN.					
Gaut, Andrew	1		2		1
Gaut, William	1	2	1		
Whittmore, Aron	2	2	5		
Drown, Thomas	1	3	1		
Robie, Ichobad	1				
Head, James	1	5	2		
Frye, Ebenezer	3	3	4		
Bartlet, Richard, Esqr.	3		3		
Kimball, Michael	2	1	5		
Farnham, David	2	2	2		
Knox, John	1	2	5		
Elliot, Jona	2	3	3		
Hutchinson, Jona	3	3	2		
Dayon, Jacob	2		5		
Dayon, Frances	1	2	3		
Brickkett, Thomas	2	1	5		
Head, Wm	1	1	3		
Moor, Robert	1	4	4		
Martin, William, junr	1	4	3		
Chickering, John	1	3	3		
Moor, John	4	1	3		
Foster, Asa	1		4		
Parker, Samuel	2	1	3		
Hamphell, Sarah	2		3		
Bickford, Daniel	1				
Harris, Samuel	3	3	6		
Mann, Daniel	1		2		
Foster, Fredrick	1	2	2		
Gautt, Samuel	1				
De Gon, Nathl	1				
Clemment, Joshua	2		3		
Jenness, John	1	2	3		
Jenness, Benjn	1				
Cochran, Margret			2		
Cochran, James	1	2	6		
Daniels, Samuel	1	4	4		
Kitterige, Ebenezer	1	1	2		
Margin, Jeremiah	2	2	4		
Cullinmore, John	1		1		
Kimball, David	2	3	8		
Foster, Caleb	1	1	2		
Foster, Moses	1	1	1		
Gile, Amos	1	2	3		
Addams, Dr. Thomas	1	3	3		
Swett, Lt. Joseph	2	2	5		
Barker, Asa	1	1	2		
Carlton, John	1	1	3		
Robbinson, Asa	2	1	3		
Carlton, Wm	3	3	3		
Greege, David	2		2		
Bartlett, Caleb	1		3		
Noyes, Lt. Samuel	1	3	4		
Noyes, Daniel	1	4	6		
Flagg, Dr. Samuel	1	2	3		
Roberson, Andrew	2	2	5		
Dow, Lucy			1		
Stickney, Antone	2		4		
McDaniel, John	2	1	6		
Connor, John	2	4	6		
McCuchin, Fredrick	1	2	4		
Bunker, Benjn	1	1	3		
Mow, Robert	1	5	1		
Kimball, Aron	1	1	1		
Robbison, Thomas	2	3	5		

PEMBROOK TOWN—con.

NAME OF HEAD OF FAMILY.	Free white males of 16 years and upward, including heads of families.	Free white males under 16 years.	Free white females, including heads of families.	All other free persons.	Slaves.
Lucas, Danl	1		2		
Ayers, John	2	2	7		
Norris, Benja	4	1	4		
Emery, Capt. Joseph	2	1	3		
Emery, Joseph, junr	1	1	3		
Pipper, Wd	2	2	3		
Holt, Wm	1	3	4		
Kimball, Wd			3		1
Cochran, William	1	4	4		
Cochran, James	3	2	6		
Cochran, James, 4th	1	1	2		
Martten, Saml	2		1		
Martten, wd., Elizabeth	1	1	3		
McDaniel, wd., Lydia		2	3		
McDaniel, Nehemiah	1		2		
Moses, Ebenezer	1	1	2		
Cochran, John	1	1	3		
Whitehouse, Sollomon	3	2	5		
Morse, Ephriam	1	3	4		
Emery, N.	2		3		
Robertson, Zeblon	1	1	2		
Lovejoy, Caleb	2	3	4		
Holt, Daniel	2	4	3		
Knox, William, junr	2	2	5		
Wate, Nathan	1	1			
Knox, William	1	1	2		
Knox, Daniel	1	2			
Knox, James	2		1		
Dudley, Trutworthy	1		3		
Knox, John, Junr	1	1	4		
Mann, James	2	2	4		
Backer, Thomas	2		1		
Kelley, Samuel	2	1	6		
Kelley, John	1		4		
Pipper, Nathan	1	3	7		
Hardy, Thomas	2	2	3		
Jones, John	1	4	6		
Holt, Fry	1	3	4		
Chandler, Timothy	2	3	3		
Marten, Robert	1	3	2		
Lovejoy, David	3		2		
Ambros, Nathl	2	2	4		
Cunningham, James	1		3		
Holt, Benjn	2		5		
Bartlett, Stephen	1	4	4		
Baker, Lovewell	4	3	4		
Calf, John	1		1		
McConnel, Saml	2	3	5		
Mann, John	1	3	1		
Simpson, Joseph	5	3	7		
Simpson, John	1		1		
Simpson, David	1				
Simpson, William	1				
Haynes, Simon	1	2	2		
Knowles, Simeon	1	3	3		
Simpson, David, jr	1		2		
French, Andrew	1	2	4		
Fife, James	1	2	4		
Head, Nath	3	2	2		
Head, John	1	1	5		
White, John	2		3		
Connor, Joseph	1	1	5		
Kimball, Samuel	4	1	4		
Lackeman, Samuel	2		4		
Kimball, Thomas	1	1	4		
Mann, Samuel	1	4	2		
Lackeman, Nathl	2	2	4		
Whittmore, Benjn	1	4	3		
Hagget, Josiah	3		4		
Wordwell, Jeremiah	2	5	4		
Connor, Elipht	2		1		
Holt, Nathan	2	1	6		
Holt, Nathan, jr	1	1	3		
Abbott, Samuel, jr	1	4	2		
Abbott, Samuel	3		3		
Ladd, John	1	2	1		
Parker, John	1	3	2		
Kenney, Thomas	1	2	2		
Barker, Elijah	2	1	2		
Farmer, Andrew	1	2	2		
Parker, Joseph	1		1		
Parker, John, junr	1	2	2		
Felps, Joshua	1	2	2		
Felps, Samuel	2		3		
Fife, William	1	2	3		
True, John	1		2		
Richardson, David	2	4	3		
Lull, Simon	1	3	3		
Calf, John	1		1		
Colby, John	2	2	3		
Cochran, Joseph	2	1	6		

PITTSFIELD TOWN.

NAME OF HEAD OF FAMILY.	Free white males of 16 years and upward, including heads of families.	Free white males under 16 years.	Free white females, including heads of families.	All other free persons.	Slaves.
Hoag, Isaac	1	2	1		
Garland, Jeremiah	1	1	5		
Garland, Jona	1	2	3		
Hanson, Sollomon	1	1	4		
Marten, Dan				4	
Dow, Jesse	2	1	3		
Dow, Phineas	1	3	2		
Sterns, John	2	2	3		
Durgin, Eliphalet	1				
Clifford, Ithiel	1		6		
Phillbrick, Saml	1		1		
Pickering, James	1	2	1		
Blazo, John	1		1		
Greenleaf, Saml	1	3	1		
Berry, Thos	1		1		
Jones, John	1		3		
Dow, Jona	1	3	2		
Jones, Jacob	2	6	5		
Yeaton, Joseph	1	2	6		
Jones, Jno., Junr	1	1	5		
Barton, Josiah	2	1	5		
Marstin, Joseph	1	2	1		
Garland, James	1	3	3		
Fogg, Saml	1	3	5		
Brown, Jonathan	1	2	5		
Brown, John	2	1	4		
Brown, John, Junr	1		1		
Brown, Moses	1	1	2		
Marston, Elipt	1	1	7		
Green, Nathan	2	3	5		
Knowlton, David	3	2	5		
Dow, John	1	4	6		
Green, Abraham	1	4	5		
Drake, James	2	1	5		
Drake, Wd	1		2		
Drake, Simeon	1				
Blake, Thos	2	1	4		
Bachelder, Eliph	1				
Yeaton, Elipht	1	2	4		
Tucker, Wd	2		2		
Fogg, Chase	1	1	1		
Watson, Wm	1	4	3		
Fogg, Jona, Junr	1	4	4		
Paige, Nathl	1	2	3		
Tucker, Jabez	1				
Lamprey, Benjn	2	4	4		
Chase, Nathl	1	4	5		
Berry, Joshua	1	4	3		
Dow, Jeremiah	2	2	5		
Berry, Wm., Junr	1	4	2		
Seavey, Isaac	1	1	2		
Yeaton, John	2	3	8		
Peasley, Elijah	2	3	6		
Towle, Jona	1	4	4		
Morill, Abither	2	2	2		
Huckings, Isaac	1	4	3		
Chase, Wm	3		4		
True, John	1	2	2		
Kerby, Charles	1		1		
Tilton, John	1	3	2		
Chase, Sollomon	1	1	1		
Durgin, Wm	2	1	5		
Norris, Joseph	1	1	1		
Green, Brady	1		1		
Chase, Jno	1	1	3		
Goss, Joseph	1	3	2		
Cram, Smith	1	3	1		
Bean, Ebenezer	1		1		
Fogg, Joseph	1		1		
Fogg, Josiah	1	3	4		
Dier, Saml	1		1		
Bickford, Thos	1		2		
Hearn, James	2	2	5		
Wells, Nathl	1	1	4		
Norris, Moses	2	2	8		
Yeaton, Danl	2	2	8		
Blake, John	2	3	4		
Elkins, Richard	1	1	5		
Potter, Saml	2	3	5		
Libbe, Isaac	2	3	5		
Green, Asael	1	1	1		
Sandborn, Edmund	3		3		
Jonson, Thos	2		3		
Bunker, Frances	2	4	3		
Tibbits, Robert	2	2	2		
Blake, Enoch	1	2	3		
Muncy, Wm	1	4	2		
Tilton, Benjn	1	2	2		
Sias, Benjn	3	4	5		
Brown, Saml	1		3		
Brown, James	1		2		

ROCKINGHAM COUNTY—Continued.

NAME OF HEAD OF FAMILY.	Free white males of 16 years and upward, including heads of families.	Free white males under 16 years.	Free white females, including heads of families.	All other free persons.	Slaves.
PITTSFIELD TOWN—con.					
Cram, Wadliegh	1	1	5		
Sias, Benjn, Junr	1				
White, Josiah	3	4	5		
Bunker, Dodifer	3	3	5		
Purington, James	2		4		
Shaw, Caleb	1	2	4		
Cram, Ruben	2	1	6		
Purkins, Jona	2	2	6		
Bachelder, Jacob	2	2	5		
Blake, Stephen	2	1	5		
Yeaton, Jonathan	2		3		
Gordon, Wm	1	2	4		
Durgin, Richard	1	3	3		
Lovet, Ruben T.	2	1	2		
Lovet, Bracket	1	2	1		
King, Saml	2		3		
King, Ausgood	1		2		
Nudd, Benja	1		3		
Prescott, Saml	1		2		
Sandborn, Timo	2		2		
Nudd, Wm	1	2	3		
James, Jabez	1	1	3		
Prescott, Ebenzr	1	1	4		
Hilyard, Timo	1	1	1		
Mason, Benjn	1	1	1		
Kenny, Jno	2	1	3		
Kenny, Jona	1				
Berry, Wm	1	2	2		
Kenny, Jno., Junr	1	2	3		
Sandborn, David	2	2	3		
Cram, Jona	1		2		
Marston, James	1				
Cram, James	2	2	7		
Sweet, Thos. R.	2	1	2		
Cram, Jno., Esqr	7		5		
Sargent, Jno	1		3		
Sargent, Edwd	1		1		
Jenness, Jno	2	2	2		
Haskel, Job	2	2	3		
Fogg, Jona	1	1	4		
Fight, James	1	1	2		
White, Nathan	2		2		
Brown, Abraham, Jur	1	1	5		
Tibbits, Saml	1				
Bean, Nathl	1		3		
Phillbrick, Jona	1		3		
Page, Cristopher	1	2	5		
Walton, Shadrick	1		2		
Perry, Saml	2	2	3		
Shepard, Joseph	1				
Morggen, Nathl	1	4	5		
Brown, Abraham	1		1		
Wille, Paul	1		1		
Morill, Malcijah	1		4		
Dickkey, Robert	2		4		
Sargent, Wd Heziak	1	1	2		
PLAISTOW TOWN.					
Ayers, Wm	1	1	2		
Ayers, Danl	2	2	2		
Ayers, Joseph	1	1	3		
Allen, Francis	1		2		
Ayers, John	3		4		
Bardley, Wm	3	1	2		
Bradley, John	1	2	2		
Bly, Benja	2	4	4		
Bly, Moses	1	4	5		
Bryant, David	3	3	3		
Bartlett, Moses	1	4	2		
Cheney, Dustin	2	1	2		
Bartlett, Danl	2		2		
Cheney, Nathl	1		1		
Bartlett, Nathl	1		3		
Chase, Parker	1		2		
Chase, Moses	1	1	1		
Clement, Christor	1	5	3		
Copps, Jona	2	1	1		
Carlton, David	2		3		
Chase, John	1	2	3		
Cooper, Jona	1		1		
Cooper, Jona, jr	1		3		
Dow, Saml	2	1	2		
Dow, Joshua	2	2	5		
Dow, Ezekiel	1	3	6		
Dow, Saml, jr	2	2	3		
Davis, Benja	1	2	2		
Davis, Moses	1		2		
Davis, Amos	1		2		
Dow, Peter	1		1		
Davis, Benja	1	1	1		
Eaton, Job	3		2		

NAME OF HEAD OF FAMILY.	Free white males of 16 years and upward, including heads of families.	Free white males under 16 years.	Free white females, including heads of families.	All other free persons.	Slaves.
PLAISTOW TOWN—con.					
Eaton, Jesse	1		2		
Eaton, Danl	3	3	4		
Flander, Ezekiel	3	1	2		
Folansbee, Simon	2		3		
Farnum, Wm	2		2		
Flint, Widow	1	1	3		
Gilman, Jereh		2	3		
Gile, Ezekiel	5	1	8		
Gile, Ruth	2	3	2		
Gile, Ruth, jr	1	4	2		
Green, Peter	1	3	7		
Hall, John	1		2		
Hall, Thos	1	3	3		
Heath, Saml	1	1	3		
Herriman, Moses	1	3	3		
Herriman, Leonard	1		2		
Herriman, Saml	3		3		
Herriman, Joseph	2		2		
Herriman, Aseph	2	2	5		
Herriman, Mary		1	3		
Herriman, David	1	4	7		
Heath, Jona	3	1	6		
Jackman, Moses	2		2		
Jeffers, John	1	3	5		
Johnson, Isaiah	1	2	3		
Kimbal, Jona	1		2		
Kimbal, Joseph	1	1	3		
Kimbal, Nathl	1	3	5		
Kimbal, John	1				
Kelley, James	1	1	4		
Noyes, Ebenr	2	1	2		
Noyes, James	2		2		
Ordway, Moses	2		1		
Peasley, Reuben	1	2	3		
Peasley, Simeon	2	3	3		
Payson, Jona	1		6		
Sawyer, Amos	3	2	4		
Stevens, David	2		2		
Stevens, David, jr	1	4	1		
Stevens, Jesse	2	3	5		
Stevens, Chase	1	1	1		
Stevens, Danl	1	2	4		
Stevens, John	1		1		
Stevens, Alexr	1	1	1		
Smith, Joseph	1	4	3		
Simmons, Moses	1		4		
Smith, Meriam	1	1	1		
Tucker, John	1		2		
Stevens, Mehitable	2		2		
White, Mary			2		
White, John	3	2	3		
Welsh, Joseph	2	3	4		
Woodard, Stephen	1	1	3		
Bradley, Thankful			3		
Simmons, Ephrm	1		2		
Roberts, Hannah			2		
Nichols, Danl	2	3	3		
Simmons, Jona	1		3		
Heath, Stephen	1				
Chiney, Widow			2		
Kimbal, Hannah		1	2		
POPLIN TOWN.					
Godfrey, Ezekiel	3	1	5		
Sanborn, Abraham	3	4	5		
Laying, Joshua	2		2		
Sleeper, Steven	4	6	9		
Clefford, Richard	2	1	6		
Lifard, Bilard D	1	1	2		
Cram, Benjamin	3	1	4		
Weed, David	1	2	2		
Flanders, Samuel	2	2	2		
Mugget, Joseph	2		4		
Davis, Jeremiah	1	1	4		
Brown, Joseph	1	1	3		
Roberson, Josiah	2		3		
Car, John	2		4		
Brown, Ephraim	2		3		
Roberson, John	1	2	3		
Chase, Thomas	2	2	2		
Brown, Jeremiah	2	1	4		
Fellows, Joseph	1		4		
Roberson, Ezekiel	2	1	6		
Davis, Nathaniel	1	1	3		
Smith, Ezarel	2		2		
Levet, Moses	3		3		
Davis, Judah		1	1		
Holbs, Joel	1	1	1		
Beedy, Thomas	1	1	4	1	
Burley, Caleb	2	3	3		
Sibley, Patience			2		

NAME OF HEAD OF FAMILY.	Free white males of 16 years and upward, including heads of families.	Free white males under 16 years.	Free white females, including heads of families.	All other free persons.	Slaves.
POPLIN TOWN—con.					
Beedy, Eli	1	2	5		
Beedy, Jonathan	3	2	2		
Collins, Joseph	1		1		
Sleeper, Sherburne	1	3	3		
Merrill, Nathan	2	2	4		
Bachlor, Nathan	1	4	1		
Taylor, William	1		2		
Litton, David	1	2	2		
Merrill, James	2	2	5		
Grig, William	1	1			1
Tassay, William	1		1		
Cluff, Jabish	2		1		
Tefethern, John R	1	1	2		
Cluff, Joseph	1	3	2		
Beedy, Ppinaus	2	2	3		
Davis, Benjamin	1		1		
Wolleymash, Joseph	1	2	5		
Brown, Nathan	3	1	5		
Brown, Daniel	2	1	3		
Brown, Enoch	3	1	5		
Hoit, Dorithy	1	3	5		
Hoit, David	4	2	3		
Abbett, Joshua	2	2	2		
Wodley, William	1	1	2		
Scribner, William	3		4		
Abbet, Ephm	1	1	4		
Brown, Jonathan	3	1	5		
Colbee, Stephen	2	1	5		
Brown, Jonathan	3	2	3		
Hobes, Stephen	1	1	4		
Taylor, Betsy			2		
Roberson, Jonathan	1	1	2		
Abbet, Joshua, ju	1	2	3		
Sanborn, Daniel	2	2	4		
Seavy, Solomon	1	2	2		
Hains, Walter	1	1	4		
Kimball, Joshua	2		2		
Smith, Enoch	2	2	3		
Kimbrel, John	3	4	2		
Cluff, Benjamin	1	1	5		
Morrill, William	1	1	1		
Hook, Elishar	2	1	3		
Tucker, James	3	1	4		
Smith, Abraham	3	1	5		
Goarding, Josiah	1	3	4		
Cenerstone, Joab	3		2		
Bodg, Benjamin	2	2	4		
Goarding, Nicholas	2	1	4		
Goarding, Benoni	1	2	6		
Wood, Asac	3	2	2		
PORTSMOUTH TOWN.					
Alcock, Joseph	1		3		
Ayers, Perkins	1	2	6		
Akerman, Walter	2		1		
Akerman, Joseph	2		3		
Akerman, Barnard	1	3	1		
Adams, Nathaniel	1	5	3		
Ayers, James	3	4	5		
Adams, William	1		2		
Atkinson, Susanna	1		4	2	
Abbot, John	1	2	2		
Abbot, John, Junr	1	1	1		
Akerman, Simeon	1	1	2		
Ayers, Jonathan	1		3		
Akerman, Nahum	3	2	3		
Ayers, John	1		2		
Ayers, John, Junr	1	1	1		
Akerman, Josiah	2	1	2		
Akerman, George	1		1		
Ayers, Thomas	1	2	1		
Ayers, William	1	1	5		
Ayers, Edward	1	1	5		
Abbot, Amos	2		4		
Abbot, Amos, Junr	1		2		
Ayers, Stephen	1	3	1		
Ayers, Dependance	2	1	4		
Ayers, Jonathan, Junr	2	1	5	1	
Abbot, George	1	4	1		
Ayers, Levi	1	1	2		
Ayers, George	1		2		
Arny, Sarah			2		
Buckminster, Joseph	2	2	5		
Beck, Samuel	3	1	5		
Brewster, William	3		4	1	
Briard, Samuel	1	1	1		
Brewster, David	2	1	3		
Bartlett, Robert	1	2	2		
Billings, Richard	1	1	2		
Butler, Alford	1	1	6		
Bennett, Winthrop	1	5	3		

ROCKINGHAM COUNTY—Continued.

NAME OF HEAD OF FAMILY.	Free white males of 16 years and upward, including heads of families.	Free white males under 16 years.	Free white females, including heads of families.	All other free persons.	Slaves.
PORTSMOUTH TOWN—continued.					
Bodge, John	1	2	3		
Brewster, David	1	2	1		
Brown, Margarett			1		
Beck, John		1	2		
Berry, Bartholomew	1	2	3		
Bartlett, John	2		2		
Bryant, George	2	1	2		
Brewster, Samuel	1				
Brackett, Joshua	1		3	1	
Bass, Joseph	1		1		
Blasdell, Abner	4	3	5	1	
Bowles, Samuel	2	4	6		
Babb, Nathaniel	1	1	2		
Broughton, Joseph	1	1	2		
Beck, Amos	1	1	4		
Barns, John	1	1	5		
Babb, Peter	2		1		
Beck, John, Junr	1	1	4		
Bigelow, Benjamin	1	1	5		
Broughton, John	3		1		
Broughton, Benjamin	2		4		
Bigelow, Benjamin, Junr	1	1	2		
Babb, Benjamin	1		3		
Beck, Joshua	2	1	3		
Boddington, Thomas	1		1		
Beck, George	1		2		
Blasdell, William	1	1	2		
Bowles, John	1		1		
Bazeen, John	1	2	4		
Broughton, Daniel	1				
Ball, Peter	1	1	1		
Beck, Thomas	1	2	4		
Babb, Philip	2		5		
Brewster, Moses	1	1	1		
Banfill, John	1	1	4		
Barns, Thos	2	5	1		
Beck, Andrew	1	4	2		
Brewster, Caleb	1		6		
Broughton, William	1	1	1		
Ball, Peter, Junr	1	2	8		
Bryant, Thomas	1	1	2		
Blunt, Arthur	3	1	2		
Bickford, Henry	1		4		
Blunt, William, Junr	2		2		
Broughton, Noah	1	1	3		
Banfill, Tobias	2	1	2		
Babb, Aaron	1	1	2		
Bird, Widow			3		
Buck, Eliza			1		
Cutts, Samuel	5	2	5		
Cotton, Joseph	1		3		
Colebath, George	2	2	4	1	
Clap, Supply	5	1	6		
Call, David	2		2		
Clapham, Mary			5	1	
Caverly, John	2		1		
Cutts, John	1	2	7		
Champney, Richard	2		4		
Champney, Joseph	1		6		
Currier, William	2	1	1		
Chadbourne, Thomas	1	2	5		
Clark, Thomas	1		1		
Cook, Widow		1	4		
Chadwick, Ebenezer	3	1	3		
Cotton, Thomas	1		1		
Cutter, Ammi R	6		5		
Curtis, Eliza	1		2		
Coffin, Edmund	2	1	1		
Cotton, Samuel	2	1	4		
Cotton, Solomon	1	1	4		
Chandler, Benjamin	2	3	3		
Clear, Philip	1	1	4		
Carter, Benja G	1		3		
Chadbourne, Mark	1	1	3		
Caverly, Charles	1	1	5		
Cambridge, William	1	1	1		
Chase, Stephen	3	2	9	1	
Cones, Peter	2		5	1	
Clark, Joseph	1	1	2		
Chase, John	1	3	3		
Chapeau, Antonio	1		4		
Caverly, William	1	1	4		
Croney, Darby	1	1	3		
Cotton, William	1		2		
Cate, Samuel	1	2	3		
Cate, John	1		1	2	
Clark, John	1		3		
Cotton, Nathaniel	2	1	1		
Drown, Benjamin	1	1	3		
Dame, George	1		2		
Dame, William	1	1	3		1
PORTSMOUTH TOWN—continued.					
Dennet, Jeremiah	1	4	6		
Dennet, Ephraim	1	2	3		
Dearborn, Benjamin	2	5	6		
Duncan, David	2	2	2		
Doe, Samuel	1	2	2		
Dennet, Thomas	1	2	1		
Driscol, Nathaniel	1		1		
Dennet, Nathaniel	2	3	4		
Dennet, John	1	1	2		
Dean, Nathaniel	2	2	3		
Dearing, Ebenezer	2		1		2
Doig, George	1	5	2		
Dimpsey, Edward	1	1	2		
Daniel, Reuben	2		3		
Drown, Samuel	1	4	5		
Davis, Theodore	1	1	3		
Davenport, John	4		4		
Dammerell, Joseph	1	1	1		
Dearing, William	2		5		
Drisco, James	1	3	6		
Driscol, Cornelius	1		1		
Day, James	1	1	3		
Dibble, Martin	1	1	2		
Dame, Mark	1	1	2		
Daverson, John	1		2		
Dame, Theodore	1		2		
Davis, John	1	1	3		
Dennet, John	1	1	3		
Drown, Joseph	1	1	1		
Davis, Edmund	1	1	1		
Eliot, Abraham	2	1	3		
Ewen, Alexander	2	2	7		
Eliot, Samuel	1		4		
Edwards, William	1	1	3		
Emerton, Henry	1		1		
Evans, John	1	5	4		
Furnald, John	1	1	1		
Furnald, Humphrey	2	1	1		
Furniss, Robert	3	2	7		
Folsom, Nathaniel	1	1	6		
Frost, John	3	3	3		
Furnald, Samuel	1	2	4		
Furnald, Randell	1	1	2		
Furnald, Gilbert	1		5		
Fitzgerald, John	1		1		
Fitzgerald, Joseph	1	1	1		
Flagg, John	1		1		
Folsom, Josiah	1	2	1		
Fowler, Michael	1		1		
Field, Michael	1	3	4		
Ferren, Moses	3		1		
Furnald, Amos	1				
Furnald, Edmund	1		3		
Fuller, Jeremiah	2		5		
Foster, James	1	1	1		
Furnald, Daniel	1	1	1		
Foss, Samuel	1	1	2		
Freeze, Jona Chase	1		1		
Furnald, William	1		3		3
Frost, Michael	2		1		
Fishley, Eunice			2		
Frost, Daniel	1		2		
Gardner, John	1		3		
Gookin, Nathaniel	3	3	7		
Gains, George	2	4	4		
Gooch, John	1	1	3		
Greenleaf, John	2		3		
Goodwin, Samuel	1	1	5		
Goddard, John	4	2	5		
Goodwin, Gideon	1		2		
Green, Mark	1		2		
Gunnison, William	2		2		
Gibbs, William	1	2	2		
Griffith, Nathaniel S	1	2	3		
Gale, William	1	2	3		
Grouard, James	4	2	4		
Gardner, John, Junr	1		1		
Grace, Charles B	1	3	6		
Gray, Thomas	1	2	1		
Grant, Martha		2	2		
Gove, Edward	2	2	2		
Griffin, James	2		3		
Grouard, James, Jr	1	2	2		
Griffith, Samuel	1	1	2		
Gates, William	1	1	3		
Gerrish, William	1	3	2		
Glass, Thomas	1	2	3		
Green, Joseph	2	2	3		
Gardner, Benjamin	1		3		
Gardner, David	1	2	2		
Gammon, David	1	2	2		
PORTSMOUTH TOWN—continued.					
Ham, William	2	1	3		1
Hart, George	1		4		
Hart, Richard	3		5		1
Hart, Daniel	4	6	4		
Ham, Robert	2		2		
Ham, Samuel	2	1	4		
Ham, Timothy	2	3	7		
Ham, George	3	2	1		
Hull, George	4		4		
Hill, Elisha	5	3	5		
Hill, Samuel	2	3	4		
Hill, James	3	5	7		
Hall, Elijah	3	3	4	1	
Hodgdon, Aaron	1	2	4		
Hart, Edward	2	5	5		
Haven, Joseph	1	2	3		
Ham, Benjamin	1	3	2		
Hilton, Henry	1	3	4		
Hart, George, Junr	1	2	3		
Hardy, Stephen	2	7	6		
Hill, Aaron	1	2	5		
Harvey, Thomas	1	1	2		
Hayley, John	1	1	4		
Harris, Abel	3	3	3		
Hobart, Samuel	1	1	2		
Hunt, Peter	2	1	3		
Ham, Ephraim	2	2	2		
How, George	3		2		
Haslett, James	1	5	2		
Hart, William	1		2		
Huntress, Joshua Lang	2	2	3		
Hutchins, Samuel	2	1	3		
How, John	1	2	2		
Holmans, George	1	2	2		
Hale, Samuel	2		3		
Ham, John	2	2	4		
Hill, Jeremiah	3		3		
How, Richard	1	1	1		
Haven, Samuel	4	4	7	1	
Haven, Samuel, Jr	1	2	4		
Haven, Nathaniel A	2	2	5		
Hall, Stacey	2	4	5		
Harold, Robert	2	1	3		
Holbrook, Robert	1	2	2		
Hasty, Joseph	1		1		
Hohn, George	1		1		
Humphreys, Daniel	2	1	5		
How, George, Junr	2		3		
Ham, William, Jr	1	2	4		
Hooker, Michael	1		2		
Hill, Elisha, Junr	1	2	1		
How, Richard, Junr	1		1		
Ham, George, Junr	1	2	1		
Hurtle, Lewis	1		1		
Hickey, James	1	1	2		
Hill, Samuel	1	1	1		
Holmes, Christian			2		
Holmes, Jeremiah	1	1	3		
Hooker, John	3		3		
Holmes, Benjamin	2	2	1		
Holbrook, Samuel	1		5		
Hall, Samuel	3	2	7		
Hall, John	1	3	3		
Hodgdon, Phinehas	2	1	2		
Ham, William	1				
Haslett, Matthew	1	2	8		
Hodgdon, John	1	1	1		
Hubbard, Leverett	1		1		1
Holman, Oliver	3	6	3		
Hill, Moses	1		3		
Holbrook, John	1	1	1		
Holmes, John	1		3		
Jaffrey, George	2	1	1		
Jackson, Nathaniel	6	1	3	1	
Jackson, Richard	4	2	4		
Jenkins, Richard	1		3		
Johnson, Jotham	3	1	4		
Jackson, Thomas	2		1		
Hayden, Richard	1		3		
Haynes, Sarah			3		
Isaac, Betty				2	
Holnes, James			2		
Holmes, William	1	1	2		
Jackson, Hall	1	1	3		
Jackson, Samuel	3	2	2		
Jackson, Daniel	1		1		
Jackson, John	1	1	6		
Jackson, Gecrge	1		1		
Jones, Joshua	2	2	5		
Jenkins, William	2	1	3		
Jones, James	1		2		

ROCKINGHAM COUNTY—Continued.

PORTSMOUTH TOWN—continued.

NAME OF HEAD OF FAMILY.	Free white males of 16 years and upward, including heads of families.	Free white males under 16 years.	Free white females, including heads of families.	All other free persons.	Slaves.
Jackson, Stanford	2		1		
Jones, James, Junr	2	1	3		
Jones John	1	2	1		
Jones, Alexander	1	2	3		
Jackson, Joseph	1	1	2		
Jackson, Samuel, Jr	1	2	3		
Jones, John, Junr	1	1	2		
Isaac, Abraham	1		2		
Jones, Thomas	1	1	4		
Jones, Samuel	1	2	1		
Johnson, Jacob	1	1	1		
Jones, Joshua	1	1	3		
Janvrin, Abigail		1	1		
Jones, Thomas	2	2	5		
Janvrin, Martha			3		
Jones, John	1		1		
Lassel, John	1	1	1		
Kennard, Nathaniel	1	2	1		
King, Thomas	1	1	2		
Leslie, Abigail			3		
Little, Sarah			3		
Low, John	1	2			
Lang, John	1		2		
Lang, Nathaniel	1				
Long, George	1	1	4		
Langdon, William	2	1	2		
Lear, John	1		1		
Leach, Josiah	1	1	2		
Low, Joseph	2	1	3		
Libbey, Jeremiah	2	2	3		
Lakeman, Aaron	2		3		
Low, Richard	2	2			
Leach, John	1				
Loud, Daniel	1	2	4		
Lang, Henry	1		1		
Leverett, Benjamin	1	1	2		
Low, Elisha	1		1		
Langdon, Woodbury	2	5	12		
Langdon, John	2		5	1	
Leighton, Paul	2	6	3		
Lang, Daniel	1	2	2		
Loud, Edward	2	2	3		
Low, Joseph, Junr	1		2		
Lord, John	1		3		
Loud, William	1	2	6		
Lang, George	1	1	1		
Loud, Thomas	1		3		
Lunt, Daniel	1		1		
Lowd, Benjamin	1		1		
Lowd, Abigail		1	4		
Langley, Elihu	1	3	1		
Loud, Joseph	1		1		
Lyel, Alexander	1	1	1		
Leach, Richard	1				
Lewis, Lydia		1	2		
Little, Sarah		1	4		
Lunt, Josiah	1	1	3		
Leighton, Luke Mills	1		2		
Loud, Mark	2	4	1		
Loud, David	2		1		
Lear, Samuel	1	2	5		
Langdon, Samuel	4	1	5		
Lang, Mark	3	1	2		
Lear, Benjamin	1				
Lear, Tobias	2		4		
Lewey, George	1	1	3		
Lock, James	1	2	2		
Lombart, Widow			3		
Mann, Peter	4	1	4		
Mendum, John	1	1	8		
Macintire, Neil	4	7	7		
Miller, Benjamin	1	2	4		
Massey, George	1	3	3		
Meloon, Enoch	3		4		
Martin, Thomas	2	1	5		
March, John	1	1	1		
Moses, William	1	1	2		
Marston, Lemuel	1	2	4		
Melcher, Nathaniel	3	3	4		
Martin, John	2	1	2		
McHard, William	1	2	5		
Magill, Robert	1				
Miller, Nicholas	1	2	3		
Miller, Robert	1	3	4		1
Marsh, John	1	1	1		
Marsh, Sarah			3	1	
McKann, Philip	1		1		
Mifflin, James	1		1		
Miller, Benjamin	1	2	5		
Miller, James	1		1		
Melcher, John	3	3	2	1	

PORTSMOUTH TOWN—continued.

NAME OF HEAD OF FAMILY.	Free white males of 16 years and upward, including heads of families.	Free white males under 16 years.	Free white females, including heads of families.	All other free persons.	Slaves.
Moses, Samuel, Junr	1	1	2		
Masuera, John	1		3		
Mountford, Timothy	2		3		
Mills, Richard	2		1		
Marden, James	1	1	5		
Moses, Samuel	2	1	2		
Melcher, Nathaniel	1	1	3		
March, Jonas	11	4	34	1	
Melcher, John	2	4	1		
Manning, Thomas	2	1	6		1
Marshall, Nathaniel	1		2		
Marshall, John	2	5	7		
Meserve, William C	1	2	3		
Masuera, Peter	1	1	3		
Muchemore, Benjamin	1	1	4		
Marden, Joseph	1	1	2		
Melcher, Tobias	1	1	3		
Munns, John	1		2		
Maccannan, William	1				
Moulton, Thomas	2	2	3		
Marden, Jonathan	3		3		
Morton, Isaac	2	3	2		
Melcher, Nathaniel	1	1	2		
Marden, Israel	2	1	2		
Moses, Nadab	1	4	5		
Melcher, James	2	1	3		
Marden, Timothy	2		5		
Marden, Jonathan	1	1	2		
Marden, William	1	1	1		
Marden, Francis	1	3	2		
Marden, James	1	1	5		
Melcher, James, Junr	1		1		
March, Margery			2		
Nelson, John	1		1		
Noble, Moses	7		6		
Noble, Mark	1		2		
Noble, John	1	1	5		
Nason, Nathaniel	1		2		
Nutter, Samuel	2	1	5		
Noble, Mark, Junr	1	1	2		
Noble, Moses, Junr	1	2	1		
Neal, Thomas	1	2	3		
Nutter, Mary			2		
Nutter, Samuel, Junr	1		5		
Neal, Josiah	1		3		
Nelson, Elizabeth		3	2		
Nelson, Thomas	3	1	2		
Nelson, John	1	1	2		
Nutter, Henry	1	1	1		
Nutter, Lemuel	2	1	3		
Nichols, Ichabod	1	4	7		
Nelson, Joseph	1		1		
Neal, Robert	2		2		
Nelson, Joseph, Junr	1				
Neal, Robert, Junr	1	1	3		
Norrie, James	2		5		
Noble, Rachel			3		
Nutter, George	1	1	2		
Neal, Samuel	1		1		
Neal, Clement J	1	1	2		
Norton, John	2	1	3		
Norris, Joseph	1		2		
Norris, Samuel	3	1	3		
Nelson, William	1		1		
Norton, Dudley	1		4		
Osborne, George J	2		3		
Osborne, George J., Junr	4	1	2		
Overton, John	1	2	3		
Orne, James	1	2	4		
Odiorne, Thomas	1		1		
Oram, Robert	1	1	1		
Oaks, Samuel	2		2		
Oxford, John	2		3		
Odiorne, Samuel	1		1		
Ogden, John C	1	2	3		
Osborne, George	2		1		
Penhallow, John	4	1	6		
Parker, John	3	3	6	2	
Palmer, John	1	1	7		
Priest, Thomas	1	3	3		
Palmer, Thomas	1		4		
Pierce, John	1	2	2		1
Parker, Robert	5	1	7		
Pickering, John	1	1	6	1	
Peverly, Richard	1	2	5		
Plaisted, William	4	1	2		
Penhallow, Samuel	1		3		
Penhallow, John, Junr	1	1	2		
Parcher, Henry	1	1	3		
Palmer, Thomas, Junr	1		3		
Palmer, William	1		3		

PORTSMOUTH TOWN—continued.

NAME OF HEAD OF FAMILY.	Free white males of 16 years and upward, including heads of families.	Free white males under 16 years.	Free white females, including heads of families.	All other free persons.	Slaves.
Parker, William	1		1		
Plaisted, George	3		2		
Peirce, Nathaniel	1	2	4		
Priest, Amos	1				
Pillar, John	1				
Peirce, Thomas	2	1	1		
Pickering, John	1	5	4		
Pearse, Peter	2	2	2		
Palmer, Cotton	1				
Peirce, John	2		2		
Pitman, Nathaniel	2	4	2		
Pitman, John	1	2	6		
Pitman, Ezekiel	3	1	9		
Place, Samuel	1	3	2		
Partridge, Benjamin	1		3		
Parker, William	1	2	2		
Plaisted, Elisha	1	3	1		
Parry, Martin	3		7		
Peirce, Daniel	1	4	3		
Preley, Charles	1		4		
Parry, Richmond	1	1	7		
Peirce, Samuel	1		6		
Pendexter, John	1		2		
Prowse, Daniel	1		3		
Parrot, John	1	2	2		
Pray, Thomas	1				
Parry, Richard	1	1	1		
Pike, Joshua	1	2	4		
Priest, Mary	2		1		
Packer, Martha			6		
Quincey, Edmund	1		3		
Reed, John	1	2	4		
Rindge, Daniel	1		1		
Russel, Eleazer	1	2	2		
Redding, John, Junr	1	3	3		
Rymes, Samuel	2	1	1		
Rice, Samuel	1	3	5		
Rogers, Daniel	2		4		
Rogers, Daniel R	1	1	6		
Roach, Thomas	2	2	3		
Reed, Luther	1		3		
Raynes, John	1		3		
Rindge, Isaac	2	1	2		
Roberts, Charles	1		2		
Reed, John	1	2	2		
Row, John	1		4		
La Rose, ——	1	1	2		
Robb, Joseph	1	3	3		
Russell, William	1	3	2		
Rouselett, Nicholas	1	1	4		
Reed, ——	1	3	2		
Renley, Charles	1	2	3		
Ryan, James	1				
Sherburne, John	1	1	1		2
Sherburne, John	1	1	4		
Sherburne, John	2		3		
Salter, Richard	1	4	4		
Simes, Thomas	4	1	7		
Seaward, Shackford	1		1		
Shannon, Nathaniel	2	3	3		
Seavey, Mark	2	2	6		
Slade, Benjamin	1	3	4		
Sheafe, Thomas	2	4	7		
Sherburne, Samuel	3	3	3		
Sherburne, Samuel	2	2	7		1
Seavey, William	1	1	3		
Storer, Clement	3		2		
Shannon, Nathaniel, Jr	3	3	2		
Shortridge, Richard	2	1	2		
Simes, Daniel	2	1	6		
Sherburne, John Samuel	1		3		
Sowersby, William	1		3		
Sheafe, James	2	2	3		1
Simpson, Adam	1	2	3		
Smith, Josiah	1	3	5		
Simpson, Thomas	1		3		
Sheafe, Jacob	1	1	2	1	
Sheafe, Jacob, Junr	2	5	7		
Stavers, John	2	1	4		
Stavers, John, Junr	1	1	1		
Seaward, Giles	1		2		
Storer, Samuel	1	4	7		
Stevens, Joseph	1		2		
Sparhawk, Widow	1	1	3		
Shillaber, Joseph	1		3		
Seaward, William	3		3		
Snell, Reuben	1	1	3		
Sherburne, Thomas	1		3		
Shillaber, Jonathan	1	1	4		
Stanwood, William	3	2	2		
Stokell, John	1	1	3		

ROCKINGHAM COUNTY—Continued.

PORTSMOUTH TOWN—continued.

NAME OF HEAD OF FAMILY.	Free white males of 16 years and upward, including heads of families.	Free white males under 16 years.	Free white females, including heads of families.	All other free persons.	Slaves.
Shereve, Samuel	2	2	7		
Seaward, John	1		2		
Salter, John	4	3	6		
Shores, James	2	1	3		
Shackford, Eleanor			4		
Sherburne, Benjamin	1	1	3		
Sherburne, Thomas, Junr	1		4		
Stoodley, Thomas	1		1		
Savory, Richard	1	4	2		
Shapley, Reuben	2	3	4	1	
Shapley, Benjamin	1				
Sargent, Edward	2		3		
Salter, John, Junr	1	2	4		
Stoodly, Guppy	2	3	2		
Seavey, John, Junr	2		2		
Shapley, John	1		5		
Spence, Keith	1	3	6		
Sheafe, William	1	1	3		
Shearman, Richard	2	3	3		
Seavey, John	2		5		
Sullivan, John	1		1		
Sheafe, John	1	1	2		
Stevens, Thomas	1				
Sellars, James	1	1	3		
Stillman, James	1		3		
Seaward, John D	1				
Sumner, Eli	1	2	4		
Stavers, William	1	1	2		
Sherburne, Nathaniel	3		6		
Sherburne, Tobias	1				
Shapley, James			3		1
Swett, Henry	1		2		
Sellars, Tobias	1		1		
Spencer, Robert	1	1	2		
Scott, William	3		1		
Sewall, Jonathan M	1	1	5		
Sherburne, Nathaniel	2		6	2	
Sherburne, Jonathan	2	1	3		
Savage, John	1	1	1		
Seavey, Thomas	2		4		
Sherburne, Nathaniel	3		2		
Seavey, John	2		5		
Stavers, Martha		1	2		
Salter, Titus	3		3		
Shores, John	1				
Shaw, Joseph	3	1	1		
Savage, Mary			1		
Sherburne, Levi	1		2		
Savage, Benjamin	2	1	3		
Sinclair, Sarah			1		
Seaward, Widow			2		
Sumner, Stephen	1		3		
Teago, Francis	1	3	3		
Thompson, Samuel	3		3		
Thompson, Samuel, Jr	1				
Thompson, Benjamin	1				
Treadwell, Charles	1		1		1
Treadwell, Nathaniel	3		3		
Treadwell, William E	1				
Treadwell, Nath., Junr	2	3	3		
True, Israel	1	1	1		
Tripe, Samuel	2	1	1		
Turner, George	1	4	5		
Tripe, Sarah	3		2		
Trefethen, James	1		6		
Thurber, Thomas	1	1	7		
Thompson, Thomas	2	3	5	1	
Tuttle, James	2	2	6		
Trundy, Thomas	1	5	1		
Tibbets, Richard S	1	2	2		
Thompson, Enoch	1	4	1		
Trickey, Joseph	1	1	2		
Thomas, William	1	1	1		
Trusdell, John	1		2		
Thomas, Thomas	1				
Tarlton, Benjamin	1	2	3		
Tucker, Elijah	3	2	3		
Tarlton, James	3	1	4		
Tucker, Joseph	1	1	2		
Tucker, George	1	1	1		
Trefethen, William	3	3	3		
Tucker, Richard	2	3	3		
Tarlton, Elias	2		3		
Tarlton, John	1	1	4		
Trefethen, Robinson	2		3		
Trickey, Thomas	1	3	5		
Tucker, Samuel	1	2	4		
Treadwell, Robert	1		1		
Thompson, Wid:	1		4		
Treadwell, Ann		2	2		
Thomas, John	1		2		

PORTSMOUTH TOWN—continued.

NAME OF HEAD OF FAMILY.	Free white males of 16 years and upward, including heads of families.	Free white males under 16 years.	Free white females, including heads of families.	All other free persons.	Slaves.
Toscan, John	3		2		
Twyman, Elizabeth			1		
Underwood, Mary	1	1	3		
Naughan, William	1	4	5		
Nerrieul, William	2		3		
Walton, Joseph	2	2	3		
Warner, Jonathan	2		6	2	
Wincol, Joseph	1		4		
Walker, Tobias	2	4	6		
Wilson, Richard	1	1	3		
Wallace, Samuel	4	1	2		
Walker, Seth	4	2	5		
Walden, Jacob	1	4	4		
Welch, John	1	1	5		
Walden, Thomas	2		1		
Weeks, Jonathan	1	3	2		
Whittier, William	1	1	2		
Wingate, Aaron	1	2	3		
Wentworth, Joshua	2	3	5	1	
Wentworth, George	1	2	5		
Whidden, Michael	2	1	6		
Walker, Joseph	2	2	3		
Weeks, William	1	3	4		
Ward, Nahum	1	1	5		
Warner, Margarett	1	3	2		
Wilson, William	1	1	4		
Walker, Gideon	2	1	2		
Whidden, George	1		1		
Wingate, Elizabeth			1		
Waterhouse, Samuel	2	1	3		
White, John	1		1		
Welch, William	1		2		
Wentworth, Elizabeth			6	1	
Whipple, Joseph	1		3		
Whipple, Oliver	2	1	4		
Woodward, Moses	4	3	6		
Woodbury, Benjamin	1		2		
Wilson, Peter	1	2	1		
Wilson, James	1		1		
Walton, Thomas	1	1	2		
Wentworth, Michael	3		6		
Whidden, Samuel	1	4	7		
White, Nathan	1		2		
Walden, William	2	3	5		
Walden, George	2	2	3		
Whidden, Joseph	2	3	6		
White, Joseph	2		2		
Williams, John	1	2	3		
Williams, Benjamin	2	1	3		
Wendell, John	1	4	3	1	
Whidden, James	3	1	3		
Walker, Samuel	1	3	5		
Williams, Widow		1	1		
Warner, Elizabeth			2		
Whipple, Nancy	1		2		
Welch, Benjamin	2	1	6		
Wood, William	1	1	1		
Yeaton, Hopley	1	3	2		1
Yeaton, William	2	3	2		
Yeaton, Robert	1		2		
Yeaton, Philip	1		2		
Yeaton, Benjamin	1	1	1		
Yeaton, Thales G	2				
Colson, John			3		
Dolly, Richard	1		1		
Holmes, John	1	2	6		
Arickson, Margaret		1	1		
Prouse, Peter	1		1		
Martin, Mary		2	3		
Beck, John	1		3		
Stanley, Hannah			2		
Hart, Ruth	1		2		
Pendexter, Edward	1		1		
Gale, Sarah	1	2	2		
Hooper, James	1		2		
Woodhouse, Rachel			4		
Peverly, John	1		2		
Ross, Sarah	1		3		
Hodgdon, Thomas	1		2		
Marshall, Hannah		1	4		
Parker, Timothy	2		1		
Welch, Keyron	1	2	4		
Gregory, Elizabeth		1	3		
Gerrish, Timothy	1	3	5		
Haymans, Mary	1	1	12		
Waters, Charles	1		3		
Seaward, Sarah		3	5		
Scott, Alexander	1		2		
Pevey, John	1				
Flagg, Anna	1		4		
Waters, Betty			2		

PORTSMOUTH TOWN—continued.

NAME OF HEAD OF FAMILY.	Free white males of 16 years and upward, including heads of families.	Free white males under 16 years.	Free white females, including heads of families.	All other free persons.	Slaves.
Bennett, Thomas	1		1		
Penhallow, Hannah		1	2		
Hale, Mary	1		3		
Hall, Samuel	1	1	3		
Lavers, Elizabeth			3		
Leach, Joseph	2		1		
Mendum, Wido			3		
Pinkham, Sarah		2	7		
Pike, Sarah			3		
Cate, Shuah		3	2		
Alcock, Phebe			1		
Wilson, Samuel	2	2	2		
Moses, Elizabeth		3	2		
Hall, Ammi R	1		4		
Langdon, Mary			3		
Currier, Deborah		1	1		
Greenough, Abigail	2	1	2		
Chadbourne, Sarah		1	1		
Parker, Rebecca	4	2	6		
Reed, Susannah		2	5		
Hart, Benjamin	2		4		
Gerrish, Samuel	1		2		
Bartlett, Anthony	1	2	3		
Buck, Andrew	1		1		
Colebath, Dudley	1	2	2		
Pascall, Elizabeth			2		
Briard, Elizabeth	1	1	3		
Phippin, Nathaniel	1	2	2		
Cullum, Peggy		3	1		
Wells, Mehitabel			3		
Fellows, Mary			5		
Hodgdon, Cæsar				2	
Adams, Peter				2	
Nanny				2	
Mercy				2	
Warner, Peter				2	
Simonds, William				4	
Shores, Pharaoh				4	
Juba				4	
Myrtilla				3	
Odiorne, Jock				4	
Romeo				2	
Saunders, Thomas	1	1	3		
Stoneman, William	1		1		
Tucker, John	1	1	2		
Senter, Elizabeth		2	1		
Mackey, Elizabeth		1	3		
Nichols, George	2		1		
Greenough, Lucy	1		2		
Grouard, Betsey		2	3		
Clough, Thomas	1		1		
Stevens, Lydia			3		
Clark, Robert	1		2		
Nutter, Lydia			2		
White, Elizabeth		1	2		
Akerman, Mary			2		
Codder, Olive			2		
Bickford, Thomas	1	2	3		
Brown, Joseph	1	1	4		
Redman, Ruth			3		
Wyat, Mary			1		
Ross, Abigail		2	3		
Shaw, Samuel	1	1	1		
Cruesey, Margarett			2		
Hooper, John	1		1		
Shute, Lucy		1	3		
Cox, Joseph	1	1	2		
Lang, John	1	1	1		
Goodroe, Charles	1	1	1		
Scot, Abigail			3		
Jackson, Jerusha			2		1
Waters, Anna		1	1		
Harvey, Richard	1				
Ryan, Mary			3		
Buck, Mary		1	4		
Griffin, Anna		2	1		
Waters, Elizabeth			2		
Dammerell, Edward	1	4	2		
Davis, Priscilla			1		
Jackman, Elizabeth			2		
Dammerell, Benjamin	1	1	4		
Snagg, Elizabeth	2		1		
Marshall, Mary			1		
Benson, Joseph	1	1	1		
Uriter, Lewis	1	1	1		
Loud, Benja., Junr	1	2	3		
Furnald, Margery	1	2	2		
Libbey, Deliverance			3		
Jenkins, William	1				
Goodwin, Bartholomew	1	1	1		
Talpey, Mary		1	3		

ROCKINGHAM COUNTY—Continued.

PORTSMOUTH TOWN—continued.

NAME OF HEAD OF FAMILY.	Free white males of 16 years and upward, including heads of families.	Free white males under 16 years.	Free white females, including heads of families.	All other free persons.	Slaves.
Coleman, John	1		1		
Seavey, Mary			2		
Pitman, Mary		2	3		
Lewis, Mary			3		
Barnes, Samuel	1		2		
Nelson, Dorothy		1	2		
Hooker, Eliza			2		
Crosby, Polly		1	1		
Muchemore, Sarah			3		
Davis, Clement	1				
Abbot, Charles	1		1		
Blunt, William	2	2	5		
Hunt, Mary			1		
Lang, John	1	1	1		
Stewart, William	1		3		
Sherburne, Susanna			1		
Severett, Elizabeth			4		
Beck, Alice		1	3		
Evans, Catharine		2	2		
Shores, Sarah			1		
Gardner, Susannah		2	3		
Blunt, George	1	1	3		
Walden, John	1	1	2		
Fitzgerald, Sarah			1		
Yeaton, Mary			1		
Lang, John	1	1	4		
Sawyer, ——	1		2		
Phillips, Widow			3		
Spinney, Widow			3		
Ham, Mary			2		
Sherburne, Elizabeth			3		
Whipple, Prince				5	
Whipple, Cuff				2	
Gerrish, Cæsar				6	
Hart, Cæsar				6	

RAYMOND TOWN.

NAME OF HEAD OF FAMILY.	Free white males of 16 years and upward, including heads of families.	Free white males under 16 years.	Free white females, including heads of families.	All other free persons.	Slaves.
Roby, Danl	2	2	1		
Robinson, Richd	1	2	5		
Cram, Benjn	2	2	7		
Norris, Danl	4	1	4		
Cram, Hannah			2		
Presmit, Ruben	1	1	3		
Fogg, Saml	2	3	5		
Cram, Ebenr	1	3	2		
Batchelder, John	2	3	4		
Osgood, Timothy	2	1	8		
Dearborn, Jonathan	1	1	2		
Dearborn, John	1	2	1		
Osgood, Ebenr	2	3	2		
Fulington, John	2		2		
Folsum, Elipt	1	4	3		
Folsum, John	1	3	2		
Hoit, Danl	1		2		
Holman, W. Jean	1		3		
Smith, Jacob	1	1	4		
Holman, Danl	1		1		
Osgood, Ebenr, Jr	2	3	3		
Todd, Danl	1	1	2		
Moore, Wm	1	1	2		
Merrell, Abige	2	1	4		
Poor, Ebenr	1	2	4		
Glitton, John	2	1	2		
Glitton, Joseph	1	3	2		
Lovering, John P.	1	1	3		
Lovering, Danl	1	1	1		
Lovering, Thomas	1	1	2		
Witcher, Aaron	1	4	5		
Joy, Nancey	2		2		
Witcher, Richd	1	4	5		
Lovering, Jonathn	1	2	1		
Peavey, Saml	1		2		
Peavey, Joseph	1		1		
Nay, Saml., Jr	2	2	3		
Gorden, Thomas	3	1	3		
Moody, Danl	1	3	3		
Moody, Clement	1	1	1		
Roby, Nathen	1	2	2		
Been, Elizh	1		2		
Bean, Thomas	1		2		
Brown, Levi	2	3	2		
Towl, Elipt	1	1	1		
Towl, Wm	1		3		
Prescut, Ebenr	1	2	2		
Osgood, Enoch	2	1	6		
Page, Robt	1	2	6		
Fogg, Josiah	1	3	4		
Batchelder, John	1		3		
Batchelder, Jon	1	3	3		
Kimbell, Amos	1		2		

RAYMOND TOWN—con.

NAME OF HEAD OF FAMILY.	Free white males of 16 years and upward, including heads of families.	Free white males under 16 years.	Free white females, including heads of families.	All other free persons.	Slaves.
Poor, Saml	1	2	5		
Moody, Clement, Jr	1		2		
Stoence, John	2	1	2		
Thansher, Danl	1	2	1		
Dudley, James	1		2		
Heneman, Asa	1	2	2		
Fulington, Ezekel	2	1	3		
Tilton, Ruben, Jr	3	1	4		
Wells, Salley		1	1		
Kast, Moses	3	2	4		
Sanborn, Jonathan	1		3		
Elesworth, Jonathan	1	2	2		
Chapman, Saml	1	3	1		
Perkins, Benja	2	1	5		
Gilman, Jonathan	1	2	2		
Gilman, Phines	1		2		
Towl, Danl	1	5	2		
Dudley, Gilman	1	1	2		
Dudley, John	2	1	2		
Dudley, Moses	1	2	2		
Smith, Caleb	1	2	2		
Richardson, Danl	2		5		
Calcut, Thomas	1	1	4		
Smith, John W	2	4	5		
Tucker, Isac	3	1	2		
Dudley, Joseph	3	1	3		
Cleford, Jacob	2	8	2		
Ela, Wm	1	2	4		
Ela, Saml., Jr	1	2	2		
Ela, Asa	1	3	5		
Smith, Joseph	1		3		
Smit, John	2		2		
Wormwood, Wm	2	1	2		
Smith, Sanders	4		1		
Smith, Jonathan	1		4		
Swein, Jonathan	1		4		
Swein, Levi	1		1		
Moulton, Josiah	1	2	5		
George, James	3	1	6		
Towl, Wm	2	1	3		
Hook, Humphre	1	3	4		
Prescut, Ruben	1		2		
Towl, Fleman	1		2		
Prescut, Stephen	1	1	2		
Osgood, John	1		2		
Hisco, Ceser				3	
Jones, Saco				4	
Hisco, Philip				1	
Wadley, Dean	1	2	2		
Waters, Thomas	1		4		
Sanborn, Noah	1		2		
Towl, Jeremiah	1	4	2		
Dollan, Clement	2	3	5		
Leavet, John	2	2	5		
Smith, Wm	1	1	4		
Roberts, Ezl	1	1	2		
Layn, Danl	2	2	3		
Ela, Saml	2	1	3		
Vermem, John	1	2	4		
Layn, Saml	2	2	2		
Griffin, Obidiah	2	3	4		
Hains, Marther	2	3	5		
Shannon, Saml	1		3		
Layn, Joseph	2		3		
Bendell, Wm	2	1	3		
Colby, Benjn	2	1	4		
Libby, Abm	2	2	3		
Clay, Danl	2	2	3		
Clay, Polley			2		
Layn, Davd	1		4		
Layn, Jacob	1	2	3		
Sandborn, Saml	1	1	1		
Matton, Judey	1	1	2		
Powers, John	2		3		

RYE TOWN.

NAME OF HEAD OF FAMILY.	Free white males of 16 years and upward, including heads of families.	Free white males under 16 years.	Free white females, including heads of families.	All other free persons.	Slaves.
Berry, Ebenezer	1	2	1		
Berry, Jeremiah	1		3		
Berry, Levi	1		3		
Berry, Timothy	1	1	3		
Berry, Jotham	1		3		
Berry, Samuel	1	1	3		
Berry, William	1	2	4		
Berry, Jacob	1		3		
Berry, Merryfield	2		3		
Brown, Jonathan	1	1	3		
Brown, John	1	4	3		
Brown, John, Junr	1		3	2	
Brown, Jeremiah	1	1	3		
Brackett, Phebe			2		

RYE TOWN—con.

NAME OF HEAD OF FAMILY.	Free white males of 16 years and upward, including heads of families.	Free white males under 16 years.	Free white females, including heads of families.	All other free persons.	Slaves.
Dow, Isaac	1	4	4		
Dalton, Michael	3	2	2		
Davison, William	3		1		
Dolbeare, Nicholas	2	3	3		
Dow, James	1		1		
Elkins, Samuel	1	3	5		
Elkins, Henry	2		3		
Foss, Rachel			1		
Fitzgerald, Daniel	1	2	3		
Foy, John	3	1	2		
Foss, Mary			1		
Foss, Samuel Dowse	1	4	3		
Foss, Nathaniel	2		4		
Foss, Job	2	1	3		
Foss, John	1	2	1		
Garland, Peter	5		5		
Garland, Levi	2		1		
Garland, John	1	3	3		
Garland, Benja	3	1	3		
Garland, Simon	2		2		
Garland, Joseph	1	1	2		
Goss, Levi	3	2	1		
Goss, James	1	1	2		
Goss, Nathan	3	1	2		
Green, Richard	1	4	3		
Gould, Mary			3		
Hall, Joseph	1		3		
Hall, Edward	1	2	1		
Hobbs, James	1	1	4		
Hobbs, Jonathan	1	1	1		
Jenness, Francis	1	1	6	1	
Jenness, John	1	3	4		
Jenness, Benjamin	2		2		
Jenness, Levi	1	2	2		
Jenness, Richard	1	2	1		
Jenness, Simon	2	1	4		
Jenness, Job	3		3	2	
Jenness, Samuel	3	1	5		
Jenness, Joseph	3		2	1	
Jenness, Jonathan	1	1	3		
Jenness, John Bean	1	2	1		
Jenness, Noah	1	2	2		
Jenness, Nathaniel	2	3	5		
Jenness, Nathaniel, Junr	1	1	2		
Johnson, Peter	2		2		
Johnson, Peter, Junr	2	1	2		
Knowles, Samuel	1		1		
Knowles, Simon	1		4		
Knowles, Nathan	2	1	2		
Libbey, Joseph	1		2		
Lang, Bickford	2	2	5		
Lear, Alexander	5		6		
Libbey, Samuel	1	3	2		
Locke, David	1	2	5		
Locke, David, Junr	1	1	1		
Locke, William	1	3	4		
Locke, Elijah	1		2		
Locke, Jeremiah	2	2	6		
Locke, Richard	2		3		
Locke, Richard, Junr	1	1	3		
Locke, Richard, 3d	1	3	3		
Locke, Job	1		2		
Locke, Joseph	2		3		
Locke, Jonathan	3	1	3		
Locke, Jonathan, Junr	1	2	2		
Locke, John	2	1	2		
Lang, Mary			2		
Locke, Elijah, Junr	1	2	2		
Mace, Haman	1	1	2		
Marden, Benjamin	3	1	3		
Marden, Benjamin, Jr	1		4		
Marden, Nathaniel	1		2		
Marden, Nathaniel, Jr		3	6		
Mason, Daniel	2		6		
Marden, William	1	2	6		
Matthes, Abraham	1	1	4		
Moulton, Reuben	1		2		
Moulton, Nehemiah	2		5		
Mace, Levi	1	3	2		
Poor, Robert	1	1	2		
Parsons, Joseph	2		4		
Perkins, James	2	1	3		
Perkins, John	1	1	3		
Philbrook, Jonathan	2	2	3		
Philbrook, Joses	1	1	2		
Philbrook, Joses, Junr	1	1	1		
Philbrook, Anna	1	4	4		
Philbrook, Reuben	4	1	3		
Porter, Huntington	2	2	2		
Rand, Joseph	2	3	3		
Rand, Joseph, Junr	1	1	2		
Rand, Nathaniel	1		7		

ROCKINGHAM COUNTY—Continued.

NAME OF HEAD OF FAMILY.	Free white males of 16 years and upward, including heads of families.	Free white males under 16 years.	Free white females, including heads of families.	All other free persons.	Slaves.	NAME OF HEAD OF FAMILY.	Free white males of 16 years and upward, including heads of families.	Free white males under 16 years.	Free white females, including heads of families.	All other free persons.	Slaves.	NAME OF HEAD OF FAMILY.	Free white males of 16 years and upward, including heads of families.	Free white males under 16 years.	Free white females, including heads of families.	All other free persons.	Slaves.
RYE TOWN—con.						SALEM TOWN—con.						SALEM TOWN—con.					
Rand, Nathaniel, Jr	1		2			Gurrill, Nath¹	2	3	5			Dustin, Caleb	2	1	1	1	
Rand, George	2	2	7			Gurrill, Widow	1	1	2			Rowell, Lemuel	1	2	1		
Rand, Samuel	2	1	3			Rust, Nathan	1		4			Rowell, Wm	1	3	5		
Rand, Thomas	1		1			Bailey, Joshua	2	2	4			Gordon, Alexr	1	1	3		
Rand, John	1	2	6			Foster, Paul	1		3			Gordon, Benja	1		2		
Rand, Ruth		4	3			Clough, Josiah	3	3	6			Belnap, Obediah	1		1		
Rand, Stephen	1	1	4			Austin, Abiel	1		2			Belnap, Nath¹	1		2		
Rendall, George, Junr	1	2	2			Austin, John	1	1	6			Dustin, Stephen	1	1	2		
Rand, William	2		1			Austin, Nathan	2	1	2			Cross, Jona	1	2	3		
Remick, Mary		1	2			Austin, Peter	1	2	1			Bailey, Moores	1	5	3		
Rendall, George	2		3			Clough, Isaac	1	1	5			Campbell, John	1	3	4		
Salter, Alexander	2	2	2			Emerson, Hannah	1	1	4			Dustin, Ebenr	1		1		
Sanders, Robert	2	1	1			Kimbal, Barnard	2	4	7			Clough, Mary			3		
Sanders, Robert, Junr	1	3	2			Ayers, Nathan	1	2	6			Dustin, David	3	1	3		
Sanders, Robert, 3d	1	2	1			Beadle, Joseph	1		1			Gorden, Daniel	4	1	8		
Sanders, Sarah		1	2			How, Ebenr	1	3	2			Woodman, Nath¹	2		3		
Seavey, Joseph Langdon	2	1	4		1	Webster, Nath¹	3	3	2			Sanders, Henry	1	3	2		
Seavey, Daniel	1	2	2			Merrill, Nath¹	1		2			Runnels, Thomas	1	1	2		
Seavey, Ebenezer	1		2			Merrill, Perley	1	5	3			Perry, Ebenr	1	3	2		
Seavey, Paul	1	4	4			Beaty, Edward	2	4	3			Rowell, Benona	1	2	3		
Seavey, James	4		1	1		Tibbett, John	1	3	3			Allen, Ann	3	1	5		
Seavey, James, Junr	3		1			Bartlett, Dan¹	1	3	3			Clark, Nath¹	1	1	2		
Seavey, Amos	1		4	2		Mercer, John	1	4	2			Townsend, Thos	1	2	4		
Seavey, William	1	2	7			Mercer, Richd	2	1	1			Ellinwood, Robert	2		4		
Seavey, Joseph	1	2	3			Page, Joseph	1	1	5			Marble, Caleb	2		2		
Shapley, Henry	4	1	2			Bigsby, Dudley	1	2	4			Marble, Sam¹	1		1		
Sleeper, Tristram Coffin	2	1	3			Mercer, David	1	2	3			Clemment, Wm	1	2	2		
Smith, David	2	2	3			Webster, Sam¹	2		5			Parker, Ebenr	2		1		
Smith, Samuel	1	1	2			Day, Sam¹	2	2	1			Hovey, Joseph	1		4		
Sanders, Sarah	1		4			Cawley, Dan¹	2	1	8			Dow, Thomas	1	4	5		
Shapley, Betsey			2			Cawley, Asa	2	3	5			Dow, Abraham	2		2		2
Trefethen, William	1	3	3			Heath, James	1	4	2			Petty, Peter	1	1	5		
Tucker, Nathaniel	2		4			Bailey, Mary			2			Chase, Sam¹	1	3	3		
Tucker, William	1	1	2			Heath, Abiel	1	1	2			Rowel, Josiah, jr	2	3	4		
Verriel, John	1	1	2			Harris, Joseph	1		2			Kelley, Nehemiah	1	1	3		
Verriel, Hannah			6			Rowell, Israel	1	2	2			Taylor, Matthew	1	4	2		
Verriel, Edward	1	3	2			Rowell, Asa	1	5	3			Bows, Widow			3		
Wallis, Ebenezer	2		2			Rowell, Phillip	1	4	2			Kimbal, Richd	3	2	4		
Wallis, Samuel	3		2	1		Bigsby, George	1	2	4			Marcy, Jona	1	2	4		
Wallis, Samuel, Junr	1	1	2			Dustin, Abigail			2			Rallins, Benja	1		2		
Webster, Josiah	1	3	3			Hall, Joshua	3	1	5			Webster, James	2	2	4		
Webster, Richard	1	1	7			Rowell, Jacob	1	1	2			Gage, Stephen	2	2	3		
Webster, John	1	2	7			Dow, Amos	1		1			Wheeler, Abijah	2	2	3		
Wells, Samuel	3	1	7			Kelley, Nath¹	1	1	3			Ober, Israel	1		3		
Williams, John Floyd	2	1	2			Robinson, Thos	1		2			Ober, John	1		2		
Yeaton, Joseph	2		2			Woodbury, Nath¹	2	1	8			Copp, Aaron	1	1	1		
						Wheeler, Josiah	1		2			Bailey, Wm	1	1	1		
SALEM TOWN.						Wheeler, Amos	1		3			Smith, Jona	1				
						Woodbury, Israel	1	4	4			Ordway, Jesse	1		1		
Purkins, Nath¹	2	3	5			Bradford, Wm	2	2	4			Carrier, Dudley	1	2	3		
Fletcher, Sam¹	1	2	5			Bradford, John	1		1			Carrier, Abiah			2		
Ladd, Timothy	2		2			Bradford, Simon	1	1	1			Harris, Martha			4		
Wardwell, Joseph	1		1			Gordon, Wm	1		2			Kelley, Esther			3		
Poor, Benja	1	1	3			Woodbury, Ebenr	1	1	4			Wheeler, Abner	1	2	4		
Gage, John	4		5			Cross, Sam¹	1	4	3			Webster, Stephen	1	4	2		
Gorden, Phineas	2	4	3			McLanghan, Thos	1	1	3			Wheeler, Jona	2		2		
Moore, Caleb	2	2	1			Morland, John	2		1	1		Wheeler, Stephen	2	1	1		
Little, Henry	2	3	3			Woodbury, Luke	1	3	3			Wheeler, David	1		2		
Beadle, Dorothy		1	2			Stevens, Wm	2	1	2			Smith, Thos	3	2	6		
Duty, Wm	1	4	3			Woodbury, John	1	3	4			Johnson, John	1		2		
Lowell, John	1		7			Merrill, Jesse	2		3			Merrill, Joshua	1	1	2		
Bailey, Jona	1	1	3			Hull, Joseph	1	1	2	1		Jones, Evan	1		1		
Hasseltine, Nath¹	1	1	4			Smith, Wm., junr	2	3	2			Morse, Moody	1		1		
Currier, John	1	1	2			Stevens, Simeon	1	2	3			Ordway, Enoch	1		3		
Pettingale, Abbot	2	4	3			Hall, David	3	3	4			Bailey, Revd Abner	2		3		
Merrill, Enoch	1	2	2			Kimbal, Oliver	1		3			Tenney, Jona	5		5		
Merrill, John	2		2			Kimbal, Oliver, jr	1	1	5			Kelley, Jona	1	1	4		
Ellinwood, John	1		3			Hall, Elijah	2	2	6			Tayler, Ceaser				5	
Wilds, Ezra	1	2	1			Thom, Wm	3	1	6			Currier, Stephen	1	1	5		
Page, Ebenr	2	2	4			Smith, Solomon	1		3			Kelley, Somes	1	1	1		
Webster, Jesse	2	3	5			Smith, Francis	1		1			Jones, Evan	3		3	1	
Simson, Alex	1	1	3			Rowles, Reuben	1	4	2			Jones, Hezekiah	1		1		
Rawlins, John	2		1			Smith, Wm	1	1	1								
Rallins, David	1	3	3			Woodbury, Elisha	1	2	4			SANDOWN TOWN.					
Campbell, Robert	2	2	3			Silver, Daniel	1	1	7								
Webster, Hannah	1	1	6			Pettingale, Wm	1		1			Davis, Daniel	2	1	2		
Nevins, David	1	3	6			Heath, Joshua	2	3	4			Fowler, Betty	2	1	2		
Kelley, Sam¹	2	1	4			Heath, John	1		2			Page, Abigail			2		
Merrill, Joseph	1	6	3			Clough, Wm	1	1	4			Tilton, Joseph	2		3		
Smith, John	3		4			Stevens, Jona	1	1	2			Griffin, Moses	1	2	3		
Kelley, Richd	1	1	3			Stevens, Jona., jr	1		3			Page, Henry	1	5	2		
Sanders, Oliver	2	3	5			Hesseltine, Jona	1	1	3			Sanborn, Sam¹	2		2		
Sanders, James	1	6	3			Clough, Wiman	3		2			Long, Ebenr	1	2	2		
Gorden, Jona	3	3	5			Thistle, Josiah	1	2	3			Hook, Abrahm	2	2	5		
Rowell, Josiah	1	1	2			Bailey, John	2		2			Tilton, Isaac	1	1	2		
Lancaster, Henry	1		1			Hastings, James	2		1			Clark, David	3	4	2		
Bailey, Dudley	1	2	4			Lancaster, John	1		4			Hook, Moses	2	1	4		
Dow, Jereh	4	1	6			Woodman, Abner	1	1	5			Towle, Caleb	1	2	2		
Dow, Oliver	3	2	4			Ladd, Daniel	4	1	5			Rowell, Wm	1	1	1		
Page, John	1	1	2			Wheeler, Warner	1	3	3			Tilton, Timy	2	3	2		
Mackanel, Elizth		1	1			Corliss, Widow			1			Fuller, Sarah			2		
Worth, Stephen	2	2	4			Whittier, Mitchel	1	4	4			Neal, Andw	1	3	1		

ROCKINGHAM COUNTY—Continued.

NAME OF HEAD OF FAMILY.	Free white males of 16 years and upward, including heads of families.	Free white males under 16 years.	Free white females, including heads of families.	All other free persons.	Slaves.	NAME OF HEAD OF FAMILY.	Free white males of 16 years and upward, including heads of families.	Free white males under 16 years.	Free white females, including heads of families.	All other free persons.	Slaves.	NAME OF HEAD OF FAMILY.	Free white males of 16 years and upward, including heads of families.	Free white males under 16 years.	Free white females, including heads of families.	All other free persons.	Slaves.
SANDOWN TOWN—con.						**SEABROOK TOWN—con.**						**SEABROOK TOWN—con.**					
Whittier, Phineas	1	1	2			Brown, Benjamin	1	2	5			Noyes, Edward	1	5	3		
French, Nath¹	3		5			Beckman, John Robinson	1	3	2			Marble, Jonathan	1	1	3		
Wells, Nath¹	1	1	3			Brown, Thomas	4	1	3			Leavitt, Benjamin	2		3		
Taylor, Benjª	2		5			Bragg, Peter	1	5	2			Leavitt, Jonathan	1		1		
Sanborn, John	2		1			Boyd, David	1	5	3			Lock, Thomas	1	2	2		
Sleeper, Sam¹	1		1			Brown, Elisha	2	2	2			Lock, Timº Blake	3	1	5		
Sleeper, John	1	1	3			Chase, Thomas	1	2	1			Lock, Simon	1		2		
Sleeper, Sam¹, 3ᵈ	1		2			Green, Daniel Chase	2	3	4			Robie, Henry	2	1	2		
Long, Stephen	1	1	3			Collins, Tristram	1		3			Row, Reuben	1	2	4		
Long, Richᵈ	1		1			Collins, Robert	3	2	5			Row, Aaron	1	3	3		
Sleeper, Ruth	1	2	2			Caldwell, Stephen	2	4	5			Silley, Thomas	1		1		
Sleeper, Sam¹, jr	1		1			Chase, Abigail	1	2	3			Silley, Jacob	1	5	3		
Crawford, Robᵗ	3	1	5			Collins, Ezekiel	1	2	1			Silley, Jonathan	2	2	3		
Sanborn, Sherburn	1	2	6			Chase, Winthrop	1	2	1			Smith, Richard	2		2		
Sanborn, Moses	2	2	3			Chase, Chrisʳ Toppan	1	1	2			Smith, Daniel	2	1	4		
Hunkin, Benjª	2	2	4			Chase, Daniel	1	3	1			Smith, John	1	4	5		
Colby, John	1	1	3			Dow, David	3	1	4			Smith, Stephen	1	1	1		
Atwood, Benjª	1	1	3			Dow, Abraham	2	2	2			True, Thomas	2		3		
Colby, Peter	1		1			Dow, Benjamin	3	1	5			True, Edward	1	1	2		
Colby, Ebenʳ	1	2	5			Dow, Jacob	1	3	1			True, Moses	1	3	3		
Pilsbury, Benjª	3	1	3			Dow, Moses	1	3	6			True, Mary			1		
Cotton, Thoˢ	1	3	5			Dow, Winthrop	1		1			Page, Joseph	1		2		
Fellows, Thoˢ	1		1			Dow, Zebulon	3	2	2			Merrill, Eliphalet	1		3		
Plumer, Kelley	1	1	2			Dow, Josiah	1	2	3			Bragg, John	2		3		
Shaw, Benjª	3		3			Davis, John	2	2	2			Row, Ephraim	1	1	1		
Gibson, Robᵗ	1	2	2			Dow, Levi	1	1	2			Dow, Winthrop	1		4		
Clough, Humphry	1		1			Dow, Israel	1	3	1			Tucker, Judith			2		
Heath, Moses, jr	1	3	3			Eaton, John	2		2			Roberts, Judith			1		
Wyatt, Sam¹	1		2			Eaton, Wimon	2	1	3			Greenleaf, Enoch	1		2		
Wyatt, Chase	1	1	2			Eaton, David	2		2			Roberts, Jonathan	2	1	5		
French, Ezra	1	1	5			Eaton, David, Junʳ	1	2	3			Norton, Joseph	1		1		
Edmunds, Thoˢ	1	1	7			Eaton, Ephraim	1	2	6			Eaton, Samuel, Junʳ	1		2		
Griffin, Theoˢ	3		3			Eaton, Ebenezer	2	2	3			Brown, Mary			2		
Showell, Thoˢ	1		2			Eaton, Joshua	1	2	4			Hunt, John	1	1	2		
Griffin, Thoˢ	1	2	2			Eaton, Thomas	2		3			Rogers, Mary			2		
Heath, Moses	3		4			Eaton, Silvanus	1	4	2			Janvrin, George	1		2		
Collins, John	1	1	3			Eaton, William	2		2								
Bailey, Joseph	1	1	2			Eaton, William, Jʳ	2	2	4			**SOUTH HAMPTON TOWN.**					
Morse, Gilbert	1		3			Eaton, Jabez	1		2			Jones, Judith	2		2		
Eaton, James	1	1	1			Eaton, Winthrop	1	2	5			Jewett, Rachel	2		4		
Kelley, Dan¹	2	2	5			Eaton, William 3d	1	2	3			Merrill, Joseph	3	3	6		
Plumer, Widʷ		1	2			Eaton, Bryant	2	1	3			French, Henry	3	3	5		
Clemens, Reuben	1	2	4			Eaton, Joseph	3		3			George, Moses	1	1	2		
Daniels, Sam¹	2		3			Eaton, Samuel	1	2	1			Collins, Jacob, jr	1	2	1		
George, Joshua	1	2	4			Eaton, John, Junʳ	1	1	2			Ordway, Prudence		1	3		
Draper, Joseph	1		1			Eaton, Reuben	1		2			Collins, Jacob	2	1	3		
George, Moses	1	1	2			Eaton, Jane	1		2			Collins, Richᵈ	1		1		
Fitts, Richᵈ	1	1	2			Fogg, Ebenezer	2		2			Flanders, Jeremiah	3		5		
Collins, Robᵗ	1	1	3			French, William	1	2	5			Pilsbury, John	1	1	2		
Fitts, Abigail	1	1	3			French, Jacob	2		2			Page, Dan¹	1	1	5		
Eaton, Ezekiel	2		2			Felch, Samuel	2	1	4			Brown, Abel	2		3		
Emerson, Peter	1	1	4			Felch, Henry	1		2			Brown, Nathan	1	3	3		
Call, Benjª	1		1			Felch, Parker	1	2	4			Brown, Benjª	1		3	1	
Palmer, Joshua	1		2			Felch, Nicholas	1	3	2			Brown, Nathan, jr	1		4		
Chase, Robert	1		5			Fowler, Ebenezer	1	1	5			Colby, Ichabud	1	1	3		
Straw, Jonª	1	1	2			Fowler, Samuel	1	1	3			Clough, Ezekiel	1		1		
Wells, Jacob	1		2			Fowler, Thomas	1		2			Flanders, Nath¹	1		1		
Wells, Timothy	1	2	6			Fowler, Jacob	2		1			Rogers, Josiah	2	3	7		
Wells, Sargeant	2	2	5			Philbrick, Joseph	1	2	2			Graves, David	2	4	3		
Sargeant, David	3		7			Green, Jacob	1		2			Graves, Wm	2	2	3		
Bachellor, Phineas	1		6			Gove, Stephen	2	1	7	1		White, Phillip	3		3		
Clough, Jonª, jr	1	2	2			Gove, Edward	1		2			Fitts, Susannah	1		3		
Clough, Wm	1		1			Gove, Moses	1	3	5			Fitts, Ephraim	4	3	5		
Clough, Jonª	2	3	4			Gove, Joseph	2		2			Flanders, Moses	2	3	4		
Clough, Reuben	1		2			Gove, Richard	3	2	3			Pilsbury, John	1	2	2		
Straw, Rowel	2		7			Gove, Enoch	2	1	2			Pearse, Humphry	1	2	4		
Sanborn, Peter	1	3	5			Gove, Winthrop	2	3	4			Clough, Benjª	2		2		
Bennet, Spencer	1	3	7			Green, Jonathan	3	2	4			Brown, Nath¹	1		1		
Hunt, Zaccheus	1		5			Green, Benjamin	2		2			Currier, Reuben	2		7		
Ingals, Nath¹	1	2	6			George, Samuel	1	1	1			Carter, Ephraim	1		2		
Huse, Jonª	2	1	5			Griffith, Gershom	1	1	2			Currier, Barnard	2	2	3		
Ingals, Widʷ		2	2			Greenleaf, Paul	1	1	2			French, Elisha	3	2	5		
Colby, Benjª	2	1	2			Green, Nathan	1		2			French, Abel	3		2		
Colby, Jonª	1		1			Gove, Levi	2	1	2			French, Obediah	3	1	5		
Percy, Charles	1	3	5			Gove, Miriam	3		3			French, James	3		2		
Chase, Benjª	1	1	4			Hardy, Bradbury	2	1	4			Sawyer, Israel	1	2	7		
Little, Sam¹	1		1			Hardy, Jonathan	1	1	4			Sawyer, Josiah	1		3		
Tucker, Jacob	1	3	4			Hooke, Joseph	1		3			Sawyer, Richᵈ	1	2	6		
Tucker, John	1		2			Jones, Samuel	1	3	3			Colby, Erv	1		3		
Flanders, Ephᵐ	1	1	2			Janvrin, John	2	1	2			French, Moses	2	4	3		
Cheney, John	1	1	4			Janvrin, James	1	2	2			Dole, Jearah	1		2		
Flanders, Benjª	2		1			Roberts, Elisha	1	2	1			Kimbal, Sam¹	1	3	4		
Perrere, John	2	2	2			Janvrin, William	1	1	1	1		Titcomb, Enoch	1	1	3		
Ferrin, Wm	2	4	2			Dow, Robert	1	4	2			Brown, Moses	1		2		
Ferrin, Alpheus	1		4			Weare, Jonathan	1		2			Woodman, Sam¹	2	3	7		
Dow, Sarah		1	2			Weare, John	1	2	3			Jones, Joseph	2	1	3		
Dow, Ely	2	1	3			Fogg, David	1	1	2			Jones, Dan¹	3	1	4		
Percy, Peter	1	1	2			Walton, Jonathan	1		1			Currier, Sarah			2		
						Walton, Samuel	1	3	4			Jones, Joseph, jr	1	2	1		
SEABROOK TOWN.						McQuillen, Abraham	1	2	3			Flanders, Barnard	3	1	5		
Brown, Isaac	1	4	6			Dow, Nathan	1		2			Rowell, Elijah	1	1	4		
Brown, John	1	2	7			Eaton, Samuel W	2		3			Barnard, Benjª	2		2		
Brown, Jeremiah	1	3	5			Perkins, Benjamin	1		1			Barnard, Benjª, jr	3	1	2		

ROCKINGHAM COUNTY—Continued.

NAME OF HEAD OF FAMILY.	Free white males of 16 years and upward, including heads of families.	Free white males under 16 years.	Free white females, including heads of families.	All other free persons.	Slaves.	NAME OF HEAD OF FAMILY.	Free white males of 16 years and upward, including heads of families.	Free white males under 16 years.	Free white females, including heads of families.	All other free persons.	Slaves.	NAME OF HEAD OF FAMILY.	Free white males of 16 years and upward, including heads of families.	Free white males under 16 years.	Free white females, including heads of families.	All other free persons.	Slaves.
SOUTH HAMPTON TOWN—con.						**STRATHAM TOWN—con.**						**WINDHAM TOWN—con.**					
Flanders, Phillip	2		2			Merrill, Joseph	1	2	3			Williams, Simon	2	1	4		
Noyes, Revd Nathl	1	2	3			Moore, Harvey	2	2	4			Curren, Marther			3		
Tewkesbury, Thos	2	2	4			Moore, Peter	2	3	3			Hall, Ebenr	2	4	3		
Currier, Chellis	2		2			Moore, Thomas	1		2			Clide, Danl	1	1	4		
Currier, Thos	2	4	1			Moore, Thomas, Junr	2	1	3			Merrell, Petter	1		1		
Currier, John	2	2	6			Moore, William	1		2			Merrell, Timothy	2		5		
Currier, Nathan	3	2	3			Merrill, Eliphalet	2		3			Parks, Elexander	1	2	2		
Brown, Saml	1	2	3			Murray, Samuel	1		3			Clide, Joseph	4		2		
Hadlock, James	2		1			Norris, Joseph	1	4	5			Clark, James	1	1	2		
Brown, Elias	2		4			Neal, Samuel	1		2			Anderson, James	3		2		
Barnard, Jacob	3	1	4			Odel, James	1	1	3			Cambell, Henney	1	1	4		
Flanders, Richd Currier	2	1	4			Piper, Jonathan	2	3	8			Gregg, Davd	1	2	2		
Barnard, Widow			1			Piper, Samuel	1	1	6			Gregg, Willm	1		1		
Colby, Thos	1	1	3			Piper, Stephen	2	1	6			Cambell, John	1	1	2		
Jones, Jacob	1	1	1			Pottle, William	4	1	7			Gregg, Davd, Jr	2		3		
Merrill, Elipt	4		2			Pottle, Samuel	1	3	2			McCoy, Willm	1	2	6		
French, Wm	1		2			Perkins, Josiah	1		2			Davidson, George	2	1	2		
Shepherd, John	1	1	6			Paul, Cæsar					5	Shad, Willm	2		2		
						Rawlings, Joshua	1		2			Eastman, Richd	2	1	1		
STRATHAM TOWN.						Rawlings, Jotham	1	4	6			Davidson, George, Jr	1	2	3		
Avery, Joshua	3	1	5			Rawlings, Nicholas	2	2	3			Davidson, James	1	3	4		
Avery, Nathaniel	1	2	2			Robinson, Jonathan	2	2	3			Willson, Hugh	1				
Adams, John	2	1	3			Rundlett, Simeon	2	2	4			Morgan, Jennet	1		2		
Adams, Nathan	1		1			Rawlings, Eliphalet	1		4			Gregg, Wm	1		2		
Barker, Benjamin	2	1	5			Scammon, Richard	3		4			McCoy, Alexander	1	1	5		
Barker, Ebenezer	2		2			Scammon, William	1	2	2			Cambell, Danl	2		3		
Barker, Ezra	2		2			Sinkler, John	1		1			Anderson, John	1	4	5		
Barker, Nathan	1	2	5			Smith, David	2	2	5			Anderson, James	3		3		
Bordman, Thomas	2	2	4			Smith, Josiah	1	2	5			Merrell, Amos	1	1	3		
Boynton, Samuel	1	1	3			Smith, Solomon	1	1	4			Cambell, James	3	1	5		
Burleigh, Edward	1	2	1			Smith, Theophilus	2	3	4			Moore, James	1	4	2		
Burleigh, Wheeler	1	1	3			Sinclair, Richard	2	2	4			Moore, Wm	1	1	3		
Calley, Samuel	1	1	3			Stockbridge, John	3	1	3			Clark, Saml	3		4		
Chase, Dudley L	1	1	5			Stevens, Sarah			2			Karr, John	1	4	5		
Chase, Josiah	3	1	4			Stevens, Joseph	1	2	3			Bettan, James	1	1	7		
Clark, Moses	6	2	7			Stevens, Nathaniel	3	2	7			Anderson, Danl	1		1		
Chase, Moses	3	3	2			Stockbridge, Abraham	2		4			Anderson, John	1	2	3		
Clark, Daniel	3		3			Stockbridge, Anna		1	2			Willson, Saml	2		4		
Crockett, David	1	4	4			Stockbridge, Jacob	1		1			Armstrong, Davd	2	2	7		
Clarkson, Thomas	1	1	5			Simpson, Nancy			3			Hamphill, Robt	3		3		
Clark, Taylor	1	1	4			Thurston, Stephen	1	1	2			Hamphill, Nathl	3	3	10		1
Clark, David	2		2			Thurston, Stephen, Jr	2		4			Ried, Mathew	1		6		
Cutler, Tobias				3		Tilton, Abraham	3	1	6			McKeen, Wm	1	1	5		
Durgin, Lydia			3			Tibbets, Ephraim	1		1			Cochran, James	2	3	3		
Dearborn, John	2	1	3			Thurston, John	1	1	5			Jemerson, Thomas	3		3		
Davis, Amos	1		3			Thurston, Josiah	1	2	6			Jemerson, John	1	2	1		
Fifield, Joseph	3		2			Veazey, Thomas	1	1	1			Emerson, John	2	1	4		
Foss, Jeremiah	1	1	7			Veazey, Thomas, Junr	1	1	3			Morrison, Robt	2	1	3		
Foss, Isaac	1	1	5			Wiggin, Samuel, Jr	4		2			Keger, George	1		1		
French, Daniel	2	4	4			Wiggin, Andrew	1	1	2			McAdams, Marcy	2		3		1
French, Thomas	1		1			Wiggin, Andrew, Junr	3	1	6			Merrell, Danl P	1	2	1		
French, Jeremy	2	1	5			Wiggin, David	1	2	4			Morland, James	1	4	3		
French, Reuben	1	1	1			Wiggin, Dorothy	2		2			Simpson, John	2	3	5		
French, Elijah	1		3			Wiggin, Jonathan	2	1	6			Noyes, Moses	1	5	3		
Fifield, Mark	1	2	2			Wiggin, Joseph	2		1			Corliss, Joseph	1	5	2		
Green, Benjamin	1	4	6			Wiggin, Levi	1	3	2			Simpson, Alexander	1	1	2		
Hill, John	3		4			Wiggin, Mark	1	3	4			Barnet, John	1	5	3		
Hoag, Enos	3	1	3			Wiggin, Nathan	1	2	3			Dinsmore, Robt	2		3		
Hoit, Daniel	1	2	3			Wiggin, Richard	3		4			Dinsmore, James	1	2	1		
Hoit, Jonathan	3	2	7			Wiggin, Penelope	1	1	3			Dinsmore, John	1	1	3		3
Jewell, David	1		1			Wiggin, Samuel	3		2			Dinsmore, John, Jr	2	1	2		
Jewell, Daniel	4	4	6			Wiggin, Simon	3		5			Dinsmore, Wm	5	3	5		
Jewett, Deborah	1	2	4			Wiggin, Thomas	1		2			Dinsmore, Robt., Jr	1	2	6		
Jewett, Jonathan	2		4			Wiggin, Tufton	1	1	3			Dustan, Peter	2	2	6		
Kelly, James	1	1	2			Wingate, Paine	3	2	4			Dinsmore, Frances	1		2		
Kenniston, Henry	2		8			Wiggin, Nathaniel	3		4			Willson, George	1	5	3		
Kenniston, Dorcas			1			Wiggin, Nathaniel, Junr	1	3	2			Gilmore, James	2	1	6		
Kenniston, James	1	1	3			Wiggin, Sarah	1		5			Merrell, John	1	1	3		
Lane, Samuel	1	1	1	1		Wiggin, Chase	2	2	6			Balch, Caleb	2	3	4		
Lane, Joshua	4	3	4			Wiggin, Walter	2		5			Dow, Asa	2	6	4		
Lane, Samuel, Junr	2	4	4			Wiggin, Mary	2		3			Morrison, Saml	1	4	2		
Leavitt, Jonathan	2	1	2			Wiggin, Moses	1		2			Morrison, John	1	2	2		
Leavitt, Joseph	3		1			Wiggin, Stephen	1	3	5			Parks, Andrew	1	5	3		
Lewey, John	2		1			Wingate, Joshua	1	1	2			Parks, Joseph	1	1	2		
Low, Jacob	4	2	4			Wiggin, Broadstreet	1	2	7			Parks, Alexander	1		4		
Leavitt, Elizabeth	2		3									Stuart, Robt	1	1	2		
Lary, Rachel			3			**WINDHAM TOWN.**						Thorn, Wm	2	4	5		
Lane, Jabez	2		4			Willson, Thomas	1	4	3			Prentice, Henney	1	3	1		
Leavitt, Anna			2			Simpson, Willm	2	3	4			Armer, Gain	4		5		
Mason, Hannah			1			McAlven, James	2	1	2			Helisengton, Philip	1	7	2		
Miltimore, James	1	2	3			Willson, Alexr	1		2			Ladd, Elipt	1	4	4		
March, George	1	1	2			Gumney, John M	1	1	1			Morrow, Alexander	3	3	6		
Marble, Samuel	3		3			Clide, John	2	1	2			Morrow, Margret			3		
Mason, Edward	1		5			Brown, Hugh	1		1			Thompson, Jonathan	2	2	6		
Mason, Noah	1		2			Davidson, John	1	4	5			Smith, Joseph	2	3	6		
Mason, Ward	1		3			Smith, Robt	1	1	1	1		Comen, Agness	1		1		
Merrill, Benjamin	1	2	4			Willson, John	4	4	6			McAlven, Marcy		1	2		
Merrill, Ford	1	2	4			West, Stinson	1	1	2			Emerson, Peter	2		3		
						Mountgumry, Marther			2			Simpson, Saml	1	2	3		
												Tempelton, Adam	2	5	6		

STRAFFORD COUNTY.

NAME OF HEAD OF FAMILY.	Free white males of 16 years and upward, including heads of families.	Free white males under 16 years.	Free white females, including heads of families.	All other free persons.	Slaves.	NAME OF HEAD OF FAMILY.	Free white males of 16 years and upward, including heads of families.	Free white males under 16 years.	Free white females, including heads of families.	All other free persons.	Slaves.	NAME OF HEAD OF FAMILY.	Free white males of 16 years and upward, including heads of families.	Free white males under 16 years.	Free white females, including heads of families.	All other free persons.	Slaves.
BARNSTEAD TOWN.						**BARNSTEAD TOWN—con.**						**BARRINGTON TOWN— continued.**					
Edgerly, Thomas......	2	1	2			Garland, Samuel......	1		3			Lock, Jethro, Jr......	1	1	2		
Morrell, Timothy......	2	1	3			Dudley, Nicholas......	4		2			Johnson, Thos., Jr......	1	1	8		
Edgerly, Ezekiel......	1		3			Straw, Ezra......	3	4	5			Otis, Elijah......	2	7	3		
Dudley, Daniel........	2	1	5			Pitman, John........	3	1	7			Leighton, Stephen......	1				
Young, Jonathan.....	1	3	1			Hill, Gideon......	1	1	2			Otis, Micajah......	2	3	2		
Chapman, Valentine.....	2	3	4			Hill, Silas......	1	1	1			Leighton, Andrew......	4	2	5		
Eastman, Ezekiel.....	2		4			Pickering, Jacob......	1	2	2			Garland, John, Jr......	2	5	2		
Marshall, Meribah.....	1	3	4			Elkins, Samuel........	1	1	1			Foss, Thos......	2		3		
Dockham, Nath^s.....	2	2	4			Avery, John........	1	4	2			Carnell, Ebenz^r......	1	2	5		
Wiggin, Nicholas.....	1	3	3			Coldbath, Dependance..	2	1	6			Otis, Joshua......	1				
Stevens, Samuel........	2		4			Adams, Ebenz^r......	1	2	4			Otis, Stephen, Jr......	1	3	4		
Clark, Benjamin......	3	1	7			Nute, Samuel......	1	2	2			Holmes, Eph^m......	1		1		
Sanborn, Edward......	1	2	2			Snell, Thomas......	2	1	5			Berry, Rich^d......	1	1	1		
Tuttle, John.........	1	4	6			Nutter, John, Jr......	2	5	1			Berry, Nathl......	2		2		
Jacobs, David........	1	2	4			Norton, John......	1		3			Young, Benj^a......	1		1		
Jacobs, Daniel, Jr.......	1	2	2			Meader, Nicholas	1	3	3			Young, Jon^a......	1	1	2		
Rand, Moses...........	2	2	7			Hawkins, John......	2	4	5			Foss, Solomon......	3	3	3		
Drew, Samuel........	1	3	5			Lammas, James......	1	1	2			Hayes, Joseph......	2	4	4		
Jacobs, Jonathan.....	1	2	4			Chesley, Samuel......	2	2	5			Hayes, Samuel......	1	1	3		
Ewers, Rufus........	1	2	5			Nelson, Samuel......	1	2	3			Stanton, Eliz^a......	1		1		
Tebbetts, Ephraim.....	1	3	3			Hodgson, Peter......	2	4	5			Stanton, Ezek^l......	1	2	1		
Munsey, Henry........	1		3			Came, Joseph......	2	5	5			Berry, George......	2	4	2		
Bunker, George.........	1	2	2			Came, James.........	1	2	1			Hayes, Paul......	2	3	5		
Bunker, John.........	1	3	1			Nutter, Benj^a......	1	3	3			Berry, Thos......	1	4	3		
Wille, Thomas........	1		3			Rand, David......	1	2	6			Hall, Joseph......	1	2	5		
Bunker, Jonathan......	1		2			Lord, William, Jr......	1	3	5			Holmes, Eph^m., Jr......	1	1	2		
Bunker, Eli.........	1	3	2			Drew, John........	2	4	3			Brock, Stephen......	2	3	4		
Bunker, Jos...........	3		5			Bunker, Jon^a., Jr......	1	1	2			Yeaton, John......	1	1	3		
Gerrish, Thos.........	1	2	4			Lord, William......	1		1			Scruten, Thomas......	2	2	4		
Jones, Stephen........	1	1	3			Peirce, Israel......	1		1			Foss, Saml., 3^d......	1	4	1		
Bunker, Thos.........	3		1			Nutter, John......	1	1	3			Hartford, John......	2	2	4		
Avery, Saml.........	1	2	4			Jacobs, Daniel......	1		1			Ham, George......	2	2	4		
Avery, David........	1	2	1			Drew, Elijah......	1		3			Ham, Benj^a......	1	3	4		
Smith, John..........	1	1	2			Lock, James......	1		1			Conner, Joseph......	2	3	5		
Tebbetts, John........	1		1			Otis, Joshua........	1		3			Littlefield, Robert......	1	3	2		
Meserve, John........	2	4	5									McNeal, Daniel......	1	2	5		
Peas, Nath^a.........	1	3	2			**BARRINGTON TOWN.**						Foss, Moses......	2	3	6		
Batchelor, Jethro.......	1	2	5									Holmes, Noah......	1		2		
Pickering, Stephen.....	2	2	5			Hayes, Benj^a......	1	1	2			Holmes, John......	1	1	1		
Sinclair, Richard......	3		1		1	Hayes, Andrew........	1	2	1			Holmes, Joseph......	1	2	1		
Sinclair, Rich^d, Jr......	1	1	4			Young, Eleazer......	1		3			Penney, John......	1	1	4		
Adams, Joseph.......	2	1	2			Young, Peter......	3	1	2			Snow, John......	1	1	2		
Adams, Ezekiel.......	1	2	4			Hayes, James......	2	1	1			Gray, James......	2	3	5		
Adams, Dudley........	1	1	1			Ham, Joseph......	2		4			Gray, Joseph......	2	4	3		
Dennett, Moses........	1	1	5			Ham, James......	1	1	1			Berry, Benj^a......	1	2	2		
Chesley, Jon^a..........	2	2	7			Ham, Clement......	2	2	5			Hill, Jon^a......	1	2	2		
Place, Joseph........	1					Jenness, Mark......	2	3	1			Otis, Nich^o......	1		8		
Hodgson, Charles......	3		3			Ham, Shadrack......	1		1			Otis, Joseph......	1	1	1		
Sanborn, Joseph........	2		5			Hayes, Joshua......	1	3	5			Hill, Saml......	2	3	6		
Brown, Thomas........	1	1	3			Garland, John......	1		2			Babb, Moses......	1	1	5		
Brown, William........	3		3			Garland, Joseph......	1	1	2			Hayes, Ezek^l......	1	2	2		
Smith, Daniel........	3	5	2			Garland, Benj^a......	1	2	1			Meader, Saml......	1	2	3		
Chesley, Aaron........	1	2	2			Hayes, Sarah......			3			Saunders, W^m	1	1	2		
Johnson, David........	2	1	4			Cloutman, Eliph^t......	3	1	1			Rowe, George......	1	1	3		
Wille, Robert........	1	3	2			Kingman, John......	2	1	5			Huckins, Samuel......	1	2	2		
Peary, William........	1	1	1			Kingman, Elizabeth.....			1			Fulker, Michal, Jr......	1	2	4		
Williams, Saml........	1	3	3			Seavy, Henry......	1		1			Fulker, Julius......	2		2		
Meserve, Nathl........	2	3	3			Seavy, Elijah......	1		2			Demeritt, Robert......	1	1	1		
Tasker, John........	2		2			Hayes, Saml........	1	2	3			Carpenter, Benj^a......	1	2	3		
Tasker, Joseph........	1	3	4			Lock, W^m......	3	2	8			Otis, John......	1	5	3		
Wille, Susanna........	1		3			Foss, Eph^m......	3	3	5			Fulker, Joseph......	1	5	3		
Emerson, Benj^a........	1	1	2			Babb, Thos........	1	4	2			Young, David......	1	1	4		
Hill, W^m...........	2	2	2			Foss, John......	2		3			Babb, Rich^d......	1	2	4		
Pitman, Saml.........	1	2	6			Foss, Joshua........	6	3	7			Berry, Stephen......	1	3	3		
Emerson, Jon^a........	1	3	5			Foss, James......	2	1	2			Rowe, James......	3	5	2		
Bryant, Joseph........	2	1	4			Foss, James, 3^d........	1	1	1			Fulker, Isaiah......	1	4	2		
Davis, Timothy........	3	3	5			Foss, John, 3^d......	1	1	1			Pearl, John......	1	1	2		
Davis, William........	2		1			Winkley, Francis......	3		3			Fulker, Charles......	1	1	3		
Davis, Jeremiah........	1	3	1			Winkley, John, Jr......	1					Young, Paul......	1	3	2		
Davis, Samuel........	1	1	1			Babb, Benj^a........	3		3			Berry, Jerem^h......	1	4	2		
Bickford, John........	3	1	5			Foss, Stephen......	1		2			Brock, Nich^o......	1	5	2		
Bickford, Jonathan	1		2			Babb, W^m., Jr......	1	1	1			Pearl, Benj^a......	1		1		
Snell, Samuel........	1		4			Foss, Hinkson......	1		1			Pearl, W^m......	1	3	1		
Hawkins, William......	2	2	4			Marden, Hinkson......	1	3	3			Willey, John......	2	1	3		
Clark, John..........	6	3	3			Marden, James......	1		1			Gray, Solomon......	1	3	3		
Green, William........	2	2	2			Marden, James, Jr......	1	1	2			Berry, Saml......	1	2	3		
Sinclair, John........	1	1	2			Foss, Jer^y......	1	1	5			Church, James......	1	3	1		
Sinclair, Joseph........	1	1	1			Church, Nathl......	2	1	2			Church, Benj^a......	1	1	3		
Elliot, John........	2	5	4			Brewster, John......	1	1	2			Tebbetts, Jerem^h......	1	1	3		
Green, John........	1	1	2			Brewster, Paul......	2		3			Tebbetts, Joseph......	1		3		
Peirce, Thos.........	1	2	3			Cator, Edward......	1	4	5			Ham, Saml......	1		2		
Munsey, Solomon......	1	3	6			Cator, John......	1	1	6			Hayes, Hezek^i......	1	1	2		
Pendergast, Stephen....	4	3	4			Gray, George......	1	2	4			Young, Stephen......	2		2		
Nutter, Ebenez^r........	2	2	4			Babb, John......	4		2			Hayes, Hezek^h, Jr......	1	2	2		
Mason, Lemuel........	1		2			How, Thos........	4		2			Leighton, James......	1	2	2		
Avery, Benjamin......	1	1	4			Brewster, Samuel......	2	1	2			Waldron, Isaac......	5	3	9		
Avery, Samuel, Jr.......	1	2	3			Hayward, John......	1	1	4			Drew, David......	2		3		
Avery, Moses........	1	1	2			Clark, Josiah......	1		1			Drew, David, Jr......	1	4	3		
Ayres, Thomas........	1		2			Foss, Isaiah......	1	4	3			How, Thos., 3^d......	1				
Ayres, Winthrop.......	1	2	3			Clark, Jacob......	1	3	5			Cate, Nich^o......	2		5		
Crocker, Solomon......	1	2	3			Howard, James......	2	1	6			Waterhouse, George....	2	3	5		
Lock, James, Jr........	1	3	2			Howard, Eph^m......	1	1	1			Cate, John......	4	1	5		
Drown, John..........	1	2	1			Lock, Jethro......	1		2								

STRAFFORD COUNTY—Continued.

BARRINGTON TOWN—continued.

NAME OF HEAD OF FAMILY.	Free white males of 16 years and upward, including heads of families.	Free white males under 16 years.	Free white females, including heads of families.	All other free persons.	Slaves.
How, Thos., Jr	1	1	1		
Watson, Benja	1	1	3		
Woodbury, Robert	1		1		
Waldron, Abraham	2	4	6		
Waterhouse, John	2		1		
Waterhouse, Benja	1	2	2		
Babb, Israel	2	1	2		
Jenks, Simeon	1	1	2		
Garland, Richd	1	2	5		
Blake, John	1	1	4		
Cate, Solomon	2		3		
Cate, Joseph	2	3	5		
Cate, Ebenzr	1	2	4		
Seavy, Wm	1	5	1		
Hale, Saml	4		1		
Caverly, Thos	4	2	4		
Hayes, Wm	1	2	2		
Pasley, Richd	1	2	4		
Pasley, Thos	2	1	1		
Brown, Nicho	2	2	7		
Brown, John	2	1	4		
Foss, Nathl	1	5	5		
Foss, George	1		1		
Sloper, Joshua	1	1	4		
Sloper, Joshua, Jr	1		6		
Meserve, Clems	2	3	2		
Stiles, Saml., Jr	1	1	2		
Stiles, Moses	2	3	3		
Stiles, John	1	2	3		
Stiles, Saml	1	1	2		
Young, Saml	2	2	2		
Montgomery, John	1		2		
Montgomery, Jona	1	2	5		
Huckins, John	1		2		
Huckins, John, Jr	1	1	3		
Otis, Thomas	1	1	1		
Otis, Hezeki	1	2	2		
Huckins, James	1	3	1		
Foss, George, 3d	2	4	5		
Foss, Richd	1	5	2		
Foss, Wm	1	3	1		
Foss, Sam, 5th	1		1		
Foss, Nathan	1		1		
Foss, John, Jr	1	1	3		
Foss, Mark	1	1	1		
Foss, Joshua, 4th	1		2		
Foss, Timothy	1	2	1		
Peavy, John	1	2	4		
Peavy, Joseph	1	2	2		
Foss, Joshua, 3d	1	2	1		
Foss, Mark, Jr	1	1	2		
Foss, James, Jr	1	1	2		
Hill, Henry	1	3	3		
Woodman, John	1		3		
Perkins, Joseph	1	3	3		
Hodgson, Amos	1		1		
Perkins, Timothy	3		1		
Perkins, Lemuel	2	2	5		
Winkley, Mark H:	1				
Jenness, John	3	1	4		
Tasker, Paul	1	1	1		
Hawkins, George	1	2	1		
Twombly, Joshua	2	2	6		
Willey, Isaac	2	1	2		
Willey, Leml	2	1	6		
Evans, Thos	1	1	3		
Evans, Edmund	1	4	6		
Evans, Leml	1	2	2		
Hanson, Ebenzr	1	1	1		
Leighton, Jededh	2	2	3		
Swain, John	2	2	6		
Boody, Joseph	1	3	3		
Swain, Isaiah	2	1	3		
Chesley, George	2	1	5		
Chesley, Danl	1		1		
Waldron, Aaron	3	6	3		
Waldron, David	1	1	2		
Caswell, Joseph	1	4	3		
Hall, Ebenzr	1	3	3		
Huckins, Israel	1	2	4		
Foss, Saml., Jr	2	1	3		
Foss, Saml., 6:	1		1		
Ham, John	1	3	4		
Hall, John	3	3	5		
Smith, Jabez	2	3	4		
Tasker, Samuel	1	1	2		
Tasker, Wm	1	4	1		
Tuttle, James	2	3	5		
Tasker, James	1	1	2		
Frost, George	1				
Watson, Nathl	2		4		
Daniels, Ephm	1	1	1		
Cook, Samuel	1		4		
Daniels, Joseph, Jr	1		3		
Cook, Reuben	1	1	3		
Cook, Peter	1		2		
Critchet, Richd	1	2	2		
Roberts, Nathl	1	2	5		
Caverly, Philip	3	5	3		
Hawkins, Benja	1		5		
Danielson, Devi	3		3		
Caverly, John	1	1	5		
Demeritt, Daniel	1	2	3		
Daniels, Joseph	2		4		
Gray, John	1		4		
Gray, Saml	1	1	3		
Davis, Jabez	1	1	1		
Tuttle, Elijah	2	2	5		
Caverly, Charles	1		4		
Winkley, Saml, Jr	1	1	4		
Evans, Isaac	1	1	2		
Drew, James	1	1	3		
Brown, Josiah	2		3		
Hanson, Nathl	1	2	5		
Hanson, Caleb	1		3		
Clark, Daniel	1	4	3		
Parsley, George	1	4	2		
Hall, Benja	2	2	6		
Waterhouse, Timothy	1	3	2		
Winkley, Saml	2	1	3		
Tuttle, Thos	2	1	5		
Winkley, Wm	1	2	1		
Caldwell, Silas	2		1		
Daniels, Clement	1	3	8		
Fowler, Wm	2		2		
Hall, Ralph	3	4	9		
Drew, Silas	2	3	6	1	
Kelley, Ebenzr	1	3	7		
Young, Andrew	1	1	2		
Young, Joseph	1		1		
Hixon, Perry	1		1		
Hall, Solomon	2	2	5		
Hart, Betty			2		
Tuttle, Daniel	1	2	3		
Jones, John	1	2	3		
Peirce, Israel	1	2	3		
Edgerly, Daniel	1	3	4		
Williams, Saml	2	3	3		
Langmaid, Saml	1	3	4		
Langmaid, John	1	1	2		
Dennie, Albert	1		1		
Sheperd, Jacob	1	2	4		
Bamford, Sarah	3		2		
Rollings, John	2	3	2		
Allison, Abraham	1	2	8		
Williams, Charles	1	1	4		
Jones, Peletiah	3	3	5		
McDonald, Wm	2		3		
McDonald, Wm., Jr	3		3		
McDonald, Wm., 3d	1	1	3		
Hill, John B:	1	4	3		
Daniels, Peletiah	2	2	8		
Mow, Peter	1		3		
Langley, Timo	1	3	2		
Chesley, James	1	2	3		
Swain, Daniel	1		2		
Swain, Micajah	1				
Swain, Richd	1		3		
Boadge, Richd	2		2		
Ayres, Mark	2		8		
Foy, Stephn	2	1	6		
Foy, John	2		2		
Roberson, Saml	1	2	3		
Swain, James	1	3	4		
Clark, James	2		1		
Clark, Moses	1		3		
Wille, Saml	1	1	2		
Wille, Benja	1		1		
Tebbetts, Peter	1		3		
Hussey, Richd	1	2	4		
Smith, Garland	3	3	4		
Haynes, Timo	2		4		
Caveno, John	2	1	5		
Caveno, Jeremh	1		1		
Libbey, Joseph	1	2	2		
Caswell, Timo	1	2	5		
Runnells, Michal	2	1	1		
Leighton, James	3	4	3		
Buzzell, Saml	3	1	8		
Buzzell, John	3	1	4		
Buzzell, Moses	1	1	1		
Buzzell, Benja	2	2	3		
Leighton, Isaac	3	1	3		
Leighton, Aaron	1	4	2		
Seaward, George	2		2		
Buzzell, Daniel	1		1		
Young, Isaac	2	3	1		
Boody, Azariah	1		2		
Boody, John	2	3	3		
Hill, John	2	4	6		
Hill, Wm	3		2		
Hill, Joseph	1	2	2		
Fernald, Isaac	2	3	7		
Seaward, George, Jr	1	1	4		
Dealing, Daniel	4	2	3		
Durgin, James	1		2		
Durgin, Thos	1	3	3		
Starboard, Simeon	2	2	6		
Starboard, Stephen	2	3	3		
Munsey, Timo	1	2	4		
Pearsy, Wm	2		4		
Gear, John	1		1		
Gear, Benja	1		2		
Gear, Saml	2		3		
Monson, Josiah	2		2		
Jackson, Ebenzr	2	2	1		
Sherburne, Isaac	2	2	4		
Sherburne, John	2		3		
Hale, Thos. R:	2	4	3		
Davis, Thos	3		3		
Balch, Benja	2	3	3	1	
Roberts, Jona	1	2	1		
Foss, Wm., Jr	1		2		
Pasley, Joshua	1				
Scott, James	1		1		
Harlott, Thos	2	3	5		
Hunskum, Aaron	3	1	4		
Evans, Wm., Jr	1	3	5		
Twombly, Moses	1	4	3		
Johnson, Joseph	1		4		
Fulker, Michal	1		1		
Rowe, Abraham	1	3	4		
Berry, Nathl., Jr	1		2		
Lord, Daniel	1	3	1		
Harlott, Josiah	1	3	3		
Swain, Jona	1		2		
Huntress, Enoch	1	2	2		
Stores, Aaron	1				
Fowler, Jona	1		2		
Jones, Abigail	1	3	3		
Buzzell, Rachel	1		4		
Ham, Esther		3	1		
Foy, John, Jr	2	3	5		
Brown, Edward	1	4	2		
Parsley, Saml	1	1	2		
Sawyer, Zaccheus	1	1	4		
Johnson, Thos	1	1	8		
Vincent, Wm	1	1	3		
Foss, George, Jr	2	3	2		
Woodman, Joseph	1		1		
Cramner, Thos	1	3	3		
Young, Moses	1				
Otis, Paul	1	3	5		
Gray, Reuben	1		2		
Caverly, Moses	2		2		
Stiles, John	1	2	3		
Parsley, John	3	7	3		
Hunskum, Aaron, Jr	1	3	2		
How, Thos	2		2		
Daniels, Elijah	1		1		
Daniels, Dodavah	1		2		
Evans, Wm	2		4		
Roberts, Saml	2		4		
Tasker, Daniel	1	3	1		
Blake, Wm	1	2	2		
Foss, John	1	1	1		
Scott, James	1		1		
Rowe, Wm	1	2	3		
Hall, Joseph, Jr	1		2		
Hays, Ebenzr	1	1	3		
Barry, George	1		3		
Gray, Solomon	1	3	3		
Hall, Elisha	1	3	1		
Hall, Elijah	1	2	2		
Hall, Isaac	3	1	8		
Willey, Thos	1	1	3		
Drew, Nathl	1	2	3		
Elliot, Wm	2		3		
Leathers, Ebenzr	1	3	4		
Bamford, Margrett		1	3		
Chesley, Ebenzr	1	2	4		
Chesley, Winthrp	1	2	1		
Leathers, Ebenz:	3	4	4		

STRAFFORD COUNTY—Continued.

CONWAY TOWN.

NAME OF HEAD OF FAMILY.	Free white males of 16 years and upward, including heads of families.	Free white males under 16 years.	Free white females, including heads of families.	All other free persons.	Slaves.
Densmore, Elijah	3		2		
Densmore, Elijah	1	1	1		
Densmore, Stephen	1	1	2		
Densmore, Solomon	1		2		
Willey, Saml	2	2	3		
Sherburne, Henry	1	1	7		
McClintock, Robt	1		1		
Hart, John	1	1	5		
Thompson, Solomon	1	2	4		
Lovejoy, Abigal	1		4		
Lovejoy, Jeremy	1	1	2		
White, Wm	1	1	1		
Thompson, John	1		2		
Canny, Benja	1	1	2		
Canny, Wm	1				
Abbot, Ephm	1		6		
Bean, Ebenzr	1	1	2		
Bean, Duglas	1		3		
Herrisman, Lenard	1	5	3		
Merrill, Amos	1	3	3		
Allen, David	1	1	5		
Merrill, Thomas	1	3	5		
Russell, Thomas	3	3	8		
King, Thomas	1	1	5		
Sparhawk, John	1				
Humphrey, Daniel	1				
Chase, John	2	3	5		
George, David	1		3		
George, Austin	1	1	1		
Harriman, Philip	2	3	3		
Lovejoy, Abial, junr	1	1	2		
Knox, Wm	1	4	2		
Lary, Daniel	1	4	3		
Hill, Charles	2	1	3		
Varnam, Benjamin	1	3	3		
Abbot, Jeremah	2	2	3		
Emery, Anthony	2	2	4		
Seavey, Jonathn	1	1	3		
Randal, Moses	3		4		
Randal, Hezah	1		3		
Thompson, Joseph	2	3	3		
Eastman, Noah	1	5	3		
Barnes, Amos	1		1		
Varnam, Ebenz	1				
McMellen, Andrew	8	1	8		
Eastman, Abiathr	4	5	4		
Loud, Joseph	1	1	1		
Springer, Saml	2	2	3		
Chadbourne, Wm	1		3		
Crocker, Roland	1	3	2		
Merrill, Jona	1	2	2		
Young, Jacob	1	2	2		
Odle, Joseph	3	2	6		
Eastman, Richd	2	2	5		
Dollaff, John	3	4	5		
Dollaff, Joseph	3	1	5		
Heath, Joshua	2	4	3		
Burbant, Ebenzr	2	3	3		
Porter, Nathl	1	2	5		
Walker, Barnet	1	2	1		
Walker, Steph	1	1	2		
Walker, Enoch	1	1	2		
Webster, Wm	1	2	1		
Walker, Timo	1		1		
Walker, Ezek	2		2		
Farrington, Jeremy	1	3	4		
Bozell, John	3	2	5		
Kimball, Richd	1	1	5		
Cross, Daniel	1	3	2		
Bayley, Thomas	1		3		
Newman, Thomas	2		2		
Edds, Isaac	1	1	1		
Howan, Saml	3	3	3		
Osgood, James	3	2	4		
Osgood, Benja	3	2	5		
Osgood, Moses	1	1	1		
Davice, Nehemiah	1				
Ross, Near	2		2		
Page, David	4	4	2		
Richard, Jo.	1		1		
Lewis, Je.	1	2	3		
Osgood, John	1	3	5		
Dunford, Eliph	1		3		
Kelly, Joseph	2	2	3		
Spring, Jedediah	1	1	2		
Page, Jeremiah	1	2	3		
Coffin, Steph	1	3	3		
Wilson, John	3		3		
Herrill, James	1	1	2		
Chase, Josiah	1	1	3		
Chase, Thos	1	1	1		
Coffin, Peter	1	2	3		

CONWAY TOWN—con.

NAME OF HEAD OF FAMILY.	Free white males of 16 years and upward, including heads of families.	Free white males under 16 years.	Free white females, including heads of families.	All other free persons.	Slaves.
Coffin, Nichl	1		2		
Smith, Caleb	1		1		
Coffin, James	1				
Coffin, Benja	1				
Steal, Wm	1	3	3		
Merrill, Enoch	2	2	6		

DOVER TOWN.

NAME OF HEAD OF FAMILY.	Free white males of 16 years and upward, including heads of families.	Free white males under 16 years.	Free white females, including heads of families.	All other free persons.	Slaves.
Brewster, Wm	1		2		
Cogswell, Amos	2	2	5	1	
Mard, Peter	1	1	2		
Tebbets, Ebenzr	2	2	5	1	
Peirce, Benja	3	2	7		
Cooper, Nathl	1	2	3	2	
Stagpole, Saml	2	3	4		
Watson, Wm	3	1	3		
Sweasy, Nathl	1	1	3		
Sawyer, Moses	2		2		
Green, Ezra	1	3	5		
Tebbets, Lydia	3	1	5		
Twombly, Wm	1	1	3		
Baker, Otis	4	1	3		
Clapham, Charles	1	3	6		
Randal, Danl	1	1	5		
Watson, Nathl	1	2	3		
Lindsey, John	1	1	3		
Ham, Nathl	1	3	4		
Watson, George	1	3	3		
Atkinson, Wm	3		3		
Tappan, Caleb	3	1	4		
Bragg, Saml	2		3		
Marshal, Lydia			2		
Rhemar, John	2		2		
Rawson, Jona	2	1	2		
Lovett, Joseph	1	1	3		
Dame, Theophilas	1	1	2		
Canney, Richd	2	1	3		
Kitteridge, Jacob	3	1	1		
Simmonds, Jona	1		2		
Neal, Eliph	2	2	3		
Peaslee, Amos	2	2	3		
Honig, Enoch	2	1	2		
Hanson, Jona	1	1	5		
Lord, Gersham	1	3	1		
Gray, Robert	6	1	3		
Libbey, Benja	3		5		
Titcomb, Benja	1	6	7		
Riley, John	1	2	6		
Friend, John	1	2	2		
Hanson, Wm	1		1		
Wingate, Moses	4	2	6		
Hodgdon, Caleb	7	1	5		
White, Timo	3	1	2		
Belknap, Joseph	1		1		
Cushing, Thos	1	3	6		
Folsom, Josiah	1	1	4		
Hanson, Anthony	2	3	1		
Osborn, Marble	1	1	3		
Hanson, David	2	3	5		
Footman, Thos	2	2	4		
Rhemack, James	1	3	3		
Watson, Isaac	3	1	4		
Gage, Jona	1	1	3		
Hanson, Elizza	1	3	4		
Hanson, John	1	1	3		
Hanson, Hannah	1		2		
Evens, Bethiah			1		
Johnson, Caleb	1	1	2		
Perkins, Elijah	2		2		
Taylor, James	1		3		
Patten, Stephn	2	2	5		
Waldron, Wm	1	1	3		
Jewett, David	1		4		
Calf, James	3	2	4		
Wentworth, Peggy	1	2	4	1	
Titcomb, John	1	2	4		
Dean, Benja	1	1	2		
Gilman, John P	4		3		
Evans, Joseph	1	1	3		1
Roberts, Stephen	1	2	1		
Gould, Isaiah	2	3	3		
Moulton, Wm. P	2		2	1	
Read, Michael	1	2	5		
Walker, Gidian	3		1		
Evens, Stephen	1		5		
Burnham, Joseph	2		1		
Young, Joseph	1	1	2		
Plummer, Joseph	1	1	1		
Shannon, Thos	3	2	9		
Horne, Heard	1	2	2		
Ricker, Wm	1	1	1		

DOVER TOWN—con.

NAME OF HEAD OF FAMILY.	Free white males of 16 years and upward, including heads of families.	Free white males under 16 years.	Free white females, including heads of families.	All other free persons.	Slaves.
Waldron, Charles	2		2		1
Smith, James	1	1	3		
Shannon, Wm	1		2		
Hanson, Sary			1		
Hanson, Ebenzr	1		1		
Eastes, Joseph	1	1	1		
Eastes, Saml	2	3	1		
Eastes, Caleb	1		2		
Walker, Mark	1	1	1		
Wingate, Joshua	2	1	3		
Kelley, Wm	2	1	2		
Hays, Ichabod	2	3	5		
Ricker, Nicho	3		3		
Yound, Ezra	2	1	4		
Eavens, Saml	3		3		
Evens, Miles	2	1	2		
Hanson, Richd	1	2	7		
Hays, Ezekel	2	5	5		
Hanson, Stephn	2	2	4		
Kelley, John	3	1	3		
Ham, Dod	2	2	4		
Twambly, Jotham	1	1	5		
Hody, Hannah	1		3		
Nute, Jona	1	1	2		
Hanson, John	1	2	1		
Hanson, Sarah	1	1	3		
Hanson, Solomen	1		3		
Hanson, Zachr	3	1	2		
Peverly, Wm	1		1		
Hanson, Anny	2	1	3		
Young, Ephm	1	1	1		
York, John	1	3	4		
Hall, John	1		2		
Quimby, Jacob	1		4		
Tebbits, Ichabod	2	3	5		
Coffin, Stephn	1	1	2		
Ingales, Jona	1		1		
Watson, Wentworth	1	3	3		
Emmerson, Wm	1		4		
Watson, Thoms	2	1	3		
Whitham, Ebijah	1		1		
Waldron, Wm	1	3	4		
Horne, Ichabod	1	3	4		
Horne, Paul	2	3	5		
Shackford, Saml	2	1	2		
Ham, Danl	1		2		
Ham, David	1	2	4		
Church, Benja	2		6		
Yound, Stephn	1	1	2		
Garland, John	1	1	3		
Ham, Ephm	2	1	5		2
Ham, Ephm., jr	1	3	2		
Ham, Marthy	1		2		
Hays, Mary	2		5		
Cushing, Danl	1	1	2		
Watson, Otis	1	1	4		
Witcher, Obediah	1	2	3		
Horne, James	2	2	3		
Horne, Isaac	2	2	7		
Baker, Ebenzr	1	1	1		
Ricker, George	1	2	2		
Chestey, Corodon	1	1	3		
Roberts, George	1	1	1		
Roberts, Abigal			4		
Conner, Mary		1	1		
Kimbal, David	1	1	1		
Ricker, Ruben	2	2	5		
Waldron, John	3	1	6		
Ricker, Saml	1		1		
Brown, Wm	6	3	5		
Sawyer, Jacob	3	1	4		
Hays, Benja	1	2	2		
Robertson, Meshick	2	4	3		
Heard, Saml	2		3		
Purrington, Zacheus	3	1	4		
Tripe, Richd	3	3	5		
Heard, John	3		4		
Sawyer, Stephn	4	5	3		
Varney, James	2		3		
Fisher, Jannalin	2		3		1
Emery, Moses	2		3		
Kimball, Ezra	2	1	1		
Varney, Paul	1	2	2		
Gage, John	1		2		3
Ham, John	3	2	4		
Trickey, John	2	1	2		
Coffin, Eliph	1	1	8		
Chase, Enoch	2	1	5		
Odiorn, John	2		2		
Horne, Wm	4		6		1
Hanford, John	1		4		
Heard, Danl	1	1	4		

STRAFFORD COUNTY—Continued.

DOVER TOWN—con.

NAME OF HEAD OF FAMILY.	Free white males of 16 years and upward, including heads of families.	Free white males under 16 years.	Free white females, including heads of families.	All other free persons.	Slaves.
Heard, Josiah	1	1	3		
Burrows, Thos	2	2	4		
Guppy, James	3	1	3		
Ham, Moses	2	1	3		
Ham, John	3	3	3		
Kimball, Richd	4		3		
Varney, Hanson	1	1	3		
Varney, John	1	1	3		
Kimball, Ezra	2	2	4		
Kimball, Paul	2	2	4		
Horne, Nathl	2	2	5		
Hanson, Thos	4	2	8	2	
Kimbal, Thos	1	2	4		
Waldron, Joseph	1	3	6		
Waldron, Richd	1	3	5		
Robertson, Timo	2	1	5		
Huzzey, Timo	2	1	3		
Huzzey, Paul	3	1	3		
Varney, Jedediah	2		3	1	
Waldron, John	1		2		
Bollo, Peter	1	2	2		
Waldron, Ephm	1	3	3		
Varney, Danl	4		4		
Varney, Joshua	1	5	3		
Varney, Shubal	1	5	3		
Varney, Amos	1	3	4		
Varney, Solomon	1		3	1	
Hartford, Nicholas	1	2	4		
Varney, Isaac	2	1	1		
Whitehouse, Joseph	2	4	2		
Land, Wm	1		8		
Varney, Nathan	2	1	5		
Varney, Ephm	1	1	4		
Varney, Bershl	1	1	3	1	
Kimbal, Ephm	1	1	4		
Wentworth, Jona	3	3	5		
Gage, John	1	3	4		
Hanson, Benja	2	1	3		
Ham, Ichabod	1	1	1		
Bickford, James	1	3	5		
Drew, Joseph	1	1	3		
Holden, Phebeus	1		2		
Foss, John	3	1	1		
Ham, Jona	1	2	1		
Varney, Joshua	1		3		
Land, Paul	1	2	2		
Ham, Ephm	2				
Door, Susannah	1		1		
Hanson, Joseph	4	1	3		
Watson, Lydia	2	2	4		
Ranson, Ebenzr	2	3	2		
Watson, James	1		3		
Perkins, Joshua	1		3		
Merrow, Thos	1	3	3		
Bantam, Ambros	5	1	3		
Pinkham, Paul	2	1	3		
Pinkham, Joseph	2	2	1		
Horne, Nathan	2	1	3		
Gage, Moses	2		5		
Roberts, Saml	2	1	2		
Crommel, Philip	1	2	2		
Bigford, Ephm	2	2	7		
Nason, Steph	1	1	3		
Young, Thos	4	1	4		
Canney, Benja	2	3	4		
Nason, John	1	2	2		
Pirkins, Adam	1		5		
Hodgdon, Moses	1	1	2		
Roberts, Aaron	2		2		
Tuttle, Wm	2	2	3		
Tuttle, Elijah	1		2		
Tuttle, James	3	2	2		
Austim, Nathn	1	1	3		
Tebbets, Jeremy	2		4		
Bigford, Jona	4	2	3		
Canney, Thos	2		3		
Hanson, Joseph	4	2	8		
Howard, Amos	2	1	2		
Hanson, George	3	2			
Varney, Robert	1		5		
Varney, James	2		2		
Austin, Stoton	2	1	4		
Varney, Elijah	1		4		
Nute, Isaac	4	3	4		
Roberts, Joseph	1	2	4		
Plummer, Ephm	3	1	4		
Pirkins, Patience			4		
Jackson, Wm	1	2	4		
Trickey, Jona	1	2	3		
Hodgdon, Anna	2	1	2		
Sise, Edwd	1		2		
Hodgdon, Shadrack	1	1	3		

DOVER TOWN—con.

NAME OF HEAD OF FAMILY.	Free white males of 16 years and upward, including heads of families.	Free white males under 16 years.	Free white females, including heads of families.	All other free persons.	Slaves.
Hanson, Miles	2		1		
Drew, Francis	3	2	4		
Stimpson, Joseph	2	1	3		
Drew, Elijah	2		1		
Drew, Joseph	1	7	3		
Peaslee, Elzabuth	1	1	4		
Jacobs, Joseph	2	1	3		
Twombly, Danl	1	3	1		
Nute, Paul	3		8		
Tuttle, Stephn	1	3	3		
Tuttle, David	1	2	3		
Tuttle, Andrew	2	3	4		
Tuttle, Ebenzr	3		5		
Tuttle, Paul	1		1		
Tuttle, Paul, jr	1	1	5		
Tuttle, Silas	3		2		
Tuttle, Isaac	1		3		
Colman, Woodman	1	1	3		
Emmerson, Dolly	2		1		
Emmerson, Michal	1	1	3		
Leighton, Wm	1	1	3		
Nute, Jona	2	1	3	1	
Smith, Daniel	3	2	2		1
Lummex, Nathl	2	1	3		
Merservy, Clemt	2	1	3		
Meservey, Paul	1	3	5		
Pinkham, Saml	1	2	5		
Jinkins, Joseph	1	2	1		
Libbey, James	2	2	4		
Hanson, Manle	2		2		
Hanson, Robert	2	2	2		
Twambly, Daniel	1	2	2	1	
Tarr, Andrew	2	3	4		
Pinkham, Danl	1	2	6		
Pinkham, John	6	3	4		
Roberts, Moses	4		4	1	
Canney, John	4		2	1	
Young, Susannah		2	3		
Clemment, Thos	1	3	2		
Clemment, Joseph	2		2		
Henderson, Danl	1		2		
Tuttle, John	1		1		
Tuttle, John	1	1	3		
Ellett, James	1		5		
Tripe, Silvanus	1	2	5		
Henderson, Howard	3	1	3	1	
Clement, Job	3	1	3		
Ham, Benja	1		2		
Pirkins, Joshua	3	6	5		

DURHAM TOWN.

NAME OF HEAD OF FAMILY.	Free white males of 16 years and upward, including heads of families.	Free white males under 16 years.	Free white females, including heads of families.	All other free persons.	Slaves.
Adams, Samuel	1	1	4		
Appleby, Joseph	1		2		
Appleby, Thos	1	1	1		
Angier, John	1		1		
Appleby, Wm	1	2	1		
Boynton, Joseph	1	4	2		
Burnham, Edward	1	1	1		
Blydenburgh, John	1		4		
Bunker, Benja	2	3	6		
Ballard, Joshua	3	2	5		
Ballard, Wm	1				
Burnham, Pike	1	1	3		
Bennett, Abrahm	1				
Bennett, John	4		4		
Burnham, Jeremh	3	1	2		
Bickford, Esther	1		3		
Burnham, Robert	1		1		
Bunker, Ephm	1	4	6		
Bickford, Reuben	2	1	4		
Burnham, John	2	3	3		
Burnham, Saml	1		2		1
Bickford, Benja	1				
Bickford, Winthrp	3		3		
Bennett, Eleazr	1	1	6	1	
Brock, Wm	2		4		
Butler, James	1				
Burleigh, Isaac	2	1	4		
Chesley, Joseph	3	1	3		
Coe, Curtis	2	3	4		
Critchet, James	1				
Chesley, Benja	2	1	2		
Chesley, Benja., Jr	2	5	6		
Crocksford, Daniel	1		6		
Chesley, Isaac	1	1	4		
Coldbath, John	1		2		
Chesley, Mary	1		4		
Cogan, Stephen	1	4	3		
Chesley, Col. Saml	2	4	1		
Chesley, Sarah			1		
Clough, Ephm., Jr	1				

DURHAM TOWN—con.

NAME OF HEAD OF FAMILY.	Free white males of 16 years and upward, including heads of families.	Free white males under 16 years.	Free white females, including heads of families.	All other free persons.	Slaves.
Clough, John	4		3		
Crummett, Jacob	2	1	6		
Crockett, Jona	2	1	3		
Daniels, Elipht	3	1	2		
Doe, Wiggin	1	3	2		
Drew, Saml	1				
Durgin, Mary					
Drew, Andrew	2	1	4		
Durell, Benmore	3	2	5		
Davis, Ephm	2		3		
Dame, George	1	1	7		
Denbo, Ichabod	2		2		
Demeritt, Israel	1	1	2		
Dame, Joseph	1	2	3		
Davis, James	1				
Davis, Daniel	1	1	2		
Demeritt, Nathl	2	1	4		
Durgin, James	1	3			
Davis, Love			1		
Doe, Benja	4				
Davis, David	4		4		
Davis, Thos	1				
Doe, Ebenzr	1	1	1		
Dame, John	1	3	7		
Durgin, Joseph	1	1	3		
Durgin, Trueworthy					
Durgin, Zebulon	3	1	4		
Davis, Levi	1		4		
Dearbon, James	2	3	3		
Durgin, Wm	2	2	2		
Durgin, Eliza			1	1	
Durgin, Stephn					
Emerson, Timothy	2	1	4		1
Edgerly, Ebenzr	1	4	3		
Edgerly, Samuel	4	1	3		
Edgerly, John	1		2		
Edgerly, Moses	1	1	2		
Edgerly, Moses, Jr	3	2	2		
Edgerly, Saml., Jr	1	2	2		
Emerson, Edward W	1	2	2		
Emerson, Joseph	1				
Frost, George	2	2	5		
Furnass, Patrick	1	3	2		
Folsom, James	1		1		
Griffin, Hannah	1	2	3		
Gillmore, James	2	1	1		
Grover, John	2	1	3		
Grant, Thos	1		2		
Hardy, Theops	1	1	5		
Ham, Thos	3	3	6		
Jackson, Laskey	1	2	3		
Jones, Stephn	3	1	5		1
Jenkins, Nathl	1	1	1		
Joy, Saml	2	3	4		
Jewett, Noah	3	2	5		
Jewell, Bradbury	1	1	3		
Jackson, Enoch	2	3	7		
Jones, Robert	1	1	4		
Knight, John	1		3		
Kent, Richd	1	3	1		
Kent, Lydia	2		2		
Leathers, Abednego	2		2		
Leathers, Benja	1	1	1		
Leighton, James	4	1	6		
Langley, Joseph	2	2	2		
Libby, John	1	2	3		
Lapish, Robert	2	4	6		
Leathers, Saml	1	1	1		
Leighton, Tobias	1	1	8		
Lapish, Robert, Jr	3	1	1		
Leathers, Robert	2	1	2		
Langley, Valentine	3	1	2		
Meserve, Timo	1	1	2		
Meader, Isaac	1	3	6		
Mathes, Valentine	4	6	3		
Mathes, Benja	1		2		
Meserve Ebenzr	1	2	3		
Muroe, John	1				
Neal, Joshua	2		4		
Nutter, Christophr	1	2	2		
Nutter, Lemuel	1				
Pinkham, Thos	2	1	7		
Pindexter, Thos	1	5	3		
Pendergast, Dennis	2		1		
Pendergast, Edmund	2	2	3		
Pendergast, John	2	1	5		
Pitman, George	1		3		
Pindar, Thos	1	4	2		
Perkins, Wm	1		1		
Pindar, Wm	1				
Pindar, Jeremh	1	1	4		
Pinkham, Abijah	1		3		

STRAFFORD COUNTY—Continued.

DURHAM TOWN—con.

NAME OF HEAD OF FAMILY.	Free white males of 16 years and upward, including heads of families.	Free white males under 16 years.	Free white females, including heads of families.	All other free persons.	Slaves.
Ryan, Michael	2	3	3		
Richards, Bartho	1	3	2		
Richardson, Joseph	1	1	5		
Spinney, Wm	2	2	2		
Sullivan, Jno	6		6		
Smith, Benja	4	1	1		
Smith, John, 3d	1		3		
Smith, Robert	1		2		
Smith, Jno	2	1	4	1	
Smith, Jno., Jr	4	1	4		
Smith, Ebenzr	1	4	2		
Stephen, Cornelius	1		5		
Stephens, Benja	2	2	4		
Stevens, John	3	1	2		
Stevenson, John	3		7		
Steel, Jona	1		3		
Starboard, John	1	3	4		
Spencer, Abednego	1		3		
Spencer, Jno	2		2		
Spencer, Levi	1	1	1		
Smith, Joseph	1	1	7		
Thomas, James	1				
Thomas, Joseph					
Thomas, Joseph, Jr	2	4	6		
Thompson, Ebenz	3	1	4		
Thompson, Ebenz., Jr	1	1	3		
Thompson, Jona	1	3	4		
Thompson, John	1	1	3		
Thompson, Edmund	1	2	3		
Thompson, Thos	1		4		
Tucker, Henry	2	3	8		
Taylor, Thomas	1	3	2		
Thompson, Benja	1				
Tripp, Benja	1		2		
Thompson, Samuel	2	1	1		
Woodman, Jona., Jr	2	5	3		
Woodman, Jona	4	4	5		
Williams, Jona	2		2		
Welch, John	1	4	3		
Wiggin, Issachar	1	5	3		
Wormwood, Joseph	4		3		
Willey, Benja	3		4		
Willey, Jeremh	1	3	3		
Willey, James	2	1	5		
Willey, Robert	1	1	2		
Willey, Theodore	3	2	4		
Willey, Jeremh., Jr	1		3		
Woodman, Jacob	1		4		
Woodman, Lemuel	1		5		
Willey, Valentine	1		1		
Young, Joseph	3	1	3		
Yeaton, Saml	1	4	5		
Watson, Henry	1		1		
Jackson, James	1	1	2		
Dealing, Abigail		1	3		
Davis, Micah	2		5		
Leathers, Ezekl	1		1		
Willey, Thos	1	2	3		
Bunker, Zachr	1	4	2		
Cromwell, Saml	1		1		
Cromwell, Saml., Jr	2	2	2		
Bickford, Jona	1	2	1		
Bickford, Eliakim	1	1	3		
Smart, John	1		3		
Smart, Bartho	1		3		
Beck, Abigail	1	1	2		
Rollings, Sarah			1		
Coldbath, Sarah			2		
Durgin, Henry	1	1	2		
Durgin, Philip	1		2		
Sharp, Abigail		1	2		
Gerrish, Peggy			1		
Dearbon, Mary		1	2		
Willey, Mary			3		
Smith, John, 4:	1	1	1		
Noble, Stepha	2	2	3		
Drisco, Sarah			1		
Bean, Ebenez	1	1	2		
Flint, Polly		1	3		
Marston, Levi	3	3	3		
Simson, Wm	1	2	4		
Banter, John	1	3	3		
Folsom, Joseph	1	1	2		
Langley, Jno	1		1		
Eastman, Wm	1	1	1		
Webster, Reuben	1		2		
Chace, Oliver	1				
Drew, Joseph	1		1		
Smith, Jonatha	1		2		
Dutch, Jno	1				
Nutter, Matthias	1	1	2		
Crocket, Jno	1		1		
Hunskum, Lucy			2		

DURHAM TOWN—con.

NAME OF HEAD OF FAMILY.	Free white males of 16 years and upward, including heads of families.	Free white males under 16 years.	Free white females, including heads of families.	All other free persons.	Slaves.
Swain, Razar	1		2		
Durant, John	1	2	1		
Parsons, Jona	1		1		
Cromwell, Mary		1	3		
Evans, Stephen	1		5		

EATON TOWN.

NAME OF HEAD OF FAMILY.					
Hatch, David	2	1	2		
Cook, Ebenez	1	3	1		
Mason, Jona	2	3	5		
Kennett, John	1	4	4		
Wickerson, Shaver	1	2	4		
Flanders, Typrus	1	3	4		
Wesherso, Josha	1	4	3		
Kineson, Josha E	1	3	3		
Banfield, Joseph	1		3		
Banfield, Saml	2	1	5		
Burk, Thoms	1		3		
Danford, Timo	1	1	3		
Danford, Thoms	1	2	4		
Danford, Saml	1	1	1		
Danford, James	2	3	5		
Danford, Thoms	3		2		
Glime, John	1		2		
Robertson, Wm	1	2	2		
Turist, Isaac	1	1	4		
Banfield, John	1	2	2		
Mooney, Jona	2	4	2		
Jackson, Saml	1	3	2		
Jackson, Philip	1	2	3		
Jackson, James	2		2		
Jackson, Ebenz	1		1		
Hill, Henry	1		3		
Jackson, James	1	3	4		
Wood, Henry	1	2	3		
Colby, Joseph	3	2	4		
Canfield, George	1	3	4		
Colby, Colman	1		1		
Piskim, Ebenez	1	3	3		
Tappan, Saml	1		2		
Brier, Saml	1	1	2		
Blasdell, Henry	3	1	1		
Gannett, Seth	2	1	3		
Colby, Habbert	1		1		
Gannett, Mathw	1	2	2		
Parsons, Josiah	1	2	2		
Washborn, Alden	1	1	2		
Wead, Henry	3	2	1		
Blasdell, Jacob	1	2	4		
Varney, Silas	2	2	5		
Hatch, Saml	1		1		

EFFINGHAM TOWN.

NAME OF HEAD OF FAMILY.					
Philbrook, Simion	1	1	2		
Davice, Eleazr	2	3	5		
Palmer, Wm	1	2	2		
Leavett, John	1		1		
Titcomb, James	2	2	2		
Hobs, Nathl	2	3	4		
Taylor, Wm	1	2	2		
Taylor, John	1		1		
Mersan, Jona	1	1	1		
Cooper, Moses	1	3	4		
Maloon, Joseph	2	2	3		
Hobs, Benja	1	1	2		
Palmer, Joseph	2	1	2		
Drake, John	1	1	2		
Drake, Ware	4		1		
Dearborne, Joseph	2	1	1		
Dearborne, Benja	1	2	4		
Clements, Job	1	1	1		
Wedgwood, Josih	1		1		
Wedgwood, John	1		1		
Leavett, Carr	1	2	4		
Dearborne, Asael	1	1	1		
Lampree, Benja	2	1	3		
Brown, Nathl	1	1	2		
Masters, Jerim	1	4	2		
Taylor, Richd	1	2	2		
Marsten, Abrahm	1	1	2		
Lord, George	1	1	2		
Costalow, John	2				1
Leavett, Jerim	1	3	3		
Taylor, Josiah	1	1	2		

GILMANTOWN TOWN.

NAME OF HEAD OF FAMILY.					
Avery, Joseph	1		1		
Avery, Joseph, Jr	1	1	2		
Avery, David	2	1	3		
Allen, James	1		3		

GILMANTOWN TOWN—continued.

NAME OF HEAD OF FAMILY.	Free white males of 16 years and upward, including heads of families.	Free white males under 16 years.	Free white females, including heads of families.	All other free persons.	Slaves.
Avery, Jonathan	1	1	4		
Allen, Reuben	2	2	3		
Allen, Reuben, Jr	1	1	1		
Avery, Saml	1		4		
Badger, Joseph	1	2	3		
Bean, Jude	2	5	4		
Batchelor, Jonathan	1	3	1		
Cogswell, Thos	3	6	3	2	
Clough, Simeon	3	1	1		
Clough, Jonathan	1				
Clark, Joseph	2	3	2		
Clough, Saml	2	4	3		
Clough, Abner	3	1	4		
Clough, Isaiah	2		6		
Clough, Daniel	1	4	4		
Conner, Jeremiah	2	1	1		
Conner, Jeremiah, Jr	1	2	3		
Chase, James	2	1	2		
Cogswell, Jeremy	2	2	5		1
Conner, Jonathan	1	1	2		
Dudley, Stephen	2	1	4		
Dudley, John	1	2	4		
Drew, Theophilus	1	2	2		
Dow, Benja	2	1	3		
Dow, Benja, Jr	1	2	3		
Elkins, Jasper	2	3	7		
Edgerly, Dorothy	2	1	5		
Elkins, Nathan	1	2	3		
Evans, Abner	2	3	5		
French, Benja	3		4		
Foss, Daniel	1	4	2		
Flanders, Jonathan	1	2	3		
Flanders, Thomas	1		2		
Flanders, Thomas, Jr	1	2	1		
Fifeild, Samuel	1	1	2		
Gilman, Jonathan, 3d	1	3	3		
Gillman, Jotham	2	1	6		
Gale, Daniel	3		3		
Gillman, John, Jr	1		1		
Gillman, Stephen	1		1		
Gillman, Edward	1	3	1		
Gillman, Antipas	1	1	3		
Gillman, Edward, Jr	2	3	5		
Gillman, Benja	1	2	4		
Gillman, Joshua, Jr	5	4	3		
Gillman, Colo. Antipas	3	1	4		
Gillman, Winthrop, Jr	2	1	1		
Glidden, Andrew	2	1	6		
Gillman, Nathl	1				
Hayes, Thomas	1	2	3		
Hill, Doct. John	2	2	4		
Hunt, Henry	1	2	3		
Hatch, Hosea	1	2	7		
Hutchinson, Elisha	1	2	2		
Hutchinson, Jonathan	2	1	2		
Hutchinson, Stephen	1	3	3		
Hatch, Samuel	1		1		
Kimbol, Trueworthy	2		3		
Kimbol, Nathl	1	4	3		
Lowger, Nehemiah	1	4	4		
Lougee, Jesse	1	1	8		
Lougee, Gillman	2	2	4		
Lougee, John, Jr	3	1	6		
Lougee, Henry	3		4		
Morrell, Lt. Jeremiah	3	1	4		
Morrell, Ephm	1		2		
Morrell, Nathan	2	4	3		
Mudget, Simeon	1	2	5		
Melcher, John	1		3		
Marston, John	1	1	3		
Meserve, John	3		4		
Morrell, Micajah	1	1	4		
Marsh, Noah	2	3	5		
Meader, David	1	3	5		
Marsh, Joseph	2	2	3		
Melcher, John, Jr	1	2	1		
Nelson, John	2		4		
Potter, Saml	1	1	2		
Potter, Thos	1				
Potter, Joseph	1	1	3		
Potter, Israel	1	1	3		
Parsons, William	1		1		
Parson, Joseph	2	2	5		
Page, David	1		4		
Porter, Emerson	3		1		
Page, Ebenzr	1				
Page, Winslow	1	2	2		
Page, True	1	1			
Page, Moses	3		4		
Page, John	1				
Page, Benja	2		2		
Parsons, Ebenzr	1	2	3		

STRAFFORD COUNTY—Continued.

GILMANTOWN TOWN—continued.

NAME OF HEAD OF FAMILY.	Free white males of 16 years and upward, including heads of families.	Free white males under 16 years.	Free white females, including heads of families.	All other free persons.	Slaves.
Rogers, John	1	3	3		
Ross, Jonathan	3	2	4		
Richardson, Jeremiah	2	1	3		
Sanborn, Deac John	3		4		
Sheperd, John	3	1	6		
Smith, Doctr Wm	3		7		
Sheperd, Saml	2	3	3		
Smith, Robinson	1	3	1		
Swain, John	1	1	1		
Swain, John, Jr	1		2		
Swain, Theops	1		3		
Sibley, William	2	4	5		
Swain, Stephen	1				
Sawyer, Maths	1	2	1		
Tilton, John	1	3	7		
Tilton, Samuel	1		1		
Willson, Capt. Nathl	2	2	2		
Willson, Nathl., Jr	1	1	1		
Wattson, Zebediah	2		3		
Young, Dudley	3	1	5		
Lougee, Pitts	1				
Edgerly, Benja	2		8		
Roberts, Silas	1		4		
Gilman, Wid. Rebecca	1		4		
Lougee, Joseph	1				
Barter, Henry	1	2	2		
Parsons, Willm., Jr	1	3	3		
Powers, Walter	1	2	6		
Fox, John	1	1	2		
Judkins, Josiah	1	2	1		
Tilton, David	1	2	2		
Jackson, Joseph	1		2		
Edgerly, John	1	1			
Clark, Ezra	1		2		
Gillman, John	2	5	5		
Perkins, Dorothy		1	2		
Bean, John	1		1		
Peters, Robinson				7	
Siveal, Moses	1				
Dean, Thos	1		1		
Glidden, John	1	3	3		
Gale, Joseph	1		3		
Thompson, John	1	3	4		
Soverain, Jonathan	1	2	4		
Odlin, Elisha	1	4	2		
Smith, Revd Isaac	3	2	5		
Avery, Josiah	2		4		
Badgor, Peasly	2	3	3	1	
Bean, David	2	4	4		
Bean, Simeon	3	5	5		
Bean, John, Jr	1	1	1		
Bean, Stephen	3	2	4		
Bean, Caleb	2		3		
Bean, Gideon	1	2	3		
Batchelor, Isaac	2	2	6		
Bede, Barzilla	2	2	2		
Brown, Saml	3	6	2		
Buswell, John	3	2	8		
Bickford, Paul	1	3	6		
Bradford, Joshua	1	3	5		
Bond, John	1		2		
Brown, Saml., Jr	1	1	1		
Copp, Simeon	2	2	3		
Courier, Charles	2	1	8		
Clifford, Joseph	2	3	6		
Conner, Jeremiah, 3d	1		2		
Dean, Benja. W	1	1	1		
Dow, Capt. Noah	1	3	3		
Dow, Jonathan, Jr	3	3	3		
Dow, Nathl	1	2	3		
Dame, Willm	1	2	4		
Dow, Jona, 3d	1		1		
Elkins, Jona	1	1	3		
Eastman, Lt. Ebenzr	2	5	4		
Elkins, John	1		1		
Elkins, James	1	2	1		
Elkins, Daniel	1	1	3		
Elsworth, David	1	2	3		
Folsom, Peter	1		1		
Folsom, Lt. Peter, Jr	4	3	5		
Folsom, Peter, 3d	1	4	4		
Folsom, Daniel	3	4	4		
Fifield, David	2	1	5		
Folsom, Joseph	1		1		
Gillman, Daniel	1		2		
Gillman, Jona	2		5		
Gilman, Saml	1	3	4		
Greely, Col. Samuel	3	4	6		
Gale, Jacob	2	1	2		
Grant, Danl	1	3	2		
Garinan, Joseph	2	2	9		
Gilman, Zebulon	1	2	1		

GILMANTOWN TOWN—continued.

NAME OF HEAD OF FAMILY.	Free white males of 16 years and upward, including heads of families.	Free white males under 16 years.	Free white females, including heads of families.	All other free persons.	Slaves.
Hutchinson, Levi	1	2	3		
Hutchinson, Dudley	2	1	3		
Huckins, John	1	1	3		
Huckins, Jos. Jr	2		3		
Huckins, Jos., 3d	1		2		
Huckins, Joseph, Sen	1		3		
Hoit, Ezekiel	1	2	2		
Hutt, Nathan	1	3	4		
Hanniford, John	1	2	1		
Jones, Joseph	1		1	1	
Jones, Richard	2	2	3		
Jones, James	1	1	2		
Kelly, Jacob	1	3	6		
Kelly, Micajah	1	2	4		
Libby, Ephm	2	2	4		
Moulton, Robert	1		3		
Moulton, Daniel	1	1	1		
Moody, Capt. John	3	2	3		
Morrell, Thomas	1	2	3		
Morrell, Joseph	2	2	2		
Mudget, Edwd. Scribner	1	6	5		
Mudget, Samuel	2	3	4		
More, Joshua	1		2		
Bean, John	1	3	6		
Merrell, Paul	2	1	1		
Nelson, Jona	1	3	3		
Osgood, Saml	2	4	5		
Osgood, Reuben	2	1	6		
Osgood, Joseph	2	2	5		
Price, Willm	3		3		
Page, Andrew	1	3	7		
Price, Wm., Jr	1	4	2		
Parsons, Abraham	1	2	3		
Prescott, Saml	1	1	3		
Rand, Lemuel	1	1	2		
Rand, Wm	1		3		
Rogers, Robert	3	3	7		
Randlett, Charles	2	6	4		
Smith, Saml., Jr	1	2	3		
Smith, Benja	3	2	2		
Stevens, Benja	2		2		
Sanborn, Jeremiah	2	2	5		
Sanborn, David	1		3		
Sanborn, Abiather	1		2		
Sergeant, Jonathan	1	1	6		
Sweat, Elisha	1	1	4		
Sanborn, Zadock	1		3		
Sweat, John	1	6	2		
Stevens, Ebenzr	1	5	3		
Smith, Abraham	1		2		
Smith, Timothy	1	5	1		
Smith, Saml	1	2	3		
Thurston, Saml	1	2	6		
Thurston, John	1	1	5		
Tilton, David	1	2	2		
Tucker, John	2		2		
Tucker, Jacob	2		2		
Tilton, Nathl	2		2		
Weeks, Mathias	5	2	6		
Wade, Edward	1	2	5		
Thompson, Wm	1	4	4		
Young, Joseph	2	1	2		
Gilman, Lt. Peter	1	2	4		
Gilman, Nichl	3	3	2		
Ladd, Nathl	2		1		
Evans, Danl	1	2	6		
Avery, Jona	1	1	5		
Lougee, Jona	1	3	4		
Badger, Enoch	2		5		
Jackson, Joseph	2	2	3		
Hook, John	1	2	3		
Perry, Mary			3		
Wallis, Ceaser				4	
Gillman, Juda	2		2		
Avery, Josiah, Jr	1				
Avery, Saml	1		3		
Ames, James	1	3	3		
Ames, David	1	2	3		
Blasdel, John	2	1	4		
Bean, Edward, Jr	1				
Bean, Levi	1	5	3		
Brown, Jethro	1		2		
Bickford, Ephm	1	3	3		
Bennett, Andrew	1	2	1		
Bennett, John, Jr	1	2	3		
Bennett, John	2		1		
Bradbury, John	1	3	4		
Brown, Ephm., Jr	1		2		
Boadge, Benja	1	1	4		
Brown, Ephm	1	1	1		
Badger, Joseph, Esq	3	2	4		
Badger, Joseph, 3d	1	1	1		

GILMANTOWN TOWN—continued.

NAME OF HEAD OF FAMILY.	Free white males of 16 years and upward, including heads of families.	Free white males under 16 years.	Free white females, including heads of families.	All other free persons.	Slaves.
Badger, Joseph, 4:	1	2	2		
Blasdel, Saml	1	3	1		
Burley, John	1	1	3		
Chace, John	1		3		
Clark, Wm	1		3		
Clark, Saml., Jr	1	2	2		
Clough, Daniel	1	3	4		
Courier, Ebenzr	1		5		
Clark, Saml	2	3	5		
Clark, John	1				
Cotton, John	2	1	6		
Cotton, John, Jr	2	4	5		
Chace, Green	1		1		
Chace, Stephen	1	2	4		
Clough, John	1	1	3		
Chapman, David	1	3	1		
Danford, Edward	1	2	3		
Wallingford, Cato				2	
Dow, Jona	2	2	4		
Davis, Malachi	1				
Edwards, John	1		4		
Edwards, William	1	6	2		
Edwards, Jona., Jr	3	2	3		
Edwards, Jona	2	2	2		
French, Israel	1		2		
Farrar, Israel	4				
Farrar, Jeduthen	1		4		
Folsom, Jonathan	1	5	5		
Folsom, John	1	2	4		
Folsom, Benja	1	1	2		
Foster, Thomas	2	2	8		
Frowhawk, Thomas	1	5	3		
Flanders, Joseph	1	1	5		
Folsom, Nichl	1	4	1		
Gilman, Saml. Folsom	2	1	2		
Flagg, Jonas	2		3		
Gilman, Wm., Jr	1	2	5		
Gilman, Wint	1	2	2		
Gale, Stephen	1	3	5		
Gale, Barthe	1	1	4		
Gillman, Andrew	1		2		
Gilman, John, Jr	1	2	3		
Gilman, Ezekl	1	1	2		
Gilman, Dudley	1	2	2		
Gilman, Levi	1	1	3		
Gilman, Jona., Jr	1	2	4		
Hoyt, Danl	2	2	4		
Hoyt, Simeon	2	3	5		
Hunt, Wm	1		3		
Hunt, Abel	1	3	3		
Hunt, Enoch	1	2	3		
Hodgson, Scammon	4	2	6		
Hadley, Stephen	1	1	2		
Hoyt, Nathan	1		3		
Hale, David	1				
James, Caleb	1				
Jones, Joseph, Jr	2		3		
James, Lt. Jabez	1	2	2		
Jewitt, Saml	1	1	2		
Jewett, Jacob	1	1	3		
Jewett, Saml., Jr	1		4	1	
James, Benja	2	5	4		
Knoles, Joseph	1	2	2		
Leavitt, Levi	1	1	1		
Leavitt, Jona	1	2	3		
Leavitt, Stephn	1	2	5		
Ladd. Saml	4	4	4		
Lougee, Wm	1	1	2		
Morrison, Daniel	1	1	2		
Morrison, Jona	2	2	3		
Marston, Caleb	1		4		
Morrison, John	1	2	6		
Morrison, Alexr	2	2	5		
Moulten, Robert, Jr	1	2	1		
Marsh, John	1	1	6		
Mason, Simeon	1	4	2		
Morrell, Ephm., Jr	1	2	4		
Marsh, Henry	1	2	2		
Maxwell, Saml	1		2		
Plummer, Henry	2	3	3		
Perkins, Jonathn	1		2		
Prescott, Jonathn	1	1	1		
Pilsbury, David	2	1	2		
Prescott, Stepha	1	3	2		
Page, David	1	2	3		
Page, Reuben	1		2		
Prescott, Dudley	3	2	4		
Bansons, John	1	1	3		
Richardson, Jery	1		2		
Randlett, Jacob	1		2		
Randlett, Jona	1	1	3		

STRAFFORD COUNTY—Continued.

GILMANTOWN TOWN—continued.

NAME OF HEAD OF FAMILY.	Free white males of 16 years and upward, including heads of families.	Free white males under 16 years.	Free white females, including heads of families.	All other free persons.	Slaves.
Rand, Filbrook	1	1	4		
Randlett, Josiah	1	2	2		
Richardson, Benja	1	1	1		
Robertson, Josiah	1		1		
Smith, Saml	1	1	6		
Sanders, George	1	1	3		
Sweasy, John	1	4	1		
Sanborn, Noel	1	5	3		
Stevens, Daniel	3		3		
Sanborn, Jona	1	1	1		
Tayler, Jeremy	1		1		
Sawyer, Josiah	1	1	3		
Smith, Ebenzr	1	2	1		
Sewall, Thomas	1	5	1		
Swain, Nathan	1				
Smith, Oliver	1		4		
King, Jeremy	1		3		
Thurston, Benja	2		9		
Taylor, Simeon	1	3	4		
Taylor, Thos	2	2	2		
Taylor, John	1	3	1		
Thompson, Jona	1	3	2		
Thompson, David	1	1	3		
King, Dudley	2	2	3		
Weeks, Josiah	2	2	2		
Weeks, Noah	1	2	3		
Weymouth, George	1	4	6		
Weeks, John	1		3		
Wadley, John	1		2		
Weeks, John, Jr	2	1	2		
Young, Joseph	3		3		
Woodman, Andrew	1		3		
Webster, Nathl	1	2	4		
King, wido Hannah	1		4		
Folsom, wid. Mehetl			3		
Gilman, Sarah	1		2		
Burnham, Benja	1	5	1		
Emerson, wid. Abigail		1	4		
Fifield, John	1		2		
Dennett, George	1	3	2		
Rowell, Wm	1	1	2		
Marsh, Isaac	1	3	1		
Dearbon, Sherburne	1	5	3		
Rowe, Jacob	1	1	1		
Taylor, Jona	2		1		
Gale, Nathl	1	1	1		
Young, Eleazer	1	1	5		
Dysa, John	1		2		
Smith, Jona	1	1	1		
Davis, Moses	1		2		
Blasdel, Jacob	1	2	1		
Gilman, Saml., Jr	1	1	1		
Shelly, Jona	1		2		
Allen, John	1	1	4		
Prescott, Wm	1		1		
Tossey, Danl	1				
Perkins, True	1	5	3		
Gilman, Wm	1	1	3		
Mudget, Benja	2	1	2		
Morrison, Wm., Jr	1	2	4		
Morrison, Saml	1	2	5		
Davis, Elijah	1	3	3		
Black, Ebenz					4
Grant, Louisa			1		
Evans, Deborah			1		
Page, wid. Judah		2	2		
Babson, Betty	1		2		
Layn, John	1	1	1		
Boyd, John	1				

LEE TOWN.

NAME OF HEAD OF FAMILY.	Free white males of 16 years and upward, including heads of families.	Free white males under 16 years.	Free white females, including heads of families.	All other free persons.	Slaves.
Sias, Joseph	3		3		
Noble, Thos	2	1	4		
Burnham, Joshua	1		2		
Emerson, Samuel	2	2	3		
Emerson, Micah	2	1	2		
Sias, John	1	3	3		
Bunker, James G.	2	2	2		
Glidden, Wm	2	4	7		
Weymouth, Wm	3	4	5		
Runlett, Charles	3		3		
Kenniston, Josiah	1	3	2		
Watson, Andrew	1	3	6		
French, Wm	2	2	9		
Meader, Joseph	1	3	3		
Thompson, Robert	4		4		
Dow, Jona	1	2	1		
Mather, Gideon	2		3		
Fox, Elijah	5	2	7		
Runnells, Jona	3		6		

LEE TOWN—continued.

NAME OF HEAD OF FAMILY.	Free white males of 16 years and upward, including heads of families.	Free white males under 16 years.	Free white females, including heads of families.	All other free persons.	Slaves.
Cartland, Joseph	2	1	3		
Dutch, George	2		3		
Moses, Timothy	2	2	4		
Brackett, James	2	3	4		
Woodman, Mary	1	1	5		
Durgin, Josiah	1		2		
Folsom, Enoch	2	1	1		
Tuttle, Thos	2	3	3		
Rowlins, Wm	1	1	3		
Smith, Saml	1	1	4		
Sawyer, Saml	1	2	4		
Burnham, Joshua, Jr	1	3	1		
White, Wm	2		2		
Rowlins, Thos	1	4	4		
Weymouth, Dennett	1	1	1		
Glidden, Saml	1	1	4		
Huckins, Simon	2	1	5		
Ladd, Jeremh	1	1	3		
Sanborn, Phineas	2		3		
Durgin, Josiah, Jr	1	1	4		
Mathes, Francis	1	1	2		
Folsom, Asa	3	1	8	2	
Tuttle, Joseph	1	1	2		
Fernald, Amos	2	1	6		
Emerson, Joseph	1	3	6		
Cartland, Tobias	1		2		
Watson, John, Jr	2		2		
Watson, Daniel	1		1		
Whidden, Ichabod	1	1	4		
Davis, Obediah	1		1		
Stevens, Hale	1	2	3		
Ordway, Nehemiah	1		2		
Emerson, Charles	1		2		
Meder, Paul	1	1	3		
Hill, Reuben	3		3		
Tuttle, George	1	2	2		
Stevens, Jona	4	1	4		
Stevens, Nathl	4	2	1		
Davis, David	2		3		
York, Thos	1	1	2		
York, Robert	1		3		
York, Eliphalet	1	3	1		
Davis, James	2		4		
Frost, Winthrop	2		1		
Tufts, Henry	2		1		
Hilton, Andrew	2		4		
Durgin, Saml	2	5	2		
Davis, James	1	3	2		
Burleigh, Josiah	2	2	8		
Burleigh, Joseph	1	2	1		
Burleigh, Saml	2		3		
Doodey, Joseph	1		2		
Tuttle, George, Jr	1		3		
Wattson, David	1	1	2		
Thompson, Jona	4	1	6		
Dame, Hunking	2	3	4		
Runnells, Job	1	2	5		
Laskey, Wm	2	1	6		
Clough, Zaccheus	3		4		
Clough, Nathl	1		1		
Langley, Samuel	1	2	1		
Jenkens, Wm	2	1	4		
Hill, Saml	2		2		
Giles, Paul	4	1	3		
Mathes, Samuel	5		4		
Follett, Joseph	3		5		
Randall, Miles	2		1		
Langley, Thos	1	3	3		
Shaw, Daniel	2	3	5		
Bickford, Micah	2		3		
Bartlett, Josiah	2	7	2		
Davis, John	2		2		
Davis, Clement	1	2	5		
Manson, Aaron	2	3	4		
Furber, Eli	2		1		
Elliot, Richard	1	3	5		
Jenkins, James	2		4		
Jenkins, John	1	2	2		
Hart, Nathl	1	2	2		
Faxon, Christopher	2		2		
Martin, Richd	1	3	5		
Critchet, Elias	1	2	3		
Runnells, Miles	2	1	2		
Randall, Ebenzr	1		1		
Randall, Thos	2	3	3		
Bickford, Ranah	1		3		
Plummer, Dodavah	2	1	3		
Footman, John	1	2	5		
Mitchell, John	2	2	4		
Burnham, Israel	1				
Randall, Joseph	2	2	1		
Shaw, George	1	4	5		

LEE TOWN—continued.

NAME OF HEAD OF FAMILY.	Free white males of 16 years and upward, including heads of families.	Free white males under 16 years.	Free white females, including heads of families.	All other free persons.	Slaves.
Randall, John	1	3	5		
Garland, Gideon	1	2	3		
Cartland, Elijah	1	2	3		
Langley, Thos., Jr	1		1		
Wigglesworth, Samuel	1		1		
Langley, Levi	1	2	2		
Chesley, Joseph	1	2	2		
Emerson, Smith	2	2	4		
Chesley, Daniel	2		2		
Randall, Wid. Sarah			3		
Leathers, Edward	1		3		
Snell, Jno	2	2	7		
Boadge, Sarah			3		
Davis, Aaron	2	4	3		
Munsey, David	2	1	3		
Jones, John	1	1	4		
Chesley, Hannah	1	2	2		
Williams, John	1		3		
Williams, John, Jr	1	1	6		
Hill, Wm	1	3	3		
Hill, Edward	2		4		
Layn, Jno	3	2	4		
Caldwell, Wm	1		1		
Randall, Simon	1	1	1		
Boadge, Josiah	1	2	1		
Leathers, John	1	4	3		
Lammas, Moses	1		5		
Clay, Joseph	2	3	1		
Williams, Isaac	1		2		
Leathers, Aaron	1	3	2		
Hill, George	1		2		
Drew, John	1	1	2		
Edgerly, James	1		2		
Clay, Samuel	1	2	1		
Williams, John 4th	1				
Demeritt, Andrew	1		2		
Small, Benja	1		2		
Hill, John	1	1	3		
Hutchins, Thos	2		1		
Glover, Jno	1		3		
Glover, Richd	1		1		
Leathers, Wm	1		4		
Small, Edward	1		3		
Davis, Jno	1	3	2		
Runnells, Nathan	2	1	3		
Follett, Jno	2		2		
Bickford, Saml	2		4		
Wiggin, Winthrop	1	1	3		
Wiggin, Thos	1	2	4		
Thompson, Solomon	2	1	2		
Randall, Nathl	1	1	1		
Sullivan, James	1	1	2		
Leathers, Paul	1		3		
Hervy, Samuel	1	1	2		
Hoit, William	1		2		
Willey, Stephen	1		5		
Palmer, Wm	1	2	2		
Sias, Phepe	1		1		
Hide, Jno	1		1		
Bunker, James, Jr	1	2	1		
French, Saml	1		2		
Veasy, Saml	2	1	7		
Stephens, Benja	1	3	4		
York, James	2	1	2		
Trefethern, Moses	1	3	1		
Tufts, Lydia			5		
Glover, Timothy	1	2	2		
Clay, Jno	1		1		
Jones, Matthias	3		4		

MADBURY TOWN.

NAME OF HEAD OF FAMILY.	Free white males of 16 years and upward, including heads of families.	Free white males under 16 years.	Free white females, including heads of families.	All other free persons.	Slaves.
Austin, Elijah	1	1	6		
Ainmet, Thos	1	1	1		
Boadge, Samuel	1		6		
Bunker, Enoch	1	2	3		
Kenney, Moses	3	2	5		
Kenny, Isaac	2	3	2		
Cook, Hezekiah	2		2		
Cook, Jedediah	1	1	1		
Cook, Remembrance	4	2	4		
Carney, John	1		2		
Demeritt, John	3	2	5		
Demeritt, Solomon	2		4		
Demeritt, James	1	1	2		
Demeritt, Eli	2	4	2		
Johnson, James	1	1	1		
Evans, Jona	1		2		
Baswell, Ezekl	1	1	3		
Clay, Saml	1	1	2		
Chesley, Philip	1	1	2		
Wingate, Betsy			3		

STRAFFORD COUNTY—Continued.

NAME OF HEAD OF FAMILY.	Free white males of 16 years and upward, including heads of families.	Free white males under 16 years.	Free white females, including heads of families.	All other free persons.	Slaves.	NAME OF HEAD OF FAMILY.	Free white males of 16 years and upward, including heads of families.	Free white males under 16 years.	Free white females, including heads of families.	All other free persons.	Slaves.	NAME OF HEAD OF FAMILY.	Free white males of 16 years and upward, including heads of families.	Free white males under 16 years.	Free white females, including heads of families.	All other free persons.	Slaves.
MADBURY TOWN—con.						**MERIDETH TOWN—con.**						**MERIDETH TOWN—con.**					
Rynes, Joseph	1		1			Crosby, Jonª	2		5			Somes, Timothy	2	1	4		
Frost, Reuben	2	1	3			Crosby, Thoˢ	1	3	5			Shepard, Samuel	3	2	4		
Tasker, Wᵐ	3		3			Crosby, John	1	2	2			Sinclair, Benjª	2	1	3		
Woodhouse, James	1	3	4			Cate, John	1	1	3			Sinclair, Thoˢ	1	3	5		
Davis, James	1		1			Cate, Simeon	1		2			Senter, Moses	5	1	4		
Boadge, Ichabod	4		4			Cass, Daniel	1	3	2			Smith, Nicholas	1	1	2		
Hooper, Wᵐ	1	5	5			Colcord, Peter	1		3			Sibley, Samuel	1	2	4		
Drew, Moses	1	1	1			Chase, Wᵐ	1	2	1			Smith, Daniel	1				
Bickford, Sarah			2			Clough, Daniel	1	1	1			Smith, Pain	3	2	5		
Pinkham, Samˡ	1		1			Dow, Ebenzʳ	3	1	5			Swain, Elias	2		1		
Leathers, Stephⁿ	1		1			Danford, Jonª	1	5	3			Swain, Elias, Jr	1	2	4		
Demeritt, Jonª	2	1	3			Dockham, John	3		6			Swain, Benjª	1	3	3		
Demeritt, Ebenzʳ	2	1	7			Dockham, Thoˢ	1	4	4			Swain, Hezekiah	1	1	2		
Drew, Joseph	3	1	3			Dockham, Samˡ	1					Swain, Abraham	1	2	3		
Drew, Wᵐ	1	1	2			Davis, Wᵐ	4	3	8			Swain, Jacob	1				
Drew, Francis	2		1			Drake, Nathˡ	1	1	2			Spiller, Samˡ	1	3	3		
Drew, Ebenzʳ	2		2			Edgerly, Jonathan	5		2			Smith, Robert	2	1	1		
Drew, John	1		1			Edgerly, John	1	1				Sanborn, Nathˡ	3	1	5		
Daniels, David	2	3	4			Edgerly, James	1	2	4			Watson, David	1	3	6		
Drew, Elijah	1	4	4	2		Eaton, Jacob	2	1	3			Wadleigh, John	1	1	5		
Davis, Samuel	2		3			Eaton, Jacob, Jr	1	2	4			Wadleigh, Nathˡ	1	2	3		
Emerson, Solomon	1	1	2	1		Eaton, Joseph	1	2	3			Weymouth, Timothy	1	1	3		
Emerson, Moses	1	2	4			Folsom, Abraham	3	1	3			Wadley, Simeon	1	1	2		
Emerson, Solomon, Jr	1	2	6			Folsom, John	1		1			Woodman, Joshua	4		3		
Edgerly, Susanna	1	1	2			Folsom, Rev'd Nichᵒ	2	3	2			Weeks, John	1	2	1		
Edgerly, John	2		3			Foss, Benjª	1	3	2			Dollar, Thoˢ	1	2	3		
Edgerly, Paul	1	1	1			Fox, Edward	1	1	6			Lowney, Wᵐ	1	2	4		
Drew, Francis, Jr	2	1	3			Farrar, Isaac	2		2			Smart, Dudley	1				
Evans, Solomon	2	3	4			Farrar, John	1	1	1			Currier, Isaac	1	1	1		
Edgerly, Aaron	1					Farrar, Stephen	1					Fogg, Stephen	1	4	1		
Gerrish, Benjª	3	2	4			Gillman, John	4	2	3			Foss, Wᵐ	1		1		
Garland, Jacob	1	1	5			Gillman, Bradbury	1	2	5			Leavitt, Nehemiah	1	3	1		
Glover, Ebenzʳ	1	2	2			Gillman, James	2	4	3			Carr, Sander	2	3	3		
Hill, Benjª	4		3			Jenness, Samuel	2	1	4			Shepard, John	1	1	2		
Hicks, Joseph	2	1	6	1		Jenness, Samuel, Jr	1	2	1			Merrill, Winthrop	1	1	3		
Hanson, Andrew	2					Jenness, John	1	2	3			Quinby, James	1	2	3		
Hill, Ebenzʳ	4	3	4			Judkins, Job	1		2			Philbrook, Nathˡ	1	2	2		
Hanson, Jonª	2		2			Kelly, Wᵐ	1	1	4			Currier, Jacob	2		1		
Hanson, Timothy	4		3			Kimbol, John	1	6	2			Blasdel, John	1		1		
Hayes, Daniel	3		3			Leavitt, Weare	2	1	4			Bryant, Benjª	1	1	3		
Huckins, Robert	2		2			Leavitt, Stephen	2	1	1			Clark, Mark	1		1		
Huckins, Robert, Jr	2		3			Leavitt, Amos	1		3			Leavitt, Samuel	1		2		
Huckins, Jonª	1	1	1			Leavitt, Levi	1	2	2			Tucker, Morris	1	1	2		
Hayes, Elihu	2	1	6			Leighton, George	2	2	5			Elsworth, William	1		1		
Jackson, James	3	4	5			Marston, Reuben	1		3			Blasdel, Thomas	1		2		
Joy, Jacob	3	2	6			Marston, Reuben, Jr	3	1	7			Richardson, Timothy	1	2	2		
Jenkins, Jonª	2	3	3			Marston, Jeremiah	1	1	3			Lithgorn, Samuel	1				
Jacobs, Seth	2		3			Meloon, Jonª	2	1	5			Sanborn, Henry	1				
Kelly, Samuel	3	1	8			Mead, Wᵐ	3	1	3			Moulton, Peter				1	4
Leathers, Jonª	1		2			Mead, John	1	4	2			Sanborn, Henry	1				
Meserve, Daniel	3	1	4			Mead, Wᵐ, Jr	1		2								
Meader, Mark	2	3	4			MᶜCrelis, James	2	3	3			**MIDDLETON TOWN.**					
Nute, James	2	2	6			Morgan, Reuben	3	1	3								
Pinkham, Stephen	2	1	5			Merrill, Moses	2	4	1			Furnald, John	2	2	5		
Pinkham, James	3		3			Nichols, James	4		3			Furnald, Abigal			1		
Pinkham, James, Jr	3	2	3			Nichols, Paul	1		2			Palmer, James	1	3	2		
Pitman, Connor	1		3			Neal, Joseph	3	2	4			Willey, Josiah	1	1	4		
Pinkham, Louisa	1		4			Neal, Joseph, Jr	1	1	1			Drew, Jedediah	2	4	2		
Pitman, Joseph	1	1	1			Neal, John	1		3			Durgan, David	1	2	2		
Meserve, Joseph	2	1	5			Plummer, Jesse	6	3	4			Daniels, Obediah	1		1		
Rynes, John	1	3	2			Plummer, Moses	1					Brown, Joseph	1		2		
Spurlin, Thoˢ	1	4	3			Peas, Benjª	2	4	5			Stanton, John	1	3	2		
Tasker, Ebenzʳ	2	1	5			Peas, James	1		2			Stanton, Charˡˢ	1	1	2		
Twombly, Wᵐ	1	1	2			Pike, Wᵐ	2		3			Austen, Nicholas	1	3	5		
Twombly, John	3	3	4			Pike, Jeremʰ	2		2			Johnson, Phinias	3	2	4		
Tebbetts, Daniel	1	1	1			Perkins, John	2		3			Tebbets, Samˡ	4	2	3		
Varney, Isaac	1	2	3			Perkins, Benjª	1	1	3			Willey, John	1	1	4		
Wingate, John	1	4	3			Perkins, Joseph	1	2	2			Stoddard, Dearron	1	2	1		
Twombly, Reuben	2	4	4			Piper, Gideon	3	1	3			Nickerson, George	1	1	4		
Wingate, Jonª	1	1	3			Philbrook, Elias	1	1	3			Coldair, Robert	4	3	6		
Young, Timᵒ	1	5	4			Pittman, Ebenzʳ	2	1	5			Drew, Andrew	1	2	1		
Young, Solomon	2	3	4			Page, Benjª	3	1	4			Johnson, Timᵒ	2	1	2		
Boadge, Daniel	2		1			Pearson, Joseph	1		1			Whitehouse, Moses	2	4	4		
Davis, James	1		1			Quimby, James	3		5			Whitehouse, Cha'l	2	1	4		
Twombly, Ezekˡ	1	4	3			Quimby, Caleb	1	3	1			Liford, Stephen	1	3	4		
Demeritt, Mary			2			Robinson, Chace	3	1	4			Roberson, Josiah	3		4		
Leighton, Jonª	2	1	2			Robinson, Chace, Jr	1		3			Pike, Jacob	3	3	6		
Tasker, Ebenezʳ, Jr	1					Robinson, John	1	2	2			Robertson, Walter	1	1	2		
						Robinson, Gideon	2	4	4			Dearborn, Margerett			3		
MERIDETH TOWN.						Robinson, Jonª	1	1	2			Hanson, Rheuben	1				
						Robinson, Joseph	2	3	4			Hanson, Rich'd	1	3	5		
Boynton, David, Jr	2	4	4			Robinson, David	1	2	4			Watson, David	1	2	1		
Bryant, Richard	2	2	5			Robinson, Winthrop	1	1	2			Whilley, Stephen	1		2		
Bryant, Robert	2	2	3			Runlett, Wᵐ	1	4	4			Wiggins, Jepa	1	1	3		
Batchelor, David	1	2	1			Roberts, Joseph	2	1	3			Wiggins, Joseph	2	2	5		
Black, Edmund	2	1	4			Roberts, John	2	1	3			Clay, Benjª	1	1	3		
Black, James	1	1	1			Roberts, Sander	2	2	3			Clay, Jonathⁿ	1	1	2		
Bunker, Jacob	1	1	2			Ray, Wᵐ	3		3			Palmer, John	2		2		
Bowman, Zadock	1	1	3			Roby, James	1		1			Kinneston, Thomˢ	4		1		
Crocket, Joshua	3	3	4			Smith, Ebenzʳ	4	1	7			Perkins, Moses	3		3		
Conner, Phillip	4		5			Smith, Lucy		2	1			Chamberlan, Thomˢ	1	2	2		
Cram, Joel	1	2	3			Smith, Jeremiah	2	1	2			Chamberlain, James	2	2	3		

STRAFFORD COUNTY—Continued.

MIDDLETON TOWN—con.

NAME OF HEAD OF FAMILY.	Free white males of 16 years and upward, including heads of families.	Free white males under 16 years.	Free white females, including heads of families.	All other free persons.	Slaves.
Willey, Wm	1	1	4		
Kent, William	2	1	2		
Edgerly, James	1		2		
Stellings, Peter	2	3	3		
Alley, Ephm	1		1		
Sanbourn, Ezekl	2	3	3		
Watson, Nathl	2	1	1		
Chamberlain, John	1	3	3		
Chamberlain, Wm	1	1	5		
Watson, Joseph	1				
Watson, Saml	1				
Wentworth, Richd	1				
Dearborn, John	1	1	1		
Sawyer, Daniel	3	4	2		
Kenneston, Waldron	2	3	7		
Hill, William	1	1	5		
Pike, Jacob	3		3		
Drew, John	3		1		
Drew, Daniel	2	2	5		
Coock, Robt	1	4	1		
Coock, Joseph	1	6	4		
Haggey, Jona	1	1	2		
Woodman, Archl	2	2	4		
Stanton, Isaih	1	2	3		
Colby, Moses	1	1	1		
Briant, John	1	2	1		
Perkins, Solomon	2	4	5		
Hanson, Timo	1	3	2		
Whitehouse, John	1	2	7		
Ellice, Joseph	1	4	4		
Ellice, Ephm	1	4	4		
Guppy, Joshua	1	1	3		
Gesh, John	2	3	4		
Baggey, Aaron	1	2	2		
Baggey, Wm	2	1	2		
Hiner, John H	2	1	5		
Bigford, Andrew	1		2		
Whitehouse, Danl	1	3	2		
Whitehouse, Jona	1	2	4		
Horne, Jethro	2	4	5		
Clast, Saml	1	2	1		
Johnson, Gidion	1	1	4		
Bennett, Archl	1	1	2		
Davice, Moses	1		3		
Bly, William	1		3		
Whitehouse, John	2	2	4		
Whitehouse, Paul	1	2			
York, Eliz'			4		
Johnson, Josiah	1		1		
Kenniston, John	3	1	5		
Johnson, Saml	1		4		
Twombly, Anna			1		
Wentworth, Moses	1	1	3		
Hix, John	1		4		
Burnham, George	1	2	5		
Garland, Thoms	1	2	5		
York, Benga	1	1	1		
Runnels, Ebenzr	1		2		
Place, Moses	1		3		
Gerrish, Paul	1		1		
Richards, Tristam	1	1	2		
Gerrish, James	1		3		
Davice, James	1	1	3		
Frost, Saml	1	2	1		
Pike, Henry	1		2		
York, Josiah	2	5	3		
Baker, Charles	1	1	3		
Frost, Nicho	2	2	4		

MOULTONBOROUGH TOWN.

NAME OF HEAD OF FAMILY.	Free white males of 16 years and upward, including heads of families.	Free white males under 16 years.	Free white females, including heads of families.	All other free persons.	Slaves.
Adams, John	2	1	2		
Adams, John	1	2	1		
Rogers, John	3		3		
Clements, Richd	3	2	3		
Cannaday, John	1	1	3		
Leach, William	1	4	3		
Lee, Daniel	1	1	4		
Rogers, Daniel	1	1	6		
Coock, Jona	1	1	3		
Malloon, Ebenzr	3		6		
Watson, Nathl	3	2	4		
Watson, Simon	1	1	1		
Garland, Peter	2	1	4		
Blake, Ebenzr	3	2	3		
Leavett, Willm	1	5	2		
Whipple, Wm	1		4		
Adams, Abner	1	1	4		
Carr, Roland	1	1	3		
Moulton, Jacob	2	3	3		
Randal, Mark	2		2		
Moulton, Smith	1	4	2		

MOULTONBOROUGH TOWN—con.

NAME OF HEAD OF FAMILY.	Free white males of 16 years and upward, including heads of families.	Free white males under 16 years.	Free white females, including heads of families.	All other free persons.	Slaves.
Brown, Blanchard	1	1	4		
Berry, James T	1	3	3		
Jennes, John	1	2	4		
Adams, Ruphus	1	2	3		
Bradbury, Ephm	1	1	5		
Brown, Danl	1	3	3		
Hutchins, John	1	3	4		
Truse, John	2	3	5		
Glidden, John	1	2	4		
Maloon, Samuel	1		1		
Lee, Ebenzr	2	1	7		
Lee, Nehemiah	3	1	5		
Truse, Joseph	1	2	3		
Blake, Enoch	1	6	3		
Burham, Saml	1	1	5		
Coock, Luther	1	1	1		
Bean, Moody	2	4	4		
Bean, John	2	3	5		
Doten, Ephm	1	1	2		
Glimes, Ezruel	1		3		
Glimes, Robert	1	1	2		
Smith, David	1	1	1		
Harriman, Jacob	1	1	4		
Blake, Paul	2	2	4		
Sanbourn, Robert	1	1	2		
Stapels, Timothy	3	1	2		
Merril, Wm	1	1	3		
Adams, Stephen	2	5	5		
Tole, Josiah	1	1	3		
Brown, John	1	1	3		
Wiggen, Andrew	1	2	3		
McNortan, Duncan	2		3		1
Goodwin, Moses	2	2	1		
Chandley, Joseph	1	2	3		
Glimes, John	1	3	3		
Chandler, Abraham	1	1	3		
Chandler, Moses	1	2	1		
Sandbourn, James, jr	1		1		
Sandbourn, James	1	1	3		
Frost, Jona	2	3	5		
Blachey, Mark	2	2	5		
Mall, Eliph	1	1	3		
Morse, Caleb	1	1	4		
Maston, John	2	2	3		
Shaw, Jerimiah	1	3	4		
Smith, Elias	4		4		
Lee, Nathn	2	1	4		
Lee, Abigal	2	5	3		
Lee, Nehemiah	1		1		
Hoit, Nathan	2	3	4		
Morse, Benja	1	1	3		
Sanborn, Amos		1	3		
Ambros, Nathl	2	3	3		
Ambros, David	1		2		
Sanbourn, John	1				
Shannon, Nathl	2	3	5		
Moulton, Edwd	2	2	3		
Emery, David	2		2		
Johnson, Daniel	1		2		
Moulton, Timothy	1	1	1		
Chadbourn, Wm	1	4	3		
Clark, Eleazr	1	3	3		
Richardson, Joseph	2	3	5		
Richardson, Joseph, jr	1		2		
Richardson, Brady	3	3	5		
Drake, Ephm	1	1	1		
Penniman, Adney	1		4		
Brown, Benja	2	1	4		
Moulton, Jona	1		2		
Moulton, John	2		3		

NEW DURHAM TOWN.

NAME OF HEAD OF FAMILY.	Free white males of 16 years and upward, including heads of families.	Free white males under 16 years.	Free white females, including heads of families.	All other free persons.	Slaves.
Collemy, John	3	4	4		
Runnels, Saml	3	3	7		
Nason, John	1		7		
Colleney, Richd	1	1	3		
Mason, John	2	2	1		
Tash, Thomas	3	2	5		
Cogswell, Joseph	1				
Moony, Joseph	1				
Mooney, Benja	1	2	1		
Allard, Shadrack	3	1	3		
Allard, Daniel	1		3		
Edgerly, John	1	1	2		
Berry, Benja	1		2		
Berry, Joseph	1	2	3		
Dugnoine, Andrew	1		3		
Nute, Isaac	1	3	2		
Doe, Josiah	1		4		
Edgerly, Caleb	2	1	3		
Willey, Saml	1	2	1		

NEW DURHAM TOWN—continued.

NAME OF HEAD OF FAMILY.	Free white males of 16 years and upward, including heads of families.	Free white males under 16 years.	Free white females, including heads of families.	All other free persons.	Slaves.
Parker, Ezekl	1	5	2		
Hanson, Nathl	1	3	2		
Homes, Ephm	1	1	3		
Homes, Ephm, jr	1	1	1		
York, Susannah		1	1		
Palmer, James	1	1	3		
Homes, Ichabot	1	1	2		
Davice, Lemuel	1		3		
Davice, George	1		1		
Davice, Nathn	1	1			
Durgon, Ebenzr	2		3		
Tash, Thomas, jr	1	2	1		
Davice, Elisha	3	2	2		
Taylor, Jeremy	2	1	2		
Willey, Josiah	2	1	2		
Durgon, Nathl	2	4	1		
Bickford, Ebenzr	1	5	3		
Doe, James	1	3	3		
Doe, John	1	2	1		
Leighton, Jacob	1		6		
Davice, Winthrop	1	1	2		
Townsend, Jacob	1		1		
Bickford, Saml	2	4	3		
Colleny, John	1	2	2		
Dearing, James	2		1		
Davice, Solomon	1	1	3		
Eavens, Moses	1	4	3		
Drew, Stephen	2	2	3		
Allard, Jona	2	3	1		
Nute, Andrew	1	1	3		
Evans, Paul	1	1	1		
Willey, Samuel	3		5		
Willey, Joseph	1		1		
Gilman, Saml	1	1	2		
Thomas, Sarah		2	5		
Bickford, John	1	2	3		
Meades, Stephen	1	1	2		
Bickford, Ebenzr	1		2		
Durgan, Joseph	2	3	3		
Bickford, Joshua	1	1	3		
Berry, Stephen	2				
Bickford, Jona	2		4		
Bickford, Joseph	1		4		
Bickford, Ebenzr	1	1	4		
Berry, John	1	2	2		
Folsom, Jona	2	3	4		
Meader, Moses	1		2		
Libbey, Abraham	1		4		
Libbey, Margarett		2	2		
Dame, Thomas	1		1		
Eavens, Joseph	2		4		
Hanson, Isaac	1	1	4		
Drew, Isaac	1	2	5		
Eavens, Daniel	1	1	2		
Boody, Zachr	2	2	3		
Hays, Jonathan	1	1	2		
French, Thoms	2	1	4		
Kelley, David	1	2	2		
Randall, Benja	2	3	5		
Bickford, Abraham	1	1	3		
Bickford, Benja	1	1	3		
Bennett, John	3	1	2		
Elkins, David	2		2		
Peavey, Joshua	2		5		
Roberts, John	2	2	4		
Jackson, Joseph	2	1	2		
Peavey, John	1		2		
Dennett, Saml	2	1	1		
Beck, Joseph	1	3	3		
Chamberlain, Isaac	1	1	2		
Chamberlain, Abra	1	1	2		
Richards, Theodore	1	1	2		
Buzzey, Ichobad	3	5	3		
Young, Thomas	1		1		
Beck, Samuel	1		2		
Pattle, Simon	1		2		
Palmer, Jeremy	1				
Drew, Benja	1				
Durgan, Daniel	1	1	3		
Peasley, Nathn	1	1	2		
Glidden, John	1	2	5		
Kenniston, Joseph	1	2	4		
Kenniston, Nathn	1	3	5		
Kenniston, Joshua	1	1			
Bickford, Andrew	1		1		

NEW DURHAM GORE.

NAME OF HEAD OF FAMILY.	Free white males of 16 years and upward, including heads of families.	Free white males under 16 years.	Free white females, including heads of families.	All other free persons.	Slaves.
Peirce, Joseph	3	1	2	1	
Chamberlain, Jacob	3	4	4		
Chamberlain, Ephm	3	2	4		
Pinkham, Clement	2		3		

STRAFFORD COUNTY—Continued.

NAME OF HEAD OF FAMILY.	Free white males of 16 years and upward, including heads of families.	Free white males under 16 years.	Free white females, including heads of families.	All other free persons.	Slaves.
NEW DURHAM GORE— continued.					
Davis, Gideon	2	1	2		
Davis, Timothy	2	3	4		
Davis, Eleazer	1	5	4		
Davis, Zebulon	1	2	5		
Glidden, Zebulon	2	2	4		
Glidden, Nicholas	1	3	3		
Stockbridge, Israel	2	6	4		
Norton, Thos	1	2	1		
Buzzell, Joseph	2	2	4		
Buzzell, Robert					
Benson, Dennis	1	1	4		
Worcester, James	1		1		
Wilkinson, James	1	4	3		
Chamberlain, Paul	1				
Chamberlain, Joseph	1				
Edgerly, Thos	3	3	5		
Bennett, Benja	2	1	4	1	
Peavy, Oliver	2	2	2		
Roberts, Joseph	3	1	3		
Roberts, Joseph, Jr	1	2	2		
Horn, George	1	1	3		
March, Henry	1				
Leighton, Jona	1	1	5		
Rowlins, John	1	2	3		
Rogers, Charles	1		1		
Rogers, Saml	1		3		
Glidden, John	2	3	5		
Glidden, Phineas	1	3	2		
Flanders, Ezekiel	3	2	6		
Flanders, Ezekl, Jr	1	1	1		
Flanders, Thos	2	1	6		
Coffin, Jona	2	4	5		
Bean, Joel	1	3	3		
Gilman, Moses	2	2	3		
Smith, Ilhiel	4	2	2		
Smith, Josiah	3	1	5		
Smith, Reuben	1	1	4		
Smith, Ezra	1		4		
Clough, Simon	1	3	3		
Moores, Jona	2		3		
Elkins, James	1	1	3		
Elkins, Samuel	1		2		
Clough, Aaron	1		4		
Buzzell, Silas	2	3	3		
Buzzell, Joseph, Jr	1	1	2		
Woodman, Jeremh	1	3	2		
Meader, Moses	1	3	3		
Palmer, James	1	1	4		
Littlefield, Obediah	1				
Horn, Wm	1		1		
Wiggins, James	1	1	4		
Libbey, Benja	1	3	2		
Chace, Jona	1	3	5		
Small, Joseph	3		3		
Benson, John	1	1	2		
Penney, Peletiah	1	1	3		
Willey, Andrew	1		3		
York, Benja	1	2	3		
Horn, Wm	1		1		
Runnells, Jack					5
Place, Jacob	1	2	4		
Dudley, Stephen	1	1	3		
Glidden, David	2	3	4		
Roberts, Ephm	1	1	1		
Leighton, Jona, Jr	1	2	2		
Place, Ebenzr	2	1	3		
Place, Ebenzr, Jr	1				
Rogers, James	1	1	6		
Hurd, Tristram	2	5	1		
Fall, Stephen	1	2	2		
Dow, Moses	1		1		
NEW HAMPTON TOWN.					
Robinson, Noah	4	3	4		
Smith, Elisha	2	4	6		
Sinclair, Jacob	1	1	3		
Ward, Mercy			3		
Veasy, Daniel	1	4	3		
Woodman, Thos	1	2	2		
Ward, Jeremiah	2	2	4		
Boynton, John	1	1	1		
Russell, Jona	1	1	2		
Cummins, Isaac	1	1	6		
Dolluff, Samuel	1		2		
Dolluff, John	1	2	2		
Fogg, Simon	1	3	1		
Harper, John	1		2		
Fogg, Phineas	3	5	2		
Smith, Nichls	2	1	3		
Smith, Joseph	1		5		

NAME OF HEAD OF FAMILY.	Free white males of 16 years and upward, including heads of families.	Free white males under 16 years.	Free white females, including heads of families.	All other free persons.	Slaves.
NEW HAMPTON TOWN— continued.					
Boynton, John	1	1	3		
Boynton, Richd	1	2	1		
Boynton, Wm	1	2	2		
Sinclivant, Jesse	2	1	3		
Duncan, Abraham	1				
Page, Daniel	1	1	3		
Warden, Thos	1	2	5		
Molton, Benning	3	2	3		
Burnham, Abraham Gli	1	1	2		
Payne, Richard	1	1	3		
Stirdivan, Chance	4	1	3		
Stirdivan, Hosea	1	2	3		
Payne, Amos	2	2	2		
Payne, John	4		3		
Cate, Enoch	1	3	4		
Moss, Moses	2	2	1		
Tote, James	4		2		
Kelsey, Moses	1	1	4		
Batchelor, Benja	1		2		
Moss, Ezekl	2	2	3		
Moss, Abel	1	1	1		
Bestor, Timothy	2	3	4		
Chamberlain, Ebenzr	1		1		
Chamberlain, Daniel	1	1	3		
Chamberlain, Ephraim	1		1		
Senter, Joseph	2	4	3		
Moor, Ephm	1	2	2		
Kelsey, Robert	1				
Kelsey, Hugh	1	1			
Tebbetts, James	1		1		
Smith, John	1	1	2		
Smith, Benja	2		3		
Taylor, Edward	1	3	5		
Herrin, Thos	1	3	3		
Herrin, John	3	1	2		
Huckins, Saml	1		2		
Mudget, Joseph	2	1	2		
Huckins, James	2	3	5		
Huckins, Benja	1	3	4		
Smith, Obediah	1	1	1		
Leavitt, John	1	3	6		
Smith, Stephen	1	4	1		
Nichols, Tom			1	2	
Smith, Jona	1		1		
Cummins, Elisha	1	4	2		
Batchelor, Simeon	1	1	2		
Glines, James	2	2	5		
Hacket, Ezra	2	3	4		
Hackett, Ephm	2				
Sawyer, Daniel	2	3	3		
Plastead, Saml	2	3	4		
Megoon, Thos	2		1		
Plastead, Wm	2	4	5		
Neley, Wm	1	1	4		
Drake, Thomas	2		1		
Dollaf, Phineas	1	2	3		
Smith, John, Jr	1	1	4		
Weeks, Nathl	1	1	2		
Smith, Benja, Jr	1	2	2		
Drake, Abraham	3		1		
Smith, Philip	1				
Marston, Jeremiah	2		4		
Hunniford, Peter	2	1	4		
Dow, Levi	2	1	6		
Walton, Simeon	1	3	2		
Sanborn, Zadock, Jr	1	1	4		
Fuller, John	1	4	4		
Sanborn, Joseph	1	2	1		
Sanborn, Zadock	3		3		
Sanborn, Benja	1	1	2		
Drake, Abraham, Jr	2	3	3		
Gordon, Enoch	2	4	3		
Gordon, Wm	1		2		
Kelling, Dudley	3		1		
Hearter, Moses	4	3	4		
Cops, Solomon	1		5		
Lyford, Nathl	1	3	1		
Goodwin, Wm	1	2	4		
Brown, Isaac	1	1	1		
Brown, Jacob	1		1		
Blake, Oliver	1	1	8		
Tilton, David	1	1	5		
Wells, Ebenzr	2	2	3		
Heath, Danl	1		4		
Tilton, David	2		4		
Tilton, Green	1	2	1		
Dudley, Hobart	1	1	1		
Dudley, Jery	1		2		
Inglass, Ebenzr	3	1	5		
Simson, Thos	1	3	3		
Kelley, Samuel, Jr	3	2	2		

NAME OF HEAD OF FAMILY.	Free white males of 16 years and upward, including heads of families.	Free white males under 16 years.	Free white females, including heads of families.	All other free persons.	Slaves.
NEW HAMPTON TOWN— continued.					
Gordon, Enoch	1	4	3		
Gordon, James	2	4	4		
Kelley, Samuel	4	2	3		
OSSIPEE TOWN.					
Ranel, John	1		3		
Davice, Rheuben	1	2	5		
Glover, Brichd	1	2	6		
Densmore, Cornelious	2	3	6		
Brow, Moses	1	1	4		
Libbey, Joseph	1		2		
Clark, Benjm	2	2	2		
Pribble, Abra	2	1	2		
Harvey, James	1		2		
Schiggell, John	1		2		
Schiggell, John, jr	1	2	1		
Kenneston, Saml	1	2	4		
Brown, Jacob	2	3	4		
Fogg, Seth	1				
Fogg, Seth, jr	1	2	1		
Dearborne, Joseph	1	1	1		
Dearborne, John	2	2	2		
Tasker, Saml	3	2	3		
Brozey, John	2		4		
Marsten, John	1				
Lear, Abigal	1		1		
Bracket, Joseph	1	3	3		
Tucker, John	1	4	2		
Hersom, Ebenzr	1		3		
Lord, Wentworth	1	3	3		
Knight, Ephm	1		1		
Mason, John	2	1	6		
Smart, Winthrop	3	3	4		
Dearborne, Levi	1	2	2		
Cooler, John	1	3	5		
Smith, Simon	1				
Folsom, Andrew, jr	1		1		
Folsom, Andrew	1		2		
Sanderson, John	2	1	2		
Warren, Peter	1	1	2		
Demeritt, Richd	1		1		
Edgerly, Jeremy	1	2	2		
Drew, Noah	3		1		
Eames, Joseph	1	1	3		
Hayley, Thoma	1		1		
Smelfurgus, Benja	1				
Sloris, Benja	1	2	3		
Fogg, Joseph	1				
Blake, Sanbourn	1	1	2		
Nay, Joseph	1	1	5		
Pitman, Joseph	1	3	4		
Young, John	1	4	5		
Goldsmith, John	2	2	3		
Goldsmith, John, jr	1		3		
Rogers, Thoms	1	1	1		
Poland, Josiah	1		3		
Lear, Saml	1	2	3		
Sias, Saml	2		3		
Keniston, John	1	2	3		
Sprout, John	1		4		
Caster, Stanten	2	1	2		
Mason, Nathn	1		1		
Lear, Saml, jr	1	2	2		
Kinneston, John	1	3	1		
Garland, Amos	1	1	2		
Garland, Joseph	1				
Moody, Jona	1	4	3		
Nutter, Saml	1	1	3		
Beachum, Richd	1	1	4		
White, Joseph	1		2		
White, John	1		2		
Door, Jedediah	1		2		
Williams, Isaac	1	1	5		
White, Timo	1	1	1		
ROCHESTER TOWN.					
Wentworth, Samuel	1	2	2		
Coason, Joshua	1	2	4		
Foss, Benja	1	2	2		
Coarson, Ebenzr	1	3	3		
Varney, Ebenzr	1				
Thomas, James	1				
Thomas, John	1				
Plummer, Ephm	1		2		
Tuttle, Wm	1		5		
Goodwin, James	1	2	2		
Wentworth, Ichabod	1	1	1		
Varney, Enoch	2	2	4		
Whautcum, Caleb	1	2	2		

STRAFFORD COUNTY—Continued.

ROCHESTER TOWN—con.

NAME OF HEAD OF FAMILY.	Free white males of 16 years and upward, including heads of families.	Free white males under 16 years.	Free white females, including heads of families.	All other free persons.	Slaves.
Ricker, Tobias	1	3	3		
Harvey, Stephen	1	1	4		
	1	3	5		
Hays, Daniel	2	2	3		
Hays, Ezecal	1				
Varney, James	1	1	2		
Nute, Jotham	1	4	2		
Nute, Saml	4	5	3		
Jinkins, Stephen	3	2	4		
Twombly, Benja	4		1		
Clemment, Job	1		2		
Varney, Benja	1	4	1		
	2	3	2		
Varney, Mordicai	2		4		
Wingate, Aaron	2	2	3		
Dorans, James	2	1	2		
Varney, Caleb	2	3	2		
Langbey, David	1	3	5		
Wentworth, Ephr	3	2	2		
Plummer, Saml	3		3		
Rollings, Joshua	1	1	1		
Rollins, Olly	1		4		
Toor, Simon	3	2	5		
Ricker, Joseph	1		3		
Hays, Daniel	1	3	2		
Hays, Ichabod	1	4	6		
Watson, Joshua	1		2		
Hays, Moses	2	2	4		
Watson, Nathl	2	3	6		
Randlett, Richd	1	1	2		
Twambly, James	2	3	6		
Horne, Moses	3		5		
Davice, Thomas	1	5	2		
Clemment, Gersham	1		2		
Rollins, Anthony	1	1	1		
Austen, Moses	1		4		
Trickey, William	3	1	3		
Kimbal, Daniel	3	2	4		
Ricker, Ebenzr	1	2	4		
Folsom, Jeremy	1	1	3		
Willard, George	2		3		
Richardson, Timo	1	2	1		
Richardson, Wm	1		2		
Tanner, John	1	1	2		
Down, Moses	1	1	3		
Down, Moses, jr	1	1	3		
Down, Aaron	2	2	1		
Richerdson, John	1	2	3		
Baker, John	1				
Hanson, Benja	1	1	3		
Hartford, Mary			2		
Hartford, Stephn	2	1	5		
Alley, Ephm	1				
Libbey, Isaac	3	1	3		
Roberts, Thomas	2	1	6		
Garland, Daniel	1	3	4		
Garland, Dudly	1	1	1		
Coock, Abra	1	1	1		
Libbey, Paul	3		4		
Colman, James	1	1	6		
Colman, Ebenzr	2		2		
Hays, Wentworth	1	1	2		
Mains, Josiah	3	2	4		
Haven, Joseph	3	4	6		
Heard, Joseph	2		2		
Duffee, Wm	3		4		
Chamberlain, Saml	2	1	3		
Heard, Trustam	1		3		
Wallingford, Aigar	2		3		
Tebbits, Henry	3	3	4		
Nutter, Richd	2	2			
Nutter, Richd	1	2	1		
Richardson, John	3	1	2		
How, James	1	4	3		
Rollins, Edward	1	5	3		
Watson, Danl	1	3	1		
Menrow, Joshua	1	2	1		
Horne, Peter	4	3	4		
Wentworth, Isaac	2	3	5		
Wentworth, Stephen	1		3		
Place, Paul	1		2		
Jackson, Caleb	1	3	3		
Palmer, Barnabas	3	1	2		
Knight, Joseph	1		1		
Knight, Joshua	1	1	3		
Richards, Jona	2	1	8		
Goodwin, John	1		2		
Goodwin, Richd	1	5	3		
Heard, Abra	1		1		
Adams, James	1	4	3		1
McDuffee, James	1	1	2		
Heard, Nathl	1		1		
Heard, Trustum	1	1	1		
Heard, Nathl	1	1	2		
Kimbal, Mary			2		
Jewet, Derborn	1	2	1		
Clark, Joseph	1	1	3		
Knight, Hatival	1		1		
Place, Mary		1	3		
Hartford, Paul	1	3	2		
Ellice, Morrice	1	2	6		
Rollins, Benja	1	1	7		
Cross, Richd	1	1	1		
Pinkham, Stephh	1		2		
Richards, Jona	1		1		
Richards, Jona	1		1		
Crockett, Eliza			1		
Hoit, Benja	2	3	7		
Hoit, Enoch	1	4	4		
Nutter, Jona	3	3	4		
Wentworth, Joshua	1	2	5		
Perkins, Soloman	3	1	2		
Hanson, Joseph	1				
Mathews, Francis	1		3		
Cushing, Peter	1	1	4		
Folsom, Josiah	1	2	3		
Clarks, James			2		
Horne, Anna			2		
Horne, Ebenezr	1	2	4		
Richards, Saml	1		2		
Dame, Joseph	1	1	1		
Calf, Daniel	1	3	3		
Pirkens, Ephm	3	2	2		
McDuffee, Danl	4	2	5		
Rogers, Danel	1	2	3		
Rann, Eleazr	3	4	2		
Henderson, Wm	1	2	2		
Wentworth, Wm	2	2	4		
Roberts, Timo	1	2	2		
Varney, Thoms	1	3	1		
Roberts, Benja	1	1	2		
Clark, Jacob	1	4	5		
Walter, John	1	2	4		
Morrison, David	1	1	1		
Runnells, Joseph	1	4	2		
Pirkins, Ephm	1	1	2		
Varney, Stephen	1		2		
Laghton, Ephm	1	1	4		
Jones, Joseph	2	1	7		
Runnels, Benja	1		2		
Jones, Saml	1	4	1		
Leighton, David	2	1	2		
Coldbath, Wentworth	2	4	3		
Leighton, Wm	1	1	1		
Rollins, Joseph	1	6	1		
Roberts, Joseph	1	3	1		
Watson, David	2	4	3		
Knight, Wm	1	1	4		
Knight, Charles	1	1	1		
Peavey, Thoms	1		1		
Peavey, Antheny	2	2	4		
Peavey, Danl	1	4	5		
Stephens, James	1		3		
Trefethern, James	1		2		
Place, Amos	3	3	4		
Roberts, John	2	4	2		
Durgan, Josiah	1	3	3		
Ham, John	2	4	4		
Colbath, Benning	3	1	1		
Caverly, Richd	3	1	1		
Stephens, John	1		2		
Stephens, Timo	1	1	1		
Knowls, Danl	1	1	2		
French, David	2	2	2		
French, Gilbert	1	2	5		
French, James	2	4	4		
French, Jona	1	2	2		
Roff, Jeremy	1	1	1		
Walker, Robert	1	2	4		
Glidden, Abigal		1	2		
Pottle, Joseph	1		2		
Wiggen, Eliza			2		
Varney, Edwd	1	1	5		
Allard, David	2	3	2		
Leighton, Saml	1		2		
Leighton, Saml	1	2	2		
Leighton, George	1	1	1		
Hodgdon, Eleazr	1	1	2		
Runnels, James	1	3	4		
Hodgdon, Jeremy	1		3		
Tebbits, Edmund	2	1	5		
Pearl, John	1	1	4		
Richardson, Lemuel	1	4	3		
Wingate, Wm	1	2	5		
Nutter, Nelson D	1	1	3		
Roberts, James	1	2	2		
Roberts, David	1	3	2		
Kenney, Joseph	1		2		
Horne, Ebenzr	1	1	3		
Murry, John	1	1	4		
Canny, Thomas	2		2		
Pearl, Ichabod	1	2	6		
Wingate, John	1	1	1		
Buzzey, Thoms	1		2		
Buzzey, James	1	3	3		
Buzzey, Henry	1	3	3		
Small, Saml	1	2	4		
Atkins, John	1		4		
Allard, Joseph	1	6	3		
Hornes, Joseph	1	1	2		
Ham, Wm	1		2		
Ham, Wm	1	1	3		
Bennett, Wm	1		2		
Leathers, Thoms	1	1	5		
Hoit, Richd	1	2	3		
Ham, Thoms	1	1	2		
Coldbath, Kershing	1	2	3		
Downing, George	1	2	2		
Wingate, Danl	1		2		
Read, Benja	1	2	4		
Thompson, Joseph	2	2	5		
Chesley, Benja	1	2	4		
Johnson, Nathl	1	2	2		
Demerrit, Paul	1	1	3		
Ricker, Ezecal	1	2	1		
Hanson, Jededias	1		2		
Wingate, Edmon	1	1	2		
Wentworth, Jona	2	3	3		
Clark, Arnal	1		4		
Downing, Joshua	2		2		
Garland, Nathl	3	3	5		
Burnham, Enoch	1	1	6		
Roberts, Moses	2	2	4		
Dame, Richd	2	1	2		
Page, Daniel	1		3		
Page, Joseph	1	2	3		
Rollins, Volantine	1	3	4		
Page, Daniel	1	1	2		
Page, Benja	1	1	2		
Chesley, James	1	4	5		
Randal, John	2	6	6		
Randal, John, jr	1	1	4		
Downs, Gersham	1	1	2		
Dame, Marry	1	1	4		
Hodgdon, Abner	1	1	4		
Varney, Eliza			2		
Dame, Benja	2		2		
Dame, Jona	1	1	1		
Varney, Thomas	2	2	3		
Varney, Ebenzr	1		3		
Hays, Moses	2	1	3		
Bigford, Josiah	2	2	3		
Varney, Moses	2	1	3		
Downing, Saml	1	2	4		
Varney, Benja	1	1	2		
Hays, Moses	1	2	2		
Place, Richard	1	1	1		
Place, John	1		3		
Heard, Rheuben	1	1	1		
Heard, Jona	1	1	3		
Dame, Jona	1	1	4		
Dame, Richard	1	2	3		
Twambly, Isaac	2	1	5		
Peake, Joseph	2	1	1		
Nute, John	1		3		
Hase, Joshua	1	2	1		
Brown, Thoms	1	1	4		
Young, Moses	1		2		
Hammock, John	2		2		
Hogdon, Alexr	2	1	2		
Bigford, John	1	1	2		
Hammock, Moses	1	2	3		
Brown, John	3		3		
Brown, Isaac	2		3		
Plummer, John	4	1	4		
Odiom, Benja	2	2	4		
McDuffee, John	4		3		
Dame, Zebulan	1		3		
Wentworth, Pheby			1		
Richardson, John	2	1	3		
Hays, Benja	1		2		
Hodgdon, John	2	2	4		
Varney, Thomas	2	2	4		
Varney, Elerzah	1	5	4		
Heard, Rheuben	2	2	3		

STRAFFORD COUNTY—Continued.

ROCHESTER TOWN—con.

NAME OF HEAD OF FAMILY.	Free white males of 16 years and upward, including heads of families.	Free white males under 16 years.	Free white females, including heads of families.	All other free persons.	Slaves.
Varney, Moses	1	3	2		
Varney, Mehipsable	1		1		
Varney, Thomas	1		1		
Cotland, Pallatiah	1	1	2		
Ham, Eph^m	2		2		
Ham, Eleaz^r	1		3		
Place, David	3	2	4		
Walker, Joseph	2		2		
Brewster, Daniel	2	1	2		
Huzzey, Danl	1	2	3		
Brewster, Danl., jr	1		2		
Leighton, Jon^a	1		2		
Brewster, John	3		4		
Heard, Joseph	1	3	2		
Furber, Richard	2		2		
Furber, Benj^a	1	3	4		
Tucker, Joseph	1	3	2		
Tucker, Hugh	1		8		
Evans, Hannah	2	2	4		
Place, James	2	1	4		
Hodgdon, W^m	2		5		
Welch, Athiel	1	1	2		
Roberson, Saml	2	1	5		
Jennens, Paul	1	1	2		
Ham, William	1	3	4		
Ginnes, Jon^a	1	1	1		
Morrison, Jon^a	2	3	4		
Drown, Solomon	2	1	3		
Meader, Benj^a	3	2	3		
Meader, Francis	2		1		
Meader, Sarah			1		
Meader, Nathl	1	1	3		
Jenkins, Isaiah	1	1	4		
Hanson, Jacob	1	4	2		
Holms, Joseph	3		3		
Varney, Tobias	1	4	2		
Meader, Jon^a	1	3	2		
Jennis, Aaron	1	4	1		
Ginnins, David	1	2	2		
Nutter, Winthrop	1	3	1		
Ginnins, Moses	1	3	2		
Meader, Joseph	2	5	3		
Kimball, Eph^m	2	4	3		
Whitehouse, W^m	1	1	2		
Meader, Eliz^a	2	3	3		
Leighton, Hatvil	2	3	4		
Furber, Rich^d	1	2	2		
Hanson, Moses	2	3	5		
Furber, Saml	1	5	3		
Ham, Francis	1	1	2		
Bigford, John	2	1	2		
Nutter, James	1	1	2		
Eavens, Benj^a	3		2		
Gray, Jeremy	2	3	4		
Hill, Eliph	1	2	3		
Gennins, Saml	1	1	2		
Gray, Saml	1	2	4		
Berry, Alex^dr	1	2	4		
Allard, Job	1	1	6		
Canney, Danl	1		1		
Drown, Saml	1	2	2		
Twambly, Jon^a	3	2	2		
Emmerson, Jube	1				
Scruton, Jon^a	1	1	1		
Pearle, Abigal			1		
Clark, Steph^n	1		2		
Pearle, Dimon	4		4		
Drown, Joseph	3	3	4		
Heard, Benj^a	1	2	3		
McKneal, W^m	1	3	6		
Drown, Saml	1	2	4		
Evans, W^m	1	1	3		
Ham, Aaron	1		3		
Giles, Joseph	1	3	4		
Henderson, Howar	2	4	4		
Garland, Ebenz^r	3	1	1		
Place, John	1	2	4		
Hays, Rich^d	1	3	3		
Place John	1	1	3		
Place, Jon^a	1		1		
Allard, Aaron	1	1	3		
Mills, Saml	1	1	3		
Ham, Stephen	4	4	1		
Seavey, Isaac	2	1	3		
McDuffee, James	3	1	3		
Bigford, Limney	3		3		
Nute, Saml	1	2	4		
Ham, Jon^a	2		2		
Hays, Joseph	1	3	5		
Ham, Izrael	1	2	4		
Whitehouse, Turner	4	3	2		

ROCHESTER TOWN—con.

NAME OF HEAD OF FAMILY.	Free white males of 16 years and upward, including heads of families.	Free white males under 16 years.	Free white females, including heads of families.	All other free persons.	Slaves.
Bigford, Isaac	2		1		
Hanson, Jacob	3	1	3		
Whetherell, John	2	1	5		
Courson, Ichabod	2	2	5		
Tebbits, Joseph	2		5		
Courson, Benj^a	1	1	1		
Allen, Saml	2	1	5		
Tebbits, David	2	1	4		
Ellice, William	2		2		
Elice, Ellaner		2	1		
Tebbets, Moses	1	1	2		
Tebbets, Robert	1	3	5		
Roberts, Heard	1	3	2		
Tebbets, Silas	1	2	2		
Trickey, John	1	5	4		
Tebbets, Ezecal	1	4	6		
Tebbets, Elezah	2	2	5		
Allen, Joshua	1	1	2		
Wingate, Daniel	3	2	4		
Wingate, Saml	3		5		
Twombley, Tobias	1		1		
Twombley, David	1	2	1		
Twombly, Saml	1	1	4		
Clark, Solomon	1	2	2		
Merrow, John	1	1	1		
Tebbets, John	1		3		
Coarson, Ichabot	2	2	2		
Twombly, Wentworth	1				
Heard, Joseph	1		1		
Hays, Nathl	1		5		
Garland, Dodipha	1	1	2		
Ellice, Jon^a	1		1		
Ellice, Jacob	1	1	2		
Ellice, Joshua	1	1	2		
Copp, Benj^a	4		4		
Plummer, Thomas	3	1	2		
Twombly, Stephen	1		2		
Trickey, Eph^m	1	1	3		
Coock, John	1	1	2		
Cloughtman, John	2		3		
Card, Thomas	2	2	5		
Wentworth, Ellahue	1	3	2		
Wentworth, Ebenz^r	2	1	4		
Hays, George	1	2	3		
Walker, Rich^d	2		5		
Twombly, Jon^a	5		5		
Maison, Rich^d	1	2	3		
Twombly, John	2		1		
Wentworth, Aaron	1	1	2		
Jons, Ebenz^r	3	3	4		
Palmer, Saml	1		2		
Pinkham, Jon^a	1	3	1		
Burgan, John	1	3	2		
Furber, Thomas	1	2	2		
Wentworth, Nicholas	1	3	3		
Palmer, Benj^a	1	2	5		
Hurtford, Nicholas	9		1		
Down, John	1				
Ricker, Ebenz^r	1	3	1		
Ricker, Timothy	1	2	3		
Wentworth, Saml S	1	2	3		
Wentworth, John	1		3		
Wingate, Enoch	1				
Wentworth, James	1		1		
Hays, Clement	1		2		
Ricker, Lem	2	3	5		
Plummer, Eph^m	1		2		
Wentworth, Steph^a	1		2		
Ham, Jon^a	1		2		
Twombly, Saml	1	1	6		
Pinkham, Nathl	1		1		
Wentworth, Dudly	1	2	2		
Pinkham, Thom^a	1	2	2		
Hays, Enoch	1	1	3		
Horne, Elijah	1	1	3		
Pirkins, Gilbert	1		2		
Door, Jon^a	1	3	1		
Door, Daniel	1		3		
Coarson, David	1	2	1		
Pirkins, Rich^d	2	2	3		
Drew, Eph^m	1		1		
Wallingford, David	1		1		
Scates, Benj^a	1	3	4		
Hait, Joseph	2	4	5		
Palmer, Willm	1	1	3		
Palmer, John	1		2		
Twombly, Eph^m	1	1	3		
Gerrish, Timothy	1		2		
Plummer, Beard	2	4	4		
Plummer, Joseph	2	1	4		
Hayes, James	1		2		

ROCHESTER TOWN—con.

NAME OF HEAD OF FAMILY.	Free white males of 16 years and upward, including heads of families.	Free white males under 16 years.	Free white females, including heads of families.	All other free persons.	Slaves.
Chamberlane, Moses	1	1	2		
Quimbey, Daniel	1	2	3		
Hanson, John	1	1	5		
Wingate, Caleb	1				
Horne, David	1	2	4		
Wingate, Ebenz^r	1				
Griffiss, W^m	1		1		
Carr, John	2	3	4		
Door, Benj^a	1	3	4		
Watson, Steph^n	1		2		
Noch, Nattan	2		2		
Chapman, Joseph	1	5	1		
Miller, Mark	4	3	3		
Door, Beniah	1	1	3		
Berry, James	1	1	2		
Berry, James	1		1		
Berry, W^m	1		2		
Whitehouse, Amos	3	2	1		
Whitehouse, John	1	2	2		
Pikes, Patty	1	1	4		
Knowls, James	3		3		
Knowls, John	1	5	2		
Ginnen, Danl	2	3	4		
Ginnen, W^m	5		2		
Coock, Jon^a	1	3	2		
McDuffee, John	1				
Kent, Ebenz^r	1		2		
Low, Phinias	1	2	3		
Low, Marry			3		
Jones, Rheuben	1	2	2		
Horne, Thomas	1	2	4		
Brackett, Isaac	1		2		
Hatch, Francis	1	3	3		
Deland, W^m	1	2	5		
Wentworth, John	1	2	2		
Dame, Jabis	4	1	4		

SANBORNTOWN TOWN.

NAME OF HEAD OF FAMILY.	Free white males of 16 years and upward, including heads of families.	Free white males under 16 years.	Free white females, including heads of families.	All other free persons.	Slaves.
Burleigh, David	2		3		
Burleigh, Josiah	1		2		
Brown, Mehitable		2	2		
Batchelor, W^m	1	1	2		
Colby, Isaac	2	3	3		
Cheney, John	1	2	2		
Cheney, John, Jr	1		2		
Cheney, Nathl	2	2	4		
Caulley, Jon^a	1	3	2		
Chapman, Elisha	2	3	3		
Copp, Solomon	1		2		
Copp, Thos	1	3	4		
Chandler, Abiel	1		2		
Cram, Dudley	2	2	2		
Colby, Ebenz^r	1		1		
Colby, Ebenz^r, Jr	1	2	1		
Emery, Josiah	3		6		
Eastman, Ebenz^r	2	5	4		
Eastman, Thos	1	2	3		
Elsworth, Aaron	1	3	2		
Fogg, Ephraim	1	1	1		
Fifield, Daniel	1	1	1		
Fifield, Daniel, Jr	1		2		
Fifield, Samuel	1		2		
Giles, Nicholas	1	4	4		
Gage, Thaddeus	1	2	2		
Gilman, Joseph	1	1	4		
Gove, Ebenz^r	2	2	3		
Grant, Nathl	2	1	1		
Huse, Joseph	2	2	3		
Huse, John	1	1			
Hasting, Timothy	1		3		
Hunking, Robert	1	2	1		
Hoit, Bernard	3		5		
Hoit, Nathl	1		2		
Jewett, Andrew	2	1	5		
Johnson, Abner	1		1		
Johnson, Brackett	1		1		
Johnson, Benj^a	1		2		
Johnson, John	2		4		
Judkins, Jon^a	1	1	3		
Judkins, Samuel	1	1	1		
Kimball, Abner	1	1	3		
Leavitt, Joseph	1		4		
Leavitt, Moses	1	1	4		
Moor, W^m	2	2	4		
Morgan, Benj^a	1	5	6		
Philbrook, Reuben	2	1	2		
Philbrook, David	2	2	5		
Perkins, Abraham	1		2		
Perkins, Jon^a	1	3	2		
Philbrook, Joseph	1		2		

STRAFFORD COUNTY—Continued.

SANBORNTOWN TOWN—continued.

NAME OF HEAD OF FAMILY.	Free white males of 16 years and upward, including heads of families.	Free white males under 16 years.	Free white females, including heads of families.	All other free persons.	Slaves.
Pearson, John	1	4	2		
Prescott, Wm., Jr	1	2	1		
Runlett, Joseph	1	1	1		
Robinson, Levi	1	4	3		
Robinson, John, Jr	1	3	3		
Robinson, Wm	1		4		
Sanborn, Josiah	4	1	2		
Shute, Thos	1	4	2		
Smith, Timothy	3	2	4		
Sinclair, Thos	1	2	2		
Sinclair, James	1		1		
Steel, Benja	3	2	4		
Sanborn, Josiah, 3d	2	2	1		
Swain, Ichabod	1		2		
Somes, John	1		1		
Smith, Peter	1	1	3		
Saunders, Peter	1		3		
Sanborn, Jona Cram	1		3		
Smith, Nathan	2	1	1		
Shaw, Josiah	1		2		
Smith, Benja	1	2	3		
Smith, Elisha	4	2	6		
Sanborn, Joshiah, Jr	2	4	5		
Taylor, William	1	3	4		
Taylor, John	2	1	3		
Taylor, Jona, Jr	1	1	3		
Thomas, Jona	2		3		
Thomas, Jacob	1	2	2		
Taylor, Jerem	1	2	2		
Whitcher, George	1	2	3		
Wheelock, Archipus	1	2	1		
Gilman, Moses	1	1	5		
Gilman, Simon, Jr	1	2	2		
Miles, Josiah	2	4	3		
Miles, Abner	1	5	1		
Gillman, Simon	2	3	2		
Dearbon, Josiah	1				
Cate, Benja	1		2		
Morrison, Jona	1	5	3		
Johnson, John	1		1		
Brown, Samuel	1	5	3		
Blake, Nathan	3	2	4		
Blake, Henry	1	1	3		
Buzzell, Noah	2	1	5		
Calley, Josiah	1	2	2		
Cass, John	1		2		
Colby, Benja	2	3	2		
Cantfield, Benja P	1	1	3		
Cally, Wm	1	1	1		
Cally, Benja	1	1	1		
Cally, Thos	1	2	4		
Chapman, John	3		5		
Caverly, Nathl	1	2	2		
Colby, John	1	2	2		
Colby, John, Jr	1	1	1		
Connor, Joseph	3	1	4		
Chandler, Nathl	1	3	4		
Colby, Richd	1		2		
Chace, Wm	2	2	7		
Chace, Jona, Jr	1	3	3		
Chace, David	1	1	2		
Chace, Ebenzr	1	1	2		
Cass, Jona	1	1	4		
Clark, Stephen	1	2	3		
Clark, Ebenzr	1		2		
Calley, Eliphalet	2	1	2		
Dustin, David	3	1	6		
Deverson, Daniel	1	1	1		
Dustin, David, Jr	1		3		
Dow, Eliphalet	2	1	3		
Dow, Chandler	1				
Caton, Wm	1	3	4		
Folsom, Theopa	2	2	4		
Harper, Wm	3	3	3		
Jaquish, Samuel	1	4	2		
Kelly, Edward	2		2		
Layn, Saml	2	5	2		
Layn, John	1	4	4		
Lang, Lowell	1	5	2		
Leavitt, Nathl	2		2		
Harper, Samuel	1		1		
Morrison, David	3		2		
Morrison, Bradbury	1	1	1		
Prescott, Wm	2		1		
Prescott, Elisha	1	2	3		
Prescott, Saml	1	2	1		
Parsons, Nathl	1	2	4		
Prescott, Stephn	1	1	1		
Prescott, Joseph	1		1		
Piper, Nathl	1	1	2		
Prescott, Joseph, Jr	1	2	2		

SANBORNTOWN TOWN—continued.

NAME OF HEAD OF FAMILY	Free white males of 16 years and upward, including heads of families.	Free white males under 16 years.	Free white females, including heads of families.	All other free persons.	Slaves.
Prescott, Joseph, 3d	1		1		
Prescott, Samuel, Jr	2	3	3		
Rollings, Jotham	1	3	5		
Rollings, Daniel	1		1		
Runlett, Wid. Comfort		3	3		
Rollings, Reuben	1	4	2		
Robertson, John	2	1	4		
Sanborn, Daniel	3	2	3		
Sanborn, Benaiah	3	2	6		
Sanborn, Jona Hobbs	1	2	5		
Sanborn, James	1		1		
Sanborn, John, Jr	1		5		
Smith, Joseph	4	1	2		
Smith, Joseph, Jr	1	2	2		
Smith, Jeremy	1	4	3		
Sufferance, Ephm	1	2	1		
Swain, Jeremh	1	1	3		
Swain, Anna			1		
Swain, Dudley	1				
Smith, Jona	3	1	2		
Smith, Noah	2	2	3		
Smith, Trueworthy	1	2	3		
Smith, Reuben	1		1		
Shaw, Josiah, Jr	1	2	2		
Swain, Ebenzr	1	2	2		
Smith, Solomon	1	1	1		
Jones, Wm. Carpenter	1	1	1		
Tilton, Daniel	1	4	3		
Taylor, Edwd	1				
Weeks, Thos	1		3		
Wadleigh, James	1	3	3		
Wadleigh, Joseph	1	1	3		
Weeks, Wm	1	1	3		
Weeks, Chace	1	1	4		
Weeks, Coll	2	2	1		
Weeks, John	1	1	1		
Thompson, Wm	1	4	3		
Hodskins, Wm	1	2	2		
Woodman, Joseph	2	4	7		
Cushing, Warden	3	2	2		
Wallis, Reuben	1	3	1		
Buzzell, Elias	1		4		
Brown, John	1	1	4		
Bamford, Jacob	2	1	3		
Burleigh Wm	2	2	3		
Burleigh, Nathl	3	1	4		
Bean, David	2		5		
Burbank, Nathl	1	4	3		
Burligh, Joseph	1	1	4		
Burleigh, Nathl, Jr	2	4	1		
Cates, James, Jr	1	3	3		
Calf, Jeremh	1	3	2		
Cross, Robert	2		1		
Cates, Elisha	1		5		
Cates, James	2	1	2		
Cates, Jona	1	2	3		
Cates, Simeon	1	1	1		
Clark, Nicho	2	2	2		
Clark, John	1	1	1		
Clark, Joseph	3	1	2		
Clark, Satechiel	3	1	4		
Clark, John, Jr	1	1	3		
Clark, Taylor	1	4	2		
Chase, Jona	2	1	5		
Critchel, Thomas	2	1	3		
Darling, Daniel	1	2	1		
Darling, Ebenzr	2	2	3		
Darling, Abraham	1	2	3		
Dearbon, John	1		1		
Durgin, Hannah			3		
Durgin, Wm	1	2	6		
Durgin, John	1	5	2		
Durgin, Wint	2	3	2		
Elkins, Peter	2		4		
Fullinton, James	3	2	2		
Fullinton, James, Jr	1		3		
Gale, Daniel	1	5	5		
Gale, John	3	1	6		
Gale, John Carter	1		1		
Garland, Jacob	1	1	4		
Gibson, James	1	1	4		
Gibson, Jeremh	1	3	3		
Gibson, Enoch	1				
Gale, Stephen	2	1	4		
Hains, James	1	2	1		
Hains, Simeon	1	2	5		
Hersey, James	1		6		
Hayes, Wid. Mary	1		2		
Hart, Saml	2	2	3		
Hersey, Jacob	1				

SANBORNTOWN TOWN—continued.

NAME OF HEAD OF FAMILY.	Free white males of 16 years and upward, including heads of families.	Free white males under 16 years.	Free white females, including heads of families.	All other free persons.	Slaves.
Hersey, Peter	2	1	3		
Hunt, Phillip	1		2		
Hunt, Phillip, Jr	1	3	2		
Hunt, Ephm	1		2		
Huse, Wm	1	2	3		
Hunt, Humphrey	1		2		
Hanniford, John	2		1		
Hayes, Wm	2	2	2		
Hersey, Wm	1		1		
Hersey, Josiah	1	1	2		
Layn, David	1		2		
Lancaster, Thos	1	3	3		
Morrison, Saml	1	2	2		
McGoon, Saml	1	1	1		
Morrison, Ebenzr	4	1	4		
Morrison, Ebenzr, Jr	1	1	1		
Morrison, John	2	2	3		
March, Joshua	2		4		
March, Moses	2	2	2		
Osgood, James	1	1	3		
Robinson, Benja	2		3		
Robinson, Benja, Jr	1	1	2		
Runlett, Reuben	1		3		
Sanborn, Josiah, 4th	1		1		
Sanborn, Andrew	1				
Sanborn, Jeremh	5	2	4		
Smith, Jacob	1	1	2		
Sanborn, Abner	2		1		
Sanborn, Hilliard	2	1	2		
Sanborn, Caleb M:	1				
Sanborn, Mary	1		4		
Sanborn, Ebenr	1	1	6		
Sanborn, Benja	3	3	7		
Smith, Henry	1				
Smart, Robert	1		1		
Smith, Stephen	1	1	2		
Smith, Benja, Jr	1	2	1		
Sanborn, John	2	1	4		
Sanborn, Jeremh, Jr	1	1	2		
Sanders, John	1	2	5		
Sanborn, Susanna			2		
Sanborn, Peter	2	2	2		
Thompson, Jona	2	1	2		
Thorn, John	4	2	3		
Tenney, Saml	1	3	3		
Thompson, Mathew	1	2	1		
Thompson, Moses	2	4	6		
Tilton, Jacob	1	4	4		
Tilton, Nathl	2	1	3		
Tilton, Jeremh	1	2	1		
Taylor, Chace	1				
Taylor, Nathl	1	1	4		
Rowen, Andrew	3		2		
Burligh, Stephn	3		4		
Elkins, Joseph	1	2	2		
Hunking, Isaac	1				
Bango, Joshua	1		1		
Durgin, Elijah	1				
Thompson, Jacob	1		4		

SANDWICH TOWN.

NAME OF HEAD OF FAMILY.	Free white males of 16 years and upward, including heads of families.	Free white males under 16 years.	Free white females, including heads of families.	All other free persons.	Slaves.
Wead, Hannah	1	1	6		
Sanderson, Ruben	1	2	4		
Watson, John	1	1	2		
Folsom, John	1	1	2		
Eastman, James	1	1	1		
Brier, Peter	1	1	2		
Kenniston, Saml	1				
Beade, Daniel	1	5	2		
Atwood, Philip	1				
Varney, Eliph	1		1		
Bean, Andrew	1				
Wead, Henry	2	2	5		
Brewer, Moses H	1	1	3		
Bean, Josiah	3	1	4		
Hacket, George	1				
Hacket, John	1	1	2		
McGaffee, Andrew	1	6	3		
McGaffee, Saml	1	3	2		
McGaffee, John	2	1	4		
McGaffee, Workman	1		1		
McGaffee, Henry	1	4	4		
McGaffee, Andrew	1		1		
Fogg, Sherborne	1	1	4		
Harriss, Saml	1				
Brown, David	1				
Willson, John	1	1	3		
Calley, Nathl	1	6	1		
Jewel, John	2	2	7		
French, Nathl	2	1	3		

STRAFFORD COUNTY—Continued.

SANDWICH TOWN—con.

NAME OF HEAD OF FAMILY.	Free white males of 16 years and upward, including heads of families.	Free white males under 16 years.	Free white females, including heads of families.	All other free persons.	Slaves.
Quimbey, Joseph	1	2	1		
Quimbey, Aaron	4	3	4		
Sinckler, Zebuland	1		3		
Colbey, John	2	4	4		
Morse, Sarah		1	4		
Quimbey, Wm	3	3	4		
Webster, Jacob	1		4		
Bean, David	3	3	3		
Coock, Cornelious	2		1		
Scrivner, John	1	4	2		
Jewell, Jacob	2	1	3		
Winslow, Saml	1	2	5		
Wells, Edwards	2				
Webster, Hezekh	1				
Beade, Jona	1	2	1		
Thracher, Joseph	1	1	6		
Gilman, Peter	1	1	3		
Bean, Hugh	1	1	1		
Webster, Stephen	3	2	3		
Altridge, Nathl	1	1	2		
Maxfield, Eliph	3	1	3		
Brier, Simon	1		2		
Muggett, Elisha	1	1	3		
Jewell, Sargent	1	1	2		
Gilman, Caleb	1	1	4		
Webster, John	3	2	5		
Beadey, Nathan	2	3	4		
Hoacey, Enoch	1	2	3		
Hoacey, Stephen	1	1	1		
Colby, Thomas	1	3	5		
Har, Joshua	2	1	2		
Burley, Thomas	1		3		
Burley, Samuel	1		3		
Hoit, Betsy		5	2		
Ettridge, Nathl	1	1	2		
Ferguson, Eleazr	1	2	5		
Prescott, Bradbury	1	2	2		
Prescott, Joshua	1	1	2		
Smith, Eleas	1		2		
Bean, Philip	1		2		
Marsten, Whithrop	1	1	3		
Smith, Daniel	1				
Ladd, John	1	5	2		
Sandborn, Jethro	1	3	4		
Bean, Benja	1	1	7		
Smith, Simion, jr	1		3		
Smith, Simion	1	5	4		
Gilman, Jona	3	1	2		
Smith, Jacob	2	3	4		
Smith, Eliph	1	1	3		
Kimbell, Sargent	1	2	3		
Ladd, Elias	1		2		
Thompson, Saml	1	1	2		
Burley, Thomas	2	3	4		
Hill, Samuel	2	1	8		
Smith, Edward	4		3		
Wallace, Ebenzr	1	1	2		
Page, Saml	1				
Burley, Josiah	1	1	1		
Atkinson, Benja	4	1	3		
True, Enoch	3	2	4		
Hogskem, Francis	1	3	3		
Ladd, Elias	3	1	5		
Furgerson, Wm	1	3	1		
Moulton, Ruben	1		3		
Tukesby, Timo	1	4	5		
Ethard, Stephen	2	3	2		
Peade, John	1	1	2		
Bean, Benja	1	1	6		
Moulton, Danl	1	3	5		
George, James	1				
Beade, Jacob	1	1	3		
Moulton, Danl	1	3	5		
Allcott, Saml	1	4	4		
Varney, Richd	2		4		
Varney, Joseph	1	2	2		
Beade, Danl	3	1	6		
Norris, James	1	3	2		
Randal, Mark	1	3	1		
Randal, Ruben	1	2	2		
Sinckler, Ebenzr	1		3		
Rice, Pheby	3	1	1		
Rice, John	1	1	2		
Telton, Jeremy	2	5	3		
Sinckler, Richd, jr	1				
Sinckler, Rich	3	1	5		
Burley, Benja	3	4	4		
Crosby, Asa	1				
Prescott, John	2	3	9		
French, Ezekal	1	2	3		
Prescott, John	1	2	2		
Scribner, Benja	2	1	8		

[SANDWICH TOWN—con.

NAME OF HEAD OF FAMILY.	Free white males of 16 years and upward, including heads of families.	Free white males under 16 years.	Free white females, including heads of families.	All other free persons.	Slaves.
Tappan, Christopher	1	1	2		
Scribner, Nathl	1		2		
Tappan, Abraham	1	1	3		
Page, Jerimy	3	1	5		
Brown, John	1	4	2		
Brown, Saml	1		2		
Choat, Jona	1	3	4		
Wead, Bayley	3	2	3		
Wead, Nathl	2	1	4		
Kenniston, David	1		4		
Blanchard, Benja	2	3	7		
Wead, Sarah		2	3		
Bennet, Stephen	1	1	1		
Page, Wm	1	1	4		
Cram, Nehemiah	1		2		
Cram, Nehm., jr	2	2	1		
Jewell, Jacob, jr	1	2	3		
Mugett, Thoms	1		2		
Mudget, Thoms., jr	1	2	4		
Vittam, Wm	3		2		
Vittam, Wm	1	3	1		
Vittam, Stephen	1	3	3		
Wallace, John	1	3	3		
Webster, Wm	1	1	2		
Webster, Joseph	1	1	3		
Webster, Jona	1	2	1		
Wead, Moses	2	5	4		
Knowls, Nathl	2	2	4		
Page, Jona	1		1		
Page, Jona	1	2	3		
Page, Moses	1	1	3		
Brown, Nathl	1	1	4		
Hubbard, John	1	2	6		
Bradbury, Ephm	1	1	6		

SOMERSWORTH TOWN.

NAME OF HEAD OF FAMILY.	Free white males of 16 years and upward, including heads of families.	Free white males under 16 years.	Free white females, including heads of families.	All other free persons.	Slaves.
Coock, Joseph	2	1	3		
Twombly, Isaac	2	1	5		
Horne, Wm	5	1	3		
Wentworth, Danl	3		2		
Clemment, Job	1		2		
Philpot, Richd	1	1	5		
Huzzey, Saml	2	2	9		
Paul, Daniel	1	1	3		
Paul, Josiah	1	1	3		
Frost, Saml	1	3	6		
Paul, Benja	1	2	5		
Philpot, Ruth			3		
Philpot, John	1	4	3		
Goodwin, Danl	1	1	2		
Robert, Nathan	1	1	3		
Stiles, John	1	2	4		
Roberts, Nathan	2		2		
Roberts, Saml	1	4	2		
Stiles, Wm	1	1	2		
Roberts, Paul	1	2	2		
Hobs, James	1	1	3		
Garvin, James	1	1	2		
Garvin, Thomas	1	2	1		
Pray, Danl	1	1	3		
Roberts, Saml	2		2		
Hobs, John	1	1	3		
Whitehouse, Enoch	1		3		
Whitehouse, Thoms	1		1		
Stagpole, Stephn	2	3	2		
Stagpole, Otis	1	3	2		
Varney, Wm	1	2	3		
Stagpole, Tobias	1		3		
Rollins, John	3	3	5		1
Stagpole, Wm	1		1		
Chadwick, Wm	2	2	7		
Pappoo, Hannah			2		
Roberts, Joseph	1	2	1		
Quimby, Jacob	1	2	4		
Quimby, Benja	2	2	5		
Lord, Nathan	1		2		
Frash, Lydia	2	1	4		
Stagpole, Lydia	1		1		
Pike, Saml	2		3		
Roberts, John	2				
Ricker, Ebenzr	5		6		1
Borce, Richd	5	3	3		
Tebbets, Rheuben	2	2	6		
Tebbets, John	2	1	3		
Whitehouse, Richd	3	3	4		
Goodwin, Noah	1	4	3		
Eaton, Trestin	1		2		
Furnis, John	1	1	3		
Eaton, Francis	2		1		
Ricker, Lydia	1		2		
Robert, Thomas	2	2	1		

SOMERSWORTH TOWN—continued.

NAME OF HEAD OF FAMILY.	Free white males of 16 years and upward, including heads of families.	Free white males under 16 years.	Free white females, including heads of families.	All other free persons.	Slaves.
Eaton, Saml	1	1	4		
Drew, John	4	1	7		
Roberts, Francis	2	3	4		
Roberts, James	2		6		
Varney, Zackeus	2	1	3		
Nichols, Thoms	3	2	7		
Wentworth, Andrew	1				
Roberts, Jedediah	1	1	5		
Wallingford, Thomas	4	1	4		
Stillson, Wm	1	2	1		
Eaton, Moses	1		3		
Mirron, Jona	2		2		
Roberts, Hativil	1	2	3		
Kenney, John	3		5		
Ricker, James	1		3		
Jones, Benja	2	1	2		
Plummer, Ebenzr	1	2	1		
Roberts, James	2	1	1		
Roberts, John	2	1	2		
Hall, John	2		3		
Varney, Joseph	1		2		
Varney, Joseph	1	3	3		
Roberts, Ebenzr	2	1	5		
Crommell, Eliph	2	1	1		
Hobs, Morris	1		2		
Varney, Saml	1		3		
Pike, Danl	2		1		
Brown, Wm	1	3	2		
Wentworth, Benja	1	2	2		
Downs, Saml	3		1		
Whitehouse, Ebenzr	1	1	3		
Pierce, Thomas	1		2		
Randal, Saml	1	1	3		
Barnald, Saml	1	3	2		
Carr, Moses	1	3	3		
Wentworth, Thoms	2	1			
Door, John	1	2	5		
Brown, Charls	1	1	5		
Ricker, David	2	3	6		
Wentworth, Saml	1		3		
Cole, John	1	1	2		
Ricker, Phinias	2		5		
Ricker, Aaron	1	1	4		
Wentworth, Joshua	1		1		
Wentworth, John	2	1	2		
Wentworth, Gersham	3	1	2		
Stephens, Aaron	2		5		
Wentworth, Drisco	2	3	5		
Wentworth, Barthl	2	4	5		
Wentworth, Evens	1		4		
Horne, Andrew	3		1		
Horne, Andrew	1	1	3		
Warrin, Francis	2	4	3		
Warrin, Moses	1	2	2		
Roberts, Benja	1		3		
Wallingford, Amos	1		4		1
Carr, James	1	2	4		
Carr, Moses	1	1	2		
Pike, James	1		2		
Pike, John	1	4	2		
Stagpole, Philip	1				
Clement, James	1	2	6		
Clement, Saml	1		2		
Wentworth, Benja	3	2	4		
Clement, Elijah	1	2	2		
Rollins, Ichabod	2	1	2		2
Rollins, Ruth	1	2	6		
Rollins, Danl	1	1	1		
Ricker, John	2	1	5		
Ricker, Danl	3	4	6		
Stephens, Moses	1	1	3		
Hammoch, Deborah			1		
Huzzey, Robert	1		1		
Austin, Stephn	1	2	5		
Austin, Danl	2				
Austin, Peter	1	3	2		
Randal, Tobias	2		2		
Wentworth, Mark	2	5	3		
Hanson, Elijah	1	5	3		
Wentworth, Benja	1				
Huzzey, Benja	1	1	2		
Brown, Joshua	1	3	4		
Horne, Saml. & Caleb	2	1	2		
Rollins, James	3	2	5		
Coal, John	1	1	3		
Teat, Joseph	1	2	2		
Brown, John	2		3		
Roberts, John	1	1	2		
Roberts, Alexr	3		2		
Wentworth, Ephm	1	2	2		
Hays, John	1				

STRAFFORD COUNTY—Continued.

NAME OF HEAD OF FAMILY.	Free white males of 16 years and upward, including heads of families.	Free white males under 16 years.	Free white females, including heads of families.	All other free persons.	Slaves.
SOMERSWORTH TOWN—continued.					
Wentworth, Benjr	2	2	3		
Roberts, Timo	1	3	1		
Burnham, James	2	1	1		
Burnham, Nathl	2	1	2		
Varney, Benja	1		1		
Baker, Sarah	3	1	2		
Marden, John	1	1	3		
Canney, Wm	2	2	4		
Coock, Ichabod	1	1	2		
Horne, Danl	1		2		
Heard, Jacob	1	4	6		
Randal, Jacob	1	4	4		
Goudy, Thoms	1	2	4		
Moore, Wm	1	1	6		
Hanson, Timo	1		1		
Marden, Baersheba		1	2		
Hanson, Tobias	1		2		
Tuttle, Saml	1	2	3		
STARK'S LOCATION.					
Starks, Samuel	1		1		
Starks, Archb	1				
STERLING'S LOCATION.					
Heath, Benja	1		3		
Sterling, Huge	2		1		
Walker, Joseph	1	2	4		
Ardua, Joseph	1		1		
Ardua, Burbank	1	1	2		
Wilson, John	1	2	4		
Wentworth, Paul	1	3	3		
Ardua, Joseph, jr	1	3	4		
Ardua, John	1	2	3		
TAMWORTH TOWN.					
Smith, Josiah	1		3		
Nickerson, Josha	2		2		
Filbrook, Jona	1	3	3		
Gilman, Izrael	1	1	1		
Clough, Joseph	1	2	1		
Field, David	1	4	3		
Gilman, David	3	1	3		
Allen, Japhat	2	1	3		
Fowler, Oliver	3		7		
Fowler, Oliver, jr	1		1		
Remmick, Enoch	3		3		
Mason, Stephen	5		3		
Hefferd, Edwd	1	3	4		
Fowler, John	1	4	7		
Gilman, Wm	1		1		
Mason, James	1		3		
Low, Danl	1	5	3		
Cheever, Wm	1	2	4		
Gilman, Benja	2	2	4		
Eastman, Wm	1		3		
Eastman, Jacob	1	2	3		
Watson, Thoms	1	1	1		
Roger, Noah	1	2	1		
Dodge, George	1	3	2		
Caster, Jonas	1	2	4		
Hall, Silvanus	1		1		
Gilman, Izra	1	1	3		1
Weymouth, Saml	1		2		
Meades, Timo	3		2		
Hackett, Hezekh	1	3	3		
Ballard, Day	1		3		
Vettam, John	1	2	3		
Folsom, Levi	1	4	2		
Wallace, John	1	3	3		
Dockham, Cotton	1	1	2		
Dockham, Mehapsuble	1		6		
Bow, John	1		1		
Folsom, Israel	2	4	4		
Jewell, Mack	1	4	3		
Stimpson Thoms	1	1	1		
Gilman, Saml	4	1	4		
Bradbury, Paul	1	2	4		
Remmeck, John	1	3	1		
Pender, John	1				
Gilman, Saml	1	3	2		
Folsom, Benja	1	1	2		
Stimpson, John	1	1	1		
TUFTONBOROUGH TOWN.					
Brown, Moses	1		2		
Dockham, James	1	1	1		

NAME OF HEAD OF FAMILY.	Free white males of 16 years and upward, including heads of families.	Free white males under 16 years.	Free white females, including heads of families.	All other free persons.	Slaves.
TUFTONBOROUGH TOWN—continued.					
Abbot, Saml	1	1	1		
Abbot, Elisha	1	1	2		
Mellen, Wm	1	2	1		
Copp, Trustam	5		3		
Young, Benja	1	2	5		
Brown, Jona	3	2	3		
Libbey, Benja	2	1	5		
Libby, Hanson	1	1	4		
Whitehouse, James	1	1	3		
Warren, Wm	1	2	4		
Nutter, Murry	2		2		
Pierce, Benja	1		2		
Lee, Ebenzr	1		2		
Brown, Obediah	2	1	5		
Moody, Abner	1	1	2		
Bean, Benja	1		5		
Graves, Phineas	1	2	5		
Moody, Edward	1	2	3		
WAKEFIELD TOWN.					
Wiggen, Jacob	1	3	3		
Rutchins, Solomon	1	1	3		
Wiggen, Simon	3	3	2		
Chapman, Saml	2		3		
Wiggen, Isaac	1	2	2		
Palmer, Jona	1	4	5		
Lingsey, Thomas	1		1		
Allen, Elijah	2	1	2		
Steel, Clemment	1	1	4		
Mannen, John	1				
Moody, Saml	1	1	3		
Chapman, Saml., jr	1	2	1		
Gilman, Jona	1	1	1		
Gilman, Peter	1	1	2		
Gilman, Dudly	1	2			
Kimbal, Noah	1	2	3		
Kimbal, John	2	4	4		
Page, Josiah	1	2	5		
Cook, Ebenzr	1	2	6		
Gilman, Andrew	2	1	2		
Garland, John	1	3	1		
leavett, Joseph	2	3	3		
Moore, Wm	1	1	2		
Hodgdon, Nathan	1				
Moore, Josiah	1	1	2		
Perry, Allen	2	5	2		
Blazo, Wm	4	1	3		
Thurstain, Oliver	1				
Thurstain, Thoms	1				
Dearborne, Marthy	3		2		
Perkins, Benja	2	4	2		
Perkins, Thoms	2	2	5		
Sherburne, Saml	3	2	6		
Piper, Asa	1		3		
Cloutman, Thoms	1	4	2		
Gain, Samuel	1		1		
Nudd, Thoms	3		4		
Young, Jona	1	2	2		
Pike, Moses	1				
Copp, David	3	5	5		
Philbrook, Elipt	2	3	6		
Wingate, John	2	2	5		
Sanbourn, Rheuben	1	1	2		
Horn, John	1	1	2		
Goudy, Otes	1		2		
Hutchins, James	1	1	1		
Hodgdon, Joseph	1	1	4		
Hall, Daniel	1		2		
Hall, Benja	1	1	1		
Sanbourn, Joseph	3		2		
Hanson, Tobias	1	5	5		
Willey, Nathl	1	1	2		
Merrow, David	1	1	2		
Edgerly, Joshua	1	3	2		
Copp, Moses	1	1	2		
Hains, Joseph	3	2	2		
Hardy, Robert	1	2	4		
Randlett, Josha	1	1	2		
Allen, Saml	1		1		
Allen, Abner	1	2	5		
Hall, Avery	2	1	3		
Allen, Saml	2		4		
Gilman, John	1	3	4		
Hill, John	3		1		
Murder, Nathl	1	3	2		
Malum, Joseph	1	2	2		
Huggins, John	1	1	5		
Horne, Daniel	1	2	3		
Quimbey, Jona	1	2	3		

NAME OF HEAD OF FAMILY.	Free white males of 16 years and upward, including heads of families.	Free white males under 16 years.	Free white females, including heads of families.	All other free persons.	Slaves.
WAKEFIELD TOWN—continued.					
Lock, Jacob	1	1	3		
Lang, Rheuben	1	2	1		
Weeks, John	1	4	4		
Allen, Joshua	2	3	5		
Watson, John	1	1	3		
Hall, Saml	2	2	4		
Kneel, Ebenzr	2	1	3		
Kneel, Walter	1	1	3		
Leavett, Edwd	1	2	3		
Dame, Saml	1	4	1		
Coock, Nathl	1	4	2		
Clark, Jacob	1	3	5		
Johnson, John	1				
Bickford, Thoms	1	1	2		
Young, James	1	2	3		
Blake, John	1	3	2		
Cook, Jona	1		2		
Cook, Peter	1	2	2		
Cook, Peter	1		1		
Wentworth, Spencer	1	4	4		
Hawkens, Stepn	2	3	2		
Derborn, Jeremy	2	2	2		
Derborn, Rheun G	2	1			
Dow, Richd	1	5	2		
Fowler, Isaac	4	4	5		
Derborn, Nathan	1	1	7		
Welch, Jacob	3	4	3		
Frisk, Jona	1	3	2		
Frisk, Joseph	1	3	2		
Burley, Jona	1	4	2		
Kelley, Philip	1	3	2		
Brown, Benja	1	2	1		
Brunt, James	2	2	4		
Hill, Ebenz	1	3	1		
Perkens, Solomon	1	2	3		
Hodgdon, Saml	1	2	4		
Plumer, Gersham	1	1	1		
Wentworth, Mark	1		2		
Wentworth, Silva	1		1		
Cook, Abrah	1		1		
Scribner, John	1	3	5		
Safford, Benja	1		2		
Gage, Moses	1				
Daniels, Rheuben	1		2		
Cook, Nathn	1		4		
Cook, Ichabod	1		2		
WOLFBOROUGH TOWN.					
Lary, Joseph	1	2	1		
Clifford, Lemuel	2	3	4		
Clefford, Athiel	1		1		
Fullerton, James	1		4		
Blake, Benja	1	2	2		
Libbey, Ruben	1	1	8		
Meader, Ebenzr	1	2	2		
Merril, Goss	1				
Thomas, Enoch	1	3	4		
Lary, Joseph	1	1	2		
Fullerton, John	1	1	4		
Horne, Ebenzr	1	2	3		
Horne, John	1	2	3		
Horne, Josiah	1	2	2		
Horne, Benja	1		1		
Horne, Benja	1	1	3		
Horne, Stephen	1	2	3		
Leavett, Josiah	1		2		
Piper, David	1	1	2		
Edmonds, Joseph	2		2		
Edmonds, Jona	1	1	4		
Wiggen, Andrew	2	1	3		
Copp, David	1	2	1		
Pipper, Thomas	1	2	1		
Hussey, Jona	2	4	3		
Lucas, John	1	3	1		
Fullington, Wm	1	2	3		
Popper, John	1	3	2		
Gould, Jeremy	2	2	1		
Tebbits, Saml	2	3			
Lucas, Andrew	1		7		
Rogers, William	1	4	4		
Tebbets, Levi	1		2		
Tebbits, Ebenzr	1				
Varney, Moses	4		4		
Basseth, John	2	1	3		
Lucas, James	1	5	1		
Allard, Henry	1	1	1		
Whitten, Jesse	1	1	1		
Lucas, Wm	2	2	5		
Chamberlain, Jasan	1	3	2		

NAME OF HEAD OF FAMILY.	Free white males of 16 years and upward, including heads of families.	Free white males under 16 years.	Free white females, including heads of families.	All other free persons.	Slaves.	NAME OF HEAD OF FAMILY.	Free white males of 16 years and upward, including heads of families.	Free white males under 16 years.	Free white females, including heads of families.	All other free persons.	Slaves.	NAME OF HEAD OF FAMILY.	Free white males of 16 years and upward, including heads of families.	Free white males under 16 years.	Free white females, including heads of families.	All other free persons.	Slaves.
WOLFBOROUGH TOWN—continued.						WOLFBOROUGH TOWN—continued.						WOLFBOROUGH TOWN—continued.					
Smith, Jacob	2		3			Furber, John	2	3	3			Jenness, Cornelious	1	3	2		
Larry, John	1		5			Snell, John	1		1			Frost, Aaron	2	4	4		
Conner, James	2	2	6			Warren, John	1	1	2			Cotton, Thomas	3	1	7		
Wiggen, Benjᵃ	1	4	1			Eaton, George	1		3			Harris, Joshua	1	2	3		
Rust, Henry	2	2	3			Stoddard, Duncin	1	1	2			Sweasy, John	1		3		
Rust, Henry	1		3			Brow, Nathan	1	1	1			Tebbets, Saml	2	1	4		
Rust, Richᵈ	1	2	3			Marsten, John	2	1	1			Goldsmith, Isaac	2	3	3		
Triggs, Wᵐ	2	2	3			Marsten, John	1		3			Hardy, Perry					
Shover, John	1	2	5			Cotten, Wᵐ	5	2	2			Kenniston, Joseph	2	3	4		
Evens, Joseph	2		2			Saltridge, John	2	2	4			Emmerson, John	2	1	7		
Warren, George	1					Tebbets, Edmond	1	1	2			Hide, Samˡ	3	6	2		
Marden, James	1		2			Cotten, Wᵐ	1	1	2								
Leavett, Elizᵃ		3	3			Drew, Isaac	4	2	6								

INDEX.[1]

[1] No attempt has been made in this publication to correct mistakes in spelling made by the deputy marshals, but the names have been reproduced as they appear upon the census schedules.

Parker, Hannaniah, 58.
Parker, Henshaw, 15.
Parker, Hezekiah, 55.
Parker, Isaac, 35.
Parker, John, 25.
Parker, John, 41.
Parker, John, 77.
Parker, John, junr, 77.
Parker, John, 80.
Parker, Jonathan, 14.
Parker, Jonathan, 25.
Parker, Jonᵃ, 47.
Parker, Jonᵃ, 49.
Parker, Joseph, 18.
Parker, Joseph, 26.
Parker, Joseph, 32.
Parker, Joseph, 52.
Parker, Joseph, 77.
Parker, Josiah, 47.
Parker, Josiah, 58.
Parker, Lemuel, 35.
Parker, Levi, 35.
Parker, Mary, 49.
Parker, Matthew, 49.
Parker, Matthew, 49.
Parker, Nahum, 16.
Parker, Nathaniel, 26.
Parker, Obadiah, 50.
Parker, Pearl, 26.
Parker, Phineas, 24.
Parker, Phinehas, 14.
Parker, Rebecca, 81.
Parker, Reuben, 22.
Parker, Robert, 11.
Parker, Robt., 39.
Parker, Robt., 49.
Parker, Robert, 50.
Parker, Robert, 80.
Parker, Samuel, 18.
Parker, Samuel, 20.
Parker, Samuel, 24.
Parker, Samuel, 26.
Parker, Samuel, 35.
Parker, Saml., 48.
Parker, Samuel, 77.
Parker, Sarah, 53.
Parker, Sarah, 58.
Parker, Silas, 22.
Parker, Silas, 47.
Parker, Solomon, 35.
Parker, Solomon, Junr, 35.
Parker, Stephen, 15.
Parker, Stephen, 46.
Parker, Thomas, 26.
Parker, Timothy, 81.
Parker, William, 18.
Parker, William, 18.
Parker, William, 40.
Parker, William, 41.
Parker, William, 47.
Parker, William, 50.
Parker, William, 67.
Parker, William, Junr. 67.
Parker, William, 80.
Parker, William, 80.
Parker, Zachariah, 37.
Parkhurst, Andrew, 56.
Parkhurst, George, 20.
Parkhurst, John, 19.
Parkhurst, John, 36.
Parkhurst, Josiah, 36.
Parkhurst, William, 50.
Parkhurt, Jesse, 58.
Parkhurt, Jonᵃ, 58.
Parkhurt, Jonᵃ, Jr., 58.
Parkinson, Wᵐ, 71.
Parkis, Phinehas, 34.
Parkman, Ezekiel, 55.
Parks, Abel, 32.
Parks, Alexander, 85.
Parks, Andrew, 85.
Parks, David, 12.
Parks, Elexander, 85.
Parks, Jonas, 12.
Parks, Joseph, 85.
Parks, Robert, 67.
Parley, Isaac, 49.
Parlim, Stephen, 56.
Parmala, Ezra, 20.
Parmala, Oliver, 14.
Parmarter, Thaddeus, 19.
Parmer, James, 49.
Parmer, Jeremiah, 49.
Parmer, John, 49.
Parmer, Jonathan, 49.
Parmer, Samuel, 44.
Parmiter, Nathl., 47.
Parrot, John, 51.
Parrot, John, 80.
Parry, Martin, 80.
Parry, Richard, 80.
Parry, Richmond, 80.
Parseval, Ichabod, 30.
Parseval, Rowland, 30.
Parseval, Rowland, Jur., 30.
Parsley, George, 87.
Parsley, John, 87.
Parsley, Saml., 87.
Parson, Joseph, 90.
Parsons, Aaron, 25.
Parsons, Abraham, 91.
Parsons, Amos, 35.

Parsons, Benjamin, 25.
Parsons, Ebenezer, 35.
Parsons, Ebenzr, 90.
Parsons, Eliakim, 13.
Parsons, James, 35.
Parsons, John, 63.
Parsons, Jonᵃ, 90.
Parsons, Joseph, 82.
Parsons, Josiah, 90.
Parsons, Mary, 74.
Parsons, Moses, 34.
Parsons, Nathl., 98.
Parsons, Stepᵃ, 76.
Parsons, Sumsbrey, 41.
Parsons, Willᵐ, 90.
Parsons, Willᵐ, Jr., 91.
Partrick, Samuel, 16.
Partridge, Amaziah, 25.
Partridge, Amos, 13.
Partridge, Benjamin, 80.
Partridge, Eli, 13.
Partridge, Eli, 2d, 13.
Partridge, Joseph, 13.
Partridge, Levi, 18.
Partridge, Simeon, 15.
Pascall, Elizabeth, 81.
Pasley, Joshua, 87.
Pasley, Richd, 87.
Pasley, Thos., 87.
Patch, Jonᵃ, 44.
Patch, Joseph, 38.
Patch, Reuben, 51.
Patch, Samuel, 16.
Patch, Saml., 51.
Patch, Stephen, 51.
Patch, Thomas, 40.
Patch, Thomas, 44.
Patch, Thomas, 47.
Patingale, Phineas, 71.
Patrick, John, 34.
Patrick, Rufus, 16.
Patrick, William, 46.
Patridge, Taby, 63.
Patten, David, 62.
Patten, James, 65.
Patten, James R., 71.
Patten, John, 18.
Patten, John, 41.
Patten, John, 56.
Patten, John, 61.
Patten, Jonᵃ, 42.
Patten, Joseph, 41.
Patten, Matthew, 41.
Patten, Nathl., 54.
Patten, Nathl., Jr., 54.
Patten, Robt., 41.
Patten, Robt., 47.
Patten, Robt., 60.
Patten, Samuel, 40.
Patten, Saml., 42.
Patten, Saml., 41.
Patten, Stepᵃ, 88.
Patten, Thos., 60.
Patterson, David, 71.
Patterson, Eleazar, Jr., 46.
Patterson, Isaac, 36.
Patterson, Isaac, 53.
Patterson, John, 71.
Patterson, Joseph, 46.
Patterson, Joseph, 76.
Patterson, Josiah, 46.
Patterson, Peter, 71.
Patterson, Peter, 71.
Patterson, Robt., 51.
Patterson, Robt., Jr., 51.
Patterson, Robt., 3d, 51.
Patterson, Saml., 41.
Patterson, Saml., 42.
Patterson, Temperance, 73.
Patterson, Thos, 71.
Patterson, William, 51.
Patterson, Wᵐ, 71.
Patterson, Williot, 54.
Pattin, Benoni, 27.
Pattin, Wᵐ, 70.
Pattington, Eleazr, 46.
Pattinson, Garvin, 67.
Pattle, Simon, 94.
Paul, Benjᵃ, 99.
Paul, Cæsar, 85.
Paul, Daniel, 99.
Paul, David, 70.
Paul, James, 26.
Paul, James, 70.
Paul, Josiah, 99.
Paulisher, Jonᵃ, 64.
Payne, Amos, 95.
Payne, Edward, 21.
Payne, Elisha, 34.
Payne, Elisha, Junr, 34.
Payne, Hannah, 30.
Payne Jesse, 21.
Payne, John, 34.
Payne, John, 62.
Payne, John, 95.
Payne, Richard, 95.
Payne, Samuel, 34.
Payne, Stoores, 35.
Payne, Thomas, 31.
Payson, Edward, 16.
Payson, Jonᵃ, 78.
Payson, Seth, 23.

Peabody, Aaron, 44.
Peabody, Abrᵐ, 76.
Peabody, David, Jr., 53.
Peabody, David, 53.
Peabody, Ephraim, 58.
Peabody, Hannah, 39.
Peabody, Isaac, 50.
Peabody, Isaac, 51.
Peabody, Isaac, 58.
Peabody, Jedidiah, 56.
Peabody, John, 37.
Peabody, Moses, 18.
Peabody, Moses, 18.
Peabody, Moses, 39.
Peabody, Nathl, 58.
Peabody, Oliver, 67.
Peabody, Saml., 39.
Peabody, Revd Stephen, 58.
Peabody, Thomas, 39.
Peabody, William, 40.
Peacock, John, 13.
Peacock, John, 17.
Peacock, Samuel, 13.
Peacock, William, 39.
Peade, John, 99.
Peake, John, 14.
Peake, Joseph, 96.
Pearce, Levi, 56.
Pearce, Nathl., 53.
Pearce, William, 73.
Pearl, Benjᵃ, 86.
Pearl, Ichabod, 96.
Pearl, John, 86.
Pearl, John, 96.
Pearl, Wᵐ, 86.
Pearle, Abigal, 97.
Pearle, Dimon, 97.
Pearly, Jacob, 60.
Pearse, Humphry, 84.
Pearse, Oliver, 72.
Pearse, Peter, 80.
Pearse, Rebecca, 58.
Pearse, William, 67.
Pearson, Dole, 67.
Pearson, Edmund, 67.
Pearson, Jacob, 67.
Pearson, John, 98.
Pearson, Joseph, 33.
Pearson, Joseph, 93.
Pearson, Saml., 44.
Pearson, Timothy M., 64.
Pearson, William, 24.
Pearsons, Caleb, 66.
Pearsons, Jonᵃ, 66.
Pearsons, Taylor, 60.
Pearsy, Wᵐ, 87.
Peary, William, 86.
Peas, Benjᵃ, 93.
Peas, Isaac, 12.
Peas, James, 93.
Peas, Nathaniel, 74.
Peas, Nathᵃ, 86.
Peas, Peletiah, 17.
Peas, William, 53.
Pease, Eliphalet, 65.
Pease, John, 65.
Peaslee, Amos, 88.
Peaslee, Elzabuth, 89.
Peasley, Amos, 42.
Peasley, Benjᵃ, 57.
Peasley, Caleb, 57.
Peasley, Ebenr, 57.
Peasley, Edmund, 74.
Peasley, Elijah, 77.
Peasley, Francis, 30.
Peasley, Humphrey, 42.
Peasley, Isaac, 55.
Peasley, Jacob, 25.
Peasley, Jacob, 70.
Peasley, John, 55.
Peasley, John, 57.
Peasley, John, 74.
Peasley, Jonᵃ, 57.
Peasley, Jonᵃ, Jr., 57.
Peasley, Joseph, 65.
Peasley, Mary, 74.
Peasley, Micajah, 74.
Peasley, Nathᵃ, 94.
Peasley, Nathl, 57.
Peasley, Nathl, Jr., 57.
Peasley, Paul, 74.
Peasley, Peter, 55.
Peasley, Reuben, 78.
Peasley, Saml., 55.
Peasley, Silas, 57.
Peasley, Simeon, 78.
Peasley, Stephen, 74.
Peasley, Timothy, 70.
Peasley, Wᵐ, 74.
Peavay, Antheny, 96.
Peavey, Benjᵃ, 94.
Peavey, Danl., 96.
Peavey, James, 73.
Peavey, Joseph, 82.
Peavey, Joshua, 94.
Peavey, Samuel, 59.
Peavey, Saml., 82.
Peavey, Thomᵃ, 96.
Peavy, John, 87.
Peavy, Joseph, 87.
Peavy, Oliver, 95.
Peck, Amariah, 25.

Peck, Ebbe, 34.
Peck, Ebenezer, 27.
Peck, Henry, 20.
Peck, Hezekiah, 20.
Peck, Israel, 32.
Peck, Jared, 14.
Peck, Mathew, 32.
Peck, Simeon, 34.
Peck, Simeon, Junr, 34.
Peck, Walter, 34.
Peckham, John, 43.
Pedengill, Jonathan, 77.
Peirce, Abraham, 23.
Peirce, Amos, 27.
Peirce, Benjamin, 23.
Peirce, Benja., 47.
Peirce, Benja., 52.
Peirce, Benja., 58.
Peirce, Benjᵃ, 88.
Peirce, Daniel, 27.
Peirce, Daniel, 43.
Peirce, Daniel, 80.
Peirce, David, 12.
Peirce, Ebenezer, 2d, 27.
Peirce, Ezekiel, 27.
Peirce, Ezekiel, 2d, 27.
Peirce, Ezra, 27.
Peirce, Israel, 86.
Peirce, Israel, 87.
Peirce, Jacob, 18.
Peirce, John, 13.
Peirce, John, 25.
Peirce, John, 27.
Peirce, John, 28.
Peirce, John, 80.
Peirce, Jonathan, 16.
Peirce, Joseph, 94.
Peirce, Joshua, 52.
Peirce, Josiah, 23.
Peirce, Nathl., 52.
Peirce, Nathaniel, 80.
Peirce, Nehemiah, 46.
Peirce, Nicholas, 25.
Peirce, Oliver, 42.
Peirce, Richard, 47.
Peirce, Samuel, 18.
Peirce, Samuel, 80.
Peirce, Silas, 16.
Peirce, Solomon, 47.
Peirce, Stephen, 52.
Peirce, Thomas, 80.
Peirce, Thos., 86.
Peirce, Timothy, 21.
Peirce, Willard, 50.
Peirce, William, 58.
Peirce, William, Jr., 58.
Pelton, John, 35.
Pelton, Joseph, 35.
Pemberton, James, 53.
Pemberton, Leonard, 18.
Pender, John, 100.
Pendergast, Dennis, 89.
Pendergast, Edmund, 89.
Pendergast, John, 89.
Pendergast, Stephen, 86.
Pendergrass, Sarah, 42.
Pendexter, Edward, 81.
Pendexter, John, 29.
Pendexter, John, 80.
Penhallow, Hannah, 81.
Penhallow, John, 80.
Penhallow, John, Junr., 80.
Penhallow, Samuel, 80.
Penney, John, 86.
Penney, Peletiah, 95.
Penniman, Adney, 94.
Pennyman, David, 27.
Pennyman, Jonathan, 37.
Pennyman, Nathan, 37.
Pennyman, Paul, 27.
Pennyman, Thomas, 26.
Percy, Charles, 84.
Percy, Peter, 84.
Perham, David, 23.
Perham, William, 43.
Perhum, Oliver, 50.
Perkens, Solomon, 100.
Perker, Daniel, 56.
Perkins, Abel, 23.
Perkins, Abraham, 35.
Perkins, Abraham, 65.
Perkins, Abraham, Junr, 65.
Perkins, Abraham, 97.
Perkins, Alexander, 14.
Perkins, Archeus, 43.
Perkins, Benjn, 82.
Perkins, Benjamin, 84.
Perkins, Benjᵃ, 93.
Perkins, Benjᵃ, 100.
Perkins, David, 38.
Perkins, David, 42.
Perkins, David, 69.
Perkins, Dorothy, 91.
Perkins, Elijah, 88.
Perkins, Henry, 12.
Perkins, Ichabod, 27.
Perkins, Isaac, 35.
Perkins, Jacob, 25.
Perkins, Jacob, 30.
Perkins, James, 82.
Perkins, Jane, 23.
Perkins, Jesse, 54.

Perkins, John, 74.
Perkins, John, Junr., 74.
Perkins, John, 82.
Perkins, John, 93.
Perkins, Jonathᵃ, 91.
Perkins, Jonᵃ, 97.
Perkins, Jonᵃ C., 72.
Perkins, Joseph, 18.
Perkins, Joseph, 25.
Perkins, Joseph, 39.
Perkins, Joseph, Jr., 39.
Perkins, Joseph, 57.
Perkins, Joseph, 87.
Perkins, Joseph, 93.
Perkins, Joshua, 89.
Perkins, Josiah, 85.
Perkins, Lemuel, 87.
Perkins, Moses, 68.
Perkins, Moses, 93.
Perkins, Peter, 35.
Perkins, Philemon, 51.
Perkins, Samauel, 64.
Perkins, Samuel, 21.
Perkins, Samuel, 35.
Perkins, Soloman, 96.
Perkins, Solomon, 57.
Perkins, Solomon, 94.
Perkins, Thomᵃ, 100.
Perkins, Timothy, 87.
Perkins, True, 92.
Perkins, William, 74.
Perkins, William, Jr, 74.
Perkins, Wᵐ, 89.
Perkison, Henery, 63.
Perlin, John, 17.
Permont, Richard, 21.
Permot, Susany, 32.
Perrere, John, 84.
Perrere, Saml Noyes, 70.
Perrey, David, 21.
Perrey, Sylvanus, 21.
Perrin, Daniel, 11.
Perry, Abigail, 58.
Perry, Abijah, 58.
Perry, Allen, 100.
Perry, Daniel, 18.
Perry, Ebenr, 83.
Perry, Ivory, 16.
Perry, Jame, 58.
Perry, James, 55.
Perry, John, 23.
Perry, Joseph, 44.
Perry, Justus, 19.
Perry, Mary, 91.
Perry, Micah, 16.
Perry, Oliver, 22.
Perry, Samuel, 12.
Perry, Saml, 78.
Perry, Simeon, 16.
Perry, Stephen, 20.
Perry, Thomas, 14.
Perry, William, 59.
Person, Danl, 57.
Person John, 56.
Person, Noah, 48.
Person, Oliver, 49.
Person, Saml., 56.
Persons, Daniel, 50.
Persons, George, 56.
Persons, Isaac, 41.
Persons, John, 65.
Persons, Jonᵃ, 50.
Persons, Jonathan, 50.
Persons, Jonᵃ, Jr., 50.
Persons, Joseph, 50.
Persons, Samuel, 65.
Persons, Thomas, 43.
Persons, Timothy, 50.
Pervear, Josiah, 69.
Peten, Absalom, 38.
Peters, Isreal, 22.
Peters, John, 56.
Peters, Richard, 22.
Peters, Robinson, 91.
Peters, William, 48.
Peterson, Benjamin, 14.
Peterson, Danl, 41.
Peterson, Ephriam, 14.
Peterson, Turner, 34.
Petingill, Asa, 76.
Pettee, Abner, 44.
Pettee, Asa, 56.
Pettee, Danl., 56.
Pettee, John, 45.
Pettingale, Abbot, 83.
Pettingale, Wᵐ, 83.
Pettingale, Jethroe, 66.
Pettingill, Amos, Jr, 54.
Pettingill, Benjᵃ, 54.
Pettingill, Benjᵃ, Jr., 54.
Pettingill, Benjᵃ, 3d, 54.
Pettingill, Carlton, 54.
Pettingill, David, 54.
Pettingill, Dudley, 57.
Pettingill, Ephriam, 66.
Pettingill, Joseph, 54.
Pettingill, Joshua, 40.
Pettingill, William, 58.
Petts, James, 26.
Petty, Asa, 32.
Petty, James P., 38.
Petty, Jedediah, 33.